# PRINCE HENRY OF PRUSSIA
## Brother of Frederick the Great

# Prince Henry of Prussia
## Brother of Frederick the Great

By CHESTER V. EASUM

PROFESSOR OF HISTORY
THE UNIVERSITY OF WISCONSIN

GREENWOOD PRESS, PUBLISHERS
WESTPORT, CONNECTICUT

# Foreword

The man principally responsible for the achievements of Frederick II of Prussia was Frederick himself. No one else earned for him the title of "Frederick the Great," *Friedrich der Einzige,* or "Old Fritz." Yet he owed much of his success to the work of his predecessors, particularly the Great Elector and Frederick William I, and much to the help his brother Henry gave him. As the rather obscure figure of the younger brother emerges from the shadow of the throne only as the light of investigation is thrown upon it, so Frederick himself takes on a new and in some ways more attractive appearance as his character is more fully revealed by the study of his relationship with Henry. Far from being discredited, he gains more than he loses as a result of this renewed scrutiny. So does Henry.

An all-inclusive list of those who have contributed to the completion of this enterprise would be far too long for the space available. For the grants-in-aid that made research travel possible the writer is indebted to the Social Science Research Council, the Oberländer Trust, and the University of Wisconsin; to the University of Wisconsin also for a very generous allowance of research leave, and to his colleagues in the Department of History for their readiness to make so cheerfully the adjustments necessitated by his prolonged absence from the classroom. The librarians and archivists who have helped him are legion; notable among them, and especially entitled to his gratitude, are those of the Harvard College Library; the British Museum; the French National Library, National Archives, and Foreign Office Archives; the German State Library and Heeresbücherei in Berlin; the Archives of the House of Brandenburg-Prussia, the Prussian Secret State Archives, and the German National Castles and Parks Administration; and, first and last, the Library of the University of Wisconsin.

The drawing of Prince Henry on the title page was made by James S. Watrous, instructor in art history in the University of Wisconsin, from photographs of the equestrian statue on the base of Frederick's monument in Unter den Linden, Berlin.

Chester V. Easum

# Contents

# Illustrations

# Maps

# ABBREVIATIONS USED IN FOOTNOTES

Berner and Volz.   Ernst Berner and Gustave B. Volz, *Aus der Zeit des siebenjährigen Krieges.*

Bisset.   Andrew Bisset, ed., *Memoirs and Papers of Sir Andrew Mitchell, K. B.*

Fr. F. O.   French Foreign Office Archives (Archives du Ministère Étrangères).

*F. B. P. G.*   *Forschungen zur brandenburgischen und preussischen Geschichte.*

Hausarchiv.   Brandenburg-Preussisches Hausarchiv, the Archives of the House of Brandenburg-Prussia in Berlin-Charlottenburg.

Jany.   Curt Jany, *Geschichte der Königlichen Preussischen Armee bis zum Jahre 1807.*

M. P.   Mitchell Papers, British Museum.

*P. C.*   Gustave B. Volz and Others, eds., *Politische Correspondenz Friedrichs des Grossen.*

Staatsarchiv.   Geheimes Preussisches Staatsarchiv, Berlin-Dahlem.

A. Schäfer.   Arnold Schäfer, *Geschichte des siebenjährigen Krieges.*

Schöning.   Kurd Wolfgang von Schöning, *Militärische Correspondenz des Königs Friedrich des Grossen mit dem Prinzen Heinrich von Preussen.*

Sybel.   Heinrich von Sybel, *Geschichte der Revolutionszeit.*

PRINCE HENRY OF PRUSSIA
Brother of Frederick the Great

# CHAPTER I

# 𝔄 𝔓𝔯𝔦𝔫𝔠𝔢 𝔬𝔣 𝔱𝔥𝔢 𝔅𝔩𝔬𝔬𝔡

*"There is an amphibious sort of creature who is neither sovereign nor subject, and who is sometimes very difficult to govern; it is what is called a prince of the blood. Their distinguished origin gives such persons a certain pride, which they call nobility, that renders obedience insufferable to them and any kind of constraint odious. If there is any intrigue, any plot or petty conspiracy to be apprehended, it is likely to emanate from them. In this state [Prussia], they are more powerless than anywhere else; but the best course to take with them is to rebuff sharply the first one who raises the standard of independence, to treat them with all the distinction appropriate to their birth, to load them down with outward honors, but to exclude them from affairs and not to trust them with the command of troops except in favorable circumstances — that is, when they have ability and one can depend upon their character.*

*"What I say of princes applies also to princesses, who ought never under any pretext whatever to meddle in government."*

THE WRITER of these lines was the king of Prussia known as Frederick the Great. The princes of the blood whom he thus described but did not name were his own three brothers, considerably younger than himself, for whom he had become responsible upon his father's death. The responsibility had weighed heavily upon him, and his authoritarian control had weighed heavily upon them; so he had frequently found them troublesome, and they had always thought themselves harshly treated. With characteristic cynicism, and plainly enough, he stated in his Political Testament of 1752 the point of view of the older brother and head of the family. Princes must not be permitted to forget that the brothers of a king were still his subjects. He seemed never to have asked himself whether his brothers could be happy in the position to which he consigned them, or whether he might have spared them the unhappiness he had himself experienced as heir apparent to the throne.[1]

Uneasy lies the head that hopes to wear a crown. Friction between the representatives of the older and the younger generation in the conduct of the business of John Doe and Son is traditional rather than exceptional. Only very rarely does an American president-elect find it possible to

[1] From the Political Testament of 1752 of Frederick II, printed in French in a supplement to Gustave B. Volz and Others, eds., *Politische Correspondenz Friedrichs des Grossen* (46 vols., Berlin, 1879–1939), cited hereafter as *P. C.* Originals of the king's various Testaments are in the Brandenburg-Prussian Hausarchiv — hereafter cited as Hausarchiv — in Berlin-Charlottenburg.

3

cooperate with his predecessor for a smooth transition from one administration to the next; and even the British have often seen their Prince of Wales discontented and unhappy.

Hohenzollern Prussia never found the ideal solution for the problem of the crown prince or Prince of Prussia. So long as the monarchy was in theory absolute, and the authority of the king unlimited and indivisible, the heir to the throne could not conveniently be invited to participate to any considerable extent either in the determination of policy or in the conduct of public business. He had to be rigorously trained for his profession and at the same time restrained from practicing it until the death of the reigning king. Soon to be a sovereign, he was still a subject. Shortly to be master of all the resources of the state, he could not yet control his own purse or household except as his king accorded him the privilege. Certain prerogatives were his, of course; but because he was the prince he was denied much of the freedom enjoyed even by his fellow subjects.

Yet the prince could never forget that he would one day be king. Had he himself been able or inclined to shut that thought out of his mind, there would have been plenty of others to suggest it to him in countless ways, usually for their own devious purposes. Since the reigning king could not live forever, there were always those interested in learning the bent and helping to predetermine the policies of his successor. Representatives of foreign powers were generous with offers of personal — usually private — loans. Discontented elements of all sorts stood ready to surround the heir apparent with sycophantic and by no means disinterested friends, filling his mind with illusions of greater power for the monarchy, or greater boundaries and prestige for the state, or the greater glory of God to be brought about by political liberalism, social or economic reform, intellectual enlightenment, or the patronage of music, the drama, and the other arts. There was always someone interested in making certain, and in encouraging the prince to resolve, that in the next reign things would be different.

The experience of the great Frederick as crown prince was no exception to this rule; nor was it a happy experience. Much of the unhappiness for which his heavy-handed father has commonly been blamed was in fact inevitable under the circumstances, and the common lot of princes so situated.

Still less comfortable psychologically was the position of the other "princes of the blood." Because they shared to a certain extent "that divinity which doth hedge a king," they were not treated quite as ordinary subjects. Frederick II in particular wished his brothers and sisters

4

to be distinguished persons; but he saw to it that the honors he conferred upon them were social distinctions only, carrying with them no political authority. So their appointments never satisfied their ambitions; their generous allowances never quite covered the expenses of their extravagant households; and they found themselves hedged out of the fields of public policy and administration which the king reserved for himself, always cautiously keeping his own counsel on affairs of state.

Frederick's three brothers were congenial but not alike; nor were they always treated alike. During the first year of the Seven Years' War, Augustus William, the eldest, passed ingloriously out of the picture. Ferdinand, the youngest, gave abundant proof of personal bravery but revealed none of the other qualities necessary in a commander of troops; so he stood thereafter only in the background or on the sidelines, referred to occasionally with sympathy as "poor Ferdinand," or with affection as "dear Ferdinand," but treated by Frederick as a person of no consequence. He was shown consideration as a member of the family, but never figured in affairs of state. Only one of the brothers, Prince Henry, and Frederick's brother-in-law Ferdinand of Brunswick, really carried any considerable share of the burden of the defense of Prussia.

Until he proved himself invaluable in war, Henry had been to Frederick only one of three rather troublesome younger brothers. The three had had much in common. All, upon the death of their father, had had to recognize in Frederick the head of the family, the supreme lawgiver of their lives, the donor of their lavish allowances; and all had resented his tutelage. All more or less ambitious (Henry perhaps most and Augustus William least), they were equally and indiscriminately excluded from all public life except the military service required of them as regimental officers; and even there they had little authority and found scant room for the exercise of initiative. Thrown back upon themselves, with houses, households, and an abundance of time on their hands and without the steadying influence of responsibility or regular occupation, they naturally fell into frivolous habits. Among the least admirable of these habits was their customary attitude of opposition to and irresponsible criticism of the king, their brother. For years before the great testing time of 1756–1757 the three younger brothers, personally very fond of one another, had formed a close combination to shut out of their lives the older one who had so completely shut them out of his. He was known among them as "the old man" long before his soldiers had learned to call him "Old Fritz," and less affectionately.[2]

---

[2] Frederick's characterization of the "princes of the blood," quoted on page 3, was written before the Seven Years' War began.

This is only one of many rather tragic aspects of the personal life of the great Frederick. He had himself never known happiness. He had, to be sure, learned as a boy to form with his favorite sister Wilhelmina the same secretive and spiteful sort of partnership against his own father that his younger brothers later formed against him. He had learned intrigue and duplicity early enough, at the knees of a mother constantly guilty of the cardinal sin of setting the minds of her children against their father. He had had most of the softness hammered out of him by the blacksmith methods of his father, Frederick William I, in a determined and surprisingly successful though ill-directed effort to make a man of him, fit to be king in Prussia. He had perhaps come closer to knowing happiness during his halcyon period as crown prince at Rheinsberg — *Frederico tranquillitatem colenti* — than at any other period in his life, however little his well-meaning, long-suffering, and in many ways admirable wife may have helped him in his search for it. But he had not learned either how to find happiness for himself or how to command it for others. Always lonely, often hungry for human affection, yearning for the warmth of close and confidential friendship even when surrounded by the most brilliant galaxy of wits, he was doomed to go his way alone.

To say that he was a wicked man for whose many sins loneliness was only too light a punishment, or that one who lives for himself alone must expect to live by himself, alone, is to make a very easy and superficial generalization about the king, but to show no real understanding of the unrelieved loneliness of the man. To say that the spiritual desert in which he dwelt in such glittering but deadly isolation was of his own making is equally easy; but such a statement is either something more or something less than the truth, for it implies that he chose to make and to inhabit such a desert; and he did not so choose.

There were persons of whom Frederick was genuinely fond. He respected the intelligence, determination, and strength of his mother, and never disregarded her. He showed her far more formal consideration than he did his wife, and mourned sincerely at her death. His sister Wilhelmina held a prominent place in his affections in his youth, and he was deeply grieved over her death in one of the darkest periods of the Seven Years' War. In subsequent years he sought compensation in the affection of his younger sister Amelia. All these he loved and lost, two through death and the third from a crippling disease which never prevented him from showing her every possible consideration but which did rob him, and his brother Henry, unseasonably of the pleasure of her society.

*Bronze Bust of Prince Henry (ca.1880) by M. Wiese, in the Berlin Zeughaus*

Reproduced by courtesy of the Verwaltung der staatlichen Schlösser und Gärten.

A Prince of the Blood

Conversation with his friends gave him pleasure; the valor of his comrades-in-arms won his gratitude; faithful service of any sort earned his respect and occasionally a curt expression of approval, perhaps even a reward. But he outlived his most valued friends, soldiers, and servitors, or found them somehow wanting and sent them away. He lost interest in his visitors from other lands and saw them no more. Elizabeth Christina was his queen but not his wife; she shared neither his thoughts nor his retreat at Sans Souci. The more he saw of men, he said, the more respect he had for his dogs, which set no price on their love or their loyalty. So dogs enjoyed great license at Sans Souci, where no man dared venture uninvited or overstay his welcome. Thus the legend grew that the lonely king despised people as he said he did, that he loved no one and was loved by none.

There was, however, one member of his family, one comrade-in-arms, one occasional consultant in politics and emissary on confidential diplomatic missions, one intellectual companion to whom he could write or speak with a freedom which he could permit himself with no other person — his brother Henry. Prince Henry resembled him too closely, and had too many of the same faults along with some of the same virtues, ever to be the perfect companion. He valued himself too highly to be properly grateful for Frederick's generosity to him. He was graceless enough never fully to requite Frederick's genuine affection for him, or to realize how incredibly patient Frederick often had to be in dealing with him. But the mere fact that there was in the world one man with whom Frederick was almost endlessly patient, and whose affection he craved and courted all his life without ever winning it, makes that man especially interesting to any student of the life of the great king; and the confidential character of their lifelong correspondence makes much of it a mine of invaluable information.

In 1752 Henry was merely one of the princes of the blood. Five years later he had earned for himself a place beside the king; and he served thereafter until the end of the Seven Years' War as second-in-command. During those years he found himself in a position more uncomfortable than that of an ordinary prince of the blood — or indeed of an heir apparent.

Although technically subordinate to the commander in chief, the second-in-command is compelled always to think of himself as potentially the commander. Willingly or unwillingly, he must sit in judgment upon every act and decision of his chief, knowing that, if some accident had befallen the chief, he would himself have had to make that decision or find another solution for the problem. Unless he is capable of the most

7

complete self-effacement, as men qualified for leadership are not likely to be, he will inevitably regard unfavorably some of the decisions made without his approval or against his advice, even though loyalty may enjoin silence upon him and impel him to make an honest effort to carry them into effect. If he is sufficiently confident of the generosity of his chief, or cares little whether he is given due credit by contemporaries as well as by history, he can devote himself without reservation to a life of selfless service. If he feels otherwise, only a miracle of self-control or a phenomenal sense of duty can hold him faithful to his trust.

After the Seven Years' War no one could forget that Frederick the Great had a brother Henry who was his worthy associate. Precisely there, however, in that family relationship and in the similarity of their inherited characteristics, are to be found the sources of personal friction. Henry himself could never forget that he was Frederick's brother — but only his brother, and one of his subjects. As restless and ambitious as Frederick himself, he had only an occasional opportunity to employ his really considerable abilities in the service of the state or to win public recognition for them. A military genius second in his day only to the soldier king of Prussia, he was still second, and conscious and resentful of the fact that he was so considered.

The accident of birth had made him only the king's younger brother, who might otherwise have been king, and who never realized that he would not have been a better king than the brother whose acts he so often criticized. Another accident, death on the battlefield or in the palace, might at any moment during a period of twenty years have made him regent and guardian of the youthful heir to the throne. So both in the army and in other affairs of state he found himself in the exquisitely uncomfortable position of the second-in-command, condemned to the punishment of Tantalus, going through two wars and through life as he has since lived in history, not as his own man, under his own name and in his own right, but as "the brother of Frederick the Great."

Younger brothers of famous men in all lands, aspiring understudies of star performers everywhere, ambitious men made restless by the consciousness of superior abilities and driven into querulous discontent by the want of opportunity to exercise them, and all students capable of sympathy for such persons will understand why such a prince was never quite content to be known only as the younger brother of a great king or as the irascible old uncle and great-uncle of two others who frequently disappointed and exasperated him by their failure to achieve the greatness that their times demanded of them.

# CHAPTER II

# 𝔉𝔯𝔢𝔡𝔢𝔯𝔦𝔠𝔲𝔰 in 𝔏𝔬𝔠𝔬 𝔓𝔞𝔯𝔢𝔫𝔱𝔦𝔰

*"History is no criminal court. It does not have
to judge and condemn; it has to understand."* — Buchfinck.

THE EIGHTEENTH of January was "coronation day" in the Hohenzollern
family calendar, the anniversary of the crowning of the grandfather of
Frederick II as the first king in Prussia. After the Seven Years' War, for
the rest of his lifetime, Frederick gave a new character to the observ-
ance of the day, celebrating it instead as the birthday of Prince Henry.

The child born to Frederick William I and Sophia Dorothea on
coronation day, 1726, was the third of their four sons. Christened Friedrich Heinrich Ludwig, he more commonly wrote his name in its French
form as Frederic Henri Louis — or merely Henri.

As a boy Prince Henry was much as Frederick had been, slender and
of less than average height but with an abundance of nervous energy,
artistic in temperament, fond of reading and of music. It was early noted
that his eyes, especially, had the same compelling quality about them
as Frederick's, whether they beamed with friendship or enthusiasm,
flashed in anger, or grew hard and cold with displeasure or enmity.

Like all his brothers and sisters, young Henry was early entrusted
to a French governess. That did not mean that their father was pro-
French. On the contrary, Frederick William was aggressively Prussian
in his general outlook and frankly Philistine in his attitude toward the
"Frenchified" ways of Frederick I and of his own queen; but he himself
habitually used a vocabulary oddly compounded of French and German,
as did most of his German contemporaries until the works of Lessing,
Goethe, and others brought home to them the realization that the Germans had at last developed a worthy national language of their own.

Prince Henry wrote many years later that a young man whose linguis-
tic repertoire was limited to any language other than French would find
his experience of the world also limited practically by the boundaries of
his own country or province. Knowing French, on the other hand, one
might travel where he would on the Continent and make himself understood in court circles or in intellectual company, or correspond with like-
minded men anywhere. So it was more important that he be taught
French than that he try to become a stylist in German. Long before the

# THE FAMILY OF FREDERICK II

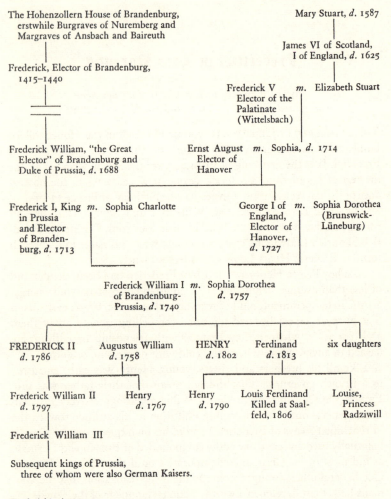

The Hohenzollern House of Brandenburg, erstwhile Burgraves of Nuremberg and Margraves of Ansbach and Baireuth

Frederick, Elector of Brandenburg, 1415–1440

Mary Stuart, d. 1587

James VI of Scotland, I of England, d. 1625

Frederick V — m. — Elizabeth Stuart
Elector of the Palatinate (Wittelsbach)

Frederick William, "the Great Elector" of Brandenburg and Duke of Prussia, d. 1688

Ernst August — m. — Sophia, d. 1714
Elector of Hanover

Frederick I, King — m. — Sophia Charlotte
in Prussia and Elector of Brandenburg, d. 1713

George I of — m. — Sophia Dorothea
England, Elector of Hanover, d. 1727 — (Brunswick-Lüneburg)

Frederick William I — m. — Sophia Dorothea
of Brandenburg-Prussia, d. 1740 — d. 1757

FREDERICK II
d. 1786

Augustus William
d. 1758

HENRY
d. 1802

Ferdinand
d. 1813

six daughters

Frederick William II
d. 1797

Henry
d. 1767

Henry
d. 1790

Louis Ferdinand
Killed at Saalfeld, 1806

Louise, Princess Radziwill

Frederick William III

Subsequent kings of Prussia, three of whom were also German Kaisers.

Frederick's sisters:

Wilhelmina, Margravine of Baireuth.
Frederika Louisa, Margravine of Ansbach.
Philippine Charlotte, Duchess of Brunswick, wife of the reigning Duke Charles, whose brother was the famous soldier, Prince Ferdinand of Brunswick. Frederick's queen was Princess Elizabeth Christina, sister of Duke Charles and Prince Ferdinand.
Sophia Dorothea, Margravine of Brandenburg-Schwedt, grandmother of Sophia Dorothea of Württemberg, who was the second wife of the Grand Duke Paul of Russia, son of Catherine II; maternal grandmother also of the Princess Louise of Prussia, daughter of Frederick's brother Ferdinand, who became (by marriage) Princess Radziwill.
Louisa Ulrika, Queen of Sweden.
Anna Amelia, Abbess of Quedlinburg.

prince had formulated these elaborate arguments, his inarticulate father had arrived silently at the same conclusion — or had permitted his wife to decide the question as one belonging to the nursery anyway.

On the military education of his sons, however, the old king had ideas of his own. Princes were born to work, and in Prussia a very vital part of their work was the military; so princes must be soldiers. If by misfortune a prince was born who was not a born soldier, he must be made into a soldier nonetheless. Frederick had found that pounding process very painful; but his father had forged him into a keen-edged and finely tempered soldier in spite of his protests and his efforts to escape; and when he became king, he prescribed for his younger brothers the same rigorous treatment that their father had thought good for them.

Their father had sent them early to the drill field and parade ground. In May, 1738, Prince Henry was named an ensign in the grenadier regiment. He must then have been about half as tall as the shortest grenadier. In December, although not yet thirteen, he was made a lieutenant. At the funeral of his father both he and Prince William were required to remain with their regiment while Frederick, in uniform, walked with "little Ferdinand" behind the funeral car. The new king was twenty-eight years old; his brothers who stood on the steps of the throne when he was acclaimed by the nobility of Berlin were eighteen, fourteen, and ten.

With the inauguration of the new reign, the second education of Prince Henry began. It also was largely military, and the new head of the family proved to be but little less exacting than the old. In fact, so far as Prince Henry was concerned, Frederick was even more severe than their father had been. The new king soon conceded that, in his own numerous quarrels with his father while crown prince, he had not always been right, nor his father always wrong. Now, *in loco parentis,* he himself became the stern parent and his young brother the rebellious prince. High-spirited, proud, resentful of tutelage, restive under the regime prescribed for him, the youngster was often a troublesome charge to one who had already forgotten that he had ever been young.

That the family history should thus repeat itself so soon, that Frederick should make so many of the same errors of overseverity in his training of his younger brother that his own father had made with him, that another youth of sensitive personality should be made to suffer more than was necessary, even as the younger Frederick himself had suffered, through overinsistence upon complete conformity without any attempt to distinguish between essentials and nonessentials — these are interesting psychological phenomena; but to Henry they were hard and unreasonable facts, and they sentenced him to an emotionally stormy youth.

Military promotions came fast enough. During the first month of the new reign he was made colonel of the Thirty-fifth Regiment, then at Spandau. Though such an appointment, for an undersized boy of fourteen, could have been only honorary, and though he was still jokingly called a "Colonel of Marionettes," he was expected none the less to do his regular garrison duty, subject at once to regular discipline as an officer and to special rules as a prince. When not actually with his regiment — and leave of absence even for a ride into Berlin could be secured only with the express permission of the king — he was kept under Frederick's own watchful eye at Potsdam.

Nor was that eye by any means blind to his nonmilitary education. On occasion the king urged him to apply himself with greater assiduity to the study of logic and of belles lettres, which he was told he would find more useful than anything else in the world. "Apply yourself, think straight, and always do your duty," was the older brother's advice.[1]

Although he was certainly interested in the French and Italian languages, French literature and philosophy, the Greek and Roman classics (in French translation), and in music, the young prince was neither steady nor industrious enough to suit the young king, and did not take kindly to correction. A letter marking a formal reconciliation[2] was likely to be followed by one revealing a new quarrel. For example: "If you love me, your love must be metaphysical, for hitherto I have never seen people show their love for one another in this fashion. . . . you hold yourself aloof from me, treat me with coldness, and show an indifference toward me which one cannot quite understand."[3]

In wartime such bickering between the brothers ceased; and four of the first six years of Frederick's reign were war years. The death of the emperor Charles VI, head of the house of Hapsburg, on October 20, 1740, gave Frederick an opening which he was quick to see and to utilize. The emperor had sought to insure the peaceful succession of his daughter Maria Theresa as archduchess of Austria and queen of Bohemia and Hungary by inducing the other princes, including Frederick's father, to enter into an agreement guaranteeing it, commonly called "the Prag-

[1] Kurd W. von Schöning, *Militärische Correspondenz des Königs Friedrich des Grossen mit dem Prinzen Heinrich von Preussen* (4 vols., Berlin, 1859), I, 44. The first three volumes of this valuable work constitute a sort of documentary history of the Seven Years' War; the fourth covers in similar fashion the War of the Bavarian Succession. See the bibliography. Hereafter cited merely as Schöning.
[2] Such as that of January 14, 1741, from Breslau: "I have been delighted to find in your letter some sentiments worthy of a prince of the blood, who, having forgotten himself, knows at least how to get back on the right road." Schöning, I, 44.
[3] Frederick to Henry, in *Oeuvres de Frédéric le Grand*, XXVI, 153 (Berlin, 1855). This is hereafter cited as *Oeuvres* and is not to be confused with the *Oeuvres posthumes*. This letter is quoted also by Andrew Hamilton in his *Rheinsberg* (2 vols., London, 1880), and by others. The correspondence between Frederick and Henry is cited hereafter as F. to H. or H. to F.

matic Sanction." For a woman thus to govern the Hapsburg dominions in her own right was in itself a startling departure from the traditional practice, which had been based upon the old Salic law. No one, therefore, thought very seriously of trying to secure for her the German Imperial crown as well; but it was a part of the family plan that her husband, Prince Francis of Lorraine, should become emperor.

Francis had a right to hope that he might be known in history by some other title than that of husband of Maria Theresa, and he had reason to expect Hapsburg support for his aspirations. Some such tempting possibilities and a duchy in Italy had been held before him by his prospective father-in-law years before, to induce him to give up his duchy of Lorraine to Stanislaus Leszczynski, father-in-law of the king of France. That had been the old emperor's contribution to another temporary solution of the perennial problem of the Polish succession, and to the ultimate acquisition of Lorraine by France.

With the moral or other obligations of the Hapsburg family to Maria Theresa's husband, young King Frederick of Prussia was in no way concerned; but as an Imperial elector he would cast one of the nine votes which would determine who the new emperor should be. His father's acceptance of the Pragmatic Sanction, on the other hand, was only one of many instances of that subservience to Austria of which as crown prince he had been ashamed and of which as king he did not propose to be guilty. He did not consider himself in any way bound by the sanction; for, he said, Austria had not kept her part of a bargain concerning Julich and Berg upon which Frederick William I had based his acceptance of it. But Frederick did not take the trouble to pretend to his own ministers that he took such legalistic arguments seriously. The only important point was that the financial and military strength of Prussia, as he had inherited it from his father, justified him in listening to the prompting of his own ambition and making an attempt at once to hoist his kingdom from the second rank among the German states, where he had found it, to the first. That could be done only in defiance of Austria. He would do it also at Austria's expense.

So he offered, first, to cast his electoral vote for Francis of Lorraine and to guarantee Maria Theresa the peaceful possession of her other hereditary states if she would cede Silesia to him. When she refused, he invaded and seized the province. He would have been considered a fool, he said, had he neglected such an opportunity.

Leaving it to his ministers to justify him as best they might, he himself crossed his Rubicon — the Silesian border — on December 16, 1740, with drums beating and banners flying. He could not foresee all the

13

consequences of that bold step, but in his youthful self-confidence he assumed that, whatever they might be, he would deal with them as they arose. He knew what he was doing, and that it was dangerous; he knew also that he would be denounced for it, but he shrank neither from danger nor from denunciation. What others called an act of aggression was to him only an act of self-assertion; he would win fame for himself, and for Prussia the position in Europe to which he thought her entitled.

Frederick had reversed his father's policy with respect to Austria, but he was carried through his first Silesian campaign by the momentum of his father's work. Only a disciplined army could have made such swift marches through the winter's mud and snow and have been fit for fighting at the end of them. Years of careful attention to every detail of military organization bore their fruit in the success with which supplies kept pace with the army. Superior equipment and endless hours of drill paid dividends in the first great battle — Mollwitz, on April 10, 1741 — when the Prussian infantry, by virtue of their metal ramrods and their ability to reload their muskets quickly and efficiently, even under battle conditions, attained a marked superiority of fire power over the Austrians, who in the excitement of battle broke their wooden ramrods or spilled their powder in the snow. Frederick William and his drillmasters had not made men into machines, but they had drilled them until they could perform, almost mechanically, certain vitally necessary operations upon which fire power and effectiveness in battle depended. Superiority of equipment and discipline bred confidence and steadiness in the ranks; the veteran generals, Schwerin and the old Prince of Anhalt-Dessau, supplied the same qualities in the high command.

The battle of Mollwitz was fought in deep snow at the end of several hours of marching. The Austrians had almost been taken by surprise in their quarters. Even so, the Prussian cavalry was dispersed, and Frederick himself left the field, thinking the battle lost. He returned hours later to discover that his father's infantry, led by one of his father's old and trusted officers, Count Schwerin, had won a decisive victory for him.

Victory brought prestige, and an alliance with France and Bavaria; the elector Charles Albert of Bavaria claimed the German Imperial throne and the others agreed to help him get it. In the face of such a coalition the Austrian government saw itself compelled to yield at some point; so at Klein-Schnellendorf, on October 9, 1741, it secretly agreed to cede Lower Silesia to Prussia if Frederick would confine his military operations thereafter to a pretended siege of Neisse.

Even without Prussia's help, France and Bavaria continued to make progress; and with Prague in their hands there was the danger that momentous changes might be made in the Empire to their advantage and without Prussia's participation. So at the end of the year Frederick re-entered the war, and in January, 1742, invaded Moravia with a small army of Saxons serving rather halfheartedly as an auxiliary corps. Forced by the failure of his requisition system and the consequent lack of supplies to retreat through eastern Bohemia, and thrown upon his own resources by the withdrawal of his Saxon auxiliaries, he was still able to fight and win a battle at Chotusitz on May 17, 1742. This victory was his own, not Schwerin's; and this time his cavalry, which he had worked sedulously to improve, showed itself equal in quality to the Austrian. His infantry was still superior to any other in Europe.

Victory at Chotusitz brought him another tempting opportunity to make a separate peace; and he saw no prospect of really effective cooperation with his allies. The treaty negotiated in Breslau in June, 1742, and confirmed in Berlin on July 28 brought him all of Silesia and the county of Glatz. For his allies he could do nothing. So the peace cost him the confidence of France and Saxony, as Prince Henry later pointed out, and the two campaigns had cost him something in men and in money; but he could show a handsome profit in such tangibles as lands, their population and resources, and the revenues they might be expected to pay.

There followed two years of peace for Prussia, during which her former allies continued their war against Austria with less and less prospect of success. First Prague and then all of Bohemia were retaken and Bavaria was overrun by the Austrians. The French were defeated by a British-Hanoverian army at Dettingen. France seemed likely to lose Alsace-Lorraine and to be no longer available as a counterweight against Austria in German affairs. Again Frederick had to decide whether he could permit great changes to be made in the balance of power among the German states, this time in favor of Austria and again without his participation. He renewed his alliance with France, announced again his support of the elector Charles of Bavaria as the rightful emperor, drew a few of the other German princes into his Union of Frankfort, and in August, 1744, again declared war — ostensibly as a defender of the Empire against Austrian aggression.

Frederick's first objective in the second Silesian war was Prague. Some of his troops were drawn directly there from Silesia; others were grudgingly permitted to pass through Saxony. All efforts to bring the Saxons into the new alliance had failed, and soon they took the field as the allies of Austria. Frederick captured Prague and pushed on far to the southward into central Bohemia, and was well pleased with himself when he had placed his troops between the Austrian army and Austria. But that also meant that the Austrians and Saxons stood between his own army and its base; and his position became untenable before theirs did. It was all he could do to win his way back to Silesia without having to fight for his life.

He did have to fight for Silesia, at Hohenfriedberg on June 4, 1745, against an invading force of Austrians and Saxons. The fighting was particularly bitter where the Prussians had a chance at their former very unsatisfactory allies, the Saxons. The Prussian victory put an end to the enemy invasion of Silesia, and Frederick followed his foes again into Bohemia but did little else until he was practically forced to fight his way out again by way of Soor on September 30, 1745. All summer he had been hoping that Great Britain would induce Saxony and Austria to make peace with him; but a winter campaign against the Saxons, marked by another Prussian victory at Kesselsdorf on December 15 (the work of "the old Dessauer," Prince Leopold of Anhalt-Dessau), was still needed to force them to it. Then, by the Peace of Dresden, Frederick was once more confirmed in the possession of Silesia and Glatz.

By his first Silesian war the young king of Prussia had acquired at Austria's expense some provinces of considerable value. By his second he had prevented Austria from indemnifying herself elsewhere in Germany, and had successfully held on not only to his new possessions but to Prussia's new position as the rival, no longer the satellite, of Austria. He knew that Maria Theresa would neither forgive nor forget; so he must stand constantly on guard to hold his gains, and might at any time have to fight to maintain his new position; but that, as he viewed it, was the law of life among nations.

Left behind, to his great disappointment, at the beginning of the first Silesian campaign, Prince Henry soon secured permission to follow the king into the field. At the battle of Chotusitz, at the age of sixteen and with the nominal rank of colonel, he served as one of Frederick's adjutants. In the second Silesian war he again accompanied the king and, as was usual with those who went where Frederick did, found himself more than once in real personal danger. In 1744, while ill in the village of Tabor, which was occupied at the time by only a small body of Prussian troops, he narrowly escaped capture by helping to fight off an Austrian raid. Near Prague, Prince William of Brandenburg was killed beside him, and his own page was wounded.[4]

After the retreat from Bohemia in the autumn of 1744 the king stayed as usual with his troops but sent young Prince Henry back to Berlin for the winter. Late in the following spring, however, the prince returned

[4] Letters from Frederick and his secretary Eichel to minister Podewils, from camp near Prague, September 12 and 13, 1744, in *P. C.*, III, 279.

to the field and as adjutant to his brother participated in the battle of Hohenfriedberg. At Soor, as a major general, he commanded an infantry brigade. The king found frequent occasion to praise his conduct. After Hohenfriedberg Frederick wrote to Podewils that his brothers Henry and William had "fought like lions." Both were made to sign with him his letter to their mother, in token that they were safe.

Prince Henry continued to earn his brother's approbation during the remainder of the summer, revealing already the peculiar genius for swift movement and for utilization of terrain that subsequently won him fame. Of his brilliant defensive action on the march from Tratenau to Schatzlar, Frederick wrote: "My brother Henry distinguished himself to a high degree on our march of the sixteenth, and his talents, of which I have so often spoken to you, are beginning to be known in the army." [5]

Obviously no nineteen-year-old boy, however talented, could have advanced at such a fabulous rate on his merits alone. In those days the king's brothers did not need to earn promotions; they had only to justify them. Until they had learned their trade, they were fairly well insured against fatal blunders by the presence at their elbows of exceptionally well-trained professional soldiers as advisers, the material out of which the General Staff was ultimately made. Prince Henry was the only one of the three cadets ever to be graduated from such tutelage, although of course both he and Frederick always made good use of staff officers trained as specialists.

Soon after the retreat from Bohemia illness overtook him again in the form of smallpox, which marked his face for life with deep and rather ugly scars. He therefore returned to Berlin before the actual conclusion of the campaign, and Frederick sent his sympathy and compliments to "dear Henry" by way of Podewils until he could himself return after the signing of the Peace of Dresden, when he invited both Henry and Augustus William to share his triumphal re-entry into Berlin.

"Dear Henry" continued to be a problem in peacetime, however, even in his military activities. As a major general and a man of twenty, he considered himself entitled to an independent establishment of his own, and was more irked than ever when he found he had reverted virtually to the status of a boy in school. As a veteran of two wars, who naturally never realized how much of his rapid advancement he owed to the fact that he was the king's brother, or how much of his success had been due to his brother's teachings and ever-watchful protection, even against his own errors in the field, he had begun to think of seeking fame as an

---

[5] To Lieutenant General Rothenburg, from Rohnstock, in *P. C.*, IV, 320; Hamilton, *Rheinsberg*, II, 10.

officer in some foreign army. After the excitement of field campaigning, the drill, parades, and inspections of garrison soldiering bored him more than ever; and he neglected them.

Membership in the *Ordre des Chevaliers Bayards,* a group of twelve soldiers *"sans peur et sans reproche,"* organized for the study of military science and the cultivation of the so-called military virtues, served to stimulate his ambition rather than to satisfy it, and so contributed to his restlessness.[6]

The prince's idea of entering the military service of a foreign power was rejected. The king explained that the organization and methods of other armies were so different from the Prussian that little of value for the Prussian service could be learned by serving in them; also that, in spite of the prince's want of zeal for the Prussian service, which made the king doubtful of his value to another power, he still loved him too much to permit him to risk his life in such fashion. He hoped Henry would submit cheerfully; but if he would not, Frederick would still "try to go on living with him as Dr. Horsch lived with his wife." [7]

The rejection of his tentative suggestion excited the prince almost as much as if he had been in earnest about it. This and similar emotional flare-ups convinced the king that the wish for a separate establishment was still premature. "After the evidence of excitability which you have recently given me," he wrote Henry, "it would be foolish for me to let you quite out of my sight, and I tell you very frankly that I have decided not to put you on your own responsibility until I see that you have achieved the necessary steadiness and firmness of character." So, although Rheinsberg had already been given nominally to the prince and Frederick was planning a town house for him, he must continue to live in Frederick's household at Potsdam when not actually with his regiment.[8] "I am very much afraid," the king concluded, "that my letter will put the mustard up your nose, but I would rather speak frankly with

[6] Frederick, Augustus William, and Prince Ferdinand of Brunswick were also members. Fouqué, as Grand Master, "knighted" Frederick. Because of this early association and of his genuine friendship for Fouqué, Frederick in his military correspondence during the Seven Years' War often addressed him as "my friend," and wrote to him in more informal and confidential fashion than to most of his other generals, Prince Henry always excepted. Fouqué, too, was less severely censured for his surrender of Landeshut than other generals, such as Schmettau and Finck, for similar failures.

[7] *Oeuvres,* XXVI, 155–157. Cited also by Hamilton, in *Rheinsberg,* II, 8–9, and by E. Maschke, in the *Jahrbücher für die deutsche Armée und Marine,* CXVII (1900), 73–74. The king did not say whether he remembered that he had himself once tried to run away from their father's service.

[8] *P. C.,* V, 553. The prince is to be seen in this period only, as it were, in a mirror — and darkly. His image and his moods are reflected in Frederick's letters to him; but so few of his own earliest letters have been preserved that he appears at best only as a rather shadowy figure. He knew even then that he would so appear, and felt resentfully that he was constantly in the shadow because Frederick stood always between him and the light.

you than to dissimulate, and I love you none the less for it; but there must be no more such scenes as the last one; and if you wish me to have confidence in you, I must be sure and certain that you know how to behave yourself. Assuring you that I am, with affection, my dear brother, your faithful brother and servant, Federic." [9]

The prince's request that he be given a better regiment, which had probably been prompted in the first instance chiefly by his desire to be stationed in Berlin and to get away from Potsdam and the surveillance of the king, was summarily rejected with the suggestion that he devote himself more seriously to improving the one he had. That admonition was not fruitful of results, and the king put Colonel von Rohr in actual charge of the regiment, while leaving the prince nominally in command as a major general. Such treatment, however well justified, was humiliating to the prince; but the king's decision was put inexorably before him: "Sir: I have considered it proper to put some discipline into your regiment, because it was about to be ruined. I am not accountable to you for my actions. If I have had changes to make, it is because they were needed; you will need to make plenty in your own conduct; but on that matter I expect to make myself clear at some other time. That is all that I have to say to you for the present." [10]

Some estrangement naturally resulted. When their brother Prince William made an ill-advised attempt to intervene on behalf of Henry, he was effectively snubbed for his pains. But within a few weeks Henry submitted and Frederick forgave him and resumed his practice of taking him along on his tours of inspection in Silesia. [11]

Two years later, when plans for Henry's marriage were fairly well advanced and when the prince could at last look forward to setting up an independent establishment, Frederick was "much gratified" to find him "greatly changed for the better, kinder and more prudent." [12]

No doubt he was. No one could stand beside Frederick II and shine in his own light. That was a lesson his brother Henry found it hard to learn, and harder still to accept as final. So until the prince learned at least to recognize it as a condition under which he must live whether he liked it or not, Frederick did not always find it easy or comfortable to "go on living with him." Compliance is always more gratifying to a masterful person than nonconformity, especially when that person is an elder brother *in loco parentis*.

[9] *Oeuvres*, XXVI, 155–157. The letter is quoted also by Schöning, I, 48–49. The king usually signed his letters *Federic* when writing in French, *Friderich* when using German.
[10] Schöning, I, 49.
[11] Letters of July 19 and August 5, 1749, in *P. C.*, VII, 23, 42, and in Schöning, I, 49.
[12] F. to Wilhelmina of Baireuth, September 16, 1751, in *P. C.*, VIII, 451.

CHAPTER III

# Rheinsberg Reawakened

*"A wife will do him good."* — Frederick to Wilhelmina of Baireuth.

FREDERICK II never came nearer to happiness, and was never himself more attractive, than while living in Rheinsberg during his last years as crown prince. This country seat, a long day's journey over the sandy roads from Berlin, was isolated enough to insure a quiet life if that was what its occupants desired. There Frederick found more than ever before or ever again the tranquillity he said he was seeking. There, in a tastefully furnished study in a tower room overlooking a lovely lake in the woods, he wrote his *Antimachiavel*. There, too, he gathered about him a group of boon companions famous for their brilliance of wit, learning, or literary gifts — Voltaire among them. There, daily, he played the flute with his own orchestra. There, in short, in partial retirement though not quite in the wilderness, he quietly completed the process of growing up in preparation for the strenuous days and heavy responsibilities ahead.

The Schloss at Rheinsberg was really neither castle nor palace, but before and during Frederick's occupancy it was converted into an attractive country house and a good deal was done toward beautifying its grounds. Then Frederick William died; Frederick became king and turned his back upon Rheinsberg and, so it often seemed, upon the philosophical prince who had lived there; and Rheinsberg went back to sleep. To Frederick it became only a memory. To the world, it has become a symbol of the singularly sensitive, highly gifted youth who had to become a man so suddenly when Frederick, the dilettante artist and potential idealist, became king of Prussia, the cynic and realist of whom Rousseau was to say: "He thinks like a philosopher and acts like a king."

The country residence thus permanently associated with the youth of Frederick the Great was quite appropriately destined to become for half a century the home of his favorite brother Henry. There Henry also came as near to contentment and happiness as he ever did anywhere. There the younger brother continued the work of the elder, enlarging the Schloss and developing a park on the shores of the lake when, following his marriage, the place was reawakened from its twelve-year sleep and made ready for a new occupancy.[1]

---

[1] Rheinsberg is today a pleasantly situated village to which the beautiful lake and excellent resort hotels draw many summer visitors. The Schloss is still maintained as a sort

20

It is surely no fault of the Rheinsberger Schloss that neither of the illustrious marriages housed there proved to be, in the generally accepted sense, "happy." Each was a marriage of policy, urged by a king for reasons of state and entered into by a prince more for the sake of the independence that would go with a separate establishment than with any hope of romantic happiness. Each was acquiesced in, obediently and in good faith, by a princess who knew what her duty required of her when her family had arranged for her a desirable match. Each was from the beginning, psychologically, a bad matrimonial risk. It was hardly matrimony, really, and certainly not romance in either case; merely a royal marriage.

Frederick's lack of enthusiasm over his own marriage, at the time when it was decided upon by his father, is frequently ascribed to the fact that he had been encouraged by his mother and his sister Wilhelmina to entertain the idea of a more brilliant English match. His father's choice of a bride from a smaller German state was therefore both a personal disappointment to him and, in his eyes, a shameful concession to Austrian dominance in German affairs. No such plausible explanation is at hand for Prince Henry's strangely indifferent demeanor as a prospective bridegroom. Romanticists, then and later, made what they could of some reports that he was already in love with someone he could not marry. Other rumors had it that, although he was not in love with anyone, he was being forced into marriage against his will. Evidence more reliable than romantic rumor indicates only that all the initiative was taken by the king and that the prince merely complied with his brother's wishes without public protest but without apparent enthusiasm.

The prince married not for love but for liberty. As Frederick, on his marriage, had escaped from surveillance and found sanctuary in Rheinsberg, so Henry hoped to do. It was this freedom, in a court of his own, that he wanted; and he wanted it so intensely that he was willing to marry to get it. The choice of a bride was a secondary matter in which he took little active interest, since the ultimate decision rested with the king in any case; he was probably surprised to be given as much of a voice in the matter as he was. It was merely one of the many occasions on which he found it more pleasant to do what Frederick wished than to refuse.

of museum. The park is now comparatively unkempt, but its former glories are easily restored by the imagination of the visitor. Frederick was there very little after he became king, although he did live there for a time during the autumn of 1750; hence the "Rheinsberg Protocol," ostensibly of October 29 of that year.

Frederick wished him to marry. He always considered it vitally important that his brothers and nephews should safeguard the succession, as he himself had no hope of doing, by filling the family with princes; and he hoped that marriage would have a steadying influence upon Henry. He had very definite ideas also about the age at which it was best for a prince to marry; Henry, at twenty-five, had reached that age. The time had come; the prince was sent to look over a rather limited field of potential candidates, and to choose himself a bride.

The preliminary eliminations had of course been managed long before by the king and his ministers. Only German Protestant ladies of high rank and proper age were considered. Those heads of states whose daughters or nieces could qualify in these respects were then invited to submit through their foreign ministries recent portraits and minute descriptions of the young ladies under consideration. The choice was thus narrowed down to a princess of Darmstadt, who subsequently proved to be already engaged and about to be married, and the four daughters of Landgraf Maximilian, a brother of the reigning prince of Hesse-Cassel. Photographs and descriptions indicated that, in beauty, spirit, and education, the second and fourth of the princesses of Hesse-Cassel were superior to the others. The queen mother decided that either of them would do, and the king agreed.

But the prince was certainly to be consulted, although until then he had taken no part in the discussion. Within the limits prescribed, he was perfectly free to choose. Frederick insisted, in fact, that he should go on an extended tour, see something of the world, including these young ladies and such others as might come his way, and on his return indicate orally, first, that it was his wish to marry, and, second, upon whom his choice had fallen. Thus he was not to be married either against his will or to anyone not of his own choosing.[2]

On tour he went, but more as a tourist than as a prince studying the marriage market. At Düsseldorf he had an opportunity to compare works of Titian, Rubens, and Van der Werff — and liked the last best. At Cologne he found the cathedral rather impressive, but it was the rich Imperial coronation robes of the elector that really awed him. He

[2] This account is based upon the correspondence of the four royal brothers, some of it published and some unpublished; upon an extremely interesting article on Prince Henry's "Brautfahrt" by Ernst Berner, in the *Hohenzollern Jahrbücher*, VIII (1904), 75ff.; and upon entries in Count Lehndorff's diary, *Dreissig Jahre am Hofe Friedrichs des Grossen*, edited by Karl E. Schmidt-Lötzen (Gotha, 1907). The manuscripts of the unpublished portions of the correspondence are in the Brandenburg-Prussian Hausarchiv in Berlin-Charlottenburg and in the Prussian Secret State Archives in Berlin-Dahlem. Berner and Volz's *Aus der Zeit des siebenjährigen Krieges* (Berlin, 1908), hereafter cited as Berner and Volz, contains excerpts from Princess Henry's diary, and is more useful for a later period than for this. See the bibliography.

was at Cassel for more than a week and wrote long descriptions of the place and its palaces without mentioning its princesses; but as a Prussian soldier-prince he could and did comment with some condescension on the maneuvers of the Hessian troops. At Ludwigsberg it was an opera, and at Ansbach a fete in Chinese style and costumes, that seemed to him worthy of extended description. At Frankfort he went to see the Golden Bull, but not as a pious pilgrim. "One goes there in order to say one has been there. The thing in itself is not worth the trouble." [3]

Of princesses he wrote not a word. Not a sign did he give that he had so much as seen one, or that he had been either favorably or unfavorably impressed by those whom he had been sent specifically to see. Frederick may have wondered, but he betrayed no curiosity. There were two eligible princesses in Cassel; he expected Henry to choose between them; then he would send a formal request for her, which her family would not refuse. People wanted establishments, after all, for their girls as well as for their boys, and families of prominence could not afford to be romantic. It was a prince's duty to marry wisely, and he hoped that Prince Henry would sooner or later recognize the wisdom of the course planned for him, and that marriage would have a steadying effect upon him. [4]

What the young prince's hosts thought of him, and to what extent he found favor in the eyes of his future bride, are matters that would not find their way into the official correspondence, which therefore reveals no more than would have been obvious without it — that the court of Hesse-Cassel was glad to marry one of its princesses to a brother of the king of Prussia. Its minister von Borcke had made that fact plain long before the prince reached home; he reported that Henry had, after brief hesitation, decided upon the princess Wilhelmina, and that the court was eager to receive the formal marriage request. Frederick refused to send it, however, until the prince had completed his tour, seen him face to face, and told him directly of his choice. Then, "on the wings

[3] Berner, in the *Hohenzollern Jahrbücher*, VIII (1904), 80–81.
[4] *P. C.*, VIII, 408, 473. Count Kalckreuth, who as an intimate associate of the prince for many years should have been in a position to know the truth but who can certainly not be accepted as an unbiased or even as a reliable witness, gives an interesting but very unconvincing explanation of the prince's failure to mention the princess. He says that Henry was already a confirmed misogynist who was being forced reluctantly into marriage by his mother and the king and who was therefore indifferent even to the choice of a princess. *Paroles du Feldmaréchal Kalckreuth* (Paris, 1844), 311–313. Kalckreuth was adjutant to the prince in the Seven Years' War and for three years thereafter. He attained his highest military rank in the campaigns against revolutionary France. His story of the prince's choice of a bride is introduced here only because it seems unwise to dismiss unexamined any plausible theory that might shed light upon the reasons for the eventual separation of the prince and princess, which is still less than half explained, and because of Kalckreuth's own personal connection with that separation.

of love," as Frederick put it, an emissary was sent off to complete the negotiations.

Only Wilhelmina of Baireuth raised again the question of Henry's attitude toward his bride. The king curtly refused to "go any further into the subject of his love or of his indifference." [5] So the matter was settled, although it was the general impression, among his intimates and strangers alike, that the prince was for some reason strangely unhappy over his approaching marriage.

What was he worrying about? Money, for one thing. Constantly tempted by the easy credit that was offered him without the asking, he had lived beyond his income and contracted a number of debts. None of them was large, but their total was considerable. The king had repeatedly warned him that a spendthrift would find his whole life poisoned by debts, large or small. Now the prince had decided upon a refinancing operation that should consolidate his numerous obligations into one, so asked the king for permission to borrow ten thousand thaler with which to clear his slate. He thought he could repay the new loan at the rate of two hundred and fifty thaler a month. To secure his brother's approval for the proposed manipulation, he argued that he had really not been extravagant, was not in the habit of running into debt, and would not do so again.[6] Certainly the prince needed money in those days. A fine house was being made ready for him in Berlin's Wilhelmstrasse.[7] Rheinsberg also, which had been given to the prince eight years before but in which he had not yet taken up his actual residence, must be renovated and refurbished. When he had entertained the queen mother and the princess Amelia there, just before taking the field for the campaign of 1745, he had had to use borrowed cooks and servants from the king's own establishment.[8]

Now he must have cooks and servants, coaches and horses, and a court of his own. Using as a model the household already set up at Oranienburg for Prince William, he drew up for the king's approval a list of what seemed to be required: a chamberlain at 400 thaler per year, and a master of horse at 300; a household staff consisting of a secretary, four pages, two house servants, and fifteen lackeys; a kitchen force of nine, headed by a *Küchenmeister* commanding a salary equal to that of the chamberlain, and ranging thence downward to a washer of silver

---

[5] F. to Wilhelmina of Baireuth, May 29, 1752, in Berner and Volz, xi.

[6] H. to F., Potsdam, June 9, 1752, in Berner's article in the *Hohenzollern Jahrbücher*, VIII (1904), 82. Berner found the king's marginal comment on this letter "quite illegible."

[7] Sometimes known as the Graf Schwerin house. It is situated diagonally across from the modern Chancellor's Palace, and is today occupied by a branch of one of the ministries.

[8] Schöning, I, 46.

and a laundress at 40 thaler per year and a kitchen maid at 38; a cellar crew of three, at salaries of 120, 48, and 24; and for the stables and coaches twenty more men and fifty horses. Four coachmen were to be paid 66 thaler each, outriders and stable boys 60. The purchase price of the horses was not estimated, only the annual cost of maintenance being considered. Then, although the prince asked for a man whose duty it should be to provide feed for the horses, the cost of that feed, making at 4 thaler per horse per month a sum of 2,400 per year, was added to the estimate by another hand than his. Perhaps he had forgotten that mundane item; or perhaps he had left it to be looked up and filled in by a secretary. The total estimated cost of the household, in salaries alone, was 5,392 thaler; including feed for fifty horses, 7,792.[9]

Concerning one appointment the prince was surprisingly slow to act and careless in action. In a hasty note to the king he suggested the appointment of "a young Riebeck who was staying at Seegefeld" as gentleman in waiting to the princess. He himself had barely seen the candidate, but the young man was recommended by Baron Retzow, and he really hadn't time to look any further. Surely only a very indifferent or a supremely self-confident bridegroom could have been so casual about such an appointment; but all his life the prince was often equally impulsive, ill-advised, and unfortunate in his choice of members of his official household.[10]

On June 25, 1752, in the chapel of the royal palace at Charlottenburg, the marriage was solemnized before a brilliant assembly of the Prussian royal family and court and representatives of other ruling houses of northern Germany. The king had spared no expense; the setting was elegant, the costumes gorgeous, and the bride lovely. It was the groom, not she, who had the air of a lamb being led to the altar to be sacrificed. All observers were struck by the "grave and serious air" with which he made his responses and the "gloomy countenance" he had worn when he received his bride on her arrival and continued to wear at the wedding.[11]

Whatever may have been the reason for his joyless demeanor, the festivities were outwardly gay enough. For two months there was a con-

[9] The German word *Reichsthaler* or *Thaler* was used at that time as if it were the equivalent of the French *ecu*, or "crown."

[10] An entry in Lehndorff's diary, three years later, indicates that Riebeck was appointed but soon dismissed, then subsequently taken into Prince Ferdinand's court. If he did abuse his patron's confidence in some fashion, he was but one of many ill-chosen intimates who did so.

[11] *Briefwechsel der "Grossen Landgräfin" Caroline von Hessen*, edited by A. F. Walther (2 vols., Vienna, 1877), I, 171; Baron Jakob Friedrich von Bielfeld, *Lettres familières et autres* (2 vols., the Hague, 1763), I, 299; Lehndorff, *Dreissig Jahre*, 25 *et passim*.

tinuous round of dinners, operas, plays, concerts, masquerades, and garden parties. Only the bridegroom was occasionally a death's-head at the feast, and he failed only rarely to take his part in the elaborate entertainments. His own house was the scene of some of the most brilliant affairs, at which he was careful to have put in a prominent place among the decorations plaques dedicated to "the best of kings and the best of brothers."

Nor, apparently, was the bride at fault. Courtiers and other observers were unanimously enthusiastic over her wit and beauty, her charm, and her irreproachable behavior. She won Frederick's hearty approval at once and retained his friendship as long as she did that of her husband. The other brothers, too, were frankly delighted with their new sister-in-law. Prince William, especially, showed her every attention and kindness and was rewarded with sympathy and understanding even in his darkest and last days. The queen mother accepted her at once as a daughter, to such an extent as sometimes to arouse the jealousy of her own daughter, the princess Amelia.

In May of the following year, 1753, the princess Henry made her first journey to Rheinsberg to take up her residence there for the summer, and wrote to the king a very graceful and tactful note of thanks for having given that "charming spot" to the prince.[12]

In those early days the princess was tactful and prudent. When others quarreled among themselves she usually managed to remain on friendly terms with both parties. She accepted major and minor parts in theatricals with equal grace and played them well. As a hostess she did her full share in winning for the house in the Wilhelmstrasse and for Rheinsberg an enviable reputation for unobtrusive hospitality and tasteful though lavish entertainment. In public and among their guests, at any rate, she let herself be guided in her conduct by the fast-changing moods of her mercurial husband. If she was not ideally happy with him, she wore no troubles on her sleeve and was careful not to confirm the world's guesses.

The world did, to be sure, soon begin to guess. Lehndorff noted that although she was always gay and animated in conversation, her face often assumed a melancholy expression when she was alone or quiet for long. The French minister de La Touche reported that the prince was strangely indifferent to his very attractive wife. And the countess Caroline of Hesse, a very keen observer, apparently remembering (while seeming to forget) that happiness which must be proved is after all im-

---

[12] May 7. The letter, with many others that she wrote to the king or received from him, is among the papers of the princess, Rep. 56, II, T, in the Hausarchiv.

perfect, observed: "The princess Henry seems content with her lot, loved by the whole royal family and always well treated by the king. So you see, my dear sister, that she is not at all unhappy. She is just now at Rheinsberg for four months with her prince; she likes it there very much, and it is said that the prince and princess amuse themselves there very well. The princes, her brothers-in-law, go there quite often." [18]

No scandal arose involving charges of extramarital love interests on the part of either prince or princess, although there were whispers and suspicions. A certain Countess Bentinck, for example, was the object of the king's strong displeasure just at the time when the prince and princess first left Berlin for the summer at Rheinsberg. Her letters to the prince certainly reveal a greater interest in him than patriotism would seem to require a lady to feel in the brother of her sovereign, and subsequently in the prince's own house a jealous rival handed her a "lantern of Diogenes" to aid her in her quest of a man. Shortly after that the countess left Prussia. A number of extremely polite letters were exchanged between her and the prince late in life in which he referred to the "follies" and she to the "joys" of their youth; but if he wrote her any letters in those first years of his married life, they have not been preserved with the rest — which is not surprising, and perhaps just as well. Neither the fate of Prussia nor anyone's happiness, unless it were perhaps that of the Countess Bentinck, was vitally or permanently affected by the incident.

The real charge to be brought, if one is to bring a charge, against the life of the Prussian court of that period is not one of exceptional license or immorality but of mere vacuity. It was dull even in its pursuit of brightness, monotonous in its farfetched efforts at originality, repetitious in its unending quest of variety. In January the court assembled in Berlin for the "carnival" and the invariable round of opera, concerts, sleigh rides, masquerades, dinners, dances, and suppers. The king participated in only a few of the more formal of these activities. In fact any affair at which he appeared, however hilarious, was likely to become very formal indeed, and at once. The others could play better without him, as when all of them represented statues to be brought to life by a magician, or when Prince Henry danced as a slave girl in the market, or all the men masqueraded in women's clothing and vice versa. Even blindman's buff was popular for a time!

In the summer months Rheinsberg offered facilities for entertainment

---

[18] To the Duchess of Baden, June 10, 1754, in *Briefwechsel*, II, 207. The very discerning countess was herself discreet and tactful enough to remain on friendly terms with both the prince and the princess all her life.

on a grander scale. So, but less often, did the residence of Prince Augustus William at Oranienburg and that of Prince Ferdinand at Neu-Ruppin. At Rheinsberg extensive improvements were constantly under way. Rustic guest houses, pavilions, sylvan grottos, and artificial ruins were scattered in studied fashion through the woods of the extensive park. Gondolas and barges ferried guests across the lake to the island called Boberow or Remusberg, or brought on the stage the characters in a pageant.[14]

Much ingenuity went into the entertainments, and many of them were very beautiful. Servants often participated as musicians and sometimes as players of minor parts, always as stage hands and extras. Leading parts were usually taken by the princes and princesses themselves or by the ladies and gentlemen of their courts, and scenarios and dialogues were often written by them specially for the occasion. The address of Prince William, arriving by boat as an ambassador from China to the court of France — it was written by Henry, who played the part of Mazarin — was fairly clever and humorous, as was also Henry's address of indictment in a mock Inquisition. All the princes were more or less musical and usually played in the orchestra when not otherwise occupied. Henry played either violin or bass; and he and his sister Amelia sometimes composed the music.[15]

In Berlin, all went regularly to Monbijou,[16] the home of the queen mother, whose influence over her children was still strong, and who did much to hold the family together. Occasionally she attended a function at one or another of their urban residences; but it was at their periodical dinners with her that they met most often as a family. At those dinners, but rarely elsewhere, appeared with them also the queen of Prussia. When Frederick dined with his mother without the others, his wife could never be certain that she would be invited. When she was, Lehndorff accompanied her. If she could not or did not protest against this neglect, Lehndorff could and did — to the pages of his diary. "The poor queen is so delighted," he wrote on one occasion, "if she is permitted to

[14] There was an ancient legend to the effect that Remus, driven from Rome by Romulus, had found a refuge there. Both Frederick and Henry, when living there, were fond of referring to themselves as "hermits of Remusberg."

[15] It was only in this halcyon period of their youth, of course, that the prince and his family could themselves participate so actively in these performances. After the Seven Years' War, entertainment was more and more professionalized; but the prince maintained both an orchestra and a company of players, and would always produce a pageant or an opera on occasion.

[16] Now a museum and, particularly for this period in the history of the Hohenzollern family, probably the most interesting one in Berlin. Here are the table and chairs from the famous "Tobacco Parliament" of Frederick William I, countless relics of Frederick the Great and his family, one of the finest portraits of his queen, and rooms preserving faithfully the furnishings and interior decorations of the period.

have ever so small a party; and I am always pleased to see her have a moment of pleasure, she has so few."[17] Princess Henry showed the queen more consideration than the others did. Naturally she never revealed whether her conduct was prompted by instinctive kindness and sympathy, by prudence (for Frederick allowed no one but himself to slight his wife), by a premonition that she and the queen were destined to have much in common, or by the fact that they already had more in common than the world supposed. Whatever the reason, she quickly won and always kept the friendship of the queen.

The three princes were especially fond of visiting and entertaining one another. In fact, during the frequent absences of the prince the others were sometimes received by Princess Henry at Rheinsberg in the same elaborate fashion as when he was there. His military duties seem already to have been more arduous than theirs; periods of regimental duty at Potsdam and Spandau, and tours of inspection in the company of the king, often kept him away from home for extended periods.

Even at home the time was not all devoted to the pursuit of pleasure. For a long time, as an intellectual exercise, Henry and William were engaged in an elaborate war game, carried on entirely by correspondence. In 1753, writing under the pseudonym "Marshal Gessler," and ostensibly — though probably not in fact — by direct order of the king, Prince Henry drew up a number of memoranda on the situation in which Prussia would find herself if engaged in a war, with France as her ally, against the combined forces of Austria, Great Britain, and Russia. He wrote out in detail the diplomatic correspondence presumed to have taken place, general plans of operations, marching orders and battle dispositions, not only for Prussia's own army of invasion in Hanover but for the Hanoverian defense force as well, and internal administrative and military reforms which he thought necessary to strengthen Prussia for the test of battle.[18]

"Marshal Gessler's" answer to the general problem of the strategical defense of Prussia, against overwhelming odds and against attacks from

---

[17] Lehndorff, *Dreissig Jahre,* 158.

[18] There is nothing startling or especially sinister about the setting of such problems in peacetime as exercises for staff officers or prospective commanders. Plans were drawn up by designated officers, to be criticized by others. A long critique of Prince Henry's "general plan of operations" was written by an aide-de-camp, von der Goltz. In 1755 General Winterfeldt made a similarly detailed and complete plan for an invasion of Saxony. See Ludwig Mollwo, *Hans Carl von Winterfeldt* (Munich, 1899), *Beilage,* iii, and page 135; also Otto Herrmann in the *Historische Vierteljahrschrift,* XXVI (1931), 365.

It was at one time, not unnaturally, supposed that Prince Henry's "Marshal Gessler" manuscripts were actually written by order of the king, as they themselves say they were; but Herrmann and Koser agree that they were not. See Otto Herrmann, "Eine Beurteilung Friedrichs des Grossen aus dem Jahre 1753," in the *Forschungen zur brandenburgischen*

several sides at once, was the same answer Frederick found in 1757 and 1758 to the same problem—with a slightly changed line-up of friends and enemies. The inferior force, he argued, did not dare stand and await attack but must act aggressively, going to meet its enemies and destroying them separately. Prince Henry's "general plan" went into details only for the invasion of Hanover, but included specific orders for a series of operations designed to hold fast and then annihilate the Hanoverian army.[19]

The prince's ideas on military matters were at that period presumably derived very largely from his personal association with Frederick (both in war and on tours of inspection), from the teachings of his old military tutor, Colonel von Stille, and from some knowledge of the opinions of Marshals von Schwerin and von Schmettau—probably gained in conversation with those experienced officers. But both on military and on civil matters he was beginning also to have definite ideas of his own, and to dare to offer frank and not always favorable criticisms of his brother's policies. He was, after all, twenty-seven years old, a major general who had participated in the campaigns about which he wrote, and a thoughtful and patriotic prince who had at least pondered over the policies he discussed and the reforms he advocated, when he drew up his remarkable "Memoir on His Prussian Majesty's Present Situation, by Marshal de Gessler, 19th November, 1753."[20] It offered Frederick a great deal of gratuitous advice, to which he paid very little attention. Clear and penetrating at times, befogged and repetitious at others, it was a revelation of the state of its writer's mind and of his own conception of his peculiar position in the state.

The easy conquest of Silesia had been due, he wrote, only to "the valor of your troops and the promptness with which you invaded." From Mollwitz onward Frederick had "played the part of a wavering prince who seeks peace without getting it and makes war without wishing it."

*und preussischen Geschichte* (hereafter cited as *F. B. P. G.*), XXXIV (1922), 239–264, and Reinhold Koser, *Geschichte Friedrichs des Grossen* (4 vols. in 3, Stuttgart, 1912–1914), IV, 75.

There was a Prussian general named Gessler who served in the Silesian wars; but Herrmann found the "Gessler" manuscripts among the prince's papers in the archives and was convinced that they were written by no other hand than that of Prince Henry himself. Certainly the prince's writing, while difficult to read, would be still more difficult for such a scholar to mistake. The use of pseudonyms under such circumstances was also a common practice, especially among the brothers of Frederick II for their criticisms of the king and his policies. It was more fun that way, and perhaps safer, although Frederick was always so fully informed about his brothers' activities that there is little doubt that he knew all about the "Gessler" manuscripts.

[19] Prussian Secret State Archives, hereafter cited as Staatsarchiv. Cited by Otto Herrmann; see note 18.

[20] Printed by Herrmann, with an illuminating introductory article and explanatory footnotes, as "Eine Beurteilung Friedrichs des Grossen, etc." See note 18.

By his desertion of the French-Bavarian alliance he had "profited nothing save to alienate the hearts" of his allies, to "make distrustful those who saw themselves obliged to deal" with him, and to "hearten the enemy by relieving him of an adversary so formidable" as the Prussian army. As his best defense against the dangers he had created, the king ought to be cultivating the confidence of the other German princes, forming them into a compact group under his leadership, and working sedulously to strengthen the state of Prussia and mold its people into "the form of a nation."

The writing of treatises on war and government could occupy only a portion of the time and energy of a prince who aspired to the status of an intellectual. Many of his happiest hours Prince Henry spent in reading, alone or with one or two of his friends: history, philosophy, the French drama, and the classics. Group visits were made to showings of the latest imported china, drawings, and finely bound books, to a demonstration of an air-pressure pump at Oranienburg and other mechanical novelties in Berlin, and to demonstrations of surgery and lectures on anatomy by the learned doctor Lieberkühn.

So the court life of the period, which at its worst seemed so petty and spiteful that Lehndorff remarked in disgust that its people need not disguise themselves much when they dressed as apes for a masquerade, had also its better moments. When not at its best, it was insufferably dull. There was an atmosphere of unreality about it; its members moved mechanically like so many marionettes, or like child actors posturing listlessly through a rehearsal on a dimly lighted stage and only now and then remembering that they were children and running off to play at hide-and-seek in the darkened wings. Between wars, the king of Prussia had found nothing better for Prussian princes to do than to pose, to play, to parade, and to beget more princes.[21]

In such an atmosphere Prince Henry could not possibly be happy. He entertained and was entertained like the others, but he counted lost most of the hours spent in company. After years of alternating between society, in which he and his brothers worked so hard at amusing themselves, and the solitude of his study, in which he worked equally hard to improve his mind, he began often to ask himself why he should labor at either task. A sense of futility grew upon him, and misanthropic expressions fell freely from his lips and pen. He was often deeply depressed.

What purpose was served, he asked himself, by all these elaborate entertainments? No purpose at all, his mind answered, except to impress

[21] Prince Henry begat no princes.

31

the provincial princelings from the minor German states, or to serve notice upon the greater courts of Europe that the Prussian king also had an enlightened capital graced by a cultured society. And why should he strive for that? He decided that he was not interested; yet he was not free to withdraw from society, because he was a prince of the blood.

Why should he study government? He would never govern; and the memoranda he wrote, offering unwanted advice, would be read only by people whose opinions were as unimportant as his own. Why study at all? The scholarship of a prince would only be praised by sycophants and smiled at condescendingly by the intellectual aristocracy of the savants, as Frederick's poems were. Why improve himself as a soldier? If war should come again, the king would command in person as usual and reap all the glory. He decided that he was not interested; yet he was not free to withdraw from the army, because he was a prince of the blood.

Ambitious enough to be restless, unstable enough to be extremely temperamental, and not yet philosophical enough to make the best of the position in life into which he had been born, he was discontented because he was so useless, and useless because he was so discontented. In short, by midsummer of 1756 Prince Henry of Prussia was well on the way to becoming a badly baffled young man, when the outbreak of the Seven Years' War made him once more a person of some significance because the king again had need of him. The king's interest in him revived quickly enough in wartime; and both the thought and the possibility of withdrawal of any sort took wings at once, because he was a prince of the blood.

In the meantime, de La Touche was succeeded as French minister to Prussia by the Duc de Nivernois, who was shown every possible courtesy by Frederick, increasingly so as the likelihood of a breach with France increased. The Marquis de Fraigne, whom Frederick subsequently called a spy and arrested in wartime in non-Prussian territory, appeared in Berlin in a subordinate post at the French legation. The Marquis de Valori followed the unsuccessful Nivernois. The old Franco-Prussian treaty was neither renewed nor strengthened. Then the noses of the French and all their partisans were put out of joint by the Westminster Convention and the coming of Sir Andrew Mitchell to Berlin.

Without realizing it, the Prussian princes had witnessed a diplomatic revolution and a new alignment of the powers of Europe. Seeking protection against Russia, their brother had become virtually an ally of Great

Britain. Bent upon the reconquest of Silesia, Kaunitz had finally succeeded in winning France over to the side of Austria. As they interpreted such of these changes as came to their knowledge, Frederick's repeated desertion of France in the Silesian wars had at last resulted in the loss of the French alliance; but they refused to believe it irretrievably lost.

Having been, moreover, on extremely good terms with the French ministers, they did not swing over readily to the pro-British attitude which was becoming apparent at court during the early summer of 1756. Lehndorff grumbled in July because the princess Henry (prudent and politic as usual) had sat with Sir Andrew and Lord Huntington at supper, and in August that everything had been decided between the king and the British minister without the knowledge of the Prussian ministers or princes. But the princes themselves clung to their French friends and their preference for a French alliance.[22]

The "princes of the blood" had been handled as the king's political testament had stated four years before that they should be. They had been generously supported in a glittering but half-idle existence that left them abundant time for quite idle speculation upon the state secrets which were carefully concealed from them, and for irresponsible criticism of policies the backgrounds of which they did not know and in the determination of which they had not shared. The war, however, was an experience in which, as Prussian princes, they were expected as a matter of course to share, even though they considered that war unnecessary, unwise, and in fact suicidal for the state. Whether any of them would prove to possess the qualities of mind and character which alone, according to that same *Testament Politique,* would warrant trusting him with the command of troops, and whether loyalty to the family traditions of obedience and service could triumph over such opinions of the cause in which they were called upon to serve, remained to be seen.

[22] Lehndorff, *Dreissig Jahre*, 270. Mitchell Papers (British Museum, additional manuscripts 6802 to 6871 and 11260 to 11262), I, 53. Some of the Mitchell letters were edited and printed by Andrew Bisset as *Memoirs and Papers of Sir Andrew Mitchell, K. B.* (2 vols., London, 1850). These will hereafter be cited as Bisset and unpublished ones in the British Museum collection as M. P. Many of them are also quoted at length by the editors of the *Politische Correspondenz Friedrichs des Grossen.*

CHAPTER IV

# 𝔗𝔥𝔢 𝔊𝔯𝔢𝔞𝔱 𝔗𝔢𝔰𝔱𝔦𝔫𝔤 𝔗𝔦𝔪𝔢

*"You then profited nothing but to alienate the hearts of your
allies and to make distrustful those who see themselves obliged
to deal with you."* — Henry to Frederick, 1753.

AN AUTOCRAT who at the beginning of his reign had pointed out to his
ministers that he possessed just then some real advantages over the archduchess of Austria and queen of Hungary, and had asked himself and
them only the rhetorical question, in effect, "Do I use this opportunity in
Silesia or do I not?" could have answered in only one way the question
that confronted the king of Prussia in the summer of 1756. Frederick
thought that, sooner or later, he must fight again for the possession of
Silesia. Therefore he chose to anticipate his enemies by seizing the initiative and assuming the offensive. His brothers thought that the war was
neither inevitable nor wise, so they tried hard through intermediaries to
dissuade him from it. Augustus William, as Prince of Prussia, tactlessly
revealed that one of his reasons for opposing it was his objection to seeing
the future inheritance of his son so put to hazard. Yet when the troops
marched out the princes marched with them, albeit without enthusiasm
or hope of victory.

The king may have thought that the war was imposed upon him by
the enmity of his neighbors; but he was surely not pushed into it by his
family or his friends.[1] The British minister Sir Andrew Mitchell reported
to his government several conversations in which Frederick represented
himself as affronted and threatened by Austria. To what extent the king
was emboldened by his treaty with Britain Mitchell could not judge, although he said he had sought to exert a moderating and restraining influence.

On one occasion Frederick exclaimed to Mitchell: "How now, Sir?
What do you see in my face? Do you think my nose was made to be
tweaked? By God, Sir, I'll not stand for it!" The Scotsman replied that
he thought no one would really be rash enough to threaten His Prussian
Majesty. If any affront were offered, his character was too well known

---

[1] The princes believed that he was pushed or tricked into it by his favorite general,
Winterfeldt; but that weird notion seems to merit no consideration except as an illustration
of the peculiar psychology of the princes and a partial explanation of their offish attitude.
See Albert Naudé, "Aus ungedruckten Memoiren der Brüder Friedrichs des Grossen,"
*F. B. P. G.,* I (1888), 231ff.

in Europe to leave anyone in doubt as to the manner in which the offense would be resented. The king of Prussia was justly famous for many great qualities; but Mitchell had never heard either patience or forbearance mentioned among the number. Frederick accepted the sally good-naturedly, but pointed to a picture of Maria Theresa and said, "There's no help for it. That lady wants war." [2]

In July Frederick claimed knowledge of an Austro-Russian plan to attack him as soon as the necessary preparations could be completed, probably in the spring of 1757.[3] Mitchell suggested that before declaring war he demand an explanation from Maria Theresa. If she failed to reply satisfactorily, he would be vindicated in the eyes of the world, and Great Britain would be put in a much better position to attempt to restrain Russia.[4] Frederick at first refused to expose himself to the danger of an insulting reply, although Mitchell argued that the haughtier the response the better. The king still refused, then did as urged, and got an answer which Mitchell called inoffensive and he himself called unsatisfactory.

So it was largely a matter of timing. If the campaign started as early as August 1, the king said, the French would still have time to occupy Hanover that autumn and take up winter quarters there; so he would wait. On August 27 he told Mitchell he would wait no longer. He did not say, and had not said, that he was going through Saxony. Mitchell learned that only from an advance copy of his manifesto.[5]

For the Prussians to go through Saxony for their invasions of Bohemia in 1756–57 was as logical as for the Germans to go through Belgium into France in 1914, and had many of the same imponderables to be weighed against it. Saxony was in the way, as Belgium was. The Elbe was vitally necessary for transport, as were the roads and railways of Belgium. Topography argued powerfully in favor of such a course in both cases, and the ostensible aggressor dared not gamble upon the continued neutrality of the ostensible victim in either. In each, the invader drew upon himself the charge of unprovoked aggression, consolidated the opposition, and made new enemies for himself.

What Saxon traitor sold the secrets of his government, by what high-handed methods Frederick seized the Saxon archives, how fully their contents confirmed what his spies had already told him, are matters of which the king has written his own official record and on which he has

[2] M. P., I, 29.
[3] Letter to Knyphausen, in *P. C.*, XIII, 115.
[4] Frederick had hoped that his Treaty of Westminster with Great Britain would insure Prussia against attack by Russia. Mitchell reported to Holdernesse on August 20 that he believed that a declaration by the British ambassador at St. Petersburg had actually restrained Russia from declaring war. Bisset, I, 200.
[5] M. P., I, 31–36.

of course been challenged by his critics. The facts essential to a study of his relations with Prince Henry are that he went into Saxony at the end of August, 1756, and that his brothers, who were among his critics, went with him.[6]

Even his nephews, the little sons of the Prince of Prussia, would have gone with him had they been permitted. According to Lehndorff the elder of them, the future King Frederick William II, was deeply chagrined when the king told him he must "stay at home and mind the dogs." No one knew then that the war would last long enough for both of those boys to see something of it before it was done. They were left behind under the care of their mother and their tutors; the provision had already been made that, in the event that both king and their father should die in the war, Prince Henry should become regent and their guardian during their minority.[7]

Saxony was not occupied without opposition; but the Saxon troops were soon rounded up and compelled to surrender at Pirna. Many of them were taken into the Prussian service, by agreement with the elector, although their officers were not to be required to serve against their will and were given no responsible commands.[8] Except for a brief incursion into Bohemia, where the battle of Lobositz was fought and won on October 1, the campaign was confined for that year to Saxony.

That was enough. The Prussians had occupied territory which was to be useful to them, though difficult to defend, throughout the war. But the Treaty of Versailles soon proved to be effective as a French-Austrian alliance, and Valori was recalled from Berlin. Frederick instructed Knyphausen to come home from Paris without taking leave. "If they want to be my enemies, very well; it is they themselves who have willed it." [9]

[6] In the library of the Berliner Schloss is a set of the posthumous works of Frederick the Great (1788 edition), several volumes of which bear numerous marginal notations in the unmistakable but almost illegible handwriting of Prince Henry. Internal evidence indicates that they were written about 1793 or 1794, although Volz dates them 1788. See his "Prinz Heinrich als Kritiker Friedrichs des Grossen," in the *Historische Vierteljahrschrift*, XXVII (1932), 392. As that was one of the most embittered periods of the prince's life, the comments are extremely caustic. Such words as "false," "liar," "heroics," and "misleading" are often used. Concerning the king's account of the origins of this war in his *Histoire de mon temps*, the prince's comments, assembled and summarized, would be about as follows: "The king was duped and pushed into the war by Winterfeldt. The treaties which he calls threats to the safety of Prussia were defensive only. He says himself that no one planned to attack him that year. He should have waited. It was his ambition and Winterfeldt's which provoked an unnecessary war." It is interesting to note that the prince worried no more than the king himself over the awful charge of being the aggressor.

[7] By the *Tutelar-Disposition* of August 15, 1756, in *P. C.*, supplementary volume (1920), xi. The younger of the princes, also named Henry, was an extremely attractive youth, universally popular, and a great favorite of the king. His early death saddened Frederick greatly.

[8] Mitchell to Holdernesse, in Bisset, I, 209–212.

[9] *P. C.*, XIII, 581–583.

Mitchell obligingly sent home a "memoir to justify the conduct of the king against the false imputations of the court of Saxony," and a "reasoned memoir on the conduct of the courts of Vienna and of Saxony," which he said were based upon "the papers taken from the Saxon archives." [10] But while such justification might be sufficient to satisfy an ally, the enemies of the king of Prussia naturally found it unconvincing.

All three of the Prussian princes and the queen's brother Ferdinand of Brunswick commanded troops in the Saxon campaign, but in subordinate capacities and with trusted professional soldiers beside them as staff officers. Prince Henry so commanded a brigade on the march into Saxony and at the siege of Pirna, and witnessed there the surrender of the Saxons.[11] In December he was off for a time on the Bohemian border with a part of the corps of the Duke of Bevern; but during most of the autumn and winter he was with the king in Dresden, quartered in the house of the Saxon minister, Count Brühl.

That was a gay and comfortable winter for those of high rank in the Prussian army. Soon many wives of officers were on their way to spend the winter with their husbands in Dresden. The princes did not avail themselves of the privilege of bringing their wives on, but sent home presents of porcelain and long epistolary accounts of one another's doings.

One outstanding event of the winter was that Frederick went to church, attending a service in the cathedral in Dresden. The whole family was agog for a time over the incident, the pious queen being especially eager to secure a copy of the sermon preached on that memorable occasion. Several copies were sent by her brother Ferdinand and others.

In January, 1757, for the only time during the war, the king went back to Berlin. He was accompanied by Prince Henry and stayed for a week. On the last day of their visit the other brothers arrived for a stay of about a month; so on January 11 the queen mother saw all four of her soldier sons together for the last time.

That was indeed a joyless visit, for there was even more reason for concern over the health of the mother than over the safety of her sons. The populace saw nothing of its king and little of his brothers; and Prince Henry's was not a romantic homecoming.[12]

[10] Mitchell to Holdernesse, in Bisset, I, 216.

[11] His correspondence with the king during that period was concerned chiefly with the choice of a new adjutant for himself, Count Henckel von Donnersmarck. He eventually had his way in the matter, in spite of some patient objection on the part of the king. Subsequently he quarreled with Henckel and chose Kalckreuth, also against the king's advice. Both of these adjutants wrote memoirs in which they did him something less than justice, although he was eventually reconciled with both and the family of Henckel owed much to his lifelong generosity.

[12] His papers contain no record of it, so the romanticist might hopefully make the best

The princess recorded in her journal that she was overjoyed but taken entirely by surprise when the king and her husband, coming directly to their mother's residence, found her there by chance. Thereafter, through the whole week, the prince neither avoided her nor sought her company in preference to that of other members of the court. On the fifth day of his visit she received a bag of brilliants as a gift from him. Early on the seventh he came to her home with his brothers, who had arrived during the night from Dresden and hurried in the morning to greet her. The next day his messenger brought her a letter from him saying that he had left with the king at seven for Potsdam. She had known, to be sure, that he was about to go. Under date of January 10 there is an entry in her journal to the effect that her heart was breaking at the thought of a second separation, after eight days of happiness in seeing the man who was the joy of her life. Yes, she had seen him; but that was about all.

If her diary is a faithful record, however, she could still sympathize with the queen mother. And who could not? Sophia Dorothea was old and ill, and her last leave-taking from her sons was hard, even for so Spartan a mother as she had learned to be. Princess Henry witnessed it, and wrote: "What an awful scene, to see that venerable woman weep! She said to me: 'My dear child, I must depend entirely upon you now. You will be my only consolation.'— My heart was so touched that I could not say a word in reply, but left at once to come home and give free utterance to my own affliction, which is extreme." [13]

With one short preliminary campaign behind them, and knowing that the real test would come with the spring, the princes naturally spent some of their leisure time during the winter in self-appraisal and in revising their estimates of one another. Who had earned promotion? Who would be promoted? Frederick did not at once commit himself; but it

of his silence if the diaries of Lehndorff and the princess Henry were equally reticent; but they are not. Long fragments from the journal of the princess are printed in Berner and Volz. The editors say that it was written by her own hand, but evidently rewritten and revised from time to time. It also gives evidence now and then of having been written for self-justification as well as for self-expression. Some of the entries were obviously not written on the day of the incident to which they refer; so she may have interpolated any number of afterthoughts, more or less in self-defense.

[13] Berner and Volz, 19. The queen mother was not just then on speaking terms with her daughter Amelia, who, although she had become abbess of Quedlinburg, still spent most of her time with the others in Berlin or Magdeburg. The queen mother's feelings, with all four of her sons facing death on the battlefield while she herself faced it at home, may well be imagined from her expression of relief when she had learned that the three older ones were all safe after Hohenfriedberg in 1745. Thanking Frederick especially for the thoughtfulness which had prompted him to have William and Henry sign with him his first letter after the battle, she wrote: "At this moment I am the happiest mother in the world. I feel as if a stone had been lifted off my heart." *Oeuvres de Frédéric le Grand* (1855 edition), XXVI, 84.

was plain that Prince William was already jealous of him, and disgruntled because he had had so little opportunity to show what he could do.[14] Prince Henry and Ferdinand of Brunswick, on the other hand, were already looked upon as the "coming men" of the group. Both showed plenty of self-confidence and optimism as to their own future; and the two were rapidly developing a strong feeling of mutual admiration and confidence, although Ferdinand had a very low opinion of Henry's entourage.

Troops fortified themselves after a fashion in one position after another, in the Seven Years' War, but did not dig themselves in on a fixed line or attempt to hold a continuous front anywhere. The war was largely one of movement in which swift marching, skillful choice of ground, and the successful solution of the ever-present problem of supply or the disruption of the enemy supply system often played a part almost as important as actual fighting, and were sometimes more productive of permanent results. The Prussians possessed the advantage of fighting on interior lines; but throughout the war they were so overwhelmingly outnumbered that they were constantly forced to utilize that advantage to the utmost, attempting to multiply their own numbers by shifting their forces to parry enemy thrusts first from one side and then from another. It was also to some extent an advantage for them that they were fighting in general on the defensive, and sometimes a triumph for them if they could merely survive by holding grimly on to well-chosen and impregnable positions.[15]

Most of the campaigning was done in the southern and eastern parts of electoral Saxony (for the southeastern district of which the regional name of Lusatia was often used), in northern Bohemia, in Silesia, and

[14] This attitude is especially apparent in his letters to Princess Henry. See Berner and Volz, *passim*.

[15] It would be possible to follow faithfully the footsteps of either the king or Prince Henry right through the war; for their truly tremendous correspondence has been so carefully preserved and edited that it is not difficult to locate either of them on practically any day or night. Schöning's *Militärische Correspondenz* contains letters of both the king and the prince, and some to and from other generals. The *Politische Correspondenz* contains only a few of the prince's letters but all of the king's to him, instructions to other commanders, diplomatic correspondence, and many of Sir Andrew Mitchell's reports. Originals and drafts are in the Hausarchiv and the Staatsarchiv. In addition to the manuscript collections and published correspondence (including Mitchell's in both cases), and biographies of Frederick II, particularly Reinhold Koser's *Geschichte Friedrichs des Grossen*, general accounts such as the official history of the war by the military history section of the German General Staff, *Der siebenjährige Krieg* (13 vols., Berlin, 1901–1914); Kurd W. Schäfer's *Der siebenjährige Krieg, nach der Original-Correspondenz Friedrichs des Grossen mit dem Prinzen Heinrich und seinen Generalen* (Berlin, 1859); Curt Jany's *Geschichte der Königlichen Preussischen Armee bis zum Jahre 1807* (3 vols., Berlin, 1929); and numerous special articles have been drawn upon for this account of the war.

in the rough country of the Silesian-Bohemian border.[16] The campaigning did, to be sure, often range far afield from those areas. Prince Henry often pushed his raiders far to the south and west, once even to the valley of the Main. Rossbach was miles away to the west in electoral Saxony, beyond Leipzig; Zorndorf and Kunersdorf were beyond the Oder east of Berlin, and Olmütz in Moravia. There were also campaigns in northern and northeastern Germany against the Russians and the Swedes, and that of Prince Ferdinand of Brunswick against the French in defense of Hanover and northwestern Germany; but the real center of interest was always where the king was or where Prince Henry served as his deputy.

From the Prussian point of view, the principal objectives of the war in 1757 and 1758 were the conquest of Bohemia, the continued occupation of Saxony, the defense of Silesia, and the repulse of Russian and Swedish invasions. After 1758, invasions of enemy territory except by raiding expeditions could scarcely be considered, and the efforts of the Prussians were concentrated more and more on retaining Silesia permanently, and as much as they could of Saxony for the duration of the war, while keeping the Mark of Brandenburg as free as possible from devastation. Sometimes, especially during the last three years of the war, their immediate war aims had to be more modest than that: merely to keep the field with forces too formidable or in positions too easily defensible to invite attack, and thus to hang on until their enemies were ready to make peace.

The Saxon campaigns were fought on both banks of the Elbe, with Dresden as their natural center. Pirna is on the Elbe above Dresden, near the Bohemian border, and Lobositz farther up, half-way from that border to the city of Prague. Torgau and Wittenberg are below Dresden on the same river, Maxen and Freiberg off in the hills to the south and southwest of the city, and Hochkirch well to the east, near the headwaters of the Spree. Görlitz, Zittau, and Lauban are in Upper (southeastern) Lusatia, Sagan farther north on the Bober, all vitally important for communication between the forces operating in Saxony and those in Silesia. Glogau and Breslau, on the Oder, were then the principal cities of Silesia, but they were usually protected by fortified towns nearer the Bohemian border, such as Landeshut or Schweidnitz.[17]

[16] See the end-paper map.

[17] This explanation, and frequent references to the map, should make it easier to follow the movements of the king and of Prince Henry, in so far as they are chronicled. The necessity of following these individuals through the war, as if they had fought it in person, will be readily apparent when it is pointed out that, except for the victories of the composite force under Prince Ferdinand of Brunswick, no battle of any major importance was won

## The Great Testing Time

In the spring of 1757 the war at once took on larger proportions. By then Great Britain and Prussia had converted the Westminster Convention into a virtual alliance; but in the meantime the Regensburg (Ratisbon) Diet of the Holy Roman Empire of the German People had declared war upon Prussia as a recalcitrant member. Frederick habitually scoffed at the "so-called army" of the Imperial states; but it was nonetheless inconvenient to have them as enemies. An Austro-Russian alliance had been completed in January, 1757, under the terms of which each of those powers agreed to keep eighty thousand men constantly in the field against him, to make no separate peace, and to make no peace at all until Silesia and Glatz had been secured to Austria by treaty. In March Frederick's sister Ulrika, queen of Sweden, saw her adopted country also join the enemies of her native state.

To the king of Prussia, thus compassed about by enemies, it seemed suicidal to wait for those enemies to unite in action against him. It was more in accord with his natural instincts, moreover, to go to seek his foe, scorning to wait and be sought. If he could deal with their numerous armies one at a time, so much the better. As soon as the season warranted it, therefore, he again invaded Bohemia.

By May 6 his men were approaching Prague, where on that date they won a great battle, although the victory brought them no advantage that was worth the price they had to pay for it. The Austrian army was defeated but not destroyed, and was driven into the city but not away from it. Prague itself was not quite surrounded; so neither army nor city could be compelled at once to surrender. The cost of that partial success was tremendous. On that day, as Frederick said, fell the pillars of the Prussian infantry, which the wastage of war made it impossible to rear anew; and that day fell also good, dependable old Schwerin, who had done so much to strengthen those pillars before Frederick became king, and to help him win many of the earlier battles upon which his reputation as a soldier had been built.

As far as Prague, in that campaign, all the king's brothers accompanied him. Newly promoted to the rank of lieutenant general, Prince Henry had enjoyed that spring his first independent commands. In the middle of April he was sent with a small force, chiefly as a demonstration to divert enemy attention from more important operations under Schwerin, to occupy Neustadt for a few days; but he sent to Frederick, as always afterward, all the information he could get about enemy forces and arrangements, including notations indicating which of these reports

by the armies of Prussia during the whole war except under the immediate personal command of the king himself or of Prince Henry.

he himself did not consider credible or reliable; and he brought back all he could carry of the beef, beer, grain, and forage which he forced the inhabitants of the district to supply.[18]

On the march to Prague Prince Henry commanded one of the Prussian columns. In the battle of May 6 he showed great personal intrepidity by placing himself at the head of the Itzenplitz regiment, plunging into and across a deep ditch partly filled with water, and on up the heights of Hloutepin, to play what the king generously called a decisive part in the fighting on the Prussian right wing.

The issue of the battle was not really decided on that wing, nor that of the whole campaign on that day; but it was a great event in the life of the prince, one never to be forgotten. It won him the praise of all. The king neglected no opportunity to proclaim that "Henry had done wonders," and Mitchell so reported to his government. His brother William, who frankly admitted that he himself was happy not to have been present at that "party," wrote to Princess Henry on May 10, "The officers admire him and the soldiers swear only by him. Heaven be praised that he survived. It is a miracle." [19]

To Kolin, south and east of Prague, Frederick went alone; all three of his brothers and Ferdinand of Brunswick stayed with the troops around Prague. Near Kolin, on June 18, in a series of stubborn attacks upon an enemy whose quality and numbers he had underestimated and the strength of whose position he had refused to consider — scorning the easier way of barring the road and waiting to be attacked — the headlong king smashed to pieces the comparatively small force with which he had gone out to prevent the relief of Prague by an Austrian army under Marshal Daun. He was to have much to do with Daun in the next few years. Having learned this day to respect that officer's ability as a defensive fighter, he had still to learn at Hochkirch more than a year later that Daun could also attack.

As he had gone alone to Kolin, so he stood alone, morally, after his first defeat. Mitchell, with the besieging army at Prague, noted that the atmosphere there was one of discouragement, discontent, and foreboding, and that the king's conduct of the campaign was openly and bitterly criticized. The unnamed critics could scarcely have been anyone else than

---

[18] Schöning, I, 65–66; *P. C.*, XIV, 516. Prince Henry's promotion had been predicted with evident pleasure by Ferdinand of Brunswick to his sister the queen of Prussia, and reported with coldly formal politeness but with no apparent enthusiasm by the Prince of Prussia to his sister-in-law the princess Henry. Although Augustus William was already a lieutenant general, the rank of general was still open to him; but the king did not see fit to advance him to it, and his disappointment made it hard for him to appear pleased even at the promotion of Henry. Berner and Volz, 403, 277.

[19] Berner and Volz, 297.

the four princes and perhaps Marshal Keith.[20] William, the Prince of Prussia, had constantly and openly predicted disaster, and seemed almost pleased when his prophecies were fulfilled. Henry wrote to his sister Amelia: "Phaeton has fallen, and we know not what will become of us. The day of the eighteenth will forever be an unhappy one for Prussia. Phaeton took good care of his own person, before the loss of the battle was fully decided." [21] That last gratuitous insinuation was entirely unfair and unjustifiable; for the king had actually exposed himself to danger far more than a responsible commander should.

How much Frederick knew about all this backbiting criticism and open pessimism, he did not reveal; but he could not have been entirely unaware of it. It must have hurt him; but in spite of that, or because of it, he required his brothers to accept more responsibility in the retreat which followed.

The defeat at Kolin was more decisive of subsequent events than the victory at Prague. The siege of Prague was abandoned and a general withdrawal from Bohemia began at once. Frederick himself was terribly downcast and almost ready to collapse when, after an exhausting ride from the battlefield of Kolin, he reached the Prussian headquarters before Prague on June 19. As he passed through the camp, although he maintained the best possible countenance, his appearance confirmed the bad news which Captain Grant had brought the night before. Inside his quarters, he at once threw himself down to rest, saying repeatedly that he wished he could die. He was able therefore only to approve without change the dispositions already made by Prince Henry, and left the active command of the retreating forces largely to him, Marshal Keith, and Prince William. The successful conduct of the retreat of the main body of the Prussian army down the valley of the Elbe to Pirna in Saxony was principally the work of Prince Henry, who was personally in command of the column moving along the right bank.[22] The king himself accom-

---

[20] Bisset, I, 352–354.

[21] E. Maschke, in the *Jahrbücher für die deutsche Armée und Marine,* CXVII (1900), 81; G. B. Volz, in the *Historische Vierteljahrschrift,* XXVII (1932), 391. This letter was captured by the Austrians and was printed from the Austrian archives by Alfred von Arneth, in his *Geschichte Maria Theresias,* V, 502 (Vienna, 1875).

[22] Frederick, in his *Histoire du guerre de sept ans,* says that the king himself made the dispositions. The prince's marginal comment in the Berliner Schloss copy of the *Oeuvres posthumes* is: "The king did nothing at Prague. No order or disposition was given by him." Cf. note 6. See also Koser, *Geschichte Friedrichs des Grossen,* II, 501–502.

Henri de Catt, Frederick's Swiss "reader" who lived at headquarters from 1758 onward as a sort of literary secretary and companion to the king, is one of those who give Prince Henry all the credit for the success of the withdrawal. He says that Frederick was quite incapacitated upon his return from Kolin, and entirely dependent upon the prince. But de Catt was not an eyewitness of that incident. He did not join the king's suite until the year after it happened. His story of the retreat is based upon a tale told him by a "well-informed

panied that column. Wherever he went, he no doubt kept an eye upon troop movements, and he was seeing his deputy commander every day; but he was too well pleased with the prince's work to interfere with it.[23]

It could not be said that the king was equally well pleased with the work of his other brother, Prince William. That unhappy man had at last been given an important command, but under extremely difficult circumstances. His troops included those that had been defeated at Kolin. Their morale was low, their discipline bad, and their cohesiveness and fighting qualities, temporarily at least, far below standard. With the prince, nominally as a subordinate but actually either as mentor or as a sort of deputy on mission, went General Winterfeldt, whom he bitterly hated and who he knew was constantly sending unfriendly reports directly to the king. General Schmettau was there, and he was the prince's trusted friend; but Schmettau disliked and distrusted Winterfeldt as much as William did, so there were quarrels and differences of opinion when the prince sought the counsel of the generals who should have been his advisers. The king himself bombarded him with admonitions and warnings which had little effect except to convince him that he was being persecuted and that Frederick was bent upon his ruin.

The prince's mission would in any case have been a difficult one. He was to withdraw with his corps into Lusatia in such a manner as to hold that region open for free communication and passage of troops between Saxony and Silesia. Actually, by want of vigilance and of resolution, he permitted himself to be cut off from both, lost enormous quantities of equipment and supplies in his precipitate retreat, and had in hand only a sadly demoralized and shattered force when the king at last removed him from command.[24]

That removal was, no doubt, amply justified and in fact inevitable under the circumstances. The brusqueness with which it was carried out

Prussian officer" during the black period following Finck's surrender at Maxen in 1759, when Frederick's personal popularity in the army was at its lowest ebb and Prince Henry's prestige at its highest. De Catt's narrative of his conversations with the officer is interpolated, both in his diary and in his memoirs, into his account of his experiences of December, 1759. See R. Koser, "Unterhaltungen mit Friedrich dem Grossen: Memoiren von Heinrich de Catt, Tagebücher von Heinrich de Catt," in *Publicationen aus den königlichen preussischen Staatsarchiven*, XXII, 279, 415. Cited hereafter as Koser, "Unterhaltungen."

[23] The king's mind and time were just then very much engrossed by diplomatic questions and correspondence. Preoccupation, rather than depression following defeat, was probably responsible for his leaving to subordinates so much more than usual of the direction of a military operation.

[24] Cf. Mitchell's journal, in Bisset, I, 361. Frederick also wrote to Marshal Keith: "If I do not hasten my march, I shall never overtake my brother; I believe they will run right to Berlin." July 27, in *P. C.*, XV, 280. The prince's troops, after his dismissal, were quarantined away from the others as if they were unclean or infected with some epidemic disease.

would be less easy to defend. The unfortunate prince was publicly disgraced. The king refused to speak to him, but sent an adjutant to tell him in the presence of his officers that, while as a general he deserved to lose his head, as the king's brother he would be let off with dismissal from his command. When he demanded a full investigation of his conduct, it was refused. When he sought permission to go to Dresden to rest and regain his health, he was told bluntly but indirectly that he might go where he would. The king had done with him.

He had already been told by letter that he would never be anything but a pitiable sort of general who knew neither what he was doing nor what he wanted. He might be qualified to handle a harem of court ladies, but never again while Frederick lived would he be trusted with the command of as many as ten men. If the king were dead, he might commit what follies he would; the responsibility would then be his own; but meanwhile he would have no further opportunity to ruin the state, or the army's reputation, or Frederick's.[25]

One of the fairest estimates of the prince's character had been written only a few weeks before by the king himself: "My brother has courage, is well instructed, and has the best heart in the world, but no resolution. With that, he is much given to worry and inclined to avoid the making of positive decisions."[26] Frederick never explained to anyone why such a man was given so important and so difficult a command, or why he was permitted to ruin his own reputation and an army before he was removed from it.

Yet up to that time one of William's chief grounds for complaint had been that he, the senior Prussian prince, had been given no responsible commands in which he could display his ability, while others junior to him in military rank had been given every opportunity. Furthermore, of his seniors in rank, Keith was being used elsewhere; and there was no reason to suppose that the margrave Karl of Schwedt would do any better than the Prince of Prussia. Marshal Schwerin would have been quite capable either of commanding that army or of serving in it as the prince's loyal subordinate and adviser, in spite of his age and military seniority; but good old Schwerin was dead. So, if he had not failed, the prince would have seemed quite the logical man for the place.

He was the logical man for the place, but not the right one. He was, and had been all along, obsessed by the idea that he was being saddled with the king's own mistakes and would be publicly blamed for the fail-

[25] July 19, 1757, in *P. C.*, XV, 257–258.
[26] Quoted in German by Maschke, in the *Jahrbücher für die deutsche Armée und Marine*, CXVII (1900), 73–74.

ure of the whole campaign. His lack of resolution in the field was equalled only by his complete want of dignity, reserve, or common prudence in public or private conversation or in correspondence. He did not bear his trials with fortitude nor his disgrace with dignity, but complained constantly and querulously of illness, fatigue, injustice, and Frederick's determination to ruin him.[27]

The king soon recovered his dignity and a certain degree of equanimity; but he never changed his opinion of the prince's conduct nor apologized to any one for his dismissal. On the day after that painful incident he wrote: "You have by your bad conduct brought my affairs into a desperate state; it is not my enemies who are destroying me, but the unwise measures you have taken. My generals are not to be excused, either for having counseled you badly or for having permitted you to make such mistakes. Your ears are accustomed only to the language of flatterers; Daun has not flattered you, and you see the consequences. . . . I say nothing against your heart, but charge you with ineptitude and bad judgment. . . . The misfortune which I foresee is partly your fault. You and your children will suffer the penalty more than I. Believe me, in spite of that, I have always loved you, and I shall die with the same feeling." [28]

Still complaining of bad health, writing to the princess Henry that he could not play a minuet on the cello without being as completely exhausted as a woodchopper, the prince stayed on in Dresden, Torgau, Wittenberg, and Leipzig until the middle of November, failing to act upon Prince Henry's suggestion that he try to redeem his personal reputation by appearing as a volunteer at the battle of Rossbach.

The younger brother had that time guessed rightly the temper of the king. Frederick wrote later to William that, while he would never again trust him with the command of an army unless he "had one too many," still not even a Prince of Prussia should find it in any way dishonorable to serve in one commanded by the king himself. Instead, he said scornfully, the prince chose to go to Berlin, where he could probably save

---

[27] See his numerous letters to Princess Henry, written both before and after his dismissal, in Berner and Volz, 305, 306, *et passim*. The princess Henry, although sympathetic, counseled him as best she could against such despair and imprudence, and against further precipitate action after he left the army. His sisters Amelia and Ulrika strongly disapproved his conduct, and lectured him for it by letter, as did practically all the family except Prince Henry and his brother Ferdinand. See also Koser, *Geschichte Friedrichs des Grossen*, II, 508–513, and Mitchell's journal in Bisset, I, 362–363. Mitchell had to dissuade the prince from publishing a defense of his conduct, which would inevitably have been also a denunciation of the king and have made the quarrel public, both at home and abroad. It was already a matter of common knowledge among the senior army officers, which was bad enough.

[28] *P. C.*, XV, 281–282.

himself from capture by some raiding party only by hiding in a fortress along with the women. "A fine role for the heir presumptive to a throne!" The king said he wished that his relatives might set others an example of constancy and honor, not one of cowardice! [29]

Nevertheless the prince returned to Berlin, dividing his time thereafter between the city and his residence at Oranienburg.[30] There he brought himself to write the king a letter of congratulation upon the victory at Leuthen. To that overture Frederick replied that he did not doubt the sincerity of his felicitations, but wished that the prince had chosen to be present and share in the victory instead of sulking in Oranienburg.[31]

It was unkind to accuse the prince of sulking. At the same time it is equally unfair to Frederick to say, as his hostile critics habitually do, that the brokenhearted prince went into hiding and died of chagrin because he could not endure his disgrace or the king's displeasure. Of course the prince was unhappy; but he lived until June 12, 1758, his demeanor indicating more anger than grief — then died of natural causes much more convincing than a broken heart. The queen wrote to her brother Ferdinand of Brunswick that he had had a stroke, following a high fever.[32] Lehndorff and the princess Henry recorded in their journals that a post-mortem examination had revealed a growth on his brain. That may have been a contributory cause of his failure as a soldier, as well as of his death.[33]

[29] *Ibid.,* 297–298.

[30] At the time of his departure from Leipzig, Mitchell described him as "much mended" in health. M. P., IV, 1. Prince Henry subsequently told their brother Ferdinand that Frederick had refused the complaining prince the services of the staff surgeon, Cothenius — which, on the eve of the battle of Rossbach, would have been surprising and unjustifiable only to a man as biased as Henry then was. Hausarchiv, Rep. 56, II, F.

[31] *P. C.,* XVI, 100–101. Prince Ferdinand of Prussia, newly promoted to the rank of lieutenant general, was at Leuthen and was praised by the king for his conduct. He had told Prince Henry that he intended to leave the service at the end of that year. After Leuthen, he decided not to retire after all, but he saw very little action in 1758 and none thereafter.

[32] Berner and Volz, 416. A month before he died the prince wrote to Prince Henry's former adjutant, Count Henckel von Donnersmarck: "Never believe that I have any thought of returning to my regiment. No, so long as the glorious reign of the [present] king shall last, I count myself as stricken off the list of those who labor to enhance his military reputation. I may have lost an opportunity to lay the foundation of my own; or perhaps destiny has done me a favor by getting me out of a situation where I should have exposed all my ignorance and incapacity. Be that as it may, here I am in retirement where I am making myself quite comfortable. Sometimes I think of the shame of being thus exiled and useless; but being convinced that I am in no way at fault, I am . . . etc." Leo A. Henckel von Donnersmarck, *Briefe der Brüder Friedrichs des Grossen an meine Grosseltern* (Berlin, 1877), 43.

[33] Only two days before the prince's death, Princess Henry had written in a letter to her husband: "I say nothing of what I have suffered during these days. You know too well what reason I have to love and esteem your brother. . . . But above all I long for good news from you; that interests me more than all else. . . . Adieu, my dear prince; may

When word of the death of their brother William first reached him, Frederick tried to be tactful in mentioning it to Henry, who he knew had been one of William's strongest partisans; but, perhaps in self-defense against a charge which had not yet been made unless by his own conscience, he permitted himself some observations upon their brother's character which Henry regarded as slanderous and which would have provoked a serious quarrel if the king had not simply refused to quarrel over it. From near Olmütz on June 25, 1758, in the midst of the worries of his hazardous and eventually unsuccessful Moravian campaign, he wrote to Henry:

I have received from Berlin the sad and painful news of the death of my brother. I am all the more afflicted by it because I have always tenderly loved him, and have attributed all the chagrin that he has caused me to his weakness for listening to bad advice, and to his hot temper of which he was not always master; and remembering his good heart and his good qualities, I have borne with patience many things in his conduct which were very irregular and in which he has failed in his duty towards me.

I know how tenderly you have loved him. I hope that, after having given way to love and nature in the first outpourings of your sorrow, you will make every effort of which a strong soul is capable, not at all to efface from your memory a brother whose image should live always in your heart and mine, but to moderate the excess of a grief which might be fatal to you. Consider, I beg of you, that in less than a year I have lost a mother whom I adored and a brother whom I have always tenderly loved; in my present critical situation, do not add to my afflictions the injury which grief may do you. Make use of your reason and of philosophy as the only aids to enable us to endure evils for which there is no remedy. Think of the state and of our country, which will be exposed perhaps to even greater misfortunes if, in the course of this terrible war, our nephews should fall into tutelage. Remember, finally, that all men are mortal, that our tenderest connections and strongest attachments do not exempt us from the common law imposed upon our kind, that, after all, our life is so short that it does not leave us time even to mourn, and that as we weep for others we may believe without self-deception that in a little while others will weep for us in our turn.

In conclusion, my dear brother, I will not and cannot write at length on the sad subject of this letter. I fear for you; I wish for you long life and good health, and I hope at the same time that the multiplicity of your occupations and the glory which you will win will serve to distract you from matters

Heaven hear the prayers which I make without ceasing, for your preservation. Do not forget, Your very devoted, Wilhelmina." Hausarchiv, Rep. 56, II, I.

The princess's journal records the writing of many letters to the prince and the receipt of a considerable number from him, particularly during the first three years of the war, very few thereafter; but nearly all of their letters to one another seem to have been lost or destroyed.

which cannot but pierce your heart, pain you, and depress you; being with perfect love and esteem, my dear brother, your faithful brother and servant, Federic.[34]

The letter was less tactful than the king intended it to be. What he said about his love for their brother seemed insincere to Henry in the light of his treatment of him, and his references to the prince's weaknesses sounded like attacks upon the dead man's character. If Frederick had lost an adored mother and a well-loved brother within the past year, so had Henry; and he doubtless considered that his own account with the latter at least would balance better than that of the king. Suggestions that he be reasonable and philosophical about a loss for which he did not at the moment even wish to be consoled, and attempts to beguile him away from his grief with observations about the mortality of man and the brevity of life which left no time for mourning, or with a reference to the glory he was to win in a war which he considered had cost him a beloved brother, seemed to him heartless.

Furthermore, although Henry did not introduce the point into the discussion just then, he could not have been at all flattered by the king's reference to a regency. Frederick's opinion that a long regency during the minority of the heir to the throne was likely to be fatal to almost any state and ought to be avoided at all costs was presumably already well known; so he was probably quite unconscious of any special personal implication when he referred in his letter to "even greater misfortunes" to which the state would be exposed if their nephews should fall into tutelage. But he must have guessed, although he probably did not then know, that in their brother's will, which he as king permitted to stand, Prince Henry was already named as executor of that will and guardian of their two nephews, and that by his own royal order the prince would become regent at once in the event of his death. It was of course only too natural for him to think that it would be a national disaster if he himself should die and be replaced by Prince Henry as regent; but it was scarcely politic for him to say so in such a manner to a man so superlatively sensitive as the prince.[35]

---

[34] *P. C.,* XVII, 79–80.

[35] The prince wrote to the king on July 4 that he had just received from their sister Amelia a number of their brother's papers, including a copy of his will written by his own hand. Prince Henry said that he regarded it as his sacred duty to comply with the request, and sought the king's permission to do so. Meanwhile another copy, after being read by the ministers by order of the princess Amelia, had been sent to the king to see whether he would confirm it. There was some question in the minds of the ministers as to the legality of its form; they were not at all sure that the king would declare it valid, and they would evidently have been ready with a legal justification of his refusal if he had chosen to refuse. Letter from Wartensleben to Prince Henry, June 22, in the Hausarchiv, Rep. 56, II, I.

The prince did not permit all these reactions to appear in his first reply; but he did refer to "feelings more powerful than his reason," which made it impossible for him to lose sight of the image of his dead brother or to dismiss the thought of the "terrible and cruel" disgrace that William had suffered. He himself, beyond fear of disgrace or hope of favor, could only continue to do his duty. "I must nonetheless assure you that I have not in any way neglected my work, though torn by chagrin and sadness. . . . My affliction will not in any way hurt your interests nor get the better of me. This does not prevent me from thinking that those who live furthest removed from the society of men are happier than princes."[36]

That reply cooled the king a bit; but he made a second attempt, if not to console his highly emotional younger brother, at least to hearten him a little:

My dear brother: Surely one would deceive himself very badly if he sought to find perfect happiness in this world, or anything that he could call perfection. You ought not then to expect it any more than any other mortal. All the evils of life have their remedies, save the death of persons dear to us. . . .

But, my dear brother, . . . one must not become misanthropic. Every man who lives in a society must try to make himself useful to that society; and more especially a prince such as you must remember that he cannot renounce the world except by leaving it entirely. . . . Do then, I beg of you, everything you can possibly imagine, not indeed to console yourself but to divert your thoughts. I am truly in pain for you, and I fear that this grief may ruin your days and destroy the little health that you have left.[37]

Still the prince refused to be distracted; and his reply revealed that it was his brother's disgrace even more than his death that was the real obstacle in the way:

I have grieved over the misunderstanding between you and my brother, and your reference to it has pained me still more. . . . If he were still alive, I would gladly shorten my days to blot out every one of those during which you were angry with him, but it is too late now for that. I shall bear my unhappiness with patience; but though fortitude may make a man master of his own actions, it need not stifle sentiment; and while one may renounce happiness and satisfaction in life, there is little virtue in indifference.

My sister of Baireuth has been on the point of death; she cannot write; I fear that she will not recover from this illness. She does not yet know about the death of my brother, and there is reason to fear that this news will dissipate such little hope of recovery as now remains.[38]

[36] July 8, 1758, in Schöning, I, 209–210.
[37] July 19, 1758, in *P. C.*, XVII, 116–117.
[38] July 28, 1758, *ibid.*, 144.

Clearly the discussion had reached a point where the man with the greater poise and self-control must be the one to drop it. The king dropped it:

My dear brother: We have enough foreign enemies without tearing each other to pieces within the family. I hope that you will do sufficient justice to my feelings not to regard me as an unnatural brother or relative. The business in hand at present, my dear brother, is to save the state, and to use every means imaginable to defend ourselves against our enemies.[39]

There, fortunately, the case was closed, so far as direct discussion of it was concerned; but occasional unavoidable questions concerning the handling of the property of the late Prince of Prussia kept his ghost on foot to haunt the correspondence of the brothers for a long time to come.

The dismissal and death of his favorite brother and his own quarrel over it with the king affected Prince Henry profoundly and disastrously His character was warped by the experience, and his whole subsequent life poisoned by the memory of it. Something — fear, self-interest, ambition, patriotism, or sense of duty — kept him faithful to Prussia and made him serve the Prussian king loyally and well for thirty years longer; but nothing — not time nor the comradeship born of dangers and high enterprises shared, nor marks of the highest confidence — could quite draw from his heart the barbed dart which entered it that day when he witnessed the public degradation of one of his brothers by another. It constituted an unseen but permanent obstacle between himself and the king to whom he stood in other respects so near; and it goaded him to many graceless acts, of which the last and the ugliest was his erection at Rheinsberg after Frederick's death of a monument "to the heroes of the Seven Years' War," on which he "made amends" at last by giving Prince William the place of greatest honor and not permitting even the name of the soldier-king to appear. In erecting that memorial to one brother who he thought had been harshly and unjustly used, he unfortunately perpetuated in stone his own lifelong grudge against another to whom he himself had often been uncharitable and unjust in his thoughts but who, in spite of all, had loved him.

To understand Prince Henry's conduct the whole picture must be recreated, not necessarily as it was but as it appeared to him. He was convinced that the Prince of Prussia, once their father's favorite son, had been persecuted and killed by the jealous king's injustice, and that Fred-

---

[39] *Ibid.*, 145. The letter is quoted in English by Andrew Hamilton in his *Rheinsberg*, II, 48. It was only a week later that Frederick had occasion to name Prince Henry again for the position of regent, commander in chief, and guardian of the boy king their nephew in the event that he himself should be killed. As that was the thing to do, he did not permit this unpleasantness to prevent him from doing it.

erick's vindictiveness would eventually rob him of his good name as well. He believed also that any other officer who might be so unfortunate as to fail, even when ordered to do the impossible, might expect precisely the same fate. So he refused to take command of the army of Prince William, on the ground that he would not build a reputation for himself on the ruins of that of his brother; and on many subsequent occasions he earned himself the name of faint-heart and pessimist by stressing in advance the difficulties in the way of an enterprise, and by angling for a promise of immunity from the wrath of the king in the event of failure. He could not or would not forget the fate of his favorite brother; and he had no confidence thereafter in the moral integrity of the king.

Rarely has the world seen such a gifted pair of brothers or such an effective working partnership; and rarely has so cordial and confidential a relationship been so poisoned by the permanent psychological effects of a single incident. This was by no means the only rift between them; but to remember it makes the others easier to understand; for the prince, with William's ghost ever beside him, remembered it always.

That the prince felt as he did, the king never quite realized; and the king was always more successful than the prince in mastering his own thoughts and emotions and turning his back upon the past when it was wiser to do so. He therefore displayed much greater patience and more tolerance in his relations with the prince than the prince ever showed for him. To be sure, as the sovereign he was safe and could afford to be magnanimous, whereas the prince, as the subject, had to contend with the added mental hazard that his fate and future were always in the king's hands. Psychologically, the prince was in the less comfortable position of the two; but it was more largely due to his attitude than to the king's that the complete mutual confidence essential to a perfectly cordial brotherly relationship was unfortunately never established.

After the general retreat of midsummer, 1757, a small Prussian corps under Marshal Keith remained on Bohemian soil. Stronger forces stood in Saxony, including Lusatia, where the Prince of Prussia had met his fate and where General Winterfeldt soon met his death — an end which Prince Henry regarded as a righteous judgment of God in an otherwise unjust world. But the issue of the year's campaign was still in doubt; and the king, as always when confronted by baffling uncertainties instead of clearly recognizable and definable dangers, was in a bad state of nerves.[40]

Should he try to make peace? To do so would be almost tantamount

[40] His frequent alternations between periods of affected cheerfulness and unaffected fits of violent temper were repeatedly mentioned by Mitchell. The news of his mother's death reached him soon after the disaster at Kolin and added greatly to his distress.

to a confession that he had failed — or perhaps even that the war itself had been a mistake; yet he could not afford to dismiss the idea without exploring its possibilities. Perhaps a separate peace could be made with some one of his enemies. Naturally Austria would be the last to consider any such proposition. France, on the other hand, might be more easily detached from the hostile alliance than Russia; and France was already threatening.

Through his sister Wilhelmina of Baireuth, therefore, he sought to discover whether Madame la Pompadour could be induced by offers of money and territory to use her influence with the king of France in the interest of peace with Prussia; but nothing came of it.[41] Meanwhile he sounded Mitchell on the possibility that Great Britain suggest to France that a general peace be made for Germany on a prewar basis. Mitchell was entirely noncommittal, and Holdernesse replied only in general and platitudinous terms.[42]

The king hoped that if peace could not be made the British would send a fleet into the Baltic. That would aid him tremendously, for his Baltic provinces were practically at the mercy of the Swedes and Russians; but Britain was not at war with Russia and had no wish to be, and in any case could not easily have found a fleet just then for that purpose. Mitchell did his best, but in time the king began to be annoyed even with him. The minister eventually suspected that Frederick's attitude was being reflected even by the servants at the royal table, where he then customarily ate with the headquarters officers. Once when he had been badly served, he observed to one of those officers, "No fleet, no soup, I see."

Poor Mitchell, as an honest messenger, found himself in an uncomfortable position. His own government reprimanded him for his failure to convince Frederick that the British could find him no fleet at the moment, and the king of Prussia scolded because, he said, British trading interests were being preferred to the protection of Britain's most valuable ally. But no fleet was sent.[43]

No fleet; but as early as the middle of July the British Privy Council had decided that it would be wise to offer him a subsidy, instructing Mitchell to discover when and in what amounts it would be acceptable.[44]

Ten days after his defeat at Kolin Frederick had tentatively opened

---

[41] Letters of July 7, 1757, to Wilhelmina of Baireuth, in *P. C.*, XV, 218–219; to Colonel de Balbi, September 26, 1757, *ibid.*, 337–338; and many others.

[42] Bisset, I, 257–259, 354–355.

[43] M. P., IV, 56 *et passim;* Bisset, I, 389–393, 401, *et passim.*

[44] Minute in M. P., XXIX, fol. 146–148; cited by Arnold Schäfer in *Geschichte des siebenjährigen Krieges* (3 vols., Berlin, 1867), I, 642–643.

that question, protesting his unconquerable aversion to accepting a subsidy and his determination never to do so unless absolutely compelled by circumstances, and insisting that he was not asking for one but merely asking about one. Mitchell, an understanding and sympathetic man, reported:

I said if he would give me leave I would write about it as from myself and in such a manner as not to commit him. To this he agreed as it imports him to know what he may reasonably expect, if the worst should happen. . . .

I must observe that it is the first time I ever saw His Prussian Majesty abashed, and this was the only conversation I have had with him which seemed to give him pain.[45]

Yet the offer was refused, although it was hailed as "a draught of comfort to one who has not had a single drop since the 18th of June." The king's reply, as reported by Mitchell, was as follows:

I am deeply sensible of the king's and your nation's generosity, but I do not wish to be a burden to my allies; I would have you delay answering this letter till affairs are settled in Lusatia; if I succeed, I will then consult with you upon the different points suggested in this letter, and give my opinion freely upon them. If I am beat, there will be no occasion to answer it at all; it will be out of your power to save me, and I would not willingly abuse the generosity of my allies by drawing them into unnecessary and expensive engagements that can answer no useful purpose.

There Mitchell added his own comment: "I was pleased, but not surprised, with the noble dignity of this answer; for I have seen the King of Prussia great in prosperity, but greater still in adversity."[46]

Meanwhile, in mid-August, Holdernesse informed Mitchell that if and when a subsidy was granted, the British government was willing that it should be "as large as ever was given at any time to the House of Austria." By the end of August, according to Mitchell, Frederick "was sorry it was now become necessary," and suggested an amount of four million thaler for 1761.[47] With that message Mitchell sent to Holdernesse a private letter in which he described Frederick's situation as virtually hopeless. "The King of Prussia marches with 20,000 effective men; the Loss of a Battle will only anticipate the Ruin of his Countries a few Weeks, the Winning of it cannot save him. I lose myself when I think of His Situation. I can see no Salvation for Him but in the Arms of France."[48]

[45] Mitchell to Holdernesse, June 22, 1757; printed from the document in the Public Record Office, London, in *P. C.*, XV, 193–194.
[46] *Ibid.*, 272–279, also from a document in the Public Record Office.
[47] M. P., XIX, 158; A. Schäfer, I, 664; Bisset, I, 271. Four millions, or £670,000, were paid annually from 1758 to 1761 inclusive.
[48] Dresden, August 31, 1757, in M. P., XVIII, 37.

While Frederick would have been glad to have the assurance of a subsidy as a reserve to fall back upon in a desperate emergency, he hesitated to sign a convention that would commit him irrevocably to the continuation of the war while there was still a possibility of peace with France; and Mitchell was not sure that Great Britain ought to insist that he continue.[49] Even after the Prussian victories of Rossbach and Leuthen, Mitchell wrote to Holdernesse: "Notwithstanding the glorious and almost incredible success of the Prussian arms, it is my humble opinion that it is still the King of Prussia's interest to make peace, as soon as he can with safety and Honour, and I am persuaded that if he does it will be with a proper attention to both." [50]

On into the year 1758, although his need of money was so desperate that by midsummer he remarked in a letter to Henry that he would soon be forced to take to the highways as an ordinary robber to find cash with which to pay his troops, Frederick continued his stubborn refusal to sign a convention, and sought to combine the subsidy question with a British pledge to send a fleet to the Baltic and more troops to Hanover. Only Mitchell continued patient, praising to Holdernesse the king's "magnanimous and generous Resolution, (not to be paralleled in the whole History of Subsidies)." For his pains, Mitchell was temporarily replaced by Colonel Yorke.[51]

Frederick's own minister in London, L. Michell, fared little better. He was scolded by Frederick for being "more the secretary of Mr. Pitt than the envoy of the king"; and Baron Knyphausen was sent to London as minister extraordinary, in the hope that two Prussians could withstand the insidious influence of the British court better than one.[52]

Neither the king of Prussia nor any of his ministers or generals was unmindful of the value of the aid offered by Great Britain in the form of subsidies; but neither he nor they thought that she would be doing enough if she contributed only money to the allied cause. Frederick wrote L. Michell: "Those people are perfect idiots as to foreign affairs, and especially as to German questions; or else they are very ill-disposed." [53]

No one disguised the fact that the ruin of Prussia seemed imminent. Still, though offered what the British called a larger subsidy than they had ever paid to a foreign prince, the king took no steps until midsummer to make actual use of it; and payment of the first year's grant was not completed until October, 1758.[54]

[49] Bisset, I, 277–279, 378.
[50] M. P., IV, 29.
[51] From Breslau, February 9, 1758, *ibid.*, IV, 58–62, 73, 77.
[52] P. C., XVI, 252–253, 293.
[53] March 26, 1758, *ibid.*, 332.
[54] Letters from the king to Finckenstein, July 7, and to Prince Henry, August 10, 1758,

Nothing ever tried Frederick's nerves like uncertainty; and never did he feel less certain of his future than in the late summer of 1757, following the failure of his invasion of Bohemia. In was then, therefore, that he began to talk of suicide, and once asked Voltaire whether a man overwhelmed by misfortune was not justified in putting an end to his own life. Without raising the pertinent question whether a man bent on suicide is likely first to consult his distant friends about it by letter, Voltaire replied that by such a step he would ruin his own name instead of making it immortal as he apparently hoped to do. In a second letter on the subject, Voltaire reminded him: "No one will look upon you as a martyr for liberty; you should be honest with yourself; you know in how many courts men still stubbornly continue to look upon your entry into Saxony as a violation of the rights of man. What will they say in these courts? That you have avenged that invasion upon yourself; that you could not endure your own chagrin at not being able to lay down the law to them. They will accuse you of premature despair, for having made this unfortunate decision in Erfurth when you were still master of Silesia and Saxony."[55]

Prince Henry, seeing the king daily and often alone, heard more of his talk of suicide than anyone else, but was even more skeptical about it than Voltaire, saying bluntly that a genuinely heroic king would be giving no thought at such a time to ways of personal escape for himself, but would be devoting himself entirely to the salvation of his state. Even if Frederick had to cede some of his territory to save the rest, argued his brother, he would not be the first prince in history to lose a province. He should therefore think more about the major interest of his people and his duty to them, and less about his own personal shame or glory.[56]

Despite the bitterness of his feelings over the treatment of their brother William, and despite his known refusal to take the king's suicide threats seriously, Henry continued meanwhile in active service and on otherwise cordial and to a certain extent confidential terms with the king. Too confidential, perhaps; for he saw Frederick too often with his guard down, storming up and down the room in the privacy of his quarters, debating with himself, and with Henry, the disadvantages of every possible course of action, and presenting a picture that contrasted sharply with the image of unshaken resolution which he quite properly tried to

in *P. C.*, XVII, 93, 158. In the whole course of the war, the subsidies totaled about 16,000,000 thaler. See Hans Rothfels in the *Historische Zeitschrift*, CXXXIV (1926), 21.

[55] *Oeuvres complètes de Voltaire*, LXV, 249–251 (Paris, 1785).

[56] Which is probably the only thing Frederick ever (except just after Kunersdorf) thought at all seriously of doing. See Rudolph Schmitt, *Prinz Heinrich von Preussen als Feldherr im siebenjährigen Kriege* (2 vols., Greifswald, 1885, 1897), I, 43; and Koser, *Geschichte Friedrichs des Grossen*, II, 530–531.

show to the world. Henry knew, if no one else did, that Frederick was sorely perplexed and uncertain of his course. The younger brother thought he saw again the "wavering prince" of the earlier Silesian wars whom as "Marshal Gessler" he had criticized for bargaining for peace without getting it, and so being compelled to continue a war he could not win. The difference was that in the first instance he had criticized his brother for throwing away the chance of a decisive victory to make an easy but disappointing peace; now he feared that the same misguided Frederick would haggle over the price of peace until he let his opportunity escape, and would then sacrifice his army and his state by continuing a hopeless war and playing for the miracle which alone could bring him victory.

That Henry should have thought as he did, under the circumstances, is less surprising than that, thinking so, he still continued to honor Frederick's commands and to execute them faithfully and well. He criticized his brother; but he neither disobeyed nor failed his king-commander.

Frederick talked boldly of staking his life and the future of his state on one more throw of the dice and attacking again at Zittau. In view of the disasters which had already overtaken the king himself in Bohemia and the Prince of Prussia, General Winterfeldt, and the Duke of Bevern in Lusatia, Henry urged strongly that the Prussian forces should stand on the defensive there for the remainder of the season. Another defeat just then, he argued, would be disastrous; and the potential advantages to be won, even by a battle victory, were not great enough to warrant the risk.

Except that the prince considerably underestimated the moral effect that another smashing victory under just those circumstances might have had, that was not bad advice; but to give it required moral courage matching the physical daring he had shown at Prague; for he was risking the king's displeasure as well as the suspicion of cowardice. Mitchell, Marshal Keith, and most of the other generals shared his opinion, but only he dared voice it.[57]

In spite of their differences in temperament, the king and Prince Henry were in other ways remarkably alike as soldiers; in fact, by virtue of their differences, the two supplemented one another almost perfectly.

[57] Nevertheless, the advice he then gave the king is seized upon as cowardly by his severest critics, Maschke and von Bernhardi, in spite of the fact that those same critics, literally with their next breath, praise the king for having been so prudent as to refrain from making the attack against which the fainthearted prince had advised him. See Koser, in the *Historische Zeitschrift*, XCII (1904), 249; Marshal Keith, in a letter to Mitchell, in Bisset, II, 463; Maschke, in the *Jahrbücher für die deutsche Armée und Marine*, CXVII (1900); Theodor von Bernhardi, *Friedrich der Grosse als Feldherr* (2 vols., Berlin, 1881), I, 116–119, 144–150; Schmitt, *Prinz Heinrich*, I, 41.

The prince was prudent and cautious, sometimes overcautious, and needed encouragement and occasional prodding from his more sanguine senior. The king attempted and accomplished the impossible so often that he sometimes forgot how to recognize the limits of the possible. On such occasions he was fortunate to have such a master of maneuver and defense as the prince to help him ward off the worst consequences of his disastrous defeats. Meanwhile their enemies learned that to attack Henry was as difficult as to meet one of Frederick's attacks — and almost as dangerous. As time went on, the two not only supplemented one another but each learned from the other; their methods were more and more alike; and they became indispensable to one another. Neither could have done what he did without the other, although neither was ever quite satisfied with the other. In spite of the personal rift between them they became in time, so far as their military campaigning was concerned, practically one dual personality, a partnership that enemy generals could not break and a puzzle they could not solve. To observe the development and success of that working combination between them makes any attempt to establish the definite superiority of either over the other, as a soldier, seem very futile indeed, and quite beside the point.

The prince heartily approved of the king's attempts to effect a reconciliation with France. He was in fact so insistent in the matter that the king had at last to remind him that making peace was more easily said than done; there must be two parties to any such agreement.[58]

In his wish for peace the prince revealed himself as something of a pessimist but certainly not a coward. He was not cravenly urging his brother to seek a peace that Frederick himself had had no thought of making, or to purchase it by cessions of territory which no patriot could ever consider. He was merely less hopeful than the king about winning the war and less fully aware of the obstacles in the way of pacification, and therefore willing to pay a higher price for peace. He thought the war could be continued only at too great a cost; the king decided that peace, on the only terms on which he could obtain it, would be too dearly bought. Therein lay the only essential difference between them. It was not a case of poltroon versus patriot.

After the battle of Rossbach, hopes of peace with France were still kept alive, and both the king and the prince showed the wounded officers among the French prisoners every courtesy. Subsequently the prince, who was in charge of them, continued to treat them with extraordinary kindness, and released several of them on parole with the understanding that they would return to France and work there for peace with Prussia.

[58] October 19, 1757, in *P. C.*, XV, 441.

This was done with the full knowledge and consent of the king, although Frederick was less sanguine than Henry about the results of the experiment.

Mitchell, who had some inkling of what was going on but who thought that the prince was acting on his own initiative and without the knowledge of the king, judged him at that time to be nothing but an ambitious intriguer, jealous of the king and aspiring to the honor of winning a peace for Prussia after the king had failed to win the war.[59]

Meanwhile it developed that the prince's military career had not been wrecked by his refusal to take command of the army of Lusatia, from which William had been dismissed, or by his subsequent refusal of another independent command which had been accepted and competently handled by Prince Ferdinand of Brunswick. In subordinate though responsible positions he continued to serve, to thrive, and to win the praise of Frederick.[60]

At Rossbach on November 5, 1757, the Prussians put an end for that year to the annual threat from the west by attacking on the march and almost annihilating the French and Imperial army of Marshal Soubise. It was a sort of "generals' battle" in which things happened so quickly that, after making his initial dispositions, the commander in chief was able to do little to direct its course. In that fast-moving action, starting as ordered by the king and proceeding necessarily at their own discretion, General Seydlitz commanded the cavalry and Prince Henry the infantry of the Prussian left wing which made the initial and decisive attack. It was the prince who placed the Prussian guns on the slope of the Janusberg to fire directly in upon the close-packed and confused masses of French and Imperial troops as they were herded ever more closely together by the Prussian enveloping movement. It was Seydlitz who pursued the scattering fugitives. Both were wounded, the general more seriously than the prince. It was all over so quickly that the French commander could defend himself at home only by reporting that his plan of battle had really been very good, but he had been beaten before he had time to carry it out.

The name of the prince was not very prominently played up in the king's official accounts of the battle; but it ran through the land at the time. His princess, whose journal and letters say that she had been terribly smitten by the news of his injury, was soon relieved and overjoyed by the assurance that he was out of danger, and for a long time

[59] M. P., IV, 2; Bisset, I, 305–306. He revised his opinion later.
[60] P. C., XV, 353.

rejoiced in his fame as a national hero. The king himself visited him in his quarters in Leipzig, and later referred to Rossbach as "your day of glory," which his own victory at Leuthen (without Henry) might match but could not outshine.[61]

The prince was then left in command in Saxony, while Ferdinand of Brunswick took charge in Hanover and Frederick himself rushed off on the headlong campaign which culminated in his victory at Leuthen and in the reconquest of most of Silesia. By the end of the year the king was again in possession of nearly all his territories, and had more prisoners of war on his hands than he could afford to feed. It was because he did not want to burden himself with more, he said, that he permitted the Austrian garrison of Liegnitz to march off home instead of demanding its surrender.[62]

What a year! It had ended well enough to enable the king to write jubilantly after the recapture of Breslau, as he had done after Leuthen, contrasting his comparatively slight losses with the far heavier ones of the enemy. So as to derive the maximum benefit from his renewed good fortune, he directed the prince to see to it that his optimistic accounts of recent events should fall as if by accident into the hands of the French prisoners, in the hope that the truth about the war would be smuggled home by them to give the lie to the false accounts published by their own government.[63]

The year, however, had taken heavy toll. The Prussian army never fully recovered from the losses it had then sustained. Recruits could be found, and were; but the replacements were always inferior in quality and spirit to the men of '57. Reliable leaders were increasingly difficult to find, for no general was fully trusted again after a few failures, and only Prince Henry went through the war without being overtaken by a major disaster; even the king could never again quite equal his exploits of that year. Many potential leaders had been killed; others had been tried and found wanting.[64] Among the few who had stood the test of

[61] See the account of the battle of Leuthen, written on December 5, 1757, in *P. C.*, XVI, 74–75.

[62] *Ibid.*, 134–135.

[63] December 22, 1757, *ibid.*, 117. Throughout the war the work of their spies and enemy activities reported by them figured almost as prominently in the brothers' correspondence as did their own movements. An attempt to deceive the enemy by the dissemination of false reports and misleading rumors was, on the other hand, always a part of their own preparation for any important move; and each of them told the other whenever possible what he was doing toward that end.

[64] The Seven Years' War was one in which even generals could get themselves killed; thirty-three of them did so, in the Prussian army alone, in the first four years. The battle of Lobositz in 1757 had cost Prussia the lives of four general officers, Prague four, Kolin and Moys one each, Breslau three, Leuthen two. Two battles of 1758, Zorndorf and Hoch-

war well enough to warrant being given greater responsibilities thereafter, the most prominent in rank and the most conspicuous for their services and ability were the queen's brother Ferdinand and the king's brother Henry.

kirch, were to cost three each, and Kunersdorf three in 1759. In 1759 Frederick complained: "One would think that the Austrians were immortal and that only ours must lose their lives. My generals are taking the Acheron at full gallop; soon I shall not have a man left." Koser, *Geschichte Friedrichs des Grossen*, III, 8; Curt Jany, "Der siebenjährige Krieg," *F. B. P. G.*, XXXV (1923), 192.

CHAPTER V

# General Commanding in Saxony

*"If we are to suffer a reverse, I should prefer that it
happen to me."* — Henry to Frederick.
*"It is a miracle that Prince Henry and his little army
had not been devoured."* — Sir Andrew Mitchell.

IN JANUARY, 1758, the king expressed the wish that, if the year then beginning were to be as bad as the one just ended, it might then be his last.[1]
In the event, it proved to be equally strenuous and somewhat less successful. It witnessed, as 1757 had done, the failure of an invasion of enemy
territory; its hard-won victories were less numerous and less productive
of results; and a brilliant late-autumn campaign was necessary to prevent
it from ending in disaster.

The year began, as the war had begun, with highhanded action on
the part of the king of Prussia. Convinced that the Marquis de Fraigne,
formerly secretary of the French legation in Berlin, was taking advantage of his position as French agent at the little court of Zerbst, he told
Prince Henry to arrest him. Henry sent a Lieutenant Borowski with four
men to do what the king had ordered, but they ran into trouble. The
Prince of Zerbst, insisting that Fraigne was not a military person and
therefore not subject to military arrest, took him into his castle under
his own personal protection, and dared the young officer to drag him out
by force. For such an undertaking the lieutenant, who had only his
orders by way of warrant for the arrest, found his force of four men
insufficient; so he returned without his prisoner.

In reporting this miscarriage of vengeance to the king, Prince Henry
exonerated Borowski; but Frederick replied that the lieutenant deserved
to be arrested for failure to carry out his orders. (The implied rebuke to
the prince, for failure to send with him a force large enough to overawe
and thus to prevent opposition, he left unstated.) Fraigne, he said, was a
spy who must be captured at any cost, even if he must be dragged from
the private living quarters of the Prince of Zerbst himself.

Next time more thorough preparations were made. Prince Henry had
insisted that, if he must make the arrest, the king must first justify it by
formally denouncing Fraigne to the Prince of Zerbst. In doing so Fred-

[1] F. to H., in *P. C.*, XVI, 198.

erick asserted that because he was a spy the marquis was not entitled to protection under international law or the usages of war. Then Colonel Kleist was sent with a detachment large enough to use force if necessary; so it was not necessary, and the Marquis of Fraigne was brought to Magdeburg as a prisoner.[2]

The incident is an interesting early example of one of the principal differences between the royal brothers, which furnished material for countless arguments between them as time went on. Possibly by nature but more probably by choice, as a calculated policy, Frederick was more ruthless than Henry. He had insisted, for instance, that the prince should adopt sterner measures for the collection of "contributions" from the little principality of Anhalt;[3] and repeatedly they quarreled over the king's refusal to believe that Saxony had been plundered to the limit when Henry said it had, and over Henry's refusal to enforce discipline by making his men "fear the cudgel."

For Prince Henry the active campaigning of the year 1758 began in February. The Prussian victory at Rossbach in November of the year before had practically destroyed one French army and scattered the forces of its German allies who had taken the field in the name of the Empire. But the Prussians had not been able to garrison the whole region thus temporarily cleared of enemy troops, and of course new incursions were only to be expected and were already being made.

Some of the states thus threatened, notably Hanover, Brunswick, and Baireuth, were friendly to Prussia. Others, preferring neutrality but unable to maintain it, were forced to contribute supplies and money to whichever belligerent could spare the troops to occupy their territories — which meant contributing alternately to both, as raiders came and went.

As soon as they had recovered from the demoralization following their defeat at Rossbach, French and Imperial troops, having already seized the Prussian Rhineland provinces of Wesel and Cleves, resumed their advance, aiming at the military occupation of the whole area on the right bank of the Weser. Not only Hanover but the Duchy of Brunswick, the western Saxon territories not included in Electoral Saxony, and the Bishopric of Hildesheim would thus have fallen into the hands of Prussia's enemies, who would then have found themselves upon the borders of Electoral Saxony and of the hereditary states of the king of Prussia.

[2] Letters in Schöning, I, 122, 128, 131, 132; *P. C.*, XVI, 164, 189, 198, 206–207; A. Schäfer, II, 55.

[3] *P. C.*, XVI, 146, 156. "Il ne faut pas ménager ces messieurs."

The defense of Hanover, and of as much as possible of the other territory in the valley of the Weser, was primarily the task of Prince Ferdinand of Brunswick, whose composite British-Hanoverian force was supplemented by some regiments of Prussian hussars. To aid him, and to ward off the danger threatening Saxony and Magdeburg, Prince Henry was sent in February and March on a swift-marching winter campaign based on Leipzig.

Since the campaign was being undertaken partly for its moral and political effect, propaganda naturally played a part in it. By Frederick's order and under protest the prince sent the French commander a letter threatening reprisals: "Sir: In view of the horrible disorders, exactions, and depredations which the French troops have committed in the [Prussian] principality of Halberstadt, I am ordered by the king to warn you that the territories of the allies of the king of France will be treated with the same inhumanity and barbarity, and that hereafter the French officer prisoners will be made to feel the effects of the improper conduct of your troops toward His Majesty's subjects." [4]

The "reprisals" argument was used also to justify the rigors of the Prussian regime in Dresden: the French, it was alleged, had abused Halberstadt, and the Russians had forced the inhabitants of East Prussia to swear allegiance to the czarina.[5]

Before the prince left Leipzig, Ferdinand of Brunswick had been told by Frederick not to demand or to expect too much of him. He was to operate in the region of Hildesheim and threaten the right flank and rear of the French army; but that was all. The king specifically warned Ferdinand that he had himself already set limits upon the number of troops Henry might take, how far from Leipzig he might venture, and how long he might absent himself from Saxony.[6] If he did nothing but frighten the French, attract their attention to himself, and draw them together and away from Ferdinand's front, he would have done all that could be asked of him.[7]

As he usually did on the eve of an enterprise, Henry needed the reassurance Frederick gave him. When he contemplated the dangers and difficulties he would encounter, which were real enough, his own physical ills and weaknesses, equally real, began to seem more important and to figure more prominently in his correspondence with the king. Finally,

[4] F. to H., January 22 and February 5, in *P. C.*, XVI, 191, 224. On April 25 the king wrote to the prince: "Let them expiate in Berlin the brigandage their compatriots have committed in my country." *Ibid.*, 401. The threat was not made good. French officers in Berlin were treated more as guests than as prisoners.
[5] Schöning, I, 126–127.
[6] F. to Ferdinand of Brunswick, January 30 and February 3, in *P. C.*, XVI, 211, 219.
[7] F. to H., February 10, *ibid.*, 236.

revealing what had probably been the principal reason for his reluctance all along, he complained of the quality of the troops assigned to the expedition, pointing out that the commander of such unreliable soldiers would be likely at any moment to be betrayed and disgraced by them.[8]

That argument the king met with the curious mixture of flattery and quiet insistence which he usually found to be most effective with the temperamental prince. A really good workman, he said, could turn out a creditable piece of work even with inferior tools, and a commander with Henry's God-given talent and genius could well undertake a task that was admittedly too difficult for an ordinary general. He was confident, he said, that the prince would prove equal to the test if he would guard his health carefully and free his mind for constructive work by brightening up a bit.[9]

Once started, the prince seemed to have forgotten that he had ever hesitated. That was his way, just as it was Frederick's. He moved out punctually at the appointed time and continued on schedule. In quick succession he occupied Regenstein, Goslar, Wolfenbüttel, and Hildesheim, and restored the Duchy of Brunswick to its fugitive ruler. The French, startled by the swiftness of his movements and confused by the skill with which they were masked, estimated his little force of eight or nine thousand men at twice its actual strength and assumed that Frederick must be leading it in person. Apparently they also believed the report spread by the prince's troops that this was only an advance guard and that a large Prussian army was following. So they retired with all possible speed behind the Weser, leaving sick and wounded, baggage and artillery, and great stores of supplies behind them. A little more than a fortnight after he had left Leipzig the prince reported to the king from Hildesheim, the high point of his advance, that he believed that in three more weeks there would be no French troops left in Westphalia except in Cleves and Wesel. But he was ordered to go no farther.[10]

He had already gone far enough to hasten the French evacuation of Bremen and Göttingen, to facilitate Prince Ferdinand's capture of Minden, and to declare a generous dividend in captured military stores and contributions from the "liberated" cities and states. Ransomed towns paid or promised to pay a total of 220,000 thaler. Those that could not pay cash had to furnish hostages. His officers handled thousands of prisoners of war and recruited many of them for the Prussian service. When ready to return to Saxony he concealed his intention and facilitated the

[8] Schöning, 1, 136.
[9] *P. C., XVI*, 236.
[10] H. to F., March 3, 8, in Schöning, I, 145–148; F. to H., March 3, in *P. C.*, XVI, 278.

withdrawal by making a short advance and spreading a rumor that he contemplated another general attack.[11]

Prince Ferdinand of Brunswick would naturally have been glad to see so useful a diversion continued; and others, reasoning from the assumption that such a success would have gone right on succeeding, have blamed Prince Henry because he did not continue his push forward. Some of his critics have alleged that he stopped because he was afraid, and that not even the king could goad him further.[12] One of his faithless adjutants was responsible for an even uglier report, that he stopped at Hildesheim for no better reason than that he was jealous of Prince Ferdinand and had no wish to contribute to his growing reputation. Neither charge is justified. He stopped, and he returned, in obedience to definite orders from the king.[13]

Certainly the king was satisfied, and said so, not only to the prince himself but to his General Directorium. During the campaign Mitchell had written to his government that the king was "much pleased" with the vigor his principal lieutenants were showing.[14] When Hildesheim was reached, Frederick wrote: "I am so well pleased with everything that I see you do that, if I were beside you to tell you at every moment what I think, it could not be more in conformity with my ideas. . . . To be sure, it would be fine if you would surround the army of Soubise, after having driven away that of Clermont; it would also be splendid if Heaven should so inspire the Imperial troops with fear that they would run away as well; but that would really be too much to ask." To Prince Ferdinand's request for further help Frederick replied bluntly: "That can't be done." And to Prince Henry: "It is not a question of going to the Rhine but of defending the Electorate, which will certainly be endangered if you do not rejoin the corps of Marshal Keith." [15]

With the triumphs of Prince Ferdinand of Brunswick the king was equally well pleased. Even before most of them had been won, he had

[11] H. to F., in Schöning, I, 136, 147.

[12] That criticism is completely belied by his correspondence with the king. See *P. C.,* XVI, 278.

[13] Count Henckel von Donnersmarck had served the prince well enough as an adjutant in 1757 and their friendship was to be revived in later years; but they had quarreled. He was a member of the expeditionary force as a regimental officer, but was in disfavor with the prince and not in his confidence. His testimony on any matter into which a subjectively formed opinion can enter is therefore entirely unreliable, especially so for just this period, although his journal is very useful as a contemporary day-to-day record of events. See his *Militärische Nachlass* (second edition, 2 vols., Leipzig, 1858), II, 19; also Schmitt, *Prinz Heinrich,* I, 57. Von Bernhardi's account, based upon Henckel's, criticizes the prince for not going farther. Count Clermont's reports and the Austrian account of Alfred von Arneth in *Geschichte Maria Theresias* indicate that the French were on the run and might have been pushed farther back if the Prussian advance had been continued.

[14] M. P., IV., 70; *P. C.,* XVI, 343.

[15] F. to H., in *P. C.,* XVI, 296–297, 320; F. to Ferdinand of Brunswick, *ibid.,* 316.

written to Prince Henry: "When I say my little prayer, I always add: 'O God, who lovest neither ingrates nor brigands, be graciously pleased to give thy servant Ferdinand all the strength of David, that he may be more than equal to all these rascally Frenchmen, Amen.' If you do not find this formula good, I would remind you that it is at least worth as much as the prayer of old Ogilvy, whom we heard braying in Latin in the Catholic church of Dresden." [16]

The king's benevolent attitude toward Prince Ferdinand and his mission was undoubtedly genuine; but such further help as Ferdinand received must come, if not directly and miraculously from the Lord, at any rate from someone other than the king of Prussia. Prince Henry and his men were needed in Saxony.

While in the midst of his Halberstadt-Hildesheim campaign, Henry had been notified that he was destined for the larger responsibility of an independent command in Saxony. He accepted the appointment without hesitation or apparent misgivings. His acceptance was modest but confident in tone, expressing his readiness to undertake the task and his pleasure at having been chosen for it. It betrayed no other sign of the relief that he actually felt at not being ordered back to the king's own army in Silesia.

The question of his health was not again raised for a long time, although ever since midwinter he had been suffering from colic, cramps, occasional fevers, rheumatism, headaches, and a persistent inflammation in his eyes. In spite of such handicaps, when he was offered an opportunity to be useful he assured the king that he would be able to do what was necessary. Both the brothers bore, throughout the war, pains and fatigues that must have taxed their frail physiques to the limit of their endurance. Mitchell was a strong man, but he could not indefinitely keep up with either of them. [17]

In his letter accepting the new appointment the prince asked only one favor — leave of absence for a few days, upon his return to Saxony, to go to Berlin and attend to some of his personal affairs. His request was politely but definitely refused. Only Marshal Keith could possibly take his place, even temporarily; and Keith was needed elsewhere. If it were

---

[16] *Ibid.*, 266. In a letter to Prince Ferdinand himself he expressed the hope that the French would soon be kicked right across the Rhine, each branded on his rump with the fleur-de-lis and with the initials of the Peace of Westphalia. *Ibid.*, 319.

[17] F. to H., *ibid.*, 267; H. to F., in Schöning, I, 148; H. to Ferdinand of Prussia, in the Hausarchiv; cited also by Otto Herrmann in the *Historische Vierteljahrschrift*, XXVI (1931), 375. The prince's complaints about his health had more to warrant them than hypochondria. He naturally made more argumentative use of his physical ills and weaknesses when discouraged or disgruntled, but the king referred just as frequently to his own. Their

a matter of money, the king said, he had already taken care of that as best he could with the limited resources still left to him, by granting the prince an additional thousand thaler per month as "special table money," and had ordered the treasurer of the Torgau war chest to give him whatever he asked for the payment of spies. So, if it were a matter of business, Frederick suggested that perhaps it would be less urgent than Henry had supposed. If he merely wanted to see his wife, he could have her come to Saxony to meet him.[18]

The prince did not act upon his brother's suggestion, although he did share his new prosperity with his wife by sending her a hundred louis d'or as a birthday present. It was apparently Rheinsberg that he wanted to see; and for that he had to wait several years longer.

The king's general plan of campaign for 1758 was no less ambitious than that of 1757, aiming again at the conquest of Bohemia but using a different approach. He himself proposed first to recapture Schweidnitz and to use that fortress as a base for a force of perhaps fifteen thousand men who should hold the mountain passes of the Bohemian border of Silesia. Then he would carry the war southward into Moravia, aiming first at the capture of Olmütz. Assuming that the Austrians would be forced to recall a whole army from Bohemia to oppose him in Moravia, he hoped that Prince Henry could then take advantage of that withdrawal to advance quickly and easily to the capture of Prague.

Until he knew that the king had captured Olmütz the prince was to confine his efforts to the defense of Saxony. That did not mean that he should stand passively and await attack. He was strongly urged, instead, to act always offensively, to neglect no opportunity to annoy the enemy by anticipating his designs and checkmating them in advance. Whenever it was clear that the enemy was in a position to compel him to give battle, he was to force the fighting, at times and on ground of his own choosing. This bold advice was tempered, to be sure, by the further admonition that he must give battle only when defeat could have no disastrous consequences. Isolated expressions urging him always to keep the initiative in his own hands and to act aggressively even on the defense could indeed be lifted from their context to indicate that the king contemplated two major offensives beginning simultaneously in Moravia and Bohemia; but the prince's instructions called as much for caution as for firmness; and the capture of Olmütz, which was to be the

exchanges of medical advice and the enumeration of their aches and pains sometimes resembled debates as to which was the more seriously incapacitated.
[18] Schöning, I, 148; *P. C.,* XVI, 306–308.

signal for him to abandon the generally defensive policy which had been enjoined upon him, never took place.

Besides defining thus his general objectives, the king gave his brother some general advice. The strictest possible discipline, he said, must be maintained. Upon flagrant offenders who deserved it the death penalty should be imposed if approved by a council of war; and examples should be made of captured deserters if desertions became too numerous. Officers must spare no effort to see that the soldiers were properly fed; and "above all, the poor wounded" and the sick must be given all possible care.[19]

Although councils of war might be used for courts-martial in disciplinary cases, the prince was expressly forbidden ever to call one to discuss his operations. In planning his movements he was to depend upon his own judgment only, and to fight or to avoid battle, to take or to yield ground, as he deemed best.[20] When notifying the prince of his selection for this important post, the king had promised not to tie his hands in any way — "for woe be unto them who would hold to the letter; for in these cases I say unto you that the letter killeth, while the spirit giveth life." [21]

No other general in the Prussian service was or could have been given such wide discretionary powers. Some of them failed apparently because they adhered too closely to the letter which killeth; but in every such case the king had given them such detailed and rigid orders because he had reason to fear that they had not enough of the spirit which giveth life. The prince too, in his orders to his subordinates, often tried to instruct them in advance for every conceivable contingency, but he usually left somewhat more to their discretion than the king did. For that reason, or else because he was less feared, he was usually better served by his generals than the king was, in crises calling for initiative or discretionary decisions on their part; but he was more often embarrassed by their failure to carry out their orders as given.

Prince Henry himself, upon receipt of his general orders, asked at once that they be elucidated upon various points. What regiments were to compose his army? Where would he find the engineers and artillery for a siege of Prague? If he must give up either Dresden or Leipzig, which should it be? If he found that Dresden could be defended for a

---

[19] The opinion was quite general in the army that the prince took better care of his men in every way than the king did.

[20] *P. C.*, XVI, 303–305; Schöning, I, 148–153. In forbidding councils of war the king probably had in mind the unfortunate experience of the Prince of Prussia, whom he had accused of demoralizing his own army in 1757 by his show of indecision in calling such councils too frequently.

[21] *P. C.*, XVI, 267.

few days only, should he defend it for that period in spite of the damage it would inevitably suffer, or should he spare the city the horrors of war by abandoning it at once if it was seriously threatened? [22]

Here the prince was being not only prudent but disagreeable; but like his fellow generals he always feared the king's displeasure in case of failure at least as much as he feared the enemy. The example of the Prince of Prussia, moreover, was a constant reminder that as the king's brother he might be made to feel the ruler's wrath all the more keenly but would never be saved from it.[23] So he needed to know more definitely just what was required of him; and he had to ask his questions while the king was still within reach.

In his question concerning Dresden there appeared again a certain humanitarianism in Henry which seemed to Frederick in wartime to be only a weakness. The prince would rather surrender a city which he believed he could not hold indefinitely than cause its destruction or subject its noncombatant inhabitants unnecessarily to bombardment. The king would have gambled on the chance that the Austrians would rather fail to capture Dresden than ruin it by firing upon it. He himself bombarded it in 1760 without capturing it, and with little prospect of being able to do so.[24]

As the king's personal representative in Saxony, Henry was much occupied with administrative matters while the enemy left him undisturbed in the early spring of 1758. The Duke of Cassel, again threatened by the French, called upon him for protection. For once the prince found that not being quite his own master had its advantages. He replied that his forces could be divided only by order of the king, and referred the request to Ferdinand of Brunswick. Presently the Duke of Gotha appealed to him in great distress because, being ordered to furnish a contingent of troops to the Empire, he feared disciplinary action by the Imperial government or Austria if he did not do so and reprisals by Prussia if he did. That problem soon solved itself. Gotha furnished the troops, and Prussia quickly captured them and took them into her service.[25]

The problem of Dresden's cash contribution the prince submitted to the king, in the form of a petition from the city officials. Frederick re-

---

[22] H. to F., March 31, in Schöning, I, 159.

[23] The fear that he would suffer the same fate the first time he failed to do all that was demanded of him, probably during that very campaign, he plainly stated in a letter to his brother Ferdinand of Prussia on April 17. Hausarchiv, Rep. 56, II, F; also cited by Otto Herrmann in the *Historische Vierteljahrschrift,* XXVI (1931), 368.

[24] After that failure Prince Henry wrote bitterly to his brother Ferdinand: "The siege of Dresden has been abandoned but half the city has been reduced to ashes; so all goes well." *Ibid.,* 370; Hausarchiv, Rep. 56, II, F.

[25] Schöning, I, 168, 182.

plied that, without knowing how much the city had already paid, he could give no definite answer; but if it had been as much as three hundred thousand thaler, he had already instructed Commandant Schmettau to accept that amount and be lenient. Then as if he could sense the prince's own attitude, even at that distance, he added: "You know that I am neither hard-hearted nor [personally] interested; but, compelled as I am at present to pay on every hand, I am forced in spite of myself to have recourse to every desperate expedient." [26]

Doubtless Frederick sensed also that once more, on the eve of a great undertaking, the prince was so much concerned about providing in advance for every difficulty which might later confront him that those difficulties were appearing larger to him in prospect than they were likely to be in fact. So he disposed of them by letter. Suppose the prince was short of wagons; he had the Elbe. Suppose some of his men were sick; so were some of Frederick's, and even more of the enemy's.[27] Let the able-bodied march under arms, and let baggage and invalids follow when God willed it. The prince thought his powder supply insufficient for a siege of Prague, but Frederick said he wished only that he had as much with which to take Olmütz.[28]

The king found out in time that the powder he had with him was not enough for a siege of Olmütz. The recapture of Schweidnitz and the invasion of Moravia went according to plan; but when Olmütz was reached on May 5, plans began to go awry. The Austrians had refused to fight a battle in the open to stop the king's advance; and since the place was well enough garrisoned and fortified to withstand for two months the only sort of siege Frederick could conduct at such a distance from his base, they still refused to risk the sacrifice of an army by sending one to the city's relief. There were less costly ways than that of ridding themselves of their enemy's presence. His replacement troops had to convoy long and vulnerable wagon trains of supplies over many miles of dangerous roads in order to reach him. These the Austrians began to cut off; and thus, by the capture of a particularly vital convoy in spite of its guard of ten thousand men, they forced him to abandon the siege of Olmütz on July 1 and turn homeward again.

Boldly the king put the best possible face upon a bad situation. The

---

[26] *P. C.,* XVI, 394.

[27] It will be observed here that General Grant was not the first soldier to get what comfort he could out of the thought that his enemy was subject to the same hardships as himself, and probably feared him as much as he feared the enemy. Frederick always minimized the strength and magnified the difficulties of the forces facing Henry.

[28] *P. C.,* XVI, 381.

capture of the city had never, in his mind, been so much an object in itself as a means of drawing an Austrian army out of the hills of the Bohemian border in the hope of destroying it, and the Austrians had refused to be drawn. Meanwhile the Russians were threatening the Mark of Brandenburg, and there were no troops in Prussia or Saxony that could be disengaged to meet them. So he must soon have returned with his army in any case.

Quite characteristically he struck boldly into Bohemia, spreading the report both through his own agents and through Prince Henry's that he was marching straight on Prague. Then he withdrew via Königgrätz, so as to spare Silesia the hardships incidental to the passage of his army. When the withdrawal had been completed, he claimed that it had been accomplished with the loss of only two men. Mitchell, who was with him, called the retreat "precipitate," deplored the abandonment of great quantities of badly needed supplies, and mentioned "the usual desertions." Henry called it the king's best-managed maneuver of the whole war.[29] It was a strenuous march, but the king finished it in a fighting mood and with his men in fighting condition, as a less able commander could not have done.

Prince Henry was not surprised by the failure of the invasion of Moravia. He had never concealed even from the king his opinion that it was dangerous so to underrate the Austrian high command. With his own predilection for warfare by maneuver and by disruption of the enemy's service of supply, he had quickly seen and pointed out the opportunity that was being offered to the Austrians to act as in fact they did, and not as Frederick had hoped they would.

It was characteristic of the prince in any discussion to stress the risks involved in a proposed line of action, and of the king to look first at the advantages he hoped to win by it if successful. In this case the king had admitted before he left Silesia that he was not quite certain of the wisdom of the move he was about to make, or sure of success; but, he said, one could never be sure beforehand. "I hope that you will agree for the present, and that you will realize that everyone, taken as he is, makes mistakes, and that he is worth most who makes the least grievous ones. That, my dear brother, is the characteristic trait of humanity. The scope of [man's] wisdom is more limited than it is thought to be; perfection is found in no one; man approaches it from one direction or another, but never attains it. You will consign me to the devil with my moralizing, but I have to do it. These truths are humiliating to humanity, but they

[29] M. P., IV, 96; Bisset, II, 31; marginal comment by the prince in the *Oeuvres posthumes,* III, 270ff.

are true nonetheless; and they do not prevent us from acting as if we were perfect." [30]

The prince, to whom personally Frederick was not the perfect and infallible king of Prussia but an all-too-human older brother, had been unconvinced by his philosophical defense of a gambler's policy, but had raised no further objection to the plan; he had dutifully created a diversion in its favor by ostentatiously collecting depots of supplies and attacking some frontier posts in a manner indicating that he was about to invade Bohemia.[31] He could not resist the temptation, however, to send after the king one thinly veiled admonition not to waste his man power in the venture. After congratulating him upon the capture of Schweidnitz, he added: "Your small losses in men in taking this place constitute another aspect of the good fortune which I hope may follow you in all your undertakings. To conquer with success, it is essential that one's forces shall not be exhausted [in the process]." [32]

With the king's entry into Moravia the prince had become responsible for the defense of both Saxony and Silesia. For his task he was given a field army of about thirty thousand men and garrisons totaling ten thousand. Both his numbers and his means seemed to him quite inadequate, but the king blithely assured him that the enemy's needs were greater than his, and that a small force could and must be more active than a large one.[33]

Instead of doing the conventional thing that Frederick suggested, trying to overcome his handicap in strength merely by superior vigilance and greater swiftness in action, the prince worked out a system of his own in defiance of the accepted rules. It was unconventional to disperse an inferior force in the face of a superior one; but he did it, spreading his little army thinly over an area which the critics, both then and since, have said was far too large. The only apparent justification for his system is that it was thoughtfully worked out to fit the terrain in which he was operating and the enemy by whom he was faced — and that it was successful. With a sleepless vigilance equal to Frederick's, he was able thus to keep more closely in touch with enemy activities than if he had permitted his forces to be confined to a smaller area. By the incessant activity of light troops operating from widespread bases he kept his opponents constantly concerned about their communications and supply depots, at the same time making it more difficult for them to disturb his own. By his wise choice of a position for it, and by careful attention to all measures of defense, he made each of his detachments safe against attack by any but an overwhelming force; when necessary he moved it

---

[30] April 5, 1758, from Grüssau, in *P. C.*, XVI, 355–356; Schöning, II, 165–170.
[31] H. to F., in Schöning, I, 182.  [32] Schöning, I, 185.  [33] *P. C.*, XVI, 400.

to another position equally inaccessible. He was constantly aware of the danger of having these detachments cut off and beaten in detail; but since to foresee a danger and worry about it in advance was one of his most characteristic habits of mind, he consistently anticipated and therefore survived such hazards. Meanwhile he held, and drew supplies from, an area considerably larger than he could have done if he had concentrated his forces.

Henry's activities in the late spring and early summer of 1758 consisted therefore of an enormous number of troop movements, changes of position, and minor engagements. He fought no general battles, won no great victories, and suffered no serious reverses. He held on, struck viciously here or there, feinted, or dodged; but he neither abandoned his general position nor gave his enemy an opportunity to attack him with any prospect of success.

One reason for his good fortune was that he was usually fairly successful in guessing not only what his enemy would probably do but also at what times he could reasonably be expected not to do anything. One such occasion offered itself in the middle of May, while Frederick was engaged in the siege of Olmütz. Henry rightly refused to believe the king's repeated reports that practically all of Marshal Daun's Austrian forces had been drawn off from Bohemia toward Moravia; and he knew that the army facing him had lately been reinforced by some troops of the Empire. Yet he thought that a fraction of his own forces, properly posted and fortified, could hold their positions without fear of a determined general attack while he himself turned his attention for a short time to Franconia.

The presence of Imperial troops in that region west and southwest of electoral Saxony was a source of constant annoyance and some danger to the Prussians; and the petty principalities there, whether willingly or not, were furnishing recruits, money, and supplies to the enemies of Prussia. Immediately after his return from Hildesheim the prince had proposed a similar swing into Franconia toward Bamberg. The king had not authorized it then, but by May 4 he was beginning to view it more favorably, provided the prince still found it feasible. Three days later, although he himself was making no progress before Olmütz, he had become convinced that the prince could, within eight days, lay a heavy hand upon the Bishop of Bamberg and others ill disposed toward Prussia, force them to return to neutrality and recall their contingents from the Imperial army, levy contributions upon them, and return to Bohemia for a practically unobstructed advance upon Prague.[34]

---

[34] H. to F., in Schöning, I, 185; F. to H., in *P. C.,* XVII, 3, 7, 18. The king's refusal to

The prince, as usual, estimated his risks with all possible care. He realized that if the Austrians were at all awake to their opportunities — and unless General von Hülsen was very much awake to his — they might easily cut off all communication between von Hülsen at Freiberg and himself in Franconia. He decided to take the risk, however, in the hope of winning advantages elsewhere sufficient to justify it.[35]

Again a military operation was to serve a political purpose. Ahead of his troops, Prince Henry sent letters to the princes of Franconia, warning them to withhold or to recall their contingents from the army of the Empire. They were frightened by his approach, but were even more afraid of Austria and the Empire. Although both Würzburg and Bamberg were occupied by Prussian troops and a contribution of ninety thousand thaler in addition to military and other supplies had been levied upon Bamberg alone, its prince-bishop told Prince Henry that he was already too deeply involved with Austria to find neutrality possible, and feared that the regiments already furnished would simply be incorporated into the Austrian army if the princes should attempt to recall them.[36]

While the war thus rolled in successive waves around and over the friendly little state of Baireuth, its princess Wilhelmina lay desperately ill. Early in May, although Baireuth had been occupied by Prussia's enemies and forced to furnish them a contingent of troops, the highspirited sister of the king of Prussia had assured him that those men would mutiny, when the time came, rather than actually fight against him. She herself secretly sent on to her brother all the information she could gather concerning the plans of his enemies, and loyally urged him always to put Prussia's interest first and not to handicap himself in any way in order to spare Baireuth. Both the king and Prince Henry had, nonetheless, been careful not to carry the war into Baireuth. On May 28 the prince, who had made a detour to see her, had to explain to Frederick that she had been too ill to write; early in June he believed she was better; in July, goaded by his own bitterness over the death of Prince William, he wrote that the news of their brother's death would no doubt destroy her last slender chance of recovery.[37]

believe that his plan to draw Daun's army out of Bohemia was not working as he had expected was evidently in Sir Andrew Mitchell's mind when he wrote the following comment, marked "private and secret," to Holdernesse, just a few weeks later: "In this Army the Spies are paid too sparingly, consequently the Intelligence is none of the best, and when there comes Intelligence which does not agree with the Hypothesis that we have formed, that Intelligence is but little regarded." M. P., IV, 96; Bisset, I, 418.

[35] Schöning, I, 192, 198.
[36] *Ibid.*, 199–213; *P. C.*, XVII, 116.
[37] Schöning, I, 193–198, 234; *P. C.*, XVII, 144–145. See also above, p. 50. She lived

Henry's visit to Baireuth promised for a time to have some political repercussions. The little capital was known to be full of French spies, and the reigning margrave, his brother-in-law, perforce to have a foot in either camp. So it was probably rather by design than upon impulse that he made there the ostensibly indiscreet remark that he heartily wished his brother the king would come to his senses and begin to think about a durable peace. Naturally the remark was immediately passed on by the margrave to the French ministry.

The seed seemed at first to have fallen upon good ground. Previous attempts by Wilhelmina had failed to open up a channel for fruitful discussions, but this new overture, coming as it did during the siege of Olmütz and while the French were still expecting that siege to succeed, was welcomed by the French minister Bernis, who at once sent to the margrave a memorandum outlining in general terms the basis of a proposed settlement. That memorandum was copied by the margrave in his own hand, so that the suggestion would come ostensibly from Baireuth and not from Paris, and then sent to Prince Henry to be forwarded to Frederick. In sending it on, Henry commented that it was "almost certain" that the project was not the work of the margrave himself but had been sent to him by someone else. While he did not very strongly urge its acceptance, he obviously hoped that it might lead to negotiations.[38]

If Olmütz had fallen, the French might perhaps have sought to induce Maria Theresa to make peace; but with the king's forced withdrawal from Moravia and Bohemia all prospect of a negotiated peace at once disappeared. No peace based upon the proposals submitted by his brother-in-law would have been accepted by Frederick in any case. Great Britain, France, and Sweden would have been asked to guarantee the final treaty, and would thereafter have been empowered to arbitrate disputes arising between Austria and Prussia. Frederick did not stress that point either in his conversations with Mitchell or in his replies to the margrave, but he was not one to submit to compulsory arbitration. How much he thought of his dying sister, and how little of the negotiations, was indicated by his exclamation: "God give me good news of my sister; that is more important to me than all the negotiations in the world."[39]

Only those immediately concerned had any knowledge of this discussion of the possibility of a peace; and only Henry and his brother

until October, when the news of her death came as another blow following the defeat at Hochkirch, as the report of their mother's death had followed Kolin the year before.

[38] Schöning, I, 229.

[39] Conclusion of letter to the margrave of Baireuth, September 8, 1758, in *P. C.*, XVII, 217; M. P., IV, 100, 137; Bisset, I, 419–420; A. Schäfer, in the *Historische Zeitschrift*, XXI, 112–124.

Ferdinand blamed Frederick for his failure to secure a settlement that was at once unattainable and undesirable in itself. But coming as it did in midsummer of 1758, when he was, as he said, "suffering unspeakably" over the death of Prince William and quarreling bitterly with the king over its cause and its consequences, this new disappointment struck him at a very bad time. To his jaundiced eye Frederick was ugly just then in any light; and he and Ferdinand soon managed to convince themselves that an opportunity to make peace had been let slip merely because the king was "not yet sated with blood." It was not without reason that other members and friends of the family worried at times lest Henry's disaffection should make him forget his duty to the state, and feared that Ferdinand was insane.[40]

The family had yet to learn that it was between campaigns and not in the midst of one that Prince Henry was likely to try to leave the service. In the summer of 1758 it was as if his mind were departmentalized, or as if he were several persons at once. One person, or part of the man's mind, joined Ferdinand in carping criticism of the king; another handled the estate of the late Prince of Prussia; a third defended Saxony, administered Prussian affairs there, and carried the war into Franconia, reporting fully and faithfully to the king at every step; and a fourth, entirely unknown until then, volunteered for new and more arduous duties. The same courier sometimes carried letters to the king from two or more of these persons oddly joined in the complex character of Prince Henry, letters contrasting as sharply with one another as did the contradictory phases of their writer's personality. He was a disaffected person, but he was also a Hohenzollern, a Prussian prince, and a soldier; so he continued to serve.

He did more. He offered to undertake the strenuous and hazardous task of going to meet the invading Russians. On his own responsibility, while Frederick was on his way back through Bohemia and therefore could not be reached for orders or asked for help, he had already taken steps to reinforce the little army with which Count Dohna was observing and trying to impede the Russian advance into the New Mark. If the situation there had become any more critical before the king returned to deal with it, he had planned to go himself with the larger part of his troops from Saxony, to add Dohna's force to his own, and to confront the Russians.

After Frederick's return the prince proposed that the king stop in

[40] Henry-Ferdinand letters, in the Hausarchiv, Rep. 56, II, F; Caroline of Hesse, *Briefwechsel*, I, 271; Berner and Volz, *passim;* Otto Herrmann, in the *Historische Vierteljahrschrift*, XXVI (1931), 368.

Silesia and by strenuous activity there if possible immobilize the Austrian troops in Bohemia, while he would himself make Saxony temporarily safe by a quick thrust into Bohemia, then dash away and try to stop the Russian invasion and return before Saxony could be entirely overrun. He would rather risk an attempt to retake the province or even Dresden, if it were lost, than try to hold it with the reduced strength he would have left if he were required to reinforce Dohna. One small corps, he said, could not simply stand on the defensive against an army.[41]

The scheme was indeed a bold one, and not entirely practical. To retake Dresden or southern Saxony, once it was lost, proved subsequently to be a very difficult task. The king, harrassed as he was, replied rather bluntly that Dohna must defend the New Mark if he could, with reinforcements from Prince Henry's army. The prince, with whatever he had left, must hold Saxony and the Elbe and look out that no considerable invasion of Brandenburg was made by way of Lusatia. Frederick would himself take care of Silesia and seek to defeat either the Austrians or the Russians, whichever gave him the first good opening.[42]

In other words, the king would himself command in those great battles which promised to be decisive. The prince did not again volunteer. He suspected that he had been refused not for fear he would lose the battle but for fear he would win it and so make the king's own military record for the year look bad by comparison. It was clear to him that while the king lived he would be given only secondary commands.

The king soon made it equally clear, however, that in the event of his death the prince would be no longer second in command but regent and commander in chief. As Frederick's oldest living brother, he was the logical man for that place during the minority of their nephew Frederick William, who had inherited his father's title of Prince of Prussia and who would become king but who was still too young to take actual charge of either government or army. So Frederick, who could also departmentalize his mind with some degree of success when necessary, went ahead and did the logical thing by appointing him, undeterred by the recent unpleasantness between them. Frederick was always too keenly and constantly aware of his responsibilities as king ever consciously to do anything, for a merely personal reason, that would undermine either the authority of the monarchy or the prestige of the dynasty. The rule of

---

[41] Schöning, I, 228–229; *P. C.*, XVII, 88. In 1760, when he was himself holding the Saxon front under very similar circumstances, Frederick wrote to Henry: "If you can furnish me with an expedient whereby I can cover this whole country and at the same time send off a detachment, I shall welcome it with all the pleasure in the world." *P. C.*, XIX, 393.

[42] *P. C.*, XVII, 117, 140.

primogeniture was to be strictly followed. Under it his nephew should inherit the throne while the senior uncle assumed the responsibility.

Frederick loved to dramatize his actions. At the same time he considered it his duty not only to serve the state as long as he lived but also to protect it as best he could, in advance, against the consequences of his death. So it was not unusual for him, in preparation for battle, to draft orders covering the steps to be taken if he should be killed. On the eve of his departure for a do-or-die campaign against the Russians, the situation demanded some such provision on his part; and he was just in the mood for it. First, he wrote to Prince Henry:

My very dear brother: I beg you to preserve for me the strictest secrecy as to all the contents of this letter, which is for your sole direction only.

I march tomorrow against the Russians. As the fortunes of war can give rise to all sorts of accidents, and it can easily happen that I shall be killed, I have thought it my duty to inform you fully of my plans, especially as you are the guardian of our nephew with unlimited authority.

1. If I am killed, all the armies must at once take the oath [of fidelity] to my nephew.

2. You must continue to act so vigorously that the enemy will notice no change in the [high] command.

3. Here is my plan for the moment: to give the Russians a good whipping, if that is possible; immediately to send Dohna back against the Swedes, and myself either to return with my corps to Lusatia, if the enemy tries to get in through there, or to rejoin the army of Silesia and send off six or seven thousand men into Upper Silesia to drive away de Ville who is infesting that region; as for you, to let you act as the occasion presents itself, the object of your greatest attention being properly the projects of the enemy, which you must always derange before he succeeds in bringing them to maturity.

With regard to finances, I believe it my duty to inform you that all the disturbances which have recently taken place, as well as those which I still foresee, have obliged me to accept the English subsidies, which will be payable only in the month of October.[43]

As for politics, it is certain that if we hold out well through this campaign the enemy, weary, worn out, and exhausted by the war, will be the first to want peace; I trust that that point will be reached during the course of this winter.

That is all that I can tell you of affairs in general; as for detail, it will be your duty to inform yourself at once about everything; but if, immediately after my death, any impatience or a too strong desire for peace were shown, that would be sure to result in [your] getting a bad one and being obliged to accept dictation from those whom we have conquered.

[43] The last of four installments was paid in October. The money had been appropriated by Parliament on April 20 and the first installment was paid later in August.

I should add to all this my itinerary, so that you may know where I shall be and where you can find me. . . .[44]

The "itinerary" was a strenuous one. Within ten days the king expected to effect his junction with Dohna; and within two weeks he promised to be at grips with the Russians. He had to march some of his men to death in the August heat to do it, allowing only ten marches and two rest days for a distance of a hundred and fifty (English) miles, but he adhered to schedule. On the evening of the twelfth day he was in camp near Küstrin and, with a great battle impending, wrote out in German another "last will" to govern the conduct of his generals if he himself should be killed.

First he gave them such purely military instructions as he could, covering in hypothetical fashion a situation which had not yet actually arisen. Then they were directed to see that the whole army at once took the oath of fidelity to his nephew, but took its orders thereafter from Prince Henry and obeyed them as if they came from the reigning king, as the prince was to be the boy king's guardian with unrestricted authority. Another paragraph, which was repeated in its essentials in several such "wills" during the course of the war, directed that no fuss should be made over the king after his death and no post-mortem examination permitted, but that he should be carried quietly to Sans Souci and buried in his garden there. A postscript instructed the generals, if the battle should be lost, to reassemble the army behind the fortress of Küstrin, draw to it whatever reinforcements they could, and prepare, "the sooner the better," again to fall upon the enemy.[45]

Frederick did not lose at Zorndorf either his life or the battle; but it was a brisk and costly bit of business. He could have forced Fermor to withdraw for the season, merely by disrupting his rearward communications and destroying his supply depots. That would have been Prince Henry's way. But such an operation would have demanded more long marches from men already desperately tired from plodding day and night through the deep, hot sands of that region.[46] It would also have

---

[44] August 10, 1758, in *P. C.*, XVII, 158. A letter of similar content, but without the itinerary, was sent on the same day to the minister Finckenstein, who was instructed not to tell even his fellow minister Count Podewils of it unless the king was killed.

[45] August 22, in *P. C.*, XVII, 183; "je eher je lieber dem Feind von frischem wieder auf den Hals gehen."

[46] Mitchell's estimate of the march was over forty-four German (or more than two hundred English) miles, counting a German mile as slightly less than five English ones. Mitchell had accompanied the king and was present at the battle of Zorndorf. His accounts of the whole campaign (M. P., IV, 106, and Bisset, I, 425) are extremely interesting. Of Zorndorf itself he wrote: "We were on the very brink of destruction. The Russians fought like devils." Frederick had joked with him beforehand about the risk he was running, asking: "If you get yourself killed, who will notify your king of our victory?"

taken time; and the king had no time to lose, nor patience for Fabian tactics. Then the Russians shelled and burned Küstrin, and that angered him. The withdrawal of their army would not thereafter have been enough. He sought its total destruction.

The king tried therefore to move around the Russians' position and then attack them in such fashion that the swamps of the Mietzel River would prevent their escape. On the afternoon of August 24 his leg-weary troops had to march from one o'clock until long after dark. At three o'clock the next morning they were again on foot, with six hours of marching yet to do before getting into position. Then from nine until it was dark again they fought against foemen stubborn enough to fall in their ranks by thousands and too stubborn to give way. By nightfall their strength was spent. Their commander could usually defy fatigue in himself and disregard it in his men, but complete exhaustion prevented them from quite surrounding their enemy or driving him from the field. The armies simply fought one another to a standstill.

Frederick had reason to be dejected; after spending men to save time he found that he had lost both time and men and must still wait for the surly withdrawal of the enemy he had tried so desperately to destroy. The Russians were stopped; but the "good whipping" they had had, such as it was, had left them unrepentant and uncowed. They would not attack Prussian troops commanded by the king in person; but neither would they run from them.[47]

A victory was at once announced, and the churches were ordered to sing *Te Deum laudamus;* but public statements about the battle were carefully edited and reticent about the cost of the victory. Frederick had lost a third of his effectives, and the Russians nearly half of theirs.

The preoccupation of the king and the sending of reinforcements to Dohna left Prince Henry with depleted forces, outnumbered more than two to one by those facing him. Without hope of immediate succor, he was charged with the defense of Saxony, the safeguarding of transport on the Elbe, and the maintenance of communications with all other sectors. It was no simple task. Beforehand he had said that it could not be done, but when actually confronted by it he undertook it bravely and in good spirit. With his troops placed fanwise on the heights of Freiberg, Maxen, Pirna, and Dippoldiswalde, the Elbe serving as their lifeline and

[47] That evening the indefatigable Frederick found the time and energy to write out in his own hand the draft of a letter to Prince Henry announcing that, although he had been "on the point of being beaten," yet he had "beaten them." He knew then neither the enemy's losses nor his own, but had been told that three Russian lieutenant generals were among the prisoners. It was a short letter, ending: "Adieu, dear brother, I am low in spirit; I embrace you with all my heart." *P. C.,* XVII, 187.

Dresden as their focal point, he waited alertly but with a great show of confidence for the Austrians' first move. "I shall do all that is humanly possible to put myself in the way of the enemy," he wrote. ". . . Although I shall be very greatly in need of cavalry here, none the less I know that it is even more urgently necessary there; and if we are to suffer a reverse, I should prefer that it happen to me, since the damage could be more quickly repaired than if fortune were unfavorable to us against the Russians." [48]

The prince was justified in his confidence that he could hold off the composite Austrian and German Imperial army, commanded by the Prince of Zweibrücken, immediately facing him in the southern border region of Saxony, although for once in his career he seriously under-estimated the size of the hostile force. [49] By incessant activity, which kept his enemy always tactically on the defensive, he managed to maintain himself without much general change of position throughout most of the month of August.

Soon a new danger threatened, from the other direction. On the day after the battle of Zorndorf Marshal Daun moved out westward from Görlitz in Lusatia, by the Bautzen road, with another Austrian force nearly twice as large as Henry's whole army. It was his intention to strike the Elbe at Meissen, below Dresden, thus cutting the prince off from his principal supply base at Torgau and depriving him of the use of the river for transport, then to work upstream and get between him and Dresden. If the prince did not then try to fight his way out of the ring thus closing in upon him, Daun would attack him from the north and the Prince of Zweibrücken from the south. [50]

Henry drew his forces a bit closer together, reinforced the garrisons of Dresden and Torgau, moved his own headquarters nearer to his front line so as to be in closer touch with the enemy — and waited. Hostile troops swarmed around him in such numbers that the *Feldjäger* who still slipped through with dispatches had to be trusted with messages to be delivered orally if the letters they carried had to be destroyed for fear of capture. But in spite of all hazards the king got word in to him that his army and Saxony were Daun's objectives, not Torgau or Magdeburg, and he got word out that he was still holding his own and was sure he could continue to do so until Daun actually took a hand. After that there would be cause for concern. [51]

[48] August 19, 1758, in Schöning, I, 247, and in *P. C.,* XVII, 182.
[49] He did not believe that it exceeded 38,000 men, although he knew that it claimed 50,000. The German General Staff history puts it at 50,000 to 51,000, Jany at 39,500.
[50] Von Arneth, *Geschichte Maria Theresias,* V, 410.
[51] Sedlitz, August 30, in Schöning, I, 250–257, and in *P. C.,* XVII, 144.

A week after Zorndorf Frederick was still trying vainly to maneuver the Russians off eastward to Landsberg or beyond, so could send Henry only advice and encouragement. As advice he had little to offer except the familiar admonition to maintain the strictest discipline in the infantry, "making them fear the stick." [52] As encouragement he wrote: "I have only infinite praise for your wise and prudent dispositions, and it would be difficult for me to add the least thing to perfect them." And again: "There is not a word to be said [in criticism] of your conduct."

By the end of another week the prince had been forced to give up Pirna to the Imperialists; but the Prince of Zweibrücken thought the position at Gamig too strong to be attacked; Daun hesitated to attack it alone; so there they stood, Imperialists at Pirna, Austrians at Stolpen, and Henry between them at Gamig, outnumbered more than four to one but apparently unafraid. Then the approach of the king of Prussia put a new face upon the situation. [53]

Sir Andrew Mitchell thought it was "a miracle that Prince Henry and his little army had not been devoured." That they had not been devoured was due not to any lack of appetite on the part of their opponents but to the prince's genius for making himself unpalatable if not inedible, and to the inability of the chef to control his fellow cooks in the preparation of the broth. If Daun and the Prince of Zweibrücken had cooperated as cordially as the Prussian commanders did, they could hardly have failed to overrun all Saxony. As the king and his brother learned by experience to count upon one another more and more confidently, they learned also in their calculations always to figure in a few enemy blunders to equalize the odds. Consequently, when the enemy failed to blunder, the Prussians books were likely to be thrown badly out of balance.

The spirit with which the royal brothers met that September crisis, in contrast with their opponents' irresolution and lack of unity, explains Mitchell's miracle. From Elsterwerda, where the king was compelled to halt to give his men a day of rest after marching twenty-four German (nearly a hundred and twenty English) miles in seven days, he assured his brother that, despite their forced march, they would arrive in condition to give a good account of themselves in battle if "His fat Excellency of Kolin" should be willing to test them. The prince, for his part, had bread, pontoons, and a supply of ammunition ready at Dresden for the use of the king's troops. He even remembered and reported that

[52] *Leur faire respecter le bâton.* The king's undisciplined East Prussian regiments had not shown at Zorndorf the steadfastness of the service-hardened veterans he had brought there with him; and that experience was yet fresh in his mind. P. C., XVII, 199, 204.

[53] Schöning, I, 257–260; M. P., IV, 115; Bisset, I, 448. De Catt's diary reads: "Went to the advance guard. Saw the army of the Empire, Prince Henry's, Daun's, and ours." Koser, "Unterhaltungen," 365.

the Bishop of Bamberg had not yet completed the payment of the contribution levied upon him in the spring! [54]

In Dresden on September 11 the brothers met for the first time in ten months, with General Seydlitz, who had come with the king, as a third party; again five days later they dined together in the king's camp at Pillnitz. Their armies were not actually united. That brought by Frederick was put to work at once in an attempt to maneuver Marshal Daun out of his fortified camp at Stolpen; but after a week of unsuccessful effort the king abandoned the attempt and resorted to a partial blockade of the Austrian position, grumbling meanwhile that the Austrian generals must all have been born in the mountains. "They no sooner see a hill than there they are, up on top of it."

As usual, comparative inactivity while he waited "for hunger to accomplish what the sword had failed to do" affected Frederick's nerves adversely, giving his weariness, disappointment, and countless difficulties an opportunity to prey upon his mind. It was a period of deepest discouragement for him. Finding more time than usual for worrying and writing, and acting instinctively on the pathetically erroneous assumption that Henry would be as sympathetic in these personal concerns as he was correct in his military conduct, he counted his woes daily in a self-commiserating fashion bordering closely upon hysteria. His was for a time, by his own account of it, the worst of all possible worlds; and the prince, who chose that occasion to remark that the war was, in his opinion, likely to last for four or five years longer, was not a very consoling confidant. Thus, unfortunately, Frederick the man, seeking sympathy from his brother, revealed all too plainly to his self-confident and critical second-in-command the doubts, perplexities, and badly shaken confidence of Frederick the king and commander in chief. [55]

Meanwhile hunger, summoned as an ally against the Austrians, sat down as an unbidden guest at the Prussian mess tables. When Henry brought it to Frederick's attention that his army was suffering from a shortage of forage he received only the sharp reply that the king's own was no better supplied and that there was no money with which to buy more. He was advised instead to give no further credence to his supply

[54] Schöning, I, 262–263, and *P. C.*, XVII, 217, 222. In spite of all his insistence upon discipline, the king grumbled that his own troops often lacked ammunition in battle because they were in the habit of throwing it away on the march to avoid carrying it.

[55] H. to F., September 19, in the Hausarchiv, Rep. 56, II, I; F. to H., in *P. C.*, XVII, 228–260. Among the special worries of the period were the increasingly critical illness of Wilhelmina of Baireuth and the threat of a Swedish raid on Berlin, which had already had to be ransomed once from the Austrians less than a year before. The Swedes did occupy Rheinsberg temporarily without doing it much damage. The costs and the inhumanity of the war were also weighing heavily upon the king since Zorndorf, as upon Napoleon after Eylau.

officers, who, the king said, had been bribed by the Saxons to protect them while they deceived him about the alleged exhaustion of their stores. There was still forage to be had in Saxony if the prince would require his officers to find it and take it.[56]

In the last week of September, after again calling his brother into conference to explain his plan, the king turned once more to maneuver as a means of getting the Austrians out of Saxony. But his spirits failed to rise as they usually did when he was actually on the move, and his talk of suicide was resumed.[57]

At last, on October 6, he managed to dislodge Daun from Stolpen and followed him eastward into Lusatia. On the eleventh he was at Hochkirch in a position with which he was by no means satisfied, but for the choice of which he blamed General Retzow's failure to seize a hill called the Stromberg, near Weissenberg, as ordered. The hill was fortified and strongly defended; but the king was angry and aggrieved because he "had not been obeyed." If Retzow had done his duty, he said, Daun would have been forced to decamp at once. As it was, as soon as Marshal Keith could bring up the remainder of his forces and a convoy of flour from Dresden, he planned to try again to outflank Daun and force him back away from Görlitz and Zittau, and then go on into Silesia. He had no thought of staying long where he was.[58]

He was not permitted to stay even as long as he had intended. Both friend and foe recognized, as he himself had done, the weakness of his position; and Daun, who had vainly sought all summer for a favorable opportunity to attack Prince Henry, found his opening at last and attacked the king himself.[59] The army was driven from its ground and badly disorganized, losing about nine thousand officers and men — nearly a third of its effective strength — and more than a hundred of its guns. Marshal Keith and Prince Francis of Brunswick, a brother of the queen of Prussia, were among those killed. The men and wagons for moving the wounded from Bautzen to Dresden had to be provided by Prince Henry.

Sir Andrew Mitchell, who had remained behind at Dresden, wrote *propria manu* and "most privately" to Holdernesse what many others thought but dared not say: "Impatience is certainly excusable in the

[56] Schöning, I, 270; *P. C.,* XVII, 268. Instead, Henry forced his enemies to feed him for a time by raiding some Imperialist convoys and supply depots.

[57] *P. C.,* XVII, 274, 280, 292.

[58] *Ibid.,* 296–297. Feeling always a certain amount of sympathy for General Retzow and for other generals in similar situations, Prince Henry wrote, many years later, the following marginal comment in his copy of Frederick's *Histoire de mon temps* (*Oeuvres,* 1788, I, 230): "All his life he blamed his errors on his allies or on his generals."

[59] October 14. Keith is said to have protested, on arrival, "If the Austrians leave us alone here, they deserve to be hanged." Bisset, II, 490–495. Prince Moritz of Anhalt-Dessau, and

situation in which the King of Prussia now stands, . . . but . . . I can
not help suspecting that the success of this surprise is owing to two causes,
the very great contempt he had of the enemy, and the unwillingness I
have long observed in him to give any degree of credit to intelligence
that is not agreeable to his own imaginations." [60] A better explanation,
which may not have occurred to Mitchell but which more probably he
left unsaid because he thought it imprudent to write it, was that since
Zorndorf and more particularly since that period of intense depression at
Pillnitz in September, the king had definitely not been at his best.[61]

It was a part of Prussia's good fortune in the war that, though both her
principal commanders had their slack periods when weariness, bad
health, or worry lowered somewhat the level of their efficiency, they
were rarely both in the doldrums at the same time. While the king
traveled his unhappy road from Pillnitz to Hochkirch, Henry had been
making hay in Saxony. Freiberg was retaken, Prussian raiders were
active over a wide area and almost uniformly successful, and the prince's
re-established position was not materially worse than the one he had
held in the spring.

Immediately after Hochkirch the king's losses had to be made good
from the forces in Saxony. Men, guns, other military equipment, food,
and forage were required. Since the prince would have had but little
left after honoring these requisitions, he urged a temporary fusion of the
two armies, or else that he be permitted to bring in person the detachment which came to join the king, leaving to someone else the command
of the remnant remaining in Saxony. The king wisely refused to abandon Saxony, even temporarily, but permitted the prince to join him
along with the replacements while General Finck took up the watch on
the Elbe.[62]

Generals Seydlitz and von Schmettau are also said to have warned the king that he would
certainly be attacked there. Count F. W. K. von Schmettau, *Lebensgeschichte des Grafen
von Schmettau* (Berlin, 1806), 392. The king's own account of the battle, to Prince Henry,
is in the *P. C.,* XVII, 305, and in *Oeuvres,* XXVI, 192.

[60] Bisset, I, 455. The hero-worship so much in evidence in Mitchell's attitude toward
the king in the first two years of the war was less and less notable as time went on.

[61] In his second letter to the prince after Hochkirch, after asserting that he would not
have lost if he had had eight battalions more, he concluded: "Adieu, dear brother; have
compassion upon the unfortunate, and remember what I told you so often a year ago"
(clearly another of his many references to suicide). *P. C.,* XVII, 307. It was during the
same anxious period that, according to de Catt, he showed the latter a golden vial containing eighteen little poison pills which he was wearing suspended from his neck on a
ribbon and concealed beneath his shirt. "You see," he is reported to have told de Catt,
"I can end the tragedy when I will." He always had a special horror of being captured and
held prisoner by the Austrians, and declared that he would certainly kill himself if taken.
See Hans Rothfels, "Friedrich der Grosse in den Krisen des siebenjährigen Krieges," in
the *Historische Zeitschrift,* CXXXIV (1926), 14–30, and Koser, "Unterhaltungen," 190.

[62] Schöning, I, 284–285; *P. C.,* XVII, 308–316. The senior general then serving in

By the time he received the king's permission the prince was ready to start, taking with him all his artillery and heavy loads of supplies but moving with remarkable speed. Although his princess, on hearing of it, considered it bad news that he had gone to join the king, and wrote that the thought of it caused her "some inquietude," he was welcomed as a lifesaver. When authorizing him to come, the king had added: "Hasten your marches. . . . Whatever you do, do it quickly. The enemy is [only] a quarter-mile away from me, and who knows even what may happen tomorrow!" While waiting, he had said to others: "Only let my brother come here, and you will see that Daun will gain no advantage over us." When reproached for having exposed himself so freely to personal danger at Hochkirch, on the ground that he must keep himself alive to save his army, he replied: "If I don't do it, my brother will." [63] Upon his arrival the prince was made a general of infantry — just when he had voluntarily given up an independent command to serve again temporarily in a subordinate capacity. [64]

In spite of any forebodings the princess Henry may have had, there followed a period of the finest possible cooperation between the brothers, during which they both approached their brilliant best. The prince had been instructed to include no Silesian battalions among the replacements, because it was necessary to fight an aggressive campaign in Silesia or lose the province for the winter; and the king was determined to go on there exactly as if Hochkirch had never happened. Such a seeming disregard of a disastrous defeat was highly disconcerting to his enemies and made them cautious even as they swarmed upon his heels. But there was hot fighting from Bautzen to Görlitz and beyond, in which the Prussian rearguard was courageously, skillfully, and successfully commanded by Prince Henry. The prince then held the frontier posts of Hirschberg and Landeshut while the king, with his flank and rear so protected, went on to the relief of the Silesian fortresses of Neisse, Schweidnitz, and Löwenberg.

Saxony was von Hülsen; and it was to him that the prince had assumed he would turn over the command; but Finck was preferred by the king because he was younger and more active. One of von Hülsen's staff officers, a lieutenant, was Baron von Steuben, who later served as inspector general in the Continental Army during the War for American Independence. See John McA. Palmer, *General von Steuben* (New Haven, 1937).

[63] Koser, "Unterhaltungen," 194, 190; M. P., IV, 140; the princess's journal in Berner and Volz, 106; F. to H., October 17 and 18, in *P. C.*, XVII, 316, 319. At the bottom of the ciphered letter of October 18, the anguished king wrote in his own hand: "Great God! My sister of Baireuth!" He had just learned that she had died.

[64] Schmitt, *Prinz Heinrich*, I, 76; Schöning, I, 290. That was his last promotion. Frederick ruled that the one higher rank of field marshal was not open to a Prussian prince, although Ferdinand of Brunswick attained it. Prince Henry was thus for many years the "senior" general of infantry in the army, and the further promotion of other distinguished commanders, such as the Duke of Bevern, Fouqué, Seydlitz, and Zieten, was blocked out of consideration for him.

The year 1757 had ended with the reconquest of Silesia as a result of the victory at Leuthen. As the year 1758 approached its end, that province had once more been reconquered in spite of the defeat at Hochkirch; but Lusatia and Saxony remained to be cleared, and Dresden had again to be rescued.[65]

Leaving Loudon to watch the king of Prussia, since he could not stop him, Daun had turned back to Saxony. On November 8, while Mitchell was wishing that Prince Henry would soon return, the prince heard from deserters that Daun was marching on Dresden, and so reported to the king, with the reservation that his informants were none too reliable. That same day, on the basis of logic alone, Frederick had decided that Daun would do nothing more that autumn. If he had intended to do anything, he would have done it already. So the king demonstrated to his own satisfaction that Dresden was safe. As the Austrians would not wish to destroy the city, they would not in any case fire upon it; so the garrison could hold it for some time, even if it were attacked. He himself and Prince Henry could therefore afford to take time to make a bid for the possession of Lusatia before their presence in Saxony would be required. It was not until a week later that he could bring himself to believe that Daun had actually returned there.[66]

Even then the king decided to clear Lusatia on his way, rather than march around it. So, moving in three columns (the king's own, Prince Henry's, and General Zieten's, which was to remain there), the Prussian mobile army swooped in from Silesia, via Lauban, Frederick's spirits soaring higher with every sleepless night and every day spent in the saddle; and Lusatia was cleared. The king had said: "I do not know whether the enemy will wait for me or not; but I am quite sure I shall see to it that he leaves"; and the result justified his reviving confidence.[67]

During the week that elapsed after Frederick first heard that Dresden was endangered and before he realized that the report was true, the city was being besieged. It was not very seriously damaged by Austrian gunfire, but the commander of the Prussian garrison, General von Schmet-

---

[65] Mitchell wrote to Holdernesse from Dresden on November 8 that Finck had been in trouble from the day Prince Henry left: "I . . . do not expect much from this army whilst it continues on the footing it now is. If Prince Henry was here it might do something." M. P., IV, 145. Mitchell's concern was shared, and his wish was supported, by opinion in the Prussian capital. Caroline of Hesse wrote on November 18 to Princess Amelia: "I shouldn't be afraid if Prince Henry were still in command of our army in Saxony." *Briefwechsel*, I, 287.

[66] H. to F., in Schöning, I, 294, and *P. C.*, XVII, 362; F. to H., in *P. C.*, XVII, 361, 376. It was of course a common trick to order a soldier to desert and tell a misleading story to his captors.

[67] *P. C.*, XVII, 373. In the same letter he again paid his compliments to the Austrian field marshal: "I hope to God that Daun gets his nose frozen and goes to the devil."

tau, ordered some of the suburbs to be burned on November 10 as a measure of defense. A week later the besiegers were gone, driven away by the approach of the Prussian king and Prince Henry. On November 20 the two re-entered the city; and the king sat down to rest for a few days in the electoral palace.[68]

For Frederick a "rest" was usually only a change of activity, and the brief period of quiet in Dresden was no exception. The old *Tutelar-Disposition* of August 15, 1757, was renewed and brought up to date, naming Prince Henry (in the event of the king's death) regent, guardian of the Prince of Prussia, general in chief, and "head of all the colleges of the state," during the minority of the heir to the throne.[69] Hundreds of thousands of thaler and two years' exemption from taxes were granted to indemnify Küstrin, the New Mark, and Pomerania for the damage they had suffered at the hands of the Russians. More than half a million (payable in the following February) was promised the army officers as an aid in re-equipping themselves for the new year. Prince Henry's bonus, if apportioned according to rank, would have been two thousand thaler. A field marshal was to receive three thousand.[70]

There were not many to be rewarded at that rate; none had been appointed to replace Count Schwerin, but now there was a new one. Prince Ferdinand of Brunswick was promoted, although he had been a general of infantry for only nine months. Along with the announcement of that promotion the king made it known by a general order that he reserved the right thereafter to promote whomever he chose on the basis of meritorious service, regardless of seniority, particularly among the general officers. That was his answer to the problem of finding effective leaders, and to the friction that had recently prevailed among the generals in Saxony because of the preference shown General Finck.

Prince Henry had also been promoted faster than his years alone

[68] M. P., IV, 149, 152, 153; Bisset, I, 463.
[69] P. C., XVII, 409; *ibid.*, supplement, xi; Volz in the *Hohenzollern Jahrbücher*, XX (1916), 177; MS in the Hausarchiv.
[70] Schöning, I, 305; Berner and Volz, 420, 427. Captains were to receive 250 thaler each, lieutenants 50. They needed less equipment, but their salaries and ordinary allowances were proportionately small. On January 4, 1760, the queen reported to her brother Ferdinand the following distribution of money:

To the queen:

| | |
|---|---:|
| for the repair of Schönhausen, considerably damaged by the Austrians | 10,000 thaler |
| for the poor of Berlin | 6,000 thaler |
| for the poor of Potsdam | 4,000 thaler |
| for the poor of Charlottenburg | 2,000 thaler |
| To the city of Berlin to indemnify individuals | 100,000 thaler |
| To the city of Berlin, as compensation for ransom paid | 1,000,000 thaler |
| To the city of Halberstadt | 200,000 thaler |
| For the purchase of grain for the spring planting in devastated areas | 100,000 thaler |

would have warranted, but his birth would have given him some protection against the jealousy of his fellow officers even if they had not recognized his ability. While his generals sometimes quarreled among themselves, none of them ever challenged his authority or his superiority. The new general order would therefore not have been necessary on his account, but if anyone had been nourishing a grievance on that point he would have learned from that order just where he stood.

After less than three weeks in Dresden the king went off to Breslau. The prince resumed command in Saxony, and had very soon recovered full possession of it. His troops formed, that winter, a chain along the Bohemian border. Mitchell, on his way to rejoin the king, wrote from Berlin to Robert Keith at St. Petersburg: "The retreat of the Austrian army and of the army of the Empire out of Saxony is one of those events which will hardly be credited in history." [71]

The same thing could have been said of the whole Prussian fight for survival in the year 1758. The king and his brother had rescued one another from some desperate situations. Together they had once more saved their state. Neither could have done it alone. To have done it at all was a triumph, and glory enough for two.

Yet no one realized better than they the emptiness of that triumph or the price paid for their glory. The prince had hated the war from the beginning and had gone on with it only because he could not extricate himself. And of that year's work the king wrote: "Our campaign is finished, and nothing has come of it on either side but the death of a great many honest fellows, the misery of a great many poor soldiers maimed for life, the ruin of some provinces, and the ravaging, pillage and burning of some flourishing towns. There, dear Milord, are exploits that make humanity shudder, the sad effects of the wickedness and ambition of a few powerful men who sacrifice everything to their unruly passions." [72]

[71] M. P., IV, 166.
[72] To George Keith, Lord Marshal of Scotland and brother of Marshal James Keith, from Dresden, November 23, in *P. C.*, XVII, 398.

CHAPTER VI

# The Miracle of the House of Brandenburg

*"I announce to you the miracle of the house of
Brandenburg: during the whole time since the
enemy crossed the Oder, when by risking a battle
he could have won the war, he has marched from
Müllrose to Lieberose."*—Frederick to Henry.

ON HIS WAY from Dresden to rejoin the king in Breslau in December,
1758, the British minister to Prussia was entertained at dinner in Magdeburg by the princess Henry. His mood and his manners being what they
were, he could not have failed to give her an enthusiastic account of her
husband's part in the campaign just then concluded. As the year approached its end it was reported that after a week or two of comfortable
living in Dresden the prince found himself again in good health and
high spirits, and that he hoped to visit his family in Berlin in January.
Entries in the princess's journal would indicate that she looked forward
with the greatest eagerness to his coming.[1]

For the prince himself the return could not have been other than a
sad one. Here was, for him, no longer the family of two years before.
The goodhearted queen showed in every possible way her gratitude to
him, not only for his distinguished services to the state but for the respect-
ful consideration he always showed her; but he never saw her without
being reminded afresh of the absence of the late dowager queen, his
mother. A considerable part of his time was spent in reading his mother's
letters and in handling over and over all sorts of mementos of her, which
had been saved by Princess Amelia for more than a year and a half. He
also showered attentions upon his widowed sister-in-law the Princess
of Prussia and upon her two boys, his wards; but he could not be with
them without feeling again the pain of the loss of his brother.

Such consolation as he found for his renewed sense of bereavement
was afforded him chiefly by the company of his sister Amelia. She it was
and not his wife whom he invited to come as far as Wusterhausen to
meet him, and to give him dinner when he arrived on the evening of
his birthday. And his wife had to take her the message! Finding but
little consolation in the fact that Amelia promptly invited her also to

[1] M. P., IV, 160; Berner and Volz, 111, 114.

91

dinner, poor Princess Henry decided to start early on the road toward Dresden and be the first to greet her husband when he stopped to change horses at some relay post before reaching Wusterhausen. Accompanied by one of her ladies in waiting, she made the fatiguing but futile journey. After a night and a day spent either in her carriage or sitting sleepless and almost entirely without food beside the fire in cramped and malodorous quarters in the tiny posthouse at Muhle, she decided that her husband must have changed his route; so she returned home, dressed, and went to Amelia's to wait with the others. Having come by the pre-arranged road, but many hours behind schedule, the belated wayfarer arrived at last, sometime after midnight, to be greeted by a great concourse of people and a semipublic supper at Amelia's.[2]

The prince was at home for a fortnight, but his wife's home was not his. Sometimes they dined together at Amelia's or the queen's, or *"chez nous,"* according to her journal. Sometimes she entertained his aides while he dined with Amelia. He brought her an elaborate gift of porcelain and charged her with packets of valuable papers to be guarded carefully for him; but he left her without a word of farewell. He made parting calls upon the queen and the Princess of Prussia; but only his aides came around to his wife, to be fed again and to take leave of her.[3]

In its private and personal aspects the second return of the prince from the war zone was as lacking in romantic thrills as his first, but he showed no disappointment. Outwardly it was more of a success. He was hailed as a hero by the people of Magdeburg and Berlin, and monopolized for a while the spotlight which would naturally have been following the movements of the king if Frederick had also returned. It was a new and pleasant experience.

From Berlin the prince returned to his post by a circuitous route via Sagan, whither Frederick had come from Breslau to meet him for a conference. They found themselves in close agreement both as to the remoteness of the possibility of peace (particularly since the fall of the French minister Bernis), and as to the wisest course for them to follow, if permitted to choose their course at all, in the coming campaign. As Frederick put it, while a sovereign or two might be expected to die in the course of the year, a real epidemic must break out among the rulers of Europe before Prussia could dare hope to find her safety anywhere but at the point of her sword; and Henry agreed. In such a situation the prince would hold that sword poised in readiness for defensive thrusts,

[2] Princess Henry's long journal entry for that day (which was presumably not written that night), concludes: "I came back home, more irritated and exhausted than I have ever been in my life." Berner and Volz, 117.

[3] *Ibid.,* 119, 421. Although she did not name him in that connection, it is quite probable

but would not willingly see the Prussian defense throw itself completely off balance and expose itself to easy counterattack by any such lunges deep into enemy territory as the Moravian invasion of the year before; and the king agreed, for the first time since the war began, to wait for one of his enemies to make the first move. He did so in the hope that an Austrian army would come out of its beloved hills into the open country where he might be able to attack it with some prospect of success and "use the little oil that was still left in his lamp." In general, the prince would again guard the Elbe and the king the Oder. For their whole field army about 110,000 men would again be available, and they could hope to find at most points two men to face three of the enemy.[4]

The "waiting" policy which circumstances seemed to dictate in all the principal war areas could be abandoned with safety only on Henry's western front. There the situation was much the same as before his Thuringian campaign of the previous year, except that the towns were better fortified and that the enemy would not for a second time be so easily surprised. Prince Ferdinand of Brunswick wished to see another diversion there, which he would always find useful; and Frederick was willing to let Henry try it again and see what he could do. Neither the king nor his brother thought he could go as far or accomplish as much as in 1758. There was too much danger of an Austrian incursion into Saxony in his absence, or of his being cut off entirely from Dresden and the Elbe if he went away too far or stayed away too long. Frederick thought that Erfurt should be about his limit. Again Ferdinand of Brunswick was dissatisfied and protested that if he could expect no more help than that, he must merely stand on the defensive; but again Henry and Frederick were in complete agreement.[5]

Again, as a year earlier, the Prussians found their worst enemies to be the rain, the cold, the mud, and the distances. The Imperial troops were driven off without much serious fighting, although there was almost constant skirmishing. Prince Henry went in person as far as Naumburg on the Saale, where he stayed for a few days in the first week of March while his generals pushed ahead; Knobloch held Erfurt for ten

that one of those aides was Kalckreuth. He had then been a member of the prince's staff for several months.

[4] *P. C.*, XVIII, 33, 731, 128; M. P., IV, 180–183; Koser, *Geschichte Friedrichs des Grossen*, III, 1–19. The conference took place on February 3 or 4. On the ninth the brothers were again at their posts, one in Breslau and the other in Dresden, and the prince was gratefully acknowledging some "new proofs of [the king's] good will." Schöning, II, 18.

[5] *P. C.*, XVIII, 732, *et passim*; M. P., IV, 189; Schöning, II, 23, *et passim*. Theodor von Bernhardi, in *Friedrich der Grosse*, I, 319, criticizes Prince Henry very severely, as usual, for not making a major enterprise out of this bit of byplay, and Maschke suggests that Frederick was sarcastic, not sincere, when he later congratulated the prince upon his admittedly small successes in it. *Jahrbücher für die deutsche Armée und Marine*, CXVII (1900), 202.

days and levied upon it a ransom of eighty thousand thaler, to be paid within eighteen weeks, and Kleist and others went on westward to Eisenach and Fulda, thus once more reaching the Weser River. The Bishop of Fulda had to ransom his town for twelve thousand thaler. Everywhere they went the Prussian troops were ordered by the prince to bring back with them to Naumburg all the grain they could find and such military prisoners as they could catch. They caught about six hundred. They were not to destroy property indiscriminately nor to make war upon civilians except by way of their purses, but some prominent persons were again carried off as hostages for the payment of the "contributions" their towns were compelled to make. The king commented, when it was finished, that although the campaign was not one of those decisive strokes by which a nation is shaken to its foundations, it had gone well beyond his expectations, and he was pleased with what it had brought him in "honor, prisoners, and money." [6]

The prince was back in Dresden by March 6, but in bad physical condition. He did not mention his health to Frederick in those days; he had no occasion to do so, for the staff surgeon Cothenius was with him and was making frequent reports directly to the king. Although he was comparatively free from pain, he had suffered for some time from exhaustion, intestinal disturbances, a persistent undulant fever, sleeplessness, and general debility. He was not suspected of malingering, for he was neither mentioning his illness nor seeking even partial relief from duty; but Frederick was impatient with Cothenius and remarked that he should be "much quicker with his cures." He naturally wanted his second-in-command to be fit for more strenuous service in the emergencies that would inevitably arise as the season advanced, so he expected the surgeon to do his duty and see to it. [7]

After Henry's return to Saxony the two brothers waited on the alert for the first enemy move. Word of such a move seemed likely to reach the prince first, for his troops were widely spread along the Saxon border, with only a mobile reserve of two regiments in hand in Dresden, and his spies were active in both Prague and Vienna. Frederick urged him to spare neither ink and paper nor men and horses in sending on immediately whatever military intelligence he could gather from any source. Meanwhile, with the prince posted in Dresden and Fouqué in Silesia, the king considered himself and the troops under his immediate command as the mobile reserve of the whole army, to be used at once at the point of greatest danger. He was thus consciously assigning to each, him-

[6] H. to F., in Schöning, II, 26; M. P., IV, 191; F. to H., in *P. C.*, XVIII, 109.
[7] Schöning, II, 25.

self and his brother, the task for which he was best fitted. He was himself essentially an offensive fighter seeking always a quick decision by battle, and his troops had been trained chiefly for the attack; Henry, as friend and foe alike had learned, was a wizard on the defense; and no one except the king himself or Prince Henry was better qualified than Fouqué for the Silesian assignment. The prince had about thirty-seven thousand men, the king forty thousand, and Fouqué somewhat less than twenty thousand.[8]

During March the Austrians did little on their Saxon front except to strengthen their fortifications and obstruct the roads along the northwestern frontier of Bohemia, from Eger to Aussig; it seemed probable that they also were planning to await an attack instead of making one. So Ferdinand of Brunswick began to urge that Henry try to repeat another of his exploits of 1758 by undertaking a second expedition into Franconia. Frederick also suggested it and announced to Mitchell that the prince was "going again to Bamberg," which would "set the French a-running" and render them inactive for two months.[9] Henry complied at once to the very limited extent of sending General Knobloch to capture Saalfeld and Hof, on the upper Saale, both of which yielded some grain and some prisoners.[10] That would prevent the sending of any French or Imperial troops from that region to Ferdinand's front on the Weser; but Henry hesitated to involve himself any more deeply there until he had first tied up the Austrians so as to make sure they would not break into Saxony while he was gone. So he formulated a bold plan for a sudden attack upon the Austrian detachments and depots in northwestern Bohemia, along the Eger and the Elbe rivers, and presented it to Frederick, with such a treatise on the possible objections to it that he seemed almost to be convinced of the impracticability of his own proposal.[11]

Frederick not only approved the prince's project but planned at once three others like it. He himself, Fouqué, and Ferdinand of Brunswick should all make similar raids simultaneously, each in his own area. All three tried — and failed. Only Henry, whose plan was more carefully matured than theirs, succeeded. Leaving behind him forces which he considered sufficient for the protection of Dresden and Lusatia, he took one corps himself into Bohemia and sent in a second simultaneously at another point. Within a week (April 11–17) he had ruined the Austrian communications and depots along the frontier and for miles up the Elbe. At Teplitz, Aussig, Lobositz, Leitmeritz, Budin, Komotau,

---

[8] M. P., IV, 202; Bisset, II, 53; *P. C.*, XVIII, 149.

[9] *P. C.*, XVIII, 139.    [10] H. to F., in Schöning, II, 39.    [11] Schöning, II, 42.

Saaz, and elsewhere his men burned such enemy stores as they could not use or carry off. They destroyed all the bridges across the Eger, a hundred and fifty boats on the Elbe, and supplies enough to have lasted twenty-five thousand horses for one month and fifty thousand men for five, worth more than a half million Austrian crowns. The Austrian and Imperial troops were so completely surprised that they tried only to escape. Most of them retreated almost to Prague, but the Prussians took twenty-five hundred prisoners with only very slight losses on their own part. All in all, it was a very profitable week's work; and Henry could congratulate himself that he had paralyzed his opposition on that front for a period of several months and thus freed himself for the Franconian campaign already proposed for him by the king and Ferdinand of Brunswick.[12]

Disconcerting though it was to the enemy and satisfying in itself, such a raid could of course serve no great strategical purpose except as it released the prince for activity elsewhere; and Frederick was as apt as Napoleon ever was at asking his subordinate commanders what they had done or what they proposed to do the *next* day. His first comment in reply to Henry's report was:

I congratulate you on the glorious, useful and fruitful operation which you have just completed; it is a fine opening for the campaign and should warrant high hopes for the future. . . . That would be excellent for anyone else, but for you it is not enough; you are to march now into Hesse and Franconia. . . . We must have troops to oppose the Russians. Dohna's army is not strong enough to fight them; there is no hope of success unless we send him 12,000 men. In my present position facing Daun, I cannot detach a single foot soldier; but if you clear away these *messieurs* of the Empire, there will be no one left facing you; so your army can furnish this detachment. . . . I give you thanks in the name of the fatherland for the good service you have done it, and take that as an indication of the efforts you will make to crown your work.[13]

Some such urging by the king was needed to set the prince again in motion. By swift action on his own initiative he had created a golden opportunity for himself; then, suffering from a renewed attack of cau-tion, he hesitated to use it. He knew he had destroyed some vitally im-

[12] *Ibid.*, 47; *P. C.*, XVIII, 149; Koser, *Geschichte Friedrichs des Grossen*, III, 20–21; M. P., IV, 201. Ferdinand of Prussia was ill again, and Frederick, reporting that fact to Henry, had added: "Our family is going entirely to the devil." *P. C.*, XVIII, 128.

[13] *P. C.*, XVIII, 179–180. De Catt says that Frederick was "extremely well pleased" with the news of what the prince had done, and "spoke of his brother and of his military talents in terms of the highest praise," saying that if his other subordinates would only do as well he would have more elbow room and could breathe better. Koser, "Unterhaltungen," 232.

portant military stores in Bohemia, but Austria had plenty of troops left there, and he would therefore have preferred to sit tight in Saxony until it became clearer whether they or the Imperialists would be the first to attack.[14] In so thinking, he was overestimating his enemies' determination and spirit of enterprise and overlooking the important consideration that the Austrian generals would be unlikely to risk any important offensive elsewhere while Frederick stood with Prussia's one sizable army at Landeshut. Knowing as he did that Frederick considered himself tied fast where he was as long as Daun stood near by, facing him, Henry failed to realize that his own recent success in Bohemia and some minor ones achieved by Fouqué in Silesia had been made easy by Frederick's mere presence and by his prestige. Fearing him as it did, the Austrian high command had centered its attention chiefly upon him. So the king and his army still constituted, potentially, what he himself had recently called them — Prussia's mobile reserve.

Frederick was therefore fully justified in overruling the prince's objections and in urging him to act promptly; but he did it tactfully, and with scrupulous regard for his brother's sensitive feelings. The Bohemian raid, he pointed out, had done the Austrians damage which it would take them some time to repair; but time in itself was of no value to Henry unless he utilized it to rid himself promptly of his enemy in the west. If he waited he might have to meet two attacks at once. If he went immediately he could expect some help from Ferdinand of Brunswick in the Bamberg region, which Frederick had already asked Ferdinand to send.[15]

Much of the king's patient pressure was wasted. It took the couriers about a week to go and return; and since he was sending one off almost every day, several of his letters urging Henry to go into Franconia at once were written after the prince had already agreed to go. Two of them followed him on his way. On April 23 Henry had written: "If you think that it would be for the good of the state that I should attempt an enterprise so desperate, never doubt that I shall do it! If not, I shall adhere to my own plan."[16]

In his usual prudent fashion the prince had been busy with systematic preparations for the campaign, even while debating its advisability; so he had really lost no time at all. He was taking with him a considerable train of heavy artillery, which Frederick had cautioned him not to forget, for the guns could present "the most convincing arguments to make the rights of kings respected." Inasmuch as he was going into territory

[14] H. to F., in Schöning, II, 50–51.
[15] Six letters, April 20–28, in *P. C.*, XVIII, 179–196.
[16] Schöning, II, 50.

already repeatedly foraged over by enemy troops, he must carry most of his supplies with him, so needed heavy guards for his long convoys. While assembling his guns, wagons, horses, and troops he had, as he said, felt it his duty to lay before the king all the hazards and difficulties of the enterprise "so as not to be reproached with having undertaken it lightly." [17]

Once he knew that the prince was really going to make the expedition, Frederick readily conceded that it was hazardous. In any other war, or for any other commander, he said, it would have been too hazardous; but they were facing such odds that they could not fight according to the rules. Besides, those rules were made for ordinary commanders, not for men like Henry. Then, with evident pleasure, the king passed on to his brother the deciphered copies of some captured Austrian dispatches, the contents of which he gleefully paraphrased as follows: "You have become the terror of the Austrians, who accuse you of deranging all their plans and consign you to all the devils there are. M. Daun is very much surprised that you who have neither papal bonnet nor sword blessed by the pope should have taken from him his apostolic supply depots." [18]

The prince started off from Zwickau on May 5, a day ahead of the schedule he had set for himself. It was rough country that he had to traverse, for he proposed to go by way of Hof and Baireuth, through the region where the Eger, Saale, and Main rivers have their sources. Over such a terrain it was not easy to take a whole army on a raid; and that was practically what he was forced to do. The Austrians had reoccupied Eger, hence a corps must be detached and left behind to hold them in place. Every pass along the route must be fought for, and then garrisoned until the return march. Some towns surrendered without resistance, but others were fortified and held out long enough to cause inconvenient delays. Despite all obstacles the whole expedition moved along with surprising speed, the subordinate commanders Knobloch, Finck, Belling, and Kleist rivalling one another in boldness and enterprise.

Four days after the start, the prince was at Hof. By the end of a week he had left Baireuth behind. On the eleventh day Knobloch drove the Imperial troops out of Bamberg and found there supplies enough to subsist forty thousand men for two weeks. Without those captured supplies

[17] *Ibid.*, 54. The fear of reproach in case of failure was still an obsession with him.

[18] *P. C.*, XVIII, 197. Frederick, who in all three of his Silesian wars liked to call himself the champion of Protestantism and religious toleration against Catholic bigotry and oppression, was never weary of joking bitterly about the hat and sword given with his blessing by the pope to Marshal Daun.

the army would soon have been hungry, for it had outmarched its own convoys. The Imperialists under the Prince of Zweibrücken left three thousand prisoners in the hands of the Prussians and retreated to Nuremberg, while Prussian detachments went on to within two miles of Würzburg, and Ferdinand of Brunswick made good his promise to send six thousand as far as Schweinfurt.

Prince Henry himself took up his quarters in the village of Sachsendorf, near by, and from there dealt again with the Bishop of Bamberg through his generals Knobloch and Itzenplitz. As a cash contribution in addition to all the supplies that had been seized, he compelled the bishop to promise to ransom his town for five hundred and thirty thousand thaler, payable in exchange on Hamburg; two hundred other persons of prominence signed the document with him. The prince agreed, on his part, to return some church silver which he had held for a year as a pledge for the unpaid portion of the enforced contribution of 1758.[19]

Again, as the year before, the prince had done all that the king expected of him; and again he was ordered to go no farther than Bamberg and to return as soon as possible. Since the Imperialists would not stand and fight, there was little possibility of destroying them utterly. That being the case, Frederick said, it mattered little whether they tried to hold on or simply ran away. The thing to do was to destroy their depots so that they could not return for two or three months, to bring back all captured guns and powder, and to burn such other stores as could not be used up or carted home. Even money contributions, while useful, were to be only a secondary objective.[20]

Henry remained in the vicinity of Bamberg for nine days, then reversed his route to Saxony, stopping only for two days at Hof to send back a rear guard to the further discouragement of his halfhearted pursuers. It was high time for him to return. Frederick had already warned him that as soon as he had passed that point on his way out the Austrians had reinforced their post at Eger and had begun sending raiders into southwestern Saxony. The Russians meanwhile were also on the move and were threatening the Mark of Brandenburg from the east,

---

[19] Schöning, II, 58–75; *P. C.*, XVIII, 272, 301; M. P., 210. Carlyle, in his biography of Frederick, acclaims this adventure of the prince as a marvelous exploit. Schmitt (*Prinz Heinrich*) considers it a very creditable piece of work. Heinrich von Bülow, who holds generally to the view that the prince was a far better soldier than Frederick and "saved the country" in spite of the king's errors, thinks that the war might have been won by making this campaign a major enterprise instead of a minor one. See his *Prinz Heinrich von Preussen, kritische Geschichte seiner Feldzüge* (2 vols., Berlin, 1805). Theodor von Bernhardi, who recognizes no gain except by a victory won in battle, treats it as of no consequence because no great battles were fought.

[20] F. to H., May 16, 23, 26, in *P. C.*, XVIII, 226, 248, 257. Frederick was lavish with his praise and later authorized his brother to reward his men by paying a hundred thaler for each captured gun and twenty each for flags. *Ibid.*, 227, 296.

and Loudon was moving into Lusatia with an Austrian corps. Frederick himself, confronted by Daun's principal army, said that he "couldn't detach even a cat" to take care of any of these other areas or to prevent Loudon from joining the Russians if that was what he had in mind. So he had good reason to treat all that the prince had done thus far as only a "very pretty prelude," and to hope that "the play to follow" would be worthy of it.

There was no long entr'acte. Allowing the men only a single day of rest, the prince at once sent Finck to the defense of Dresden and Generals Hülsen and Itzenplitz with fifteen thousand men right across the Mark of Brandenburg to Dohna at Landsberg. Those men had to traverse two thirds of Germany, from southwest to northeast, almost without a halt, and in five weeks' time. The prince himself, with what he had left, quickly chased the Austrians out of Saxony again and threw them on the defensive in Bohemia by spreading reports that he intended to attack them there and by acting as if he meant to do so. Frederick was so pleased with the aptitude his prize pupil was showing that he placed himself and his pupil for once in the same category: "Daun is very angry that you did not go on to Nuremberg. . . . They take us both for hot-headed fools; but they will get to know us, and [that] although we have no papal bonnets we do have the congenital intelligence which is worth a great deal more." [21]

During the month of June Frederick was unable to do anything with his vis-à-vis Daun but to coin new nicknames for him (such as "my big blessed beef," "His Holiness," "Semper Augustus," etc.) while he waited for him to move and Daun waited for the Russians and the harvest. Henry easily kept Saxony clear and occupied some posts in Bohemia. Both watched closely the course of events in western and eastern Germany, and both guessed wrong as to their outcome.

In the west Ferdinand of Brunswick had to meet an attack by the French and Imperial forces, and called for help. They both thought he had lost his head and would surely be defeated,[22] but he won a decisive

[21] *Ibid.*, 283. The Imperialists had been ordered to retreat from Nuremberg if attacked; and the Austrians, Frederick believed, had hoped that Henry would go on there or beyond, and so permit himself to be cut off from Saxony. Frederick to Secretary von der Hellen at the Hague, June 4, *ibid.* 289.

To General Schmettau, in command of the garrison at Dresden, the king wrote: "When my brother returns, you have nothing to fear for Lusatia." *Ibid.*, 296. He warned his brother himself, however, that his growing reputation would make his succeeding enterprises more difficult; for thenceforth their enemies would assign only their best officers to command against him, and would be careful to run no unnecessary risks where they faced him. *Ibid.*, 301.

[22] The king wrote Henry that he, who was still "driving away our enemies as the wind scatters chaff," should write to Ferdinand and tell him how to do it; Ferdinand, he said, needed to learn. *Ibid.*, 327; Frederick to Ferdinand, *ibid.*, 356, 360.

victory at Minden on August 1. Dohna's campaign against the Russians, concerning which they had been fairly confident in June but less hopeful in July, ended in disastrous defeat between Kai and Züllichau on July 23. No help would have been available for Ferdinand in the west if he had needed it; but Saxony had to be still further denuded of troops to try to stem the tide of invasion in the east.

First it was necessary, if possible, to prevent the Austrians from sending a corps through Lusatia to join the Russians. With that end in view the prince proposed on July 7 that he move most of his troops east to Bautzen, so that he and the king could hold Daun and Loudon between them. Two days later, before he had had time to get his brother's letter, the king suggested the same thing, but Henry was already on his way when that suggestion reached him. Within a week, leaving behind a few small units which could do little but "watch" the Austrians under Brentano and garrison the city of Dresden, he had shifted the main body of his army from Plauen, at the extreme southwestern tip of Saxony, to Bautzen in the southeast. Loudon was driven back to Lauban by Prince Henry and Eugene of Württemberg when he made a move toward Sagan, apparently to join forces with the Russians.[23]

The Russians had needed no help. First Frederick sent his adjutant general von Wobersnow to coach Dohna, then Wedell to replace him, with orders to attack. On July 24 he instructed him not to attack after all unless he could catch the Russians at a disadvantage, but that letter arrived too late; for on the twenty-third Wedell offered battle between Kai and Züllichau and was badly beaten, losing eight thousand men, including General von Wobersnow. Some unusual demoralization was also evident, for two Prussian regiments ran away without fighting. The king exonerated Wedell and told him to think no more about the disaster, but only about what to do next. Fatalistically he remarked that he had expected it; those fellows were all afraid.

It would probably be unfair to say that Frederick was himself afraid, but a spirit of hopelessness was more and more noticeably weighing him down since the failure of his attempt in June to induce George II to invite their enemies to a peace conference. He was still fighting, but desperately, with his head down and his eyes closed. It was in that dangerous

---

[23] *Ibid.*, 386, 396, 404, 407, 420; Schöning, II, 108–119. Such cooperation was possible only because just then the two brothers were thinking and acting so much alike that each anticipated the other's thoughts.

The incessant character of the prince's activity is indicated by the fact that practically half his letters to the king during the month of July were written between midnight and three in the morning; and he always wrote them out in full, himself, however hurried or weary he was. Frederick himself was still held fast at Schmottseifen, where he had been for so long that he said he knew the terrain of that whole area as he knew his garden at Sans Souci.

mood that, instead of sending his coolheaded brother to dispose of the Russians as he had said he intended to do, he suddenly decided to go himself. Henry might stop the Russians, but that would not answer the purpose. They must be destroyed; and for that sort of work — in spite of Zorndorf — Frederick would rather trust himself than anyone else.

To exchange roles without loss of precious time, the brothers had to exchange armies as well. The king's own troops could not leave their position without releasing Daun and leaving Silesia open to invasion. So Frederick ordered the prince to be in Sagan by July 28, going on ahead of his troops if necessary but being sure that they should arrive there not later than the twenty-ninth, when the king would come up from Schmottseifen to take command of them. Henry was in Sagan on the twenty-eighth, and his troops with him.[24] So he did not wait there for Frederick. With only a small escort of hussars, sufficient for his personal safety because Frederick had the roads along the Bober all guarded and fresh horses waiting at every relay post along the way, he set out before daybreak on July 29 for Schmottseifen and arrived there at two o'clock in the afternoon. It was the brothers' first meeting in nearly five months, but a two-hour interview had to suffice. By four o'clock the king was off to the north by the route just traveled by the prince, riding on through the night until he reached Sagan at two o'clock the next morning.[25]

Although these changes were made with all possible secrecy and speed, they gave Loudon his opportunity. As the victorious Russians approached the Oder in the direction of Frankfort he slipped away with an Austrian corps to join them. Frederick was not far behind, but could neither intercept nor overtake him. Marching night after night over sandy roads and resting but little in the heat of the August days, both the king and his men were badly worn down by fatigue, always one of the soldier's deadliest enemies, and were therefore already near the breaking point when they brought their human foe to bay at last in a strong position at Kunersdorf, a village a little to the east of Frankfort-on-the-Oder, on August 12.[26]

[24] Again he had anticipated his orders and was on his way with a long day's march already behind him when he got Frederick's letter of July 24. In his marginal comments in the king's history of the war he said he went to Sagan without orders, which is not strictly true; but he gained a day by starting without them.

[25] *P. C.*, XVIII, 455–462; M. P., IV, 233. On July 29, while awaiting Henry's arrival, Frederick drew up for him a memorandum containing some brief general instructions and later, in response to his questions, added a few bits of specific information about the special qualities of some of his officers and prominent natives of the neighborhood. He also wrote to Count Finckenstein that he must not be bothered with any more public business for a while, for he would have no time for it.

[26] The Austrian generals then with the Russians believed that, because of the shortage of supplies and equipment, the Russian army would very soon have gone back across the

The Russian position could best be approached from the south or the east. Frederick chose to approach it from the east so that his enemy must fight with his back to the Oder and with his way of escape practically cut off by the swamps along the right bank of the river. He crossed at Oetscher, below Frankfort, leaving General Wunsch there with a detachment to guard the army's baggage and to make sure that the Russians could not escape over the bridges there. With the rest, which by that time included Finck and his corps from Lusatia and Wedell and the remnant of the army recently defeated at Kai, he set out again, as at Zorndorf, on an exhausting move around his enemy's position. It was nearly noon the next day before his first regiments had dragged themselves and their guns through the pine woods to the positions from which they were to attack. They had then been on their feet for nine hours and were suffering from hunger and thirst and the burning heat. It was a man-killing march, and only the prelude to a murderous battle. The king complained of the inferior quality of those troops, and they were not the men of Prague or of the Zorndorf campaign of 1758. Yet none but good soldiers would have fought at all after such exertions and privations.[27]

In their initial frontal attack the Prussian grenadiers secured a foothold on the Mühlberg, near Kunersdorf village on the left flank of the Russian position; but there they were stopped. The king had planned to use only a portion of his force in the principal attack, holding back the remainder as a reserve with which to follow up a victory or insure an orderly retreat if defeated; but before the afternoon was over he had used up all the men he could find, first in a desperate bid for victory and at last in a stubborn attempt to fight off defeat. Both he and his generals exposed themselves to danger with a reckless daring that approached foolhardiness; in the later stages of the battle he seemed to be actually trying to get himself killed.[28] By late afternoon his reserve was gone, and with it his hope of victory; by sunset he had no army left. In the night he found shelter across the Oder in the village of Reitwein; the other fugitives straggled back to Oetscher, seeking the protection of

Vistula for the remainder of the year without waiting to be attacked; but Frederick could not know that, and he did know that an Austrian corps under Hadik, released by the withdrawal of Finck from Lusatia, was in an excellent position to march straight to Berlin. So he thought he must attack immediately. Besides, he was in an attacking mood.

[27] The king had no proper maps of the region, and his local guides failed to inform him adequately of the nature of the ground over which he must march and fight. His men paid with their lives for his ignorance.

[28] Lieutenant General Itzenplitz and two major generals were killed; Generals Seydlitz, Hülsen, and Knobloch and virtually all the general staff officers were among the wounded; and Frederick thought that his own life had been saved by a snuffbox in his pocket, which was flattened by a bullet.

Wunsch's fortunate troops, who had not had to fight that day. Wunsch, who had been left there to prevent the escape of the Russians, had to close the bridges to prevent the further flight of his demoralized compatriots. The next day, August 13, they were in better order; they recrossed the river without enemy interference and destroyed the bridges. Fortunately for Prussia, the Russian commander Saltykov was neither a Frederick nor a Napoleon, so did nothing "the next day" or the day thereafter.[29]

If he had been pursued, Frederick might have pulled himself together instinctively to resist attack. Left unmolested, he collapsed. He had pushed himself far beyond the limits of his physical endurance; his nerves, which had clouded his judgment and darkened his outlook for a month, gave way at last under the strain, and for once even his courage deserted him. Those were the darkest days of his life. After all his grandiloquent declarations that he would conquer or die, he found himself still alive and unwounded but overwhelmingly defeated, with his weapon broken off short in his hand. In despair he flung it from him and decided to die. He would wait two days, while Prince Henry was notified of his new responsibilities as regent and commander in chief; then he would destroy himself. In the night of August 12–13 he wrote to his minister, Count Finckenstein:

I attacked the enemy today at eleven. We pushed them back to the Jewish churchyard near Frankfort. All my troops were engaged and did wonders,[30] but the cemetery cost us a prodigious number. Our troops were thrown into confusion; I rallied them three times; at length I thought I was myself about to be taken prisoner, and had to abandon the field of battle. My clothes were riddled by bullets, and I had two horses killed under me; it is my misfortune that I am still alive. Our loss is very considerable; of an army of 48,000 men I have not three thousand. At this moment, while I write, all are in flight and I am no longer master of my men. You in Berlin will do well to think of your safety.[31]

It is a cruel reverse, I shall not survive it. The consequences of the affair

[29] The Prussian and Russian forces engaged at Kunersdorf numbered about 45,000 and 60,000, respectively. The 19,000 Austrians present did comparatively little of the heavy fighting; they lost only one man out of eight, whereas the Russians lost one of four, but what they did came just at the decisive moments and turned the tide. The Prussians lost nearly half their numbers and had, that night, no effective strength left. Their losses in guns were also very heavy.

[30] Later he wrote differently on that point, saying that he was on the point of winning a brilliant victory when suddenly, without reason, his "wretched infantry" lost heart and ran away.

[31] Government and court again moved to Magdeburg at once. Frederick wrote next day that private individuals who could do so should get out of the city and go to Hamburg, taking with them their money and all articles of value they could carry.

will be worse than the affair itself. I have no resources left and, to tell you the truth, I consider that all is lost; I shall not survive the ruin of my country. Farewell forever. Federic.[32]

Next day he turned over to General Finck the command of the army then reassembling on the west bank of the Oder. To minimize so far as possible the immediate moral effect of the change, he told the general that he was making it only because of a serious attack of illness, and only until he should recuperate. He told the general in so many words that the army was "no longer in a condition to fight the Russians," but suggested that an attack on the Austrians under Hadik might delay, if it could not prevent, an attack on Berlin. Finck must "report on everything" to Prince Henry, whom the king said he had made *Generalissimus* of the army, and take orders only from him. The army must swear allegiance to the king's nephew, Frederick William.[33]

On the third day after Kunersdorf, August 15, the king's secretary Coeper secretly asked Finckenstein, "for the good of the state and of the king," to come to headquarters and try to hearten their ruler, who he said was still "in a state of discouragement infinitely painful to all who had the honor to approach him." Coeper himself did not think the situation quite so desperate as Frederick seemed to consider it, and clearly hated to see his master acting as if the end of the world had come.[34]

Coeper's solicitude was really superfluous, and Finckenstein was not needed. On the fourth day, August 16, the king had recovered and resumed the active command which he had never in fact completely given up. To his great surprise his enemies were giving him time to reorganize his troops, to bring guns and munitions for them from the Berlin arsenals, to get a grip once more on his own habitual steadfastness and resolution; and time was life itself.

So he staggered to his feet. With reviving strength and courage returned also the will to live. The tempting thought of self-destruction

<hr/>

[32] *P. C.*, XVIII, 481.

[33] *Ibid.*, 482, 483. This is as near to abdication as the king ever came. If any order declaring Prince Henry commander in chief was ever promulgated, it must have been lost. The first direct word the prince received from Frederick after Kunersdorf was a dictated dispatch written by Coeper on August 18.

The last paragraph of the king's "Instruction for General Finck" reads, "Diesses ist der eintzige Raht, den ich bei den Unglücklichen Umbstanden im Stande zu geben bin, hette ich noch ressoursen wehre ich darbei gebliben." It is quoted by Hans Rothfels in his "Friedrich der Grosse in den Krisen des siebenjährigen Krieges," in the *Historische Zeitschrift*, CXXXIV (1926), 14–30, and by Koser in his *Geschichte Friedrichs des Grossen*, III, 35.

[34] *P. C.*, XVIII, 485. If the end of the world had come, it would presumably have found the imperturbable Coeper still at his field desk, pushing the king's pen for him as if one more royal order, properly put on paper, would countermand the decree of Destiny itself.

gave way once more to his sense of duty; and perhaps unconsciously he announced his spiritual recovery. "At the moment when I told you of our misfortune," he wrote Henry, "everything appeared desperate; that is not [to say] that the danger is not still very great, but count [upon it] that, so long as my eyes are open, I shall sustain the state as it is my duty [to do]." [35]

How profound had been the darkness through which he had just passed was revealed by his concluding words: "Picture to yourself all that my soul has suffered in this cruel crisis, and you will easily judge that the torment of the damned does not approach it. Happy are the dead! They have escaped from their sorrows and are free from trouble. Federic."

But the worst was past. By September 1, still alive and encouraged by the prompt and helpful activity of his brother and the continued comparative inactivity of his enemies, he was able almost to begin to believe in his good fortune. Slightly incredulous even yet, but himself again, he wrote to the prince from Waldow: "I have your note of the 25th, and I proclaim to you the miracle of the house of Brandenburg: during the whole time since the enemy crossed the Oder, when by risking a battle he could have ended the war, he has marched from Müllrose to Lieberose." [36]

[35] August 16, in *P. C.*, XVIII, 488. Lost in transit or destroyed to avoid capture, but printed from the retained draft in Frederick's own hand. The first clause quoted refers to an earlier letter that the king evidently thought he had written, but of which neither original nor draft has been found.
[36] A short march of no significance. *Ibid.*, 510.

# CHAPTER VII

# 𝔐𝔞𝔵𝔢𝔫

*"To attack, one must first find a way."*— Henry to Frederick.

THE "miracle of the house of Brandenburg" was the logical result of three phenomena: the remarkable spiritual recovery of the king of Prussia, bickering and mutual distrust among his enemies, and the promptness and vigor with which his brother Henry came to his rescue. The first of these phenomena, the unproclaimed miracle of self-mastery by which the great Frederick pulled himself together and set himself again on his feet within a few days of such a complete moral and physical collapse, resolutely confronting the invader once more with a reconstructed army, almost matches in magnitude the proclaimed miracle of Prussia's deliverance to which it so materially contributed.

Immediately after the battle of Kunersdorf the Scotsman Loudon, commanding the Austrian corps then serving with the Russians, pointed out to the Russian commander Saltykov the desirability of prompt and aggressive measures to utilize the advantages they had won. His plan was to give Frederick's shattered army the *coup de grâce* and march at once on Berlin while there was no one to stop them. But Saltykov refused to budge. He had been angry even before the battle because Daun had sent only a detachment to join him, instead of coming with his whole army. He was angered still further by the fact that at Kunersdorf it was Russian and not Austrian troops that had had to bear the brunt of the fighting. In two campaigns, he said, Russia's finest army had been seriously depleted by three hard-fought battles; and before he demanded further sacrifices from it he would be pleased to see his Austrian allies make some real contribution to the common cause.

Then Quartermaster General Lacy, a Russian-born Irishman, was sent from Daun's headquarters to try, where the Russian-born Scotsman had failed, to reach an agreement for joint action. He carried some alternative proposals. The Russians, further reinforced by a second Austrian corps under Hadik, should march on Berlin while Daun held off Prince Henry; or the Russians should hold the king of Prussia on the Oder while the Austrians seized either Berlin or some Silesian fortress. In either case both the king and Prince Henry should be prevented from sending succor to Dresden, which the army of the Empire should then

easily capture. But Saltykov was too suspicious. He demanded both reinforcements and supplies before he would agree to do anything. Food
supplies meant more to him than a subsidy. His men, he said, could not
eat money.

Next Daun went in person to Guben to deal with him, on August 22.
By then the Austrian field marshal had discovered that Prince Henry did
not propose to leave him free to choose his course; and he and his government had become convinced that the destruction of the prince's army
should be the primary objective of the allies for the remainder of the
season. It was the one pillar of the Prussian defense still unshaken; on
it rested Prussia's last hope. They should therefore concentrate upon it.
So it was agreed that Daun should simply hold the prince on the northwestern border of Silesia and Saltykov should hold the king on the Oder
until Dresden was captured. With Dresden, Saxony would fall into the
hands of the Austrians and the Imperials, as Leipzig, Wittenberg, and
Torgau had already done. Then Daun and Saltykov would cooperate in
a campaign to blot out Prince Henry's army and take possession of some
fortresses in Silesia where they could spend a comparatively comfortable
winter.[1]

Daun was slow and cautious; but he was far too able a strategist not
to realize what an opportunity was his. His failure to make better use
of it was due not only to his own weaknesses and lack of cooperation
from his ally but to the manner in which Henry took the play away from
him. So the three factors which worked "the miracle of the house of
Brandenburg" were not isolated phenomena but were closely interre-
lated.

The prince had almost literally stepped into his brother's shoes at
Schmottseifen, late in July. He had taken over the command of the
king's own army and along with it the royal quarters, kitchen, servants,
and riding horses. Never before had he commanded so large an army,
nor one of such excellent quality; yet he was outnumbered two to one by
Daun, and further threatened by Hadik's corps in Lusatia.[2]

By mid-August he had been without word from the king for ten

[1] These plans obviously discounted the king and his nondescript little army far too
heavily. If his enemies had united or even acted jointly against either him or the prince,
the king counted upon joining forces with his brother, and thought that then he could
battle both of them on even terms, though not with equal numbers. Letter to Finckenstein,
August 23, in *P. C.*, XVIII, 496, 497. Furthermore, neither of them relished the thought
of another battle with Frederick, and Daun had been ordered by his empress to avoid one.
Saltykov, on the other hand, under pressure from home, soon began again to urge a joint
attack upon the king; and it was that — or the seizure of Berlin as an alternative — which
Daun had in mind in September when he started off via Spremberg, whence the prince
turned him back to Bautzen.
[2] The prince's old complaints that the king habitually took the best regiments and the

days. Soon rumors of the most disturbing sort began to reach him, but still no message or reliable news from his brother. Fully realizing the responsibility that would fall upon him if Frederick was defeated, he could still do nothing but prepare for the worst and take his cue from his immediate enemy, who would probably be better informed than he.

During that very trying time he was being closely watched by Sir Andrew Mitchell, whom he had taken over along with the other appurtenances of great headquarters, and who accompanied him instead of the king for the rest of the campaign. On August 15 Sir Andrew reported to Holdernesse: "In this horrid State of anxious and disheartening Uncertainty, I need not mention to Your Lordship the Perplexity and Doubts of the whole Army, but I cannot help admiring the Magnanimity, Prudence, and Firmness of the Commander-in-chief, who has already taken his Resolution, though he delays in putting it in Execution in hopes still of hearing from his Brother." [3]

By the seventeenth the rumors of Frederick's defeat were too persistent and apparently too well grounded to be any longer disbelieved, and Prince Henry was ready to move instantly to the rescue; but he could not simply disregard Daun and his army and turn his back on them. [4]

Then at last the first messages from Frederick came through. The prince at once sent off that "note of the 25th" which his brother found so encouraging and answered by proclaiming "the miracle of the house of Brandenburg" on September 1. Logically assuming that the Austrians' first step would be to send reinforcements and supplies to Loudon and the Russians, Henry said he would do his utmost to prevent it. Probably for fear that his courier would be captured, he gave no details of his plan but said he had one and would do his best to carry it out; and for Frederick that was enough. [5]

lion's share of all supplies, leaving him to get along as best he might with second-rate regiments, third-rate recruits, inadequate supplies, and worn-out horses and guns, ceased for a while to be heard. Instead, it was Frederick who complained constantly of the quality of the troops he had to lead. He blamed them for his defeat at Kunersdorf, and said later that the best of them were unequal to the worst of those of former years; he called them trash and a rabble of cowardly dogs, and said that only a fool would lead such men into battle. Apparently forgetting that it was with those very men that he ordinarily expected his brother to get results, he said that he himself feared them more than he did the enemy. He also reproached the prince, later in the season, for not accomplishing more than he was doing with their "finest army."

[3] M. P., IV, 237. De Catt, who had also remained at headquarters, recorded that all sorts of rumors were current among the generals — that the king had been defeated, that he was dead, that the Russians were in Berlin, and so on. Prince Henry's quietly confident bearing, he says, did little to discourage the rumors, as the generals were certain that the prince had had bad news and was putting on so good a countenance only to conceal it. Koser, "Unterhaltungen," 247.

[4] M. P., IV, 239; XLIII, 3, 5.

[5] But not for von Bernhardi. He says that the prince had "as good as nothing at all"

Leaving the fortified camp at Schmottseifen occupied, the prince moved swiftly with a small mobile force to Sagan on August 29, and pushed his advance guard on into Lower Lusatia to Sorau. Surprise and consternation struck the Austrian headquarters and Vienna. By deliberately drawing all their attention upon himself, and by his seizure of the roads through Sagan, the prince prevented the Austrians from sending either men or supplies to be used against his brother, although he himself soon found his position there untenable and had to retire a few miles south toward Görlitz.[6]

On September 9, hearing that Dresden was about to fall, Daun moved off north to Spremberg, temporarily abandoning his earlier project to concentrate on the destruction of the prince's army, and planning either to join the Russians in an attack upon the king or to go on to Berlin. When he learned that Daun was at Spremberg, Frederick wrote almost frantically to his brother, "You must act." He suggested an attack either upon the Russian base at Guben or upon a detached Austrian force at Sorau. His letter was written on the twelfth, and on the false assumption that Prince Henry was still at Sagan. Actually the prince moved immediately when Daun did. Resorting to his old familiar tactics, he himself blocked Daun's way while he sent detachments to cut him off from Bohemia. On the eleventh his generals took Görlitz and Zittau and destroyed the supply depots there; next day they captured another, and seven hundred prisoners, at Friedland; on the thirteenth they intercepted an Austrian supply train of a hundred wagons. Meanwhile the prince, though heavily outnumbered as usual, completely outfaced his principal enemy. On the fourteenth Daun was in retreat toward Bautzen, with the Prussians bringing in hundreds of prisoners, horses, and wagons taken in running fights with his rear guard.[7]

On September 15 Daun was at Bautzen and the prince at Görlitz. Neither Berlin nor Frederick was in any immediate danger, and the proposed junction of the principal Austrian and Russian armies had dwindled away to a meager detachment of ten thousand men sent by Daun, whom Saltykov found it difficult to feed and whom Loudon had eventually to drag painfully home to Hungary by way of Poland. As the prince's army had proved to be the principal obstacle in their way

in mind when he marched to Sagan, and that the Austrians greatly overestimated his ability and spirit of enterprise. Bernhardi, *Friedrich der Grosse*, I, 419.

[6] On September 8 Frederick erroneously reported that five regiments of infantry had just come from Daun's army to join the Russians, but did not blame Henry for having failed to prevent their departure. "Don't worry about me," he wrote; "you take care to protect Silesia." *P. C.*, XVIII, 524.

[7] Yet, when a few days later an Austrian detachment of 10,000 men (12,000, according to Frederick's estimate, which Koser accepts), originally destined for service in Saxony, was sent to reinforce Loudon and the Russians instead, the king grumbled that the prince

ever since Kunersdorf, the Austrians returned to their original plan to destroy it or put it out of the way, and then to seize a fortress or two and settle down in Silesia for the winter. Saltykov was furious at Daun's failure to fight his way through to join him, and called it a breach of faith and a betrayal; and he consequently refused to do anything aggressive thereafter, or even to besiege Glogau as he was repeatedly urged to do.

Up to that point nothing had been required of the prince but to protect Silesia and to prevent Daun from joining the Russians, and he had done both; but from that time on additional tasks were assigned him. Although the king was in even less danger on the eastern front than he supposed, and in spite of the victory of Ferdinand of Brunswick at Minden, things had gone badly for the Prussians in the west, and Saxony was about to be lost.

At Dresden General von Schmettau as commandant found himself responsible not only for the city and its garrison of thirty-seven hundred men but for an arsenal, enormous quantities of uniforms and other military equipment, a war chest of 5,600,000 thaler in coin, and a hospital full of sick and wounded. On August 24 he received a letter written by the king ten days before (on the second day after Kunersdorf), which instructed him to capitulate on the best terms he could get, so as to save his war materials and treasure, if he was not sure he could defend himself successfully.

Meanwhile the king, having rehabilitated himself and his army in the face of his surprisingly unenterprising enemy in the east, was sending off such detachments as he could spare to redeem the situation in the southwest. First General Wunsch recaptured Wittenberg and Torgau and went to the relief of Dresden. On September 5 the harassed commandant of the beleaguered city, von Schmettau, received the king's letter of August 25 which ordered him to defend himself at all costs; and on the same day he learned that Wunsch was nearly there. But on the evening of the fourth, giving up hope of holding the city any longer against an attacking force of thirty thousand men and seventy heavy guns, and obeying the only instructions he had up to that time received (the king's unhappy letter of August 14), he had capitulated on terms which permitted his garrison to march out of the city, taking all royal property with them. Relief had come just one day too late, and Dresden was lost for the duration of the war.[8]

"stood too far off" from his enemy and made it easy for him by not watching him closely enough! *P. C.,* XVIII, 555. Although they were both writing almost every day, only about one letter a week was yet getting through to either. When Frederick wrote that, he knew neither where Henry was nor what he had been doing.

[8] *P. C.,* XVIII, 529–530; Schmettau, *Lebensgeschichte des Grafen von Schmettau,* 444; Schöning, III, 549.

Wunsch and Finck soon retook Leipzig, but all they could do thereafter was to hang on in the neighborhood of Meissen until Prince Henry returned to Saxony.

Until the fall of Dresden Frederick had thought that Wunsch and Finck could take care of Saxony, and had repeatedly assured Prince Henry that he need concern himself only with Silesia.[9] But from mid-September on, although he said that if Henry had a better idea he would approve it, he began to urge the prince to work around to the north of Daun's position at Bautzen so as to be able the better to protect Berlin and help Finck in Saxony.[10]

As was so often the case, Henry thought he must first insure himself against after-the-event criticism by pointing out that, where he was, he stood between Daun and Silesia, which he thought was their enemies' real objective and which he had all along been told must be his own first care. He further argued that so long as he kept Daun handcuffed he would be carrying out his own principal mission; and he could do that where he was as well as anywhere else. Furthermore, he stood at the moment considerably farther away from Saxony than Frederick did, in Lower Lusatia, and would have to make an extremely hazardous march right around Daun's army in order to reach it. Even if he made the move successfully he must disclaim any further responsibility for Silesia; for Daun would still be free to decide whether to follow him to Saxony or merely to march, virtually unopposed, straight ahead into almost any Silesian city he might choose.

Frederick of course knew all that; but he felt sure that Daun would follow the prince and that the major field of operations could so be transferred once more to Saxony, which he was determined to reconquer before cold weather ended the campaign. If Daun did as he expected, he could himself defend Silesia against Loudon and the Russians.

As usual when the king insisted, he had his way. And as usual he wisely left all the details of the execution of his great strategical plan to his brother.[11] On September 19 Frederick withdrew to the southeast, via Sagan, keeping pace with the Russians and blocking their road to Glogau. On September 23 Marshal Daun moved eastward from Bautzen with more than fifty thousand men to undertake the task assigned him as his principal mission no less than a month earlier — to attack Prince Henry's army of about thirty thousand, which he thought was then near Görlitz. On the evening of the same day the prince also moved off east-

---

[9] Letters of September 4, 5, 8, in *P. C.*, XVIII, 514–524.
[10] *Ibid.*, 544ff.
[11] *P. C.*, XVIII, 557; von Bernhardi, *Friedrich der Grosse*, I, 433. Mitchell was much perturbed over the risks the prince must run in attempting to march right around Daun's

ward to Rothenburg, ostensibly either retreating into Silesia or running away to join the king. Instead, during the night, he turned sharply to the northwest. Covering eighty kilometers in two successive night marches, he rounded Daun's old position and suddenly reappeared on the twenty-fifth at Hoyerswerda on the Elster, northwest of Bautzen. An Austrian corps there was taken entirely by surprise. With the loss of only forty-four men, killed and wounded, the Prussians captured the Austrian General Vela and eighteen hundred of his men.[12] Daun dashed back to Bautzen in such haste that he was reported to have lost three thousand men by exhaustion or desertion on the way; then, guessing the prince's destination, he went straight for Dresden. In his anxiety over Saxony he forgot all about Silesia for the season, just as Frederick had anticipated.

Daun was also capable of swift movement, and he had all the advantage of the interior line, shorter route, and better roads; but the two armies reached the Elbe almost simultaneously, at the end of the month. Daun crossed to the left bank at Dresden and joined the troops of the Empire under the Prince of Zweibrücken in an attack upon General Finck, near Meissen, forcing him back to Strehla. There Prince Henry came up, after crossing the river at Torgau, and stopped the retreat. Daun feared to attack him, and a council of war in the camp of the allies decided that Daun was right.

So, after ten days of strenuous marching, the two principals faced one another again, but on different ground and on different terms. The odds had changed from two against three to two against four; for Daun had gained considerably more, numerically, by his junction with the army of the Empire than the prince had by adding Finck's force to his own.[13] The problem of supplies was also more serious for the Prussians than it had been. At Görlitz they had been fed from the well-filled Silesian fortresses. In Saxony they had the use of the Elbe again, but their usual supply depots in that region had but recently been retaken from the enemy, and they naturally did not find them full; so they had to draw rations from Magdeburg.

Yet the prince felt fairly confident at first, and thought he could main-

numerically superior army. He thought that the king insisted upon the move chiefly for fear Daun might join in an attack upon Glogau. M. P., IV, 249; Bisset, II, 93.

[12] *Der siebenjährige Krieg* (German General Staff work), XI, 149. Mitchell called the march "almost incredible." Of the action at Hoyerswerda he wrote: "I had the pleasure of admiring the coolness and presence of mind with which his R[oyal] H[ighness] gave his orders during the action, and the humanity and goodness with which he treated his prisoners after the action was over." M. P., IV, 249; V, 5; Bisset, II, 94–103.

[13] Daun had 60,000, the Prince of Zweibrücken 23,000. The prince had 40,000, including Finck's corps. The whole area south of Berlin and west of Silesia was subject to his orders.

tain himself without help. If, on the other hand, the Russians would be good enough to go away and leave Frederick free to send him some reinforcements, he promised to recapture Dresden and put Daun out of Saxony before cold weather set in. His army was equally confident and in excellent condition.[14]

But for the prince, with such an army (even without reinforcements), merely to defend himself was far from being enough to satisfy the king. "Daun is making fools of us," he wrote. "He isn't going to attack you. . . . He means to take Leipzig. That you must not permit, for the result will be that Magdeburg will be ravaged again." [15]

The prince, who also thought that Leipzig was in danger, sent off one detachment after another to cover it; but as that weakened his main body at Strehla considerably, and as Daun began sending heavy detachments around his right flank, he himself found it necessary to retreat toward Torgau. Before he made the move he reported it to the king, in a mood of deep discouragement: "The enemy is behind me and the roads are blocked. . . . I cannot fight on all sides at once. . . . To attack, one must find a way. . . . I have not time to tell you everything I have tried to do, or why I have not done it; but truth compels me to say frankly that although I shall do all that is humanly possible, I doubt that, without some unforeseen event, I shall be able to hold Saxony. . . . That is an unpleasant truth; but it is exactly as I tell you. If the enemy uses his advantages I cannot maintain myself, whatever I do. There remains then only the hope that he will not use them, and that some unforeseen event will alter the situation." [16]

What actually happened, which after his extensive experience with the same opponent need not have been unforeseen by the prince, was that Daun made very little further use of his advantages. By a night march on October 16–17 the prince escaped from the Strehla position where he had been so nearly surrounded and took up another a little nearer Torgau. The next Austrian corps sent around him to threaten his rear gave him one of those openings for which he was always on the alert; and he attacked it, front and flank, and almost annihilated it.[17] With that the Austrian offensive came to a standstill. During the whole

[14] Von Bernhardi, *Friedrich der Grosse,* I, 449; M.P., V, 7.
[15] October 11, in *P. C.,* XVIII, 589.
[16] *Ibid.,* XVIII, 600. Von Bernhardi characteristically quotes all the gloomiest passages of the prince's letter, and omits the last sentence. *Friedrich der Grosse,* I, 451. The prince also complained that the terrain of the region was unfavorable for its defense — which had been one of the reasons urged on him by Frederick for acting on the offensive there.
[17] At Pretsch on October 29. The Austrian commander, the Duke of Arenberg, admitted a loss of 4,000 men, including one lieutenant field marshal. Von Arneth, *Geschichte Maria Theresias,* VI, 53. The prince had planned to surround Arenberg's corps of 16,000 men in Dommitsch and to destroy it completely; but the Austrians got word of the attack and

month of October, by their joint efforts and with more than twice his numbers, the allies had succeeded in pushing him back only three miles. Then he himself counterattacked and in one week regained all the ground he had lost.

Frederick, meanwhile, was in a frenzy over the way things were going. He was less badly outnumbered than his brother was but, since his were not first-line troops, he could do nothing to hasten the withdrawal of the Russians except to interfere as much as possible with their service of supply. He was forced therefore to play precisely the part he always found most hateful — that of an idle and helpless spectator. If anything ever worked on his nerves more adversely than that, it was his gout; and he had a very severe gout attack just then. Both feet, one knee, his left hand — and his temper — were badly affected; and Henry did not find his letters pleasant reading.

The king had, moreover, again heard rumors that France and Great Britain might make peace that winter. If they should, he must enter the conference with a pawn in hand, to be exchanged for a war indemnity. The military possession of Saxony must be that pawn. He was therefore obsessed with the idea that Prince Henry must attack Daun and recapture Dresden at once. When he heard that Henry contemplated a withdrawal from Strehla he fairly exploded: "I have received your letter of the 16th of this month. I don't know what can be troubling you all of a sudden, with the finest of my armies. The terrain between Leipzig and Torgau is level, and there you can attack the enemy. If you will never risk anything you can never do anything. . . . When circumspection is pushed too far it becomes timidity, and can lead to the greatest misfortunes. . . . Buck up your courage, for the love of God, and take care that your head doesn't fail you at a time like this."

Four days later he said bluntly that he disapproved of Henry's conduct and his choice of a position in "that hole at Torgau," and continued: "Since you crossed the Elbe, my dear brother, you have not been the same man. Finck has filled your mind with his gloomy ideas. I beg you, for the love of God, to think differently and with more nerve."[18]

No one but Frederick seemed to think at the time that his reproaches were deserved. His cabinet secretary Eichel wrote secretly and confiden-

took to flight; so the fighting had to be done in impromptu fashion along the roads and the success was not quite complete.

[18] *P. C.*, XVIII, 601–604. How the sensitive and self-willed prince would take that kind of advice and such a scolding can well be imagined — coming as it did under just those circumstances from a man who in that whole year's campaign had himself attacked no one except at Kunersdorf, and then with the most disastrous results; but it may have done something to spur him on to his savage counterattack at Pretsch. More than thirty years later he was still smarting from it, and remarked to a foreign visitor: "The only 'art of war' my brother ever understood was to battle."

tially to Finckenstein: "His Majesty does not seem to me to have any accurate idea of the present state of affairs in Saxony, which is surely critical. Everyone must do the prince the justice [to concede] that no one could have done better than he has done, or worked harder, or spared himself less. As for my own insignificant self, I still hope for the best." [19]

Mitchell was also still hopeful, though he considered the crisis a serious one. The king of Prussia, he said, was still alive and might yet work wonders. As for the prince, he "has shewed very great military talent, and though his constitution is not robust, he is indefatigable. I observe but one failing, which is in the blood; he exposes his person too much and upon slight occasions. His character and temper of mind are entirely different from his elder brother, and yet in many respects they resemble each other." [20] "H. R. H. has fairly owned to me that more is asked of him than is possible to perform. . . . If notwithstanding these and other Disadvantages H. R. H. can still keep possession of Saxony, it will be one of the most extraordinary Events that has happened in this or perhaps in any other War." [21]

On October 24 the Russians at last moved off into Poland.[22] Frederick at once initiated through Mitchell an attempt to induce their government to make a separate peace, either by bribing some ministers or by suggesting that, as Great Britain and France were about to make peace, Russia might as well do so.[23] But even if he had taken his own suggestion seriously, the prospect of peace would only have spurred him to greater efforts to win, before it came, a pawn of some considerable exchange value.

Unable to travel because of his gout, he sent off General von Hülsen at once with a substantial reinforcement for the army in Saxony. Then, partially recovered but still unable to walk or to ride, making his men carry him in a sedan chair "like the relics of a saint" when not riding in his carriage, he followed with another small corps. Couriers rode on ahead with word that, although he was reduced to a mere skeleton and kept alive only by good will, he was "flying thither on the wings of patriotism and duty." The prince would have preferred that he stay away.

[19] *Ibid.*, 601–602.
[20] Private letter to the Duke of Newcastle, from Torgau, October 22, in Bisset, II, 106–108.
[21] "Most Secret" letter to Holdernesse, October 22, in M. P., V, 9–12. Mitchell, and perhaps Eichel also, would naturally reflect to a certain extent the prince's own views, unless he was obviously wrong or had alienated them in some way.
[22] Loudon, whom Frederick had nicknamed "the Arch-bear-leader of the Empire," went with them, then turned homeward and made his way with great difficulty around Silesia through Poland to Moravia.
[23] M. P., V, 22–26; Bisset, II, 108–110.

Frederick was in no fit physical or psychological condition to take over the command. As a semi-invalid parading his infirmities and the tattered condition of his clothes, praising himself and expecting his associates to praise him for the fortitude he was displaying, he did not inspire confidence. Living in solitude, and working at French verses or other literary efforts several hours a day to distract his mind while finding only five minutes at most for the dictation of the most vitally important military dispatch, he did not readily regain confidence once lost. The army had given thanks after Kunersdorf, when it learned that he was still alive; its officers looked hopefully to him for reinforcements after the withdrawal of the Russians; but they did not rejoice over his coming to Saxony in person.

No one dared tell him he was not wanted; but Frederick was well aware that he was not being warmly welcomed. Hence, once he had heard that the prince had assumed the offensive, his letters took on a propitiatory tone. He would bring a reinforcement with him, he said, and carry his own food; he would be a burden to no one, and none need complain of his coming. He asked Henry to believe that he was not coming like Pompey to rob Lucullus of his glory after a conquest was practically complete. He was far too just for that, and wished only to increase the prince's glory by contributing to it.[24]

Frederick had said beforehand that he would try only to create a diversion in favor of the prince by acting independently "as a partisan" on the right bank of the Elbe; but it would have been contrary to his nature to do otherwise than to go directly to general headquarters and supersede the prince at once — which he did. Prince Henry, informed that a note would reach the king at Hirschstein on the Elbe above Torgau, drew up memoranda showing the exact status of his affairs and the course of future action which he would recommend, and took them with him when he went in person to give an account of his stewardship.[25]

Hard campaigning had reduced his army to thirty-three thousand

---

[24] Letters of November 5 from Glogau and November 10 from Spremberg, in *P. C.*, XVIII, 622, 625.

[25] November 13. One of the legends surrounding the relations of the royal brothers has it that Frederick, at their meeting at Hirschstein, praised Henry as the only one of his generals who had never made a mistake — *der fehlerlose Feldherr*. In the light of their letters the story is incredible. If Frederick ever used that phrase, it must have been after the war. The army, however, would just then have been quite ready to accord the prince that title. Its confidence in him was undiminished and unbounded. His whole campaign since July, according to de Catt, who had followed him through it, was generally praised by his officers as a masterpiece, equal in maneuvering skill and in resourcefulness to the best that military history could offer. When de Catt rejoined the king, Frederick said to him: "My brother has handled his bark very well indeed. There, my dear fellow, is a steersman!" Koser, "Unterhaltungen," 252.

men, including the reinforcement with which von Hülsen had joined him five days before.[26] He therefore recommended the concentration of the Prussian forces on the left bank of the Elbe and the continuance of the operations in which he was already engaged and achieving considerable success. By constant though cautious pressure and successive flanking operations he had already maneuvered Daun back to Meissen, and by sending Finck around his left flank to Nossen had cut him off from Freiberg. If permitted to continue along that line he hoped soon to drive him right through Dresden and then back into Bohemia.[27]

Henry never ceased to believe that he had had the situation well in hand before Frederick arrived, and that he would soon have won a brilliant success if the king had never come. In fact Frederick accepted his plan of campaign, and the only difference between his pursuance of it and Henry's was that he was less methodical. His gout was still in his blood, and in his splenetic impatience he forgot all caution. For him it was not enough that Daun should get out of Saxony, even under Prussian escort; he must be kicked out, and in such fashion as to feel for a long time thereafter the pain and ignominy of the kicking.[28]

So the Prussian advance continued, with renewed vigor. On November 14 Daun had to evacuate Meissen and draw back to the immediate environs of Dresden, and next day Frederick ordered General Finck once more around the Austrian left flank to Maxen, where he was to interfere all he could with enemy supply trains or small parties, but to let large or fight-minded units pass by.[29]

If de Catt is to be believed, Frederick and Prince Henry quarreled bitterly when the prince went in person to headquarters to protest against anyone's being sent to Maxen as things then stood. The prince, de Catt says, left the king's quarters in a very angry mood, announcing to the world his determination to quit the service at once. "Since you are absolutely determined on it, very well," he was reported to have said to his brother; "but if trouble comes, as come it must, then take upon yourself the responsibility for the disaster to the state." To his fellow officers, according to the same witness, the prince said further: "I spoke to him as a true patriot and a good brother, but he would not listen to me. If

[26] Daun had then nearly twice that number of Austrian line troops. If Croats and other irregulars and the army of the Empire are counted, he had nearly three times as many.
[27] *P. C.*, XVIII, 627–631; von Bernhardi, *Friedrich der Grosse*, I, 456–467; M. P., V, 19.
[28] F. to H., November 12, in *P. C.*, XVIII, 628. "Je suis encore fort faible, je n'ai presque point de sommeil, j'ai encore un reste de douleur sourde dans les jambes qui m'empêche de m'en servir comme il faudrait. Je ménage toutes mes forces pour une journée d'arrière-garde, afin que cet homme, qui a accumulé sur sa tête tous les symboles de la vanité humaine, ne sorte pas de la Saxe sans être éconduit solonellement à grands coups de pieds au derrière."
[29] F. to Finck, in *P. C.*, XVIII, 639. The detachment consisted of about 15,000 men.

## Letter from Frederick to Henry

Frederick's letter of December 14, 1759, with the king's signature and with Henry's exasperated comment on the letter written across it (see page 121). Reproduced by courtesy of the Staatsarchiv.

the army were only placed a little more to the right, nearer Dippoldiswalde, the danger would not be quite so great." [30]

Finck's was in fact an exposed position, one sure to be dangerous unless the enemy were simply on the run. Once more Daun was offered an opportunity. Within two days he had troops closing in from all sides upon the hapless Prussians at Maxen. The king knew by the eighteenth that the enemy generals Sincere and Brentano were supposed to be moving on Dippoldiswalde and Maxen, and warned Finck, but indicated that he did not himself take the threat very seriously. [31] He did not order a withdrawal; and he let thirty-six hours elapse before he sent von Hülsen to open a line of retreat for Finck via Dippoldiswalde, on November 20. Finck reported from Maxen confidently enough on the eighteenth that he did not expect to have any general engagement there. [32]

Mitchell was worried, although the king and his general seemed not to be. The king, he said, professed that he was not seeking a major battle, but acted as if he were trying to surround a compact and greatly superior force by stretching his own inferior one, very thinly, right around it. Mitchell feared that, by rashly pushing the enemy rear guards too vigorously, he might yet bring upon himself the general engagement which he said he intended to avoid, or lose some of the detachments he was pushing out so far and so boldly. [33]

Mitchell was said to have remarked to someone at headquarters that

[30] Koser, "Unterhaltungen," 259. De Catt had rejoined the king's suite as soon as Frederick arrived in Saxony. His devotion to his patron had never been questioned, although he had also become an admirer of Prince Henry while accompanying him from late July to mid-November of that year. Under date of November 18 he wrote in his diary and in his memoirs: "Finck is lost; you will see"; but there is nothing to prove that either entry was actually written on November 18.

[31] From Willsdruf, near Dresden, in *P. C.*, XVIII, 651. The letter, as dictated, read: "Ich überschicke Euch hierdurch die Einlage, den Rapport des Generals Zieten, aus welchem Ihr alles ersehen werdet, und überlasse dieses alles Euern Dispositiones und nöthigen Anstalten." And the postscript: "Er wird entweder mit den Reichers oder mit Sincere einen Gang haben. Friderich." Finck testified later, at his court-martial, that he had attached greater importance to the king's appended comment than to the contents of the note itself, and had understood from it that he was to stay where he was and be on his guard, but that he was in no very great danger. Von Bernhardi, *Friedrich der Grosse,* I, 462.

[32] He afterward maintained that he had gone there only under protest, and when forced to it by repeated and positive orders of the king; but that contention is not borne out either by his written orders or by his reports.

[33] "Secret" letter to Holdernesse, November 20, in M. P., V, 29. Again Mitchell may well have been reflecting the views of Prince Henry, with whom he was then on very good terms, or of the officers of the prince's entourage, who rarely hesitated to criticize the king. Kalckreuth, in *Paroles*, 199, says that they freely predicted disaster from the day of Frederick's arrival. The king, on the other hand, according to Kalckreuth, was exultant over the first rearward move Daun made thereafter, even though Daun was only continuing a retreat already forced upon him by Prince Henry. "You see!" Kalckreuth reports Frederick as exclaiming, "They are afraid of me!" But Kalckreuth, it must be remembered, was at best a very spiteful creature.

"if Finck had done the right thing he would not have dined at the king's table again for some time, but his corps would have been saved." In other words, he should have got out of Maxen while he could, with or without orders.[34]

He had been warned in time, if he had taken his warning more seriously; and on the twentieth Generals von Hülsen and Kleist were near at hand, trying to reopen the road through Dippoldiswalde. He may have heard of Frederick's bitter references to the "gloomy ideas" with which he was supposed to have infected Prince Henry a month before. His own knowledge of the king would have led him to expect censure if he retreated without sufficient cause, and rescue if he boldly faced it out. He was not ordered to retreat, nor very sharply warned; so he stayed where he was. On the twenty-first Daun, Sincere, and Brentano practically surrounded him with twenty-five thousand men. A part of his troops scattered and escaped; the rest tamely surrendered. Frederick was stating only the bitter truth when he told him that until then no one had ever heard of a whole Prussian corps' laying down its arms in such fashion without fighting.[35]

The moral effect of the surrender was proportionately far greater than the purely military consequences of the loss in men and guns, heavy though that loss unquestionably was. Knowing that it would be so, the king exclaimed when told of it: "My God! Is it possible? Have I brought my bad luck to Saxony with me?"[36]

It would be as manifestly unfair to throw all the blame for the disaster at Maxen upon any one person as it was historically inaccurate for Frederick to blame it merely on his bad luck. The king had shown a lamentable lack of prudence in sending Finck into such a position, and

[34] Kalckreuth, *Paroles,* 202–206.

[35] *P. C.,* XVIII, 657. "Es ist bis dato ein ganz unerhörtes Exempel, dass ein preussisches Corps das Gewehr vor seinem Feind niedergeleget, von dergleichen Vorfall man vorhin gar keine Idee gehabt. Von der Sache selbst muss Ich annoch Mein Judicium suspendiren, weil Ich die eigentlichen Umstände, so dabei vorgegangen, noch gar nicht weiss."

[36] Koser, *Geschichte Friedrichs des Grossen,* III, 46. To de Catt he burst forth in self-pity: "You see how unlucky I have been, . . . abused by my father, shut up in solitary imprisonment for three months at a time. . . . Misfortune has always pursued me; I have never been happy but in Rheinsberg." *Ibid.,* 48; "Unterhaltungen," 262, 408. To Prince Henry he wrote a year later: "If we succumb, let us date our destruction from that infamous adventure at Maxen." *P. C.,* XX, 5.

De Catt soon picked up a story current at headquarters, where rumors are often thickest, that Frederick had admitted in a letter to Henry that he wished to Heaven his gout had got worse instead of better and had lasted about a week longer; then he would never have come to Saxony and Maxen would never have happened. Incredible now, the story seems to have gained some credence at the time. Its very existence is evidence not only of credulity but of demoralization in the higher ranks. Koser, "Unterhaltungen," 267, 409.

General Wunsch was one of the prisoners. From Dresden his captors permitted him to send off a letter to his wife in which he blamed neither the king nor Finck but his own "damned cowardly soldiers," who, he said, had "run away as if the devil were after them." Frau General Wunsch dutifully sent the letter to the king, who acknowledged it in kind

an amazing want of enterprise in failing to warn him properly or to rescue him promptly. Finck was justly censured by court-martial after the war, not for treason or dishonorable conduct, but for failure to take the obvious precautions necessary to evade the crisis, or to show the proper resolution in meeting it.[37] For the third cause, the collapse of the morale of his men, Prince Henry himself may well have been in some measure responsible, for he apparently did nothing to prevent his own unconcealed dissatisfaction from spreading to all ranks.

To the prince, of course, only one cause was apparent: the insane rashness of Frederick. Bitterly resenting what he considered unjust criticism of his own conduct, he had not only been superseded but had then had to see his excellent plan of campaign pirated by the king as if it had been his own inspiration, and wrecked by carelessness in execution. Worn out by weeks of the most strenuous exertion, he had at last seen all his efforts brought to naught by a single colossal blunder, not his own. Wild with rage, he wrote across the bottom of a letter from Frederick: "This letter which [was as] usual accompanied by one in cypher, was written the 14th of December at Freiberg where the king was. I received it at Unkersdorf, where my quarter was. I have no confidence whatever in these reports;[38] they are always as contradictory and uncertain as his character. He has thrown us into this cruel war, and only the valor of the generals and soldiers can extricate us. Since the day that he joined my army, he has spread confusion and misfortune in it;[39] all my efforts in this campaign, all the good fortune which favored me, everything is lost through Frederick."[40]

The fires of the prince's anger were fed from many sources, and his

and courtly fashion and promised to try at the end of the campaign to secure her husband's release by exchange. Eichel sent Finckenstein an extract of the letter, but asked him to see that the general's "rather naive expressions," which had presumably been written "in his first rage" after capture, did not become generally known. They might start some ugly rumors, he said. *P. C.*, XVIII, 671, 691. It is beyond question that the morale of the whole army in Saxony was much higher before Frederick's arrival there than after.

[37] He was deprived of his commission and imprisoned for one year in a fortress, a form of restraint much less humiliating than criminal imprisonment. Many of his friends, and all the partisans of Prince Henry in his quarrel with the king, promptly and unquestioningly added Finck's name to their lists of "victims of the king's injustice." The public at first blamed him. On January 5, 1760, Henry wrote to his brother Ferdinand: "Foolish babblers, the Berliners! Finck alone, they think, is guilty! Those sheep's-heads will always draw false conclusions until the Russians or the Austrians open their eyes for them in Berlin itself. You see, dear Ferdinand, how easy it is to speak disparagingly of a man when one knows only half the story." Hausarchiv, Rep. 56, II, F; Otto Herrmann in the *Historische Vierteljahrschrift*, XXVI (1931), 368.

[38] The usual reports on troop movements and apparent enemy intentions, which the two exchanged almost every day.

[39] The command was turned over to the prince again after Maxen. He commanded at great headquarters while Frederick acted almost "as a partisan," as he had previously suggested, but around Freiberg instead of on the other side of the Elbe.

[40] *P. C.*, XVIII, 696; *Oeuvres*, XXVI, 203. See the facsimile facing page 118.

resentment only grew as his sympathizers tried to soothe his wounded vanity. His brother Ferdinand of Prussia sent him an anonymous letter purporting to be "from an officer in the Prussian service," accusing Frederick of habitual rashness and unnecessary wasting of men's lives, comparing Henry's record favorably with his, and concluding with the statement that it was the unanimous opinion of the officers of the army that if Frederick had stayed away from Saxony there would have been no surrender at Maxen, Dresden would already have been recaptured, and Saxony would have been cleared of enemy troops as successfully as in 1758.[41]

Although Henry countenanced Ferdinand's personal disloyalty to Frederick, and was himself angry enough to share it to a certain extent, no one could question even then his loyalty to Prussia; and neither friend nor foe could find another flaw in his performance of his military duties. In an attempt to profit from their success at Maxen, and to extend the limited area to which they were still confined in Saxony, the Austrians felt out the Prussian positions at various points during the remainder of the month of November, but were met everywhere by an alert and determined resistance. Frederick hoped that a shortage of supplies would yet drive them back to Bohemia before the end of the year. "The last bundle of straw and the last bit of bread," he said, "will determine which of us two remains in Saxony."[42]

His own troops had already come, in fact, almost to their last bundle of straw and their last armful of firewood. As the cold increased and the snows set in, those of them who had to hold the line of advanced posts, with only tents for shelter, suffered untold hardships. While Frederick wrote to the queen from Freiberg that he must apparently "go through the winter with one foot in the stirrup," Prince Henry (in general command at Willsdruf) did what he could to ameliorate the soldiers' lot by putting most of them into cantonments, reducing to a minimum the number encamped on outpost duty, and relieving the outposts every day. He also exerted himself to the utmost to secure firewood and to improve

[41] Hausarchiv, Rep. 56, II, F. See also Otto Herrmann in the *Jahrbücher für die deutsche Armée und Marine*, Nos. 554–555, 1917. Clearly the writer expected the prince to agree with the extraordinary views expressed in his letter; otherwise he would never have dared to send it. "Men are strange creatures," wrote de Catt in his diary. "Some take pleasure in abasing the king in order to elevate the prince, and vice versa; but is that reasonable?" Koser, "Unterhaltungen," 405.

[42] The depth of his discouragement, and its effect upon his usual predilection for battle as the most effective means of securing a real decision, is indicated by the essay he wrote at about that time on the character and military talent of Charles XII of Sweden. In that essay he said that battles were usually fought only as the last resort of generals who had failed to achieve their purposes by less costly methods and therefore knew nothing else to do. See Otto Herrmann in the *Historische Vierteljahrschrift*, XXVI (1931), 365, and Koser, "Unterhaltungen," 256.

the food supply. That his efforts were appreciated was certified by Mitchell: "The unwearied Pains he takes to have the Soldiers well supplied with everything, justly acquires him the affection of the whole Army." [43]

The Austrians, of course, with one battalion of each regiment also under tents, found the weather just as cold and the problem of supply no less difficult. At the end of the year they abandoned Dippoldiswalde, which Frederick had threatened a few days before without daring to attack. Frederick reported the event, but grimly. Immediately before it happened he had written that there was nothing more they could do but hope for an enemy blunder from which they might profit. "My courage is used up. . . . Our affairs are desperate." On the day after, he wrote to Henry: "We are more lucky than wise. Dippoldiswalde is abandoned. . . . May Heaven help us; we have great need of it." [44]

The king had reason for discouragement. To be sure, the British House of Commons had just voted to renew his annual subsidy, in response to a great speech by Pitt. And, but for the loss of Dresden and a part of southern Saxony to the Austrians and part of Pomerania to the Swedes, he still held practically the same territory as at the end of the previous year. But his resources were approaching exhaustion, and the numbers, quality, and morale of his troops had never been so low. Perhaps worst of all, he was in serious danger of losing his greatest asset (outside himself) — the services of his brother Henry.

The prince's prestige had grown enormously during the year, both in the Prussian army and in the Austrian. The Prussian agent Benoît reported to the king from Warsaw in December that the news of the surrender at Maxen was partially counterbalanced in the minds of the Austrian high command and government by the firmness of the Prussian defense just after it. "This," he wrote, "consoles me, as well as the tributes which our enemies pay to His Highness Prince Henry. The couriers who have come here from the Austrian army say unanimously that one cannot imagine how they fear this prince, or the respect that Daun and all his generals have for him." [45]

Frederick knew his brother's value and was aware of his dissatisfaction; but presumably he did not know how near he was to losing him.

[43] To Holdernesse, December 16, in M. P., V, 41.
[44] P. C., XVIII, 728–730.
[45] P. C., XVIII, 698. When de Catt sought to cheer the king by an enumeration of the victories won that year by the armies of Prussia or of her allies — Minden, Hoyerswerda, Pretsch, Münster, and Quebec — Frederick revealed by his reply that he was sensitive on that point because all of them had been won by commanders other than himself. "Yes, that is something; and it would have been more, my friend, if I (poor devil) had been successful anywhere at all." Koser, "Unterhaltungen," 291. But that is not a sufficient basis for the belief, to which the partisans of the prince clung for many years, that by the end of the year 1759 Frederick had become so jealous of Henry's growing popularity with the

He had probably not seen Ferdinand's scurrilous letter "from an officer in the Prussian service," and could not have known that Henry had answered it without reproach: [46]

You are very kind, my dear Ferdinand, to credit me with the salvation of the Fatherland; but even if I had all of the ability which you so generously ascribe to me it would be useless to me, as I can do nothing against the Will that drags us along. Whoever commands under the king loses by it in honor and reputation, and it is a miracle that I have come out of the affair as well as I have. I shall no longer lay myself open to [injustice from] him, all the less because in the course of a long war I could never withstand him, and the foolish and impetuous man would again nullify the successes of others. 'The State,' my dear brother, is a name used to throw sand into the eyes of the public; it is a knave who claims every achievement as his own and to whom therefore one sacrifices one's services.[46]

Ferdinand had, in fact, had reason to expect his remarkable communication to be more favorably received than it deserved; for only five days after Maxen, Henry had written to him: "I am resolved to end my military career with this campaign." What had happened to Finck, he said, would happen to anyone who failed, though the king himself might be entirely responsible for the failure.[47]

All who failed had been discredited. First their brother William; then Dohna, Wobersnow, and Schmettau; and now Finck; and he had himself had his share of unearned censure in October, escaping more only by taking the offensive and turning the tide of the campaign. But who could expect to be consoled and comforted for failure, when survival itself was at stake? Not least among the ways in which Frederick earned his title of "the Great" was by his ability to stand up, year after year, under such a burden of hatred as he had to bear, and to retain and make good use of such a disaffected subordinate, the more particularly when that subordinate had reason to think himself abused.

army and of his prestige in the eyes of the enemy that he considered him a dangerous professional rival thereafter, and discriminated against him in every possible way in order to enhance his own reputation as Prussia's one matchless and indispensable *Feldherr,* or field commander. Such a charge seems to be quite without justification and to need no refutation, although the prince himself was at times tempted to believe it.

[46] December 20, in the Hausarchiv, Rep. 56, II, F. See also Otto Herrmann, in the *Historische Vierteljahrschrift,* XXVI (1931), 375.

[47] *Ibid.* Not even Frederick's most ardent admirers can close their eyes to the fact that to Maria Theresa he was always "that wicked man," and that most of continental Europe, during the first half of the war, called him "the Monster of the North."

CHAPTER VIII

# 𝕱𝖆𝖇𝖎𝖚𝖘 𝕾𝖊𝖈𝖚𝖓𝖉𝖚𝖘, 𝕮𝖚𝖓𝖈𝖙𝖆𝖙𝖔𝖗

*"I shall face without fear whatever may happen, and
endure it without despair."* — Henry to Frederick.
*"I shall try indeed to attack Prince Henry if an oppor-
tunity presents itself; but he has always so far taken
such advantageous and inaccessible positions that it has
been impossible to do battle with him."* — Saltykov.
*"We absolutely cannot any longer evade battle. . . .
By temporizing, we risk our certain destruction."*
— Frederick to Henry.

THROUGHOUT the winter months beginning the year 1760 Prince Henry
continued to entertain the thought of retirement, but without bringing
himself actually to the point of offering his resignation. Instead, he
asked for and received an extended sick leave, and spent the months of
February and March convalescing in Wittenberg with Cothenius in
constant attendance and reporting directly to the king. The doctor
diagnosed his trouble as "a kind of flying gout," and seemed not to
take it quite so seriously as he had done the late-winter illness of the year
before. The prince was unquestionably exhausted and ill and in real
need of recuperation, though his condition was no doubt made worse
by his disheartenment and not improved by his half-formed decision to
use it as an excuse for retirement unless the king made peace that winter.

During January especially, the thoughts of both the brothers turned
longingly toward peace; and Mitchell was greatly exasperated because
he could not make Frederick believe that France and Great Britain were
not on the point of making a separate treaty.[1]

Prince Henry urged his brother to take advantage of any opportunity
to extricate his country from its desperate situation, of which Frederick
himself had just said on the occasion of the New Year that the trials of

[1] *P. C.*, XIX, 22. "The King of Prussia, amidst all his great and superior qualities, and
with the most penetrating understanding, is by no means exempted from the common
weakness of humanity, of believing with wonderful facility whatever is agreeable, and with
the greatest difficulty whatever is contrary to his wishes or interest."
  Although Mitchell seemed not to know it, the two powers were in fact discussing the
possibility of making a separate treaty, in which France soon stipulated that Prussia could
not possibly be included, refusing even to consider negotiating with her without the consent of Austria and Russia, and insisting upon being left free to continue her aid to Austria.
*Ibid.*, 292–293.

the past and present were exceeded only by those obviously in store for the immediate future. Surely, Henry urged, after three and a half years of heroic defense of his state, he could never be reproached for making peace, even at the price of some slight cession of territory. Since such a step would obviously be dictated by duty and patriotism, to save the state from complete destruction, it could not be considered in any way dishonorable and only the king's vanity would suffer from it.[2]

Frederick did not resent the advice, but he preferred to cede other people's territory rather than his own. To Finckenstein he intimated that he would be willing to evacuate Saxony if the French would give back his Rhine provinces, and would raise no objection to Austria's indemnifying herself by taking some part of Bavaria, or to Saxony's having Erfurt.[3] But he would not buy deliverance from disaster by the cession of any Prussian territory; and without that there was no hope of peace.

When Prince Henry left his headquarters, Mitchell felt called upon to explain "secretly" to Holdernesse that his departure would probably revive reports that he was about to leave the army. The prince, according to Sir Andrew, had been "really indisposed, and a good deal out of Humour since the unhappy Affair of Maxen," and might have "dropt some expressions" indicating an intention to retire; but he would never do that while he was so badly needed as then.[4]

Mitchell knew whereof he spoke; for he had just received a letter from the prince in which the latter sought to justify himself in his friend's eyes. He said he had just got permission from the king to go to Wittenberg for rest and recuperation. As to his part in the next campaign he made no clear statement, but indicated that, if not asked to do the impossible and if not treated too inconsiderately, he could be counted upon to devote all his powers to being as useful as possible. But as things were just then he hoped he would not be blamed for "preferring retirement to an insufferable situation."[5]

[2] Schöning, II, 221; Schmitt, *Prinz Heinrich*, II, 6; von Bernhardi, *Friedrich der Grosse*, II, 69.

[3] *P. C.*, XIX, 65; M. P., V, 56–60. More specifically, in April, he outlined to his minister in England, for Pitt's benefit, his ideas of proper terms concerning Prussia in any separate peace that France and Britain might make. France should furnish no further aid or subsidy to Sweden or to any other enemy of Prussia; France and Great Britain should guarantee Prussia's possession of all territories held at the beginning of the war, whether she still held them at the end of it or not; Prussia should not be asked to make any cessions of territory or to pay any indemnities; France should evacuate and turn over to him in good faith whatever Prussian fortresses or territories she held at the time of making peace. *P. C.*, XIX, 290–292.

[4] M. P., V, 59–60; XIX, 69.

[5] M. P., V, 56, 62; XLIII, 9, 11. Volume XLIII of the Mitchell Papers consists entirely of the minister's correspondence with Prince Henry; but from it Bisset published only one of the prince's letters. He said it was the only one he could read. It proves to have been written at dictation by a secretary, on a day when the prince was too ill to hold a pen.

Others, less well informed, were less sure of the prince. Among those was the pious queen. "May God guide Prince Henry," she wrote to her brother Ferdinand of Brunswick, "and grant that he may think of his country and choose the proper course." [6]

The queen had guessed that the prince was irritated by the continued uncertainty as to where he was to command in the next campaign. He complained bitterly to his brother Ferdinand that he had been told first that he would command in Silesia, then that he would not, then again that he would: "The good Sire is a bit confused. He doesn't know what he wants. . . . I have had quite enough of his damned war, and wish the devil had taken the man who started it, on the day when he set his army on the march." [7]

If he had only had the charity or the sportsmanship to admit it, the prince knew quite well why the king had not yet made the final assignment of commands for the year; for Frederick had submitted to him for criticism and amendment his conception of the whole diplomatic and military situation and of the strategy he hoped they might be able to follow. A plan to maneuver Daun out of Saxony was agreed upon, and the king called it "your idea." [8]

During February and March the prince was handling for Frederick, through Baron Bielfeld, the negotiations for the bribery of certain Russian ministers and generals, and for setting up a secret service in Russia and Poland to furnish information on enemy plans and movements there. A special agent, Colonel de Pechlin, was sent to St. Petersburg; and the British minister there, Keith, was authorized to spend a million ducats of Prussian money for the same purpose. Frederick was for starting with the man of greatest influence. "Peter Schuvalow," he wrote Henry, "is the one who controls everything; buy him, and all the rest of the troupe are ours." They succeeded ultimately in "buying" only General Tottleben and another officer or two. By bribes and promises of land and a pension after the war in Prussia, those officers were induced to do what they could to mitigate the harshness with which the Russians habitually treated all occupied territories and their populations, to slow down troop movements, and to send information to Prince Henry

---

[6] Berner and Volz, 429.

[7] Hausarchiv, Rep. 56, II, F; Otto Herrmann, in the *Historische Vierteljahrschrift*, XXVI (1931), 372. It should be remembered that Prince Henry was by no means the last soldier to admit, as a frightful war went into its fifth year, that he had "had quite enough" of it. Nor was he the last to go on with it nevertheless, though he cursed the man who he thought had started it.

[8] Schöning, II, 246, 249; *P. C.*, XIX, 91, 233–241. In such quiet times the couriers often carried from one to the other a book to read, or some philosophical comment on their reading.

through a Jew named Sabatky. Sabatky's secret service system in Poland, thus created and maintained by Prince Henry, proved its usefulness throughout the year.[9]

Early in April Frederick notified his brother that he proposed to assign him the Silesian and Russian fronts for that year. Still hopeful of peace with France, he said that he preferred on that account to remain in Saxony himself, so that he would be more closely in touch with Ferdinand of Brunswick and in a better position to take immediate advantage of any favorable turn of events. He did not admit, even tacitly, that he had "had quite enough" of fighting the Russians, although he did say that he was so badly fagged out that he needed to conserve his physical energy more carefully than he had been doing, and that diplomacy might serve their purpose better than fighting. "An old head, full of experience, with a young and vigorous body," he said, was going to be needed; but as things were going, he feared he would "soon have neither the one nor the other."[10]

Since it was already known that a joint Austro-Russian campaign for the conquest of Silesia had been agreed upon, the prince was to command not merely an army or a sector but all the troops on the whole eastern front. For as long as he could stay in Lusatia he was to control Fouqué in Silesia, but only that long. If Frederick succeeded in bringing Denmark into the war (which, fortunately for him, he was never able to do), Henry was to command the Danish troops as well as his own, using them principally in Pomerania, around Danzig, and in East Prussia.

Frederick assured him that he was to be entirely his own master: "I give you full powers without restriction; I do not know how I could do more; I shall give you my general ideas orally when I talk to you, and leave everything else to you. I shall be [only] too happy if I can manage to take care of the task left to me [here]."[11] At best, he added gloomily,

[9] *P. C.*, XIX, 140–147, 171, 249, 308; Bisset, II, 136 *et passim;* M.P., V, 62–119. The king was very generous in his allocation of money to maintain the service, and said often that he considered it well spent. The bills of credit sent to Keith to be spent in St. Petersburg, and de Pechlin's cipher code, were returned unused; but Prussian spies were busy in Poland, and even more active in Vienna, throughout the war.

[10] Letters of April 6 to 26 in *P. C.*, XIX, 240, 246–249, 301. While the prince rested at Wittenberg, the king had worked with unremitting industry right through the winter at the task of recruiting and equipping his army. There was no rest for him. Mitchell was amazed at the completeness with which, by the end of March, the regiments in Saxony had been brought up to full strength and re-equipped. M. P., V, 85, 95.

[11] *Ibid.*, 263. The prince's written commission was entitled: "Pleinpouvoir und völlig allergnädigste Autorisation S. K. M. wegen des Dero Bruder, des Prinzen Heinrich Liebden, aufgetragenen illimitirten Commandos über dasjenige Corps d'armée, so S. K. M. zur Campagne gegenwärtigen Jahres in denen Gegenden von Hinterpommern zusammenziehen werden." It was dated at Freiberg, April 12.

only a *deus ex machina* could save them that year from their numerous enemies.[12]

Time and again Frederick repeated his suggestion that the prince come to Meissen to meet him; but he carefully refrained from using his royal authority, as under the circumstances he might excusably have done, and ordering him to come. At last, ten days after he had received his first notice of his new appointment, the reluctant prince agreed to a conference; and on April 18 the two met at Meissen. Mitchell reported that they spent "many hours together" there planning for the year, but Henry was back in Torgau on the nineteenth and in Berlin two days later.[13]

The British minister was greatly pleased and more than a little relieved by Prince Henry's return to active service. His opinion of the prince was much more favorable than it had been two and a half years before. After having accompanied him through the last half of the 1759 campaign, he considered him "in every way equal" to the command of an independent army. But he was glad that Frederick and Henry were not together; for, he said, "there cannot be two suns in the same firmament."[14]

Through most of the month of May Prince Henry was at Sagan, where the troops for the eastern front were assembling. The line he would have to hold stretched from Landeshut, where Fouqué was stationed, along the Bober and the Oder to the Baltic Sea. To defend it against 20,000 Austrians and 60,000 Russians he would have about 40,000 men or 55,000 including Fouqué's. That would be none too many; but Frederick had only 40,000 under his own immediate command in Saxony with which to face a total of a hundred thousand Austrians and Imperialists. The Prussian total, on all fronts combined and including garrisons, could not be raised over 118,000 at the beginning of the campaign. "There are our utmost efforts," Frederick had written. "May it please

[12] Frederick still hoped that his ally would arrange a peace with France, or that he could himself make either a Danish or a Turkish alliance, or both. Although he could not have foreseen the death of the Russian empress Elizabeth, the friendship of the new czar Peter proved eventually to be of greater value to him than either of those alliances could possibly have been; so the Angel of Death had ultimately to serve as *deus ex machina*.

[13] Dates established from Prince Henry's journal in the Prussian Secret State Archives. Most of the journal entries are extremely short and sketchy. That for April 18 is merely: "At Meissen with the king."

The prince traveled fast for an invalid. He was in Berlin for only a day or two, and was back in Torgau within six days, but visited Potsdam and reported to Frederick upon the excellent condition of the gardens at Sans Souci. Neither of the brothers was able until the end of the war to return again to the beautiful spot he loved best — the prince to Rheinsberg or Frederick to Sans Souci. The princess Henry was with the court in Magdeburg while her husband visited Berlin.

[14] M. P., V, 94; Bisset, II, 158; *P. C.*, XIX, 278.

Heaven to bless them so as to put an end at last to this fatal and well-nigh unbearable war!"[15]

May passed quietly by, and both the brothers were grateful for the quiet. The king, hoping that before the end of the month he might succeed in concluding an alliance either with Denmark or with Turkey, and so bring another army into the field to distract the attention of his enemies, was not at all eager to draw them down upon himself in the meantime. Prince Henry had been told plainly that, whenever he had to leave Sagan for the Polish front, Fouqué and the Bohemian border of Silesia would become Frederick's problem, not his; but he was determined nonetheless to stay where he was as long as he could. At the end of May Loudon crossed the border to lay siege to the fortress of Glatz. Further than that he dared not go, although he was the boldest and most aggressive of all the Austrian generals. His prudence was justified; for Prince Henry at once directed Fouqué to hold on to Landeshut as long as he could without being surrounded there, but to retire to Löwenberg if necessary, and to join the prince in an immediate attack upon Loudon if the latter should venture further toward Breslau.[16]

Fouqué, afraid of being caught in the mountains around Landeshut with the county of Glatz in Loudon's possession, retreated nearly to Schweidnitz in a fashion which both Henry and Frederick condemned as overhasty and unjustified. Whether the prince should leave Sagan, go to Fouqué's support, and try to drive Loudon away became then a question of some moment, which he submitted to the king and which Frederick answered in the negative. He ordered the prince not to let himself be drawn so far away from Glogau, to keep his eye on the Russians, who were already approaching the Vistula, and to leave Fouqué and Silesia to him. Fouqué got his orders thereafter directly from the king — plenty of orders, but no help.[17]

If the king had been better informed, help for Fouqué might well have been found. Either Prince Henry or Frederick himself might have furnished it. There would have been time enough. But underestimating Loudon's swiftness of movement and overestimating the speed of the Russian advance, Frederick ordered the prince to leave it to him. Then he himself waited for reinforcements (Prussian troops recalled from

---

[15] F. to H., in *P. C.*, XIX, 238, 260. The prince's reply to his brother's prediction that, without the intervention of a *deus ex machina*, disaster must almost certainly overtake them that year was: "As I have completely unburdened my heart to you on that subject, and as there is nothing else that I can do, I have made my decision. I shall face without fear whatever may happen, and endure it without despair, my spirit strengthened by a clear conscience." Von Bernhardi, *Friedrich der Grosse*, II, 69.

[16] Schöning, II, 306.

[17] Letters of June 1 to 6, in Schöning, II, 301–313, and in *P. C.*, XIX, 386–395.

service with Ferdinand of Brunswick). He realized as keenly as anyone the short-term character of any plan he could make, and said himself that he was "losing his head more than three times a day," but seems to have hoped that word of his impending treaty with Turkey would stop the Austrians from taking the offensive.[18]

On June 10 the presence of the Russians on the Vistula forced the prince to move off to meet them. His first tentative choice of a new base for his operations had been Küstrin, but on Frederick's advice he decided on Landsberg instead. His general plan was, if the Russians should come on in separate columns, to try to destroy first one of them and then the other, provided that he could find wagons enough in the region to solve his transport problem.[19]

Again Frederick assured him that he was his own master, but never ceased to make suggestions; and on one very important point, more cautious for once than his brother, he overruled him. Prince Henry proposed to paralyze the Russians' advance by a bold attack on their principal base at Posen, as he had served the Austrians along the Eger the year before. Frederick did not, in so many words, refuse his permission, but said that the thing could not be done. The distance was too great, and there was too much danger that the raiders might find their retreat cut off. It would be much better for the prince simply to hold his force together, wait for the Russians to come on in separate columns, and then battle one or the other of them. After his own experience with the Russians, and knowing his brother as he did, he did not demand that he destroy the whole invading army, but merely that he prevent it from gaining a foothold anywhere in the New Mark or in Silesia.[20]

The prince gave up his own project without being able to carry through that of his brother. Such an attempt to impose one man's method upon another could promise little success at best; and in this case the Russians, who had feared nothing so much as precisely such a raid on Posen as the prince had planned, refused to play into the hands of the Prussians by coming on in separate columns as Frederick had assumed they would.[21]

---

[18] *P. C.*, XIX, 395, 400. Again: "I shall not dwell upon my own troubles, but I assure you I am in no bed of roses. May Heaven help us; for human prudence falls short in situations as cruel and desperate as ours." *Ibid.*, 404.

[19] *Ibid.*, 348, 413, 418.

[20] *Ibid.*, 419, 422; Schöning, II, 322–324. For such a purely defensive mission it might have been wiser to leave the prince entirely free, actually as well as nominally, to choose his own methods.

[21] Schmitt, *Prinz Heinrich*, II, 40. Frederick also refused just then to consider a proposal which someone submitted through Prince Henry, that the peasants of the region should be armed for a people's rising against the Cossacks. The king said he had tried that in East Prussia two years before, and had sent in old officers as leaders, but had not

By the middle of June the prince was in Frankfort on the Oder, and from then until the middle of July in Landsberg, from which base Frederick had said he would have an opportunity to attack the Russians on the march.[22] General von der Goltz commanded his second column at Drossen, while Forcade after a short period of failure succeeded at last in putting an end to the plundering of Pomerania by Tottleben.[23] Both Pomerania and the New Mark had already suffered heavily at the hands of the Cossacks in the two preceding summers. "The countryside is so denuded of carts and horses," wrote the prince, "that one could not believe it without having seen it; most of the land is uncultivated, and one sees few seeded fields. It is a very touching spectacle, the misery that prevails everywhere here."[24] But on July 5 he was able to report that both provinces had been cleared of invaders and were temporarily safe.

Meanwhile Fouqué lost Landeshut. Displeased by his hasty withdrawal from that post at the beginning of June, Frederick had sharply ordered him to retake it at all costs and to hold on to it. What hurt the general even more, after he had for years enjoyed the special friendship and confidence of the king, was the postscript added by Frederick personally to his ciphered letter of June 14: "My generals are doing me more harm than the enemy; they always go wrong." Stung by his master's criticism, the general went back to Landeshut. From there he reported on June 19 that Austrian detachments were occupying the heights and the passes surrounding him; but he refused to move again. "Since Your Royal Majesty has repeatedly ordered me to hold this post, I shall stay here and hold it to the last." He had food enough to last his men for a month, but no hope of a rescue unless it came from the king's army in Saxony.[25]

On June 22, fearing that Fouqué would do just what he was then

been pleased with the results. In the same letter the king admitted that he could not remember very well just what he had done during those dark days following Kunersdorf, the year before: "As for that fund of sixty-odd thousand crowns, destined at one time for the use of Dohna's army, I greatly fear that it no longer exists. I have a confused idea in my mind that after the unfortunate affair of Kunersdorf I used all the rest of that fund to pay the army or to buy horses or supplies, . . . although I cannot recall the circumstances well enough to tell you for certain." *P. C.,* XIX, 421–422.

[22] Because of their habit of carrying six weeks' provisions with them in wagons, the king thought the Russians would be found most vulnerable when on the march, as then their baggage trains were more vitally important to them than their supply depots. He had given similar advice to Dohna, Wobersnow, and Wedell in 1759. Yet he himself had never been able to catch the Russians on the march, although he had twice attacked them in defensive positions of their own choosing.

[23] Frederick had recommended Goltz to the prince, and had said that he would be a better man for an independent command than Forcade, who had "la peur au ventre." *P. C.,* XIX, 405.

[24] Schöning, II, 333, 347; Schmitt, *Prinz Heinrich,* II, 44.

[25] *P. C.,* XIX, 421; Schöning, II, 332, 335. The last words of the king's dispatch to Fouqué have been rather freely translated because they were written in figurative French

actually doing, Frederick sent him new orders exactly like those Prince Henry had given him three weeks earlier: to give up Landeshut if he must, in order to save his army and still to be in a position to defend Breslau. By then it was already about a week too late. It was fatal for Fouqué's army when its very able general ceased to use his own judgment and began, not blindly but stubbornly, to obey orders instead. On June 23 he was attacked by Loudon's men from all sides. He himself, expecting to die like Leonidas, was wounded and captured. About five hundred of his men managed to fight their way out; the rest were killed, wounded, or forced to surrender. The king had tried to play the part of the Supreme Intelligence from too great a distance, and the general had adhered too closely to "the letter that killeth." [26]

The loss of Landeshut was less hurtful to the Prussian cause than Finck's surrender at Maxen had been. Fewer men were lost, and Fouqué had at least put up a fight. Loudon, to be sure, was highly elated and reported to Daun that nothing could prevent the capture of Breslau. From Prussian documents captured with Fouqué's headquarters he said he had learned that Prince Henry could not have more than thirty thousand troops with him, and he was sure that with that number the prince would never be able to stop the Russians. Furthermore, if the Russians would just handcuff the prince for a little while, he would take Breslau himself. But Loudon was oversanguine. His own colleagues, Daun and his quartermaster general Lacy, were jealous of him and not inclined to exert themselves overmuch to help him. Saltykov was too much afraid of Prince Henry to be the man to put handcuffs on him. Tauentzien, commandant of Breslau, was not to be intimidated. And Prince Henry himself ultimately entertained his adversaries with a few surprises.[27]

But while the loss of Landeshut was not fatal, no one but Loudon found the news of it very encouraging. Frederick, at first, could see no further hope for Prussia unless Turkey should declare war on Austria. "The Turks are supposed to be on the move," he wrote Henry. "If this is true, we are saved; if not, we are lost." [28]

Repeatedly he admitted that he was at his wits' end and could no longer do anything but make mistakes—doing "things which at any

that does not lend itself readily to literal translation. The implication was that the generals always bungled their tasks and did the wrong thing; "ils manoeuvrent toujours de travers."
[26] After the peace there was an official investigation of his conduct, but he was less severely censured than Schmettau or Finck.
[27] See von Arneth, *Geschichte Maria Theresias*, VI, 131ff.
[28] *P. C.*, XIX, 462. In the same letter he complained of "Fortune's persistence in persecuting" him. To Ferdinand of Brunswick he wrote that the events of the next month would decide his fate, and that in view of the too-great superiority of his enemies, things could hardly fail to go badly. *Ibid.*, 474–475.

other time would be contrary to reason and to the rules of war." However he racked his brain, he said, he could not make a really good decision; so he was forced to act at random.[29] While in that mood, he decided to march to Silesia, and warned the prince that all communication between them was likely to be cut off for some time; but after ten days of marching and countermarching, during which more than a hundred of his men died from the heat and from fatigue, he turned back from Reichenberg and laid siege to Dresden.

The prince was left in an uncomfortable position and an unhappy frame of mind. It was in that same desperate mood that Frederick had gone off to Kolin, to Hochkirch, and to Kunersdorf; and Henry feared he would again gamble and lose. "A thousand times the quarter hour," he wrote to his brother Ferdinand, he regretted that he had foolishly consented to command again in that campaign. The wise and fortunate ones were those who had got out of the service and got away from the war (as Ferdinand had done). He had helped several of them to do so, and had "not belabored them with pretty phrases about the Good of the State, Performance of Duty, The General Welfare or such things, either."[30] As for the Turks, he would believe in the reality of an alliance with them only when he knew it was signed, and in the military value of such an alliance only when shown that an Austrian army had actually been withdrawn from the Prussian front and sent to Transylvania.[31]

For three weeks the prince held his troops together on the Prussian-Polish border, waiting for Saltykov to come on. Anticipating that he would soon find it necessary to operate in the Polish province of Posen, he issued on July 1 a proclamation claiming that the presence of Russian troops in that technically neutral territory, then and in past years, gave Prussia the right to oppose them there, as the Treaty of Wehlau had

[29] Letters of June 29 and 30, *ibid.*, 476, 477. Mitchell sent home just then a "most secret" report reading, in part, as follows: "Things cannot remain long in this situation, and what I dread most is, that the King of Prussia, in attempting to do more than he is able, will miscarry in the whole; for I find that, notwithstanding what has happened in Silesia, he is still thinking of keeping a footing there; and I have observed that every resolution he has lately taken has been in some sort dictated by the news received from that province, and therefore for some time past he does not seem to have acted with the same consistancy [*sic*] and connection which he has hitherto done." M. P., V, 112; Bisset, II, 162.

[30] Hausarchiv, Rep. 56, II, F; Otto Hermann, in the *Historische Vierteljahrschrift*, XXVI (1931), 375. Seydlitz had not yet returned to active service since being wounded in the hand at Kunersdorf. When he did return, after an absence of a year and a half, he joined the prince's army and never fought again under the immediate command of the king. He had come very close to insubordination at Zorndorf, at Hochkirch, and at Kunersdorf.

[31] Mitchell was equally skeptical. On June 23 he wrote to Pitt: "These vague and loose Assurances have made I think too deep an Impression on the King of Prussia's Mind. He

already given her the right of transit. To calm the fears of the inhabitants, and as a bid for their friendship, which might be very valuable to him, he assured them in his proclamation that he would keep his troops under strict control and would see to it that all supplies taken were paid for in cash.[32]

Then, returning to his own tactical methods, he spread out his forces and sent most of them into Poland to seek out more closely the actual position of the Russians. Frederick at once warned him that it was too dangerous so to scatter his strength when the enemy was so far superior in cavalry and other mobile troops. Concentration was the only safe policy, he advised. Yet he assured the prince that the Russians would never attack him and that he, on the other hand, must aim at the destruction of their wagon trains.[33] The prince refused to pay any further attention to instructions so inconsistent and self-contradictory, and went his own way thereafter so far as tactics were concerned. What worried him most was the fear that Lacy or Loudon, whom no one stood ready to prevent, would destroy his principal supply base at Frankfort (on the Oder), as he would have done in their place; but that, fortunately, did not happen.

During the last half of July, with the Austrians on the move in Silesia and the Russians in western Poland, Frederick was himself occupied near Dresden. From there he tried his best to keep in touch with what was happening elsewhere, and to give such directions as he could; but he was too far away. Fortunately he did not quite forget that he had given the prince full powers to do as he saw fit; so it was suggestions and criticisms that his couriers carried halfway across Germany, not categorical orders; but he would have been wiser to send fewer couriers for a while, especially since his own failure at Dresden made him increasingly irritable and his criticisms grew steadily sharper and sharper. Both in their tone and in their effect, they resembled more and more closely those of the unhappy pre-Maxen period of the year before.

The general trend of the Russians' slow movement was southward through Posen. Parallel with them, always between them and Silesia, moved Prince Henry. Learning that they were establishing a new base at Kalisch for use during a siege either of Glogau or of Breslau, he suggested that Tauentzien dash out from Breslau and destroy it; but Tauentzien was afraid to make the attempt for fear Loudon would come up

flatters himself that if the Turks begin to act the Austrians will be obliged to desist from their Attempt upon Silesia." That situation did not "appear in the same light" to Mitchell; but meanwhile, he said, he was trying to restrain the king from wrecking himself with no help yet in sight. M. P., V, 113.

[32] Schmitt, *Prinz Heinrich*, II, 44; *P. C.*, XIX, 481.   [33] *P. C.*, XIX, 499.

from Glatz and attack Breslau in his absence. On July 24 Frederick wrote that Henry should entirely disregard Saltykov for a while, drive Loudon away, and then return to a strong position somewhere between Glogau and Breslau and wait for the Russians. What the Russians might have been doing in the meantime was a question that was never answered; for the prince made no attempt at the time to act on the suggestion, and the king himself withdrew it the next day.

Before Prince Henry received either of these dispatches, Loudon had already captured Glatz, on July 26, and was ready to move on Breslau. As the prince himself conceived his problem, there was not much to be done with Loudon just then. His own army, weakened by detachments to cover the northern part of his front, did not number much over thirty-six thousand effectives. Saltykov had sixty thousand and Loudon twenty thousand. To go to Silesia too soon would be simply to hand over Frankfort and Berlin to the Russians; to attack the Russians would be to risk another Kunersdorf. If he should go off in pursuit of Loudon, instead, and should come up with him in a position not too strong to be attacked, Loudon would simply run away; and the Russians would meanwhile have marched into Glogau without opposition. His only real success so far, he said, had been to prevent the enemy from doing anything; and that was about all he could hope to do. If Loudon and Saltykov knew their business and did their duty, he could probably not go on indefinitely doing even that, for they would attack him from both sides at once. "This drives me to despair," he wrote; "but it is the simple truth, which I cannot conceal from you. . . . I wish with all my heart that I could turn this enterprise over to someone more skillful than I seem to be." He promised, however, that when his two enemies came closer together he would swing from one to the other, prevent their union if he could, and if possible keep them from taking either of the Silesian cities at which they seemed to be aiming.[34]

The crisis developed around Breslau in the first week of August; and in spite of his pessimism the prince proved with the aid of Tauentzien to be equal to it. On August 1 the Russians crossed the border east of Glogau; Prince Henry's army passed through that city; Loudon summoned Tauentzien to surrender Breslau to him; and Tauentzien defiantly refused. The Austrian commander hoped that the Russians would at least hold Prince Henry off his back while he took the city, but he planned to let them have no other share in the conquest. Saltykov, for his part, having little confidence in Loudon and none at all in the Austrian higher command, and afraid to attack the prince in spite of his over-

[34] Schöning, II, 369.

whelming numerical superiority, made some trifling excuses about bread-baking and a shortage of other supplies, and halted for two days near the border.

During those two days Prince Henry was almost incessantly on the march. On August 1, the day they crossed to the left bank of the Oder, his men marched more than four German miles. Two days later he was at Parchwitz, northwest of Breslau, and had driven off Loudon's detachment under Caramelli, which had tried to stop him there. He wrote to Frederick that if Loudon had occupied that post with a stronger force it would have been hard to get past it — which was true. Another truth, which he did not trouble to write, was that Loudon had been surprised by the swiftness of his attack — and not without excuse, for in three days he had marched his men eighteen German miles, an average of nearly thirty English miles a day. The last march, from Gramschütz to Parchwitz, had been made in a single twenty-four-hour stretch, with only two rest periods of a few hours each, during which the men fell out in marching order beside the roads.[85]

Breslau was saved. On August 2 Loudon had not again pressed his demand for a surrender but had tried to induce Tauentzien to capitulate on his own terms and march the garrison out of the town. It would have been a new drama of disaster similar to Schmettau's capitulation at Dresden with rescue almost at hand; but Tauentzien refused. On August 3, with Prince Henry on his heels, Loudon had to abandon the siege and save himself. The prince pursued him as far as Striegau without catching more than a few hundred of his men, left a small rear guard to keep an eye on him, recrossed the Oder at Breslau on the eighth, drove the Russians away from the northeastern approaches to the city, and camped between them and it. Within another week, alarmed by the approach of the king of Prussia, the invaders were retreating slowly northward toward the border. They had not only gained no foothold; except during August, they had scarcely set foot on Prussian soil.[86]

It was one of the most brilliant exploits of the whole war; but unfortunately the man who executed it and the one who reported it seemed to be two different persons. The letters which went off to the king attributed its success chiefly (and honestly) to the failure of the Russians to use their numerical strength and their opportunities, and to Loudon's oversight in failing to send a stronger force to occupy the important post at Parchwitz. His enemies might in truth have made it much harder for the prince, and he could not believe that they would not yet do so. He

---

[85] Von Bernhardi, *Friedrich der Grosse*, II, 90.
[86] Schöning, II, 376; Schmitt, *Prinz Heinrich*, II, 60–66, 75–90.

had had so little license to win that he could not forget how near he had been to losing. Then the letters which came from the king in the thick of things, all of them a week old before they arrived, were only an irritant. When the affair was virtually finished, there came one warning him that he must look out for Breslau! Almost daily, while he was spending twenty hours of the twenty-four in the saddle, shuttling back and forth between enemies, he had a letter from Frederick exhorting him to rouse up his courage, to bestir himself, and to *do something!* [37]

[37] *P. C.*, XIX, 536; E. Maschke, in the *Jahrbücher für die deutsche Armée und Marine*, CXVII (1900), 215. Only a lively imagination can conjure up a true picture of the work of the hard-riding couriers or *Feldjäger* in that war, and the most hardened statistician would probably go insane if he attempted to estimate how many miles they must have covered, going at top speed over all sorts of roads, in all kinds of weather, and often with manifold dangers added to their physical hardships. It was only justice that they were often quite generously rewarded for their rides. But it would have been better for Prussia and for the relations between the king and Prince Henry if most of the dispatches they carried in July and August, 1760, had gone astray or had never been written.

# CHAPTER IX

# Achilles in His Tent

*"I think H. R. H. carries his Resentment too far,
though I must fairly own that he must be more or
less than Man not to feel sensibly what has happened to him."*— Sir Andrew Mitchell.

THE LETTERS which so irritated Prince Henry in midsummer, 1760,
were written by a man too far away to know until several days after the
event what was actually happening, and driven almost to desperation by
his own more immediate problems and by continued failure to attain
his ends. Through the last half of July Frederick maintained his siege
of Dresden without success, although when he began it he had expected
to be in possession of the place within a few days.[1]

When its defender, Maguire, refused to evacuate the city at once, the
king did not hesitate to fire upon it, first with his fieldpieces and then
with siege guns as soon as he could bring some up from Torgau for that
purpose. During the second week of the siege several bad fires added to
the sufferings of the inhabitants and to the repugnance with which
Mitchell viewed the whole proceeding, more particularly as the worst
fires occurred after everyone but Frederick had conceded that the siege
was hopeless.

One of the things to which Mitchell objected most strenuously was
the shelling of a church. Frederick's "Relation" of the siege says that
four cannon were firing upon the Prussian batteries from the church
tower. Mitchell wrote that there was a report, "whether true or false"
he did not know, that an artillery observer had been seen in the tower,
signalling to the Austrian batteries. The worst of the fires spread from
the burning church. Nearly two thirds of the city was reduced to ashes.[2]

---

[1] F. to H., in *P. C.*, XIX, 486. There was perhaps a note of sarcasm in the prince's
reply of July 20: "I am waiting eagerly for news of the capture of Dresden. I have the
honor to congratulate you in advance, for according to the letter with which you honored
me . . . it could not hold out for more than two days." Schöning, II, 359.

[2] *P. C.*, XIX, 510. "I cannot think of the bombardment of Dresden without horror,"
wrote Sir Andrew in his report, "nor of many other things I have seen. Misfortunes naturally
sour men's tempers, and the continuance of them at last extinguishes humanity. . . .

"I have had many private conversations with His Prussian Majesty, and have been an
eye-witness to many things which I wish had never happened; I have even ventured to
speak freely upon several occasions but all the consolation I had was, that what I said
gave no offense. Your Grace shall be informed of every particular, if ever I have the happiness to see you, for they are not fit to write." M. P., V, 114–121; Bisset, II, 168–186.

On July 23 Frederick admitted to Henry that the siege had failed. For its failure he blamed the slowness of his subordinates in bringing up the siege guns from Torgau, although they had then been there for a week. Yet he persevered for eight days longer, and marched away from the city only upon the approach of Marshal Daun on August 1. Then, on the same day on which the Russians crossed the Silesian border, he himself headed for that province with thirty thousand men, depending upon Daun to go with him, and leaving General von Hülsen with twelve thousand to hold what was left of Saxony if he could.[3]

As Frederick marched eastward from Dresden, through Lusatia and into Silesia, Daun retired before him, barely fast enough to keep out of his way, and Lacy followed on his heels. It might have looked as if they were formally escorting him to a junction with Prince Henry, although that was the one thing they were ordered at all costs to prevent. Bolder than her generals, Maria Theresa urged Daun to attack, absolving him in advance in case he should do so and be defeated. Still the march continued without a battle until a third Austrian army, Loudon's, could join the lion-hunt. Then finally, near Liegnitz on August 14, the three commanders screwed one another's courage to the sticking point.

Nearly two years had passed since Daun had last dared to attack an army commanded by the king of Prussia in person. That had been at Hochkirch; and another Hochkirch or a second Maxen seemed to be in prospect. The three Austrian armies, totaling eighty thousand men, had Frederick's little force of less than thirty thousand practically surrounded and cut off from the fortress of Schweidnitz from which he must soon draw supplies. Whether they knew it or not, he had bread enough with him to feed his men only four days longer, and hunger would soon have forced him to try to fight his way out.

The Austrians had planned to make a joint attack soon after daybreak on the fifteenth; but as the first of their three armies, Loudon's, moved into position a little before sunrise it blundered almost into the Prussian camp. Frederick had again deceived them by quietly making in the night another of his sudden and otherwise apparently pointless changes of position. Almost before anyone but the king of Prussia knew what was happening, he had escaped his second Maxen and won a second Rossbach. In the dim light of the dawn, so quickly that neither Daun nor Lacy was able to bring any effective help to their distressed colleague (although Loudon afterward complained very bitterly against them for their failure to do so), and with a loss of only 639 killed and 2,757 wounded or missing, he threw Loudon's troops into complete con-

[3] *P. C.*, XIX, 514; M. P., V, 121, 123–127; Bisset, II, 178, 187.

fusion. Loudon's casualties were considerably heavier than the Prussian, and five hundred of his men and eighty guns were captured. The Austrians then drew off southward toward Schweidnitz; and Frederick, remaining on the battlefield of Liegnitz only long enough to gather up his wounded and the serviceable equipment no longer needed by the dead, made off the same day to Neumarkt, thence shortly to Hermannsdorf, a few miles southwest of Breslau. From there Mitchell wrote home that the army was still in good condition in spite of its exertions, that it had lost very little of its baggage on its strenuous and hazardous march, and that victory had given the men new strength and spirit. Mitchell himself had killed several horses in keeping pace with them, had lost some of his own baggage, and had been instructed by the king to destroy his cipher codes and papers before Liegnitz for fear of capture.[4]

The moral effect of Liegnitz was in fact tremendous in both camps. Victory had at last perched once more on Prussia's banners, and Frederick was himself again. Fully aware of that fact, disheartened and bickering among themselves, the Austrian generals were disinclined to attack him again and withdrew from a threatened seige of Schweidnitz at his approach, while Czernichev went back across the Oder with the reinforcement of twenty thousand Russians with which he was to have joined them.

Immediately after the battle of Liegnitz, in order to make sure that Czernichev would withdraw, Frederick tried to trick him into doing it. From Parchwitz he sent off a letter addressed to Prince Henry but intended for Czernichev, instructing its bearer to get himself captured by the Russians with the letter not too well concealed on his person. In the dispatch the king announced, ostensibly to his brother, that he had just won a great victory over the Austrians, that Loudon had been mortally wounded, Daun and Lacy had fled, and he and Prince Henry must at once round up Czernichev between them and destroy his detachment before he could rejoin Saltykov. In a spirit of mischievous fun, like Tom Sawyer enjoying one of his own jokes, he added: "I only hope this letter reaches you promptly."[5]

[4] M. P., V, 127–129; Bisset, II, 194–204, 233.
[5] Von Arneth, *Geschichte Maria Theresias*, VI, 448; Schmitt, *Prinz Heinrich*, II, 100–105. One or the other of the Russian commanders seems to have sent the letter to Loudon. Von Arneth found it among the family papers in the possession of Freiherr Olivier von Loudon. In it Frederick more than doubled the number of Austrian casualties and exaggerated by half the number of guns and flags he had captured. That was done for effect. He seems, however, to have believed that Loudon had been mortally wounded; for both then and two days later he repeated that statement in letters to General von Hülsen and Prince Ferdinand of Brunswick, whom he would have had no reason or wish to deceive. Before Czernichev could have seen Frederick's letter, he had already heard directly from Loudon that the latter had been defeated but was unhurt. Frederick himself was told by a deserter, nearly a week later, that Loudon had only rolled on the ground in his rage,

If Czernichev was actually deceived by the king's rather transparent ruse, it would only have hastened his retreat. There would have been little point in his going on to join a beaten army after the quarry had already escaped and the hunt had been abandoned. Furthermore, the hunter had become the hunted; and, for fear of joint action by the king and Prince Henry against either or both of them, the two Russian commanders would have reunited and retired as they did, either with or without further prompting from Frederick.

Geographically the king and his brother were close enough together, within a week after the battle of Liegnitz, to have been able to act in concert; but spiritually and in their opinions they were by then unfortunately so far apart that real cooperation between them no longer seemed possible.

The storm clouds had been slowly gathering for weeks. After giving the prince unrestricted authority and promising him a free hand on the eastern front, the king had in practice continued to shower him with advice and criticism which usually arrived too late to be relevant but which he could neither quite disregard in action nor dismiss from his thoughts. The first half of August had been an extremely trying time for them both. Their exertions had been almost superhuman, their nerves were on edge, and their tempers were unleashed. While the pressure from outside was still on them — until the prince had driven first Loudon and then the Russians away from Breslau and until Frederick had regained at least a moral though not a numerical or strategic advantage over the Austrians in Silesia after Liegnitz — the brothers merely argued about their differences. Once that crisis was past, they precipitated a new one by quarreling.

The deeper and more significant of those differences was one of opinion and, under the circumstances, was of a somewhat academic nature. They were debating general strategy at a time when they were both so completely at the mercy of events that little freedom was left them in the choice of a policy. It would have been wiser for them merely to recognize that condition and keep quiet about a difference of opinion on such a matter; but they were too articulate for that, their courier service was good, and forbearance from sharp speaking was less than ever notable among their virtues. So, while each did what he had to do, they debated what they ought to do or to have done.

While the prince was in practice, just then, no less bold than the

bemoaning the loss of his guns and cursing Daun for not coming to his relief. "I do not care for heroes who roll in the dirt," was the king's comment to Prince Henry. *P. C.*, XIX, 555. Just how much effect Frederick's stratagem actually had on Czernichev's course of action would be hard to determine. Von Arneth does not say that the trick did not work,

king, and in private no more gloomy in his view of their general situation, a fundamental disagreement developed between them in the field of general strategy. On paper at least, Frederick still talked the bolder type of warfare even when he could not practice as he preached. He had had to sit still in Saxony while Fouqué was lost at Landeshut, then had marched and countermarched through the first half of July without fighting a battle or going anywhere, and had spent the last half of July in a fruitless siege of Dresden; but meanwhile, more and more insistently, he had demanded that the prince should seek a decisive battle against the Russians.

On July 25 he wrote from his camp near Dresden: "In the situation in which we find ourselves, I and you, my dear brother, it is indispensably necessary that there shall be a decisive affair, either on your part or on mine. We absolutely cannot any longer evade battle; I beg you to impress that on your mind. . . . If not, we shall dry up on our feet and consume ourselves; and, in the end, things will be a great deal worse than they are now. So let us put that down as said, and let pass no proper occasion to come to a decision; by temporizing, we risk our certain destruction." [6]

That letter reached the prince just as his own affairs approached a crisis on the Polish border of Silesia, and added something to his perplexity. He knew he could not force Loudon to battle, and he dared neither attack the Russians nor turn his back on them, at least until they and Loudon were closer together. He had already explained all that, and had sent word (by a courier who met Frederick's somewhere on the road) that he considered it something achieved merely to have prevented the enemy from accomplishing anything.

While Frederick demanded a decision, the prince still wished to defer one if possible, since it was admitted by both that any decision that came just then would very probably be unfavorable to them.[7] If the Prussian cause was really doomed to die, as each of them said he believed it was,

and leaves the reader free to suppose that it did. Czernichev, when he later served for a time with Frederick as an ally, found it politic to permit Frederick also to suppose so. That, however, is no proof. Bülow (*Prinz Heinrich,* 171) says that it worked; von Bernhardi doubts it. Any general should have known that, while it would be to the king's advantage to spread exaggerated reports of his victory, he would certainly never have let one of his couriers be captured with a paper still on him which announced a plan to attack Czernichev in conjunction with Prince Henry if he had really intended to do what he said.

[6] *P. C.,* XIX, 521. The king went on to announce his decision to march to Silesia rather than "sit there with his arms crossed, while all his states were exposed to the greatest dangers." When he started his march, he told de Catt that he was being forced to make it because Henry would not act as he should. Koser, "Unterhaltungen," 434.

[7] "You will see," Frederick predicted to de Catt as he started for Silesia. "It will be as I have told you; I cannot hold out beyond the end of August or September. I have too many enemies." Koser, "Unterhaltungen," 431–434.

Frederick argued that the end might as well come a little sooner as later. He would at least go down fighting, though he carried down with him in his fall the very pillars of the Prussian state. Prince Henry, on the other hand, definitely preferred to die later rather than soon, counting it another triumph whenever the end of a day found him still alive, his army intact, and Prussia's downfall not yet an accomplished fact.

On July 29, after a summer of gloomy indecision in which he had repeatedly admitted that the best he could do, himself, was to try to choose the least hazardous of several dangerous courses open to him, Frederick reproached the prince for pessimism and indecision! "It pains me to see from your letters that you look at everything from the worst side. I beg of you in the name of God, my very dear brother, not to picture everything to yourself in the blackest and most hopeless fashion, not to throw your mind into a state of indecision and uncertainty, but to make a decision, let it be what it will — which indeed I must leave entirely to you — then when you have chosen a course of action, whatever it may be, follow it with vigor and without further self-questioning." [8]

That letter was written in answer to one in which Henry, although he admitted that he was "driven to despair" by the difficulties of his situation, had announced his decision, contrary to Frederick's advice, to stay close to his major enemy, the Russian army, until he found himself near enough also to Loudon to drive him away without leaving the Russians too long unopposed. Yet he was accused of timidity and indecision! The accusation hurt him all the more because it unfortunately reached him just at the moment when, having already made sure of the safety of Glogau, he was marching his men off their feet in his dash to the relief and defense of Breslau. It could not have been delivered more inopportunely.

On August 5, with Loudon off his back but ready to threaten Frederick's, and with the Russians pushed away from Breslau but not out of the reckoning, the prince again surveyed his situation and found it still far from satisfactory. Although his success had been so swiftly won at the end, and won by so narrow a margin that he could scarcely realize it, he had accomplished his principal mission. He had prevented the junction of Loudon's and Saltykov's armies; he had successfully defended Pomerania, Frankfort, Glogau, and Breslau in turn; and he had prevented the Russians from securing a permanent foothold any-

---

[8] *P. C.*, XIX, 490, 527. Frederick had himself just written to Ferdinand of Brunswick that he expected to be entirely ruined within a month, and to Finckenstein that, since it was merely a matter of perishing four weeks sooner or four weeks later, one might as well die in August as in September or October. *Ibid.*, 524–525. Yet he reproached Henry for pessimism!

where on Prussian territory. But he saw the situation too much as a whole to be content with a performance that might enhance his personal reputation while it left the state still in danger; and he saw only too clearly that the dangers which had been warded off were, after all, still there—and almost as threatening as ever. Though none too sure of their ground, all the major Russian and Austrian armies still stood on Prussian soil. Worst of all, the letters he had been receiving from Frederick throughout the weeks just past had wounded his personal and professional pride and had indicated to him that at one really vital point he had failed. He had not satisfied the king.

When Frederick learned what the prince had done during that first week of August he was ready as ever with praise of it. To the vice-commandant of Glogau, for example, he held out the hope that affairs would soon take a decided turn for the better and that Silesia would shortly be freed, "with God's help and through the incomparably fine conduct of my brother." [9] But by that time the nagging sharpness of his dispatches had driven Prince Henry beyond his limit.

Such a state of affairs was not entirely creditable to either of the brothers. If Frederick could have learned to withhold his sharper criticisms until he knew whereof he wrote, or if he had used his correspondence with Henry more for legitimate official purposes and less as an outlet for his own overwrought feelings, he would not have goaded his brother as he did. If Henry had studied the date lines of the king's dispatches more closely, and if before reading one of them he had gone back over his own far enough to recall to his mind just what information had reached Frederick before he wrote it—and what had not—he need not have been quite so sensitive as he was. If his mind had been less clouded by his emotions, he might have reminded himself that, as king and commander in chief, Frederick had a right to criticize him if any one had; but even then he would have drawn a distinction between justifiable criticism and pointless faultfinding. His task was hard enough without that. When its most difficult phase was successfully completed, just after the relief of Breslau, he decided that it was in fact too hard; and without waiting for Frederick's change of tone which was sure to follow his receipt of the good news, he offered to give it up.

"If I had foreseen the difficulties which I have encountered in this campaign and which I still foresee," he wrote, "I should have asked you to excuse me from a task which I consider it practically impossible to accomplish." [10] As a matter of fact, about the only thing which he could have been expected to do and had not done was to win the unqualified

[9] *P. C.*, XIX, 540.  [10] August 5, in Schöning, II, 376; *P. C.*, XIX, 540.

and outspoken approval of Frederick, to which in his earlier and easier campaigns he had become accustomed. He had never stood criticism well. Here, about to take his turn at going into the doldrums, he thought he could no longer endure it. So, knowing that he could escape it only by leaving the service, he offered to leave.

Frederick answered, six days before the battle of Liegnitz, as if he were entirely unconscious of the real reason for his brother's request, and as if he supposed that he had only to appeal to Henry's pride and ambition as he had so often done.

It is not difficult, my dear brother, to find people to serve the state in comfortable and prosperous times; good citizens are those who serve it in a time of crisis and misfortune. Enduring fame is grounded upon the accomplishment of difficult tasks; the more difficult they are, the more they honor [those who do them]. I do not therefore believe that what you have written me can be your serious intention. Certainly neither you nor I can be responsible for events in our present situation; but when we have done all that we can, our own clear consciences and the public will do us justice. . . .

Publish it there that I am sending you 10,000 men; tomorrow I shall put into circulation here a report that you are sending me that number. Federic.

[P.S.] I congratulate you, my dear brother, on all the great advantages which your foresight, your vigilance, and your swiftness in action have won for us.[11]

Frederick's kingly letter of August 9 did its work, and Henry remained at his post as long as he had an independent command; but on that point also he was soon overruled. Frederick decided to unite the two armies. Henry protested that such a fusion would be a suicidal blunder. The king's contention was that neither of his armies alone was strong enough to do anything but stand on the defensive. United, they might yet do something decisive against the Austrians. The Russians, he thought, could be virtually dropped out of the reckoning, for he had convinced himself that they were already preparing to return home and would do nothing more that year.

Prince Henry, who was in touch with the Russians, urged as strongly as possible that his army should be kept intact and should continue to operate between them and the eastern cities of Prussia as it had been doing all summer. Otherwise, he predicted, the Russians would march straight to Berlin. "You must set an army against an army," he argued in effect. "To concentrate now against either of your enemies is simply to leave the other free to do as he will." While he continued to send de-

[11] *P. C.,* XIX, 540–541. Four days later he wrote again: "I congratulate you on all the advantages you have won, for which the credit is due entirely to you." *Ibid.,* 543.

tachments around both flanks of the Russian army to restrict its foraging area, and to prod it along on its retreat, he warned the king that if only a small corps were left to watch it they would soon find it established in the Mark of Brandenburg, whence they might not be able to dislodge it that winter.[12]

Unable to dissuade Frederick, Henry asked that he at least be left all his troops for ten days longer, as he believed that Saltykov was heading for Glogau. To that Frederick agreed, again suggesting the adoption of precisely the tactics the prince was then using and had already described to him.[13]

Henry was right in thinking they had not yet seen nor heard the last of the Russians, and that Glogau was their first objective. Frederick was right in thinking that nothing worried any of their enemies quite so much as the thought of having the two Prussian armies close enough together to be combined quickly for joint action against one of them. On August 27 Saltykov had reported to his own government:

> In the meantime I shall move by a series of short marches down the Oder so as to force Prince Henry to follow me and thus to disengage *M. le comte* Daun and facilitate his operations against the king of Prussia. I shall try indeed to attack Prince Henry if an opportunity presents itself; [but] he has always so far taken such advantageous and inaccessible positions that it has been impossible to do battle with him without exposing Her Imperial Majesty's army to an obvious danger.[14]

So the prince maneuvered the Russians away from Glogau and out of Silesia, but on August 29 he was ordered to leave Lieutenant General von der Goltz with twelve thousand men to watch them, and to bring the remainder of his army to join the king at Hermannsdorf. That was too much for him. He sent the troops; but he himself sat down in Breslau, pleading illness. Eichel stated the facts, prudently and without prejudice, to Finckenstein: "The prince will stay in Breslau, feeling indisposed with an attack of fever — at which the king is very angry, never having been in greater need of help than just now." [15]

It would have been greatly to Prince Henry's credit if, in spite of all, he had been able to second the king again as loyally and as gloriously as

---

[12] August 19, in Schöning, II, 388; Schmitt, *Prinz Heinrich*, II, 108.

[13] *P. C.*, XIX, 557–558. "I know that what I ask is almost impossible, in view of the enemy's superiority in light troops," the king added; "but I am relying entirely upon you, and am quite sure that you will do everything you can to deliver us from those barbarians. Let us have patience and see how all this will turn out; we shall need a great deal of good luck yet, and I confess to you that I am prodigiously distrustful of my star."

[14] Schmitt, *Prinz Heinrich*, II, 107; M. P., V, 130. Saltykov was soon replaced by Fermor, and Fermor by Buturlin.

[15] *P. C.*, XIX, 567–568.

he had done in the period following Hochkirch nearly two years before; but he was not equal to it. It would be easy, but manifestly unjust to him, to explain his refusal on the ground that his self-esteem was hurt and that, after three years as an independent commander, he was too proud to serve again as a subordinate. Such a charge would contain an element of truth, which Mitchell had put, long before, into his statement that there could not be two suns in one firmament; but that explanation would itself be much less than half the truth.

The prince was a skilled soldier and a patriot. As such, he had definite opinions about the military policy proper for Prussia just then, and all his patriotism as well as his self-esteem was enlisted in support of those views. He was unalterably convinced that the concentration of Prussia's forces, upon which Frederick was just as unalterably determined, was a fatal mistake and would sacrifice all the favorable results of a year's fighting, just as he thought Frederick had done by overruling him in the Maxen matter of the year before. Such a concentration, he argued, would convert the Prussian army into a sort of hedgehog or armadillo which might itself be immune to attack but which could protect Prussian territory at but one of several simultaneously threatened points. He had tried to dissuade the king, but had found argument as useless as it had been before Maxen. He knew that if he refused to obey orders, or carried his protests too far, he would at once cease to be the king's brother and would be dismissed from the service in disgrace as Prince William had been. So he chose what seemed to be the only way open to him to show his disapproval of what the king was doing. In refusing to budge from his position, he showed all the self-confidence and the independence of judgment needed in an independent commander or in a good second-in-command; but his capacity for self-effacement could not stand the strain of the double test put upon it by his brother's order and the policy of which it was a part.

His illness was real but not serious; he had gone on in spite of worse ones many times, and would do so again. Alleged as the reason for his retirement, it was only a pretext and deceived no one.[16] His best friends

---

[16] In a letter to his brother Ferdinand in December, advising him not to return to active service, he made the revealing remark: "You can always feign an illness." Hausarchiv, Rep. 56, II, F. Kalckreuth says simply: "He said he was sick." *Paroles,* 225. His wife confided to her journal in October, after he had moved from Breslau to Glogau: "The Prince is ill at Glogau; he has left the army entirely. I have foreseen this event, and it displeases me very much." Berner and Volz, 199.

Various references to the princess in Henry's letters to Ferdinand indicate that the growing estrangement between them had gone rather far already, and had become worse just then. She probably reproached him for his conduct; but her letters to the king that year on the occasions of the New Year and of his birthday departed somewhat from her usual formula for them, as if she were trying to propitiate him on her husband's behalf without

deplored his retirement, although they did not condemn him for it, while Prussia's friends were deeply concerned over it for fear it would prove permanent. Foremost in both categories stood Sir Andrew Mitchell, who, worn out by his attempt to keep pace with Frederick, joined Henry in Breslau and soon accompanied him to Glogau. In a "private and most secret" letter to the Earl of Holdernesse, Mitchell wrote on November 10:

My Lord: It is with sincere and deep concern that I must acquaint your Lordship of an Event which I think likely to happen, and which will be extremely detrimental to His Prussian Majesty's Affairs and to the Common Cause. What I allude to is a Total Rupture between the King of Prussia and his Brother Prince Henry. . . .

H. R. H. has great Abilities, is much beloved by the Army, and H. P. M. will find it difficult to reimplace him by any other Commander. I think H. R. H. carries his Resentment too far, though I must fairly own that he must be more or less than Man not to feel sensibly what has happened to him, in this, as well as at the End of the last Campaign.[17]

While spiteful persons did what they could to keep the brothers apart, and only Mitchell exerted himself much to reconcile them, Frederick

mentioning his name. Hausarchiv, Rep. 56, II, T. Frederick replied with perfunctory but otherwise perfect politeness, without mentioning Henry, and sent the princess a handsome gift of porcelain the next time he was in Saxony.

[17] M. P., V, 144. The middle portion of the letter, of which the first and last paragraphs are quoted above, gives Mitchell's characteristically sportsmanlike but rather incomplete version of the whole affair:

"Since the End of August last when the K. of Pr. drew off the greatest Part of the Army that was commanded by his Brother and acted against the Russians, P. H. being a little indisposed threw himself into *Breslaw*. As I had frequent opportunities of seeing that Prince and was honoured with some degree of his Confidence, I soon found that Want of Health was but a Pretense for his Retreat. The real Cause was the Resentment he bore that the King his Bro. had in Effect superseded him in his Command, and he called to mind on this Occasion what happened to him last year before the Affair of *Maxen*, from [which] he concluded that as he could be of no Use in the Army where H. P. M. was, he was resolved never to serve under him, and added that his Duty to his Country, in its deplorable Situation, was the only Motive that had induced him to accept even the Command of a separate Army, during this campaign, for that from the Beginning he foresaw that some Disgrace of that Sort would happen to Him, from the Incompatibility of his Brother's Temper.

"I do not trouble your Lordship with a Detail of the Arguments I made use of to disuade [*sic*] H. R. H. from his Resolution. They were directed to heal, to soften, and to apologize for the K. of Pr.'s Conduct towards him, but all that I could say produced no Effect, and I soon found that Jealousy and Ambition have more power over military minds than Reason and Interest.

"During the whole time H. R. H. remained at *Breslaw*, he corresponded regularly with the K. his brother, and wrote him freely his Opinion concerning the Plan of Operations. The K. of Pr. pressed him very much to join the Army before he marched into Saxony, which H. R. H. declined on pretense of Health, and came to this Place, about a Month ago, when the Residence at *Breslaw* was no longer safe, since which no Letters have passed between the Brothers, and H. P. M. has not even notified the late Victory of the 3rd [at Torgau] to him, but H. R. H. has done wisely, and wrote a Letter of Felicitation to the K. of Pr. upon it. What Effect this may have I know not, but I fear what has passed will widen the Breach and heighten the Differences which have long subsisted between the Brothers."

went into the Silesian hills with his army, alone. The British minister, when he was worn out, could retire to a fortress town for a rest. Prince Henry, free from the moral compulsion which forbids the leader to falter, and lacking the last reserve of spiritual strength released in Frederick by the mere fact that he was king, could sulk like Achilles in his tent. But Agamemnon must go on.

Frederick went on also because it was his nature to do so. He was fighting without hope of victory — which to Prince Henry seemed only a sinful sacrifice of men's lives; but while his mind told him that his cause was dead, his will carried him forward from where his mind left off; and when his will failed, his fighting instinct kept him on his feet. If someone had put a bullet through his brain, he would have fallen forward, his hands clutching the ground. A king like Frederick cannot quit; and such a fighter is hard to kill.

In his own eyes, an egoist can do no wrong; so Frederick, who was both egoist and king, never entertained the idea that anything he had said or done might have been responsible for his brother's defection. Unable to accomplish any of the purposes which had been his sole justification for consolidating the armies, he repeatedly and rather pathetically urged Henry to recover and return to active service so that he could separate them again.[18]

The prince meanwhile had been sending on regularly all such military information as came to his ears and volunteering his opinions, admittedly largely guesswork, as to what their enemies' plans might be. In Saxony, however, the intentions of the Imperial army soon ceased to be a matter either of guesswork or of opinion. By the middle of September General von Hülsen had been driven back from Strehla to Torgau and was in imminent danger of losing his grip on Saxony. Within another ten days he had had to abandon both Torgau and Leipzig, and the Imperialists had burned a part of Wittenberg. On the nineteenth Prince Henry suggested to the king that a detachment be sent to Saxony before it was too late. Although he did not plainly say so, he apparently had himself in mind as its leader. The king replied that such a detachment would have to "pass in review before the whole Austrian army" before reaching its destination, and would inevitably be destroyed.[19]

Instead Frederick waited two weeks longer and then decided to march his army into Saxony; but even then he had to go first to the relief of Berlin. Goltz's little corps of observation, already too weak to do much to obstruct the movements of the Russian army and still further weakened by having to send off a detachment under General Werner for

---

[18] *P. C.*, XIX, 581, 605.    [19] *Ibid.*, 591.

the relief of Kolberg, could do nothing more than report on the invaders' progress when, precisely as Prince Henry had predicted, they decided to march on Berlin. Fortunately for Prussia, Tottleben commanded the cavalry of the advance guard and Czernichev the infantry of the raiding force, while Fermor remained with the main body of the army at Frankfort on the Oder. When their preparations were first reported to him, Frederick thought them only a bluff (*Schreckpulver*), to frighten the Prussians and appease the Austrians, who were constantly trying to goad their allies into action; but when Goltz reported that they were actually on the move, he replied: "The farther I read in your report of the 30th the worse it was. You acted as an honorable man, however, in writing me the simple truth." [20]

Hülsen from the southwest, Stutterheim and Prince Eugene of Württemberg from the north, Goltz from the southeast, and Seydlitz from leave for convalescence, the Prussian generals rallied to the defense of the capital; but they could not long delude themselves into believing that they would save it. The Austrians, on the other hand, were unwilling to see the Russians capture it without their help and keep all the ransom money to be collected from it; so Lacy was also sent off posthaste for Berlin. Frederick knew when Lacy started his march, but thought he was going to Saxony. [21]

Although Lacy marched as swiftly as he could, the Russians got there first. The city capitulated to Tottleben and Czernichev on October 9 and was in the hands of the invaders for three days. In return for a gratuity (*Douceurgelder*) of 200,000 thaler to be distributed to the soldiers in cash on the day following the capitulation, the Russian commanders agreed to hold their men under strict discipline and not to demand quarters for them. The city had to agree also, however, to a ransom of 1,500,000 thaler, a part of which was to be paid within six days and the remainder within two months. Trade was permitted to go on (officially) undisturbed, and the Russian troops behaved reasonably well. [22]

On October 7 Frederick wrote to Prince Henry from Bunzwelwitz in Silesia that he was about to march but did not know where; he must be governed by circumstances; but "conquer or die," he declared, was his device. First he moved toward Berlin; and at the news of his approach,

---

[20] *Ibid.,* 604; XX, 3.    [21] F. to H., October 3, *ibid.,* XX, 5.
[22] The invaders agreed to accept the ransom in "light" money — that is, in the adulterated coin then current. Frederick reimbursed the city in the following April. Lacy was more severe with the suburbs. From Potsdam he demanded 60,000 thaler (18,000 in cash and the balance in exchange on Hamburg), and 5,427 thaler as gratuities. Charlottenburg was assessed for 15,000 thaler; and Austrian troops and Saxons serving with them plundered the Charlottenburg palace. The palace at Schönhausen also suffered some damage. A. Schäfer, II-2, 83, 85; M. P., V, 141.

although he was still many miles away, the Russians decamped from the city and retired in great haste via Frankfort to Landsberg. Then he turned toward Saxony, whither Daun had gone in the meantime and whither Lacy had retired from Berlin.[23]

On the evening of November 2 Frederick led his tired army into camp within easy striking distance of the position occupied by the principal Austrian armies under Daun and Lacy on the heights of Süptitz just west of Torgau. Calling his generals into conference, he told them that he had summoned them not to ask for their opinions but to give them their orders for an attack. They were all tired of the war, he said; so was he himself; then let them put an end to it the next day by breaking Daun's army to pieces and throwing the pieces into the Elbe.[24]

Frederick's plan of battle at Torgau was startling in its novelty and its boldness. Although outnumbered, he divided his army, leaving General Zieten to attack Lacy from the south while he marched around the Austrian position, as he had marched around the Russians at Zorndorf and at Kunersdorf, and attacked Daun from the north. The plan was doubly hazardous because it depended for its success upon the cooperation of two widely separated units between which no direct or quick communication would be possible. Not even a "zero hour" was set for the beginning of the action. Zieten was simply to attack when the sound of guns told him that the king was attacking.

Fortunately no one had to march blindly or half at random as Frederick had been compelled to do at Kunersdorf. The king had at his elbow an engineer-officer from von Hülsen's corps who knew every road and bypath; and many of the regiments, when serving under Prince Henry a year earlier, had occupied the very positions which they now had to attack. They could therefore find their way in the dark — which was fortunate; for before they were finished they had to do precisely that. They were handicapped, however, by the weather. It was a bitterly cold, wet day, and their first attacks were delivered in a heavy rainstorm driven by a raging wind.

Frederick was badly beaten that day; in fact, he was beaten three times, but he attacked four times. When darkness set in, after the repulse of his third assault, he drew off his shattered regiments to the cover of some woods to reorganize them, hoping that the Austrians might withdraw during the night and leave him in possession of the battlefield. Daun also thought it safe to leave and let the surgeons take care of a

---

[23] *P. C.*, XX, 14; M. P., V, 137; von Bernhardi, *Friedrich der Grosse*, II, 156–157. The Russians soon continued their retirement and recrossed the Vistula.

[24] Jany, II, 579. The story is based on the journal of the king's aide-de-camp, Major von Gaudi.

wound in his leg, received some hours earlier, and sent off a messenger to Vienna announcing a great victory. Then Zieten made himself felt.

That famous general of hussars had been unable to dislodge Lacy, but had attacked him vigorously enough to prevent him from aiding Daun. Then, unhampered by the darkness because his men were fortunately so familiar with the terrain, he worked around to his left until he had re-established contact with the king's troops and from there, in the darkness, attacked the Austrians from the flank!

Quickly sensing what had happened, Major von Gaudi prompted von Hülsen to join in the attack; and soon, with all their drums beating and every gun in action that could be brought back into position, the king and his whole army returned to it. The action lasted till nearly ten; and when some of Lacy's regiments at last came up, all they could do was to cover the retreat of Daun's army (under the command of O'Donnell because of the marshal's wound) over the Elbe by the bridge at Torgau. All night long bands of stragglers wandered through the woods, taking one another prisoner and plundering the dead and wounded as they lay half frozen in the mud. Next day Lacy also retreated up the Elbe, and both parts of the Austrian army again took their old positions around Dresden where they had stood the year before.

For Frederick it was a Pyrrhic victory, almost as costly as Kunersdorf had been. He had lost about seventeen thousand men, nearly half of the combat strength of his infantry and a third of that of his whole army. Several of his most dependable regiments were reduced to one battalion each, and the "Prince Henry" regiment had to be combined with another to form a battalion. Of the total losses, only about seven hundred men were listed as "missing." Three thousand were prisoners of war. The Austrians lost about ten thousand killed, wounded, and missing, and seven thousand prisoners. Frederick was so moved by his losses that he forbade the publication of any report of them.[25]

Yet the king cannot be accused of having fought the battle of Torgau gratuitously — or without tangible results. Daun and Lacy had been ordered not to give up Saxony without the most determined resistance, and would not have given way without a battle. His dearly bought vic-

[25] Jany, II, 594–595. Jany found only one copy — and that among Prince Henry's papers. If it was the one mentioned by the king on November 12, it was unreliable. See page 155. Frederick himself said of it later: "Il y en a beaucoup que j'ai supprimés, à cause que toutes choses ne sont pas bonnes à dire." *P. C.*, XX, 87–89.

Frederick was hit that day and suffered a painful contusion on his chest but no serious injury.

At his last interview with Zieten many years later, finding the old general in worse physical condition than himself, the king insisted upon standing during their conversation while requiring his "old friend and comrade" to be seated. He had always shown in many ways his gratitude for the general's distinguished service.

tory that day, furthermore, won back for Prussia all of northern Saxony; and at the beginning of December his troops found their ardently longed-for winter quarters on the old line, Meissen-Freiberg-Chemnitz. Frederick wintered in Leipzig, and Dresden remained in the hands of the Austrians.[26]

On the Silesian front, only Glatz had been lost; and Prince Henry would again have been safe enough in Breslau; but he continued to intern himself in Glogau, rarely leaving his quarters and seeing almost no one, entertaining himself chiefly with music and reading. Throughout November Mitchell stayed there with him, despite Frederick's invitation to accompany him on the march to Saxony, and of Eichel's efforts to "rescue" him from the prince's influence. When the Scotsman did leave, it was to Magdeburg and not to Leipzig that he went; but from there, both directly and through Finckenstein, he continued to work for a reconciliation of the brothers. He told the prince plainly that both Berlin and Magdeburg were full of "infamous rumors" which he had denied but could not kill, and that Henry and Henry only could save the state from the harm that they might do. Early in December, when he was himself on the point of going to headquarters at Leipzig, he urged the prince to meet him there and make his peace with the king.

The prince replied that his health was not yet equal to such a trip and he doubted that anything would be gained by it.[27] He did, however, make an overture of another sort, by working with Schlabrendorff for the reorganization and improvement of the spy system already in operation in Russia and Poland.[28]

His health would have stood any trip he chose to make.[29] In his correspondence with Frederick, however, it continued to serve a double purpose, furnishing him a pretext for staying away until he could be fairly sure on what footing he could return, and giving Frederick something

[26] To Countess Camas, who had known him since his boyhood, Frederick described his circumstances and himself on November 18 as follows: "I swear to you it is a dog's life such as, except Don Quixote, no one but me has ever had to lead. This constant labor and ceaseless confusion have made me so old that you would scarcely recognize me. My hair is all gray on the right side, my teeth are breaking off or falling out, my face shows wrinkles like the folds of a woman's dress, my back is bent like a bow and my countenance is as sad and downcast as that of a Trappist monk. I am preparing you in advance for all this, so that if you should ever again see me in the flesh you will not be too badly shocked by my appearance. Only my heart has not changed and will preserve, as long as I live, its feelings of respect and deepest friendship for you, my good Mama." Reinhold Koser, *Aus dem Leben Friedrichs des Grossen* (Berlin, 1916), 45.
[27] M. P., V, 140, 146; XXVIII, 78; LIII, 13. Princess Henry entertained Mitchell in Magdeburg and, he said, showed him every possible courtesy; but there was nothing she could do directly, either with her husband or with the king.
[28] P. C., XX, 149.
[29] On December 1 he wrote to his brother Ferdinand that he was well enough — "Je me porte la la." Hausarchiv, Rep. 56, II, F.

about which he could keep on writing solicitous letters so as to show his continued good will. The older brother meanwhile chose indulgently to accept the fiction so as to save the prince's face for him whenever he should return.

The news of the battle of Torgau reached Prince Henry through other channels several days before he had word of it directly from the king; but, prompted by his better self, or possibly by Mitchell, he sent off a letter of congratulation anyway without waiting for the personal report which reached him only on November 11.

In that report Frederick greatly exaggerated the Austrian losses and minimized his own. A few days later he explained that he had falsified the figures not in order to mislead Henry but because he had thought it more likely than not that the courier would be captured by the Austrians and, if he was writing for their benefit, he had wanted to make a good story of it. If they found it discouraging, so much the better.[30]

The Austrians were in fact discouraged, but not to the point of offering to negotiate for peace, as Frederick had hoped they would do. Disappointed there, he turned again to Great Britain and instructed Knyphausen in London "to pull him out of Purgatory" if possible by getting the British somehow to induce France to withdraw from the Grand Alliance against him.[31] When that hope also faded, although he grumbled that he had little reason to be grateful to the heavy coat that had saved his life at Torgau, he turned to preparation for another campaign as to a task laid on him by an inexorable fate.

Would he have his brother's help in that campaign? He knew he would need it, but he waited for Henry's sense of duty to bring him back to his proper place. The prince meanwhile, as much at odds with himself as with Frederick, tried vainly to free himself from a nagging sense of delinquency by boasting to their brother Ferdinand that he had taught the king a lesson and could return to active service if and when he chose, but would do so only if offered an independent command on his own terms.[32]

[30] *P. C.*, XX, 46, 74.     [31] *Ibid.*, 76–77.     [32] Hausarchiv, Rep. 56, II, F.

CHAPTER X

# 𝕿𝖍𝖊 𝕽𝖊𝖇𝖊𝖑'𝖘 𝕽𝖊𝖙𝖚𝖗𝖓

*"To blush at that, one must be ashamed of having
been born a man."* — Henry to Frederick.

THE first months of each calendar year were necessarily devoted by
all of the belligerents to rest and recruitment; and at the beginning of
the year 1761 the Prussian forces were in even more need of reconditioning than usual. Frederick himself was again attacked by gout and up to
March 1 had left his quarters in Leipzig only once, while Henry kept
equally close to his in Glogau. Even Mitchell was exhausted and found
himself physically unable to make the campaign with them when it
eventually opened.

The recruitment of the Prussian army was slower than the recuperation of its leaders. On paper, it was to consist of a hundred and twenty-seven thousand men. In practice, it could barely be brought up to a
hundred thousand. Saxon peasants, prisoners of war, deserters from the
Austrian and Imperial armies, camp followers, and freebooters unfit to
wear the uniform or bear the name of soldiers were used to fill up the
rosters of the decimated regiments or of the newer irregular units called
"free battalions"; but the rosters were always better filled than the ranks
— especially in the free battalions, which Mitchell said were "composed
of the very dregs of mankind." [1]

Acceptable officers were harder to find than recruits; but even in that
extremity the king would not resort to wholesale promotions from the
ranks. Some foreigners attracted by his fabulous reputation were commissioned as volunteers, and many a youngster of the *Junker* class was
given the rank and title of an officer far ahead of his time and without
the training or the experience which alone could have made a dependable
officer of him. Observers in the Prussian camps were sometimes shocked
by the schoolboy character of the games in which these prematurely
transplanted scions of the Prussian nobility sought to amuse themselves;
and Frederick himself once tweaked the ear of one of them, saying that
he had just wanted to see whether the lad was yet dry behind the ears!
"Our people must be blind if they think they are protected by real

[1] M. P., VI, 112. Most of the free battalions were in Prince Henry's army, usually; and
his percentage of regular regiments was proportionately low.

156

armies," wrote Prince Henry to his brother Ferdinand; "but out of Austrian prisoners and little Prussian boys perhaps two armed forces of some sort will be got together."[2]

Among the senior officers promotions might keep pace with casualties, but only because they could proceed at whatever pace the king chose to set for them. The development of men fit for such rapid promotion could not be so accelerated by royal order. A few men such as Wunsch, Kleist, and Goltz, all of whom had served most of the time under Prince Henry, had come on very fast; but not many. Already the king was paying a great deal of attention to staff work and to the training of officers, and after the war he was to pay still more; but as Prince Henry, writing as "Marshal Gessler," had pointed out before the war began, the old system was not well adapted to the training of generals for independent commands. With Seydlitz still out of service because the disease from which he was suffering made every wound unconscionably slow to heal, Zieten was the only good cavalry commander left among the old officers, and Kleist was just beginning to be recognized among the newer ones. The situation demanded the maintenance of a second army, but the system had produced no one but Prince Henry capable of commanding it or of accepting the manifold responsibilities that such a command entailed.[3]

From that time on, no matter what the king might say or how strongly he might argue in favor of a swift conclusion by means of one all-decisive battle, the only kind of war that Prussia could possibly fight was the cautious defensive which Prince Henry had advocated all along. The army was "no longer in a condition to fight every day; so the king had to conserve the energies of his troops for the most important and most decisive occasions."[4]

The recruitment of his financial resources was a more serious problem than ever. He had already done almost all he could do by debasement of the coinage, but he refused to increase the tax rates. Those rates were already high; and the rise in prices and the decline in the value and purchasing power of the currency were themselves a form of taxation.

Britain would renew the subsidy, he knew; but as Mitchell's sympathies were being perceptibly transferred from the king to his subjects and the inhabitants of the occupied areas, he could not depend upon the Scotsman to plead his cause quite so eloquently as in years past. Mitchell

[2] Hausarchiv, Rep. 56, II, F; Otto Herrmann, in the *Historische Vierteljahrschrift*, XXVI (1931), 375.

[3] M. P., V, 192.

[4] Von Bernhardi, *Friedrich der Grosse*, II, 281, quoting the General Staff history of the war.

reported in fact that Frederick did indeed need money, but that it would never do to accept his estimate of how much he needed.[5]

Saxony had already been drawn on all too heavily. The king's demands there, Mitchell said, were exorbitant, and his punitive measures for their enforcement were "equally ruinous to the country and to the officers employed upon that service, who, when they have once tasted the sweets of plunder, cease to be soldiers." [6]

The composite army under Ferdinand of Brunswick was nominally in Frederick's service and pay but was actually supported largely by British subsidies. When the estimates of the amount necessary for its maintenance were being made, Mitchell was, as he said, "at open war with the Prussian ministry" over them, objecting that his government was being "greatly over-charged." The Prussians were asking for a hundred and sixty-seven thaler per man; the canny Scot thought a hundred and fifty thaler should be enough, but surmised that Frederick expected to have his demand scaled down.[7]

The return of Prince Henry would be worth more than any subsidy; but at the beginning of the year Mitchell could still see no sign of that. On January 3 he wrote to Holdernesse:

It gives me the deepest concern to acquaint your Lordship that I see yet no appearance of making up the breach between the King of Prussia and his brother Henry, which, if it lasts, will have the worst of consequences.

I have laboured underhand with the Prussian ministers here to bring about a reconciliation, but they have made no progress. They are well disposed, but timid, even in matters where fear of offending ought not to operate.

His Prussian Majesty has never once named his brother to me, and I [have] thought it my duty not to seem to know anything of the difference between them.[8]

A reconciliation was nearer at hand than Mitchell knew. An ex-

---

[5] On the first of those points Mitchell wrote on January 3: "The sufferings of the King of Prussia's subjects in Brandenburg, Silesia, and other provinces have been so great that I fear he will be able to draw very little from those provinces for the support of his army during the ensuing campaign. What resources he may have to supply this defect, besides the revenues of Saxony, are unknown to me." M. P., V, 165; Bisset, II, 212.

[6] M. P., V, 165–170. A demand for a contribution of 2,000,000 thaler (subsequently reduced to 1,100,000) from the town of Leipzig and the plundering of the Schloss at Hubertusburg were reported by Mitchell with disapproval.

[7] M. P., V, 175, 188; VI, 18; Bisset, II, 219, 223. Frederick claimed positive knowledge that France would pay Austria as a subsidy that year the cash equivalent of 24,000 men.

The change in Mitchell's attitude may serve as a partial explanation of the readiness with which Frederick and Cothenius agreed in the spring that the minister would probably find the campaign of 1761 too strenuous for him, and had therefore better not try to take the field with headquarters as usual; but in midsummer Mitchell was seriously ill for several weeks.

[8] M. P., V, 165; Bisset, II, 212.

change of amenities on the occasion of their birthdays in January broke the ice enough to encourage the prince to write a studied defense of his own behavior, and to make his first open bid for a return to the service. With obvious effort he began by trying to put his reasoning upon a general philosophical basis, but soon frankly admitted that he was speaking simply for himself.

To ask the impossible of men, to require them to stifle the pride with which they are endowed by nature, to demand of them sacrifices beyond their human powers, is to put them into the cruel position where they must either attempt what they cannot do or be forced to confess their inadequacy.

Pleading thus the cause of humanity, I plead my own; for I recognize that I have been prey to all the weaknesses inherent in the imperfection of our human kind. I do not blush to confess this before your judgment seat; for, to blush at that, one must be ashamed of having been born a man.[9]

As an indication that he was ready to leave Glogau, the prince reported that he had prescribed a regime of daily walks for himself in the hope of building up his strength, and might ask soon for permission to go to Spandau to recuperate. Frederick knew well that if Henry went to Spandau just then the country would at once be filled with rumors that he had gone there as a prisoner; so the permission was not granted. Then, although he still complained of stomach cramps, headaches, and nervous debility which he said made him doubt that he could make another campaign, Henry hinted that his strength might be equal to a trip to Leipzig if his presence there promised to be in any way useful.[10]

The invitation to headquarters for which he was obviously angling was not at once extended. Tantalizingly Frederick reported a Prussian-Hanoverian victory over the Imperial army at Langensalza and dwelt optimistically upon the possibility that France might make a separate peace — letting the prince assume, if he would, that perhaps he would not be needed after all.

Clearly Henry must go the whole way; Frederick was not coming to meet him. So he went, reporting that, while still far from well, he was considerably better than he had been — and asking outright whether Frederick would again have need of him and be able to "employ him as in the past." In other words, if he were again offered an independent command, he would be glad to return.[11]

At last Frederick had him where he wanted him. Without commit-

[9] Schöning, III, 16.
[10] February 17, *ibid.*, 18–20.
[11] *Ibid.*, 21; von Bernhardi, *Friedrich der Grosse*, II, 278.

ting himself on the question of the independent command, saying only that they must decide in conference how to meet their situation, he invited the prince by all means to come along to headquarters. The war, he said, was not over yet. Certainly the prince would be needed, like every good patriot, to join in a final effort to win a decent peace by continuing a determined defense. Exercise and a purposeful and significant occupation would be the best cure for his lingering illness. Yes, yes, come along. But come by way of Berlin and Wittenberg, as the bridge at Torgau had not yet been rebuilt.[12]

The invitation, cordial though it was, was not quite satisfactory to the prince without the reassurance for which he had asked. He waited several days before answering it, pleading as his excuse an inflammation in his eyes. He would start at once, he said, traveling light and leaving his equipage in Glogau; but he would wait in Berlin for further instructions. Frederick's letters had painted a very hopeful (though, in the event, illusory) picture of the general diplomatic situation; so, said the prince, "as I hope that the number of your enemies will diminish and that the Austrians, left by themselves, cannot oblige you to divide your forces, then in that case I suppose that you will have no need of my services." Apparently, uncomfortable though he was in retirement, he would refuse even to go on from Berlin to headquarters unless he were promised a command of his own.[13]

On March 28 the prince left Glogau for Berlin, where he spent the first half of April. Lehndorff, then in Magdeburg with the court, heard that the inflammation in his eyes was still so bad that he went nowhere and received no one except Ferdinand and his doctors; but it did not prevent him from continuing his correspondence with the king concerning their intelligence service on the Russian front.[14]

The assurance that he sought, however, as to what would be demanded of him if he returned to active service was still not forthcoming. So he had to explain apologetically that he had not sought to pry into his brother's royal secrets but had merely wished to know in what field and capacity he would probably be serving, so as to make his personal arrangements accordingly. He would therefore come to headquarters and make his bow, after which he would either retire or cheerfully accept an assignment, as the king might wish.[15]

---

[12] *P. C.,* XX, 273.    [13] Schöning, III, 24.

[14] The dates of the prince's movements are established from his journal in the Prussian Secret State Archives, Rep. 92, B, III, 138. Lehndorff's comment is from the supplement (*Nachträge,* I, 296) to his diary, *Dreissig Jahre.* The letters mentioned are in Schöning, III, 26, and in the *P. C.,* XX, 317.

[15] Schöning, III, 28. It is obvious that the king was determined to bring the prince to terms without bargaining — and that he had at last succeeded in doing so. Although he

Either the prince had been thoroughly humbled for the time being or some of the rumors then current at headquarters — that he was again to command in Saxony while the king went to Silesia — had already reached his ears. On April 18 he wrote an affectionate farewell note to Ferdinand and left Berlin for Wittenberg. On April 19 he met the king at Meissen, where they both stayed for nearly two weeks and where Henry was again put in command of the troops in Saxony.[16]

Frederick's instructions for the prince's information and guidance were as detailed and as specific as they could well have been made. The war chest was in Leipzig, the pontoons in use at Strehla, the surplus baggage wagons and heavy guns at Wittenberg. In case of retreat, all must be got off in good time to Magdeburg. The king stated confidently that the French and British were on the point of making peace. When that was done, Finckenstein was immediately to notify the prince, who would then form a plan in concert with Ferdinand of Brunswick for the use of the troops so released from the northwestern front. An offensive against the Austrians and Imperials in the Eger region seemed to Frederick to promise the greatest profit.

In general the prince was directed to stand on the defensive, contenting himself with the maintenance of the *status quo* in Saxony — which Frederick predicted would not be difficult, as Daun had recovered from his wound and would apparently again command the Austrians on that front. If Daun, however, should turn with the larger part of his army from Saxony to Silesia, then the prince must leave certain designated regiments and free battalions in Saxony under the command of General von Hülsen and hasten with the rest of his army by way of Sagan to join the king. Problems which could not be covered by written instructions Frederick dismissed with the words: "There is nothing positive to be said on these matters, and nature has endowed you with so much intelligence and good sense that you will know how to make your own decisions."[17]

Either the prince had suddenly lost confidence in his own judgment and had turned to complete dependence upon the king or his old desire to insure himself in advance against *ex post facto* criticism was still strong upon him; for he was not content either with the lengthy instructions he had received or with the latitude promised him in cases which they did not cover. As soon as he had had time to study them at length

refused to tell Henry so, he had already written to Ferdinand of Brunswick that he intended to go to Silesia and that Prince Henry would again command in Saxony.
[16] H. to Ferdinand, in the Hausarchiv, Rep. 56, II, F; Prince Henry's journal, in the Staatsarchiv, Rep. 92, B, III, 138; Kalckreuth, *Paroles*, 235; M. P., V, 206.
[17] *P. C.*, XX, 348–350.

he asked for more specific orders on nine different points, and concluded his request with the comprehensive general question: "I take the liberty of asking you also to tell me whether it is your intention that I shall hold myself scrupulously to the instructions you have given me, or whether I should act according to the course of events."[18]

The king replied briefly and pointedly to the nine articles, but did not take the trouble to renew the general grant of discretionary authority he had already made.[19]

Meanwhile word came from Silesia that Loudon, after giving due notice of the termination of the winter armistice, had assembled his army near Glatz and compelled General Goltz to retreat from Landeshut to Schweidnitz just as Fouqué had done the year before. Loudon had then taken Landeshut and several other posts in that region. The king's proposed march to Silesia could therefore be delayed no longer, so he set out on May 2.[20]

The withdrawal of more than half of the Prussian troops from Saxony compelled the prince at once, in obedience to his instructions, to reduce the area over which those remaining were spread. So he called in the garrisons from the advanced posts around Freiberg and collected his forces in a fortified camp near Schlettau, southwest of Meissen, in a position locally known as the *Kätzenhäuser*. There they could keep an eye on Daun's army near Dresden, and from there their patrols were soon operating as actively as ever in the Freiberg region from which their garrisons had just been withdrawn. Daun's troops were held where they were, in a state of suspended animation. Prince Henry was glad enough to be left alone; for he had suffered another attack of stomach cramps and fever which kept him in bed for a week and confined him to quarters for a fortnight.[21]

Fortunately both the king and Prince Henry were able to spend the first half of the summer in watchful waiting. Frederick's position at Kunzendorf near Schweidnitz kept Loudon confined to the mountains of the Silesian border, while Daun's army remained inactive around Dresden. Meanwhile, in order to be as well prepared as possible for whatever might happen, the brothers continued to compare ideas as of old.

---

[18] Schöning, III, 39.

[19] *P. C.*, XX, 359. The prince had under his command, most of the time during the spring and early summer, from 30,000 to 36,000 men. Daun had from 50,000 to 55,000, and was joined during the summer by 15,000 men from the Imperial army and in the autumn by 20,000 more from Loudon's. On June 20 Mitchell reported that the prince's army had a "paper" strength of 43,000 but numbered only 28,000 effectives. M. P., V, 217.

[20] Mitchell went as far as Strehla with the king, then returned to the prince's headquarters at Meissen. M. P., V, 209.

[21] Schöning, III, 43; M. P., XLIII, 15. Cothenius attended him, and Mitchell and Prince Ferdinand visited him.

Frederick was sure that Daun would soon leave Saxony and join Loudon in Silesia; for, he argued, if Great Britain and France should make peace, Austria would make a desperate last effort to reconquer Silesia before a general cessation of hostilities could follow. Prince Henry respectfully adhered to his opinion that Daun had no intention of leaving Saxony that year; but he repeatedly assured his brother that, if he ever learned that Daun had actually taken the road for Silesia, he would also start there the same day.

In that case, what should be done about Lusatia? The prince pointed out that, if the Russians should advance through Poland again for a junction with an Austrian army in Silesia as they were expected to do, and if he and Daun should move eastward simultaneously toward the storm center, he must either hurry on through Lusatia to a junction with the king or stop there to defend the region at the risk of being caught between Daun and the Russians. He would personally choose the second of those alternatives, he said. Frederick would have had him go to meet the army that approached him first, and wipe it out before it was in a position to join the other; but even if he joined the king, Frederick assured him, he would still retain his separate command.

Suppose Daun, instead of moving to Silesia, should undertake a major offensive in Saxony as soon as the Russians had joined Loudon with troops enough to prevent the king from rescuing his brother? In that case Frederick did not see how Saxony could be held at all, but thought that the prince must give it up and fight only in Lusatia or in the Mark of Brandenburg. Henry was more confident, and hoped he could hold most of the ground he then held.

Occasionally, but happily not too often, they returned to their old argument about the comparative merits of a delayed decision and a quick one, though neither cherished the delusion that any decision then to be anticipated could well be other than unfavorable to them. Bad news could wait, so far as Prince Henry was concerned. If they could postpone long enough the evil moment of their dissolution, he argued, they might yet be alive and able to enjoy their good fortune if a new day should ever dawn for them. He not only preferred that that dawn should find him alive rather than dead but seemed more hopeful than the king that it would eventually do so.

Little warning from his brother was necessary to restrain Frederick from attacking Loudon that spring. Henry did once venture to suggest that it would be more prudent to permit Loudon to waste some men in a fruitless siege of Neisse than to attack him in a fortified camp just to prevent such a siege. Frederick replied: "I have learned from painful experience at Kunersdorf and Torgau how much it costs and how risky it is to attack fortified positions; and these considerations will lead me to avoid such attacks if I can." [22]

One of the reasons for Frederick's notable loss of enthusiasm for the attack was his lack of confidence in his troops. On that point he got no sympathy from his brother, who was quick to remind him that, although his troops were no doubt inferior to the men of old, he had nonetheless taken with him all the most complete and most reliable regiments, leaving Henry in that respect much worse manned than himself. Frederick dropped that subject at once. [23]

Only over the matter of foraging for supplies did serious friction threaten to develop; and there also it was Frederick who first checked himself. On June 1 Henry reported that he had food and forage left for less than six more weeks, and that he was as badly inconvenienced by lack of wagons as by a shortage of supplies. Frederick professed to see no reason why his brother's army should not live off the country by foraging in Saxony as his own had done during the previous summer. That was precisely the trouble, the prince replied. The country had been picked bare in 1760 and no new crops had been planted for 1761. If his supply line of boats on the Elbe should once be cut, he said, his army would soon be starving; and the fault would be Frederick's, not his. He had given warning in good time.

The king ordered his commissary to give the prince whatever he must have for two weeks, but again commanded the prince to use no Prussian supplies for which substitutes could be found by foraging in Saxony. He would himself forage where he was, he said, if he were not on his own territory! [24]

Another of the so-called amenities of war which came up for discussion was the treatment of officers among the prisoners of war. There were then seven hundred Austrian officers and seven thousand Austrian soldiers being held in Magdeburg alone. Prince Henry asked for permission to let a dozen of the disabled officers go on parole for a few months to the baths in Bohemia for the sake of their health, pointing

[22] H. to F., May 20, in Schöning, III, 55; F. to H., May 24, in *P. C.*, XX, 412.
[23] *P. C.*, XX, 446; Schöning, III, 83.
[24] Schöning, III, 70–85; *P. C.*, XX, 442, 451. Soon afterward Frederick authorized the prince to requisition horses and wagons from the Magdeburg area. In fact, he reproved him for not having done that on his own responsibility, without waiting for any other authorization; for in such desperate situations, he said, "necessity knows no law." Schöning, III, 95, 124.

According to Mitchell, "The Prussian *Commissariat de Guerre* early in the Spring falsely reported to the King their Master, that everything was compleat, and to enrich themselves have risked the Ruin of the Whole. H. R. H. Prince Henry and the Army under his Command have suffered much by this unsuspected Treachery of the Commissaries." M. P., VI, 15.

out that similar privileges had often in the past been granted to wounded Prussians and that some Prussian officers had been permitted to go home on parole. Frederick refused permission, however, on the ground that the Austrians had recently been refusing such requests.[25]

By the middle of June, through troop movements and the reports of spies in Poland and Vienna, the Russian plan of campaign for the year began to become apparent. One army under Romanzov laid siege to Kolberg, which was defended by General Werner and Prince Eugene of Württemberg. A second and larger one, under Buturlin, was to advance again through Poland and join hands with Loudon in Silesia. As soon as the threat began to take definite shape, Frederick talked with all his old resolution about his way of meeting it. "I know all the hazards of battles," he wrote to Prince Henry; "but in spite of all that, you may count upon it as certain that I shall never permit the enemy to surround me at his ease but that I shall go first to seek him wherever I may find him." [26]

The king admitted a few days later, however, that if he had "just one more army" he would find it easier to accomplish his purpose. He supposed he would have to create one by sending Zieten with a detachment to join the small corps of General Goltz in Lower Silesia and to go on from there into Poland.[27] With equal forces, he said, Henry's cautious war of position, being more sure, would no doubt be better than the attack; with such unequal ones, boldness was their only choice.[28] But while continuing to talk his own kind of war, he also continued, perforce, to fight Henry's kind.

Greatly outnumbered, especially in cavalry, Zieten found himself unable either to stop the Russian advance or effectively to delay it. Within two weeks Frederick recalled him, leaving only General Knobloch with a corps of observation at Hundsfeld near Breslau to report on the invader's movements.[29]

During the first week of July, while they awaited the outcome of the campaign in Poland, Prince Henry seemed much more cheerful over the general outlook than the king. Drawing upon his own knowledge of the region where Zieten would have to operate, he suggested a number of

---

[25] M. P., V, 215; Schöning, III, 100. Frederick later objected particularly to the way in which Fouqué was treated while a prisoner.

[26] P. C., XX, 456. Early in July Tottleben's treason was discovered, and Prussia lost his services. *Ibid.*, 513.

[27] *Ibid.*, 463. Goltz died on July 1, just when the expedition was about to get under way, so Zieten had to take complete charge of it. When he reported the general's death to Prince Henry, the king added: "His loss comes all the more *mal a propos* because I have scarcely a subject left to replace those whom I lose." *Ibid.*, 501.

[28] P. C., XX, 490; Schmitt, *Prinz Heinrich*, II, 152.

[29] P. C., XX, 522.

good defensive positions for him and expressed confidence that if they committed no fatal blunders and showed the proper "constancy" they would yet see the end of their troubles that year.[30]

Frederick replied less hopefully: "It will be, according to all appearances, with Loudon that we shall have to examine into the question whether 'all is well'; and it is going to be answered with arguments that make me inclined to believe that all is *not* well in this miserable world in which we live." His soldiers, he said, were getting fat in idleness, but they would find work enough to make them lean again before the end of the autumn.[31]

[30] Schöning, III, 112, 123.

[31] *P. C.*, XX, 517, 519. To Zieten he wrote: "Das Ding hier sehr kraus zu werden anfänget." *Ibid.*, 525.

# CHAPTER XI

# 𝔖talemate

*"It would betray a very limited knowledge of my char-
acter to think me coward enough to carry out such an
order."*— Prince Henry to Ferdinand of Prussia.

DURING the last half of July, while his men were already getting their
regular exercise once more, the king engaged in a complicated series of
maneuvers in Upper Silesia, designed to occupy Loudon and if possible
to drive him away — at any rate to prevent his junction with the Russians whom Zieten had been unable to hold off. That left Prince Henry
responsible for the defense in all other areas, and the commandants of
the Lower Silesian fortresses were directed to place themselves and all
state resources at his disposal if Daun and he should transfer their activities to that region.[1]

The prince showed no sign of shrinking from his task. Both he and
Frederick were better men when they were on good terms with each
other. Their troubles did not miraculously melt away in the sunshine of
their mutual brotherly love, but they were far better able to deal with
them, and more likely to do it successfully. Their situation was no less
critical in midsummer of 1761 than it had been a year or two years before, except that before Maxen and after Liegnitz they had quarreled
and the magic was gone from their touch, while in 1761 their confidence,
in themselves and in each other, had somehow been restored. So their
courage and their capacity for cooperation and enterprise reached again,
by some strange triumph of the spirit over circumstances, the same high
point to which they had risen when the two were taking turns at snatch-
ing one another from the abyss in the autumn of 1758 — while their
enemies had lost confidence in themselves and in one another and found
effective cooperation impossible.

The remarkably close intellectual and spiritual kinship between the
brothers was clearly revealed in their official correspondence. Some con-
trasts between them appeared in an amazing exchange of philosophical

[1] If Daun remained in Saxony the prince was still instructed to do likewise. The detachment commanders in Pomerania, Brandenburg, and Lower Silesia, who had been reporting
to him regularly all summer, were to take their orders from him while the king was on
the move.

essays about the nature of man. Henry's essay has not been preserved; but Frederick's, in the form of a letter, ran as follows:

My dear Brother: The human race owes you a statue for the handsome apology which you make for it. It lacks just nothing, — except that it is not convincing; and I shall return, my dear brother, to my opinion that the best of men are [only] the least vicious. I have learned by experience to know this featherless biped, and . . . you must concede that good characters are rarer than the conjunctions of planets or the appearance of comets.

Do not think, however, that love grows out of tenderness. Unless I deceive myself, I believe it is a compound of instinct, the senses, and the needs of nature. Sentiment mingles in, I know not how, with the necessity to love which drives us on and which has for its object, after all, only a brutal sensuality. It is a necessity in adolescence, and becomes a habit in maturity. Do not accuse me, however, of a too austere morality, for I regard love as the most amiable and the most excusable of the weaknesses of men.

You tell me to look for virtue in the huts of the poor; but the men who inhabit them, are they without passions? That is what leads to the perfect virtue; and one finds it as rarely in thatched cottages as in palaces. Just reread if you please, my dear brother, the *Maxims* of Larochefoucauld; he will plead my case more eloquently than I can.

Perhaps you think that Monsieur Loudon is making an ill-humored grumbler of me. I do not deny that there may be something in that, and that if we had beaten him thoroughly I should think more favorably of the human race. We have eighty-three days to live through which will be difficult and painful; I count them on the ends of my fingers, I toil and I labor. It is natural to feel [most] that which touches us [most] intimately; thus it is said of a general that when he was well quartered he would exclaim: "There, now! The army is well encamped!" Everyone behaves in very much the same way. I do not approve of it, but such is the nature of man; if a man has a heart and some sensibility, we must forgive him the rest. I wish, my dear brother, that you would do that [in my case], begging you to believe me, in perfect amity, my dear brother, your faithful brother and servant. Federic.[2]

Try as he would, however, Frederick was unable to prevent the junction of Loudon's army with that of Buturlin; so all that was left for him to do was to fortify himself in an easily defended camp at Bunzelwitz, where he promised to "singe their noses for them" if they should ever be so foolhardy as to attack him. He could make it cost them thirty thousand men, he said, if they did; but they did not attack. His own position, however, narrowly constricted and almost surrounded, maintaining a precarious contact with the outside world only through Schweidnitz, was far from comfortable. There he was held as one besieged for nearly six weeks.[3]

[2] *P. C.*, XX, 563.
[3] *Ibid.*, 608, 611. "No hay, no oats, no meat, no beer," summarizes Bülow's description of the king's situation at Bunzelwitz. Bülow, *Prinz Heinrich*, 259–263.

The proposed Austro-Russian attack upon Frederick never materialized, partly because he was showing himself at that time as great a
master of defensive fighting as he was already known to be of the offensive, partly because his enemies had long since learned to fear him at
all times, and partly because of friction between the allies. Buturlin was
never satisfied with the way in which the Austrians kept their bargain
to find food and forage for his army; and neither he nor Loudon could
ever feel sure that, if he made an attack, the other would not somehow
fail to support him.[4]

At last, on September 10, Buturlin pulled away with the larger part
of his army and marched off to Poland, leaving only a corps of twenty
thousand men under Czernichev to winter with the Austrians. As Buturlin withdrew, a Prussian detachment under von Platen attacked one of
his wagon trains, burned five thousand wagons and took eighteen hundred prisoners, then ranged on into Poland, destroying Russian stores at
Kloster Paradies and near Posen valued at half a million thaler. Von
Platen then went on, via Landsberg, to join the defenders of Kolberg.
Prince Henry offered to send a detachment to reinforce him for that
task, but Frederick clung to his belief that that would not be necessary.[5]

With Buturlin gone, Frederick considered the campaign in Silesia
finished. He knew he was not himself in a position to start anything, and
assumed that Loudon was not.[6] So he thought it safe at last to move
from his position at Bunzelwitz, where his supply problem was becoming increasingly difficult, out into more open country.

Instead of permitting himself also to be drawn out into the open,
Loudon surprised Frederick and the garrison of Schweidnitz by making
a bold night attack upon that reputedly impregnable fortress. Troops
were assembled for the enterprise so swiftly and so secretly that Frederick, although he was only a few miles away, got no word of it and did
nothing to prevent it. The assault was made at three o'clock in the morning on October 1, without artillery preparation and without the firing
of a shot even by small arms, which might have aroused the garrison
more quickly to meet it. Even so, the defenders of the place must have
failed to maintain the proper vigilance or they could not have been so
taken by surprise or have permitted a force which outnumbered them
only three to two to capture so strong a fortress by assault. They offered
some resistance, but it was neither well organized nor uniformly good.

[4] Mitchell reported to Lord Bute on October 3: "The superior Talents the K. of Pr. has
shewn in the Conduct of a Defensive War accompanied with very difficult and discouraging
Circumstances do him as much Honour and will perhaps be attended with more real Advantage than the Gain of several Battles, the Fruits of which he has seldom been in a
Condition to reap." M. P., V, 238. The news of the loss of Schweidnitz on October 1 had
evidently not yet reached Magdeburg where Mitchell then was.

[5] Schöning, III, 160, 164; *P. C.*, XX, 618, 625.

[6] *Ibid.*, 630. His letters do not reveal whether he knew immediately that some of the

The Austrian casualties were nearly twice as numerous as theirs. By the surrender Prussia lost, in addition to casualties, forty-five hundred men as prisoners, three hundred guns, a war chest of a hundred and fifty thousand thaler in coin, supplies worth more than half a million thaler — and all the trouble and expense of a long siege which it cost Frederick the next year to recover the place. It was one of the most valuable fortresses in Silesia.[7]

The king had intended to return to Saxony in the autumn and to winter his troops there, so as to spare Silesia the hardship of sustaining them both winter and summer; but the loss of Schweidnitz compelled him to remain in that vicinity for the protection of the province. So the numerous problems of the defense in all other areas except Kolberg were left in the hands of Prince Henry. His method of meeting them all summer had been to put up a bold front with the nucleus of his forces in his strong defense position in the *Kätzenhäuser,* thus holding his principal enemy in check while meeting one minor threat after another by sending out detachments.

Three times in the course of the summer Kleist or Seydlitz drove back the Imperialists on the southwestern front; but they always ran away too fast to be caught in any great numbers or destroyed as a force, and no Prussian detachment could ever be spared for long to garrison the regions thus cleared. In August, at the request of Ferdinand of Brunswick, the prince sent a detachment to occupy Wolfenbüttel, to threaten the flank of the French army in Hanover, and to cover Magdeburg against attack from the west. The move also freed Halberstadt and resulted in the withdrawal of the French from the Duchy of Brunswick. In the same month, hearing that the Swedes north of Berlin were about to receive a reinforcement of six thousand men, the prince sent off the younger Stutterheim to help Colonel Belling drive them back into Pomerania. In September Lacy made a move that seemed to threaten Berlin from the south, but the prince quickly thrust another detachment between him and the city and turned him back.[8]

Sending off so many detachments inevitably reduced the prince's army to a mere fraction of its nominal strength. There were many times when a more enterprising enemy than Daun might have attacked him to advantage, as his good defensive position and the usual bold front were almost his only means of salvation. At such moments he occasionally voiced to his brother Ferdinand his dissatisfaction with Frederick's

Russians had remained with Loudon or whether he assumed that they had all gone with Buturlin.
[7] M. P., V, 241; von Arneth, *Geschichte Maria Theresias,* VI, 245; P. C., XXI, 6, 9.
[8] Schöning, III, 141–164.

"public information service" and the way in which he used it to maintain the spirits of the people. The strictest possible censorship was maintained in the armies, officers and men alike being forbidden to mention in their letters either military operations or conditions in the camps. The king did not propose, he said, to have them spreading bad news which, after all, might not be true. There was therefore little left by which to check the authorized version of the reports which he himself put into circulation.[9]

One of those inspired reports which appeared again and again at regular intervals was to the effect that Daun was about to leave Saxony. In one of his own uncensored letters to his younger brother, Prince Henry told Ferdinand to pay no attention to such fairy tales, as Frederick was in the habit of peddling them around to lull the people into a false feeling of security. The prince objected also, privately to Ferdinand, to Frederick's habit of making his task appear so much easier than it actually was. After making the necessary detachments, he said, he frequently found himself with no more than one fourth of the numbers that the newspapers said he had.[10]

There were times when the old discontent and discouragement gripped at him as they had done a year earlier; but fortunately it was to Ferdinand and not Frederick that he voiced them. "Only a man caught in the midst of it," he wrote in September, "can realize the exhaustion of our resources, the pitiable condition of our troops, or the stupidity of those who command them." He would rather be a peasant pushing his handcart through the mud and living on roots and salt — or a galley slave — than go on indefinitely as the general in command under such conditions.[11]

One of the conditions which caused him most serious concern was the inferior quality of his troops, and particularly of his irregular volunteers. These so-called "free troops" were utterly undependable. At the end of August one whole battalion of them deserted its colonel, killed its major, and went over first to the Imperialists and then to the French with flags, guns, and war chest. It should have felt quite as much at home in one place as another; its colonel was a Frenchman who had come into the Prussian army from the Russian, and most of its men had joined it by desertion from the French. Early in October a "Swiss corps" sent by the

---

[9] *P. C.,* XX, 513; Schöning, III, 115.

[10] Hausarchiv, Rep. 56, II, F; Otto Herrmann, in the *Historische Vierteljahrschrift,* XXVI (1931), 371–376. If the Austrians had been naive enough to believe any of those reports about his strength, which of course reached them regularly through their spies, it would have made the prince's task much easier in fact as well as in appearance; but it never occurred to him that they could be so gullible.

[11] *Ibid.*

prince to serve under von Bohlen around Halberstadt surrendered to the French "without firing a shot and without necessity." Instead of considering himself well rid of such rubbish, as he might have done, the prince felt the defection all the more keenly because, already weak at all points, he was being forced to weaken himself still further by sending off so many detachments.[12]

Yet he went on, saying nothing to anyone but Ferdinand about not going on. He did not claim to have done much himself, but considered it an achievement to have survived and to have prevented his enemies from doing anything.[13]

It was not lack of numbers that kept the principal enemy, Daun, inactive all summer, but want of confidence in himself, and his wholesome respect for the prince's fighting qualities. Before he would agree to undertake any offensive action the cautious field marshal demanded in midsummer that forty-five thousand troops be sent him from Loudon's army in Silesia. When about half that number had been sent and his government tried again to prod him into action, he offered his resignation, which was not accepted. If given all of the reinforcements for which he asked, he would promise no more than to occupy the Erzgebirge and the Freiberg region that autumn.[14]

Early in October Prince Henry knew and reported that Daun was being reinforced from Silesia, although Frederick refused for two weeks to believe that any Austrian troops had been withdrawn from his front. When finally convinced that the movement had taken place, he regretted that he could send Henry no equivalent, but suggested that as a substitute the prince should publish a report that von Platen had completed the relief of Kolberg and was on the way to join him. Without making the obvious reference to his own experience at Schweidnitz, he also warned his brother to be on his guard against night attacks.[15]

During the last week of October Daun, with his army built up to seventy-five thousand men, felt himself strong enough to make a series

[12] H. to F., in Schöning, III, 154, 180, 183. The temporary reverses to which these desertions were only incidental did not shake Mitchell's confidence in Prince Henry. He was still sure that the prince would "do everything in his Power to send the necessary Succour." Again, a week later, he praised what he called the prince's "great calmness" in the face of a general attack by the Austrians. "He sees and feels all the Difficulties of his Situation," Sir Andrew wrote to Lord Bute, "but He has taken his Resolution and I know He will abide by it." M. P., V, 240, 242.

[13] M. P., XLIII, 23; Schöning, III, 141, 170.

[14] Von Arneth, *Geschichte Maria Theresias*, VI, 241–250.

[15] Schöning, III, 178; *P. C.*, XXI, 38–41. Ever since the fall of Schweidnitz Frederick had been finding things all over Germany for von Platen to do whenever he should have finished at Kolberg; but the idea of using him as a threat while his principal task was still unfinished was an entirely new inspiration. The prince did not ask in just which of his posts von Platen's ubiquitous ghost-soldiers should serve as an *Ersatz* garrison.

of attacks upon the prince's position, aiming at the possession of the Erzgebirge.[16] The first tentative efforts were easily repulsed, but everyone in the Prussian camp supposed that they must be only the preliminaries of a general and more determined offensive. Prince Henry reported to the king that he could take care of his front without difficulty but might find himself in serious trouble if Beck came in from Bautzen with yet another corps of fifteen thousand men and struck him in the flank or rear. Beck came on, but fortunately did less harm than the prince had feared; so when on November 5 all his advanced posts were attacked at once he was able to maintain himself without any change of position except that he moved his headquarters from Schlettau to Barnitz, a little nearer to his right flank where the principal attacks were being made and where the greatest danger seemed to be.[17]

Meanwhile Prince Henry had received from the king no reinforcements at all, some advice upon which he had no thought of acting, some bad news which only confirmed his own gloomy predictions, and some rumors of good news which he could not bring himself to believe.

The advice, which reached him along with the warning that he could expect no help from his brother, was to attack. "You will do all that you can to sustain yourself," wrote the king. "You must simply fall upon whichever one of them you can best get at; that is the only way you can disengage yourself from the others."[18]

The bad news was that Kolberg had fallen. The prince had offered months earlier to send troops to its relief but had been told by Frederick that they would not be needed. He had repeatedly thereafter expressed his concern over the safety of the city while Frederick, who could no longer afford to think too much about any disaster which had not actually happened, had continued to be at least outwardly optimistic about it. On October 27 the prince wrote to Mitchell that it would be a miracle if the city did not have to surrender. Ten days later Frederick conceded that its situation was hopeless. "The reports from Pomerania put a knife at my throat," he wrote to Prince Henry. While von Platen stood by to help as he might, Prince Eugene fought his way out of the city to save his army, then failed in an attempt to break in again and reprovision the place. Both sea and land approaches to it were then in enemy hands. On December 16 it surrendered.[19]

The good news which Prince Henry could not bring himself to believe was that Frederick's years of hopeful effort and liberal expenditure

---

[16] Letter from Daun to Lacy, printed from the Austrian archives by von Arneth, in his *Geschichte Maria Theresias*, VI, 469.

[17] Schöning, III, 202-215; M. P., VI, 3, 4.   [18] *P. C.*, XXI, 63.

[19] M. P., XLIII, 27; V, 243; XXVIII, 118; *P. C.*, XXI, 62, and the first hundred pages, *passim;* Schöning, III, 210-238.

of bribe money in Turkey were at last about to bear fruit, and that a Turkish corps could be expected to appear in Hungary in the spring. The Austrians would then be forced to choose between Hungary and Bohemia, as they must inevitably lose one or the other. A score of times in the past two years, usually when no other hope was in sight, the king had written about that possibility.

Prince Henry had never believed that any help would come out of Turkey. At last he gave utterance to his disbelief. "I hope you will find whatever consolation you can in the present sad state of affairs," he wrote; "but all the same I must frankly admit that, as for me, the prospect of the appearance of the Turks in Hungary does not offer me any. That is a nation which one cannot think of as engaged [in the war] until it actually is so; and anyway it is a long time from now until June." [20]

The king was still sure that the period of disappointments was past and that at last his hopes were about to be justified. So the prince replied in December that he had too much respect for his brother's opinion to wish to contradict him. It would be splendid if the story should prove to be true. He therefore regretted only his own inability to believe it, or to keep himself from wondering what Prussia's enemies might yet do before the Turkish intervention could be changed from a beautiful dream into a reality. Near the end of the year Major von Anhalt was sent to Saxony with several missions, one of which was to convince Henry that Frederick was "not indulging in foolish notions or idle fancies"; but no Turkish soldiers materialized to make the prince doubt, even a little, his own disbelief. [21]

Whenever Frederick mentioned the Turkish matter to his brother he repeated his injunction to observe the most absolute secrecy about it, saying that he had not mentioned it to a soul but Henry and did not wish the Austrians to hear about it until the latest possible moment. It was well known in Vienna, however, that he had for a long time been working for a Turkish alliance; and the effect of that knowledge was merely to strengthen the determination of the Austrian government to improve its position in Saxony before it was too late.

The government in Vienna was more determined than the commanders in the field. Their general attacks of the first week of November had been fruitless. Then for a week all activity was suspended because of heavy rains and impassable roads. On November 14 the general offensive was resumed, but it resulted only in the capture of Döbeln. That village was then neutralized at once, for Seydlitz, when he lost it, threat-

[20] Schöning, III, 215.    [21] *Ibid.*, 240; *P. C.*, XXI, 138.

ened otherwise to set it on fire. So, while Prince Henry was preparing to meet the more determined attacks which he was still expecting, the whole affair degenerated into a scramble for winter quarters.

Winter quarters in a given area meant men, money, and supplies drawn from that area — "three things," Frederick said, "without which one cannot make war." [22] So Frederick, who always urged his brother to draw his forces more closely together when there was fighting to be done, began to urge him to spread them out more widely for the winter and to restrict the area occupied by the enemy. As a step toward that end he recommended an attempt to recapture Freiberg. If it could not be taken by direct attack, he thought, the Austrians might be flanked out of it by the capture of Chemnitz.

With only a slight change of scene, that was just what he had himself been trying to do two years before when he pushed Finck into Maxen and lost him there. The prince might have found some such operation feasible if von Platen had been able to free himself from the fighting around Kolberg and join him with the only reinforcement possible; but although Frederick "hoped" from week to week to be able to send him, he did not arrive until January.

Prince Henry agreed with his most trusted subordinate, Seydlitz, that the post at Freiberg was too strong to be attacked without von Platen's help; and he did not intend to be pushed into attacking it. "Even if someone should wish that I should," he wrote to Ferdinand, ". . . it would betray a very limited knowledge of my character to think me coward enough to carry out such an order."

Frederick had also mentioned several times the desirability of retaking Dresden that season. As to that, Henry wrote to Ferdinand: "If I could get possession of the city, I should do it without writing him any letters about it; if I cannot do it, none of his screaming and none of his orders will move me one step forward." He was very proud, just then, of the fact that he "never received a royal order" any more, but only suggestions or requests. When writing to the sycophantic Ferdinand — but fortunately only then — he seemed sometimes to forget that he was, after all, only the king's younger brother, subject, and subordinate. [23]

The coming of cold weather brought a welcome respite to the troops on the right bank of the Elbe, where Generals Linden and Lacy ar-

[22] *P. C.,* XXI, 80; Schöning, III, 223.

[23] Hausarchiv, Rep. 56, II, F; see also Otto Herrmann, in the *Historische Vierteljahrschrift,* XXVI (1931), 376. Although Henry's personal attitude toward the king, as revealed in his letters to Ferdinand, was not admirable, his military talents were never more brilliantly displayed than that year when, fighting his own kind of war, with pitifully inadequate means, he had successfully defended an enormous area and had stopped all his enemies in their tracks. Napoleon, who often spoke very highly of the prince's military

ranged a truce for the winter which Prince Henry approved on behalf of the king of Prussia. It was agreed that neither side would resume hostilities without giving the other twenty-four hours' notice. West of the Elbe there was more or less continuous activity throughout the winter, although the season was, as Mitchell said, "extremely rude," and the endurance of the soldiers in the advanced posts was severely tested.

The prince did what he could, as he had done two years before, to lessen the hardships of the winter campaign by quartering as many of his men as possible in villages and cantonments behind the line, by relieving every day those on outpost duty at the front, and by bringing up the booths from the Leipzig fair as shelters for them. Frederick feared that the advanced posts were not being strongly enough garrisoned, and wrote on December 23 that he was greatly relieved to know Daun had been so kind as to leave the prince undisturbed in such a position; but it had been "a very foolish mistake" on Daun's part, he said, to do so.[24]

The prince's position was in truth not comfortable, with his men cramped together in an area too small for foraging, yet too large to be easily defensible; but Daun's was not much better. The Austrian government was compelled that winter, in the interest of economy, to reduce the size of its army. Regiments were cut down to two companies each and men from the companies so broken up were used as replacements in those remaining, so as to save the expense of raising and training new recruits. Officers deprived of their commands by the reorganization were retired on half pay until they also should be needed as replacements. The total reduction amounted, on paper, to twenty thousand men and five hundred officers.

Frederick and Prince Henry both found it almost inconceivable that any government should take such a step in wartime; but they naturally found it encouraging. Perhaps the war would not, after all, go on forever; and perhaps they might yet outlast their enemies. So there was a genuine feeling of relief beneath the formal politeness of the special letters they exchanged on the occasion of the New Year, although Frederick's penciled comment on the face of the one he had just received from Henry was only: *"Compliment obligeant."*

ability, praised especially his campaign of 1761 and rated it as his best one. Montholon, *Mémoires de Napoléon*, V, 329. See also Hamilton, *Rheinsberg*, II, 58.
[24] *P. C.*, XXI, 138.

CHAPTER XII

# Deus ex Machina

*"There, thank Heaven! Our rear is free."*—Frederick to Henry.

On January 5, 1762, the empress Elizabeth of Russia died. When the news reached Breslau a fortnight later, no one knew what the policy of her successor would be; but it was natural for Frederick to hope that Prussia would gain rather than lose by the change. Prince Henry also hoped the event would provide them a port of refuge from the storm, but warned the king that he must expect the new Russian government, like any government at any time, to be guided only by its own conception of its own interests.[1]

The appearance of that faint gleam of light on the eastern horizon did not in fact mean to either of the brothers that the long night of war had ended. It was merely their first convincing promise of a new day. If the dawn of that day was to find them in a position to enjoy its sunshine, there remained much to be done in the meantime. They agreed that they should conserve their energies and resources and concentrate upon recuperation and defense.

If Henry could make a truce with Daun, let him do it. It would be pointless to spend the whole winter fighting for a few more villages for winter quarters, when those to be won were as wretched and impoverished as those already held. The king hoped that Magdeburg would not again be in danger; but if Henry could refortify the place without spending more than the amount of his carefully prepared estimate, let him go ahead with it. If a new bastion was indispensably necessary for the defense of Wittenberg, let it be built.[2]

There were other problems less easy to solve. One of those was the use to be made of the troops that had been released for other service by the unfortunate termination of the Kolberg campaign. Prince Eugene of Württemberg wintered with his corps in Mecklenburg-Schwerin, where he busied himself so industriously in the raising of men, money, and horses as to evoke a sharp protest from the British government,

---

[1] *P. C.*, XXI, 190; Schöning, III, 269.
[2] Schöning, III, 270–285; *P. C.*, XXI, 217, 249. Because of Daun's unaccommodating attitude, the truce was not concluded, although Lacy had made one with General Linden and Loudon one with Frederick in Silesia.

since King George had some interests there which he thought were being injured.

Von Platen's corps was placed at Prince Henry's disposal after the surrender of Kolberg; the king cheerfully explained that he could not feed it in Silesia. The prince left it near Berlin until January for fear of another Russian raid on the capital. Thereafter, it spent a restless and cheerless winter fighting the Imperialists and Saxons for quarters and food on the Thuringian border of Saxony. Having wintered it, after a fashion, the prince would have liked to keep it; and some sharp words were exchanged when he found that the king expected to take it away from him in the spring. He warned Frederick that to withdraw von Platen would mean simply to turn over to the Imperialists the area which that general's corps had occupied, for he "would not have a cat left to oppose them." [3]

Frederick replied on March 8 that he was not taking the corps away that day or the next. (They would bring their appetites to Silesia with them, and would still eat too much before the spring campaign opened.) But he reproved Henry for protesting, and accused him of thinking only of himself. If he viewed the problem as a whole, he said, the prince must see how badly those troops would be needed later in Silesia. The prince replied in turn that, while it might be wrong for him to think only of himself, he must think first and chiefly of his own task; and that task was by no means simple. Frederick, he said, could at least concentrate whatever troops he had, while he (the prince) had three widely separated posts to hold. When the time came he sent the troops as ordered, although he described the situation in which he was left as "nothing less than laughable." [4]

As a partial replacement for von Platen's corps, Prince Henry was promised that of the Prince of Württemberg whenever it should have finished its winter harvest where it was, and some new "free corps" were raised. Since efficient and reliable commanders for the new units were not available, and General Wunsch had especially distinguished himself as a commander of such troops — until they ran away and left him to be captured by the Austrians near Maxen in November, 1759 — Prince Henry asked the king to try to secure that general's release by exchange. The king would have been glad to arrange it if he could; but the whole problem of the exchange of prisoners, even of officer prisoners, had been involved for more than two years in a tangle of argument and mutual recrimination. Though no exchanges were taking place, prisoners of war were being more strictly controlled on both sides, and each belligerent

[3] Schöning, III, 292.     [4] *Ibid.*, 294–311; *P. C.,* XXI, 283, 323.

claimed the right of reprisal while accusing the other of atrocities.[5] The British minister, Mitchell, sought to use his influence to secure an exchange and better treatment of prisoners in general. Prince Henry answered him that in that matter the king had tied his hands. His own views were favorable to the exchange, he said, and his inclinations and personal practice had always been to show his prisoners of war every courtesy and to treat them with all possible leniency. Privately and in his correspondence with Ferdinand he blamed Frederick for the harsh treatment meted out to them on both sides; the king of Prussia, he said, had always been the one to set the evil precedents — the first to break the international laws of war, then first to claim the right of reprisal and to make everyone unnecessarily miserable by the senseless practice of a barbarous harshness.[6]

Probably the principal reason why the exchange was not agreed upon was that it would have been to Prussia's advantage if made upon a man-for-man basis, and Marshal Daun had advised his empress-queen to be in no hurry about agreeing to an exchange by which she would lose more than she gained.[7]

The paucity of good general officers was again keenly felt in another connection when, late in January, Prince Henry was confined to quarters by a violent fever and was compelled to consider the question of a second-in-command for the army in Saxony. Unless the king supplied or designated someone else, he supposed he would have to follow the rule of seniority and fall back upon Forcade if an emergency requiring action should arise at a time when he was himself not available. He had made good use of Seydlitz for raids and other special missions during the year just past; but Seydlitz's health was also so poor that he often said of himself that he did not know what he was doing, and the prince could not always depend upon him.

Prince Henry was not at that time offering his resignation or asking to be relieved, although for six weeks he was entirely incapacitated by fever, nervous exhaustion, and general debility. Once for about a week,

[5] M. P., XXVIII, 129.

[6] *Ibid.*, VI, 15; XXVIII, 119–132; XLIII, 29–46; Hausarchiv, Rep. 56, II, F; Otto Herrmann, in the *Historische Vierteljahrschrift*, XXVI (1931), 369.

[7] The marshal's recommendation was made in the form of an answer to a direct question on that matter, and was embodied in one of his reports on the battle of Torgau. It is also an interesting example of the mixture of languages then common, even in official reports, in the German-speaking countries: "Il y a du pour et contre. Gewiss ist dass der Feind bey dieser Auswechselung mehr als wir profitiret, car tant soldats qu' officiers et surtout generaux vaillent plus que les notres, ainsi on tirera plus de profit que v. m. dont la plupart de ses generaux prisonniers ne sont pas des grands heros. Jedoch muss es doch einmahl darzu kommen und die doppelte Ersetzung kostet dem aerario ungemein, jedoch il ne faudroit pas se presser und die Sache von selbsten an sich kommen lassen." Von Arneth, *Geschichte Maria Theresias*, VI, 454–455.

for the only time during the whole war, he was unable to write, although even then he dictated letters to the king and to Sir Andrew Mitchell, and routine matters were handled directly between his staff and Frederick's. The king, deeply engrossed in foreign affairs, neither appointed a second-in-command for the army in Saxony nor answered the prince's question on the subject. He simply relied upon the prince to recover and do his duty (or to do his duty and recover). All winter he spoke without explanation or elaboration of the two armies as "mine" and "yours," and of what they would do, "you" in Saxony and "I" in Silesia.[8]

Prince Henry, as he entered upon the new year, also assumed as a matter of course that he would continue to command in Saxony, although the old differences of opinion as to what Prussia could and should do still came to light occasionally in his correspondence with the king. Early in January Frederick sent Major Anhalt to him to explain a grandiose plan of campaign for the year. As the major had had a hand in drafting it, the prince felt more free to criticize it openly than he would have done if it had been entirely the king's own work; and he found in it plenty to criticize.

The major's plan was drawn up before the death of the Russian empress, so presumed the continuance of Russia as a belligerent. It was based also upon the further assumption that Turkey would actively enter the war. Thirty thousand Tartars and eighty thousand Turks were to invade Russia in March, eight thousand Tartars would join Frederick in Silesia, and one hundred twenty thousand Turks would invade Hungary. After sending off the necessary troops to oppose their new enemies, the combined Austrian and Russian forces in Silesia could not amount to more than fifty-five thousand men, against whom Frederick would assemble eighty thousand. In Saxony, Austrians and Imperialists together could not number more than thirty-five thousand, while the prince would have fifty thousand. The king would therefore be able to recapture Schweidnitz at once, clear Silesia, and invade Moravia while the prince retook Dresden, cleared Saxony, and invaded Bohemia. The Austrian government must then lose either Moravia or Bohemia, unless it saved itself by making peace.[9]

---

[8] Schöning, III, 225, 272–283. The king had written to Prince Henry in the preceding November that Krockow, Hülsen, Linden, and Kleist were all better officers than any he had with him in Silesia; but early in 1762 both Hülsen and Kleist were ill and wishing they could find an honorable way to retire from the service. As to the prince's illness, Frederick filled his official ciphered reply with expressions of polite concern, but added in his own hand: "My fever, my dear brother, sends greetings to yours. I hope that their correspondence will soon cease; for the sooner we can get rid of them the better." *P. C.*, XXI, 91, 208.

[9] Projet zur künftigen Campagne, so mir Se. Königl. Majestät Allerhochst befohlen,

Prince Henry refused to permit the Turks to enter in any way into his calculations until they had actually entered the war. He therefore refused to take seriously any of the details of von Anhalt's communication, but asked him bluntly: "What shall we do if the Turks do nothing?" The major could not answer his question; so he asked the king.[10]

Frederick replied that the prince need not be so skeptical, nor think him a fool for believing in something which had admittedly been slow in coming to pass but which was sure to happen eventually. Through Benoît, his secretary of legation in Warsaw, he said, he had entirely reliable information that the Turks were arming. He admitted, however, that if they should fail him he did not know what could "delay or conjure away" the destruction of the Prussian army.

Yet in contemplation of that last desperate emergency the king returned to the thought of his strategy of 1760. If no help came from outside, he said, he would assemble all his troops in a single army and hurl himself with all his weight against first one foe and then another. If by such means he could destroy an enemy army or two, he might then redivide his own to confront those that remained. He knew all the objections Prince Henry would make to the plan; but, he asked, was it not after all simply a matter of perishing either in detail or in mass? And was it not about as well to do one as the other?[11]

The prince, as always, preferred the slower to the quicker way of dying. Frederick, just as he had said, knew in advance what the character of his reply would be, and probably wondered only in what new form it would appear. Henry wrote:

The decision you say you intend to make in this case seems to me to be one of the most desperate; for if you assemble all your forces into one army you cannot feed them, the abandoned provinces will be occupied by the enemy, and the supply depots established in them will be plundered. . . . Even if you regain a province after it has been ravaged by the enemy, you cannot subsist an army in it. . . . Experience moreover has taught us that it is not so easy to blot out an army, . . . [and an enemy army, defeated but not destroyed, could easily take refuge in one of the fortified posts readily available throughout the war zone.] . . .

I concede all the inconveniences of trying to set an army against every enemy army, but as it is a matter of perishing [anyway], one needs only to know which is the slower form of death. If the term is extended, there is then some hope that some unforeseen event may happen; and as for that, I firmly believe that we can hold off our enemies for a longer time by opposing them

Ew. Königl. Hoheit sowohl mündlich als auch schriftlich bekannt zu machen." Copy drafted by Major von Anhalt, Leipzig, January 7, 1762. *P. C.*, XXI, 152–154. Neither Prussian army ever approached the numbers of the major's estimates.
    [10] Schöning, III, 261; *P. C.*, XXI, 171, n.2.    [11] *P. C.*, XXI, 171, 183.

with troops than by leaving them free to do as they please while we concentrate to attack some one of their armies.

A skillful doctor tries to keep his patient alive if he cannot cure him, so that when he dies he has at least the consolation that he has followed Galen's rule and the precepts of Hippocrates. I think, then, that some bodies of troops confronting the enemy would at least hold them off for a while; and that is all we can do or hope for in our position.[12]

To Prince Henry's reference to Galen and Hippocrates the king replied: "You know there are two doctors in Molière [La Fontaine?], Doctor So Much the Worse and Doctor So Much the Better, and that it is impossible for these two ever to be of the same opinion. Here I have an invalid to treat who has a raging fever. In a desperate crisis, I order an emetic for him, and you want to give him anodynes. But as we have not yet come to that extremity, I ask you to think quite seriously of all that Anhalt has told you."[13]

The prince recognized that his brother was ready to drop the subject, and so was he himself; but that final reference to the Turks drew from him one more thinly veiled warning. Hope, he said, as the last thing to come out of Pandora's box, might serve a man as a final consolation in time of trouble; but it might also be mistaken for something more reliable than it really was, and so had often betrayed men into a labyrinth from which there was no returning. When Frederick informed him that he was planning to send General Werner with a corps of troops into Moravia, and predicted that the general would easily make his way into the province, the prince replied that it was not how an invading force would get into Moravia that worried him, but how it would ever get out.[14]

The king at last gave up the attempt to convince his brother that Turkish participation in the war was anything more than a pipe dream. They would never think quite alike, he conceded. No two thinking persons ever did. Certainly the prince, in particular, would never be saved by his faith in Mahomet; but they would yet see Frederick's faith justified.[15]

So another troublesome question was disposed of simply by dropping it. It was not imperative that answers be found in January to either question — whether the Turks would invade Hungary that year or what the Prussians should do without them. The problem of supply, however, could not be evaded. The solution of this problem depended largely upon the way in which Saxony was to be treated — and that in turn brought

---

[12] Schöning, III, 264–266.   [13] *P. C.*, XXI, 191.   [14] Schöning, III, 268, 336.
[15] *P. C.*, XXI, 301. No material help ever came from Turkey.

to an unfortunate climax a fundamental difference, both of opinion and of character, between Prince Henry and the king.

Frederick was the more modern of the two. Throughout the war the prince had advocated and practiced the humanitarian and the king the totalitarian principle. The younger brother had sought in every way to mitigate, where he could, the horrors of war. The elder, when he considered it necessary to defend himself, usually advanced the plea of bitter necessity or claimed the right of reprisal to justify his ruthlessness; but if he had ever taken the trouble to elaborate a theoretical defense, he would have argued further that a ruthless and aggressive war is really more humane in the end, as it shortens the ordeal and thus reduces the total amount of suffering entailed by it.

Frederick had never quite lost the sensitiveness which had marked him as a youth. It still showed itself occasionally in quick flashes of sympathy for his long-suffering soldiers or for other victims of misfortune.[16] In order not to be distracted by it he had had to school himself against it, although it made him miserable; and when he was miserable on that account he was more savage than ever. For the same reason he had had consciously to blind himself to the stark destitution which prevailed in the devastated areas, and to the horror that broods over a battlefield. But as the war entered its last year he seemed to have succeeded in making himself both blind and callous wherever he chose to be so. He had learned by then at least to act as though he were entirely insensible to the promptings of humanity. Prince Henry had not; nor had he tried to.

Forced, if he was to survive at all, to draw men, money, and supplies from wherever he could find them, Frederick had throughout the war depended and drawn heavily upon Saxony for all three. As all three were delivered unwillingly and grudgingly, he knew that the Saxons would do in that direction only what they must, and that their pleas of inability to do more must be rather heavily discounted. So he adopted the policy of unrelenting sternness because he thought it would be the most effective.

Prince Henry, on the other hand, who commanded in Saxony more than half the time and who was charged when in command there with the administration of his brother's policy, permitted himself to be influenced in action much more than Frederick was by his natural feeling of sympathy for the unfortunate Saxons. He deliberately took the edge off some of the sharpest of the regulations, and used his own discretionary

---

[16] Note, for example, his remark to de Catt on July 28, 1760: "For the soldiers there is little glory to be won. From the very beginning, they get more blows than bread." Koser, "Unterhaltungen," 432. See also his letter quoted at the end of Chapter V, page 90.

powers to make exceptions and grant exemptions which Frederick thought unwarranted. In short he refused, or tacitly failed, to pick the bones of the country quite clean, even when ordered to do so. He defended his leniency not only on humanitarian grounds but as the policy that would ultimately pay best. "If we reduce this country to a desert," he said in effect, "no one can subsist here — neither Saxons nor Prussian armies. You may be willing to let the peasants starve amid the ruins of their huts, but you must feed your soldiers; and if they leave nothing alive here, you will have to feed them hereafter entirely out of your own pot. We don't need any more advice from you about how to squeeze blood out of a stunted turnip that has already been squeezed again and again. Send us something we can eat." [17]

Frederick was unconvinced because he thought he could not afford to agree. War was a hard business, in which a man simply handicapped himself by being softhearted. "We need money," he wrote, as if that explained everything and would end the argument. In the autumn of 1761 only the loss of Schweidnitz had prevented him from marching most of his army into Saxony to winter it there in order to spare Silesia, which he said could not furnish subsistence for it both summer and winter — and that in the face of Prince Henry's vigorous protest that there was already one army in Saxony, and that it alone was more than the country could feed. One of the king's stated reasons for wishing to be in Saxony in person that winter was that more men, money, and materials would be forthcoming if he were there to see to it. Henry had been a fool, he said, to believe the lies told him by the Saxons with the connivance of dishonest Prussian supply officers whom they had bribed to protect them.[18]

There was dishonesty in the Prussian service of supply, but the king was one of its principal victims. Purchases were reported far in excess of deliveries.[19] Half-filled depots were reported as full. Peculation was common and often went unpunished. Officers in charge of foraging parties were constantly tempted to engage in private plundering or bribetaking,

---

[17] A steady refrain in a score or more of his letters in Schöning, particularly those of the winter of 1761–62 in Volume III. Almost daily that winter long wagon trains left Magdeburg with supplies for Prince Henry's army, to supplement what they could find in Saxony. M. P., VI, 34. On February 5 the prince wrote angrily to the king: "It is not advice that we need, but effective relief." Schöning, III, 278.

[18] Another score or more of letters, particularly those of September 25, 1761, and March 4 and 14, 1762. *P. C.*, XX, 626; XXI, 277, 297. "Quant aux affaires de la Saxe, mon cher frère, il nous faut de l'argent."

Silesia had unquestionably suffered. Mitchell wrote to Bute from Breslau in April: ". . . this country, as well as his hereditary dominions, are exhausted to such a degree, that the bare description would move the hardest heart and extort compassion from the most insensible." *Ibid.*, 406.

[19] On March 10 an officer of Prince Henry's staff reported that of 1,284 horses ordered

and soldiers could not be restrained from either. The "free corps" were composed largely of officers and men who had nothing in common but the fact that they had all volunteered for an arduous service, not for fighting or for glory but for gain. Most of them were not even Prussians. Sir Andrew Mitchell was not far wrong when he said that many of them had ceased to be soldiers — except in that many of them never had been soldiers. Prince Henry revealed a shocking state of affairs when he wrote to Ferdinand that he had been offered some lovely china, paintings, and other household furnishings, in a sale of the effects of a "free corps" leader, but had refused to "shame his house by participation in thievery."[20]

Men who robbed either the Saxons or the king of Prussia found a determined enemy in Prince Henry; but they were too numerous to be disciplined as they deserved without the wholehearted support of the king; and Frederick was disinclined to believe that either kind of robbery was being committed, having made up his own mind that Henry was simply being imposed upon by the Saxons.

Sir Andrew Mitchell, who for years had condemned the severity of the king's Saxon policy, was moved to a new outburst (to Lord Bute, however, not to Frederick) when the Prussian commissary officers demanded four million thaler from the town of Leipzig in January, 1762. "The Harshness, Severity, Avarice and Injustice of Pr. commissaries, under Colour of executing the Orders that they have received, cannot be exaggerated by Discription, but H. R. H. Prince Henry does everything in his Power to mitigate, check, and control their iniquitous and flagitious Proceedings."

Sir Andrew was especially indignant over the character of the officers used for such work. The one in charge of collections in Saxony, he wrote, was a turncoat Saxon named Dyrhern, already distinguished for "every act of unrelenting Barbarity that Man can be guilty of, besides exacting very large Sums for his own Use, over and above the Contributions. . . . the most worthless, the most profligate, and the most hard-hearted Rascal now living."[21]

---

for his wagon train, only 180 had been delivered; and of 287 teamsters supposed to have been hired for it, not one had put in an appearance. Schöning, III, 298. Frederick replied merely that he had issued orders to cover all that; if they were not obeyed, he could not help it. The prince must himself apprehend and punish the guilty persons. When he had been in Saxony the year before, he said, he had found plenty of everything. *P. C.,* XXI, 298.

[20] Hausarchiv, Rep. 56, II, F; see also Otto Herrmann, in the *Historische Vierteljahrschrift,* XXVI (1931), 370. On May 15 the king ordered that thereafter all officers found guilty of trading in government property should be cashiered and sentenced to fortress imprisonment for life. By falsifying their lists, he said, officers both in his army and in Henry's had been securing possession of rifles and other military equipment and selling them to the free battalions. *P. C.,* XXI, 439–440.

[21] M. P., VI, 31, 143, 151.

When Prince Henry reported such cases — carefully maintaining the polite pretense that the supply officers must have violated or exceeded their instructions, as the king could not possibly have sanctioned such conduct — Frederick replied bluntly that he had sanctioned it. The French, he said, had treated Hesse and the southwestern provinces no better, and the Russians had done worse. War always brought such evils in its train, and he was in no position to obviate them. As further justification he pointed out that he was more desperately in need of money than Prince Henry seemed to realize.[22]

At last, in complete exasperation, Frederick decided in the middle of March to take the administration of the occupied territory entirely out of Prince Henry's hands. He was angry enough to forget restraint in a letter of criticism much sharper than any he had written since those which goaded the prince into retirement a year and a half before. Forgetting that he had himself, only three months since, told his brother that Daun had been a fool to leave him undisturbed in a position so widely extended and so weakly held, he wrote:

The principal reason why things don't go as they should is that you don't occupy enough ground; you are too much constricted. . . . If I could be in Saxony for three weeks, I think I could arrange everything for you; but as it is impossible for me to go two steps away from here, I shall send you Anhalt with orders to the generals to oblige them to do their duty. . . . Your misguided indulgence for the Saxons will ruin my affairs. The Saxons howl over nothing; but I shall reiterate again the orders to my officers to double the executions, without which we shall get nothing at all, and my affairs will be ruined. You ought to support my views instead of placing obstacles in my way, especially when necessity compels me to act thus.[23]

Again the prince was superseded. Only partially, to be sure; but this time it was not by the king in person but by a staff major, a mere aide-de-camp! The experience was all the more humiliating to him because Anhalt had by that time taken General Winterfeldt's place in his prejudiced mind as the king's evil genius, and he hated him for it. The major was a well-trained soldier and a trusted favorite of the king; but his fellow officers not only envied him on that account but disliked him for the arrogance with which, on his many missions as proconsul, he superseded his seniors and ordered them and their subordinates about,

[22] Schöning, III, 289; *P. C.*, XXI, 277.
[23] *P. C.*, XXI, 297. Two days later, softening the message only by sending it through staff channels instead of personally, he notified the prince that Anhalt was to "investigate and arrange for" the whole matter of levies and contributions, following only the orders already given him by Frederick himself. *Ibid.*, 298.

always in the name of the king. Staff officers have rarely been popular with officers of the line in any army.[24]

Hateful though the situation was, there was not much that Henry could do about it but to resign. While he waited for the major to arrive he wrote to the king's secretary, Eichel, to say that if the orders von Anhalt was bringing with him proved upon examination to be in keeping with the tone of Frederick's recent letters, there would be no other course open to him. In that case he hoped that Eichel would try for the sake of their old friendship to see that his release was granted and that he was permitted to retire with decency and dignity, and without being humiliated or disgraced.[25]

He could also be unpleasant to Anhalt; and he was, although he dared not carry that too far. "Three rascals have been sent here to complete the plundering of Saxony," he wrote to Ferdinand, "among them M. Anhalt. I have received him as a matter of duty, but sent him on to Leipzig without offering him anything to eat or drink."[26]

The major's orders proved not to be quite so bad as he had feared; so he said nothing to the king about resigning until Frederick stung him again, at a new and entirely unexpected point and over a comparatively trifling matter. Some Austrian troops were being transferred from the Saxon front to Silesia. Henry got word of the shift through a spy, and reported immediately. He understood that eight regiments were making the move. Frederick wrote that there had been seventeen regiments instead of eight and took him sharply to task for the "too noticeable discrepancy," which he said might have had fatal consequences. Henry replied hotly that his spy, who had said there were eight, might have been ill-informed but had apparently made the report in good faith. Later he sent Frederick what he said was the official Austrian list of the regiments involved. There were six regiments of infantry, three of dragoons, and some cuirassiers.[27]

[24] In his *Histoire de mon temps* (*Oeuvres*, 1788, I, 283), Frederick compared the republican form of government unfavorably with the monarchy on the ground that, in a republic, generals are always tempted to seek their own fortunes instead of serving the state with true and unselfish devotion. Prince Henry, reading that passage many years later, made the marginal comment: "What a lie! Under kings also. Look at your Prince Leopold, your Winterfeldt, your Anhalt. There are a lot of petty apes who made their fortunes under you!"

Many a man owed or thought he owed his loss of the king's favor to some unfriendly report made by Anhalt. Prince Ferdinand of Brunswick quarreled with him soon after the war and withdrew from the Prussian service. Another officer who retired shortly after the making of peace, following a quarrel with the all-powerful aide, was Staff Captain von Steuben.

[25] Schöning, III, 307.

[26] Hausarchiv, Rep. 56, II, F; Otto Herrmann, in the *Historische Vierteljahrschrift*, XXVI (1931), 370.

[27] Schöning, III, 306–313; *P. C.*, XXI, 310, 323, 330, 337. By the tone of his letters and

That should have ended the argument. It was undignified and foolish for a king and his brother to seize upon so small a matter and to go on worrying it after it had lost all its point. But both were ill. The war had been working on their nerves for nearly six years, and their protective covering of emotional self-control had been worn very thin. Coming as it did in the midst of their quarrel over the treatment of Saxony, Frederick's challenge of the accuracy of his brother's reports brought Henry at last to the point of asking permission to resign from the service.[28]

The king refused to let him go, and seemed surprised that he should ever have been so forgetful of his own honor, reputation, and duty to the state as to have entertained the idea of going; but, realizing at last how needlessly they had been irritating one another by saying too much rather than too little, he proposed that they limit their correspondence thereafter to the necessary exchange of military information and the conduct of public business.[29]

Again he got what he wanted. Prince Henry stayed on. "I am very happy over the decision you have made," wrote Frederick when informed of it, "and I do not doubt that, by and large, your health is governed by your determination." [30]

While the king wrangled with his brother over the treatment of Saxony, and then sought a reconciliation with him and the withdrawal of his resignation, he was wrestling mightily with the problem of his relations with Russia, a problem made doubly difficult for him by the attitude of his ally, Great Britain. He wanted a peace with Russia. The British wanted a general pacification and feared that Russia's withdrawal

by obvious implication, the king virtually accused the prince of concealing the magnitude of the enemy troop movement so as not to have to send him too many reinforcements to compensate for it.

[28] H. to F., March 30, April 11 and 18, 1761, in Schöning, III, 311–322, 324; to Mitchell, in M. P., XLIII, 50, and in Hamilton, *Rheinsberg*, II, 54; *P. C.*, XXI, 337; Schmitt, *Prinz Heinrich*, II, 203.

[29] "I have learned from my limited experience in the world that honest frankness often does not pay, and that silence is better. Therefore I shall write you only on such matters as the necessities of public business absolutely compel me to bring to your attention, which you will not take amiss; on the contrary, Your Vivacity will be grateful to me for my patience, which you put to strange proofs." *P. C.*, XXI, 337, 371, 381, 382.

[30] *P. C.*, XXI, 407, in a postscript added in the king's own hand to a ciphered letter. In the manuscript in the Prussian Secret State Archives, it reads: "Je suis bien aise de la résolution que vous avez prise, et je ne doute point qu'à quelques exceptions près, votre santé ne dépende de votre bonne résolution." In preparing the document for publication the editors of the *Politische Correspondenz* have thought it necessary to interpolate the word *que* after *dépende*, acknowledging the interpolation in the usual way by printing the word in brackets read "votre santé ne dépende [que] de votre bonne résolution." As there is nothing in the manuscript at the point indicated — no illegible word, no erasure, no blot — to warrant the interpolation, the *que* must have been considered necessary to complete the sense of the king's statement. It seems, however, not to

would only encourage Frederick to continue the war in the hope of making some conquests to compensate his people for their efforts and their losses.

Even before he knew that the Russian empress had died, Sir Andrew Mitchell was convinced that Frederick would not be willing to make peace with Austria on any terms which Austria would be willing to accept. By secret negotiations in Vienna his government discovered that Maria Theresa's attitude was much the same as Frederick's. Neither had yet won advantages sufficient to enable him or her to compel the other to make peace, or suffered quite enough to be compelled to ask for it. So Mitchell's first reaction to the news of the death of the empress Elizabeth was a premonition of further trouble rather than a feeling of relief. "One Thing I cannot help fearing," he wrote, "[is] that the King of Prussia's lively Imagination, which generally carries him too far, may on this Occasion lead him to abandon all Thought of Peace, if he ever had any."

A little later, increasingly suspicious because the king conducted his negotiations with Russia in secret and refused to make any statement of his final war aims, Mitchell hinted to Lord Bute that Great Britain might use the power of her purse to force Frederick to be reasonable. Neither Russia nor Prussia, he said, had any money left. "It will therefore be in the King's power to render any treaty or convention, that may tend to prolong the war, ineffectual, if his Majesty should disapprove of it." [31]

Prince Henry was equally anxious lest Frederick let slip his priceless opportunity to make peace with Russia. Until Sir Andrew left Magdeburg to join the king's headquarters in Breslau he used Henry as an intermediary to transmit his suggestions: Frederick should release at once, without ransom and without insisting in advance upon an exchange, all Russian prisoners of war then in his hands, and should suspend all "executions" and moderate his demands for contributions in the little state of Zerbst, in which the czar was still interested. From Robert Keith in St. Petersburg to Mitchell to Prince Henry to Frederick passed

be needed for that purpose; and although it does not completely change the meaning of the passage, it intensifies it considerably and makes it sound much more disagreeable than Frederick presumably intended. With the *que* interpolated, the postscript is a scolding; in the original it could better be interpreted as encouragement. Although Frederick was often sharp-tongued and tactless, it seems highly improbable that he would have welcomed the interpolation.

[31] M. P., VI, 39, 69. By these two letters of January 21 and March 7 Sir Andrew seems, whether he realized it or not, to have become to a certain extent a party to a policy which he afterward denounced to Finckenstein as dishonorable. What Mitchell and his government feared most was a treaty of alliance in which Frederick might promise to support the czar's doubtful claim to Schleswig, at the expense of Denmark. Peter still called himself Duke of Holstein-Gottorp.

also the suggestion that the czar would be highly pleased to have the Prussian Order of the Black Eagle conferred upon him. This was done, and he was made honorary commander of a Prussian regiment as well. All these things the prince warmly recommended on his own account, although he told Mitchell he was not at all sure that Frederick would listen to reason in the matter of men or horses from Zerbst.

The prince was encouraged by what he heard of the pacific disposition of the new czar to hope that peace would be quickly made "unless the devil took a hand in the negotiations." Mitchell feared not only the intervention of the devil but "all sorts of clever tricks" to which he suspected that Frederick would resort in an ill-advised attempt to reap the utmost advantage from his favorable situation.[32]

They need not have worried. Frederick was peace-minded enough where Russia was concerned. He made, and would have made without any prompting from them, all the concessions to the czar that they suggested. He went, in fact, much further than that, sending Bernhard von der Goltz and Count Wilhelm Friedrich von Schwerin to St. Petersburg with instructions to make peace at once at any price demanded, barring only the cession, without compensation, of any Prussian territory; they were further directed to offer the czar an alliance on his own terms. Mitchell was asked to furnish passports for the plenipotentiaries but did not see their instructions and would not have believed them genuine if he had seen them.[33]

In his negotiations for peace with Russia Frederick had to work without the aid of two of his best British friends whose sympathy and support had throughout the war been invaluable to him. He had alienated Sir Andrew Mitchell, and Pitt was out of office. Worse than that, a report reached him through Goltz that Lord Bute of the British ministry was working against him in St. Petersburg.

Goltz reported in March that the Russian ministers had, by order of the czar, shown him and permitted him to copy the report made by Prince Galitzin (or Golicyn) of a conversation he had had in London with Lord Bute, shortly after the death of the Russian empress. Galitzin

---

[32] M. P., VI, 44–52; XXVIII, 135–145; XLIII, 44–48; Schöning, III, 277. Prince Henry missed his guess completely as to the prospects of the new czar. He knew that plots against him were to be expected, but thought his bids for the favor of the nobles would be successful and would insure him sufficiently against the malcontents. M. P., XLIII, 46.

[33] *P. C.*, XXI, 234–236, 312–313, *et passim*. On March 17 Sir Andrew wrote privately to Lord Bute that Frederick was constitutionally incapable of authorizing "any man living" to negotiate or sign anything whatever without first bringing or sending it home to be examined by him. For that reason, said Mitchell, "I am inclined to think that this peace exists only in the King of Prussia's imagination, which indeed, is most fruitfull and lively, and affords him much comfort by overlooking or at least diminishing every obstacle and difficulty which might oppose or retard the accomplishment of his wishes." M. P., VI, 67; Bisset, II, 275.

reported that Bute had said it was well realized in Britain that, in view of the exhaustion of his treasury and of his states, Frederick could not properly hope to make peace without buying it by some "reasonable sacrifice" of territory. The British government, he said, had instructed Mitchell six weeks since to bring it to Frederick's attention in quite unequivocal terms that it was time to think seriously of making peace; but Mitchell had been unable to induce him to answer because he was still nourishing such "chimerical hopes" of victory.[34] The British government had wished all along to preserve the king of Prussia from total ruin, but could not wage war forever just to please him. It hoped therefore that the new czar would be in no haste to make peace with him or to withdraw his troops from Prussian soil, since to do so would prolong the general war when all the world, save the king of Prussia, wanted peace.[35]

Sir Andrew Mitchell knew at the time nothing about the Bute-Galitzin interview. He still assumed that "the usual subsidy" would be paid again that year, but was extremely impatient with Frederick for letting him know only that he was negotiating with Russia, while keeping him entirely in the dark about the course of the negotiations and the character of the proposed settlement. Great Britain, he argued, had been too frank and faithful an ally to deserve such treatment; but he could not break down the wall of reserve with which Frederick had surrounded himself, while Finckenstein professed to know no more than he about what was happening.[36]

While the British and Prussian governments were exchanging official recriminations and mutual accusations of lack of frankness and friendliness, Mitchell was instructed to lodge a formal complaint also against

[34] Mitchell had indeed tried unsuccessfully to induce the king to state his peace terms, but he had received from his government no such drastic orders as Bute is quoted as describing. He had been unable, however, to settle a long and acrimonious dispute dating from January, 1761, over the amount of financial aid that Prussia might still expect if Britain made a separate peace with France. Frederick had asked originally that the annual subsidy of 4,000,000 thaler (£670,000) be paid as usual and that Britain continue also to support (but turn over to him for his use) the German troops to be released from the army of Prince Ferdinand of Brunswick. His largest total demand, subsequently reduced, was for 9,000,000 thaler for 1761. Only the usual 4,000,000 was paid that year, and nothing thereafter. See Carl William Eldon, *England's Subsidy Policy towards the Continent in the Seven Years' War* (Philadelphia, 1938), page 136 and table facing page 160.

[35] *P. C.,* XXI, 311–312, 320. Prince Galitzin's dispatch was dated from London, January 26, old style, or February 6, new style. It was on January 21, new style, that Mitchell expressed to Bute his fear that Frederick would "abandon all thought of peace, if he ever had any."

[36] M. P., VI, 73–95. Excerpts from several of Sir Andrew's letters of the period are printed in Bisset's second volume. On May 9 he wrote: "I pay my court almost daily to the King of Prussia, and am always received with great civility, but I see he industriously avoids talking of affairs, and his minister Count Finckenstein . . . follows his master's example." *P. C.,* XXI, 426.

Frederick's diplomatic representatives in London for their "imprudence, indiscretion and impertinence" and their generally intransigent and anti-British attitude. At almost precisely the same time Frederick was scolding them for having forgotten that they were Prussians, and accusing them of having sold out to the British![37]

Frederick had had Goltz's report on the Bute-Galitzin interview in his possession for a month before he told the British minister about it, and then he waited a week longer before he permitted Finckenstein to show Sir Andrew a copy of it. Although willing to let it serve as a partial explanation of his attitude during the past weeks, he refused even then to state his ultimate war aims or to say what use he would make of another subsidy if it were granted him.[38]

When Mitchell challenged him on the matter, Bute admitted readily enough that he had talked with Prince Galitzin at the time alleged, but denied in substance virtually all the rest of the report. He had had no thought of abandoning Frederick, he said, or of discontinuing the subsidy, but had been interested chiefly in securing a general peace if he could. Meanwhile Spain's entry into the war had complicated Britain's problem by forcing her to think of the defense of Portugal, while Prussia's was about to be simplified by the withdrawal of Russia and Sweden. He had therefore thought himself justified in asking what Frederick's war aims were, but had got no answer, so had been led to insist that the subsidy, if paid, should not be used merely to prolong the war.[39]

Although Mitchell's own reports may well have contributed very materially to Lord Bute's evident distrust of Frederick, he was furiously angry at what he considered a shameless betrayal of Britain's ally; and the secretary's lengthy denial convinced him only that the Galitzin-Goltz report had been accurate and that the charge was substantially true. Moved either by his anger or by a politician's feeling for the main chance, he stepped quite out of character as a minister and spoke to Finckenstein in an extremely (but perhaps deliberately) indiscreet fashion as man to man.

Having been ordered to read to Finckenstein a translation of his letter from Bute, he did so. Then he said flatly that he was ashamed of the thing and had read it only under compulsion. He bluntly disowned the

---

[37] M. P., VI, 90; P. C., XXI, 318. "Je crois, Messieurs, que vous êtes les commis de Bute. Il paraît bien que vous n'êtes pas Prussiens. Votre père, Knyphausen, avait pris de l'argent de la France et de l'Angleterre, pourquoi il fut chassé. Vous aurait-il légué cette coutume en héritage?"

[38] M. P., VI, 94–97. Excerpts in Bisset, II, 283–286. The king assured Mitchell, however, that he had never questioned the minister's own personal loyalty to himself or his friendship for Prussia. He only wished that everyone were equally honest and virtuous, he said; the world would be the better for it. P. C., XXI, 486.

[39] Bisset, II, 299–306.

writer of it, sending word to Frederick that Bute was no proper spokes-man for the British people, and would be out of office before November. "Speaking as a free man and an Englishman rather than as a minister," he expressed the opinion that Bute must have gone insane to act in a fashion at once so faithless and so completely contrary to good policy, and deserved to lose his head on the scaffold for it. As for himself, he professed to be still as completely devoted to Prussia's interest as ever, and hoped that Frederick would continue to favor him with his confidence and that the whole matter would be righted by the ministry within a few months.[40]

Meanwhile Frederick, in the manner of an injured innocent, had ad-dressed himself directly to King George.

Monsieur my Brother: M. Mitchell has just arrived. He has brought me Your Majesty's letter, and has handed me the documents of a negotiation which your ministers have undertaken in Vienna. Although I had had these documents for a long time, but quite different from the ones I have just received, I must believe that these latter ones are authentic. I must, however, say in frankness to Your Majesty that it is not the usual practice of allies to open negotiations without the knowledge of their confederates, and to treat concerning their interests without consulting them. Nor can I conceal from Your Majesty that there has come to me from a very reliable source [a report of] a conversation of one of your ministers with Prince Galitzin, ambassador from Russia, the contents of which seem to me even more singular than these previous procedures. This has pained me so much the more because I had flattered myself that nothing could change my cordial union with England, and that it would at least be remembered that I was drawn into this war as a result of the envy aroused by the alliance I had contracted with the king your grandfather. I beg Your Majesty therefore to order your ministers in future not to treat with my enemies without my knowledge, and not to touch upon things that interest me except in so far as I shall first have given my consent.

My situation is becoming more favorable as my peace with Russia and Sweden is on the point of being concluded, and as the Emperor of Russia has seen fit to give me of his own volition a guarantee of all my states as I held them before the war. I do not doubt that Your Majesty will be doubly pleased by this as you have given me the same guarantee and as my situation thus becomes more favorable, — which encourages me to hope in this campaign to reduce my enemies to reason and to oblige them to make a reasonable peace. I am with all esteem, Monsieur my Brother, Your Majesty's good brother, Federic.[41]

---

[40] Mitchell to Grenville, in M. P., VI, 108; Finckenstein to the king, in A. Schäfer, II-2, 749. Sir Andrew may have been indulging in histrionics rather than in hysterics that day; but his account of the interview, while it tells less, is otherwise entirely in agreement with Finckenstein's.

[41] P. C., XXI, 413-414. Professor Walter Dorn, whose opinion rightly commands great respect, has pointed out that it was the Duke of Newcastle who had forced Bute's hand in

So Bute, still bickering for terms before he would throw a life line to a swimmer in distress, suddenly found himself shouting vainly at a man already rescued by someone else. Some of Frederick's failures began at last to turn to his advantage. If he had been able to bring Denmark and Turkey into the war as his allies against Russia, as he had tried so long and hard to do, Russia might not have made peace so readily. As it was, the new czar Peter III was free to follow his own inclination; and he was inclined not only to make peace with Frederick but to form an alliance with him. While the period of negotiation seemed long to a man burning with eagerness to see it ended, the steps leading to an agreement were quickly taken.

At the end of January, 1762, Frederick reported to Prince Henry that Czernichev was leaving with the Russian troops that had wintered with Loudon, and exclaimed: "There, thank Heaven! Our rear is free. . . . I hope that this news will put you in good humor." [42]

On May 20 Schwerin arrived in Breslau with a copy of the treaty signed in St. Petersburg fifteen days earlier; and within another week salutes had been fired in the camps and the *Te Deum* had been sung in the churches all over Frederick's dominions. In the midst of the rejoicing,

the matter of the secret negotiations with Austria and who had thus been chiefly responsible for the indiscretions at Vienna of which Frederick was fully informed before the thought of a Russian alliance had occurred to him. Professor Dorn and J. H. Rose agree that Prince Galitzin, himself violently hostile to Prussia and already aware of the "feelers" put out by the British in Vienna, wished to deter his master from tying himself in any way to a man already hopelessly beaten and abandoned by his own ally. Hence he may consciously or unconsciously have colored his account of his interview with Bute in such fashion as to make it appear to be much more of a betrayal than the British minister intended. Viewed in that light, Bute would appear rather as a blunderer than as a betrayer; but in Prussian eyes he was both.

The same writer has further pointed out that, if Galitzin did not misquote Bute, then what the minister said in that private interview was quite inconsistent with his publicly expressed views on the same subjects and with his own written reports of the conversation. But Professor Dorn has written a far better defense of Bute than Bute himself ever wrote. Mitchell was not alone in finding the minister's written denials and explanations unconvincing. In any case the real turning point of the whole affair was Frederick's definite bid for a Russian alliance; and he made that bid because he believed that Bute had betrayed him as Galitzin said he had.

That step of Frederick's was, in turn, equally decisive for the British cabinet. While it had refused some months earlier to renew the subsidy convention, it did not finally decide until April 30 not to pay the subsidy for 1762; and Bute had tried meanwhile by threatening to withhold payment to drive Frederick away from his Russian alliance and to force him to agree not to support Russia against Denmark. In doing so, however, he had succeeded only in making himself ridiculous by trying to intimidate a man a thousand times bolder than himself, by threatening to withhold a subsidy upon which Frederick had already ceased to depend and which he had long since forbidden his ministers to mention again. Walter L. Dorn, "Frederick the Great and Lord Bute," in the *Journal of Modern History*, I (1929), 529–560. See also Walter L. Dorn, *Competition for Empire* (New York and London, 1940), 376–377; Eldon, *England's Subsidy Policy towards the Continent during the Seven Years' War*, 144–151; and J. H. Rose, "Frederick the Great and England," *English Historical Review*, XXIX (1914), 267–275.

[42] *P. C.*, XXI, 212–213.

the peace signed with Sweden at Hamburg on May 22 was announced but went almost unnoticed.

For the sake of the effect that a good story of Prussia's reception of the news might have upon the impressionable czar, the king directed Prince Henry to see to it that the details of his army's official celebration, particularly the number of guns fired in salute, were correctly reported in the Berlin newspapers. The celebration included, in addition to the gun-firing, a *Te Deum* and a banquet for the generals, at which toasts were drunk to the czar, his ministers, and his marshals. All these items were duly reported for foreign — especially Russian — consumption.

The prince was further directed at once to "divulge adroitly" a rumor to the effect that a corps of thirty-five thousand Russians was to be sent through Lusatia for the retaking of Dresden. At the same time he was told in confidence that eighteen thousand had been promised for use against the Austrians in Silesia.[43]

Mitchell heard indeed that Frederick had not found it easy to dissuade his overzealous new comrade in arms, Peter III — recently named honorary commander of a Prussian regiment, recipient of the Order of the Black Eagle, *et cetera, et cetera* — from taking the field himself at the head of his troops; but he managed it. The king had abundant reason for the evident relief and self-congratulation with which he wrote to Sir Andrew: "Fortune is beginning to change her attitude toward me. I hope that it may continue so until the end of the year; then we shall attain this winter an honorable and, please God, a durable peace."[44]

The god had come out of the machine and saved him; and he was ready to admit that he had stood in need of salvation.

[43] *P. C.,* XXI, 448; Schöning, III, 342–348; Schmitt, *Prinz Heinrich,* II, 224. Apparently the prince thought that a story about 15,000 Russians would be easier for him to tell or for the Austrians to believe than one about 35,000. At any rate, he reduced the number when he told the tale.

[44] *P. C.,* XXI, 486; M. P., VI, 103, 112. Mitchell's letters cited here were dated May 23 and June 27. The former, the draft of which was written in his letterbook on the reverse side of the page on which another of May 23 was completed, was wrongly dated June 23, and is printed under that date by Bisset (II, 311). By June 23 it had lost its point.

# CHAPTER XIII

# Break-Through on the Mulde

*"I have myself been giving thanks to God for the victories which . . . His Highness the most worthy Prince Henry has won in Saxony. If only the outcome of this whole campaign might be such that the other enemies of His Majesty the King would also be forced to yield him his objectives, and that peace would soon follow!"* — Eichel to Finckenstein.

ENCOURAGED though he was by the providential dynastic change that had converted Russia from an enemy into an ally, and by what he knew of the exhaustion of Austria's financial resources, Frederick would have been happy to make peace whenever Maria Theresa offered him a treaty leaving him in possession of all his prewar territories. That day, however, had not yet come. Such a settlement was still to be won only by conquest — by victory in a final peace drive (*Friedensturm*) that would induce Austria's other allies also to desert her and would compel even the stouthearted empress to recognize the hopelessness of the task she had set herself.

For that supreme effort the king of Prussia and his brother Henry summoned their last reserves of moral and physical energy, threw into the scales the last gleanings from their recruiting areas, and demanded of their war-weary officers and men the ultimate exertion that was to bring them peace. The greater concentration of troops took place in Silesia, where the king continued in command; but there was more movement and more decisive action on Prince Henry's front in Saxony.

The prince was the first to take the offensive. He found his opportunity when the Austrians, alarmed by rumors that some Russian troops would be sent to join Frederick in Silesia, transferred some of their own from Saxony to redress the balance on their eastern front. On May 12, near Döbeln on the Freiberg fork of the Mulde, west of Meissen, Henry attacked the extreme left wing of the Austrian army, commanded by Major General von Zedtwitz. His purpose was to destroy that corps and so to drive a great wedge between the Austrian and the Imperial armies.

His plans were made with all possible care. Through spies and from deserters he knew that the Austrians facing him customarily spent the night under arms, then called off the stand-to at daybreak and retired at six or seven o'clock to get some sleep. He therefore assembled his storm troops shortly before dawn, concealing them behind hills or in ravines and woods, and ordering them to keep absolutely quiet and not to break cover until their prospective victims had had time to retire as usual and get to sleep.

Orders were not perfectly obeyed. The troops were nervous; some of them made too much noise, and the Austrians grew suspicious and were more alert than usual. Then somone broke cover prematurely and the attack was precipitated an hour ahead of schedule.[1] From that point onward, however, everything went according to plan. The Prussians crossed the Mulde at four points. Von Zedtwitz himself was captured. His corps lost half its men as casualties or prisoners, and the rest fled through Freiberg to Dippoldiswalde. The prince's army drove through between the Imperial and Austrian positions so far that its rear and flanks were dangerously exposed; but it was enabled for a long time to prevent the two enemy forces so separated from re-establishing contact.

Not content with merely driving a dangerous salient into the enemy line of posts, where neither side made any attempt to maintain a really continuous line, the prince moved swiftly to crumple up the Austrians' crippled left wing. On the third day of his offensive he recaptured Freiberg. On the fifth he took the heights of Pretzschendorf, within artillery range of Dippoldiswalde. As the spearhead of his attack advanced, however, he was compelled constantly to weaken it by leaving detachments behind to protect his own communications and to widen the base of the salient by pushing the Imperials back westward from Chemnitz while he was driving the Austrians in upon themselves, eastward, from Freiberg.

To exploit his gains to the fullest, he needed strong reserves of men and fresh horses; and he had neither. Both enemy armies were thrown into great confusion and Serbelloni, in command of both but fearful for Dresden, begged in vain for reinforcements from Silesia; but Prince Henry received no reinforcements either, and Serbelloni clearly had no thought of abandoning either of his intrenched positions — Plauen in the southwest or Dippoldiswalde near Dresden. The Prussian offensive had practically spent itself when Colonel Bandemer, going beyond his orders in an attempt to get possession of Chemnitz, was punished for his temerity by the Imperials under Prince Stolberg and driven back to Öderan with proportionally heavy losses in both men and guns.

[1] For years afterward there was a feud between Seydlitz and Kleist, the former accusing the latter of opening the engagement prematurely in order to claim subsequently more than his share of the credit for it.

The prince repaired that damage as quickly as possible by sending more troops under two of his finest offensive fighters, Seydlitz and Kleist, who retook Chemnitz and drove the Imperials off into Franconia. Prince Stolberg made Baireuth his headquarters thereafter until the middle of July. Bandemer was removed from command of his detachment and replaced by Kanitz, to whom Major Anhalt was attached as "adviser." There was then for a time little to be feared from that sector, but no spectacular success was to be anticipated.[2]

The immediate effects of Prince Henry's limited May offensive were consternation in Vienna and rejoicing in the camp of the king of Prussia. Maria Theresa was deeply disheartened by it.[3] Frederick was appropriately delighted, and attributed the success of the drive to "the grace of Heaven and the prince's good arrangements"—always an effective combination. But Frederick and his brother were in a better position than the empress-queen to know that the offensive had reached its limit. It was tantalizing to the prince to see such an opportunity go only half-utilized for lack of men and horses; but Frederick could not or did not find them for him, and said that he had expected from the beginning that the enemy would "try to hold firm" at Plauen and Dippoldiswalde—as indeed he had. The prince knew equally well when it was time to stop. From Pretzschendorf on May 20 he reported that his forces had been reduced by sickness, desertion, and casualties to a total of less than thirty thousand effectives and that, unless he was considerably reinforced, he could do no more for at least four weeks than hold the position he then held; and he would be lucky if the Austrians let him do that.[4]

He was not left undisturbed. In the night of May 31–June 1 the Austrians counterattacked all along the line. They took some prisoners at Dippoldiswalde, but were stopped without gain elsewhere.

Reinforcements were hard to find. Some troops, to be sure, which had been occupied in the north were about to be released for use elsewhere by the signing of peace with Sweden; but the prince got only part of them. Colonel Belling's corps came to him, and proved to be a valuable

---

[2] Schöning, III, 338–361; Schmitt, *Prinz Heinrich*, II, 218–226. It may well be imagined how assignment to such an obscure post must have irked the self-confident Major Anhalt, accustomed as he was to proconsular authority over generals and princes in critical situations. Frederick soon recalled him to Silesia.

Kalckreuth wrote many years later that if Prince Henry had followed *his* advice and pushed forward more aggressively he could scarcely have failed to take Dresden immediately; but Kalckreuth is not always convincing. *Paroles,* 243–244.

[3] Letter from d'Ayasasa to Daun, Vienna, May 26, in von Arneth, *Geschichte Maria Theresias,* VI, 478.

[4] *P. C.,* XXI, 463; Schöning, III, 347–349. Frederick's army was then more than twice as large as Prince Henry's and was confronted by an Austrian one slightly, but not much, larger than itself. Marshal Daun had superseded Loudon in command of the forces facing Frederick.

## Page of a Letter from Henry to Frederick

Last page of Prince Henry's letter of May 20, 1762, reporting on his crossing of the Mulde, estimating his losses, and asking for decorations with which to reward certain officers who had specially distinguished themselves (see page 198). Frederick's notes for his reply of June 11 are written across the top of the page (see page 200). Reproduced by courtesy of the Staatsarchiv.

accession of strength, its units being "complete" in numbers and equipment and still quite fresh in comparison with the regiments that had seen years of more strenuous service; but the king himself took the Duke of Bevern's corps, similarly released from Stettin. Belling's arrival, furthermore, was offset by the appearance, on the other side of the line, of Austrian reinforcements.

Quite aside from the fact that further reinforcements for the army in Saxony were hard to find, the king did not consider them urgently necessary. He was content that the prince should stop where he was during June and utilize his time by bringing up siege guns, pontoons, and supplies for the greater adventures that were to follow whenever the way to them should be opened up, not by a resumption of the offensive in Saxony but by the further intervention of their *deus ex machina.* Czernichev, Frederick said, would soon be with him; then the Austrian army in Saxony would be weakened by withdrawals to strengthen that in Silesia, and Prince Henry could take Dresden at will. The failure of the Turks to appear in Hungary and pull the Prussian chestnuts (if not the Prussians themselves) out of the fire, he thought he could explain on the ground that they had been afraid to involve themselves in a war with Austria for fear of being attacked by Russia; but he had induced the czar, he said, to make an announcement of policy that should allay their fears. With the Turks operating in Hungary, Prince Henry could go on from Dresden to Prague with the greatest of ease. That might not happen until September, he conceded in his letter of July 13; but "better late than never." [5]

All the prince could do meanwhile was to keep strong cavalry patrols incessantly active on his exposed right flank, which would serve the double purpose of protecting his own position and preventing the junction of the two enemy armies with which he had to deal. So, both jointly and separately, his rival raiders Seydlitz and Kleist were kept constantly busy, ranging sometimes beyond the borders of electoral Saxony into northwestern Bohemia.

Such work, while obviously useful, was hard on horses; and on June 21 the prince's staff had to appeal to the king's for more and better help from the remount service. The mounted regiments, it was reported, depleted though they were, had more men than horses; yet Colonel von Stechow of the remount service, giving the king's orders as his excuse, had refused to send them any more horses. Should cavalrymen continue to be useless or to march on foot, the prince's headquarters bluntly asked,

[5] *P. C.*, XXI, 470; XXII, 26. "Il vaut mieux tard que jamais." The Russians appeared only at the end of June; the Turks never did.

or would the king change his orders to Colonel von Stechow and permit them to be remounted?

The king replied with equal bluntness. He could not go on indefinitely conjuring up horses by the thousand, out of nothing — or armies, or men. He had already spent nearly two million thaler for horses during the past winter, and owed three million to the Berlin contractors as it was. The officers must do their duty better, and take better care of their horses! He did not say just how he supposed it would affect the morale or usefulness of an officer to be given a difficult mission involving hard marching, knowing that he would be scorched by the prince if he spared his horses and by the king if he did not.[6]

Except that Colonel Belling was sent to him from Pomerania shortly after the middle of June, the prince's requests for more men with whom to exploit his success and continue his offensive were just as brusquely refused, although there was virtually no activity at that time on the Silesian front. The Austrian army in Saxony was considerably strengthened at the same time, so that the prince was again facing odds of two to one; but Frederick professed not to believe it. Henry reported that General Stampach had brought seven Austrian regiments to strengthen Serbelloni; only five, said the king. Henry estimated Serbelloni's total strength at sixty thousand, Frederick at forty thousand. In estimating Henry's strength Frederick insisted upon adding in the newest recruits, even those who had not yet learned how to fire their muskets, and on counting only battalions and squadrons, not men actually available. On that basis he insisted on June 11 that the prince could not have less than forty-four thousand effectives present out of a total paper strength of sixty thousand (although on that same day he wrote to Baron Goltz in St. Petersburg that the army in Saxony did not number more than thirty-four thousand). The prince had said that it was under thirty thousand. Sir Andrew Mitchell estimated it at twenty-six thousand effectives.[7]

The Prussian supply problem was made doubly difficult by the shortage of horses and by extraordinarily low water in the Elbe. The larger

[6] Schöning, III, 367; *P. C.*, XXI, 562; Schmitt, *Prinz Heinrich*, II, 240. In the first week of July Kleist returned to Freiberg from a raid around Teplitz in Bohemia, with two hundred horses and a herd of beef cattle captured from the Austrians, and a fund of ransom money squeezed out of the Bohemian towns; but raids were not always so profitable, and could not be depended upon as a source of supplies.

[7] Schöning, III, 362–364, 473; *P. C.*, XXI, 524; Bisset, II, 314. At the same time that he was appealing to the lists to prove the presence of men whom the prince could not see in the ranks (and apparently without realizing how completely he was vitiating his own argument), Frederick was complaining that officers were quite commonly falsifying their daily returns, reporting deserters as "sick," and claiming more men than they had so as to make a profit by drawing maintenance money for men not actually present. His poorly paid captains normally made their living by feeding their companies on a cash-allowance basis at so much per head.

boats could come no higher than Wittenberg, and small ones only to Torgau; so a long haul was still necessary. Neither of the brothers, mercifully, said anything further just then about living off the country in Saxony.

In spite of all his difficulties, however, Prince Henry found work for Belling and his comparatively fresh troops as soon as they arrived, by sending them with Seydlitz in the third week of June to push the Imperials farther off to the west. It would have been better to deal more decisively than that with an army that was rather a nuisance than a menace; but not even Seydlitz could destroy an enemy he could not catch. The Prussians went beyond Chemnitz as far as Zwickau on the west branch of the upper Mulde, with Count Stolberg retiring before them. Then Stolberg tried to force Seydlitz to retire by threatening his rear in turn; but Prince Henry left Seydlitz where he was and sent out Kleist to protect him, and Stolberg again retreated. For the king's old motto, "always on the alert," Prince Henry seemed to have substituted a new one, "always on the march"; but by their ceaseless activity his mobile units enabled him to hold a widely extended and lightly garrisoned chain of posts, and to hem into a restricted area the numerically superior forces of his principal enemy. It requires constant vigilance and hard riding to surround a large army with a smaller one and still avoid disaster.

The prince was in fact living dangerously and avoiding disaster often by the narrowest conceivable margin. On June 27, while Seydlitz and Kleist were both far away to the west, the Austrians tried to take advantage of their absence by attacking those who were left. The attack was made at two points simultaneously, near Willsdruf and Frauenstein, so that neither sector could send help to the other; but the prince quickly arrived in person at one of the threatened points and sent help to von Hülsen at the other, and both attacks were beaten off. Henry reported to Frederick that he was "depending more and more upon the large number of our guns" for that sort of thing; but then and always he was paying close attention also to the choice of his position and the defensive organization of his terrain.[8]

Three weeks later Prince Stolberg attempted to re-establish contact with the Austrians south of Dresden; but Kleist, who was already in Bohemia on another raid, turned westward from Teplitz to meet him, and Seydlitz and Belling swarmed upon his left flank and rear. Stolberg considered himself fortunate to escape to Baireuth, and most of his army retired to Nuremberg. The only way for them to rejoin the Austrians,

---

[8] Schöning, III, 367–376; von Bernhardi, *Friedrich der Grosse*, II, 587. Both the brothers, in the course of the war, made great improvements in their use of the guns; and the prince developed into an excellent artillerist.

obviously, was to make a longer detour through the interior of Bohemia; and they did not bring themselves to the point of doing that until a month later, in August.

By that time the Russians had disappeared from Silesia, reappeared, and disappeared again. Those that had wintered with the Austrians were withdrawn when Czar Peter III made peace with Prussia. Then at the end of June, under the same commander, Czernichev, a corps of about twenty thousand returned and placed themselves at the disposal of the king of Prussia. Quite characteristically he lost no time in showing them to the Austrians, going out at once on a reconnaissance with the first detachment of Cossacks to arrive. They attacked some Austrian outposts, took a few prisoners, and called it an auspicious beginning.[9]

Sir Andrew Mitchell rather sourly observed that those foolish fellows who were so proud to serve under the eyes of the great soldier-king would probably have their fill of it before the end of the campaign; and certainly Frederick intended that they should be far more useful to him than they had ever been to the Austrians. He had determined, as his first objective for that year, upon the recapture of Schweidnitz; but he could not approach that fortress while Daun's army held the hills around it, and the Austrians were so well posted that he did not dare attack them where they were.[10]

But however cautious he might have become, Frederick could not continue to be himself and fail to utilize the temporary numerical superiority that the presence of his Russian auxiliaries gave him during the first half of July. In order to maneuver Daun off to the southward, away from Schweidnitz, so as to prepare the way for an attempt to recapture that fortress, he pushed some troops through between it and Landeshut, right into Bohemia. There, around Braunau and Trautenau, he turned the Cossacks loose to do their worst, hoping that Daun would be drawn away from the defense of Schweidnitz by concern over Bohemia and over his own service of supply.[11] The Austrian field marshal did in fact shift his troops around from the north of Schweidnitz to the southwest, but did not abandon the fortress. Hoping to make the new position untenable for him, Frederick moved around with him from Bunzelwitz to Seitendorf, not far from Burkersdorf.

[9] M. P., VI, 112.

[10] The king had gone over at last, definitely and completely, to the policy of limited risks and modest objectives, depending upon another year of discouragement to bring Maria Theresa to the point of making peace; while the prince, with less than half as many men, sought the decisive victory which would drive her to it at once. *P. C.,* XXI, 442, 490; XXII, 41, 201.

[11] "Brannte alles nieder, was Feuer fangen konnte," says Bülow, in *Prinz Heinrich,* 318. See also *P. C.,* XXII, 40.

It was a tedious business, but he thought he could not prudently hurry it. Then he found that he must hurry in spite of the risk, for his time was cut short. Czernichev brought him a message that struck him, he said later, like a thunderclap. The czar had been dethroned, and the empress-regent Catherine II had ordered Czernichev to separate his army at once from that of the king of Prussia and to bring it home! On the very eve of battle, the king was to lose a fourth of his troops!

He could not let them go like that. Even if they did no actual fighting, their very presence on the day of decision would be helpful; or, conversely, the news of their departure would so hearten the Austrians and discourage the Prussians that the king would scarcely dare seek a decision. So it was imperative that Czernichev remain, if only for a few days longer. Frederick pointed out to him that at least three days would be needed to set up supply depots for his troops to use on their march to Poland; and the gift of a jeweled sword and fifteen thousand ducats in gold may have helped him to see the cogency of the king's contention. He agreed to wait three days before obeying his empress's order.

On his third day of grace, July 21, the king attacked one wing of Daun's position at Burkersdorf. The Russians took no part in the fighting; but Daun could not be unmindful of their presence, and was handicapped thereby in his defense. With the loss of the heights of Burkersdorf, his Dittmannsdorf position had also to be abandoned; and he retired southward, leaving Frederick free to begin his siege of Schweidnitz.[12]

Then Czernichev could depart in peace, reluctant though Frederick naturally was to see him go. The king's reluctance was in fact so well understood by that kindred spirit who had assumed direction of Russian affairs, Catherine II, that in anticipation of it she had ordered Saltykov, in East Prussia, to delay his evacuation of that territory and to compel its inhabitants to swear allegiance to her. Subsequently she disavowed what her general had done, explaining that he had acted in the belief that Frederick would detain or disarm Czernichev's corps, and that reprisals would therefore be necessary to secure its release. That redoubtable German princess had studied statecraft in a hard school since her marriage to the degenerate Russian grand duke, and had learned never to wait for fate to determine the outcome of any of her affairs which she could manage for herself. It was fortunate for Frederick that she judged it more profitable to remain neutral than to enter the war against him; and he spent an uneasy ten days after Czernichev's departure before he knew that that had been her decision.

---

[12] The Prussian losses totaled about 1,600 men. Among the 1,200 prisoners and deserters who fell into Frederick's hands were a number of former Prussian soldiers who had been impressed into the Austrian service. He also captured thirteen guns. Jany, II, 630.

He tried hard at first to prevent the public from learning that the czar had been dethroned, although he informed Prince Henry of it at once.[13] Some time elapsed before it became known that poor foolish Peter had been liquidated, and meanwhile everyone speculated on his fate and on the reasons for it. Prince Henry, writing to his brother Ferdinand, permitted himself some very bitter witticisms on the subject: "Some say that he was killed, others that because of his obvious admiration for His Majesty [the king of Prussia] he had been declared insane. I have always considered poor Peter rather foolish but well-meaning. Now if such is to be the fate of well-meaning fools, what will become of the wicked?"[14]

If treaties had been tantamount to troops, the loss of the Russians would have been balanced by the acquisition of the Turks as allies. On August 4 Frederick wrote Henry that his defensive treaty with Turkey had been signed at last, and that his newest ally was going to assist him by carrying the war at once into Hungary. He would himself immediately send off his ratification of the treaty, and they would soon see its effect upon the conduct of the Austrian army. Henry could then take Dresden and possibly Prague, and could in any case winter his army in Bohemia. He would himself proceed at once with the siege of Schweidnitz, and winter in Moravia. "This will bring us peace, my dear brother," he concluded, "but we shall not get it until toward next spring."[15]

Prince Henry still believed in self-help only. "You notify me of the signing of the treaty with the Turks, [and] I congratulate you. Permit me, however, to add that I have more confidence in [one] heavy gun that you plant before Schweidnitz than in all the diversions in the world."[16]

A month later Frederick conceded that Henry had been right "not to expect a diversion on the part of the Turks." All he had got out of it was two riding horses and a pair of richly caparisoned dromedaries, and the fun of describing to Henry the sensation they created when they arrived in camp; and all the Turkish army had done had been to take a short stroll on Turkish territory near the border.[17]

While Frederick settled down to his siege of Schweidnitz, he would have been glad to see his brother move directly on Dresden; but Prince Henry, although he was making preparations for a siege, preferred to try

---

[13] M.P., VI, 117; *P.C.*, XXII, 42. Frederick must have indicated somehow that the prince should not trust a third person even to decipher his letter; for the interlinear decoded draft of it in the Staatsarchiv is in Henry's own hand, nearly half of its words illegible or left standing incomplete as soon as they began to take recognizable shape.

[14] Hausarchiv, Rep. 56, II, F; Otto Herrmann, in the *Historische Vierteljahrschrift*, XXVI (1931), 373.

[15] *P.C.*, XXII, 110.

[16] August 9, in Schöning, III, 401.

[17] August 13, September 8, 9, 12, in *P. C.*, XXII, 132, 200, 203, 209.

again his favorite old system, attempting to break up the Austrians' service of supply, and so to compel them to retire from the city without his having to shell it. So he sent Seydlitz and Kleist once more into Bohemia in the first week of August, to raid the great supply bases at Lobositz and Leitmeritz (on the Elbe, half way to Prague); but they got only as far as Teplitz. There they found Prince Loewenstein in a position in which their cavalry was practically useless. Seydlitz insisted upon waiting for their infantry to come up — which gave Prince Loewenstein a day in which to strengthen his defenses. Then they attacked and were repulsed with rather heavy losses. The friction and jealousy already existing between Seydlitz and Kleist were intensified by the incident, for each blamed the other for the failure.

Prince Henry was momentarily disheartened by the reverse, but early in September, learning that Hadick — whom he did not "consider very redoubtable" — had replaced Serbelloni as commander in chief of the joint Austrian and Imperial armies, he was thinking again of carrying the war into Bohemia and capturing Dresden by maneuver instead of by siege. How boldly he could follow out his plan, he wrote, would depend upon what risks Frederick was willing to let him run.[18]

Frederick was disinclined either to take or to authorize any avoidable risks. The direct approach to Dresden, followed by a siege if necessary, would be best, he thought. Until both Schweidnitz and Dresden were in their possession, any incursion into Bohemia would be too dangerous for either himself or the prince. It was, to be sure, imperative that Dresden should be taken: the county of Glatz had been held by the Austrians for more than two years and he had no hope of retaking it by force of arms; so he must have Dresden in hand as an equivalent to exchange for it in the negotiations of the coming winter. (A battle-victory would have served as well; but he had ceased to think of that.) To make sure of Dresden, he said, he was thinking of bringing his whole army to Saxony as soon as he had finished at Schweidnitz. Asked outright for his opinion, the prince suggested a number of alternatives which made it quite clear that, while he would welcome reinforcements, he was no more eager to see the king come to Saxony in person than he had been in 1759.[19]

September was a very trying month. Prince Henry watched with no apparent dismay while the storm clouds gathered and Hadick made extensive preparations to attack him; but the nerves of his generals began to crack. Seydlitz and Kleist had become bitter personal enemies as well as rivals. Only a little while before, Generals von Platen and Meyer had

[18] Schöning, III, 426–427.   [19] *P. C.,* XXII, 209, 232; Schöning, III, 443–450.

drawn their swords in a quarrel. Each wounded the other, and faithful old von Hülsen was also hurt when he tried to part them. The prince put them both under arrest at once, but soon had to restore them to their commands because he had no one to replace them. He thought it his duty to report the incident, but was inclined then to drop the matter and forget about it as soon as possible, attributing it chiefly to the overwrought nerves of men too long continuously at war; but the king would not permit him to pass over such a breach of discipline in silence. The reprimand he dictated, which the prince was ordered to deliver verbatim to General Meyer, the junior disputant, was a masterpiece of its kind. It reviewed Meyer's whole career and recalled every blunder the hapless wight had ever committed. If accurate, it was a remarkable feat of memory on the part of the king; but it went beyond the bounds of truth when it stated that the army still had scores of generals who knew their business better than Meyer and who could well be used to replace him. The unhappy general would probably have asked nothing better than to be replaced if that had meant for him the end of the war.[20]

In the king's own army, as the siege of Schweidnitz dragged on and degenerated more and more into a matter of burrowing into the mud, the officers' morale was equally low. Frederick had not the genius for siege operations that he had for the tactics of open-field fighting, nor the patience that such a siege required. He had at first put Tauentzien and Lefebvre in charge of the Schweidnitz operations. Tauentzien was justly famous for his defense of Breslau, and Lefebvre was supposed to have no equal as an engineer except Gribeauval (who was, unfortunately, defending the place); but soon the king was cursing Tauentzien for an ignorant devil who knew nothing about fortifications, and Lefebvre for one equally ignorant of engineering. He was so irritated by their failure that he sometimes refused to speak to them for days at a time, requiring the ubiquitous Major Anhalt to add to his own personal unpopularity by repeating to them orally the stinging messages he dictated. Eventually he took over the immediate direction of the siege in person; but it progressed no better as a result.

Since an assault was too costly to be considered, and successive bombardments had exhausted their munitions without profit, the besiegers had turned to mining operations; but the cold rains of the early autumn season turned the surface into mud, and the miners were made doubly miserable by subsurface drainage and frequent cave-ins. Tauentzien was on the point of placing Major Signoret of the miners' corps under arrest when he found to his dismay that the major would rather be under arrest

[20] *Ibid.*, 406; *P. C.*, XXII, 170.

than go on trying to mine that fortress; so he forced him to go on mining. To hold all his officers to their duty better, Frederick gave orders that every general must spend twenty-four hours of every day at the point of greatest danger in his sector, and exposed himself almost as recklessly. Yet the fortress that only the year before had been lost to Loudon in an hour — the fortress which Mitchell called "one of the worst fortified places in Europe," and which the king had expected to recapture in less than two weeks — withstood him for sixty-three days. It surrendered at last only on October 9.[21]

The king's exceptional irascibility during that period may properly be attributed only in part to his failure to take Schweidnitz as quickly as he had expected, or to the rate at which Prince Henry's cavalrymen were wearing out their horses. During August and September he was also following apprehensively the course of the separate peace negotiations then being conducted by France and Great Britain. He knew just enough about what was happening there to fear the worst for his Rhineland states.

Sir Andrew Mitchell had informed him that France was willing to evacuate Hesse, Brunswick, and Hanover. That much Great Britain would have demanded for herself. France proposed, however, in the interest of her ally Austria, to continue to occupy Prussia's Rhineland territories, Wesel, Cleves, and Geldern, until the general peace. The British had countered with the suggestion that both parties withdraw from German soil, and that thereafter no more troops be furnished or supported by either.[22]

Although Mitchell told him the content of the British reply in the same interview (August 2) in which he reported to him the nature of the French proposals, Frederick could not forget the discontinuance of the subsidy or the Bute-Galitzin incident, and so could not be convinced that Great Britain would ever safeguard his interests at any cost to herself. Hence he replied that the French need not pretend to make a virtue of evacuating Hesse or Cassel, as they had already been driven out of those states by Ferdinand of Brunswick. The British, he said, should hold on to Paderborn and Münster until they had forced the French to agree to mutual and complete evacuation of alien territories then held; but he

[21] It had cost Frederick, in dead and wounded, 86 officers and 2,929 men, and the defenders 85 officers and 3,472 men. It brought him in as prisoners 3 generals, 17 staff officers, 219 other officers, and 8,474 men. It still contained also more than 100,000 pounds of powder and 200,000 pounds of meal. Schöning, III, 466; Jany, II, 633; M. P., VI, 152.

[22] M. P., VI, 119–124. It had already been agreed between Britain and Prussia that some Hanoverian troops were to be furnished Frederick, nominally in his pay and service; so a way could have been found to continue his subsidy in secret if the British ministry had chosen to continue it. France found a way to continue her payments to Austria by claiming the right to pay up "arrears" of subsidies already promised.

reserved the right to settle directly with Maria Theresa, and only with her, all questions in dispute between Prussia and Austria.

He did not say that he had instructed Knyphausen and Michell, in London, to do what they could underhand, by inciting political pamphleteering or other subversive activities, to secure the overthrow of the ministry. They had also tried hard but vainly to pin Grenville down to a promise to make the evacuation of all Prussian territory a prerequisite of any peace settlement even between France and Britain.[23]

On September 18 Mitchell wrote Frederick a long and extraordinarily sharp protest, complaining of his refusal to state his peace terms or to accept British mediation between himself and the empress-queen. It was almost an ultimatum. His government, Sir Andrew said, had already rejected three French proposals as not sufficiently favorable to Prussia; but, unless the king of Prussia announced peace terms acceptable to Great Britain and accepted British mediation between himself and Austria, he would be left to seek his own salvation without further assistance.[24]

The Prussian reply was a wordy and in some parts rather specious defense of the king against any and all charges of bad faith, ingratitude, or insincerity as an ally — and a reminder that such charges should not be made by a ministry with the Bute-Galitzin conversation in its own record. The Prussian government, it continued, did not recede a step from its fundamental position that its quarrel with Austria must be settled only by direct negotiation with Austria, and that the terms of its alliance with Great Britain obligated the British ministry to insist upon the complete and immediate evacuation of Prussian territory by the French.[25]

In spite of Sir Andrew's self-righteous attitude, Britain failed Frederick again in the end. Her treaty with France, signed November 2, provided only that the French should evacuate Prussian territory "as soon as possible." Complete restoration and immediate rather than eventual evacuation of her territory, and the cessation of subsidy payments to

[23] *Ibid.*, 127, 131; *P. C.*, XXII, 135, 114, 117. Mitchell called the king's suspicious attitude "hurtfull to his own Interest and . . . unsuitable to the friendly and generous Openness with which His Majesty [the king of Great Britain] has acted since the Beginning of the Negotiations." In May, 1760, Great Britain had broken off a peace negotiation with France because France had refused to include Prussia in it. See J. H. Rose in the *English Historical Review*, XXIX (1914), 263.

[24] M. P., VI, 139–145.

[25] *Ibid.*, 145–158. Finckenstein's note fills nine long pages in Mitchell's letter book. Sir Andrew thought Frederick had intended to write his own reply to the note, but "finding the Facts suggested in it of an obstinate Nature, and that it would be difficult to justify his own conduct, set in opposition to that of the King, he directed his Secretary of State to make the best answer he could, which, however, I have reason to believe, has been revised and corrected by his Prussian Majesty."

Austria, would have been worth much more to Prussia; for by the Franco-Austrian Convention of Fontainebleau, on November 5, it was agreed that all French artillery, munitions, and other supplies would be turned over by the French *to the Austrians,* if Austrian or Imperial troops could come and get them; also that the old subsidy would be paid up and a new one granted for 1763, disguised as arrearage payments, which might be continued and increased if the war should run on through 1764.[26]

From that time onward the perfidy of the English was a fixed idea in the minds of both Frederick and Henry. It might, to be sure, have been to Prussia's advantage if the king had frankly told the British ministers, both in the early spring when he was negotiating with Russia and again when terms with Austria came into question, that he had no thought of continuing the war in the hope of converting it into one of conquest. He was not the man, however, to make any such announcement. He wanted peace, but he had to make it himself and in his own way. Convinced as he was that terms which he would call honorable and find acceptable were to be had only as the fear of his sword dictated them, he would say or do nothing that his enemies could interpret as a confession of weakness or of weariness. So he would not state his peace terms. As for mediation, he would not trust the British or any other government either to keep his secrets or to handle his affairs. Rather than that, or rather than encourage Maria Theresa by letting her know how he longed for peace, he permitted himself to be left in the lurch by an ally that believed, as Prince Henry had more than once mistakenly believed, that he was continuing the war by choice.

[26] *Ibid.,* 159; Bisset, II, 334; A. Schäfer, II-2, 711–713, 757. Finckenstein protested to Halifax on December 27, in the name of the common interests of Britain and Prussia, of the Protestant religion, and of liberty in Germany.

# CHAPTER XIV

# Friedensturm bei Freiberg

*"At half past six on the morning of the 29th, the army began its advance. Battle of Freiberg. Camped at Freiberg."*—Prince Henry's journal entry for October 29, 1762.

Fortunately for Prussia, the fate of her Rhineland provinces was determined not in Silesia nor in Fontainebleau but on the battlefields of Saxony, and not by Frederick's pen but by the sword of Prince Henry. In that final series of moves it was Hadick who called the first play; but Prince Henry called the last one.

Hadick had been sent to Saxony with orders to attack. His first step had been to call in most of the troops of the Empire, although they had to come by a circuitous route through Bohemia to reach him. His second was to concentrate his forces south of Dresden, thus giving the Prussian patrols greater freedom of movement but at the same time threatening the prince's principal position. His third was to draw reinforcements from Daun's army in Silesia and eastern Bohemia. The prince knew quite well, through spies in Dresden, just what his vis-à-vis was doing, but he waited with an air of complete self-possession for him to make his first move.[1]

That move was made in a series of holding and flanking attacks, from September 27 through September 30. While attacking all along the line, so as to hold the Prussians fast and prevent the shifting of reinforcements to the point of greatest danger, Hadick made good use of his authority as generalissimo to bring the principal weight of the Austrian and Imperial armies to bear from two directions at once upon the prince's exposed right flank. There Prince Henry had placed some of his best troops and his boldest generals, Seydlitz, Kleist, and Belling; but that wing was beaten back to Brand, just south of Freiberg.

The prince himself could not be everywhere at once; but, like Frederick on similar occasions, he tried to be. As Mitchell had said years

[1] Mitchell's confidence in the prince was still unshaken. He complained to Grenville on September 15 that Frederick no longer kept him informed about events in Saxony; but four days later, reporting on what he had heard through other channels about the reorganization and strengthening of the Austrian forces there, he added: "[But] the superior Capacity, Vigilance and Activity of H. R. H. Prince Henry who commands in that Electorate remove almost every ground of Apprehension of Danger in that quarter." M. P., VI, 138, 142.

before, it was in the blood; and where he was present, his presence was felt. On the third day of the offensive, Bahr's battalion on the left of his line lost its footing and was compelled to retreat. "I was present," says the prince's report laconically. The battalion counterattacked, and gained and held a better position in front of its old one. On the fourth day the prince in person checked the retreat and established a new point of resistance near Brand. His position was still dangerously extended — from Meissen through Freiberg to Brand — thinly held, and partially surrounded by an enemy that outnumbered him three to two in totals and more than two to one around Freiberg; but his losses had not been heavy and the situation had never at any point got entirely out of hand.

With obvious regret but without apology, he reported to the king that he had given ground but had kept his forces in hand. The enemy turning movement had threatened to cut off his only line of retreat, he wrote, and, with no reserves available, he had had to try to stop fifteen battalions with four. Both armies had been three days and nights in bivouac and Henry himself had "gone three nights without lying down, on horseback day and night," although he had been confined to his bed by illness for eight days before the battle began.[2]

Hadick found his reputation greatly enhanced at home, as he had managed by a combination of fighting and maneuvering to force "the master of maneuver and of defense," Prince Henry, out of a position he had held all summer; but the Prussians were not correspondingly downcast. Eichel wrote to Finckenstein, five days before the retaking of Schweidnitz, giving thanks to God that such a soldier as Prince Henry was commanding in Saxony, and wishing that the king might give as good an account of himself in Silesia.[3]

The king himself wrote the prince that the Freiberg position into which he had been driven was superior to the one at Pretzschendorf which he had been forced to abandon — provided he fortified it adequately. He uttered no word of blame for the retreat, nor of criticism, save that the prince was still trying to cover too much ground. Concentrated positions were better, he said; in such an extended one the prince was in danger of being beaten in detail.[4]

The prince was well aware of the danger of having his widely sep-

[2] Schmitt, *Prinz Heinrich*, II, 256–259; Schöning, III, 455–457. The prince's whole position still covered approximately thirty English miles.

[3] *P. C.*, XXII, 253; Schmitt, *Prinz Heinrich*, II, 258.

[4] *Ibid.*, 251–266. He had probably forgotten that his last comment on that subject had been: "You don't cover enough ground"; but then he had been talking about foraging, and now it was a question of defense — as it had been when, earlier still, he had said "You try to cover too much."

arated posts attacked separately and destroyed; but he preferred to run that risk while keeping in close touch with his enemy rather than leave Hadick free to maneuver at will without his knowledge. He was confident also that he had evolved the system best fitted to the hills and valleys of the region. So, without making any change in his dispositions in response to Frederick's criticisms, he replied: "I am quite of your opinion that compact positions are better than extended ones; but one must take one's position *not as one would wish but as the terrain permits.*" He had plenty of patrols out, he said, to give him timely warning of any enemy movement; so instead of waiting to be attacked he would "go to meet" the new danger, or would have ample time to evade it by retiring to another position.[5]

The first half of October passed rather quietly, while Hadick prepared for a new drive and the prince made what he thought were adequate counterpreparations to meet it. On the first day of the renewed offensive, October 14, he did resist it successfully enough, and reported that night that he had lost no ground and no prisoners, had had only a few hundred men killed and wounded, and had taken several hundred prisoners. Attacks had been made all along the line; but those on the left of his position where von Hülsen was in command, and on the center where he had commanded in person, had been of a secondary character only. His exposed right wing, under Syburg at Brand, had again had the hardest fighting to do, and was obviously in danger; so that night the prince himself moved over there with such reinforcements as he could muster by drawing them out of the lines elsewhere. He had no real reserves left.

The second day's battle was far worse than the first. Again the principal weight of the Austrian and Imperial forces was thrown against the prince's right flank, while holding attacks were made all along the line. At Brand several successive assaults were repulsed; but in the darkness of the early evening the prince, who had himself narrowly escaped capture, was obliged to withdraw to Reichenbach — losing both Brand and Freiberg, one whole regiment and one battalion of another as units,

[5] Schöning, III, 472. The italics are Prince Henry's own. The self-restraint that Henry displayed in answering Frederick was sadly lacking in the comments on the king which he permitted himself to make at this time to Ferdinand, to whom he always showed his ugliest side. For example, he exclaimed on October 5 that at last the world would realize that he had a real army facing him, and not the mere 16,000 men that "that scoundrel" had publicly said. "I have never had a very high opinion of the merits of a certain man, but . . . after six years during which I have been in a much better position to know him he has inspired in me only the greatest contempt and indignation. I have every reason to look upon him as the most wicked and most miserable of creatures. I have made no secret of my opinion, and the Personage is well aware that I know him [for what he is]. That is the reason why I can often speak rather boldly. . . . Nonetheless, after the Peace, I must expect to be persecuted by the Personage, for he is too vain, too envious and wicked

and a total of approximately two thousand men in killed, wounded, prisoners of war, and deserters. Von Hülsen, with the center and left sections of the army, had to retire to the old Schlettau-Kätzenhäuser positions. It was the worst day's fighting of the whole war for Prince Henry. He admitted to Frederick in his report the next day that it had been fortunate for him that darkness had set in when it did, enabling him to withdraw under its cover without still heavier losses.[6]

It was undeniably a reverse of a serious nature, but hardly serious enough to be called a major disaster or to prevent the prince from winning in subsequent years a legendary reputation, based on Frederick's alleged praise of him, as Prussia's one general who never blundered — *der fehlerlose Feldherr*. In his report to the king he scorned either to gloss over the facts or to apologize for them, although he was obviously expecting some criticism and trying to answer it in advance. On a large piece of rough, uncut paper and in great haste he wrote a full and faithful account of it, and concluded:

I shall do everything possible to maintain myself on this side of the Mulde, but I need more men and cannot offer resistance everywhere. I am sorry to give you this disagreeable news; and I should be sorrier still if I had to reproach myself with any negligence; but I have not spared myself and I have done my full duty; as to that, I can call the whole world to witness. . . . The only thing that hurts me is to see myself obliged to give you this disagreeable news. . . .

I received yesterday the letter in which you ask me for some miners: I shall do all that present circumstances permit in this matter.

I have here neither paper nor equipage; you will therefore pardon me for writing you in such haste and a little in disorder. One does not have a perfectly free mind after such cruel fatigues, especially when one's worries and exertions have been in vain.[7]

On the next day, October 17, he counterattacked, "to let the enemy know that the reverse we have suffered has in no way disheartened us," and regained some small part of the ground lost. Every day, he said, he would feel the enemy out enough to make sure of his position and to delay, if possible, any further attacks upon his own.

Meanwhile, Schweidnitz having fallen, reinforcements for both sides

not to avenge himself upon me for the service I have done him." Hausarchiv, Rep. 56, II, F; cited also by Otto Herrmann, in the *Historische Vierteljahrschrift*, XXVI (1931), 371.

[6] That admission is quoted by von Bernhardi, in *Friedrich der Grosse*, II, 603, but without its context.

On October 23 Frederick wrote to Ferdinand of Brunswick that Prince Henry's army was 20,000 men short of its nominal strength, and his own 8,000 to 10,000 short. *P. C.*, XXII, 287.

[7] Schöning, III, 479; *P. C.*, XXII, 281; Frederick had asked him to find some miners in Saxony for use in Silesia, on a six-year contract basis.

were en route from Silesia to Saxony. Frederick had sent Major Count Henckel von Donnersmarck ahead of the Prussian detachment of twenty thousand men being brought by General Wied, to tell the prince in detail about its numbers, equipment, and probable march route, and to explain to him several suggested ways in which he might use it. The king himself would go on to Leipzig to arrange for supplies and contributions from there and from the area to the westward, leaving Prince Henry in charge of the military operations around Dresden.

It was obvious to all that the year's campaign would come to a climax near Dresden — and soon. At all costs the Prussians must at least maintain their position there. If they were to hope for peace that winter, Frederick reasoned, they must recapture Dresden. Prince Henry, without specifically saying so, was already maturing in his mind as an alternative project the idea of seeking a decisive battle-victory that would compel Austria to ask for peace.

To the difficulty of choosing between those alternatives was added the problem of timing the steps necessary for the attainment of either objective. The prince correctly estimated that, because the Austrians held the interior line and had therefore a shorter road to travel, the reinforcements which Prince Albert of Saxony was bringing to Hadick would arrive several days before Count Wied could get there. It could then be taken for granted that Hadick, when joined by Prince Albert, would attack Prince Henry immediately, anticipating Wied's arrival. Even if he waited, he would gain more than the prince could from the delay, as his reinforcement was the stronger of the two. The prince therefore made the bold but prudent decision to attack before either reinforcement could arrive.

So presented, his decision would appear to have been merely the only possible answer to a problem in simple arithmetic. But it was really not so simple a matter; the prince's mind and character were far too complex to permit him to solve such a problem on a purely mathematical basis. His emotions and some personal considerations figured also to some extent in his solution.

On October 19 he had sent Count Henckel to the king to explain to him the various projects he had in mind, one of which was a counter-attack at Freiberg. Frederick replied that at least a "demonstration" ought to be made somewhere, and that Henry might possibly be able to retake Freiberg without waiting for Wied. If he failed at Freiberg, he might add Wied's force to his own and either try again there or return to his older project of an incursion into Bohemia.[8]

[8] Schöning, III, 482; *P. C.*, XXII, 285. Wied's name was sometimes written as Neuwied.

On the twenty-fifth, still without actually announcing that he had determined upon it, the prince finally outlined to Frederick his Freiberg project. Bridges were ready for the use of Wied's detachment and all arrangements were made for provisioning and using it when it arrived; but he did not know yet when that would be. Hadick, on the other hand, was said to be already receiving reinforcements, which were being so placed that they could move easily into either Freiberg or Dresden. The longer he waited the harder it would be to recapture Freiberg, and that place was too badly needed as winter quarters to be left in enemy hands.[9]

On the day of the battle of Freiberg Frederick wrote a dispatch recording his full approval of the prince's intention to fight it.

Three other considerations entered into Prince Henry's decision to attack when he did. The Austrian and Imperial troops were industriously fortifying themselves in Freiberg, and daily strengthening their grip upon it. Then on October 22 he was attacked all day long in all his advanced posts; and, while he held his ground everywhere, he was clearly in danger of having the initiative taken entirely away from him. And finally, another of Frederick's acid postscripts was eating into his skin.

On October 21, when he received his brother's first report on the reverse at Brand, the king had dictated an official dispatch admirable for its restraint though patently studied in its moderation; but he could not sign it and send it off without adding the comment that someone — he did not know exactly who — must have failed to do his duty, or the machine would not have broken down as it had done. If he had been at Freiberg, he said, with that number of troops and in a position so easy to defend, he would have defied anyone in the world to dislodge him — provided his troops had done their duty.[10]

In his correspondence with the king Prince Henry gave no indication of the effect of that postscript upon him; but a telltale phrase in a subsequent letter to Ferdinand revealed it plainly enough: "He thought I was whipped (*battu de l'oiseau*), and began to insult me."[11]

So sensitiveness, pride, and the angry resolve to show Frederick that he was not "whipped" — as well as mathematics and other military considerations — played their part in bringing the prince to the point of making, without waiting for reinforcements, an attack that took everyone but Frederick by surprise.[12]

---

[9] *Ibid.*, 297; Schöning, III, 487.

[10] *P. C.*, XXII, 281. The prince had reported that two of his regiments had not behaved as they should.

[11] Hausarchiv, Rep. 56, II, F. The letter is cited also by Otto Herrmann in the *Historische Vierteljahrschrift*, XXVI (1931), 368, 379; it was written just after the battle of Freiberg.

[12] Even Frederick had expected him to wait for Wied. *P. C.*, XXII, 294. Some of his critics have said that Henry attacked when he did because the detested Major Anhalt was

The broken character of the country around Freiberg, and the number of natural and man-made obstacles to be evaded or overcome, compelled the prince to send his men forward in four separate columns, which were moved into their jumping-off positions during the night of October 28–29. Prince Stolberg, in command of the joint Austrian-Imperial force in the town, was warned by a deserter, so got his men under arms shortly after midnight, but was unable to get up any reinforcements. So, as they stood, the defenders numbered about thirty thousand and the attackers twenty-four thousand or less.

The prince's plan of battle was something of an innovation in that it involved cooperation between four columns acting simultaneously but more or less independently. It has been freely criticized because it was so complicated, and therefore dangerous. Actually it was an adaptation of Frederick's old practice — to deliver his principal attack with only one wing of his army as he had done at Burkersdorf — the difference being that the prince proposed to attack on both wings at once. That suited the ground over which he had to operate, and although the plan was subsequently condemned by von Clausewitz and Napoleon, it has always had at least one thing to be said for it: it worked.

The position to be attacked was a line of fortifications on the hills northwest of the town of Freiberg, facing northwest. In front of the principal position was an extensive wood known as the Spittelwald, made practically impassable by felled trees and other obstructions. East of Freiberg, roughly from south to north, flowed a small stream, the east fork of the upper Mulde. On the southern edge of the town was the key to its defenses, a position called the Three Crosses.

Not even Frederick himself had ever planned a battle which aimed more plainly at the total destruction of the enemy army. The prince's intention was that Seydlitz, with the strongest column, should make a detour around the southwestern edge of the Spittelwald and approach the Three Crosses from the south. There the principal attack was to be delivered. The younger Stutterheim meanwhile should advance through the Spittelwald as best he could, while his brother, "old" Stutterheim, made the secondary attack by moving along the eastern side of the wood, between it and the Mulde, and striking the Austrian postion from the north. So Stolberg would find himself caught between the jaws of a pair of pincers which, as they closed upon him, exerted their greatest

with Wied and he feared that Anhalt might be credited with any victory won after his arrival; others that he feared that Frederick, in spite of his promise not to do so, would supersede him again as in 1759 if he waited. Neither accusation seems justified.

Count Henckel, his former aide, however, was one of those who congratulated him early in November upon having won his victory just in time to avoid being robbed of the credit for it.

pressure at their points. If he failed to stop "young" Stutterheim's advance through the Spittelwald, his position would be pierced in front; while if he permitted himself to be too much distracted by the frontal attack, the points of the pincers would meet behind him and cut off his retreat. The rear of the attacking Prussians, on the other hand, was to be protected by their fourth column, under Forcade, whose only duty was to see to it that they were not interrupted in their work by the untimely arrival of Austrian reinforcements.

It would be very remarkable if such a battle could have been fought without some change of plan; but the changes which the prince found necessary were amazingly slight. He accompanied the Seydlitz column, on his extreme right, where the hardest fighting was to be expected and had in fact to be done. As he approached the town from the southwest after rounding the Spittelwald, a body of Austrian troops was discovered on the heights near Brand, south of Freiberg, in a position to threaten his right flank and rear if he went on and left it there. So he had to leave a detachment of approximately equal strength to block it out — which weakened his attacking column perceptibly, just at the moment of the attack.[13]

Everything depended upon the subordinate commanders. They did not attain perfect coordination of all arms and all units, but they came surprisingly near it. Seydlitz, the peerless leader of cavalry charges, was not always equally fortunate when forced to conduct infantry operations as well; but that day he distinguished himself in both capacities. Captain Kalckreuth, the prince's aide-de-camp, showed considerable resourcefulness in carrying out the prince's orders to arrange for liaison and cooperation between the columns of the two Stutterheims. Everyone who had it in him had an opportunity to distinguish himself: the prince used all the men he had, with the exception of the two detachments detailed to protect the rest from interference, and the action lasted three hours.[14]

Forcade found nothing to do, for the Austrians beyond the Mulde left Stolberg to his fate. First at the Three Crosses before Prince Henry, Seydlitz, and Kleist; then on their northeastern flank before "old" Stut-

[13] It is one of the legends of Freiberg that General Kleist told the prince he knew the commander of the Austrian detachment at Brand, General Meyer, well enough to wager his life on it that he would simply stand there and watch whatever happened, without coming down off his hill. Whether the story be true or false, that is precisely what General Meyer did. His only contribution to his country's cause that day was to show himself, and so to hold one Prussian infantry brigade out of action.

The prince, who found the Austrian left wing stronger than he had thought it, has been blamed by unfriendly critics for not originally making his own right stronger than it was; but in the event the work of "old" Stutterheim's column proved to be almost equally important.

[14] From 5:00 to 8:00 A. M. Prince Henry's journal, quoted at the head of this chapter, differs from other accounts as to the hour of its beginning.

terheim; then in the center, the defenders gave way and got back across the Mulde in great confusion. Before the middle of the forenoon the Prussians were in possession of all the day's objectives and had reoccupied their old camps on the heights of the Mulde east and southeast of the town of Freiberg. If Forcade had shown the same energy and initiative as the others and cut off the retreat of the fugitives when his first mission had clearly lost its point, the victory would have been more complete. As it was, the Prussians took 79 officers and 4,340 men as prisoners, 28 guns, and 11 battle flags. Their own losses were about 1,400, dead and wounded. Enemy casualties, killed and wounded, had been about twice as heavy. The striking disparity in the numbers of battle casualties is evidence of the skill with which the attackers had used the woods and the broken ground (which might have been considered obstacles) for their concealment and protection as they advanced. They had shown not only a new flexibility in attack but a new economy of men.[15]

Prince Henry's two epistolary reports on the battle of Freiberg, written that night, were less laconic than his journal entry but, even so, wasted few words. The story he had to tell the king gained more than it lost in effectiveness from his self-contained understatement:

My very dear brother: It is a joy to me to give you the agreeable news that your army has won today a considerable advantage over the combined army of the Austrians and of the Empire. . . . I made two real attacks and two false ones. The enemy offered a stubborn resistance but the sustained valor of your troops prevailed, and after three hours' firing the enemy was obliged to give way everywhere. . . . They intended to attack me, as of tomorrow, but they will hardly be thinking of that just now. General Wied will cross the Elbe tomorrow, I believe; that comes just at the right time for me.[16]

To his brother Ferdinand he wrote with less restraint:

Here is some unexpected news for you. Heaven has assisted me, and the army has won a complete victory. . . . I saw the moment when all was lost, and that moment was terrible; but nothing gave way, [and] the courage of the officers and the exactitude with which my plan was executed — everything contributed to my good fortune. . . .

The king will be greatly surprised. He thought I was whipped, and began to insult me. I did not say a word to him [in answer], and went ahead with my plan — but it is God who has made it possible, and the valor of the men — among others that of General Seydlitz who fought with the infantry.

---

[15] "Now *there was* a battle!" was the comment which Kalckreuth said he had heard everywhere in the Silesian army when he carried the news of Freiberg to the king; "great success and small losses! Here we are made to crack our heads like dogs, to no purpose." *Paroles,* 273. The Austrian losses both in prisoners and in casualties were much heavier than the Imperial, because they had fought more stubbornly.

[16] Schöning, III, 491; *Oeuvres,* XXVI, 295.

Pardon me if I give you no details. Borck can tell you those, and I am so overwhelmed by fatigue, and so fully occupied still, that I can do no more.

Adieu. My compliments to your Princess; tell her that it is impossible for me to write to her, and that she must not impute that to any want of attention on my part. Henri.[17]

Next day, while Belling and Kleist followed up the retreating Austrians, their commander found time to write to Sir Andrew Mitchell:

My greatest satisfaction is that our own loss was not excessive and that, at least, blood was not poured out extravagantly. We had at most 1,700 men killed and wounded, which is a special favor of Providence; for the firing was lively and long-continued, and it is incomprehensible to all who witnessed the day's action that it did not cost more. . . .

It is the Austrians who have suffered most heavily; we have very few prisoners from among the Imperial troops. It is known that the enemy intended to attack me the 30th; this is verified by papers captured with their equipage.

I have sent no special messenger to inform the king your master of this event; but I hope that the king [of Prussia] will discharge that obligation. You are too familiar with the rules governing my conduct to disapprove of my using a certain amount of finesse with respect to the king with whom I have to deal. . . .[18]

The prince's letter to the king was carried by his aide-de-camp, Captain Kalckreuth. Kalckreuth was himself mentioned in it as having been "ordered to help conduct the attack by way of the Spittelwald," for which he was promptly promoted on Prince Henry's recommendation. The prince also wrote of him: "My aide-de-camp is fully informed and can tell you whatever you may wish to know of our present situation." [19]

If Kalckreuth then told the king what he subsequently told the world about his own part in the battle, and if Frederick believed him, it is not surprising that he was made a major at once. In his reminiscences,

---

[17] Hausarchiv, Rep. 56, II, F; quoted in part by Otto Herrmann in the *Historische Vierteljahrschrift*, XXVI (1931), 379. If the victor of Freiberg wrote a letter to his own princess that night, it has not been preserved either among his papers or among hers; but she celebrated his victory with a grand ball as soon as the news of it reached Magdeburg. Her guests danced till four in the morning. Lehndorff, *Dreissig Jahre, Nachträge*, I, 359.

[18] M. P., XLIII, 54–55. It was customary for one monarch to send the other by special messenger an immediate report of an event of more than ordinary importance. Mitchell had also sometimes sent Prince Henry similar reports of British victories, and had asked for special accounts of the prince's campaigns, which he as intermediary had sent on to King George. But it would have been an extraordinary procedure for a subject of one king to address himself directly to another monarch as Prince Henry evidently thought of doing. Fortunately he also thought better of it.

[19] Three adjutants, Lieutenants von Schwerin, von Klinckowström, and von Hausen, were made captains. Seydlitz and Kleist were especially praised for their conduct. The prince also recommended von Anhalt for promotion soon after he arrived with Count Wied. *P. C.*, XXII, 307; Schöning, III, 492–494.

published after Prince Henry's death, he modestly claimed for himself very nearly all the credit for the victory. According to Kalckreuth the older Stutterheim's attack was planned by the prince as only a demonstration. It was Kalckreuth who on his own initiative, in the midst of the action, had prevailed upon Stutterheim to attack in earnest — and so decided the issue. The prince, he claimed, had publicly acknowledged his indebtedness to him and had written the king that Kalckreuth was responsible for the victory! The king, according to the same fanciful account, refused to believe that such a battle had been fought and won until the story had been retold from beginning to end. Then he dictated a long and decidedly unfavorable critique of the prince's whole campaign, which the new-made major was ordered to repeat to his chief when he returned to Saxony; but the generous Kalckreuth was far too loyal and sportsmanlike to do that; so he kept it to himself and confided it — and his own disobedience of the royal command — only to his *Paroles* after the other principals were dead.[20]

Certainly there was no faultfinding in Frederick's written responses to the good news. The first, which Kalckreuth carried back with him, was all graciousness:

The arrival of Kalckreuter and of your letter, my dear brother, has taken twenty years off my age. Yesterday I was sixty, today eighteen. I bless Heaven that it has preserved you in good health and that things have come off so happily. You have done right to anticipate those who were about to attack you, and by your wise and sound arrangements you have overcome all the difficulties of a strong post and a vigorous resistance. This service you have done the state is so important that I cannot adequately express my appreciation of it, and must wait to do it in person. . . .

I have ordered the firing of salutes from Lauban to Frankenstein and Neisse, to celebrate your victory and to return, with better justification, the compliment of the Austrians who gave us the same unpleasant serenade the 26th of last month. If fortune favors our designs on Dresden we shall unquestionably have peace this winter or next spring, and we shall extricate ourselves honorably from a difficult and perilous situation in which we have often found ourselves only two steps from total destruction. By this victory, you alone will have the glory of having struck the final blow against Austrian obstinacy, and of having laid the first foundations of the public felicity which will grow out of the peace.[21]

Frederick's second letter, written two days later, showed his relief even more plainly: "All our hills have re-echoed the sound of your vic-

[20] Kalckreuth, *Paroles*, 252–254, 273–274; Schöning, III, 499.
[21] P. C., XXII, 303; *Oeuvres*, XXVI, 259. Von Crousaz attributes to the king the follow-

tory. To make the thing more touching, the guns have fired loaded projectiles wherever our posts were in touch with the enemy. This bit of gallantry will not be to their taste but it is tit for tat, and you have given me great pleasure by providing me so soon with an occasion to pay them off." [22]

The king instructed Rexin at Constantinople to tell the Turks that Prince Henry had captured a hundred officers and eight thousand men, forty guns, and eight flags. Writing to the Duke of Bevern, he cut all those figures exactly in half; for Goltz in St. Petersburg he reduced them only twenty-five per cent. Statistics, after all, meant little at such a moment to him or to anyone else; only the fact of the victory, and its probable effect upon the Austrian government, was of any real significance. [23]

That effect was paralyzing. The empress-queen's almost indomitable will was broken at last and she fully shared the disheartenment of her generals. "The damage is not so slight," she conceded. To regain Freiberg would be so costly that it would mean the ruin of the army. To hold Dresden, seventy to eighty thousand men would be needed; and no one knew where they could be found. To ask the army to spend another winter cooped up between Dresden and Dippoldiswalde, under conditions even worse than those of the past two winters, seemed at once heartless and useless. In a general sense, neither side could attain anything more than "peace without victory"; but for Prussia, peace through victory in the last great battle of the war was almost within reach. [24]

Because they realized that the full fruits of the victory would be reaped only if they showed themselves able and ready to follow it up, the king and Prince Henry did not wait for information about the immediate effect of Freiberg upon Austrian morale, but turned their minds at once to plans for a further offensive. The prince moved on through Freiberg to Pretzschendorf, but until Wied's corps became available on November 4 little could be done except to keep in touch with the retreating enemy and feel out his position at Dippoldiswalde. Wied then took over von Hülsen's part of the line while von Hülsen joined the prince, and Kleist was sent once more into Bohemia. He was aiming at Leitmeritz again

ing eulogy of his brother: "The highest praise that one can give Prince Henry is the narrative of his deeds. Those who understand such things readily discern in them that happy mixture of prudence and boldness which alone can make a complete and a great warrior." H. von Crousaz, *Prinz Heinrich, der Bruder Friedrichs des Grossen* (Berlin, 1876), 4. (The quotation, however, stands undocumented.)

[22] *P. C.*, XXII, 307; *Oeuvres*, XXVI, 260. He also said that he was "infinitely happy" that the prince's losses had been so light. "That is nobly done," he wrote, "not to water your laurels with our tears."

[23] *P. C.*, XXII, 302, 305.

[24] Von Arneth, *Geschichte Maria Theresias*, VI, 345–346.

but could go no farther than Saaz, where he destroyed stores worth nearly a million gulden. Then, as bad roads and weather combined with enemy resistance to stop him, Prince Henry recalled him to Chemnitz and told the king that he thought the campaign on that part of the front should be considered closed for the year. The Austrians were confined once more to their old Plauen and Dippoldiswalde positions, but were still in possession of Dresden.[25]

While he was making his way from Silesia to Saxony, the king had been heralded every day by couriers who could ride faster than he, bearing letters in which he discussed with Prince Henry whether they should turn their attention for the remainder of that season to Bohemia or to the smaller states of the Empire. They agreed that if Kleist's Bohemian raid should reach the great supply base at Leitmeritz and lead to the evacuation of Dresden, that would be of incalculable value to them because it would probably bring them peace almost at once. As soon as Kleist was stopped in Bohemia and recalled to Saxony, on the day on which the Berlin churches were singing their *Te Deum* for Freiberg, the prince proposed that Kleist be sent into Franconia. A prolonged raiding expedition into that area, he wrote, could easily reach Bamberg and Nuremberg and might help materially to hasten the coming of peace by causing the lesser states of the Empire to desert their Austrian alliance and recall their troops, as Austria could not protect them. If the peace offensive failed and the war had to go on, Kleist could find winter quarters there and raise men, money, and supplies for the next year's fighting.[26]

Before he knew the outcome of the Bohemian venture, and before he could have received his brother's letter proposing a new campaign in Franconia, Frederick had proposed precisely the same thing as an alternative, alleging identical reasons for it and using very nearly the same words.[27]

On November 11, after an interview with Prince Henry, he instructed his agent Plotho at Regensburg to warn the men representing the other states in the Imperial Diet there that Kleist was coming and would be

[25] Schöning, III, 496. While Kleist was gone, Wied had pushed ahead from the *Kätzenhäuser* and taken a new position on the Landsberg, but he was recalled from it by Frederick. He had been ably assisted in the enterprise by von Anhalt and von Prittwitz. Prince Henry had protested that he thought the new position too dangerous, even before he knew that it had been given up, and before he realized that both the taking and the abandoning of it had been ordered by Frederick. Although the prince remained nominally in command, some worse conflict of authority and confusion of orders must soon have arisen if active hostilities had continued — unless Frederick either took over the command or learned better not to interfere with it. *Ibid.*, 501–508.
[26] November 7, from Freiberg, in Schöning, III, 504.
[27] November 4, from Sprottau, in *P. C.*, XXII, 306.

ordered to treat as enemy territory all states that still had troops in the field against Prussia. Only those that recalled their troops and made an immediate peace with Prussia would be spared.[28]

Only a week after his return from Bohemia, the hard-riding Kleist was off for Franconia; and another week later, on November 29, he was in Bamberg. Nuremberg, Würzburg, Rothenburg, and smaller towns of the region soon saw his war-hardened horsemen come and go; and Ratisbon, pathetic substitute for a capital but the only one the Empire had, found him at its gates. Tradition tells that his men watered their horses in the Danube near there as a gesture of defiance to Austria and Empire alike.

Several of the states made peace. Others complained bitterly because Austria refused to release their troops, yet failed to protect them; but their complaints were useless. Nothing but peace with Prussia would save their towns from being levied upon for millions of thaler in ransom money, or the countryside from being plundered, or their substantial citizens from being carried off as hostages. Cynics have indeed suggested that Frederick was better pleased when they failed to make peace promptly enough, and so put themselves at his mercy, than when they stayed his hand by a timely compliance with his demands. Certainly that phase of the war paid him a profit, both directly and indirectly.

The indirect profit was in the form of pressure upon Austria to make peace. On November 20, from Meissen, Frederick wrote to Prince Henry joyfully and gratefully:

The Austrians have asked for a convention for the winter. . . . Once this convention is made, there is nothing to prevent the troops from going into quarters at once. The readiness which the Austrians have shown to listen to reason on this occasion is a result of the good lesson you taught them at Freiberg. We must always call upon you to give lessons in manners to our disdainfully arrogant enemies. I shall inform you on all the points upon which the commissaries agree; at least, we shall enjoy some solid repose during the winter.[29]

[28] *Ibid.,* 315.
[29] *P. C.,* XXII, 334. In the same series of letters the two defenders of the Prussian state were exchanging comments on its prospective ruler. Prince Frederick William, who had been with Frederick at Schweidnitz, was visiting Henry's headquarters at Freiberg. His uncle had permitted him to visit the pit-mouths of some of the mines of the region but had not thought it wise to let him go underground. He had found his nephew "polite and attractive"; he commented favorably on the young man's "free and engaging manner" and the military training he had evidently got from Frederick during the campaign, and spoke with astonishment of his "enormous" size. Frederick had written long before that he and Henry were "both pygmies beside him." Frederick wondered how Henry would keep the young fellow amused. The prince would rather dance than anything else, the king said; but there would not be any dancing partners at Freiberg, even after the signing of an armistice. Schöning, III, 513–515.

Relief was in sight! Rest for the weary soldiers, rewards for the prince, and for the king the lifting of such a load from his shoulders that he felt no need of other compensation or of the repose that he was never to find while he lived.

He began showering honors and rewards upon his brother as soon as they met at Meissen, on November 9. Since so many of their previous meetings and discussions, like the meeting of flint and steel, had struck off sparks and led to explosions, every friendly reporter of this one considered it news and hastened to assure those interested that this time nothing of that sort had happened. Henry confided to Ferdinand that everything had gone off admirably. Frederick had made no attempt to dominate the interview, had been gracious to everyone, and had granted everything that was asked of him.[30]

It would have been tragic indeed if that interview had been spoiled, as so many others had been, by some gaucherie or outburst of temper on the part of either; for the prince came to it at his own repeated request, wearing laurels, and the king bearing gifts. Frederick ordained that the prince should be attended always thereafter by a bodyguard of twenty-four hussars — a guard equal to his own, and an honor which he shared only with Prince Ferdinand of Brunswick. He made him a present of two fiefs, the bailliages of Wegeleben and Westerburg, worth ten thousand thaler a year, with the right of survivorship going to his wife, Princess Henry. He also approved all the promotions and rewards recommended by the prince, and the next day rode out with him and Seydlitz to view the battlefields around Freiberg and to hear again their accounts of that day's work.[31]

On November 24 an armistice was signed by Austria and Prussia. Frederick told Prince Henry of it the next day, saying that it was as advantageous as they could hope for, and calling it again "a consequence of your success, which has made the fiercest of mortals compliant and conciliatory."[32]

Released from field service, and with his troops already in winter quarters and busy with their annual reconditioning, the prince took up his residence in a country house belonging to Count Bünau at Dahlen, near Hubertusburg. From there he followed the course of the peace negotiations as best he could, from Frederick's frequent confidential accounts of them. He would have been glad to go to Berlin for a fortnight,

---

[30] Hausarchiv, Rep. 56, II, F. Sir Andrew Mitchell and the queen of Prussia also passed along reports which had reached them to the effect that the interview had "gone off very well." M. P., VI, 160; Berner and Volz, 448.

[31] *P. C.*, XXII, 332; Schöning, III, 501–508; M. P., VI, 160, 161. The fiefs of Wegeleben and Westerburg had fallen vacant on the death of the margrave Charles of Brandenburg.

[32] *P. C.*, XXII, 349.

but the king's permission for that was not granted until after the turn of the year.

Nearly five years before, he had written to Ferdinand: "If we only do our duty, we can look on with indifference (if we are still alive at the end of the war) while the men of blood repartition Europe." But on November 24, 1762, he indicated to Sir Andrew Mitchell that he would not hesitate to go to Leipzig if Frederick wanted him there. Otherwise, he would welcome the opportunity to sit down in Dahlen and recuperate from the buffeting he had had to stand during the past seven years of campaigning.[33]

However firmly he might say either to himself or to others that he wanted only an opportunity to retire and rest, he could not be content with the role of an observer during the peace conference; but the king would not use his own brother as a plenipotentiary where only a messenger was wanted and where young Hertzberg would do as well; and Prince Henry would never have been a perfectly satisfactory interpreter of another man's ideas in any negotiation, even if Frederick had been willing so to use him. Frederick, on the other hand, was constitutionally incapable of using either Henry or anyone else in a genuinely confidential advisory capacity in matters of such character or such importance.

So although Prince Henry was invited to royal headquarters in Leipzig for a few days in the middle of December, he went only as a distinguished guest.[34] The war was over; and with it had ended, although it took him years to realize it, that period of his life during which his unique usefulness to the state had earned him the right to stand in the sun beside the king. With the signing of the armistice, the soldier-prince was no longer so imperatively needed; and although he was not yet thirty-seven years old he was already about to enter into the long twilight of a life spent in the shadow of the throne and of his own heroic deeds.

[33] Hausarchiv, Rep. 56, II, F; M. P., XLIII, 55.

[34] It was probably there and then, if ever, that the incident occurred to which he subsequently owed the proud title of *der fehlerlose Feldherr*. According to the oft-repeated story, Frederick, at a great banquet for his generals, reviewed the career of each of them in the war, admitting and criticizing his own errors as freely as any — then offered a toast to Prince Henry as "the only one of us who, in the course of the whole war, has never made a mistake." The king may have offered just such a toast. If he did, however, it is impossible not to suspect that there was a certain amount of irony in it, although he was so happy over Freiberg that no praise was too high, just then, for the man who had won that decisive battle.

CHAPTER XV

# 𝔥𝔬𝔪𝔢-𝔠𝔬𝔪𝔦𝔫𝔤

*"I am . . . a stranger here."*—Frederick.
*"I am not in any way attached to anything in Berlin; the memory of the past is very painful to me, and the life that one leads there [now] seems quite insipid."*—Henry to Frederick.

FREDERICK's peace terms were simple. He had only to state them once, briefly, and adhere to them while Count Kaunitz estimated the cost of another year or two of war, weighed the danger of a Turkish invasion of Hungary, and brought his colleagues and the empress-queen to the point of confessing their failure. Frederick would cede no territory, not even Glatz; but when Austria was ready to concede that point, peace was possible at any time; and Austria had as good reason as Prussia to wish that it be made quickly.

Unless Russia should intervene! Before formal negotiations had begun, Frederick had received a letter from Catherine II that ostensibly offered her friendly services as a mediator but looked ominously like a threat. In it the empress reminded the king of Prussia that she had been and still was in a position to ruin him, and said she hoped he realized how difficult it had been for her to avoid being drawn into the war.[1]

Catherine would evidently have liked to have a hand in drawing up the peace treaty—a concession which Frederick had no thought of making either to her or to any other outsider. Yet he dared not offend her. He devoted three days of serious thought to his reply; choosing not to risk an outright refusal of her offer of mediation, he pretended merely to defer his acceptance of it.

Naturally, he wrote in self-justification. He knew, he said, that the British, after having failed so shamefully to safeguard his interests in their own preliminary treaty with France, had revived at St. Petersburg their old accusation that he did not really want to make peace. "There are some kinds of peace, Madame," he replied to that charge, "to which I am opposed, because they are contrary to the dignity and the glory of any sovereign, no matter who he may be. . . . Up to now," he said, the number of my enemies has put me into no position to make peace; and as long as these enemies announced openly that they proposed to exterminate

[1] A. Schäfer, II–2, 759–760.

226

the very name of Prussia, I could not have consented to a peace unless I were either frightfully irresponsible or completely imbecile.

As the Empress-Queen now finds herself almost isolated, it is to be hoped that she will entertain more moderate ideas. I have envisaged this war, Madame, as a great conflagration which one can finally extinguish only by getting rid of the combustible materials which serve to nourish it. . . . I have been the injured party in this unhappy war, and I have very ardently wished to see it ended in an honorable fashion, and above all that the structure of the peace should not be just plastered over but should be durable.

As the injured party, the king went on to say, he considered himself in a better position than any other belligerent to ask for damages; but out of the goodness of his heart, for the love of peace and for the sake of humanity, he would demand only the complete restoration of his territories. Who was the better friend of peace, he asked — the Austrian seeking conquests or the Prussian who sought only to hold what was his? The French were about to evacuate his Rhineland provinces and he had troops ready, he said, to retake possession of them; but he had heard that the Austrian government was planning to send troops from Flanders to try to anticipate him. As soon as that matter had come to a head, he averred, he had intended to ask the empress of Russia to mediate in the interest of peace — which he was, however, "obliged to defer today," not knowing yet just where he stood.

He concluded his letter with a long paragraph in praise of peace and of Catherine, its high priestess:

I have revealed to you, Madame, all that I have on my heart, fully persuaded that your Imperial Majesty will not abuse [my confidence], and that you will be convinced that an honest peace, far from being repugnant, will be very agreeable to me, but that I should prefer death to a shameful peace that dishonored me. There is nothing more praiseworthy than Your Imperial Majesty's readiness to work for peace; the benedictions of all Europe will be heaped upon you, among which I beg you to be so good as to give mine a prominent place. I do not doubt that there are ways to satisfy everyone and the Saxons, as Your Imperial Majesty very well says, provided that one has to deal with conciliatory and peace-minded spirits; [and] Your Imperial Majesty's good advice will contribute not a little to take the stiffness out of certain spirits [now] too unyielding. Finally, Madame, Your Imperial Majesty inspires in me a complete confidence; I rely entirely upon your precious friendship, which I beg you always to conserve for me, assuring you of the high consideration and distinguished sentiments with which I am, Madame my Sister, Your Imperial Majesty's good brother,

Federic.[2]

---

[2] December 22, in *P. C.,* XXII, 409–410.

Provided that his pen could protect him from outside interference, the king knew he could deal directly with Austria and Saxony, confidently and without haste. On December 30 negotiations were begun at Hubertusburg between Freiherr von Fritsch representing Saxony, Collenbach representing Austria, and the Prussian Ewald Friedrich von Hertzberg. As Collenbach was little more than a mouthpiece for Kaunitz, and Hertzberg a messenger for Frederick, much time was sure to be consumed in correspondence between conferences; but Frederick was in no hurry. Hertzberg was instructed to demand only the restoration of the *status quo ante bellum,* to be as conciliatory as possible on all points except demands for the cession of any Prussian territory, and to be especially careful to say nothing that could offend the empress of Russia; but he was to make no gratuitous concessions. He was to demand no indemnities for Prussia, but to point out that it was only Frederick's moderation that restrained him from asserting such a claim. And he was to avoid hurrying the negotiation, so that the Prussian troops would not have to be withdrawn from Saxony before the end of February.[3]

Before the negotiations had begun, Frederick was able to predict both their duration and their outcome. The really important points, he said on January 1, 1763, were "almost agreed upon"; only the details had yet to be settled, though the negotiation might be drawn out until the end of February and the evacuation of Saxony not be completed until March.[4]

Prince Henry had demonstrated throughout the war that as a military organizer and administrator he had not an equal in the whole Prussian army unless it was Frederick himself. Nothing, therefore, would have been more logical than that the command of the troops during the armistice, their withdrawal from alien territory, and their return to a peacetime footing upon the conclusion of peace should all have devolved upon him while the king concentrated first upon diplomacy and then upon the countless other problems of reconstruction. Neither of the brothers, however, could quite forget their bitter quarrels over the treatment of Saxony, or the prince's repeated offer to resign. Frederick, furthermore, was so tremendously relieved at the prospect of peace that he felt quite capable of handling the whole problem of demobilization and reconstruction singlehanded. Hence, having ceased to be indispensable, the prince found himself at once a supernumerary, and a little in the way. The army, which had needed two heads in wartime, could do better with only one in peace; and obviously that one must be the king.

[3] Hertzberg's précis of his instructions is printed by Schäfer, II–2, 762. All the concessions he was authorized to make were to be kept *"au fond du sac"* as long as possible.
[4] Schöning, III, 526; *P. C.,* XXII, 429, 430.

Prince Henry was therefore free to go home, but it was a joyless home-coming for him. The princess was in Magdeburg with the court, and there she celebrated his birthday anniversary without him by inviting in a few guests — only a few, according to Lehndorff's account, because everyone there was in such an impoverished condition that an ostentatious affair would have been out of place. The prince himself was in Berlin, where he celebrated Frederick's birthday but not his own.

From Berlin he went on to Rheinsberg, where disappointment and further disillusionment awaited him. During his absence Baron Reisewitz, who had been in his service for many years, had been commissioned by him to complete the extensive improvements of buildings and grounds which he had planned before the war but had had to leave unfinished. Upon his return he was not only dissatisfied with the way in which the work had been done but found that Reisewitz had gone heavily into debt, abused both the prince's confidence and his credit, misappropriated considerable sums of money, and forged his signature. Soon after the prince's return to Berlin Reisewitz died suddenly at Rheinsberg. The official notice stated that he had had a fever. Court gossip called it suicide.[5]

In the middle of February the court returned to Berlin; and Prince Henry, whom Lehndorff was by then calling "the scourge of our enemies," was there to receive the queen. It was a period of great scarcity and high prices in the capital, but economic miracles were expected whenever the king should be able to return; and in the meantime Prince Henry, as the victor in the last great battle and the first to return, was acclaimed wherever he went as the savior of his country. The people of Berlin had to wait a long time yet for their first opportunity to cheer their king.

It was, after all, quite in keeping with his character and with his place in the life of his people that the First Servant of the State should be the last to return from the war. Working — not tirelessly, but unremittingly — in his headquarters in Leipzig, with his thoughts running ever forward to meet and wrestle with the problems of reconstruction, never backward over the trials or the triumphs of the immediate past, Frederick the battler was already revealing himself as Frederick the builder. The hard-bitten old *Haudegen* whose image was and is familiar to all the world was giving way already to the *Vater des Volkes,* the patriarchal figure of the hard-working patriot-king that was to become even more familiar and dear to the minds of millions of Germans than that of the victor of Rossbach and Leuthen.

[5] Lehndorff, *Dreissig Jahre,* 452–453; M.P., VI, 174, 183; Richard Krauel, "Prinz Heinrich von Preussen in Rheinsberg," *Hohenzollern Jahrbücher,* VI (1902), 15.

Prince Henry during that period had only an occasional glimpse of the peace conference at Hubertusburg or of life in Leipzig, as Frederick found time to describe them to him. At the same time the king was unconsciously describing himself in metamorphosis — cynically tolerant of the weaknesses of others, confessing many of his own but working ahead in spite of them, complaining of weariness but never stopping to rest. He had not shunned danger in war, and he would not shirk his duty in peace.

In response to Prince Henry's letter of congratulation on his fifty-first birthday anniversary he wrote: "I am getting old. . . . Soon I shall be useless to the world and a burden to myself. It is the fate of all creatures to wither with age; but for all that, one must not abuse the privilege [of age] and drivel about it." [6]

Although the treaty of peace had not yet been signed, Henry heard on February 2 that its essential points had been agreed upon and that the signing would be only a formality and would take place within a week. "You know too well my way of thinking," Frederick wrote, "to believe that I have signed a shameful peace or anything prejudicial to posterity. I believe that we have made the best peace possible in the present circumstances." [7]

A week later the prince received from Frederick a confidential report on the terms of the Treaty of Hubertusburg. All boundaries between Prussian, Austrian, and Saxon territories were to be re-established as before the war. As a gesture of complaisance and to mollify the spirits of the Austrian royal family, Frederick, as elector of Brandenburg, had agreed to vote for the archduke Joseph II in the next Imperial election. (Maria Theresa had thought she was making a very material concession when she offered to give up the title of Duchess of Upper and Lower Silesia. So long as he retained Silesia and Glatz, Frederick cared very little what titles she or anyone else kept or dropped.) Final ratifications of the treaty would not be exchanged before February 25, so the last of the troops would not get home before April. Then to set their house in

---

[6] *Ibid.*, 482. The war had aged him noticeably; but he could not find time really to grow old.

[7] *P. C.*, XXII, 497. Sir Andrew Mitchell's suspicions were unduly aroused when Prince Henry showed him what the king had written about the treaty. He could not imagine Frederick's writing the words just quoted unless he had actually made some cessions of territory and felt compelled to defend himself for having done so. M. P., VI, 185; Bisset, II, 339.

When he finally saw the treaty itself, on March 7, Sir Andrew wrote the king a letter of congratulation, filled with the most fulsome praise: "I have long recognized Your Majesty as the greatest of warriors, but today when you have known how to give tranquillity to Germany in so short a time and in so few words, I admire Your Majesty as the most skilful negotiator who has ever lived. Permit me, Sire, speaking for myself, to felicitate you upon an event so glorious and honorable for yourself and so advantageous for the human race." M. P., VI, 196; A. Schäfer, II-2, 762.

order, as the king assumed Prince Henry had already begun to do at Rheinsberg! [8]

The magnitude of the task of reconstruction which lay ahead was already evident to Prince Henry, to whom Frederick's promise to show great results within a year sounded like a vain and ignorant boast. "The work that you will have to do," he said, "to remedy the evils that war has caused will be no small task. I am, nevertheless, assured that the pleasure of re-establishing order and abundance and bringing back the golden age will serve you as compensation for the pains you have suffered." [9]

The king was in fact concentrating so closely upon the first steps to be taken that he had not yet realized what a long way he had still to go, and he was somewhat oversanguine about it. With unutterable relief he had turned his back upon the war, and confidently he faced the future. Blind to any but his own conception of the paramount interest of the state, and refusing to look too long at the obstacles along any path he chose to take in its service, he suddenly announced his decision to re-establish the debased currency of his realm: "Our money will all be put on a better basis in the month of June; I shall pay off all the state debts between now and then; after that, I can die when I please." [10]

On February 15, while getting off "couriers to all the courts," the king sent one also to his brother with a message eloquent in its brevity: "Peace is signed." In the words of the prince's reply, "Never was courier received with greater joy than he who arrived yesterday evening to bring me word of the peace. The letter which you have been so very kind as to write to me on this occasion," Henry went on, "has confirmed the good news, and has given me the joy of realizing quite vividly the magnitude of the triumph you have won in terminating so burdensome and so many-sided a war without losing any of your territory. It did not look as if things could end as they have, and I cannot help but repeat how fully I rejoice with you in this fortunate event. . . . I hope not only that you may some day see everything restored to its former splendor but that you may thereafter [live to] enjoy the fruits of your labor." [11]

[8] *P. C.,* XXII, 514. Kalckreuth maintains, on his own credence only, that Frederick failed to notify the queen of the conclusion of the negotiations, and that she got her first word of it from Prince Henry, who sent Kalckreuth at once to carry this letter to her. He says further that she received both him and his message graciously, without revealing by the slightest sign that she saw anything unusual or that there was anything lacking in such a procedure. *Paroles,* 318.

[9] Schöning, III, 532.

[10] *P. C.,* XXII, 523. On June 1 new currency began to be issued which Mitchell said was considerably better than that of wartime but still below the prewar standard in value. The period of adjustment was one of great hardship for the poor, and for months the army seethed with discontent because it was still being paid at the prewar rate in wartime currency of greatly diminished purchasing power. M. P., VI, 223, 231.

[11] Schöning, III, 536; Schmitt, *Prinz Heinrich,* II, 293.

Tacitly admitting the obvious fact which the gloomy prince had suggested — that he had been fortunate to lose none of his territorial possessions — the king openly refused to mourn over having acquired no new ones. "I do not personally regret that peace should be made on the terms already known to you," he wrote Henry. "If the state had acquired some new province or other, that would no doubt have been a good thing; but, as that did not depend upon me but upon fortune, that idea does not in any way disturb my tranquillity. *If I repair properly the ravages of the war, I shall have been good for something; and to that my ambition limits itself.*" [12]

The one categorical imperative which Frederick invariably recognized and never denied or sought to evade was his sense of duty. "It is my duty in this situation . . . ," he wrote again, "to work. If ever in my life I can do the state some service it is now, by raising it again from destruction and, if it is still possible, by correcting abuses and effecting reform where necessary. The task is vast and manifold, but if Heaven accords me a few more days of life, I shall complete it; if not, I shall mark out a course which others may follow if they see fit." [13]

The details of the king's "vast and manifold" plans for reconstruction were of course not given in his letters to his brother; but some of their general outlines were sketched there and the prince was assured that every plan had been worked out in full detail and orders issued for its execution. Yielding again to his old temptation to consider already accomplished anything he had once planned and ordered, Frederick promised that changes would at once become apparent. Unused army stores would be released to relieve the food shortage and to depress the extortionate distress prices then being charged for foodstuffs. All conceivable government aid would be immediately available for the rehabilitation of agriculture and the rebuilding of the towns and villages. Within two years not a trace of the war would be visible.[14]

Blandly ignoring the effects of the depreciation of the currency (except as he announced his intention to put it back at once upon a better footing), he was still as proud as ever of his refusal to levy new taxes, and scornful of any monarch who would do so in time of distress. "What a man!" he commented when reporting that one of the first acts of the king of Poland and elector of Saxony, upon regaining possession of the electorate, had been to levy new imposts. Prince Henry denounced such taxation as ill-advised, oversevere, wrong in principle, and altogether un-

---

[12] *P. C.*, XXII, 529. The italics are the author's.

[13] *Ibid.*, 534. Prince Henry, as regent, would have been one of the "others" to whom the king here referred.

[14] Although he tried hard enough, he could not quite hold to so rapid a schedule; but he worked for years along the lines indicated. Only the social and economic rehabilitation

reasonable; and Frederick agreed that it was nothing less than inhuman for Saxon tax collectors to follow right on the heels of the retiring Prussians; but they did not reopen the old question of the justification of their own exactions there.[15]

While he waited for exchange of ratifications of the treaty and planned for reconstruction, Frederick surveyed also the whole field of foreign relations and decided that his policy should thereafter be one of cautious reserve. As for Austria, he understood that (largely as a result of Prince Henry's last campaign, he said) both Kaunitz and Maria Theresa were thoroughly tired of war and disposed to re-establish and to maintain friendly relations with him. Yet it would always be wise for Prussia to remember the fable of the cat and the mice, "The cat is still a cat, no matter what it does."

His relations with Russia were, for the moment, reasonably satisfactory to him just as they were. He feared Catherine far too much to be willing to risk her enmity, but he would "make haste slowly" in courting her friendship.

France had already made peace with Great Britain and recemented her friendship with Austria. All the powers were more or less exhausted and weary of war. Hence Frederick hoped that the peace, which was about to become general, would last out his time. If it did not, France and Great Britain would, he thought, be the first to break it. In that case Prussia's wisest policy would be to make no alliance with either — and let them destroy each other if they would. One state's disaster might be another's boon.[16]

On March 1 he was able at last to report that he was to entertain that day, at Dahlen, the Austrian and Saxon negotiators who were to bring with them the signed and ratified copies of the Treaty of Hubertusburg. "Messieurs Fritsch and Collenbach are coming here after dinner today like Noah's doves with the olive branch in beak. You may believe that they will be well received, for the news that they are bringing makes it worth the trouble."

He would himself be unable to return to Berlin for another month; but, cheered by the certainty of peace, he was able to jest about that. He

of the undistinguished thousands of discharged officers and soldiers (many of them cripples) was seriously neglected.

[15] *P. C.*, XXII, 529, 534; Schöning, III, 537–539. Considerable numbers of Saxon *émigrés*, driven out by taxation and hard times, found homes in Prussia. Prussian soldiers were also permitted after the signing of the armistice to marry Saxon women, provided the brides were strong and healthy, brought with them substantial dowries, and were willing to accompany their husbands on their return to Prussia. Frederick reported to Prince Henry that deserters from both sides were guilty of some brigandage in Saxony as the armies withdrew. *P. C.*, XXII, 547.

[16] *Ibid.*, 534, 538, 540.

would take care, he said, not to arrive on April 1 for fear his compatriots should take it as an "April fool's" joke and make fun of him.[17]

March 30 was the date eventually set for Frederick's home-coming from Silesia, where all the intervals in a series of triumphal entries and receptions had been filled in by the examination of reports, accounts, and estimates of the quantities of seed and building material and of the sums of money needed for the first steps toward reconstruction. He had written to the queen that he would have supper that evening with the family, but he had neither ordered nor forbidden a public reception. Because he had ordered none, he seems to have anticipated none; but for once the burghers of Berlin thought they should act on their own initiative and arrange a triumphal entry for the returning monarch.

All day the populace was out in the streets, buzzing with excitement. All afternoon soldiers and townspeople watched the route by which the king was expected to re-enter the city, waiting for an opportunity to cheer him as he passed. As he still had not appeared when darkness approached, torches were handed out so that he might be lighted through the crowd and that the effect of the triumphal arches and other decorations would not be lost; but Lehndorff says that thousands of people returned to their homes "angry and embittered."

Those who stayed out faithfully to the last were doomed to an even greater disappointment. Toward nine o'clock the king finally appeared at the Frankfort gate, but in no mood or condition to play the part of the returning hero. He had traveled that day approximately seventy-five (English) miles over very bad roads. A halt at the battlefield of Kunersdorf had consumed some time and had not cheered his spirit much. All day long, wherever he stopped at a relay post to change horses, he had been surrounded by crowds of his subjects praying for miracles, and bedeviled by officials asking for favors either for themselves or for their districts. And at the end of the ride he was expected to change from his traveling coach to a great gilded one, specially provided by his faithful Berliners, and parade the torchlighted streets of his war-impoverished capital like the Roman conqueror of a new province!

The next day he did it, to please them; but that night he could not. Phantom hosts of the dead from Kunersdorf and Torgau would have paraded between him and the cheering populace, and the torches would have lighted up once more in his memory the smouldering ruins of Küstrin and Dresden.[18]

[17] *Ibid.*, 540. On the same day he wrote to d'Argens: "I do not wish to arrive there on the first of next month; the facetious might make fun of me and shout 'April fish' at me." *Ibid.*

[18] Two weeks before his return he had revisited Torgau, and in a letter to Prince Henry

So he only let them greet him at the gate; then as the cavalcade made its way into the city with the triumphal chariot in its midst, the king in his service-battered old traveling carriage dropped off the rear end of the parade and made his way as quickly as possible, by obscure cross streets and bypaths, to a side entrance of his palace, where he slipped inside unobserved.

He gained thus a little time to refresh and compose himself before going to meet the members of his family and the distinguished representatives of civil and military officialdom, of the nobility, and of the diplomatic corps who had been waiting all afternoon and evening in the anterooms of the palace to receive him. When he did at last appear he singled out Prince Henry for his first and most effusive greeting — which was presumably not difficult to do, as everyone, the prince included, was expecting him to do that. Then his other brother, Ferdinand; then came Ferdinand of Brunswick, and a public acknowledgment of gratitude for his splendid services. Then he asked Prince Henry who the other gentlemen were, and the prince presented them. To the Dutch minister, who had offered an asylum to Berliners when the Russians were in the city, he was especially cordial. To the Danish representative he paid very little attention. Mitchell, his erstwhile companion on many a weary mile of road and on more than one actual battlefield, was greeted with civility, but that was all. As soon as the introductions were over he retired to the family apartments.[19]

"Madame has grown fatter," was Frederick's first word of greeting to his queen after all those years of absence, according to Lehndorff. With Countess Camas, who had earned his enduring gratitude by understanding and sympathizing with him in his youth, he was much more demonstrative. At supper he sat with his sister Amelia on his right and the Princess Henry on his left, but he ate in silence and left it to Prince Henry, who sat on Amelia's right, to carry the burden of the conversation. It was nearly midnight when he arose from the table and, after standing apart for a little while with his sister and Princess Henry, dismissed the weary family gathering by withdrawing to his own rooms — alone.

Alone, in privacy and in silence, but not in peace! Closer than the ghosts of the men of Kunersdorf and Torgau that had ridden the roads with him for years, closer than the princes, generals, and diplomats in

had referred to the battle there as one which through the intervening years had given him "some very bad quarter-hours." The letter is mentioned in a footnote in the *Politische Correspondenz*, but is not printed there —"Mon neveu a vu aujourd'hui le champ de bataille, qui, pendant plus de deux années, m'a fait passer de bien mauvais quarts d'heure." Schöning, III, 543; *Oeuvres,* XXVI, 271.

[19] M. P., VI, 203, 216; Lehndorff, 456–460; Koser, III, 170–174.

his anteroom, more real to him than the surviving members of his family at that specter-haunted home-coming supper table, there had crowded around him unbidden, all evening, the faces and the spirits of those inseparable from the memory of his war-killed past. Old Schwerin, shot down as he defied the Austrians to stop him at Prague. Marshal Keith, who died as he dared them to drive him from his place at Hochkirch. General Goltz, of whom he had said: "I never had a more faithful friend." Prince William, who failed him, and for whose unhappy end he knew his other brothers still blamed him. Margrave Charles, whose death had made providentially available the lands and revenues with which Prince Henry was rewarded for his victory at Freiberg. Wilhelmina, his best-loved sister, who had written from her deathbed that he must not spare Baireuth to his own hurt or at Prussia's cost. His mother, who after every battle had rejoiced first over the survival of her sons and only then asked whether a victory had been won — and for whom he mourned afresh as Prince Henry had done on his first return after her death. All these and many more were gone; but his memories of them so filled the atmosphere around him that those who had replaced them seemed somehow guilty of trespass. "But for the buildings," he wrote soon thereafter to his sister of Sweden, "I am as much a stranger here as if I were in London." Never in his life had he known such loneliness as then — with all Europe agape at his achievements, all Prussia waiting to acclaim him on his tours of inspection, and all Berlin outside his palace windows to welcome him home from the war.

Within the next few days there were public celebrations enough to take some of the edge off the people's disappointment over Frederick's home-coming; but the economic miracles they had expected of him were slow in coming to pass. The Jews, whom he had used often for the thankless tasks of manipulating the currency and procuring supplies (and even for purchasing surplus Russian army stores in Poland), were popularly suspected of wholesale profiteering and were blamed and hated for all the hardships incidental to the postwar deflation. "Jews and Christians," wrote Sir Andrew Mitchell, "are striving with equal Zeal and Ardour who shall have Share in the Spoils of the People, but it is hoped that the King of Prussia's Wisdom, Sagacity and Penetration will disappoint the flagitious Designs of the Money Brokers of whatever Denomination." But the British minister in his critical mood could see little virtue or ultimate utility in the king's generous grants of money to the devastated towns and provinces for reconstruction purposes. "Mere Palliatives and Acts of Ostentation," he called them.[20]

[20] M. P., VI, 206, 208, 234; Lehndorff, *Dreissig Jahre, Nachträge,* I, 369. One of several

The numbers of the discontented were swelled by many veterans of the war, officers and soldiers alike, both those retained in the military service and those dropped from it. Men discharged from the army in the interest of economy felt that they had been disinherited; those retained in it and paid in depreciated currency after the new money had begun to be issued thought they had been cheated. Discipline, which had inevitably been relaxed somewhat in the field, was at once tightened up again upon the return to garrison duty, and was found doubly irksome. Even the all-important wartime position of the armed forces was redefined by a general order which reminded the army that it existed for the defense of civilians and of their property, not for their exploitation or abuse, and threatened any officer or soldier guilty of imposing upon or abusing a civilian with punishment of the utmost severity. When Generals Finck, Schmettau, and Fouqué returned from imprisonment in Austria they were at once put under arrest to await the formation of the courts-martial that were to investigate the reasons for their failures.[21]

So Lehndorff wrote in his journal: "One sees people who are pleased and others who are not"; and Mitchell reported that while the profiteers erected triumphal arches and sang praises to the king, the people "who want Bread and have long felt the Calamities of War, are grown mutinous and almost outrageous." Things had indeed gone so far, Sir Andrew wrote secretly to the Earl of Halifax just three weeks after Frederick's return, that papers had been posted up on some of the most prominent street corners denouncing the king as a tyrant who deserved to meet the fate of Peter III of Russia, and calling for the redress of grievances under the "more humane" Prince Henry![22]

Sir Andrew thought that the very existence of this movement of protest had been successfully concealed from the king, and that no steps had been taken to apprehend or punish the anonymous culprits responsible for it. Nor is there anything to indicate that Prince Henry knew anything about it. If either or both of the brothers had had any knowledge of such a movement their home-coming would have been even more tragically disappointing than it was, and their relations with one another would again have been embittered just when they should have been, and were in most respects, at their best.

firms to go bankrupt in Berlin that year was that of Gottkowski, who had been particularly active in raising ransom money for the city during the war. The king bought a porcelain factory from him in September, to enable him to save something from the wreck of his fortune. F. to H., in *Oeuvres*, XXVI, 284.
[21] M. P., VI, 205, 210, 215.
[22] *Ibid.*

CHAPTER XVI

# 𝕭𝖊𝖙𝖗𝖆𝖞𝖆𝖑

*"I propose to keep silence."*—Prince Henry.

ALTHOUGH the thought of dethroning Frederick and putting his brother Henry in his place cannot have occurred to any but the "lunatic fringe" of the malcontents, the prince was popular in those days; and outward appearances, superficially viewed, would indicate that he ought to have been happy. He was beloved by the army — and deservedly so — for his unwearied watchfulness over the welfare of the men he had led during the war, and honored by it as the victor of Freiberg.

Frederick treated him publicly with all the distinction possible, and made his birthday anniversary the greatest family holiday of the year, the one occasion on which he would himself wear his full royal regalia and let gold plate be used for the family dinner. At the annual carnival, the high point of the social season for the court and for the whole capital, there were two "high tables" rather than one: that at which the king sat was inevitably the first, but Prince Henry presided in outwardly equal state at the second.

Privately, although it was naturally less heavy than in wartime, their correspondence was continued on a regular weekly basis and in a confidential, friendly, and often humorous tone indicative of the fullest intimacy and of some real affection.

During the war both had often voiced their homesickness and their longing for quiet by saying they wished they could "go home and plant their cabbages in peace." Both, once home from the war, busied themselves with building and planting. Frederick made plans at once for the magnificent New Palace in Potsdam that was to convince the world that he still had some resources and ambition left, and that served as one of the royal and Imperial residences as long as the House of Hohenzollern ruled in Prussia and in Germany. Prince Henry busied himself with the renovation and enlargement of the buildings at Rheinsberg and with the further development of the park there. Both were enthusiastic gardeners; and almost every courier who rode with a message from one to the other carried some gift — melons, grapes, exotic fruits grown with great care under glass, some new imported vegetable that had just been nursed to maturity, a bottle of choice wine, or something of the sort.

238

*Prince Henry's Palace in Berlin*

*Sans Souci, Frederick's Palace in Potsdam*

Occasionally it was a gift of greater intrinsic value — samples of rare French glass sought out by Henry for Frederick, or word from the king that he had paid up all of the margrave Charles's debts, which might otherwise have been chargeable against the margrave's lands that he had given to the prince after Freiberg.

Always they exchanged polite inquiries about each other's health, comparing their physical ills and their symptoms, consoling one another with the thought that, since their gout was apparently hereditary, they must learn to endure it with such fortitude as they could summon. Each recommended on occasion his favorite remedy for whatever ailed the other at the moment, although neither of them expected either himself or his brother ever to enjoy really good health again. "My hypochondria sends counsel to yours," wrote Frederick; and the prince replied that he was gradually "learning to live with" what the war had left him of the rather poor physique with which he had been endowed.

Frederick's "*gazettes de Sans Souci*," as he called his letters to Henry, usually contained a serial commentary, often highly humorous, upon the events of the day all over Europe. Sometimes they were a strange mixture of the important and the trivial. On October 9, 1763, for example, the king showed much more personal concern over his "poor dog" Alcimène which was about to die than over the inconsiderate king of Poland who had just "died like a fool" at a time most inconvenient for his fellow sovereigns, and left it to the living to find a successor for him.[1]

Nor was the king merely using current events as material with which to fill up his "*gazettes de Sans Souci*." Self-sufficient though he was in many ways, one of the most imperative needs of his nature was for someone to whom he could occasionally unburden himself. No minister or army officer would do, nor any subject. No foreigner, however distinguished, could be quite fully trusted. His beloved dogs would listen but could not answer him. So his brother Henry, with whom pretense was as unnecessary as it was useless, was still in this strange fashion indispensable to him.[2]

In November, 1763, Berlin was visited by a Turkish embassy which had to be lavishly entertained at Frederick's expense. The king grumbled to Henry about the ceremonial, the expensive gifts, and the extravagant compliments which had become the order of the day, but relieved

[1] Schöning, III, 569; *Oeuvres*, XXVI, 288. Prince Henry's own connection with the question of the Polish succession, which did nothing to increase his affection for Frederick, will be discussed in the next chapter.

[2] Something of this sort is suggested by G. B. Volz in an article, "Der Plan einer Mitregentschaft des Prinzen Heinrich," in the *Hohenzollern Jahrbücher*, XX (1916), page 182.

his feelings by writing humorous descriptions of the "Turkish craze" that had struck Berlin.[3]

The Turks were still in Berlin when Prince Henry came in from Rheinsberg in December, so he also entertained them at a grand ball — where one of them declared that he had "never seen so many pretty women all in one heap" in his life. But no useful alliance with Turkey resulted, so king and prince alike considered their effort and their money wasted, and Frederick sighed with relief when he was rid of the strange guests who, he said, had been "eating his ears off." [4]

All sorts of persons, most of them seeking appointments, asked Henry to intercede for them with the king. He recommended one of his courtiers, Count Lamberg, for an ecclesiastical position in Silesia on the ground that the king would find it desirable to have "some dependable fellows" among the clergy there. Of the candidate's spiritual qualities nothing was said.

Another of the prince's protégés, a young Paléologue, was recommended for a similar position chiefly on the ground that he had been refused a position in Baireuth on account of his religion; and Henry was even quicker than Frederick to take up arms against any form of religious intolerance. He thought, moreover, that their sister Wilhelmina had once befriended the young man. That was enough. "I can use your Paléologue," Frederick replied, "provided that I know what sauce to serve with him. If he is only a beast, we shall have to put a chain on him in the Silesian clergy and make a canon of him; if he is fit for anything better than that, I shall try to find a place for him wherever I can." [5]

Occasionally Frederick asked Henry to nominate someone for a position. In July, 1763, for example, their favorite nephew, the younger Prince Henry, was given a new tutor chosen from among several whom Henry had suggested at Frederick's request. "He is so amiable that it would be murder to put him into bad hands," was the king's comment.[6]

Both brothers were happy to relax after the superhuman strain of the war years; yet neither of them could readily adjust himself to his new condition. Both confessed themselves disturbed by a certain restlessness and a sense of unreality. Which, if any, of their three contrasting lives was the real one — the prewar period which seemed so idyllic as they looked back upon it, those awful years during which the war had been the only reality, or the quiet but not quite satisfying period of readjust-

---

[3] Schöning, III, 576–579; *Oeuvres*, XXVI, 295–296. Henry meanwhile was reading about Turkey in the letters of Lady Mary Montagu.
[4] One of the gifts brought by the visitors was a fine Arabian horse for Prince Henry.
[5] Schöning, III, 542, 564; *Oeuvres*, XXVI, 282–284.
[6] Schöning, III, 558–559; *Oeuvres*, XXVI, 276–277.

ment that followed it? "My sister [of Schwedt] and I talk over old times," wrote Frederick to Henry in July, "much like the old French lieutenant-colonels talking of their ancient feats of arms; but all that is only a dream; there are events of these [later?] times that seem almost like fairy tales to me but that are nonetheless very real." [7]

To the prince, especially in Berlin, life was both unreal and empty, in spite of the honors heaped upon him. In September, in recognition of his known fondness for theatrical performances, "The Democrat at Court" was presented in his honor in Charlottenburg; but he wrote at once to ask permission to follow the king back to Sans Souci, as he found the atmosphere of the capital stifling and unendurable. "I am not in any way attached to anything in Berlin," he wrote; "the memory of the past is very painful to me, and the life that one leads there [now] seems quite insipid." [8]

Frederick promptly invited him to come to Potsdam at once and to stay as long as he chose. He had himself "retired to his vine" there, he said. He would show his brother the sketches Guillelmi had made for the paintings that were to adorn the ceilings of his new palace in Berlin; they would read and talk and enjoy the gardens to their hearts' content. Although he was offering nothing else by way of entertainment, he did promise a most cordial welcome and "cheerful countenance as host."

Far different from this picture were the visions that arose at once in the minds of watchful observers who knew only that the two old soldiers were again putting their heads together out at Potsdam. There were those who remembered what had happened when the prince, with his brother Prince William, Marshal Schwerin, and the other generals, had been summoned to Potsdam in midsummer just a little more than seven years before. Immediately rumors were on foot and couriers made ready to mount their horses. Danzig was to be annexed. A partition of Poland between Russia and Prussia was in prospect. Hanover was to be occupied to collect an unpaid balance of the old subsidy (which Mitchell denied was due). It was true that the artillery purchased a few horses at about that time and recruiting was resumed; but the prince's visit to Potsdam, made at his own suggestion, was utterly without military or political significance, although he stayed for ten days or longer. [9]

If the world had only known how completely Prince Henry had been reduced in fact to the legal status of head of a regiment, it would have worried less than it did about an innocent visit on his part to Potsdam;

[7] Schöning, III, 563; *Oeuvres,* XXVI, 281.
[8] Schöning, III, 565; *Oeuvres,* XXVI, 283–285.
[9] M. P., VI, 241–242; Schöning, 567; *Oeuvres,* XXVI, 286.

but outsiders may well be excused for failure to understand what the prince himself had not yet fully realized. The footing on which he really stood, although his name still headed the list of generals of infantry, was made fully clear to him only at the May reviews of 1764 at Spandau. There "Prince Henry's regiment" had the post of honor, and the prince stood at its head *without the spontoon*. The spontoon was a sort of wooden staff or half-pike carried as a sign of his rank by an infantry officer of the line, and the prince himself had carried it before the war as other regimental commanders did; but, having distinguished himself as a general of armies during the war, he had apparently resolved never to carry it again. To do so would, in his mind, signify acceptance of what he considered an undeserved reduction to the ranks. So in silent protest he made himself conspicuous by appearing on parade without it.[10]

The king of course noticed the omission, knew that it was as deliberate as it was obvious, and recognized it for what it was — a challenge of his own tacitly assumed position that Prussia had again only one army and the army only one commander, and that his old wartime second-in-command was nothing in peacetime but a soldier with the name of a prince, the title of a general, the position of a colonel, and the privileges that the king chose to accord to him — no more. Although he said nothing about it, he showed his resentment plainly enough; his correspondence with his brother was confined for a year thereafter to the necessary messages on special occasions. In July, when their sister the Duchess of Brunswick brought her daughter Elizabeth to be betrothed to the Prince of Prussia, he instructed Frederick William to send Prince Henry a special invitation to attend the festivities; but he himself sent no personal letter directly, and the haughty Henry refused to come.[11]

Prince Henry was not invited to accompany the king to the Silesian maneuvers that year, as he had done regularly before the war. Seeking a reconciliation, he went to Spandau to await Frederick's return and wrote for permission to see him then. He was refused, and returned to Rheinsberg bitterly disappointed. At the carnival in January Frederick reserved the usual place for him at the head of the other high table, but the prince did not attend. Frederick, on the other hand, did appear at a dinner given by the prince in celebration of the king's birthday anniversary.

It was only at the May reviews of 1765, a full year after the original incident, that the rebel's complete submission was publicly made mani-

[10] Kalckreuth says that he had tried before the review to find out through his adjutants and Frederick's whether the king would resent the irregularity. Anhalt helped to trap him by permitting him to believe that Frederick would not object. *Paroles,* 318–325.

[11] Hausarchiv, Rep. 48, I. Just afterward Frederick refused to permit Henry to accept an invitation to visit their sister Ulrika, the queen of Sweden, basing his refusal ostensibly upon

fest and his unspoken apology accepted. There he stood at the head of his regiment, stiff as the spontoon itself, with the hated symbol of his reduced status in his hand. Seeing that, the king spoke to him graciously and invited him to hand the spontoon to another officer, mount a horse, and accompany him on the review. Once he had given that outward sign of recognition that he was really only an ordinary infantryman and, as such, subject to the same regimentation as his fellow officers, he was free once more to ride as prince beside the king. The discipline of the army and the principle of subordination had been menaced but were saved again.[12]

The prince found some solace for his wounded feelings in the attentions he received when he visited Carlsbad for his health in June and July of that year — absenting himself from the wedding of his nephew and niece, the Prince of Prussia and Elizabeth of Brunswick, as he had previously stayed away from their ceremonial betrothal.[13]

Several months in advance Frederick had quite graciously consented to the Carlsbad trip. They must expect the Austrian court, he said, to send all sorts of people to spy upon the prince; but as they would find nothing but a harmless invalid taking the waters for his health, that need cause no one the least concern. He advised the prince, however, to disarm suspicion by notifying the Austrian minister beforehand of his intention to visit the famous Austrian town. Neither of the brothers seems to have anticipated the reception that was in store for the traveler.[14]

The journey proved to be a triumph. The prince was greeted with acclaim and heaped with benedictions as he crossed Saxony, where his efforts to help the luckless inhabitants survive the war had not been forgotten. At Teplitz and at Carlsbad spies were presumably plentiful enough in his entourage; but the two companies of grenadiers sent by the empress to serve him as a guard of honor were much more in evidence. At peace with Prussia, Maria Theresa spared neither effort nor expense in being polite to the brother of Prussia's king. The peasants had been turned out to repair the roads over which he was to travel. A house was provided as a residence for him. The royal theatrical troupe was sent from Vienna to contribute to his entertainment. Everywhere, by order of

the prince's bad health, the expense of such a trip, and the danger of arousing suspicion in Sweden or in Russia. *P. C.*, XXIII, 435, 484.

[12] M. P., VII, 35; Lehndorff, *Dreissig Jahre*, 469; *Nachträge*, I, 399, 427. Kalckreuth attributes to Prince Henry a remark to the effect that never since the spear with which the Savior's side was pierced had a slender spit of wood created such a commotion. *Paroles*, 324–325. About a year later Mitchell, writing to the Earl of Chatham, said of Frederick: "Though upon some occasions he laughs at formalities, yet no man is more tenacious of them in whatever he thinks touches his rank, dignity, and consideration." Bisset, II, 364.

[13] He had no great liking for either of them, and no confidence in them.

[14] Hausarchiv, Rep. 56, II, F; *P. C.*, XXIV, 128.

the empress, he was received with the same honors accorded by protocol to an Austrian archduke or to her own son, the king of the Romans. The prince enjoyed the experience, and found the waters beneficial.[15]

Upon his return home in August, 1765, Prince Henry's position seemed to leave nothing (except a useful and soul-satisfying occupation) to be desired. Rheinsberg had been greatly beautified, with funds supplied largely by the king. When Frederick returned from Silesia in September Henry was on hand to welcome him. Frederick greeted the prince very cordially, much to the relief of all interested observers, and carried him off at once to Sans Souci for a long, quiet visit. When the king planned a trip to Torgau to meet Joseph II of Austria, in June of 1766, he invited Henry to accompany him.[16]

By 1766, also, the prince's new palace in Berlin was ready for occupancy.[17] But the splendid new residence was never a home. Seven years of absence and the war had completed the estrangement of Prince Henry and his wife, to whom he had been strangely indifferent even in the earlier years of their marriage. After his return she had always shown herself reluctant to go out to Rheinsberg with him, and his aversion for Berlin had grown in part out of his active dislike of some of the numerous friends with whom she was always surrounded there; for she was still beautiful and popular. Both prince and princess were high-spirited, proud, and increasingly sharp-tongued; and the old queen mother, who had been genuinely fond of her daughter-in-law and whom Henry had always hesitated to displease, was no longer there to keep them from quarreling.[18]

It was, then, no unspoiled Eden into which Kalckreuth insinuated

[15] Letters of Henry to Ferdinand from Carlsbad, in the Hausarchiv, Rep. 56, II, F, and of the countess Caroline of Hesse to her husband, in *Briefwechsel*, I, 69; Lehndorff, *Dreissig Jahre*, 473; *Nachträge*, I, 427. Frederick instructed his ministers to send to the empress, through diplomatic channels, a "very obliging compliment" as an official message of thanks for the courtesies shown the prince by her order. He also authorized Prince Henry to write her a personal letter, and instructed him as to the etiquette to be observed in addressing her. *P. C.*, XXIV, 235, 258.

[16] *P. C.*, XXV, 140, 161, 172; M. P., VII, 43, 48. Joseph did not keep the appointment, so at Kloster Zinna, on the Saxon frontier, the brothers turned back. There were rumors to the effect that the king had met the emperor secretly there. Mitchell thought it more probable that he had made the trip only to set the rumors running.

[17] The palace stands at the foot of Unter den Linden, on the north side of that street, quite near the royal Schloss. It has been used as the principal building of the Friedrich Wilhelm University, or "University of Berlin," ever since that institution was founded. See the illustration facing page 238.

[18] In March, 1763, the prince had already confessed to Lehndorff that he could no longer easily bring himself to make new acquaintances, although many of the best of his old friendships, when renewed, had lost their savor for him. "Even the princess his wife," Lehndorff's journal continues, "is estranged from him in consequence of the long separation, and he spends the evenings usually alone or with one or two persons while his wife entertains company in her apartments." Lehndorff, *Dreissig Jahre*, 453.

himself — if Kalckreuth was the serpent; but, although the exact degree of his culpability would be difficult now to determine, there is little doubt that the prince's adjutant was the immediate cause of the final separation. Kalckreuth had always been a scheming and deceitful rogue and trouble-maker, and he finally precipitated some serious trouble between the prince and the princess. Wilhelmina was banished from Rheinsberg forever, and from 1766 onward was assigned separate quarters in one wing of the palace in Berlin, while Prince Henry, when he was in town, occupied the other wing. Beyond that, nothing was done to disgrace her or to make a scandal. Kalckreuth was sent off to garrison duty at Königsberg — a form of exile from which he was not to return during the twenty years that Frederick had left to live.

The chief culprit's own comment on the case was written many years later, in connection with his account of the battle of Freiberg. There Kalckreuth says the prince acknowledged publicly at the time that that victory was entirely due to his work as adjutant, and assured him that so long as he had so much as a single thaler left he would gladly share it with him. Then the chivalrous Kalckreuth adds: "The jesters who have believed the tale that I was the princess's lover have said that I took him precisely at his word — which was a joke." [19]

It was commonly believed and widely told at the time that the princess had been betrayed by a letter of hers to Kalckreuth which had fallen into the hands of her husband — that she had admitted to the prince having been unfaithful to him, and that he was restrained from divorcing her only by Frederick's cooler counsel. Invoking reasons of state and family interest to strengthen Prince Henry's natural reluctance to let such a matter become public, the king was believed to have appealed successfully also to his brother's personal pride, on the ground that a strong man goes his way regardless of the thorns that a light-minded woman may put in his path. [20]

The prince went his way — in silence. Although he never revealed whether he had been wounded more deeply by the misconduct of which he believed his unloved wife to have been guilty or by the faithlessness of his trusted adjutant, he was obviously hurt; and he nursed his injury for many years. He maintained a modest establishment for the princess for the rest of his life, but saw her thereafter only when they met at some court function once or twice a year; then he only bowed to her coldly

[19] ". . . ce qui était bon pour rire." *Paroles*, 253.
[20] There are many secondary accounts of the incident, all very much alike. This narrative has followed most closely that of F. R. Paulig, *Friedrich der Grosse, König von Preussen. Neue Beiträge zur Geschichte seines Privatlebens, seines Hofes, und seiner Zeit* (Frankfurt a. Oder, 1892), which is Volume III of the series *Familiengeschichte des Hohenzollernschen Kaiserhauses*.

without speaking. When it was necessary, he wrote to her on business matters with a devastatingly formal politeness. Many years later, as an old man with all anger spent, he agreed to a formal reconciliation with Kalckreuth; but beyond stating in his last will that he harbored no grudge against his wife and wished for her such comfort and happiness as she could still find at such an advanced age, he made no other public admission of his haunting doubt whether his treatment of her had been either just or merciful.

And the princess went her way — but not in silence. Since she was not to be divorced or publicly disgraced, she was not banished from the court, and Frederick was pointedly polite to her at those semipublic family gatherings which she still attended. Soon after her repudiation by her husband she had occasion to thank the king for some new tapestries just hung in her wing of the palace divided against itself, and assured him that his goodness to her was her only consolation.[21] To others she complained bitterly that she had been falsely accused and unjustly treated; but few except her self-contained companion in obscurity, the queen of Prussia, and the generous-hearted countess Caroline of Hesse dared to show her the sympathy they secretly felt for her, or to discuss the subject with the angry prince. The king himself, of course, would have dared anything he thought desirable; but he did not choose to re-open the question.

Through the countess Caroline, three years after the separation, the princess sought a reconciliation. The king had by that time decided to divorce the Prince of Prussia from his first wife; the prospect of an immediate remarriage and the hope of insuring the succession in the direct male line made a divorce in the family seem more urgently necessary for dynastic reasons and therefore less ugly or disgraceful from other points of view than it would have been in Prince Henry's case; and the countess was bringing her daughter Frederika to be Frederick William's second bride. As Wilhelmina was her warm and intimate friend and had herself come to Prussia from Hesse as a bride less than twenty years before, both ladies hoped that her experience could be drawn upon to guide young Frederika aright.

The position of Princess of Prussia would undeniably be difficult, wrote Wilhelmina to the countess Caroline, but the girl who was about to take it must not be discouraged. She should remember to be prudent and reserved in her responses to the king and all others, but she should

---

[21] Hausarchiv, Rep. 56, II, T. She continued to write him letters of congratulation or of condolence when events furnished occasion for them, and to receive brief but kindly replies from him, for the rest of his life.

be cheered in advance by the knowledge that Frederick William was not likely to treat her unkindly. "The prince is incomparably good-hearted; that is a great deal in itself. [But] she must never ask where he is, never; he detests having people inquire into what he does. And above all, no umbrage at anything; this point is essential. The princess should never speak to him first in public, but should answer him always in a gay and friendly tone. Even in public, let him notice that she is attached to him, and he will soon love her more than anyone else. I do not know anyone more responsive to affection than this prince; he has really some admirable qualities." [22]

Then came her own call for help: "Four weeks from now I shall embrace you. This hope quickens within me a feeling of true and living joy, a sensation unknown to my soul these three years. Perhaps you will find an opportunity to make more tolerable the time I have left to live by the signs of friendship which you show me in the presence of certain persons, letting them see that you are still my friend. Surely that will make them reflect. I am sure, dear princess, that my situation arouses your sympathy; I am put to hard proofs; I stand them better than I should have believed." [23]

The countess knew better than to attempt either intervention or mediation. Princess Amelia, who professed some sympathy for Wilhelmina, although she conceded that Henry had a real grievance as well as a grudge, had warned her against it; and the prince himself had given her to understand that it would be useless. Knowing and in no way resenting the fact that she was his wife's friend as well as his, he broke in that one case his otherwise invariable rule never to discuss his marital affairs with outsiders:

For the last three years I have entirely broken off all relations with her. My intention is to inform you of the facts, not to accuse her or to justify myself, but there is no person whom I mistrust as much as her. Anything that might injure me, anything that could wrong me — I may reckon on her never to neglect an occasion to render me services of this sort. It follows that her intimate friends cannot be mine, and that any very marked confidence in her shown by your protégée [the bride-to-be of the Prince of Prussia] would make me very cautious as to the services which I might render her. I implore you, Madame, in the event of my having the happiness of seeing you here, to act as you have always done — to suspend judgment between us two; but should one party speak too strongly against the other, then but not sooner to inform yourself thoroughly. I propose to keep silence.[24]

[22] *Briefwechsel*, I, 150. Evidently a wife should seek to please!
[23] *Ibid*. Part of the letter is printed, in English, by Hamilton in *Rheinsberg*, II, 323.
[24] *Ibid.*, 323, 331.

He not only kept silence; he required others to keep it. Only once did anyone have the temerity to break it in public. On that occasion, although the luckless offender was no less a personage than the future queen of Prussia, his wrath blazed up in a scene which became the talk of the town; and the impulsive Princess of Prussia, who had only sought to do her Hessian kinswoman and friend Wilhelmina a service, was sternly rebuked by her mother for her rashness.

"You have had a very lively scene with Prince Henry," wrote the redoubtable countess Caroline to her daughter; "I have never, however, ceased to remind you of the obligations you are under to this prince. I have written you and I have conjured you to show yourself devoted to him on every occasion, and not to affect too great a friendship for the princess in his presence or where he is concerned. The prince is a man of superior merit, but he does not pardon when one fails him. Was it for his niece, a person of twenty years, to give him lessons on his feelings for the princess? You know how well I love her, and I am on a far more familiar footing with the prince, after knowing him for twenty years, than you are; but I should never dare to speak to him on such a subject. . . . Your scene with the prince will be the talk of Berlin." [25]

Repeatedly the distracted countess warned her daughter that she must not again offend the prince and must conciliate the princess Amelia by seeking counsel and guidance always and only from her, as Frederick had stipulated before her marriage that she must do. Otherwise Caroline feared that the princess Henry would be hurt rather than helped by the younger woman's misguided efforts to defend her. [26]

When Henry's sister Ulrika, the queen of Sweden, revisited the home of her youth some six years after his separation from his wife, she sought privately but vainly to bring about a reconciliation of the estranged pair. She found, as others had, that it was quite possible to remain on friendly terms with both but impossible to bring them together. If Henry ever asked himself whether he had judged his wife too hastily, or considered making any change in their anomalous way of living, he gave no outward sign of it. Countess Caroline, recognizing what she knew she could not change, again cautioned her daughter accordingly: "He is a great prince, but he does not forgive."

[25] *Ibid.*, 96. Mother knew best.
[26] *Ibid.*, 102, 110. "Ménagez, au nom de Dieu, la princesse Amélie."

# CHAPTER XVII

# The Polish Succession

*"There is a war on in Europe in which I am not taking part."*— Frederick to Voltaire, May 24, 1770.

THE FIXED PRINCIPLE of Frederick's foreign policy in the decade following the Seven Years' War was his determination to maintain the position Prussia had won among the powers, but to do so without being drawn into another war before he was ready for it. Openly and truthfully disavowing the thought of attacking anyone, he still found it necessary to seek an imposing alliance as insurance that he would never be attacked. He considered it axiomatic that Maria Theresa's personal animosity, together with Austrian jealousy and hatred of Prussia, would preclude the possibility of any cordial Austro-Prussian combination. France he neither feared as a potential enemy nor esteemed very highly as a potential ally. In Britain he had no confidence whatever. Russia, however, loomed larger in his field of vision than all the others combined. Zorndorf and Kunersdorf were not soon to be forgotten, nor had he ever denied even to himself that the timely death of the czarina Elizabeth had been one of the strokes of fortune that saved him from destruction in the late war. So, largely because it was Russia that he feared most, it was Russia's alliance that he courted.

Seeking the surest way to Catherine's favor, Frederick resolved in advance to support her policy in Poland and her candidate for the Polish kingship whenever that throne should fall vacant. As early as April, 1763, word had come back from St. Petersburg that the Russian empress was favorably disposed in principle toward the idea of an alliance with Prussia — to be concluded as soon as the "domestic affairs" of both monarchies were in order — and "grateful to the king of Prussia for his readiness to support her views in the matter of the Polish succession." [1]

By thus committing himself in advance to the support of the Russian policy in Poland, Frederick closed another door in the face of his brother Henry. Early in October, 1763, he notified the prince of the death of Augustus III, king of Poland and elector of Saxony, and of the illness of one of his favorite dogs, in a tone indicating that one loss was about

[1] M. P., VI, 224, 228. Mitchell's report was based upon statements made to him in Berlin by the Russian minister, Prince Dolgoruki.

as important to the world — and to Henry — as the other: "And now the king of Poland has died like a fool! I confess to you that I do not like these people who do everything at the wrong time. I hope, however, that this election will pass off without resulting in any new troubles. I have a domestic grief: my poor dog is about to die. I must console myself with the thought that if death does not spare crowned heads, poor Alcimène could expect no better fate." [2]

Frederick probably knew that his brother was, or might be, taking something more than an ordinary patriotic interest in the question, but he was careful not to say so to Henry. The prince himself was equally circumspect, and left all discussion of the matter to his friends; but rumors of his being offered the Polish throne were soon current, and continued to circulate for many years.

The stories started as soon as word came that the king of Poland had died. Prince Henry himself was called upon by General Gadomski, who brought to Frederick the official notice of that event, and was told that a strong party of Polish noblemen proposed to support him as their candidate in the forthcoming election. What was to come of it, Lehndorff confided to his diary, only the future would show. Very little would come of it, Mitchell thought, although the prince had every personal qualification for the position and well merited the honor; Austria would never agree to it, especially during Frederick's lifetime, and Frederick himself would rather deny Henry that doubtful distinction than forfeit the friendship of Russia. [3]

Mitchell guessed Frederick's attitude accurately enough. Frederick wanted a long peace, and would naturally not choose to offend two empresses simultaneously. He had done that once, some years before, and once was enough. Russia's friendship, with an alliance, was worth more to him than Poland would be — even with a Prussian king — if it brought him Russia's enmity. So he did his best to suppress the movement, branded as "false" a report from Warsaw that the throne was to be offered to his brother, and sharply ordered his counsellor of legation in Warsaw, Benoît, to pay no attention to such "fabrications." [4]

While thus rather ostentatiously withholding his support from any rival candidate, Frederick virtually invited Catherine to name one of her own. He even suggested that she might send in troops if she provided

---

[2] October 9, in *Oeuvres*, XXVI, 288; Schöning, III, 569.

[3] M. P., VI, 243, 250; Lehndorff, *Dreissig Jahre*, 469; *Nachträge*, I, 383.

[4] P. C., XXIII, 220. In the same dispatch he made it equally plain that no Saxon claims would have his support either. He obviously expected both messages to be passed on to Russia's Warsaw representative.

herself beforehand with a pretext by having the Czartoryski party ask her for protection. She had only to inform him of her purposes, he indicated, so that he would not in his ignorance, despite his good intentions, blunder into some course counter to them. In the meantime, "having no definite agreement" with Russia, he confessed to Catherine that he hardly knew how to answer the communications of the dowager electress of Saxony on the subject. In other words he was willing to support Catherine's policy in Poland, but she must let him know what it was, and she must make it worth his while by joining him in an alliance.[5]

The king carefully refrained from pledging himself too definitely until he was sure of his *quid pro quo* — the treaty of alliance signed on April 11, 1764. By the terms of that treaty, as a part of the price of the insurance he thought he was getting, he agreed to support Catherine's candidate, Stanislas Poniatowski, who was eventually elected king of Poland on September 7. By then the question of Prince Henry's candidacy had again arisen and again been quashed. Frederick adhered consistently to his policy of officially supporting the Poniatowski candidacy, but he did so in the face of a bold Polish effort to tempt him away from it.

A certain General Mokranowski, acting as confidential agent of the "grand general of the crown," Count Branicki, appeared in Berlin on July 24 and sought an interview with the king. Under the pseudonym of "Captain von Kersky, a dealer in Polish horses," he was admitted to the king's presence at Potsdam the next day. There he appealed first to Frederick's pride, asking why the king of Prussia, who always took the lead and went his own way elsewhere in Europe, should seem content to play second fiddle in Poland and to support without question a policy dictated by another. Why had he himself not given Poland a king, his brother Prince Henry, for example, who was endowed with so many kingly gifts of mind and character and whom the Poles themselves would have welcomed?

The king turned the question aside as if it were purely incidental to the principal issue — as in fact it was — with the offhand remark that his brother "would not want to turn Catholic." He easily divined that Mokranowski's real mission was to complain against the pro-Russian party and against such active Russian intervention as was taking place, to induce him to intervene in opposition, and as a last resort to secure his protection for the Branicki group if the Russian influence should in the end prove too strong for them. This comfort he refused them, advising them in friendly fashion to compose their differences, accept the

[5] Frederick to Catherine, October 7, 1763, in *P. C.*, XXIII, 141.

inevitable, and forget their foolish fears. The allied powers, he said, intended only to establish the liberties of the kingdom, not to suppress them.

Having thus, as he hoped, put Mokranowski and his associates "back on the right track," he sought to prepare the way for their restoration to the fold of the well-disposed by sending at once to St. Petersburg a report which discreetly omitted all reference to his making his brother a candidate or intervening in any way except as mediator, and included only the general's written propositions concerning an anti-Russian or "patriotic" confederation and an eventual reconciliation of the parties, with his own answers thereto. He then instructed Count Solms, his privy counsellor of legation at St. Petersburg, to suggest to the Russian minister, Count Panin, the advisability of treating the Branicki-Mokranowski group with all possible moderation, lest the Turks or some other ill-intentioned outsiders should find a pretext for intervention.[6]

Intervention was indeed the rule in Poland during the reign of the shadow-king Stanislas, and the distinction between the well-disposed and the ill-disposed lay largely in the point of view. At the insistence of Prussia and Russia, Protestants and Dissidents (adherents of the ortho-

---

[6] *P. C.*, XXIII, 446–449. In February the king had induced Poniatowski to promise a starosty each to Gadomski and Mokranowski, and had emphasized the necessity of winning Branicki's support. *Ibid.*, 243, 276.

The story of Prince Henry's having been "offered the Polish crown" has been told in many varying versions. Bouillé and most of his other early biographers say that two such offers were made and that Frederick, supposing that his brother knew nothing of them, specifically ordered the Polish messengers to go home at once without seeing or speaking to the prince. Princess Castellane Radziwill, in her introduction to Princess Louise of Prussia's *Forty-five Years of My Life* (New York, 1912), says that Frederick refused Mokranowski's two offers "solely through jealousy" of Henry, whom he feared as a rival. (Princess Louise was Henry's niece, a daughter of his brother Ferdinand. Her husband, Prince Radziwill of Poland, was one of those interested.) Hamilton and Maschke (*op. cit.*) seem to have accepted the Bouillé story. The version here given is based upon the written testimony of Mokranowski and Frederick themselves, as found in the Saxon and Prussian archives and in the *Politische Correspondenz*, much of which is presented and reviewed by Dr. G. B. Volz in his "Prinz Heinrich von Preussen und die polnische Krone," in the *F. B. P. G.*, XVIII, 188–201.

Five years after the event General Mokranowski told his tale again, in Paris, to the Prussian Baron Goltz, who at once reported it to Frederick. The king replied that although Mokranowski had certainly come to see him at the time indicated and might well have made him some such proposition, it was "out of the question" that he should have replied simply that his brother did not want to turn Catholic; which all seems to mean that, while he may have said that, he had not and could not have said *only* that. *P. C.*, XXIX, 86.

In November, 1770, while the prince was in St. Petersburg, the Polish Count Wielhorski approached the Prussian secretary of legation in Paris with a new proposal to make Prince Henry hereditary king of Poland with French support, as one of the activities of a renewed Franco-Prussian alliance. If the suggestion was seriously meant, it may have indicated a hope that the Russian-Prussian combination in Poland might be broken up. Frederick replied only by cautioning Sandoz Rollin that the Poles were not to be trusted, and that Choiseul had probably sent this one to him merely in the hope of tricking him into some indiscretion. *P. C.*, XXX, 282.

dox Greek Catholic church) were guaranteed the same rights there as Roman Catholics. In protest against that concession and against continued Russian domination, the Confederation of Bar was formed and a futile bid was made for Austrian support. Russian troops were sent in instead, the confederation was suppressed, and its fleeing adherents were pursued by Russian troops across the southern border into Turkish territory. From 1768 to 1774 Russia and Turkey were at war.

By the terms of his alliance with Russia, Frederick had to pay her a cash subsidy as a war aid; but so long as hostilities were confined to the two original belligerents, he was not otherwise involved, and could laugh gleefully, more than a year later, at Voltaire's apparent surprise that he was permitting a war to be fought in Europe without taking part.[7]

He did not intend to take any active part if he could avoid it; even the payment of the subsidy was irksome enough, and he lived in constant apprehension lest he find himself more deeply involved.

[7] May 24, 1770, in the *Oeuvres complètes de Voltaire*, LXV, 403.

CHAPTER XVIII

# The First Partition of Poland

*"There are no powers that cannot be friends while making treaties that promise their mutual aggrandizement."*—
Henry to Frederick, December 1, 1769.

THE LONGER the Russo-Turkish hostilities continued, the greater grew the danger that Austria-Hungary, alarmed by some Russian success, might enter the war to keep so powerful and potentially dangerous a neighbor out of Wallachia and Moldavia. Prussia would then be obligated to fight as Russia's ally. So Frederick, although he carefully refrained from making the first move, even diplomatically, was glad to invite the young emperor Joseph II to meet him on Prussian soil for a personal interview. The matter was first broached by Austrian initiative in November, 1768, but the meeting did not take place until the following August, when the king's presence in Silesia for the usual inspections and maneuvers furnished a pretext and Neisse a convenient meeting place.[1]

Prince Henry, informed of the proposed interview two months in advance and again invited to accompany the king, looked forward to it even more optimistically than did the king himself.[2] In it he thought he saw the possibility of a real *rapprochement* between Prussia and Austria, and in such a move an opportunity for Frederick then to compel Russia to accept his advice along with his money, and probably to "pacify the east and the north" by inducing her to reduce her demands on Turkey and assume a more conciliatory attitude toward Sweden. Frederick, on the other hand, while quite willing to go and see what manner of man the energetic young emperor might be, was too cautious to promise himself any such great success. He would be a long time dead and forgotten,

---

[1] *P. C.*, XXVII, 441–445. In June, 1766, Frederick and Prince Henry had traveled together as far as the Saxon border, expecting to meet Joseph at Torgau, but had turned back when word reached them that the young emperor would be unable to keep the appointment. They always supposed that they had Kaunitz and the emperor's mother to thank for that disappointment. M. P., VII, 43, 48; *P. C.*, XXV, 140, 161, 172; *Oeuvres*, XXVI, 304. See *supra*, page 244, note 16.

[2] The prince's accompanying his brother might have been looked upon as a routine matter, inasmuch as everyone considered him the king's obvious alternate or substitute as field commander in case of war. Although the world presumably did not know it, he was in fact so designated in the Political Testament of the year before.

254

he feared, before that youngster could ever succeed in freeing himself from leading strings.[3]

At Neisse, from August 25 to August 28, the brothers vied with one another in honoring their distinguished guest, while he divided his attention between them. There were rides, reviews, dinners, and — in spite of the emperor's official incognito — an elaborate exchange of gifts and compliments.[4]

Judged only by its immediate results, the conference could not be called exceptionally fruitful. Frederick tried hard to convince his guest that he was no longer the ambitious and aggressive youth who had given Austria such good reason to distrust him in the past; but Joseph wrote in his journal that "the old hostility" was still a part of the nature of the man with whom he had been exchanging compliments and professions of friendship for the past four days.[5]

Joseph suggested some partial disarmament, and stated roundly that Austria had forgotten all about Silesia; Frederick hinted at joint action for the "pacification" of Poland; but the emperor had been so thoroughly warned and coached beforehand by Kaunitz, and the king was so cautious by nature, that it would have been quite impossible for either of them to say anything that the other would accept at face value. So it is not surprising that the net political product of the meeting was an agreement that both powers would remain neutral if the threatened French-British war should become a reality or if any other new war should break out in Europe.

Prince Henry, as a member of Frederick's retinue and a guest at his table, was a silent listener through some but not all of his interminable conversations with the youthful scion of the house of Hapsburg. After their return home, the prince permitted his imagination to catch fire when Frederick told him that plans for the return visit were already being made and that he looked forward to a long series of interviews

[3] *Oeuvres*, XXVI, 316–319; *P. C.*, XXVIII, 316; XXIX, 10.

[4] Joseph asked particularly to be permitted to see the Seydlitz regiment. Stories were presently in circulation to the effect that the emperor had displayed a certain preference for Prince Henry's company and consequently had so irked the king that the prince would certainly not be permitted to accompany him on an eventual return visit, even if he were invited by Joseph to do so. Such stories seem to deserve little credence. When the return visit took place Henry was already absent on a far more important and congenial mission. See Friedrich Oppeln-Bronikowski and G. B. Volz, *Gespräche Friedrichs des Grossen* (Berlin, 1919), 140–142, and Volz in *F. B. P. G.*, XVIII, 153.

[5] *P. C.*, XXIX, 41ff. How quickly both the illustrious protagonists could relax after being on their best behavior for days is indicated by their contrasting accounts of the invitation to a return visit. "He was a very curious object to see once," Joseph wrote; "but God preserve [me] from a second; he threatens to come to Kolin some time to return the visit." Frederick, on the other hand, wrote to Finckenstein: "He has asked me to come to Bohemia to see his troops, and did it so politely that I have promised to come next year to

in which he would work step by step toward the establishment of a better understanding with the land of his ancient enemies. Why, Henry asked, should not Frederick and Joseph, like Octavius and Anthony, divide Germany between them? Provided that it were done while Russia was too fully occupied in Poland and Turkey to be able to interfere with its execution, he thought the thing quite possible.

Frederick thought otherwise. Joseph, he said, was too young and impulsive to be at all dependable. Joseph's mother, on the other hand, might live and have a voice in state affairs for many years yet; and she would not soon break her thirty-year-old habit of hating the king of Prussia. Furthermore it would be another fifteen years before the state of the Austrian treasury would permit that power to embark upon any ambitious new project. And finally, Frederick said, he was himself already too old for any important new venture.[6]

The king was in fact "too old" only because he was not feeling venturesome at the moment. What he wanted most urgently just then was the conclusion of a peace between Russia and Turkey that would release him from the payment of those "accursed subsidies." He could use that money to far better advantage elsewhere, he said; and he wanted to use it quietly, in his own way, in peace. Prince Henry, on the other hand, with no official responsibility to weigh him down and hold his feet on the earth, was free to permit his mind to play with the idea of some very considerable territorial acquisition for Prussia — such as could be made only while all Europe was disturbed by wars and threats of war, and should therefore be made while the Russo-Turkish conflict was still in progress. Thus, he reasoned, those subsidy payments which had so far been a total loss might yet be converted into a profitable investment.

So he replied to the king that Louis XIV had lived to be over seventy and that Frederick, then only fifty-seven, should not think of himself as "old." One ought never to be too old, he urged, to embark upon a new undertaking in the interest of the state. As for the traditional Austrian enmity, there were no powers that could not be friends while making treaties that promised their mutual aggrandizement. If it were undertaken while Britain was still immobilized by political and France by financial difficulties, and while Russia was otherwise occupied, the thing would not only be feasible, he argued, but would not even be dangerous.[7]

whatever camp he chooses." But of the emperor himself he wrote: "He is a man consumed by ambition; . . . restrained for the moment by his mother, he is beginning to chafe under the yoke he is wearing. . . . One may count upon it in any case . . . that Europe will be ablaze when he is master." *Ibid.*, 53.

[6] H. to F., November 22, F. to H., November 26, 1769, *ibid.*, 223–224.

[7] *Ibid.*, 235; *F. B. P. G.*, XXXV, 209. The letter is dated December 1, 1769.

Without asking just what acquisitions his brother had in mind, the king goodnaturedly adhered to his prudent decision not to give his life-long rival and erstwhile victim an opportunity to betray him. The body of Louis XIV and of many another great man, he said, had outlived his brain. Instead of risking everything in an attempt at cooperation with Joseph, he preferred to prompt Maria Theresa to try to discover in Constantinople whether she and he might work together as mediators for the making of peace between Russia and Turkey.[8]

But even so, he had already had to assume one new responsibility involving a new risk against which he wished to protect himself if possible. Returning from Neisse almost empty-handed, he had felt himself obliged to renew his Russian alliance. As part of the price of that renewal he had had to agree to effect a "diversion" in Swedish Pomerania if the Swedish constitution of 1720 were overthrown or if Russia were attacked by Sweden. That part of the treaty was secret, of course, so could not well be made the subject of ordinary correspondence. But he wanted his sister Ulrika, the queen of Sweden, to know about it, so he decided to send Prince Henry to tell her of it, to make to her such explanations as might be necessary, and to bring back a confidential report on the seriousness of the troubled situation there.[9]

Not that the king would have been at all averse to the acquisition of Swedish Pomerania. He had offered to buy it once, in May, 1765, but had quietly dropped the subject when told that it was not for sale.[10] He simply did not want to be compelled to fight there in any war not of his own making.

A personal invitation from Queen Ulrika could always be had for the asking. Twice already, in 1764 and in 1768, she had urgently invited the younger brother to come in lieu of the older, and twice she had been politely but firmly refused by Frederick. On the first occasion she was told that neither the prince's health nor the king's purse had yet recovered sufficiently from the strains of the late war. When the second invitation arrived, the prince was in Holland visiting his niece Wilhelmina, wife of William IV of Orange, and that fact served the king as a pretext

---

[8] *P. C.,* XXIX, 235.

[9] Volz in *F. B. P. G.,* XXXV, 196; Richard Krauel, *Prinz Heinrich von Preussen als Politiker (Quellen und Untersuchungen zur Geschichte des Hauses Hohenzollern,* Band IV, Reihe III, Berlin, 1902), 17. The Swedish constitution of 1720 had put some paralyzing restrictions upon the royal authority without setting up an effective parliamentary government to replace it. Catherine II wanted that constitution preserved because a considerable Swedish parliamentary faction was then in her pay and she thought (wrongly) that she would be better able in that way than otherwise to hold her own against the French influence which was also active there. The young crown prince, later Gustavus III, was believed to be one of the "French" party, and Frederick feared that his nephew might provoke Russia to the point of open war.

[10] *P. C.,* XXIV, 193–194.

for refusal. When it suited his purpose to have his brother make the trip, however, he instructed him to write and ask for a renewal of the invitation; and the "ostensible" letter from Ulrika arrived in due course.[11]

The trip was made during late July, August, and September, 1770, in truly regal style, at the king's expense as far as Stralsund. Thereafter the prince was entertained as Sweden's state guest with all the honors that would have been done Frederick himself. Frederick had stipulated that beforehand. As to the traveler's confidential mission, the king wrote to his sister: "He is my other self, and you will do well to give full credence to whatever he may say to you on my behalf."[12]

What the prince had to say to his sister on his brother's behalf was that attempts to strengthen the monarchy or to win the support of France for it were all very well so long as they were not carried far enough to offend Russia; but Russia must not be offended. What he reported to Frederick was that the Swedish monarchy was actually so weak, and the whole government so paralyzed by factions, that it mattered very little whether it was pro-French or pro-Russian.

From a personal point of view, the visit was highly enjoyable. Absent from her homeland since her marriage twenty-six years before, and saddened by personal and political quarrels at court, the lonely and unhappy Ulrika welcomed her brother's personal ambassador with all her heart. Half the members of the family had died since she left it, and Sweden and Prussia had been at war; but she rejoiced nonetheless in Henry's presence while the members of her entourage admired his courtly manners and the world-ranging sweep of his conversation. With his nephew, soon to become king as Gustavus III, Henry was less successful. Heedless of Russia's susceptibilities, that prince was off for Paris in quest of a French alliance soon after his illustrious uncle's departure.[13]

[11] *P. C.*, XXIII, 435; XXVII, 363, 368; XXIX, 277, 325, 353. Prince Henry's enemies have accused him of angling for this invitation behind the king's back. Such a suspicion might easily arise from the wording of the letter he wrote to his sister on January 1, 1770, asking her to "send me an answer I can show, and let the king know that you want to see me." As a matter of fact, Frederick had already written the day before to Count Solms, privy counsellor of legation at St. Petersburg, that the prince was being sent to Ulrika "to try to inspire in this princess some sentiments more in accord with her true interests"; and the prince himself referred to his letter a little later, in one to the king, as "the letter which you told me, my very dear brother, to write to her." The letter is quoted from the original in the Staatsarchiv by G. B. Volz in *F. B. P. G.*, XXXV, 200. The invitation to visit Catherine II was quite another matter.
[12] *P. C.*, XXX, 37. The prince was authorized in advance to accept whatever Swedish decoration his sister might be able to procure for him. *Ibid.*, 59.
[13] Circumstantial but rather highly colored accounts of the prince's Swedish mission are given by O. G. de Heidenstam in *Une soeur du grand Frédéric, Louise Ulrique, reine de Suède* (Paris, 1897), 332–337, and in the *Mémoires du comte de Hordt* (2 vols., Berlin and Paris, 1789). De Hordt, a Swedish officer in the Prussian service, accompanied the prince both to Stockholm and to St. Petersburg.

Before Prince Henry had left Stralsund en route to Sweden, a letter was on its way from Catherine of Russia to Frederick seeking his consent to her proposal that she invite the prince to visit her also before he returned home. The Russian empress had been duly notified, well in advance, of his Swedish journey and its purposes; but she may well have been consumed with curiosity concerning its results. She knew, moreover, that while Henry was in Stockholm Frederick was "returning" the emperor Joseph's visit of the year before, and sitting in conference with him and with Kaunitz in Moravian Neustadt. Naturally eager to know how her interests had fared in those conversations, she welcomed the opportunity to learn what she could in direct conversation with the brother who had been with the king of Prussia at Neisse and who had gone as his personal spokesman to Sweden.[14]

The first initiative had been taken, however, not by Catherine but by Henry himself — he had asked for the invitation without Frederick's knowledge. So, although the project suited the king's purpose admirably, it came to him as a surprise.

Prince Henry's decision thus to get himself invited to St. Petersburg without Frederick's previous knowledge or consent, and there to gamble with Catherine for stakes that Frederick himself had called too high, was in many ways the boldest stroke of his life; but it was a natural outgrowth of his discussions of policy with his brother after their journey to Neisse in 1769.[15] Unable to induce the king to take even the first steps toward the seizure of West Prussia, he had decided to take them himself and virtually to make Prussia a present of the province!

Almost immediately after his Swedish journey had become a certainty the prince took advantage of Prince Dimitrii Galitzin's presence in Berlin to send word secretly to the Russian vice-chancellor, Prince Alexander Galitzin, that he would welcome an invitation to visit the Russian court, provided only that his brother should never know he had asked for it. Catherine replied at once through the same confidential channels that she would have preferred to have him come in summer when she could entertain him better, as she had practically to hibernate in winter, but that she would be happy to have him at any time and would send her yacht to fetch him from Stockholm if he wished.[16]

---

[14] On June 17 Frederick had written to Henry: "My little journey to Moravia will make more of a pacifying impression upon the empress of Russia than all the troops and all the reviews in the world." *P. C.,* XXIX, 520; *Oeuvres,* XXVI, 320.

[15] See the letters of November 22 and December 1, 1769, cited in notes 6, 7, and 8, *supra.*

[16] Letters of February 20, March 8, and May 1, 1770, quoted from the *Sbornik* of the Imperial Russian Historical Society (Vol. XCVII, pp. 34, 66ff.) by G. B. Volz in *F. B. P.G.,* XXXV, 197ff. Until he was convinced by these documents, even Dr. Volz had sup-

True to her bargain, on July 30, new style (July 19, old style), Catherine wrote to Frederick as if she were only then yielding to an impulse which had been making itself felt more and more strongly ever since she had learned that Prince Henry was to be in Sweden that summer. She could not possibly permit anyone, she said, so closely connected with Frederick himself and for whom she cherished feelings of such admiration and esteem to come so near to St. Petersburg without asking him to come to see her also. She would be particularly happy to renew her acquaintance with Prince Henry, whom she had met during her girlhood in Germany. In short, she was waiting only for Frederick's consent. If that were given, her happiness would be complete, and an invitation would go off to the prince at once.

The king replied, in a letter even more heavily larded with flattery than hers, that he was sure neither stormy seas nor rock-bound shores would stop the prince from coming. Far from withholding his consent, he pretended only to envy his brother the privilege of conversing face to face with such a princess.

On the same day he wrote to Prince Henry:

I have just this moment received a letter from the empress of Russia of which, my dear brother, I am sending you a copy. She asks for you so urgently that it is a journey which I do not believe that you could refuse to make. I well understand that it will perhaps not give you all the pleasure possible,[17] but one must make a virtue of necessity; you will arrange all that as you see fit. If you need money, let me know, and I can get 8,000 thaler to you at St. Petersburg.

You know well, my dear brother, how necessary it is to handle that woman carefully.[18] If you can reconcile her with my sister of Sweden, that will be an achievement and will please me very much. In general, I commend to you everything affecting our interests. You will get to know there plenty of people whom we shall need to use. You will please pay the empress on my behalf the most flattering compliments, and say all that you can about the admiration she inspires everywhere; in short, do whatever seems proper. You will have time en route to collect an arsenal of pretty speeches which you can use as the occasion calls for them. If she wants to give you her order, you

---

posed that the invitation was unsolicited. See his articles in *F. B. P. G.*, XVIII, 155ff., and in the *Historische Vierteljahrschrift, Sonderabdruck*, XXVII (1932). Other writers have convinced themselves that neither of the brothers was at all surprised by it, although both of them pretended to be.

[17] Only five months had elapsed since the prince, in expressing his sympathy with Frederick over the necessity of paying seemingly endless subsidies to "so barbarous a nation" as Russia while deriving no benefit from the expenditure, had referred to Catherine as "a sovereign whose character does not inspire friendship." Quoted by Volz in *F. B. P. G.*, XXXV, 210.

[18] ". . . il faut ménager cette femme."

must accept it.[19] Finally, I fully depend for everything else upon your good judgment to make good use of every opportunity that may present itself there.

I am much annoyed not to have known this sooner; I could have told you many things.[20]

Nearly three weeks later, after he had had time to send Prince Henry a special cipher to be used by himself only, he was able to speak his mind and his second thoughts more plainly.

The empress of Russia, my dear brother, wants to see you at her court. You judge rightly that she wants only to listen to your blandishments and to display herself to you in all her glory. You must then agree with her ideas and try to praise her adroitly upon every possible pretext, such as her grand designs, her wise measures, her successes due to her vast genius, the magnificence and refinement of her court, etc. I trust that you will find occasion to free my sister of Sweden, so far as you can, from blame for the grievances that the empress thinks she has against her, and to do whatever you can to mollify her spirit.

As for me, you will talk to her about my admiration for her qualities of greatness and about how infinitely I value her friendship; and as for the present war, after having overwhelmed her with praises, if that is possible, you will add that her moderation in the peace will crown her magnificent work. Perhaps you can adroitly draw either out of her or out of Count Panin the conditions upon which she will be willing to make peace, saying at the same time that I have never said anything to you about it. I believe that a dearth of money is making itself felt there, and that this consideration may render Russia more tractable in the matter of peace. If this is true you may perhaps get some idea of it from the foreign ministers resident at that court, as well as of the state of their revenues, an innocent enough question on the lips of a foreign prince on his travels who simply seeks to learn what he can.

. . . If you speak of my journey to Moravia, you may say that, the emperor having made me the first visit, I should have been considered a very rude person if I had not returned it. . . .

In conclusion, my dear brother, however disagreeable this journey may be to you, I look upon it as inevitable under the present circumstances, especially in view of the advances which the empress of Russia has made to you. Please burn this letter after you have read it; the matters it contains are too important. It must not go with you into the country where you are going, where cleverness is carried much further in matters of curiosity of this sort than is permitted elsewhere.

Federic.

P. S. For God's sake, burn this, my dear brother.[21]

---

[19] The princess Henry had been sent the Order of Saint Catherine five years before, with Frederick's consent and cordial approval. *P. C.*, XXIV, 178, 207.

[20] August 12, 1770, in *P. C.*, XXX, 72–74.

[21] *Ibid.*, 94. Undated draft in the king's own hand, marked only "Chiffre á mon frére

Frederick hoped, through Prince Henry, to prevent further friction between Russia and Sweden which might involve him, and to induce Russia to make an early and moderate peace with Turkey. Then he would be freed from the necessity of paying "those accursed subsidies" and from the potential danger of involvement in another war against Austria. On these matters the prince was authorized "without question" to speak in the king's name. Poland, however, did not figure in their correspondence at all until long after Henry's arrival in St. Petersburg, when Frederick told him that in one of his rare letters to the empress he was urging her to settle the Polish question by conciliation without waiting for the end of her war with Turkey.

On October 15 Frederick announced to his brother the establishment of the "sanitary cordon" across West Prussia which eventually resolved itself into a military occupation. "You have nothing to fear from the plague on your return; I have had a cordon drawn from the principality of Teschen and the New Mark via Tuchel and Marienwerder [to include] all of [East] Prussia, with which the cordon secures me communication, so that you may pass by way of Danzig with perfect safety, which without that would be a matter of great inconvenience." [22]

The idea of acquiring Danzig and West Prussia was not new. In a political memorandum drawn up nine years before he became king and in his political testaments of 1752 and 1768 Frederick had repeatedly pointed out the advantages to be gained by thus filling in the gap (not yet known as a "corridor") between Brandenburg and (East) Prussia. He had also permitted himself in those testaments to dwell briefly on the potential value of Saxony and Swedish Pomerania. All three were discussed merely as possible ultimate fields of expansion, not designated as the objectives of proposed campaigns of conquest.[23]

It was Prince Henry, then, not the king, who had West Prussia definitely in mind as an immediate acquisition for Prussia in 1770, and who engineered his Russian visit with a view to getting it, in the face of Frederick's stated belief that no such gain was then possible and that no such venture would be justifiable at that time.

On May 6, nearly three months before the prince left home, the Austrian minister Nugent had suggested to Frederick that he might well give some thought to the advantages to be derived from the acquisition of

Henri," in the Staatsarchiv, Rep. 92, B, IV, 4. The date is supplied by the editors of the *Politische Correspondenz* from the ciphered draft.

[22] *Ibid.,* 191. There was in fact a pestilence in Warsaw concerning which the king's letters to de Rohd, his minister to Austria, would indicate a great and constant concern throughout the winter.

[23] *Politische Testamente Friedrichs des Grossen (P. C.,* supplementary volume), 215, and *F. B. P. G.,* XXIII, 128.

West Prussia and Ermeland, a small enclave of Polish territory almost entirely engulfed by East Prussia.[24]

Frederick turned the proposal aside without showing (to Nugent, at least) any great interest in it; but Prince Henry, when he was told of it, was at once all on fire again. "I admit that my imagination was struck by this idea," he wrote to the king, "the first time you honored me by telling me the (rather vague) propositions that were made you. But, if this is only a vision of mine, it is none the less such a pleasant one that I find it very difficult to renounce it. *I want to see you lord of the Baltic coast,* sharing with the most formidable power in Germany the influence which these two, combined, could have in Europe. If this is [only] a dream, it is [at least] a very happy one, and you may well believe that the interest that I take in your glory makes me wish it were true." [25]

"I see, my dear brother," Frederick replied, "that in the political field you do not suffer from want of a good appetite; but I, being old, have lost that of my youth. Not that your ideas are not excellent; but a man must have the wind of fortune in his sails to succeed in such an enterprise, and I dare not flatter myself that I can do it." It must be remembered, he pointed out, that Russia and Austria were rivals and enemies of Prussia, not friends, and would not readily consent to her aggrandizement.

Certainly they would not, Henry replied, if the matter were not broached until after Russia had got her hands free by terminating her Turkish war; but if they were offered reciprocal gains while that war was still in progress he thought he could guarantee their consent.

"If one could carry out your ideas, my dear brother," Frederick conceded on July 4, "certainly great advantages to the state would be realized from them." But he neither authorized nor apparently expected the prince to make the attempt. This time it was Henry who went boldly ahead while Frederick held back from excess of caution.[26]

Opportunities for confidential conversation with Catherine herself were more numerous and more favorable than Henry had anticipated. Openings for fruitful political activity were thus created by his unquali-

[24] G. B. Volz in *F. B. P. G.*, XVIII, 187; Koser, *Geschichte Friedrichs des Grossen*, III, 313. What Kaunitz had in mind, although Nugent naturally did not say so, was some sort of exchange for Silesia, and also the hope of disrupting the Prussian-Russian alliance by inciting Prussia to some overbold aggression in Poland.
[25] Italics are the author's. This letter of June 22, 1770, is not printed either in the *Oeuvres* or in the *Politische Correspondenz*, but is quoted from the original in the Staatsarchiv by G. B. Volz in *F. B. P. G.*, XVIII, 187.
[26] H. to F., *ibid.* Frederick's letters of June 25 and July 4 were not available when the appropriate volume of the *Politische Correspondenz* was published in 1903, but were printed on the cognizance of Dr. Koser in the *Sitzungsbericht der Akademie* in 1908, p. 286, and in the *Hohenzollern Jahrbuch* of 1909, p. 40. They are quoted by Dr. Volz in *F. B. P. G.*, XXIII, 72.

fied personal and social success. He was not universally admired in Russia but he was generally popular at the court. Catherine not only honored him as Frederick's brother but liked him personally and enjoyed his company. As one of the enlightened despots of the day, she loved to discuss philosophy and literature; to pose as a connoisseur and an amateur of music, painting, and sculpture; to listen to learned papers in her new Academy of Sciences (of which the prince became honorary president); and to try her hand on occasion at the drafting of a theoretically perfect code of laws. She was proud of her acquaintance and her voluminous correspondence with several of the more famous French and German intellectuals of the time. And in all these fields her guest could meet her on her own ground; Voltaire was less a stranger to him than to her, and Friedrich Melchior Grimm had been his guest at Rheinsberg only the year before.

The hardships of the sea voyage from Sweden and the overland journey across Finland had been considerable, but the honors with which he was received at the Russian border and the elaborate provision made for his comfort from that moment onward made them seem unreal in retrospect. Frederick remarked, after reading his full account of the arduous journey and of his magnificent reception at the end of it, that he seemed to have gone through Purgatory and at last to have got to Heaven. He lived sumptuously in a palace provided by the empress; when the weather began to turn cold she took care of his health by sending him a fur coat trimmed with sables and black fox; on his birthday anniversary she showered him with gifts and honors; and every day he was free, if he chose, to eat dinner and supper at her table. At the informal suppers in the "Hermitage" and in the long evenings of conversation that followed them, both of the friendly duelists were likely to be at their best.[27]

Nor was either of them likely ever to forget that it was a duel and not a sentimental interlude, however platonic, in which they were engaged. The prince found it easier to praise the empress than he had supposed it would be, and conscientiously followed his instructions on that point. "We have reason to think that incense is not displeasing to her," he had written to Frederick before his arrival; and he burned it generously.

[27] A detailed reminiscent account of the Russian mission, from the point of view of a member of the prince's entourage, is to be found in the *Memoires du comte de Hordt,* previously cited. Shorter but more useful accounts are given in Dr. Richard Krauel's *Prinz Heinrich von Preussen als Politiker,* already cited, and in the same author's *Briefwechsel zwischen Heinrich Prinz von Preussen und Katherina II von Russland* (same series, Volume VIII, Berlin, 1903). The best sources, however, are still the letters of the principals and the scholarly studies, based upon those documents, by Reinhold Koser and G. B. Volz. See the bibliography and numerous footnote citations.

Even though it involved "saying things that he did not think," he was determined to "handle that woman carefully." [28]

Handling her carefully, however, was not to preclude his attempting to influence her course of action. "The most useful thing you can do for our own good and that of Europe," Frederick wrote bluntly, "will be . . . to persuade those people, if you can, not to reject the mediation of the court of Vienna [in the matter of peace with Turkey] and not to impose intolerable conditions on the Poles." [29]

The prince was unable to persuade Catherine to agree to the mediation of the Austrian court between herself and the sultan. She had already promised to avail herself of the services of Great Britain, she said, if any mediation promised to be useful. Neither the British nor the Austrian offer was accepted. Once at least, however, Henry thought he had induced her to choose the more moderate of two possible courses. She asked him privately one evening whether in his opinion, if peace were not made, she ought to let her army "cross the Rubicon" — that is, the Danube. He pointed out in reply that such a step would be certain to arouse Austria and Hungary against her and that, while of course the king of Prussia would in every emergency remain faithful to his alliance, there would be no advantage for him in such a war, and his attention would in any event be rather fully engrossed by the French, who would no doubt support Austria. Furthermore, he asked, could Wallachia and Moldavia furnish supplies enough to support such an army after it had crossed the river? And what was the nature of the country in which it would have to fight? "Then I must make peace," Catherine remarked. Frederick fully approved of his brother's part in that little bout of wits and nerves.[30]

The king was equally gratified by Henry's personal success with Catherine, and repeatedly advised him to stay in Russia just as long as he considered that anything useful was to be accomplished by doing so. To win the personal confidence of the empress would, he urged, be a public service of incalculable ultimate value to the state. Even Orlov might have his uses; and anyone who promised to be useful was to be carefully cultivated. Only once did Frederick complain; and then it was simply because of the extravagant cost of the gifts the prince was dis-

[28] *P. C.*, XXX, 149.    [29] *Ibid.*

[30] Staatsarchiv, Rep. 92, A, I, 13. Excerpts from the prince's letters are in the *P. C.*, XXX, 255, 256. So went glimmering another highly hypothetical crown for Prince Henry, talked of by others as a potential aspirant to so many and actual seeker and wearer of none. There were rumors on foot in Poland that Catherine intended to set up a kingdom for him by conquering and combining the provinces of Wallachia and Moldavia. Frederick called the proposal "chimerical." Neither Henry nor Catherine ever mentioned it in their correspondence. *Ibid.*, 171, 173.

tributing so freely. An emperor or a king of France, he pointed out, would have given out largesse less freely, and a more experienced hand at that business might have got better results and paid less for them. Those Russians were costing him enough already in subsidies, without this new expenditure for bribes! [31]

To emphasize his brother's status as his personal spokesman in Russia, Frederick himself discontinued for the duration of the prince's stay his old practice of writing on rare occasions directly to the empress herself. Thus freed from the restraints which personal and diplomatic courtesy would have imposed upon him, even if common prudence had not enjoined them, he gave frequent and emphatic expression to his dissatisfaction with Catherine's policies. On October 26, angered by her failure to accept his suggestion of joint Austro-Prussian mediation between her and the sultan, and by her demand that he instruct his representative in Warsaw to support whatever policy she might indicate to hers, he told Henry to make it plain to Panin that he was not in the habit of taking orders so blindly from anyone. "I am resolved," he wrote, "not to get myself involved either in the peace or in the affairs of Poland, and to be only a mere observer of events; those people may either accept us or reject us as mediators, but they shall not openly make sport of us."

By mid-November he was ready to refuse further subsidies if Russia stubbornly insisted upon going on with her Turkish war. "The Turks are asking for peace . . . ," he wrote. "Under the terms of this alliance I have paid subsidies, but if they insist upon continuing the war now I am under no obligation to pay any more; and I shall not in any way sacrifice the welfare and the interest of the country which it is my duty to govern, for the sake of another power's big ideas of conquest. There is a pill for them to gild! . . . I made the alliance with Russia for my own advantage, . . . not to fight under their auspices a ruinous war which does not interest me either in black or in white." [32]

[31] *P. C.*, XXX, 270; *Oeuvres*, XXVI, 336. Such frankness would scarcely have been possible, even for Frederick, in a letter sent through the ordinary diplomatic channels. He and Henry conducted a regular exchange of letters by way of Count Solms, their privy counsellor of legation, whom neither of them fully trusted. This they called their "ostensible" correspondence and, on the theory that it would all be read by Russian spies or shown by Solms to the Russian ministers or their agents, they filled it with praises of Catherine and all her works — and her workers. In letters in Prince Henry's special cipher, sent by way of the Prussian banker Schutze, they said what they meant. A comparison of the letters sent by either of them on the same day, through the two different channels, is often highly enlightening.

[32] *P. C.*, XXX, 219, 234, 271, 275; *Oeuvres*, XXVI, 330, 336. During this same period he was saying in almost every dispatch to his men in Warsaw, Vienna, and St. Petersburg, and to his principal minister Finckenstein, that he proposed to remain a mere spectator in Poland. If Russia kept a foothold there, he wrote to Finckenstein on October 30, Austrian hatred and jealousy of her would only increase — "so much the better for us." *Ibid.*, XXX, 225.

By the time Prince Henry received that last angry protest from the king he was too deeply involved in other matters to think of presenting any such ultimatum. With Solms of Prussia and Panin and privy councillor von Saldern of Russia, he had by that time embarked on the circuitous round of exploratory conversations that led them eventually to the first partition of Poland.

By the end of October he had drafted a "plan for the pacification of Poland," based upon a memorandum drawn up at his request by Count Solms. That plan presupposed the continuance of the elective monarchy and of the *liberum veto,* but looked toward joint Prussian, Russian, and Austrian supervision of Polish affairs. Austria was to guarantee and protect the Roman Catholics, Russia the Dissidents, and Prussia the Protestants.

So far, the prince had not outrun the king. On the very day on which the first of these conversations was taking place, Frederick wrote to Henry that if Russia would propose a plan tolerable to the Poles and submit it to him and to Austria, and if it seemed reasonable to him, he would suggest to Austria that Austria and Prussia should induce the Poles to accept it.[33]

But the prince went right on. Being careful not to commit his government specifically to anything and admitting frankly that he was exceeding his instructions, he broached to von Saldern the possibility of a triple alliance, to include Russia, Prussia, and Austria. Such an alliance, he pointed out, could soon compel Turkey to make peace.

Too soon, perhaps; for if Turkey had been quick enough she might have escaped from the war before her enemies had time to agree among themselves as to the spoils to be plucked from her, and they must then have looked elsewhere for their "compensations." But Prince Henry was already looking elsewhere, and his suggestion of an alliance was only a "feeler" to test out the possibility of joint action in Poland.

Frederick's reply to the prince's report on his conversations of October 30–31 with Panin and von Saldern ran true to form: no crossing of the Rubicon, no new convention of any sort, a quick peace with Turkey.[34]

Meanwhile the prince's idea was at work in all three capitals. Russia still feared Austro-Hungarian intervention in her Turkish war; then why not turn the young emperor Joseph's attention toward Poland instead? Frederick objected to paying further subsidies which, "like money thrown into the river," brought him no return; then why not let him go

[33] Staatsarchiv, Rep. 92, A, I, 13; *P. C.,* XXX, 261, 267, 230; *Oeuvres,* XXVI, 330.
[34] Staatsarchiv, *loc. cit.; P. C.,* XXX, 269, 318. In the same letter, on the assumption that the prince would soon be on his way home, he asked him to have a look at the garrisons and the rebuilt fortifications around Königsberg as he passed.

and get something for his money in Poland, provided of course that Russia herself also found compensation there for any potential gains she might have to forego elsewhere? Frederick need no longer fear being drawn into a war against Austria on the Danube if he were drawn instead into a joint enterprise with her on the Vistula. Once the three courts began to weigh the two complementary propositions, both suggested by Prince Henry, that a joint enterprise involving all three was possible and that Poland was a potential field for it, the making of the first concrete proposal for a partition became largely a question of time and circumstances only.

That proposal was made by Catherine to Prince Henry, just at the moment when her alliance with Frederick seemed to have run upon the rocks and to be on the point of breaking up completely. The prince had been absent from St. Petersburg for nearly a fortnight, from December 24 to January 6, on a journey to Moscow undertaken at Catherine's insistence and with Frederick's approval. Not long before his departure he had been told at last by Count Panin the terms on which Russia would be willing to make peace with Turkey, and had told the count at once that he thought them far too severe. Frederick's reactions, when they eventually came in by courier, proved to be even more unfavorable than Henry had predicted. To Catherine the king elaborated politely his reasons for urging upon her a more moderate course. To the prince he wrote that, although he regretted that such unpleasantness had had to arise while Henry was still in Russia, there was evidently nothing to do but give up and come home at once. "Those people," he declared, wanted war, while he himself was ready to retire from the game and let them play it alone if they insisted upon playing it in that fashion.[35]

The prince was very critical of Frederick's tactics in the matter. The king should have opened negotiations as mediator, he thought, in spite of his disapproval of the terms proposed, and have left it to the Turks or the Austrians to raise objections in the course of the discussion. His chief concern, however, was not over the success or failure of the Russian-Turkish peace negotiations. It suited him better that they should fail. He preferred that Russia should be at war for another year and still in need of an ally, so that Prussia's value to her would be enhanced. All that seriously disturbed him was the fear that Frederick's tone would offend Catherine and wreck the plan for a partition of Poland which was already taking shape in St. Petersburg.

[35] The drafts of Frederick's letter and memorandum to Catherine are in the Staatsarchiv, Rep. 92, B, IV, 4. In the *Politische Correspondenz* (XXX, 370–374), they are printed from the archives of the Russian foreign office. F. to H., in the Staatsarchiv and in *P. C.*, XXX, 355, 357, 384, *et passim; Oeuvres*, XXVI, 344ff.

Things were beginning to happen far too fast for the means of communication then available. Frederick's memorandum admonishing Catherine on the subject of her proposed peace terms had been on its way for just a week, and its journey was still less than half completed, when the empress remarked casually to Prince Henry one evening that the Austrians had seized two starosties in Poland, taken over their legal and financial administration, and quartered troops on their frontiers. Then, as if half jokingly, she asked him: "Why should not everyone take some also?" The prince replied that while the king of Prussia had drawn a sanitary cordon across a part of Poland, such a cordon did not constitute occupation of it. "But why not occupy it?" asked Catherine smilingly.

A little later in the evening Count Czernichev broached the same subject to him: "Why don't you take Ermeland?" he asked. "After all, everyone ought to get something." [36]

Although he very soon discovered that Count Panin was opposed to Russian participation in such a venture, Prince Henry could already see the king of Prussia, if not yet actually "lord of the Baltic shore," at least well on the way to large and easily won territorial gains. Frederick showed little interest in the project. For six months Austrian and Hungarian troops and officials had been occupying certain districts in southwestern Poland and administering them on the basis of a very ancient but newly revived claim on behalf of the queen of Hungary; but Frederick had refused officially to believe that that occupation meant anything more than his own sanitary cordon in the northwest — which he said officially meant nothing at all. Throughout the month of January, 1771, after the Austrians had slightly extended their occupied area, rumors of a partition of Poland had flown thick about his head, but he had given them no countenance. On January 8, while Catherine was suggesting a partition to Prince Henry, the king of Prussia was writing to Solms that whether Russia made an early and decent peace with Turkey was the only question of any major importance. [37]

To Prince Henry's excited after-midnight report of January 8 on his momentous conversation with the empress, the king replied as if that sort of thing were a regular weekly occurrence in his life, and as if he found it rather boring. The last war had exhausted Prussia, he said; she was not ready for a new one, so must run no risks. As for Ermeland, which was dangled before his eyes, he wouldn't give six sous for it. He thought it better to wait and see what might happen. With others at

[36] H. to F., January 8, 1771, in *P. C.*, XXX, 406, and in *Oeuvres*, XXVI, 345. The original document is in the Staatsarchiv, *loc. cit.* See the map facing page 271.

[37] Staatsarchiv, *loc. cit.* See also his correspondence with Benoît in Warsaw, Rohd in Vienna, and Finckenstein in Berlin, *ibid., passim.*

war, the gains ought to be for the neutrals rather than for the belligerents; and he meant Prussia to be one of the neutrals. It would in any case be dangerous, and an unpardonable blunder, for Frederick to contribute in any way to the aggrandizement of Russia. Russia was already too powerful for her neighbors' peace of mind.[38]

After reflecting on the matter for a week, he again waved the suggestion aside — but much less decisively: "As for taking possession of the duchy of Ermeland, I have abstained from it because the game is not worth the candle. The piece is [cut] so thin that it would not pay for the complaints it would provoke; Polish Prussia, though, would be worth while, even if Danzig were not included, for we should have the Vistula and free communication with the kingdom [of Prussia], which would be an important item. If it were [only] a matter of spending some money, that would be worth while; indeed one might well spend freely. But when one snatches eagerly at scraps, that gives one an appearance of covetousness and insatiability which I do not chose to have attributed to me any more widely than it already is in Europe."[39]

It was of course West Prussia, Ermeland, and Danzig, not merely Ermeland, that the prince had had in mind from the beginning; and immediately upon his return home he took temporary charge of Prussia's foreign correspondence with a view to getting them. He arrived in Berlin on February 17 and in Potsdam on the morning of February 18, 1771, after a journey of two and a half weeks by way of Memel, Königsberg, and Danzig; in spite of the unfavorable season he had traveled almost as fast as the dispatch riders were in the habit of doing.

He had good reason for haste. There were things to be said to the king of Prussia that only he could say. He had to change the king's mind for him — and he changed it. Up to the very day of Henry's homecoming, Frederick had been determined to hold aloof; from that day onward he turned all the energies of his remarkably resourceful mind to the vigorous prosecution of a plan which until then he had thought too dangerous to be countenanced. No other of his servants was ever able to persuade Frederick to reverse himself so completely or so suddenly on a matter of such major importance; and none was ever permitted, even temporarily, so to take the play out of the king's hands.

The two were in conference in Potsdam from the eighteenth to the twenty-fourth of February. During that time it was Prince Henry who coached Finckenstein in the drawing up of a long document that went over Frederick's signature to Catherine. He drafted a memorandum to

[38] January 24, 1771, *ibid.*, 407. Sent through the border-postmaster Witte in Memel. The prince left St. Petersburg, laden down with costly gifts, at the end of January.
[39] *Ibid.*, 418; *Oeuvres*, XXVI, 349.

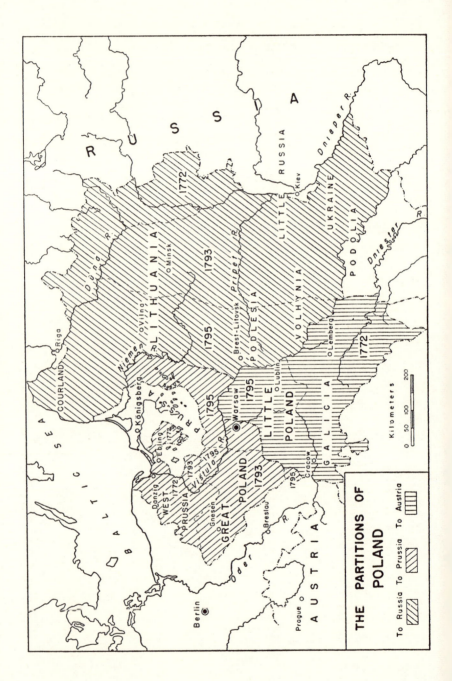

THE PARTITIONS OF POLAND

To Russia   To Prussia   To Austria

Solms in St. Petersburg instructing him to broach the partition question again and to push Prussia's claims vigorously, and continued for some time thereafter to coach Solms directly. He censored even the king's personal reply to the polite note that Catherine had asked him to carry to Frederick on his return.

When he went in from Potsdam to Berlin Prince Henry was authorized by the king to grant an interview to the Austrian minister van Swieten and to advise him as to what he considered the proper position for Austria and Hungary to take with reference to the Russo-Turkish peace negotiations. Three weeks later, after Henry had gone to Rheinsberg, Frederick wrote to him: "I have not yet received from St. Petersburg an answer to the long dispatch which I sent there, my dear brother, after you had approved it. We must be guided by this answer in our little projects of acquisition which, if they succeed, my dear brother, will be entirely due to you." [40]

The success of the project was in fact due to Prince Henry, in that it was he who overcame the king's hesitation by convincing him that it would be safe as well as profitable to go ahead with it. That change in Frederick's estimate of the situation was accomplished principally during Henry's week at Potsdam immediately after his return; but he continued his efforts to insure its permanence by correspondence. On March 5 he wrote that, although an army of sixty thousand men was said to be assembling in Hungary, it would never be used for fear of Prussia. "You hold the balance between the Russians and the Austrians," he urged, "and the former will agree in the end to some advantage for you, my very dear brother, as the price of the peace you will be in a position to get for them, while if the Austrians should notice that you intend to make some gains, no other choice will be open to them but to take something also. . . . I hope that you will realize my hopes." [41]

Once well embarked upon the enterprise, the king carried it through without much further help from his brother, except that in 1776 a special emissary was needed to seek in St. Petersburg a settlement of some of the secondary problems arising from it. Then the prince was called upon to undertake his second Russian mission. In the interim the king went his own way. The prince advised that he reach an agreement with Austria first, and that the two then impose their will upon Russia; Frederick thought it wiser to reach an agreement first with Russia and let the

---

[40] *P. C.*, XXXI, 29; *Oeuvres*, XXVI, 350. See also *P. C.*, XXX, *passim*, 446–484; *F. B. P. G.*, XXXV, 208; Koser, III, 322.

[41] Staatsarchiv, *loc. cit.; F. B. P. G.*, XXIII, 124. In August, 1771, he advised Frederick, if Russia seemed reluctant to concede him his proper portion, to threaten to remain neutral in case of an Austro-Russian war. That, he was sure, would bring Catherine to terms. Krauel, *Prinz Heinrich von Preussen als Politiker*, 21.

Austrians make the best of it. Maria Theresa might then protest all she would; Joseph would not let himself be left out of the partition.[42]

Austria, on the other hand, would have preferred to delay the "pacification" of Poland until after the termination of the Russo-Turkish war; but on that point Frederick went right over to Prince Henry's old position, encouraged Russia to seek a "glorious" peace rather than a quick one, and was content to see the war go on until Poland had been partitioned.[43]

Prince Henry's greatest service to the cause during the seventies was his maintenance of friendly personal relations with the Russian empress. With the knowledge and warm approval of Frederick, who read their letters regularly, the two carried on a fairly voluminous and, with all due allowance for its extravagantly polite verbiage, a rather cordial correspondence in which Catherine usually signed herself "Your Royal Highness's good sister and sincere friend." [44] Not infrequently a letter was accompanied by a gift — a copy of something of Voltaire's that she had said she wanted, or of the journal of Peter I that Henry had got printed for her; a costly painting supplied by Frederick and carried home by Count Orlov after a visit to Berlin and Rheinsberg; or some other souvenir to keep their carefully cultivated friendship alive.

The year 1771 was one of the happiest in the prince's life. He spent his time chiefly in Rheinsberg, elaborately entertained by a completely staffed theater, a well-trained orchestra, his books, his extensive correspondence, and an unending succession of more or less distinguished guests. In May came the youthful king of Sweden and his younger brother, and it was their uncle Henry who must show them Berlin and Potsdam, Sans Souci and the "New Palace," while their uncle Frederick worked at more serious matters. In the autumn their mother and sister came to return Henry's visit of the year before; he was the obvious one to meet them when they first set foot on Prussian soil, and to serve as their host during much of their visit — largely at Frederick's expense, as usual.[45]

---

[42] In order to make the fullest possible use of an incident in the Polish area occupied by the Austrians — an incident of the type which he had until then steadfastly refused to notice — he furnished Rohd (in Vienna) on February 27 with documentary evidence of it, and then added: "You will not forget to touch up this matter in rather striking colors [*un peu fortes*] in a detailed and separate report which you will send me on the subject, so that I may make the use of it that I plan to make." *P. C.*, XXX, 484.

[43] F. to Solms, in *P. C.*, XXX, 482.

[44] Hausarchiv, Rep. 56, II, I. This archive contains the originals of her letters and the retained drafts of his. They have been edited and printed by Dr. Krauel in his *Briefwechsel zwischen Heinrich Prinz von Preussen und Katherina II von Russland*, already cited.

[45] *P. C.*, XXXII, 249; Krauel, "Prinz Heinrich von Preussen in Rheinsberg," in the *Hohenzollern Jahrbücher*, VI (1902), 19; Heidenstam, *Une soeur du grand Frédéric*, 366. Ulrika stayed until August, 1772.

It was during that sunny year that Voltaire gave Prince Henry, in a letter to a third party, the complimentary title "the Condé of the North." "He has won the hearts of all Europe," the French cynic continued. "All that you tell me of the life he leads at Rheinsberg confirms my idea that the arts and glory have sought refuge in the north." [46]

From time to time bulletins came from the king informing him of the progress of negotiations for the partition. They were usually cheerful enough — as for example that of October 7, 1771, which reported: "I am very happy . . . to have conformed to your way of thinking. I have looked at these matters through precisely the same eyes as you do, and have done precisely what you advised. I sent the courier yesterday . . . I have tried to find out whether we can include Danzig in the portion that falls to us. It is certain that if we do not get it now we must never think of it again." [47]

The prince had little to worry about that year except his fear that he might not be given full credit by posterity for his share in what he thought was one of the greatest triumphs in the history of Prussia. He was much more perturbed than he had any good reason to be by the fact that Frederick, who in the spring had assured him that the credit was "wholly" his, had changed his phrase by October to "equally." [48]

For fear that Frederick might some day entirely forget how important his contribution to the great work had been, the prince eventually felt it incumbent upon himself to secure the written testimony of the Russian empress on the point. Frankly admitting that he craved fame and wanted the document for the sake of his own reputation in history, he intimated to Count Solms in April, 1772, that he would be glad to have a letter in Catherine's own hand bearing witness to the vital significance of his work. Waiting until after the signature of the partition treaty and writing ostensibly to thank him for his part in making it possible, she gave him again just what he wanted. Complimenting him upon his ability to bring not merely three heads but the crowned heads of three great powers under one hat — "witness this treaty" — and quite willing (possibly for reasons all her own) to let him bear her share as well as his own of their divided responsibility for the somewhat dubious enter-

[46] Quoted by Bouillé, in *La Vie privée*, 150. This was presumably a caustic reference to the papacy.

[47] He did not get either Danzig or Thorn. The prince alternated between anger because he thought that he himself could have got them and concern for fear Frederick might wreck the whole negotiation by insisting upon them.

[48] The same letter into which the offending word had been dropped as if inadvertently went on at once to say: "It was you who laid the first cornerstone of the building. Without you I should not have thought that I could make any such plans, not knowing well before your trip to St. Petersburg how favorably that court was disposed toward me." *P. C.*, XXXI, 426; *Oeuvres*, XXVI, 354.

prise, she added: "Your Royal Highness was the first to broach this grand affair." Soon afterward, she told him again that he could "be regarded as the prime mover" in it.[49]

He was therefore not quite content, although a thousand thaler per month was being paid out of its revenues into his private purse, when Frederick referred to the province on June 12, 1772, upon his return from his first tour of inspection there, as "this Prussia that I am getting, in a way, at your hands." First it had been "entirely" his work, then "equally," and at last only "in a way." [50]

The potential value of the province was apparent to the king at first glance. So was its need of development. What he said about it depended, naturally, upon his audience. To Prince Henry he wrote: "It is a very valuable acquisition and highly advantageous from a political as well as from a financial point of view; but in order to arouse less jealousy I am saying to all who will listen that on all my tour [there] I have seen nothing but sand, fir trees, heather and Jews. It is true that this morsel [of territory] is going to make me plenty of work, for I believe that Canada is as well administered as this Pomerelia. No order, no system; the towns there are in a deplorable state. For example, Culm should have eight hundred houses; there are not a hundred standing, and their inhabitants are either Jews or monks; and there are still many paupers there." [51]

The prince would probably have been pleased if his brother had turned over to him some of the work of organizing the new province, as well as a share of its revenues. Again and again, as when Frederick complained that he would far rather plant flowers than struggle with figures and financial problems all day, Henry replied that he would prefer some occupation more active and significant than rustic gardening. He was not content merely to have a dozen trees and a few flowers planted one season and then to wait and see what they would do the next. Life is empty, he hinted, for those who have only to vegetate in solitude with nothing to worry them but the weather and the verdure. Those who work are the ones to be envied, not the idle.[52] But his pleas went unheeded; between crises the king found little for him to do. He was still Prussia's highest-ranking emergency soldier but one to be called out only in emergencies, an ambassador extraordinary to be sent only on extraordinary missions — then to find himself again reduced to the passive role of sounding board for some of the king's ideas.

[49] Krauel, *Prinz Heinrich von Preussen als Politiker*, 22; Krauel, *Briefwechsel*, 96, 99. A dual agreement between Prussia and Russia was signed on February 17, 1772, the tripartite treaty on August 5.
[50] "en quelque façon." *P. C.*, XXXII, 249.
[51] *Ibid.*    [52] *Hohenzollern Jahrbücher*, XX (1916), 185.

CHAPTER XIX

# 𝔓otential 𝔠o=regent

*"I shall not die tranquil with respect to the interests
of the state unless I see you in some manner made
guardian."*—Frederick to Henry, February 10, 1776.

IN 1775 the question of the Bavarian succession began to loom up on the
European political horizon. The death of the elector Maximilian III
Joseph, while not yet expected momentarily, was already the subject of
widespread speculation. That event, whenever it occurred, would throw
open the succession either to the childless Karl Theodore of the Palatinate
or to Duke Karl of Pfalz-Zweibrücken, next in line among the aspirants.
It was scarcely to be expected that the restless young emperor Joseph II
would let pass such an opportunity to advance Austria's interests in
Germany by supporting the claims of the highest bidder.

A generation earlier, Frederick himself might have been on the alert
and interested in such a situation on behalf of Prussia; in fact, he had
been; but by the summer of 1775 he was old and ill, and interested only
in "growing his cabbages" in peace and waging war on poverty in West
Prussia and Silesia. Fifty-four new villages he had set up in Silesia that
year, he boasted to Prince Henry; there would be sixty-three more in
the next two years if he lived that long. Even death was not to find him
sitting with his arms folded![1]

Death would find him soon, though — at least so he thought, or pretended to think. "The problems being prepared for us in connection with
the Bavarian question," he wrote, "will be for my successors to solve, no
doubt, just as my father often said that it would be my task to take up
his claims on Julich and Berg."[2]

Death was not looking over the king's shoulder as he wrote; he had
eleven more years of life and labor left; but gout was in the hand and
arm that guided his pen, and the thought of death was almost constantly with him. No concern over his own spiritual salvation or the
ultimate welfare of his soul found its way into the written expression of
his thoughts. Nature would merely destroy what she had herself created; the elements of which his body was composed would return
whence they had come, and he would be no more. But the material well-

[1] *P. C.*, XXXVII, 189; *Oeuvres*, XXVI, 371.   [2] *P. C.*, XXXVII, 154; *Oeuvres*, XXVI, 370.

being of the undying state of Prussia caused him infinite concern. His spirit might die with his body or live on in a world that he knew not yet; but his ideas must live on in Prussia and guide that state aright. So his "fourteenth attack" of gout, from which it took him several months to recover and the effects of which he said he expected to feel for the rest of his life, turned his thoughts more and more to plans for insuring the continuance of his own influence in Prussia after his death.

Such plans hinged upon Prince Henry, because the king was deeply disappointed in his nephew Frederick William, Prince of Prussia and heir apparent. The young man was tall and strong, and knew how to be personally agreeable when he chose to be. As an overgrown boy, in the closing campaign of the Seven Years' War, literally under fire from two sides at once — from the enemy's guns and from the critical eyes of one or the other of his old-soldier uncles — he had shown the physical courage characteristic of the men of his family. Although never quite able to conceal his greater fondness for the very attractive younger brother Henry, Frederick had then entertained high hopes for him.

Subsequently Prince Frederick William had been carefully inducted by the king's ministers into the business of the various departments of government, but the effort was wasted. Frederick, in spite of his disinclination and all his revolts, had been made into a trained administrator and soldier by his father; after that his own genius, unflagging industry, and courage had made him great in both fields. His nephew, however, had neither his toughness of moral fiber nor his keenness of intellect; and he hated work. So precisely where Frederick's father had made some of his worst mistakes — in the training of his successor — Frederick also failed. When old King Frederick William I was most afraid that Crown Prince Frederick would never be a man fit to become king in Prussia, he went to work, hammer and tongs, to make such a man of him. When King Frederick decided that Crown Prince Frederick William was a fool, he could find no time for his further training, gave him no share in the handling of state business and very little information about it, and so left him free to give himself up entirely to his follies.

As a substitute, Frederick planned in 1776 to fall back upon his own brother, Prince Henry — not as king nor even as regent but as an indispensable adviser and tutor of the new king. The prestige of the monarchy rested so firmly upon the hereditary principle that he would not have thought it wise to set that principle aside; but if he could be sure that his successor would do the right thing and be restrained from wrecking the state by some foolish blunder, then it need not be set aside. Prince Henry would still be young enough to serve the state for years. Prince

Henry was, in Frederick's opinion, the only man in Prussia fit to command her armies; and his mind worked so much like Frederick's own that he would perpetuate the essentials of Frederick's policy if anyone would. He, then, was to be chosen as intellectual and spiritual heir apparent to the king. The legal heir to the throne was never consulted on the question.

Before the matter had ever been broached to Prince Henry by the king, the French minister Pons had anticipated that something of that sort might be done, and was already viewing the prospect with alarm. "While doing justice to the merits of Prince Henry," he reported to his government, "to the extent of his knowledge and to his military talents, I fear his character — proud, despotic, and closely resembling that of the king of Prussia — and just as arbitrary if he had the authority in his own hands. . . . We shall have always to fear the influence of his character, which is [only] too likely to follow the same principles as his Prussian Majesty; we shall see the same spirit direct the negotiations, we shall be forced just as we now are to guard ourselves against all the subtleties which the king of Prussia has made his political instruments, and I do not think that we ought to have much more confidence in the validity of the engagements he would contract." [3]

During the winter of 1775–76 the king's gout confined him to Potsdam, making it impossible for him to go into Berlin for any part of the annual court carnival. Even the celebration of Prince Henry's birthday, usually the high point of the carnival, had to take place without him. In his stead he directed their younger brother Ferdinand to preside as his personal representative and in his name. "Say to our brother all the most tender and affectionate things you can possibly think of," he wrote to Ferdinand. "I shall certainly not disavow you."

On February 2, disturbed by published reports of greatly increased military activity in Bohemia, Prince Henry wrote to the king for further information. "What you have heard about the Austrians has some foundation in fact," Frederick replied. "I shall tell you the truth of it as I get it through secret channels. They believe that I am approaching my end, and they are strengthening their troops in Bohemia so as to occupy Saxony immediately and invade this country. That will surely happen if I die, and my big boob of a nephew, unless he bestirs himself at once and shows some nerve, will be roughly handled. But nothing can overcome his natural indolence, and I am obliged to leave all provision for the

[3] December 16, 1775; quoted from the archives of the French ministry of foreign affairs by G. B. Volz, in *F. B. P. G.*, XIX, 460. Pons feared that the prince's influence would always steer his nephew's policy away from any liaison with France, in favor of a permanent Russian alliance.

future to whatever your prudence can do for the good of the state, and the rest to the uncertainties of fate." [4]

On February 6 the king offered to take his brother more fully into his confidence than he had ever taken anyone else:

The attack of gout that I have suffered has now left me; but I must guard against a relapse. Your friendship (*amitié*) alone would have cured me, my dear brother, without any medicine.

It is certain that the Austrians are planning what I told you, and the expedient that you suggest . . . is admirable; but you can win the confidence of [our] nephew, in which I shall consider it my duty to assist you. [5]

I can instruct you as to all our affairs and their interrelationships, about which no one, even among the ministers, now knows; and that will make you personally so indispensable that everyone will have to come to you for information and ask for your help. I believe this way infallible, and I hope that for the love of this state which all our ancestors have served you will not refuse to try to sustain it, especially since you are the only one of whom the state can expect true service. [6]

On February 10 followed a more definite proposal: "I shall not die tranquil with respect to the interests of the state unless I see you in some manner made guardian. I look upon you as the only one who can sustain the glory of the house and become in every respect the stay and pillar of our common fatherland. If I once have the pleasure of talking with you I can explain my ideas more fully as to the means of making this project succeed." [7]

The prince accepted the invitation with alacrity and went at once to Sans Souci for a series of conferences with the king, of which no written record was made but which were indirectly mirrored in Frederick's next letter, on February 18:

As for me, after . . . having devoted my life to the state, I shall make an unpardonable mistake, my dear brother, if I do not try so far as is within my power not at all to reign after my death but to provide that a person of your

---

[4] *P. C.*, XXXVII, 449; G. B. Volz, "Der Plan einer Mitregentschaft des Prinzen Heinrichs," *Hohenzollern Jahrbücher*, XX (1916), 181. On March 1 he wrote that unless he died suddenly he would have to spend his last moments on preparations for a defensive war to be begun immediately after his burial — condemned by fate to be a soldier to his dying gasp. *P. C.*, XXXVII, 500. Baron Riedesel, his representative in Vienna, doubted that the Austrian government had any such warlike intention. People there, he said, were much more concerned over the Prussian-Russian alliance and over Prince Henry's proposed mission to St. Petersburg. *Ibid.*, XXXVIII, 7.

[5] The letter in which Prince Henry made the suggestion to which the king here referred, as well as his answer to this one, seems to have been lost or destroyed. Apparently he had offered to lend a hand with the Prince of Prussia, whose guardian he had once been.

[6] *P. C.*, XXXVII, 458; *Oeuvres*, XXVI, 375.

[7] *P. C.*, XXXVII, 465; *Oeuvres*, XXVI, 376. Excerpts from all three letters are printed in German translation by Volz in the *Hohenzollern Jahrbücher*, XX (1916), 181–182, and in English by Andrew Hamilton in *Rheinsberg*, II, 85–86.

wisdom shall participate in the government, so that by your good counsel and advice you may compensate for the negligence, imbecility, and weakness of a creature incapable of governing himself, much less others.

In this . . . I have only the state in view, for I know very well that even if the heavens should fall it would be all the same to me the moment after my death. Convinced of your friendship for me, I have opened my heart on this matter, about which I have been thinking for a long time. I thank you a thousand times for the pleasure you have given me by being willing to do as I wish; and if heaven could be moved by our prayers I should ask that it pour down upon you its richest blessings.[8]

As late as September, 1776, still obsessed by the thought of death and of an Austrian attack upon Prussia following his demise, he wrote again to his brother: "The Austrians are unquestionably trying to embroil us with the Russians in order that, with their hands freed in this direction by my death, they can fall the more heavily upon our tall fool [of a nephew]. Good God, what is to come of all this if the good Lord does not preserve your life and health! You will be, my dear brother, like the shield of Minerva that turned bullies into stones when they would attack fools. But let us not becloud our imagination by trying to foresee the future. My consolation is that I shall be as completely untouched by what happens then as I was while fire and flame encompassed our country during the Thirty Years' War." [9]

Although he sought thus to make certain that Prince Henry would step forward as the savior of the state and guardian of its true interests, continuing unofficially to tutor their nephew even after his succession, it was not an official regency that the king had in mind. He had always thought that the succession ought to be so regulated that the throne would never be long occupied by a boy king during whose minority the country would have to be ruled by a regency. A king in tutelage was no king, in his opinion. Yet he was himself proposing that a king who was no longer a minor should submit indefinitely to tutelage, and do it while still seeming to be, and continuing legally to be, his own master. To have permitted himself to be so treated, the new king would have needed to be fully as foolish as Frederick thought him, and more nearly spineless than he actually was.

[8] *P. C.,* XXXVII, 476; *Oeuvres,* XXVI, 376.

[9] *P. C.,* XXXVIII, 339. And again on September 10, 1777: "I know very well that a dead man cannot defend himself, but I have made so many arrangements in advance that, if our lout of a nephew will only follow your advice, it will be possible to get to Dresden ahead of the Austrians." Prince Henry replied that even if the Austrians were planning an attack upon Prussia, which he did not believe, they would surely be too prudent to make it immediately after Frederick's death while the army, the fortresses, and the treasury were still in good condition, but would wait instead for his successor's neglect to cripple them first; but the king clung to his obsession. *Ibid.,* XXXIX, 319, 325.

The king was well aware of the inconsistency and the imperfection of the solution he was recommending but, as usual when confronted with a problem that baffled him, he chose the answer that seemed least open to objection, embodied that answer in a memorandum, and called the problem solved. The result in this case was his *Exposé du gouvernement prussien,* written for the guidance of his brother, not his nephew. The regent, he wrote, must enjoy great discretionary power. He must be free to act. A council of ministers would tie his hands and be as fatal to him as frequent councils of war to a general commanding in the field. It could only destroy his effectiveness and lead to the formation of factions, whereas the state's only salvation was to be found in the preservation of the principle of leadership.[10]

Such a plan to make necessary a virtual regency for Prince Henry following Frederick's death could have been put into practice only if Frederick had continued up to the last moment to keep him, and only him, fully informed about all important affairs of state. Even then it would very probably have been wrecked by the easily understandable opposition of the new king, who could not under any circumstances submit or seem to be subject to further control either by the dead hand of one uncle or by the driving hand of the other.

In the event, Frederick himself gave up the idea within three years, after Henry had quarreled with him over his handling of the same Bavarian question which, along with his illness, had first caused him to think of it. Thereafter he kept his thoughts to himself, sharing them rarely with his brother and never with his nephew.

[10] *Hohenzollern Jahrbücher,* XX (1916), 176. The *exposé* gave most of its space to military and foreign affairs, presumably as a sort of *aide-mémoire* or digest of what the king had told his brother in conference.

# CHAPTER XX

# Second Russian Mission

*"The Indians say you must worship the devil to keep him from hurting you."*—Frederick to Henry, July 20, 1775.

DURING the years 1776 and 1777 the king's avowed intention to make Prince Henry his virtual though not his legal successor served as a basis for the most cordial relations between them. Together they watched events in America, shedding no tears over Britain's misfortunes and being tempted to take no premature chances out of sympathy for the rebel Americans. Together they followed reports on the health of the elector of Bavaria and tried to predict the effect his death would have on the balance of power among the German states. And together, in order to be able to deal more decisively with the question of the Bavarian succession whenever it should arise, they tried first to finish up the interminable debate with Russia over the Danzig question and the boundary lines of their new provinces recently taken from Poland.

Because he had been in Russia and because he was still carrying on a fairly lively correspondence with the empress, Prince Henry continued to serve as senior consultant on all Russian questions. In May, 1773, Countess Caroline of Hesse-Darmstadt was about to undertake a journey to St. Petersburg, where her daughter Wilhelmina (subsequently called Natalie in Russia) was to become the bride of Catherine's son Paul; Catherine wrote Henry that "his" apartments were to be assigned to the countess as her living quarters, and asked him to do what he could to send her to Russia strongly predisposed in favor of that country and of its actual and prospective rulers.

The empress need not have worried much on that point, and probably did not. Any mother as ambitious for her daughter as the countess Caroline would have been ready to approve of less pleasing persons than Catherine and her son, with such a brilliant marriage in prospect. She showed no undue curiosity about the character of the young grand duke. He would one day be czar of all the Russias, and she was therefore sure in advance that he was an intelligent, attractive, and virtuous young man and that Wilhelmina would find him a kind and loving husband.

What the countess wanted from Prince Henry was coaching. When she started off in due time she carried in her luggage a small fortune in gifts—far more than she could afford except as a promising speculation—and in her hand a list (prepared by Prince Henry) of the persons to whom they were to be given. He had written her also a personal letter of introduction to the empress. During her stay she and Catherine, seeking common ground and subjects for polite conversation while waiting for a decent interval to elapse between the first meeting of the prospective bride and groom and the wedding which they had themselves planned long beforehand, talked much about the prince, his first visit there, and Catherine's hope that he might soon make another.[1]

Then on the eve of his birthday, 1774, Catherine asked the prince outright to pay her a second visit, sweetening the invitation with the statement that such men as he ought to live for several centuries for the benefit of mankind and enjoy unbroken happiness all their lives so that others would be encouraged to emulate their example. To be sure, there were a few other things to be got out of the way first—peace with Turkey; a visit which the young king of Sweden was for the third time proposing to make; the departure of Diderot, who was there at the time; a year's residence in Moscow for Catherine herself; some rebellions which she had to suppress but did not mention; and so on.[2]

For two years the trip was the subject of a voluminous correspondence. There was therefore plenty of time to discuss it with Frederick beforehand. Often but not very convincingly the prince professed reluctance to go. Just as often Frederick urged him to set his personal preferences aside and do what seemed to be his duty to the state. No Prussian prince, he said, could do his country a greater service than the maintenance of friendly relations with Russia. Prince Henry's personal credit there, furthermore, ought to be maintained; for after Frederick's death their nephew would need all the help Henry could give him, there as elsewhere. Frederick would therefore gladly pay for the trip and for "the usual presents," although he anticipated that the total cost might be as much as fifty thousand thaler.[3]

"As things stand between you and the empress," wrote the king some months later, "I believe that you can hardly get out of making this jour-

[1] Hausarchiv, Rep. 56, II, I; Caroline von Hessen, *Briefwechsel*, I, 145, 343, 377, 379, 435; Krauel, *Briefwechsel*, 111, 113.
[2] Krauel, *Briefwechsel*, 118–154, *passim*. The prince invited Diderot to travel by way of Rheinsberg on his way home.
[3] September 11, 1774, in *P. C.*, XXXVI, 20; *Oeuvres*, XXVI, 366. The prince's second Russian mission is the subject of an interesting twenty-page essay by Robert Stupperich, "Die zweite Reise des Prinzen Heinrich von Preussen nach Petersburg," in the *Jahrbücher für Geschichte Osteuropas*, III, Heft 4, pp. 580–600.

ney. . . . If you refuse her, that will mean breaking with her; and you know . . . the Indians say you must worship the devil to keep him from hurting you." [4]

A journey which the prince was happy to undertake, an experience which he would have missed only with the greatest regret, was thus designated a patriotic duty and gave him new opportunities to assure the king that any activity or service, however insignificant, was preferable to the idle and useless life he was then leading at Rheinsberg.

As on his previous Russian pilgrimage, the prince was to combine diplomatic business with pleasure. The new boundaries resulting from the first partition of Poland had yet to be finally drawn, and the three partitioning powers were still jockeying for position in Warsaw. Therefore, on the eve of his departure from Berlin, April 20, Prince Henry asked the king to give him a complete list of the Austrian regiments then in Galicia and Lodomeria. He could speak much more convincingly to the Russian empress on that subject if he were in a position to be specific. Frederick saw the point, and supplied the information at once.

At Riga, en route, the prince was met by the Russian minister to Poland, Stackelberg, the principal mediator between the shadow government in Warsaw and the powers participating in the partition, and he seized the opportunity to talk boundaries with him. The most critical matter discussed was the Danzig question. Frederick had long coveted that city, along with Pomerelia or West Prussia, but had at last had to admit to himself and to Henry that his demand for it was sure to be refused. So Henry claimed as a substitute the trading rights which he said the people of Pomerelia had always enjoyed there. Stackelberg rejoined that those same trading privileges had always caused friction and hinted that Prussia might be granted three or four hundred thousand thaler as compensation if she would give them up. Prince Henry, able as usual to try out a proposal by saying what he chose, subject always to subsequent ratification or repudiation by Frederick, countered with the opinion that his brother would not sell his Danzig rights for such an amount in cash, but that he might perhaps consider as a substitute the absorption of additional territory on his Silesian border if it were worth as much as four hundred thousand per year. [5]

[4] July 20, 1775, in *P. C.*, XXXVII, 122; *Oeuvres*, XXVI, 369.
[5] H. to F. from Riga, April 5, 1776, in the Staatsarchiv, Rep. 92, B, IV, 9. Well-selected excerpts from nearly all the prince's reports are printed along with the king's answers to them in the *Politische Correspondenz*, Volumes XXXVII and XXXVIII; but they are excerpts only, so far as Prince Henry's letters are concerned. The same is true of the *Oeuvres*, Volume XXVI. The letters printed by Krauel in his *Briefwechsel*, on the other hand, are reproduced in full.

Some similar line of argument, the prince thought, would be likely to do the most good and give the least offense when he got to St. Petersburg and had to deal directly with Catherine and her ministers. What did Frederick think?

Frederick thought the man on the ground must judge for himself what tactical position to take. The one thing of supreme importance was the maintenance and strengthening of the Russian alliance. Although they might have to yield to her wishes sometimes at considerable cost, they needed Russia; and their posterity might need her even more urgently. So if it were clearly necessary to give up all claim on Danzig, then do so; if some compensation could be secured elsewhere, very well; but Russia's friendship must be retained. All else he left to Prince Henry, whom he was again calling his "other self." [6]

A boundary settlement was eventually made, similar to that suggested by the prince to Stackelberg at their April meeting in Riga, the last important exchange of memoranda on the subject taking place between the same two spokesmen after Henry's return to Berlin in July.[7] In the meantime, Polish affairs had figured in many a quiet conversation in St. Petersburg, but had been pushed somewhat into the background by a new crisis of a personal nature.

Prince Henry reached the Russian capital on April 13, and was received with every honor and mark of distinction which his previous experience there could have led him to expect, the grand duke Paul and his consort as well as the empress doing everything in their power to make him welcome. Ten days later the grand duchess summoned her family and physicians to her bedside in haste: an heir to the throne was to be born. But neither mother nor child could be saved, and early in the evening of the twenty-sixth, her fourth day of labor, Natalie died.

At such a time, "friends of the family" are either useless or indispensable, and Prince Henry was indispensable, especially to the highly emotional, half-hysterical grand duke. At all hours, day and night, he was available and was frequently called upon to calm the youthful husband or to confer with Catherine. He was their constant companion and confidant. No other person stood so high in their esteem. It was said at the

---

[6] "Vous, qui êtes un autre moi-même, vous me remplacez à Petersbourg." The quotation is from his letter of May 9, in *P. C.*, XXXVIII, 77–78. The instructions paraphrased above were written April 14 (*ibid.*, 25), and repeated, with only slight variations in wording, again and again. Once the king went so far as to say that Prussia's affairs in Russia were in such good hands that he had ceased to think about them and was merely waiting for the prince to come home and tell him the outcome. May 21, *ibid.*, 107.

[7] The memorandum transmitted by Prince Henry had been sent to him on July 22 by Frederick. *P. C.*, XXXVIII, 232.

time, with some exaggeration, that he had saved the young grand duke's life.[8]

It would be easier to think that the chance presence of the family's princely guest had been instrumental in saving Paul's sanity. He was an unsteady individual at best. But the dispatches that went off in rapid succession to the king of Prussia, first from Count Solms and then from the prince himself, reveal that the grand duke and his mother (under the steadying influence of Prince Henry, of course) were at no time so overwhelmed by their sorrow as to be unable to think of the future.

Before she died poor Natalie was said to have urged her distracted husband to choose a second wife from among the princesses of the Prussian house; and Paul was not too distraught to see the wisdom of her advice. Before a merciful death put a belated end to her hopeless fight for her own life and that of her child, her successor had already been chosen; Prince Henry had been authorized to notify the new grand-duchess-designate of the privilege that was to be hers, and to secure the consent of her family.

That consent would normally have been easy enough to obtain. The grand duke's choice, guided by his mother's advice and the counsel of the friend whom fortune had brought to their court just when he could prove most useful, had fallen upon Prince Henry's grand-niece, the princess Sophia Dorothea of Württemberg. It was not at all an illogical selection, for the number of princesses eligible by birth for such a marriage and available without notice would always be limited. Sophia Dorothea had, moreover, been one of the princesses most seriously considered as a possible bride for the grand duke Paul before his first marriage, and had been dropped from the list only because Catherine then thought her too young. Her name would therefore almost automatically head the new list if a second shopping expedition into the marriage market had to be made; and Frederick gave Henry his word of honor that, without his once mentioning her, everyone in Europe thought at once of the princess of Württemberg as soon as it became known that Natalie had died.

It was only by acting with a celerity worthy of their war days that her aging great-uncles saw to it, however, that the chosen lady was still available. She had to be stopped almost literally on the way to the altar, for she had been engaged since March to the hereditary prince of Hesse-Darmstadt, brother of the late grand duchess her predecessor; but

---

[8] See Count Solms's report of April 26, in *P. C.*, XXXVIII, 86. "They tell me that the Russians swear by your name only," remarked Frederick. *Ibid.*, 84.

stopped she was, by the simple expedient of inducing Prince Ludwig to release her from her promise to marry him. With soldierly directness and without a moment's loss of time, the king made it plain to Prince Ludwig that it would be best for all concerned that he should choose another bride. No one expected Ludwig to refuse; but when he tried rather tactlessly to make sure first of the amount of cash he would be paid for his complaisance, Catherine asked Prince Henry to take him in hand. Writing as an old friend of Ludwig's mother, the countess Caroline, the prince was careful to express his sympathy for the young man who had just lost a sister and was then asked to give up his fiancée also in the interest of the Russian dynasty; but he went on to point out that Ludwig was expected not only to release the young lady but to see to it that her parents accepted the new offer without raising any objection to the necessary change of their daughter's religion. Thus, but only thus, might young Ludwig earn the gratitude of the grand duke and his mother the empress, and might hope also to induce them to forget certain charges of misconduct which they were still holding in abeyance against him on account of some injudicious behavior of his during his last visit to Russia.[9]

Before Prince Henry's letter could have been received, Baron von Riedesel was on his way to St. Petersburg with the disappointed Ludwig's formal consent to the change. On his return journey the distinguished messenger brought his friend, as balm for wounded feelings, a legacy of a thousand rubles from the late grand duchess, his sister, and word that he had been granted a pension of five thousand by the grand duke. He had asked for ten thousand.[10]

The undisguised realism with which the prince of Hesse-Darmstadt was handled was based upon two very practical considerations: a prospective Russian czar in quest of a bride found his freedom of choice more narrowly restricted than the prince of one of the minor German states; and Prussia could not let pass such an opportunity to use a dynastic marriage for whatever it might be worth to give new meaning to her Russian alliance.

The bonds of that union had become irksome to both parties. There had been bickering over boundaries in Poland; the king of Prussia had

[9] Hausarchiv, Rep. 56, II, I; Krauel, *Briefwechsel,* 155. Frederick wrote to his brother that he had been "touched to the point of tears" by sympathy for poor Ludwig's plight; and Prince Henry wrote the king that he had included the threats in his letter to Ludwig only because Catherine and Paul insisted upon it, and had veiled and softened them all he could. *P. C.,* XXXVIII, 77, 106. Prince Ludwig had at one time held a brigadier general's commission in the Russian army but had had to resign it in consequence of a sharp quarrel with Potemkin. Stupperich, in the *Jahrbuch für Geschichte Osteuropas,* III, 591.

[10] H. to F., May 21, in the Staatsarchiv, *loc. cit.* The letter is cited in *P. C.,* XXXVIII, 135, but this part of it is not printed there. See also Stupperich's essay, just cited, page 590.

not been uniformly successful in keeping his nephew, the young king of Sweden, in line; and the termination of the Turkish war nearly two years before had materially lessened Catherine's fear of Austria and hence her dependence upon Frederick. It was Prince Henry's task to knit that alliance together once more, and he did a creditable repair job, although the fabric was never again as good as new.

Among the obstacles in his way were a noticeable improvement in Russia's relations with Austria and some supposed intrigues fostered by France; and he was surprised to learn upon his arrival in St. Petersburg that the grand duchess Natalie was suspected of having been politically active in a fashion contrary to the Prussian interest. A certain Count Rasumowski, known to be a member of the Austrian party, was said to have somehow induced her to use all her influence over her impressionable husband on behalf of Austria. She was thought also, prompted by Rasumowski, to have suggested to the grand duke some of the ideas that he thought were his own, to which he clung so stubbornly in opposition to his mother's wiser plans for his guidance. The prince heard and believed these tales, some of which were substantiated by letters found among Natalie's papers after her death. Hence he felt no compulsion either to explain or to excuse his apparent heartlessness in giving direction to the choice of a second bride for the grand duke while the daughter of his old friend Caroline of Hesse-Darmstadt lay dying.[11]

It was less difficult, therefore, for the prince to recognize the hand of a beneficent destiny in the untimely death of the young grand duchess than it would have been if she had been a faithful friend of Prussia. It was made easier for others also when a post-mortem examination revealed that because of an unsuspected anatomical malformation the unfortunate Natalie could never have given the Russian dynasty the heirs it demanded of her and therefore, being unable to answer the principal purpose for which she had been called there — as Count Solms so tastefully put it in his report to Frederick on the night of her death — could never again have been happy in Russia if she had lived. Sooner or later she would have had to agree to a separation from her husband so that some other princess, one capable of motherhood, could take her place. So death, which brought her release from torture, saved her also from years of dreary living; and all concerned could console themselves or quiet their consciences — whichever was needed — by telling one another that God knew best.

The whole unfortunate affair put a heavy strain upon the nerves of

[11] *Ibid.;* P. C., XXXVIII, 148, 228.

all involved, and particularly upon those of the young husband bereft of his beloved. What then could be more natural than that, for the sake of his health and emotional equilibrium, he should travel for a while? And who could be a more fitting companion for him than his mother's true and tested friend, the brother of the king of Prussia, who had stayed so faithfully by his side out at secluded Oranienbaum during the first period of official mourning? As soon as etiquette permitted him to leave he would go home with Prince Henry, who had delayed his own departure simply out of consideration for him. If fate should decree that somewhere there he should chance to meet that little princess Sophia Dorothea of Württemberg of whom he had heard so much — well, stranger things had happened.

Fate was in fact already hard at work — finding able instruments in the king of Prussia and his brother Henry — making the most careful and detailed arrangements for that chance meeting. Prince Henry had at once been delegated by the empress to make the formal request in her name for the hand of his grand-niece, and had sent by way of Frederick a letter of exchange for forty thousand rubles provided by Catherine to make it easier for the Württembergers to be in Berlin at the appointed time and subsequently to make the trip to Russia. For fear the young lady or her parents might raise some objection to her compulsory conversion to the Greek Catholic faith, the prince told his brother to remind them that Henry IV had considered Paris well worth a mass.[12]

Frederick was indeed so eager to impress their visitor with the magnificence and cordiality of his reception that Prince Henry had to caution him against being overeffusive. In general, he wrote, the thing should be carried off with all possible éclat; but if Frederick simply duplicated in receiving the grand duke the honors which Henry had received in Russia, that would be enough. If one went but a single step farther to meet these Russians than etiquette demanded, he warned the king, it would be taken as an admission of inferiority and they would all immediately become insufferably arrogant. Frederick faithfully accepted his advice, even as to the choice of quarters for the guests in the Berlin palaces and the number of lackeys to be assigned to each.

At Königsberg the grand duke and Prince Henry, traveling together but in separate carriages, each with his own cavalcade of escorts, were met by General Lentulus as personal representative of the king, and by Counts Dönhoff and Dohna. There, at Paul's request, they reviewed a regiment of Prussian troops. Every meal they ate between the border and

[12] *P. C.,* XXXVIII, 76, 84, 129; Stupperich's essay, page 590. Frederick also contributed ten thousand thaler toward the cost of the trousseau and of the visit to Berlin.

Berlin was prepared and served by men specially sent from the king's own kitchen and cellars to provide for their comfort. At every town along the way guns boomed in salute, bells were rung in welcome, and some sort of reception or spectacle had been arranged. When they reached Berlin the number of their postilions with trumpets was doubled — making forty in all — and the grand duke made a ceremonial entry into the city in the great state coach, under an elaborate arch of triumph, between lines of people curious to behold him and ready to cheer.[13]

For a feverish fortnight the same breathless tempo was maintained through a ceaseless round of ceremonials in all the principal family palaces — Berlin, Charlottenburg, and Potsdam in turn. Through it all Frederick was plagued with anxiety lest some accident befall his guest or some illness overtake him for which he himself might be blamed, or as a result of which his Russian alliance might suffer. He had much more reason to fear the effects of sheer exhaustion, but it all went off quite smoothly. Once some plaster fell from the ceiling of the state dining room during a banquet; but no one was hurt, and Frederick hastened to head off the rumors that might otherwise have spread by spreading the story himself. Some of the Russians in Paul's suite were thought by their hosts to be rather arrogant, but no serious unpleasantness occurred.

Very nearly all the available members of the Prussian royal family were assembled to assist in the entertainment of their distinguished visitor. Among them — adequately chaperoned by her parents, of course — was the king's grand-niece, his mother's namesake, Sophia Dorothea of Württemberg; and the delight expressed by all interested observers considerably exceeded their surprise when she and Paul fell in love at first sight. Soon it was generally known that complete plans had been made for her journey to Russia and for their eventual marriage.

When the grand duke was ready to leave Berlin, having got what he had gone there for, he and his fiancée first went together for three days to Rheinsberg. As they approached their destination they were met by Prince Henry and his brother Ferdinand, who had come some miles along the road to meet them; and thence at every turn they were greeted again, as Paul had been on his first arrival in Prussia, with peasant dances or other carefully staged pastoral scenes in one Potemkin village after

[13] The journey is described at great length in the *Memoires du comte de Hordt*, II, 265–272, 276–277, and by J. H. Ch. Oelrichs in his *Ausführliche Beschreibung der Reise des Grossfürsten Paul Petrowitz von St. Petersburg an den Kgl. Preussischen Hof* (Berlin, 1776), and again but more briefly by Stupperich, in the *Jahrbuch für Geschichte Osteuropas*, III, 580–600.

another. At Rheinsberg itself a new Parnassus had been built as stage and background for a Greek play, with accommodations underneath for the chorus; a great gilded gondola (Ulrika's gift on her last visit) carried the party across to the island called Remusberg, and all the rococo resources of the place were mobilized to offer them truly regal entertainment.

At the conclusion of his Rheinsberg visit the grand duke went home to Russia without returning to Berlin. Prince Henry accompanied him as far as Schwedt, then hurried back to his other guests who had remained in Rheinsberg. Soon Sophia Dorothea also took the road to Russia, duly coached by her uncle Henry as to what she might expect to find there and what would be expected of her. In September she arrived in St. Petersburg and was acclaimed by Catherine as "perfectly charming." At her wedding in October she became the grand duchess Maria Feodorovna. In the first four years that followed, both she and her husband wrote occasionally to Prince Henry assuring him that their marriage was a perfectly happy one and thanking him for having brought it about.

It was true that Paul sometimes referred to his "black butterflies" or moods of discouragement and revolt against the idle futility of the life to which his mother had condemned him — Catherine had no more confidence or reason for confidence in her heir apparent than Frederick of Prussia had in his.[14] Catherine herself, however, was the person whose moods and whose attitude toward Prussia interested Frederick most vitally, and it was for its effect upon her that he was most highly pleased with Prince Henry's work on his second Russian mission; for in his brother's personal friendship with the empress he saw Prussia's best insurance of security on her eastern frontier.

"This confidence that the empress has so rightly learned to have in you," he had written in May, "is the surest guarantee of the union of the Russians and the Prussians. If it should happen also that eventually someone whom I shall not name should make some foolish blunder, you will always be in a position to set things right again."

And again in June: "Your close personal connection with the empress and the grand duke will enable you to act as mediator some time between that court and the nephew, in case the latter does anything foolish — and that may very well happen." [15]

The king's hopes were only partially fulfilled. Alliances needed something more substantial than personal friendship to hold them together,

[14] Hausarchiv, *loc. cit.* Excerpts are printed by Krauel in *Briefwechsel*, 165–173.
[15] *P. C.*, XXXVIII, 97, 135; *Oeuvres*, XXVI, 382.

even in the days of the enlightened despots. When Prince Henry took the field at the head of a Prussian army in July, 1778, for his last campaign against the Austrians in Bohemia, the empress wrote him that the prayers of a great part of Europe were with him and the eyes of all the world upon him; but Frederick found her willing to interest herself actively only in the restoration of peace.[16]

During that war a new and permanent (though fortunately not a total) estrangement developed between the brothers, so that it was "the nephew" instead of Prince Henry who went to St. Petersburg in the autumn of 1780. Like everyone else who had gone there from Prussia in the four years just past, he carried a letter of introduction from Prince Henry; but those missives had by that time lost most of their magic. Catherine was not favorably impressed by the nephew, so wrote that she feared he had been bored, having found no one in Russia half so brilliant as the uncles with whom he inevitably compared all others.[17]

Frederick William's visit did nothing to strengthen the alliance. It had lived out its time and he was not the man to resuscitate it; and Prince Henry, who had twice infused new life into it, was seldom smiled upon by Catherine or anyone else while being frowned at by the king of Prussia.

[16] At Teschen, May, 1779. For Catherine's letter to the prince, see Krauel, *Briefwechsel,* 173, 175.
[17] *Ibid.,* 177–178.

# CHAPTER XXI

# 𝕿𝖍𝖊 𝕭𝖆𝖛𝖆𝖗𝖎𝖆𝖓 𝕾𝖚𝖈𝖈𝖊𝖘𝖘𝖎𝖔𝖓

*"The truth often lies hidden and becomes known only when there is no longer time to listen to it. As long as I live and have the honor to merit your confidence I shall speak the truth even at the risk of displeasing you, which would be for me the greatest of misfortunes."*—Henry to Frederick.

THE QUESTION of the Bavarian succession and of Prussian policy concerning it was quickly transferred from the realm of hypothesis to that of practical politics at the end of the year 1777 by the death of the elector Maximilian III Joseph of Bavaria and the accession of the pro-Austrian Karl Theodore. One of the first acts of the new elector was to cede to Austria certain parts of Lower Bavaria and the Upper Palatinate, which were at once occupied by Austrian troops. Austrian hegemony in Germany, challenged a generation earlier by a restless young king of Prussia, seemed about to be reasserted by the equally ambitious young emperor Joseph II.

No one was very much surprised. The crisis had been foreseen for years, and Frederick had often discussed with Prince Henry how best to meet it when it came. The prince, bolder than his brother while diplomatic rather than military maneuvering was still in question, had urged him in the summer of 1775 to deal directly with Joseph at least long enough to drive him out into the open. If Joseph were willing to make a mutually advantageous bargain in the matter, he argued, Frederick might get all of electoral Saxony as compensation for his compliance. If the emperor refused to bargain, Frederick would at worst have found out where he stood and could govern himself accordingly, building up a "stop-Joseph" coalition and demanding as pay for his services in it a guarantee of the succession to Ansbach and Baireuth, which he might then cede to Saxony in exchange for some part of Lusatia. Henry urged, however, that in order to harvest any such gains as these the king set boldly to work well in advance of harvest time by invoking the agreement made at Neisse. Joseph had there proposed that he and Frederick consult each other in any emergency thereafter. Well, here was an emergency in which the emperor could not consistently refuse to talk. Try him! If he should refuse he would be put at a disadvantage. If, on the other hand, Frederick waited until the prospective crisis had become a fact and Austrian troops were already in possession of all or a part of Bavaria, he would himself be caught at a disadvantage with a burdensome war on his hands in which, Henry warned him, he could expect no effective assistance from Russia.[1]

Frederick had thought it more prudent not to commit himself. When the matter first came up for discussion between him and his brother in the summer of 1775 he seemed to think that it would be Henry rather than he who must eventually solve the problem. He said repeatedly that he expected to die before Maximilian Joseph did, and that he preferred to leave his successors' hands free as their father had left him free to do what he could with the family's claims to Julich and Berg. Still ignorant of the plan for a co-regency already taking shape in the king's mind, Prince Henry then tried to convince Frederick that, if he did not hope to outlive the elector of Bavaria, that was just one more reason why he should make every effort to settle the question of the Bavarian succession by negotiation with the emperor before he died; but the king said he preferred to leave the matter to his "successors."[2]

Two years later, less than three months before the death of the elector, Prince Henry still adhered to his belief that cooperation between Prussia and Austria was possible if Prussia would seek it, because Austria would not dare again to arouse Prussia's determined opposition. "One does not destroy two hundred thousand men. The last war clearly proved that," he wrote. The combined forces of Prussia and Austria, he urged, would on the other hand be omnipotent in Europe. The two states could divide Germany between themselves whenever they chose.[3]

Frederick, while still unwilling to attempt to negotiate before the death of the elector, was by that time ready to concede that it might be worth a trial afterward — provided, of course, that the influence of Kaunitz and Maria Theresa were not too strong, and provided that Frederick himself were still alive. If he were not, then the character of "the nephew" would itself invite trouble for Prussia.[4]

[1] Various letters, July to September, 1775, in *P. C.*, XXXVII, 202–227, *passim*.
[2] *Ibid*. It will be remembered that the king's gout was extraordinarily painful in 1775 and 1776 and that he was then planning a virtual regency for Prince Henry, to follow his death. So he would naturally have been willing to leave more to his brother's discretion than to their nephew's. The co-regency plan was not divulged to Prince Henry until February, 1776.
[3] *P. C.*, XXXIX, 318, 341.
[4] *Ibid.*, 342; *Oeuvres*, XXVI, 399, 400. "These women live on so persistently!" he exclaimed, " . . . Dame Theresa will bury us both — me and the elector of Bavaria." As to his successor: "Je veux croire que, si l'électeur de Bavière décédait pendant ma vie, peut-être l'Empereur voudrait s'arranger avec moi; mais pensez, je vous prie, que je suis vieux et infirme et qu'il ne faut plus compter du tout sur mon existence; qu'on méprise souverainement notre neveu; que, s'il est possible, on le prend encore pour moins qu'il est

When the long-anticipated cession of some Bavarian territory to Austria had become a fact, in January, 1778, Prince Henry ceased at once to urge haste and began to counsel caution, for he feared that Frederick might turn unwisely from cautious to hasty action. "I am making marvelous progress in patience," Frederick replied. "I am developing the *sang-froid* of old Marshal Wackerbarth, and shall soon turn into a statue; so I hope . . . you will be pleased with me." [5]

The prince accepted his brother's badinage good-naturedly as welcome evidence of good health and gay spirits, and proceeded doggedly to outline once more his estimate of the situation. If the matter were properly handled, Prussia must gain something from it in one or the other of two alternative ways. If the emperor preferred not to fight Prussia they might yet negotiate with him. If he were bent upon war they would do well to delay its outbreak while they built an alliance against him and organized the legal defenses of their position. In either case, while playing for time by offering to negotiate, they must hide their resentment of his action. [6]

One item which the prince overlooked was that, while dissimulating to deceive the emperor, the king would surely be suspected of dissimulation by others with whom he tried to ally himself. Frederick found a way around that difficulty by permitting Prince Henry to serve as his left hand and carry on officially "secret" negotiations with Cobenzl, the Austrian ambassador in Berlin, while he himself offered the right hand of fellowship to Austria's potential enemies. If neither hand seemed to know just what the other was doing, both could work more effectively.

Each knew at all times, privately but not officially, all about what the other was doing. They agreed that their best legal case could be built upon a claim that the emperor had violated the constitution, his own coronation oath, and the Treaty of Westphalia. Frederick should take pains therefore to appear as spokesman for the princes of the Empire, if only they could be aroused to the point of asking for his intercession. The Prince of Pfalz-Zweibrücken was the one worst hurt. He must be encouraged to protest; then Frederick could support him.

Neither cherished any illusions about the courage or the national-mindedness of the petty princes of Third Germany. Those little fellows would simply sit with their arms folded if they could, Henry pointed

en effet, et que sa mauvaise réputation lui attirera les plus mauvaises affaires. Cet animal est incorrigible; je fais ce que je peux, pour le tirer de la crapule et de la mauvaise compagnie dans laquelle le vit. Car voilà ce qui le décrie et qui attirera sûrement une cruelle guerre à ce pauvre pays."

[5] *P. C.*, XL, 54.   [6] *Ibid.*, 66; Schöning, IV-2, 2.

out, and watch the two most consequential German states cripple each other. Nothing was to be done with them and nothing need be done for them. Far from fighting in their interest, Frederick had no right to fight at all except for the aggrandizement of Prussia, though the protection of Bavaria, Saxony, or Zweibrücken might serve as a plausible pretext.

It was already too late to prevent the Austrian occupation of Bavarian territory, but Austria might still be asked what it would be worth to her to be permitted to continue in peaceful occupation of it. In the meantime, by careful handling of France, the active aid or at least the benevolent neutrality of that nation might be secured.[7]

The king promised to continue his "fruitless" negotiations with Austria as long as possible and not in any event to do anything "precipitately." The prince at the same time continued, through intermediaries suggested to him by Frederick himself, his own indirect and ostensibly underhand conversations with Cobenzl. The principal difference between the brothers was that Frederick expected his negotiations to fail while the prince still believed that more could be gained by bargaining than by war — in spite of Joseph's known boast that what Kaunitz had gained with the pen he would know how to hold with the sword.[8]

One of the first fruits of what Frederick had called in advance a fruitless negotiation was the offer of Julich and Berg as the price of his complaisance.[9] The prince would not only have listened to the proposition but would have written then, with Frederick and Joseph as co-authors, a chapter in German history which he was eventually to write with much less distinguished collaboration twenty years later. What he proposed was nothing less than the secularization of the ecclesiastical states of southwestern Germany. The Catholic House of Hapsburg would, he conceded, ordinarily be reluctant to sanction such a "pious" enterprise, but he was sure it would overcome its reluctance rather than give up any of its ill-gotten gains; Prussia, on the other hand, could claim church lands as compensation for Austrian usurpations, and should do so. The clergy need not suffer. The bishop of Würzburg, Salzburg, Bamberg, Fulda, or Paderborn, for example, could well be pensioned by his new sovereign and grow old in his diocese just as before, while state and people were blessed by the change.[10]

[7] Schöning, IV–2, 2. Henry later remarked that such protests as the lesser princes of the Empire had made against Austria's usurpation were nothing more than the croaking of so many frogs. If Austria should toss them a few thousand florins they would all join a chorus against Prussia. *Ibid.,* 9.

[8] Prince Henry's first intermediary was his former chamberlain, Count Leopold Lamberg, who was Cobenzl's brother-in-law. When Lamberg left Berlin Baron Dodo von Knyphausen took his place as messenger.

[9] ". . . pour m'associer à son brigandage." *P. C.,* XL, 130.

[10] Schöning, IV–1, 46; IV–2, 16; *P. C.,* XL, 137.

The king refused to be tempted. Prussia's ultimate interest, he argued, could be best served by restraining once for all the ambition of Austria, which would otherwise grow more and more despotic and would work changes in the Empire to Prussia's detriment. Such a long-range objective was of far more vital significance than any immediate acquisition of territory by doubtful title could possibly be. He could therefore not afford to accept land as a gift if it were given under circumstances that would restrain him from opposing Austrian aggression and defending the German constitution.[11]

Finding his "beautiful dream" rejected as impractical, the prince felt himself compelled to justify the frankness with which he had spoken of it. "I cannot help but speak frankly to you, my very dear brother," he explained. "The truth often lies hidden and becomes known only when there is no longer time to listen to it. As long as I live and have the honor to merit your confidence I shall speak the truth even at the risk of displeasing you, which would be for me the greatest of misfortunes."[12]

Frankness bred frankness. "I know quite well that it is only our own interest that compels us to act at this moment," the king replied; "but we must be very careful not to say so. Even if there are some gains to be hoped for, we must keep them hidden like murder and, if fortune favors us, ask only to be indemnified for the costs of the war."[13]

The prince knew that he was engaged once more in an argument he could not hope to win. "Since the month of January I have been convinced that you would make war," he grumbled, "but I have thought that some of Austria's suggestions could lead to an appeasement. . . . I still see then several ways by which you can achieve your purpose more surely than by war, the success of which one can never determine in advance with any certainty, or the consequences that it may entail."[14]

It was a foregone conclusion that if war came the prince would command an army again as he had done in the Seven Years' War, but no thought of martial glory beguiled him from his pacific views. "If I were thinking only of myself," he wrote, "I should prefer war, in which I can be something; but I would rather be nothing, provided that the state and you, my very dear brother, who are but one, are happy."[15]

Frederick and the state, who were but one, were sedulously preparing for war while the preliminary diplomatic sparring went on to its fore-ordained conclusion. On or about March 20, 1778, at a Potsdam conference similar to that which had immediately preceded his invasion of Saxony in 1756, Frederick divulged his plan of campaign to Prince

---

[11] *P. C.*, XL, 138, 202 *et passim.*   [12] Schöning, IV–2, 17.   [13] *Ibid.*, 31; *P. C.*, XL, 224.
[14] Schöning, IV–2, 33; *P. C.*, XL, 264.   [15] Schöning, IV–2, 35.

Henry, the crown prince, Frederick Duke of Brunswick, and the ministers Finckenstein, Hertzberg, and Schulenberg. Bohemia was to be invaded from Silesia and Saxony simultaneously, Saxony having just agreed to furnish troops and to permit them to serve under Prussian direction. Prince Henry would command on the old familiar Saxon front a composite force only slightly smaller with the Saxons counted in than the all-Prussian army based on Silesia and commanded by the king in person. Whichever invader first encountered the principal Austrian resistance was to take up the defensive while the other attacked. Both, if successful, would push right on to the Danube — the prince via Prague and the king via Pressburg. Horses were already being purchased for the army, routes and bivouac stations for marching regiments were being selected by staff officers, and other routine preparations were going on apace.[16]

The argument between the king and his reluctant associate commander then passed into a new phase. It was less concerned thereafter with the question whether war was inevitable than with guessing when it would come. The frugal prince, who had refused until then to buy himself any field equipment for a campaign which he had hoped to avert, quickly made a will and began to build up a personal headquarters staff and to study the tables of organization of the troops he was to command. (One of the omissions which he quickly noted and which Frederick promised to correct was the appointment of an auditor general.) He could not, however, bring himself to believe that hostilities would begin as soon as Frederick expected unless Frederick himself began them. When the king warned him that an Austrian attack upon Dresden was imminent he offered to bet a hundred bottles of Hungarian wine that no such attack would take place within the next three weeks. Frederick accepted the wager and thought when he left for the front that he would win it; but no Austrian invasion of Saxony was attempted.[17]

At a final conference in Berlin on April 5, just before going to join his troops, Frederick authorized his brother to assure Cobenzl through Baron Knyphausen that his warlike precautions did not necessarily mean

[16] *Ibid.*, 270. The choice of the prince to command the composite Saxon-Prussian army was an eminently logical one. He was thoroughly familiar with the terrain and was much more popular with the Saxons than the king was. Ever since the Seven Years' War he had been nicknamed *der sächsische Herrgott,* and Frederick was wise enough to capitalize on the esteem in which his brother was held by the Saxons without being deterred by any such petty considerations as jealousy. See also Krauel's article "Prinz Heinrich von Preussen in Rheinsberg," in the *Hohenzollern Jahrbücher*, VI (1902), 23.

[17] Schöning, IV–1, 67; IV–2, 44; *Oeuvres*, XXVI, 412; *P. C.*, XL, 340, 354, 378. Frederick paid the bet with good grace, but argued that the invasion had been anticipated and so had been prevented only by the promptness and vigor of his own countermeasures.

war and that negotiations had not yet become purposeless, so Cobenzl need not leave Berlin unless recalled by his own government. To the authorized message from the king the prince added one of his own to the effect that his brother was not half so eager for war as he pretended to be and that just then, when he was away from the evil influence of his ministers, would be the best possible time for the emperor to approach him directly with a person-to-person communication if Austria genuinely wished to keep the peace.[18]

Clearly the prince must all along have been trying hard to deceive either himself or Cobenzl. In continuing to communicate with the Austrian diplomat after the king had left Berlin, he pretended to be acting behind Frederick's back; but Frederick had eyes in the back of his head. When Henry said that Frederick had not decided to fight and did not wish to do so, he was saying something that he assuredly wished were true but something that, as his letters reveal, he knew was at least half false; so he was not himself deceived. He was merely trying to disarm Cobenzl and get one more offer out of him or the emperor. If he succeeded, and if war were averted by the new offer, he would have won a great diplomatic victory in spite of Frederick's skepticism, as he had done once before in the matter of the first partition of Poland. Even if he were able only to induce his brother to delay a little longer, every day gained was to Prussia's advantage. At worst, he was doing no harm. Prussia's military preparations were going right on, while this final finesse might delay Austria's.

He knew that it was only a finesse. Frederick wrote to him from his army headquarters at Schönwalde: "We are scribbling away a marvelous amount of paper; but when the ink is exhausted the sword will have its turn, and it will decide all this more quickly than the sharpest-pointed pens." Yet he kept Cobenzl convinced that Joseph had but to address Frederick directly and all would be well. "No one wishes peace so ardently as he; no one knows the king better," reported Cobenzl to Kaunitz on April 14.[19]

On the Austrian side of the border there was no more general enthusiasm for the war than on the Prussian. Joseph was the only one who contemplated it without the most serious misgivings. Maria Theresa was manifestly most reluctant to see it undertaken. Lacy and Loudon, the two old war horses who were to be charged with the fighting of it (neither born an Austrian), would have preferred to live out their days in peaceful retirement. So for the sake of some delay Kaunitz prevailed

[18] Cobenzl to Kaunitz, and H. to F., April 6, in *P. C.*, XL, 364–370, 377.
[19] *Ibid.*, 389–392.

upon his master to act upon Prince Henry's suggestion and write directly to Frederick. Since both monarchs were with their troops near the frontier, they were close enough together for a letter to be written one day and answered the next.

The emperor feinted with an offer to support Prussia's claims to the succession to Ansbach and Baireuth and intimated that he would not oppose an exchange of that claim for land elsewhere not contiguous with Austrian territory.[20]

Frederick parried with legal and moral arguments. The emperor, he said, could not control the succession to a state or to the fiefs of the Empire. Frederick's own claims therefore needed no sanction other than that of the laws of the Empire, while as a member of the *Corps Germanique* he found it his duty to defend weaker members of that body. He was involved also as a guarantor of the Peace of Westphalia and of the Treaty of Hubertusburg; those treaties had been violated by Bavaria's deal with the emperor.

The king knew that Joseph would find his reply unsatisfactory, but to prolong the discussion he went on to put in a claim for damages on behalf of Zweibrücken, Saxony, and Württemberg, the legitimate expectations of which he said had been prejudiced by the Austro-Bavarian bargain.[21]

The emperor replied sharply to what he bluntly called the king's "long tirade." To correct what he called "an error of fact," he claimed that in making his agreement with Bavaria he had been acting not as emperor but only in his hereditary capacity as archduke of Austria, and had been quite within his rights; so no outside interference was warranted. The allodial claims of Saxony and Württemberg were conceivably legitimate subjects for litigation before a properly constituted court or for adjustment by direct negotiation, but the Duke of Zweibrücken had no rights in Bavaria while his relative the elector Karl Theodore was alive and was authorized to speak for him.[22]

Frederick in reply used up another marvelous amount of paper in confessing himself unable to reconcile the facts with the law and the treaties. He had already told Prince Henry that he thought the correspondence would go about three rounds and no more. He wanted it to take that long, because "when one has said the last word there is nothing

[20] *Ibid.*, 392–394. Only Lower Lusatia could have been secured from Saxony under those conditions, as Upper Lusatia touched Bohemia.

[21] *Ibid.*, 394, 396.

[22] *Ibid.*, 407. The emperor ended his rather bellicose note with a hollow-sounding plea for peace. As one soldier to another, he appealed to Frederick not to "put four hundred thousand brave fellows to butchering one another — and for what? To what end?"

more to say." The last word would be a declaration of war, and he was not yet quite ready for that; but after a third rather perfunctory exchange of letters, on April 19 and 20, the two principals let their seconds in the foreign offices in Berlin and Vienna take up the quarrel once more at long range.[23]

While engaged in his last-minute correspondence with the Austrian-born German emperor, Frederick waited in vain for a personal letter that would clarify his relations with the German-born empress of Russia. Catherine was his ally, but he was by no means sure that she would give him any effective help. In an attempt to secure her support he had written her a long personal letter on February 13; he had sent as a special envoy to her court a young Count Podewils (carefully coached by Prince Henry) to supplement what the experienced Count Solms could do there; and Prince Henry, to whom Catherine was still writing occasionally, had transmitted several messages for him; but his own letter went unanswered.[24]

On June 30, "at the moment when he was again on the point of leaving his homeland in order to defend it," Henry wrote to the empress again. His hopes rested, he said, on the righteousness of Prussia's cause and on the dependability of her troops, but the enemy's resources were abundant and the war was sure to be burdensome and hazardous; so his heart was heavy. The king of Prussia had offered just and equitable terms of peace and had carried moderation as far as possible, but he was being pushed into war in spite of himself. The prince knew that the empress must look out first for the welfare of her own people; but he hoped that, if such a course were shown to be compatible with her Russian interest, she would join in the defense of a legitimate cause in Germany and make herself its arbiter, so that justice and equity might yet prevail.[25]

Catherine replied promptly and cordially:

Monsieur my cousin: The prayers of a large part of Europe will accompany Your Royal Highness in the glorious career that you have undertaken anew in the defense of your country as your letter of June 30 announces. Even the indifferent are interested in the deeds of heroes; their friends share with them all their trials. I see with pleasure that Your Royal Highness has

---

[23] *Ibid.*, 419, 433, 441.

[24] F. to H., June 29, in *P. C.*, XLI, 229; Schöning, IV–2, 88. Other letters are scattered through the first eighty pages of Schöning (IV–2), the *Oeuvres*, XXVI, 404ff., and the *P. C.*, especially XL, 93, and XLI, 22. Several of Catherine's letters to Prince Henry were lost, so do not appear in Krauel's *Briefwechsel*. Many of the prince's letters to the king written during the late spring of 1778 were also lost or destroyed and have to be reconstructed from Frederick's replies to them.

[25] *P. C.*, XLII, 531, supplement for the year 1778. The letter is printed from the original

for a long time counted me among the number of your friends and of those of your country, and that you do not doubt my desire to see the peace re-established; my acts will on no occasion give the lie to these sentiments.[26]

Count Solms reported to Frederick from St. Petersburg that the prince's letter had been responsible for a favorable change in Catherine's attitude. Her ministers assured him that she was contemplating an active diversion in Galicia or Podolia or both. The prince was fortunate in being able to send the king her letter on the heels of the courier carrying the report of his brilliantly successful advance into Bohemia in the first week of August, and this diplomatic success seemed fittingly to crown a military achievement.[27]

"You have done much more, my dear brother, than you think," Frederick wrote. "You have swept away an enemy corps in Bohemia; that is a great deal. But your letter to the empress of Russia has accomplished more than a battle. She has resolved at once to declare herself openly in our favor. . . . She will force the house of Austria to re-establish equity and justice in Germany. What do I not owe to you! You may be sure that the memory of this will be effaced only by my death and that . . . my gratitude will not be unfruitful."[28]

The prince himself said that he was disappointed in the letter. Russian troops could not be depended upon. Either they would effect no diversion at all or they would do it too late to do any good. A strong declaration at Vienna would have been worth more to Prussia, he thought.[29]

Frederick had said virtually the same thing to Solms a few days before, and their skepticism was well founded. In October Catherine sent one general, Kamenskoi, as a volunteer to be attached to Prince Henry's headquarters for the duration of the war.[30] No troops were ever sent; but the danger of active Russian participation in the war was, of course, a constant threat to Austria and lent weight to Catherine's eventual offer of mediation.

The war of 1778–79 against Austria was essentially a political rather than a military maneuver; and again the king and his second-in-

in the central archive in Moscow; it is not in Schöning or in Krauel's *Briefwechsel*. It is not now apparent that Frederick ever saw the final draft of the letter, but he was glad to have it sent. On July 1 he wrote to Finckenstein that he hoped a letter from his brother might induce the empress to do something in Prussia's favor. See *P. C.*, XLI, 238.

[26] Hausarchiv, Rep. 56, II, I; *Briefwechsel*, 173; *P. C.*, XLI, 387. The grand duke Paul, to whom the prince had also written, sent a letter along with his mother's. Both were written on July 13, old style, or 24, new style.

[27] An account of the campaign is given in the next chapter.

[28] *P. C.*, XLI, 323; *Oeuvres*, XXVI, 438; Schöning, IV–2, 108.

[29] Schöning, IV–2, 113; *P. C.*, XLI, 366.

[30] *P. C.*, XLI, 501, 519, 535.

command were in direct disagreement as to the policy that dictated it. Frederick, the older, was willing to fight a war which he considered necessary to prevent Austria from regaining among the German states the position of leadership of which he had deprived her in his youth. Posing as the protectress of her weaker neighbors, Prussia could well be content, he thought, with her own enhanced position among them without claiming any new territory for herself. Prince Henry, on the other hand, much younger than the king and more susceptible to temptation when an opportunity to seize some land for Prussia seemed to beckon to the adventurous spirit, could have countenanced some gains for Austria on a take-and-let-take basis if Prussia were duly "compensated" at the expense of some of the smaller German states. He always believed, however, that if Austria were merely to be checkmated, that purpose could be better achieved by diplomacy than by war. The king had no right, he thought, either to fight or to take risks for any other object than the territorial aggrandizement of Prussia.

CHAPTER XXII

# 𝔉𝔞𝔯𝔢𝔴𝔢𝔩𝔩 𝔱𝔬 𝔄𝔯𝔪𝔰

*"Nothing is more discouraging than when the
sovereign is ill disposed toward those who serve
him."*— Henry to Frederick.

PRINCE HENRY's dramatic announcement of June 30, that he was again
on the point of leaving his country in order to defend it, was no mere
figure of speech. He left Berlin the next day and spent the month of
July in Saxony, organizing his command and planning his invasion of
Bohemia. His task was in several ways more difficult than those of which
he had so brilliantly acquitted himself in the Seven Years' War. One
of his most serious problems was the result of a new development. More
artillery and heavier guns were to be used, hence more horses were
needed — which in turn called for longer wagon trains and complicated
the whole problem of supply. Roads and mountain passes that had been
used again and again by small mobile units of 1758–62 were found
inadequate by the ponderous armies of 1778. In his earlier campaigns,
moreover, usually on the defensive, the prince had commanded a unified
force against a miscellaneous conglomerate of badly co-ordinated opponents; in 1778 he had to lead a composite army in an attack upon a
well-unified one. His enemy, furthermore, stood behind elaborate fortifications in carefully chosen defensive positions similar to those in which
in the Seven Years' War the prince had himself successfully defied attack
for months at a time, against apparently overwhelming odds. So it was
not easy for him to attack. Yet it seemed wiser for him to make the principal attack than for the king to do so. Frederick was faced by the same
problems of supply and terrain as the prince, and by the same well-
fortified enemy. The Austrians, remembering their history and apparently expecting Frederick to do most of the attacking himself, had massed
about eighty thousand men under Lacy opposite the king and only about
sixty-two thousand under Loudon opposite Prince Henry. The element
of surprise might also be worth something.[1] So the brothers exchanged
roles again, or continued in effect the exchange of 1762; and the victor of
Freiberg began again where he had left off.

[1] Jany, III, 109, 117. The two principal Prussian armies numbered approximately
87,000 men each.

He began brilliantly. First he collected most of his troops around Plauen, southwest of Dresden. Then, by ordering a certain Jewish contractor whom he suspected of being an Austrian spy to establish an enormous supply depot at Freiberg, he did what he could to strengthen the Austrian assumption, of which his own spies had informed him, that he would move by the west bank of the Elbe on Aussig. As a further indication that that would be his objective he ordered General Möllendorff to make a short but showy advance in that direction, and so compelled Loudon to shift his forces westward to meet the threat there.

Then, quickly throwing three pontoon bridges across the Elbe between Pillnitz and Pirna, he crossed to the east bank and went into Bohemia by way of defiles and passes of the Lusatian mountains which had been left practically unguarded because they were considered impassable. The mountain roads and the rapid going took heavy toll of horses and wagons, and the strain of directing the hazardous venture told heavily on the prince's own slender reserve of nervous and physical energy; but a great deal of ground was gained, and thousands of prisoners were taken with very little loss of life.

Within a week the prince's Saxons had captured Gabel, and his Prussians were in possession of Zwickau, Niemes, Neuschloss (near Leipa), and Leitmeritz. He could use the Elbe as a supply line as far south as Königstein, Lusatia was well covered, and only a supporting attack on Frederick's front was needed, he thought, to drive Loudon completely out of his prepared positions in Bohemia.

If he had gone on as boldly as he had begun, he might have dislodged Loudon without the king's help. The redoubtable old Scot was no longer quite the Loudon of Kunersdorf or Liegnitz; and the impressionable Joseph, who was with him, was ready to run. But the prince's own weaknesses and the inevitable difficulties of his situation stopped him. Once stopped, he was beaten; for the supplies he could carry with him or haul over the mountain roads after him were insufficient to feed his men and horses unless they were generously supplemented by foraging or from captured stores; and his army could not long subsist by foraging or by seizing enemy stores unless it continued its rapid advance.

The king's difficulties were equally serious. His service of supply was even less efficient than his brother's, because it was less carefully organized and less closely watched, and because he depended more heavily upon pillaging the countryside for sustenance from the moment he crossed the border. He had gone a little way into Bohemia early in July, intending to feel out the enemy position and, if he found it too strong to be attacked, then to send troops into Moravia. That move would, he hoped, compel Lacy also to send off detachments in that direction which might be attacked on the march; or the principal defense force might be so weakened that he could attack it to better advantage.

Again, as Daun had done in 1758, the Austrians refused to oblige him. Lacy stood fast with his whole force; Frederick felt himself compelled to keep his own army intact in the presence of Lacy's, yet he could find no avenue of attack up which he could drag his heavy guns in numbers sufficient to give him the necessary superiority of fire power at the critical point. So he made no serious attacks and did nothing except to shift his camps slightly now and then to simplify the increasingly difficult problem of subsistence by foraging. As a part of the Austrian defense plan the peasants were ordered to destroy everything edible and all growing crops and to flee as the Prussians approached. The orders were only imperfectly obeyed, but wherever the invading armies (especially Frederick's) did not find a desert they soon made one. Dysentery and dearth of decent food meanwhile thinned the ranks of the king's army while battle losses continued to be negligible.

By late summer the campaign had degenerated into a "potato war" on the part of the hungry soldiers and a battle of words between the Prussian commanders. The prince, up to the day he joined his troops, had fought against the war with all that was in him. Frederick had frequently given way to his natural irritation at his brother's grumbling, and as early as April 17 had told him sharply that if the war was not to his liking he had only to ask to be excused from participation in it, as their brother Ferdinand had already done.[2]

Repeatedly during the early summer Frederick had reproached the reluctant Henry for his pessimism and had accused him of conjuring up imaginary dangers and obstacles that might never have to be met, while the prince made no secret of his opinion that the king was making a blunder of the first magnitude by fighting at all when so much more could have been gained without fighting.

When in the middle of July the prince outlined his plans for a surprise invasion of Bohemia by the Rumberg-Zwickau route Frederick gave the project his unqualified approval and promised to second it actively in every way possible. "A god must have inspired you," he wrote. He further promised not to push just then his own old Moravian project; Prince Henry had threatened to abandon Bohemia at once if he did.

In the first week of August, while the prince's men were pouring into enemy territory at an incredible rate, the king could not praise them highly enough to express his satisfaction. "I fear that the emperor will

[2] Schöning, IV-2, 54; *Oeuvres,* XXVI, 422; the letter is not in the *P. C.*

be a little annoyed with you, my dear brother," he wrote; "but at this price I do not doubt that you will be glad enough to merit his further displeasure. Someone burned a hundred wagon-loads of grain for us today, but that is a mere trifle and you have put a good plaster on the wound. So I shall think nothing more of it. May Heaven preserve your precious days!" [3]

There the peak was reached. On his way into Bohemia the prince had written: "In spite of the success of this enterprise, I would not attempt it again if I were offered three kingdoms. With a thousand men and two guns, the whole army could have been stopped." Again: "God forbid that an army should be obliged to retreat through there." And again: "If we lose the roads to Lusatia it will be impossible to get the army out without losing it. One cannot force those passes twice with impunity." His proper path forward was opening up for him, but he had given way to the fatal weakness of looking backward. [4]

Although it is not now apparent that he was in any desperate need of it, the prince began to call desperately for help. Let Frederick only make one serious attack from where he stood, or let him send just one small army corps to effect a junction with the Saxons on Prince Henry's left wing, and Loudon would be forced to abandon his position; but the king did neither, Loudon dug in where he was, and Henry began to tell how ill and how completely exhausted he was — and to plan a retreat.

The illness was genuine. The prince's physical endurance had been very severely taxed; but his indisposition was induced at least in part by disaffection and by what he called, in a letter written fourteen years later, "an epidemic of disputes" — *"la disputérie fut épidémique."* Frederick, he felt, was again demanding the impossible and refusing to listen to reason.

Certainly the king's comments were not only caustic but inconsistent. He bluntly blamed his brother for his own failure: "You are making me attempt things of the utmost difficulty, to try to get things again on to a favorable footing." No one need worry about Lusatia, he wrote. Suppose a large enemy corps should gain access to that province; it could

---

[3] August 6, in *P. C.*, XLI, 320; Schöning, IV–2, 106; *Oeuvres*, XXVI, 438. The letter in which he said that the winning of Catherine's promise of support was worth more than the ruin of an enemy army corps or a battle won was written two days later. See page 301, *supra*, for this letter.

[4] *P. C.*, XLI, 318, 328; Schöning, IV–2, 108. On August 22 the king replied to some of these complaints: "Don't talk to me . . . of defiles and mountains; I have them here every quarter-mile like those in the Alps! But by dint of hard labor I am improving the roads, and that is all that is still preventing me from striking my blow." *P. C.*, XLI, 383. When the Duke of Württemberg was transferred in October from Henry's army to the king's to take the place of a general who had died, Frederick reported that his arrival had occasioned a long debate as to which army had had the worse roads and suffered the greater hardships, and he had then decided that the honors had been about even. *Ibid.*, 514.

find no sustenance there and would consider itself fortunate indeed if it could get back into Bohemia. (Yet Lusatia had not been occupied, fought over, or foraged by hostile troops.) Frederick insisted at the same time, on the other hand, that if Prince Henry would only recross the Elbe at Leitmeritz (into territory from which the Austrians had just been driven and which they had systematically made into a desert as they left it), he would find forage there in abundance! The king said so because he wished to believe that it was so. No one but Prince Henry dared tell him it was not, and Prince Henry himself could not make him believe that it was not. He had resolved, by making his men forage for their food, to spread between the border and the Austrian camps a wide belt of devastation that would serve almost as well as a wall to protect the Saxon, Lusatian, and Silesian frontiers against a winter attack. As a measure of economy and as a form of economic warfare, he wanted to make both his armies eat at the enemy's expense all summer. It would have been more convenient if they could simply have stopped eating.[5]

After all their argument it was Frederick who first found it necessary to seek greener pastures. On September 8 he moved from Lauterwasser to Wildschutz for the sake of forage, and within a week had confessed to Henry that "hunger itself" and "the frightful disorders that take place among the foraging parties" would drive him out of Bohemia by the twentieth.[6]

In the fourth week of September the king retreated to Schatzlar; but the prince's army, he then seemed to think, might as well winter in Bohemia, west of the Elbe. Starting on the thirteenth, the prince did indeed cross to the west bank at Leitmeritz without being molested by the enemy; but eighty loaded munition and supply wagons got mired in the mud as a result of unseasonably heavy fall rains and had to be destroyed. On the twenty-first, knowing that Frederick himself was already on the way out, he proposed that he also withdraw. On the twenty-fourth he began his retreat.

[5] *P. C.,* XLI, 385–389. "Appendix à mon frère: Un mois de fourrage pour votre armée me coûte, mon cher frère, 400,000 écus; deux mois de fourrage que l'on prend sur l'ennemi font 800,000 écus, et il faut que nous épargnons à présent chaque sol, pour avoir le dernier écu en poche quand la paix se fait; cela décide presque autant des affaires qu'une bataille."

[6] *Ibid.,* 418, 423, 431. Foraging was certain, by its very nature, to be subversive of discipline; but the prince had all along been less troubled by fights among his own foraging parties than the king had, as he had from the beginning assigned each unit its own area and held it strictly within the bounds set upon it, while the king had adopted such regulations only late in the campaign and as a last resort. Schöning, IV–2, 144.

On August 8 the king had sent the following gentle admonition to one of his colonels: "Aber den Officiers vom Husaren-Regiment Rosenbusch und v. Brehmer könnet Ihr nur sagen: der Teufel solle sie alle holen, wenn sie nicht mehr Ordnung halten und ihr Devoir besser beobachten würden. Ich würde Kriegsrecht über sie halten lassen und sie alle mit einander cassiren. Und dem Obersten v. Brehmer könnt Ihr sagen, dass wir bald von einander Abschied nehmen würden."

The withdrawal was carried out exactly on schedule with all of his old skill and attention to careful staff work. Everything possible was done to make pursuit difficult, and the few attacks that were made upon him were beaten off by a resolute rear-guard defense. The end of the month found him back again in Saxony and not at all apologetic about having gone there; but he was sharply rebuked by Frederick for his "horrible loss in horses"—three thousand of them, worth a hundred and fifty thousand thaler! The king also refused his repeated request for two thousand thaler to enable his officers to replace their lost or ruined equipment.[7]

The farewell tour of a virtuoso adds few laurels to his crown if he is already too old when he undertakes it. So it was with the king of Prussia and his brother Henry, virtuosi of the battlefields of the Seven Years' War, when late in life they rode out once more to a return engagement with Austria. The new drama was played on the scenes of their former triumphs, the settings and supporting casts were similar, the foils who played opposite them were in several cases the same—but their successes were not overwhelming. The most unfortunate revelation of the whole experience was that their nerves and tempers were no better able to stand the strain of further campaigning than were their aging gouty legs. Neither of them ever recovered from the wounds inflicted upon his spirit by the other, and neither was compensated for his personal loss by any new soldierly prestige won at the expense of their common enemy. The prince was once on the point of achieving a tremendous military success but did not achieve it, and attributed his failure to Frederick's refusal to support him properly at the critical moment or to supply him afterward. The king's own campaign was a dismal failure, a dreary anticlimax for a military career such as his had been, and he was furious with his whole world.

The inevitable post-mortem discussion of the campaign, as the armies settled down in winter quarters, went rapidly from bad to worse. Frederick was justifying his extraordinary parsimony as a necessity, since another campaign was in view, while Prince Henry had already resolved never to fight another. Frederick complained constantly about costs, but said he had no time to reorganize his purchasing department or to investigate the work of his supply officers, who, the prince said, were robbing him shamefully every day, especially in the buying of horses.

---

[7] Schöning, IV-2, 155-170; *P. C.,* XLI, 441, 461, 491, 507. One who distinguished himself during the retreat, as he had done throughout the campaign, was General Möllendorff, who subsequently commanded against the armies of the First French Republic. Frederick sent a decoration for him rather grudgingly, thinking that Henry had overrated him.

*Portrait of Prince Henry by Anton Graff, 1778*
Reproduced by courtesy of the Verwaltung der staatlichen Schlösser und Gärten.

*Portrait of Frederick II by Anton Graff, 1781*
Reproduced by courtesy of the Verwaltung der staatlichen Schlösser und Gärten.

From a favorable comment on their nephew's conduct in the field, Prince Henry got perhaps his first intimation that the co-regency plan had gone glimmering from the king's mind. "I ought to tell you also that . . . I am highly pleased with our nephew," Frederick had written. "He has turned over quite a new leaf and has changed astonishingly for the better. I begin to take heart." Seeing his own peculiarly confidential position threatened, Henry began to lose heart.[8]

Then Frederick, despite the volume and variety of work with which he was harassed, began to append ugly little personal notes in his own hand to the more formal and fairly correct official messages dictated to his secretaries. He had no time to read reports on minor patrol skirmishes, but he took time to tell Henry so, quite harshly, when the prince with his usual thoroughness reported one.

He also found time to excuse himself for his own want of success on the ground that he was "not one of those fellows who sit with their arms folded and prefer an easy and useless repose to a fruitful activity," and had certainly done all that one man could, but had been "badly seconded."[9]

Prince Henry could not fail to take such criticism personally. "It pains me," he replied, "to see you complain that you have not been well seconded. Those upon whom that [charge] falls are no doubt very unfortunate not to be able to satisfy you; but in that case, if I may be permitted to speak with my customary frankness, it will be better for you and for them if you will choose others in whom you have more confidence. Among the great number of officers whom you have trained in war and peace there must be some who will earn your approbation. Those who have lost it, however, must lose their natural usefulness from the time when they perceive that they no longer merit your favor. Nothing is more discouraging than when the sovereign is ill disposed toward those who serve him."[10]

Frederick acknowledged the receipt of the letter, but quickly steered away from personalities and gave no sign of having noted Henry's irritation except by exerting himself to inject a bit of humor into the informal note which he wrote as usual to accompany his next official letter. He apologized for mentioning the capture of only a hundred of the enemy; they refused to stand fast anywhere, so it was hard to catch any great number of them, he said. He joked also about several conflicting rumors as to where the emperor was just then. "Of one thing I am

[8] Schöning, IV-2, 181, 185; *P. C.*, XLI, 543.
[9] Schöning, IV-2, 186; *Oeuvres*, XXVI, 460; *P. C.*, XLI, 563.
[10] Schöning, IV-2, 191.

certain; he must be somewhere, and not in two places at once — like God in the mass." [11]

But the harm was already done. The prince also avoided personalities for some weeks, then on December 3 asked to be relieved of his command. Reason dictated his belief, he said, that peace was assured for the spring. It was clearly not to Austria's advantage to continue the war, and France and Russia would be glad to gain such cheap credit as they could by using their influence to end it. Meanwhile, even in Dresden in winter, he found the command of an army too burdensome. He did not pretend to be suffering from any specific disease but said that he had found his general health unequal to the strain of active service. He had thought in the spring that he could do what was needed, and he found it humiliating to have to confess in the autumn that he had been mistaken; but his enfeebled constitution and used-up nerves would compel him to retire as soon as Frederick could find a substitute to take over the command of his army. He knew, he said, that resigning meant "going back, so to speak, into oblivion and losing all the honors of a post of command." He professed also to fear that his services in eleven campaigns and in time of peace would be forgotten; yet he insisted that he could not go on.[12]

The king gave his gout as his reason for not replying for two weeks. (He would naturally not want a secretary to know anything about the resignation unless he were ready to accept it.) When he was again able to write he expressed the hope that a careful regime and moderate exercise would restore the prince's health and enable him, after all, to retain his command. In a second letter he dwelt upon the difficulty of finding a substitute. Only the hereditary Duke of Brunswick could be considered for the place, and he was indispensable just then in Upper Silesia. "Persons like you are not easily found," Frederick explained, and asked his brother out of loyalty to remain at his post.

To the prince's hysterical outburst that he feared he would be forgotten the king replied with kingly dignity: "What you say . . . would be all right in the mouth of a man who had never distinguished himself; but I take the liberty of telling you that these suggestions are unworthy of you, unless one is to suppose that the public is unjust and that I am the most ungrateful of men; and I hope that you do not think that of me." [13]

Slightly mollified, the prince conceded that he could of course handle

---

[11] *P. C.*, XLII, 1, 2. A few days later he remarked, referring again to the volume of his correspondence, that his presence in Breslau would be a boon to the paper industry there, though it might do no other good than that.

[12] Schöning, IV–2, 209; *Oeuvres*, XXVI, 466; *P. C.*, XLII, 102.

[13] Schöning, IV–2, 210, 213, 216; *Oeuvres*, XXVI, 470; *P. C.*, XLII, 133, 147.

his work for a few weeks longer during the quiet season which permitted him to defer some of it for a time when necessary, but he made it a point of honor to serve notice then so as to avoid the appearance of resigning in the face of an opening campaign later. Frederick had already decided to accept his resignation if another campaign had to be fought; he had designated their nephew the Duke of Brunswick as Henry's successor and written an elaborate dossier of instructions for him; but he was not yet ready to say so, because he would not have chosen to make the transfer until March. So, while keeping the young duke fully informed of his intentions, he only grumbled to Henry: "It is true that at a certain age tranquillity is preferable to action. Everyone can do as he likes but me; my destiny requires me to run my course in the harness that I have to wear, and I must submit to it." [14]

Prince Henry also submitted to the king's will and remained with his troops until he marched them home in the latter half of May, after the signing of the Treaty of Teschen. Meanwhile, during the negotiation of the peace, he and Frederick had gone on exchanging letters almost daily, and a final unfortunate quarrel had so embittered them both that the king ceased to consult or to confide in him in important state affairs. He, for his part, vowed never again to offer Frederick his services either in war or in peace.

The breach already existing between them was widened by the prince's failure to evince enthusiasm over the preliminary terms of peace when Frederick announced them to him. They were, to be sure, "nothing very glorious," as the king conceded when he sent them. Any enterprise could be called glorious if it succeeded, the prince replied; and it could be said to have succeeded if it had accomplished its object. The war had apparently done that. Yet, since it had added nothing either to the wealth or to the territorial extent of Prussia, he wished it had never had to be fought, or that a solution might have been found by which Prussia would have profited. [15]

Their most serious quarrel was a result of the prince's meddling once too often in matters concerning which the king was willing enough to keep him informed but in which he had not been invited to take any active part. One of the last questions remaining in dispute between the negotiators at Teschen was the amount of the indemnity which the

[14] Schöning, IV-2, 217; *Oeuvres,* XXVI, 469, 470; *P. C.,* XLII, 121, 159–162, 169. Frederick was at that time only beginning to recover from a severe attack of gout. He was barely able to walk, and one hand was still disabled.

[15] Schöning, IV-2, 261; *P. C.,* XLII, 420. Frederick replied rather sharply that to have compelled Austria to give up her usurpations, and to have taught the other states to look upon Prussia as a counterweight to Austrian despotism, was profit enough.

elector of Saxony was to receive. Frederick had demanded four or five million thaler for him. Bavaria, at the emperor's behest, had offered one million. Henry was afraid that Frederick would fight another costly campaign, as he had repeatedly said he would do, rather than require the elector to reduce the amount of his claim. So he himself got hold of the Saxon prince and induced him to say that he would accept two millions if more was not to be had without further fighting.[16]

To the prince himself, as always, what he had done seemed perfectly reasonable. Frederick had pretended that he was fighting for Saxony, but Henry knew better than to believe him and was at the same time less ready than he was to endanger any tangible Prussian interest for the imponderable advantage to be gained by courting the confidence of the smaller states. He was himself, moreover, less fond of the Saxons than ever, after paying what he thought were exorbitant prices for quarters and maintenance in Dresden through the winter, and after rejecting as unreasonable their demand that he pay duty on everything brought into the country for the use of his army. And he was in a position to deal directly with the elector by word of mouth, as Frederick was not.[17]

Frederick did not welcome the intervention. "Whatever you do, . . ." he wrote, "you must be patient, for it is impossible to be quite sure of anything about the negotiation at Teschen until I receive a reply, the 15th or 16th. If it is as I want it, we shall have peace; if Austrian arrogance prevails, we shall have war and, in that case, I shall at once send the hereditary prince [of Brunswick] to Dresden so that you can, as you wish, take care of your health. I ought to add that all appearances point toward a rupture of the congress and that I must therefore be more on my guard than ever. Be so good then as to wait for such news as I may be able to send you without disturbing the elector of Saxony with useless suggestions more prejudicial than favorable to [our] affairs."[18]

The prince's only immediate reply directly to the king was that he was too well known to be accused of lack of virtue and had courage enough to endure misfortune, but that that incident ended his career.

---

[16] *P. C.,* XLIII, 14. Prince Henry had once suggested to Frederick that if the elector of Bavaria could not be compelled to pay the full amount, then the heir apparent, the Duke of Zweibrücken, might be induced to obligate himself to pay it when he came into his inheritance. Frederick replied that if he had already been forced to turn beggar he might consider such a suggestion, but he had not yet been reduced to that extremity. "Si la Saxe n'obtient pas une satisfaction honnête, personne à l'avenir ne voudra s'allier avec la Prusse, ainsi j'insiste raide sur ce point: ou qu'on indemnise la Saxe, ou je continue la guerre. Voilà les paroles sacramentales de cette négociation." *Ibid.,* XLII, 509.

[17] Schöning, IV–2, 203. Without Prussian help, he had said all along, Saxony could not hope to get a village or a thaler; she should be reminded of that fact if she asked for too much. *Ibid.,* IV–2, 234.

[18] Schöning, IV–2, 272; *P. C.,* XLIII, 14.

To others, then and later, he denounced the king in unmeasured and unconsidered terms. To Baron Friedrich Melchior Grimm he wrote in May that he had had so much experience of injustice in the thirty-nine years just past (Frederick's reign up to then) that he should have learned to bear it without indignation, but had not. Never again would he draw sword for such a king.[19]

No one needed to draw sword again for Frederick. He had fought his last war. The news, when it came from Teschen, was good. The elector of Saxony was promised his four millions, Austria returned most though not all of the land she had annexed, and Ansbach and Baireuth were eventually, in 1791, incorporated into the state of Prussia.[20]

Prussia had made good the last military challenge she was to offer to Austria until Bismarck's day. When Frederick again had occasion to lead the opposition to Austria in Germany he did it by resuming the role of defender of the Germanic constitution and taking steps toward the formation of a league of German princes. His success on that later occasion was largely due to the boldness with which he had dealt with his most formidable rival in 1778–79, and to the restraint with which he had refrained from imposing upon other German princes or from dictating to his allies at the peace conference as his brother had urged him to do.

A considerable part of the price the king paid for such political advantages as he won for Prussia in the war, however, was the loss, for some years at least, of whatever was left of Prince Henry's affection for him. In spite of the younger brother's resentment of the elder's tutelage in his youth, despite the devastating effects of their quarrel over Frederick's treatment of Prince William in 1757, nearly forty years of service to the same state through all the vicissitudes of war and peace had so knit the two together that after their separation neither was ever quite the same man again. They had worked in double harness too often and too long; beneath all their bickering, the bond between them was too strong to be broken without pain and permanent injury to both.

For a while Frederick kept up appearances. He invited Henry to meet him in Berlin when he returned there from a tour of Silesia just after the

---

[19] The originals of some of Grimm's letters and retained drafts of Prince Henry's are in the Hausarchiv, Rep. 56, II, I. See also G. B. Volz, "Prince Heinrich als Kritiker Friedrichs des Grossen," in the *Historische Virteljahrschrift*, XXVII (1932), 396–400.

[20] When John Quincy Adams was in Berlin in 1797 he was told by Lucchesini, an official in the foreign office, that Prince Henry had himself aspired to the succession to Ansbach and Baireuth and had taken it amiss when Frederick arranged for them to be incorporated into the monarchy. C. F. Adams, *Memoirs of John Quincy Adams*, I, 240. Dr. Richard Krauel, in his *Prinz Heinrich von Preussen in Paris während der Jahre 1784 und 1788–89* (Berlin, 1901), mentions a similar story.

Mr. Adams's journal records a more favorable impression of Prince Henry than of any other prince. Adams, *Memoirs*, 210.

war, and after a few months he resumed his old habit of writing weekly letters. "I love my country, my relatives, and my friends," he wrote to Henry in October, 1782. "When anything bad happens to them, I feel it and share with them their misfortune. Nature has made me so, and I should not know how to change. . . . Chase nature out through the door and she'll come in through the window." [21] But several years elapsed before their correspondence again assumed a political character, while by occasional bitter remarks to others the king made it quite clear that Henry's resolution never again to offer him his services would not be put to a test.

As for Prince Henry, resentment of Frederick's treatment of him became a monomania with him, an obsession of the ugliest and most hateful sort. It overcame his natural reserve and inherent good taste to such an extent that he thrust it upon strangers and shocked and offended distinguished foreigners by parading it before them. He nourished it and cherished it, and let it twine itself about him until it choked out of his life the happiness he might otherwise have known in those years of retirement. He never seemed to realize what a monstrous thing it had become — or how it would hide his better qualities from succeeding generations as it hid them from most of his contemporaries.

[21] *Oeuvres*, XXVI, 491.

CHAPTER XXIII

# Prince without Portfolio

*"I have spent half of my life wishing to see France, and now I shall spend the other half regretfully looking back at it."*— Henry to the Duc de Nivernois on leaving Paris.

"WE BOTH hang loose on the bough and shall soon drop off," wrote Frederick to Henry when reporting to him the death of their sister Frederika Louisa, margravine of Ansbach, in February, 1784. He had himself just had to be bled. His blood, he said, was "as badly disordered as the British Parliament." [1]

Prince Henry had quickly settled down after the War of the Bavarian Succession into an old man's regime at Rheinsberg. His mornings he usually spent alone, devoting hours to his voluminous correspondence and walking a good deal, but carrying his note pads with him on his walks so as to write down his reflections as they came to him. In the afternoon he had someone read to him. French literature and the current French offerings in the fields of history and political science were read most, and guests were free to listen in or not as they chose.

Guests were numerous, and among them there were often some persons of considerable distinction. Enjoyment of Frederick's favor was not a prerequisite for admission, so there was some justification for the Rheinsberg circle's being called "the court of the disaffected." From twenty to forty people met around the dinner table at six o'clock and watched or provided the entertainment that followed. [2]

Some ladies were generally among the guests and were treated with elaborate politeness by their host, who enjoyed their company if they were conversationally gifted and who valued their contribution to the brilliance of his court; but none of them could ever flatter herself that she meant anything more to him than that. It was essentially as monkish

---

[1] *Oeuvres*, XXVI, 500.

[2] In 1780 the court numbered more than a hundred persons, exclusive of guests. Johann Schulz took Salomon's place that year as director of music. Salomon, who subsequently made a reputation in London, had built up an excellent orchestra. Elaborate plays and pageants and some of the operas of Gluck, Sacchini, and Piccini were also presented. The prince's company held together and showed in Berlin for a time after his death. Kraucl, "Prinz Heinrich in Rheinsberg," *Hohenzollern Jahrbücher*, VI (1902), 21.

a milieu as Frederick's then was, and any lady who arrogated to herself any special privileges soon found that she had none left.[3]

Twice the prince had declined his sister Ulrika's urgent invitation to return to Sweden to mediate some of her endless quarrels with her son Gustavus III. He hated ceremonial and he needed his rest, he had said; and Frederick, when appealed to by Ulrika, had answered that he would not send him if he felt unable to go. Fear of involvement in the squabbles of his relatives prompted him to refuse also an invitation to visit his niece Wilhelmina of Holland in 1781; but she followed him to Spa and saw him there.[4]

Periodical visits to Spa were to become a part of his routine. He found its waters healthful because its society was pleasant. Many prominent people came there, and he was always a marked man among them. Only on his summer visit of 1782 was he outshone by a celebrity greater than himself.

That celebrity was the emperor Joseph II. The two were ostentatiously polite in public, entertained each other at dinner, and had several long and confidential conversations. The emperor assured the prince, for Frederick's benefit, that he desired nothing more than to live for the rest of his life on the most friendly terms with Prussia. It was only Kaunitz, he said, who had ever made him act or appear otherwise.

The prince immediately informed his brother that Joseph was about to go to Paris but could stay there for only four or five days before returning to Hungary for an August encampment of troops. After his own return to Rheinsberg he sent the king a more detailed report on the conversations. He then conceded that the emperor had seemed to be speaking freely, frankly, and without affectation, yet he confessed that he himself believed little of the message he was commissioned to transmit. He had found Joseph much better informed than when they had met at Neisse twelve years before, but also less "open" and impulsive, and regretted that he had not felt free to draw him out more.[5]

Joseph's own reports to Kaunitz indicate that the prince made more

---

[3] Life at Rheinsberg in the later middle period of the prince's residence there has been most fully described by Count Lehndorff, the Marquis Bouillé, Richard Krauel, and Andrew Hamilton, in books already cited; in the letters of Count Bielfeld and Baron Grimm; and most recently in English by A. E. Grantham in *Rococo* (London, 1938).

[4] *P. C.*, XLV, 1, 128; XLVI, 78, 139; Krauel, *Prinz Heinrich von Preussen als Politiker*, 28.

[5] *P. C.*, XLVI, 89, 118, 158; see also Henry's letter to Charlotte of Brunswick, quoted by Krauel in *F. B. P. G.*, XIII, 387. Bouillé, who is not always reliable, says that Joseph suggested to Prince Henry at that time that Austria and Prussia divide Germany between them, and that the prince welcomed the suggestion but showed himself wiser and more prudent than the emperor as to time and method. It was Frederick, according to Bouillé, who rejected the whole proposal because he was too old to disturb his own tranquillity by undertaking so ambitious a project. Bouillé, *La Vie privée*, 216.

of an effort to draw him out than he felt free to report to Frederick. According to the emperor's version of the interview, Henry hinted that the old king of Prussia could not possibly live much longer and that, as adviser to his nephew, he would himself be the guiding spirit of the new regime. More cordial relations between the two countries could then be expected to result. But Joseph suspected a ruse. These outspoken differences between the king and his brother were all staged merely for effect, he wrote, to trick the unwary foreigner into some indiscretion. The two had lived under one hat much too long, he reasoned, to entertain such widely divergent ideas.[6]

Despite the comfort in which he lived, and the satisfaction he derived from his occasional visits to a fashionable watering place, the self-exiled master of Rheinsberg was often restless. There beside his lovely lake and among his groves and gardens, his books and his friends, he was the center of a well-ordered universe; but it was a small world for any man who had ever known or imagined a larger one. As years of quiet restored his strength, his mind ranged far afield. His refusal to go again to Sweden or to Holland was due rather to disinclination to fight any battles but his own than to ill health or dislike of travel or of ceremonial.

Ceremonial as such, it is true, he had always found tiresome, and he had avoided it whenever possible. To be treated as a person of distinction, however, was always as incense to his nostrils — especially to be so treated by persons of distinction. He had often had that experience, but not often enough. Year after year, as he maintained his isolated little center of culture and refinement at Rheinsberg, there grew within him the desire to visit in the flesh the capital of his cultural and intellectual world, where he had so often wandered in spirit — to live as a person of distinction among persons of distinction in the glamorous city of light whence emanated the styles and standards that he had emulated all his life without ever having seen them at their source. He would go to Paris. In midsummer of the year 1784 he went.

An invitation from Louis XVI was easily obtained. Already known for many years as the most ardent Francophile in Prussia, the prince had only to let someone whisper to the French ambassador that he was contemplating an extended journey that might include France if he were invited — and the invitation was assured.

So as not to startle Frederick too seriously and thus risk a refusal of leave to go, he asked first only for permission to visit southwestern Ger-

---

[6] Volz in the *Historische Vierteljahrschrift*, XXVII (1932), 393; Krauel in *F. B. P. G.*, XIII, 385. The emperor may have been oversuspicious in this instance, but after the experience he and Cobenzl had had only four years before (see Chapter XXI) he would have had little reason to be overtrustful.

many and Switzerland. Some time later he requested his brother to get him authorization, through diplomatic channels, to visit Lyons. Then, after his departure, the French minister d'Esterno presented a letter from the king of France inviting him to Paris. Frederick assented readily to each request, and would no doubt have done so if they had all been presented at once without finesse. He was happy to have his brother go where he would, and hoped he would enjoy himself.

Henry enjoyed himself as he had never done before. Not even his first visit to St. Petersburg had equaled this new experience. Traveling under a transparent incognito as the Count d'Oels,[7] he avoided all the tiresome formality that he wished to avoid and enjoyed a freedom commensurate with the unofficial character of his tour; yet everyone knew who he was, and treated him like a king.[8]

Goethe was one of those to greet him in Weimar, and reported that he had been "very gracious."[9] In Geneva he made the acquaintance of Necker, among others, and in Lausanne that of Edward Gibbon. "His military conduct is praised by professional men," wrote Gibbon later; "his character has been vilified by the wit and malice of a demon; but I was flattered by his amiability and entertained by his conversation."[10]

At Lausanne a letter from Frederick overtook him, bringing his official passport to Lyons and Frederick's cheerful permission to accept the French king's invitation, also enclosed, to visit Paris and Versailles as well. Everything was working out according to plan, and the prince was happy.

From the time Henry left Geneva, arrangements for his journey were entirely in the hands of Baron Grimm, sent by Louis XVI to see that he visited all — and only — the right places and met the right people. The people whom he most wanted to meet were those prominent in

[7] He owned some large estates at Oels in Silesia.

[8] The principal sources of information concerning the tour are: the reports of Count d'Esterno from Berlin and those of Baron von der Goltz and Count Mercy, Prussian and Austrian ministers in Paris; the "Prussian Correspondence" in the archives of the French Ministry of Foreign Affairs; the correspondence of Baron Grimm; various contemporary memoirs; Prince Henry's letters to Frederick and to his brother Ferdinand in the Staatsarchiv and the Hausarchiv, respectively; and the *Gazette de France* for the period covered by his visit. Interesting accounts of the visit are Krauel, *Prinz Heinrich von Preussen in Paris während der Jähre 1784–89;* Chevalier de Larivière, "Le Prince Henri de Prusse à Paris en 1784 et en 1788," in the *Revue politique et littéraire*, 4ᵉ Serie, XVI (1901), 334–340 and 393–398; and G. B. Volz in pages 440 to 449 of his extended critical essay, "Die *Vie privée* und die ältere Literatur über den Prinzen Heinrich von Preussen," *F. B. P. G.*, XIX, 423–462.

[9] That was their second meeting. Dr. Krauel suggests that Prince Henry may well have been the person whom Goethe had in mind when he described in *Wilhelm Meisters Lehrjahre* a prince combining in his own character the hero, the army leader, and the courtier. Krauel, *Prinz Heinrich von Preussen in Paris*, 5.

[10] *The Autobiography of Edward Gibbon* (London, 1896), 331. The "demon" mentioned is presumably Mirabeau, as will appear later.

musical, dramatic, literary, and scientific circles. Whether by arrangement or not, he was everywhere received in the most flattering fashion possible.

At Lyons an official welcomed him in the name of the king. The archbishop gave a dinner for him and prompted Madame de Rochebaron to entertain him at a fete. He visited the factories which the emperor Joseph II had found very impressive only two years before; but the factories were forgotten when he met the famous Madame Vestris of the Comédie Française. He was thrilled by the applause which greeted him when he entered the theater and followed him when he left. He attended a session of the Lyons Academy, heard himself eulogized, and found himself not insensible to eulogy. His admiration for the French people reached new heights. He had been flattered before, by experts; but he had never been fed on such a varied diet of flattery, so cunningly prepared and artfully served by such masters of the art. His letters to Ferdinand were lyrical in their praise of these people who knew so well how to be polite.

A similar welcome awaited him in Dijon.[11] From there he went on to Paris, where he found lodgings prepared for him at the Hôtel de la Chine; but his journey's end was reached not at his hotel but at the opera, where he sat that evening in the box of Marshal Biron.

Baron Grimm continued to serve as social secretary and publicity manager. But his task was not difficult; persons of high and low estate were cordially friendly to the prince wherever he appeared. His features were already fairly well known in Paris, for a bust by Monnot had attracted some attention there the year before. Soon Houdon was known to be making another. The story of his military exploits had gained color with repetition through the years; and the part he had played at Rossbach could easily be forgiven him in the light of his subsequent kindness to French prisoners — particularly after he publicly congratulated Marshal Soubise upon the courage shown by the French troops and confessed that "my brother was lucky that day." It would have been impolitic for Paris to be ungracious to the brother of the king of Prussia. To have failed in gratitude or ungrudging hospitality to France's most faithful Prussian friend and admirer would have been blind unreason.

Paris did not fail. At a sitting of the French Academy, Marmontel acknowledged and advertised Prince Henry's presence by pointing out the happy coincidence that a "prize of virtue" was about to be awarded "in the presence of virtue crowned with glory." The prince became a regular attendant at the Academy for the duration of his visit. Knowing

[11] *Gazette de France*, No. 68, August 24, 1784.

his interest in the Count of Turenne and noting his admiration of one of the general's portraits, Madame Vigée-Lebrun made a miniature copy of the picture on a snuff-box and gave it to him. Beaumarchais read him an unpublished play (which he thought queer, and which promptly failed when produced); but he greatly enjoyed the fiftieth performance of *The Marriage of Figaro*. Madame Vestris, who had recently been disciplined for her refusal, on the pretext of a sore foot, to dance for Gustavus III of Sweden, returned to the stage; and Prince Henry had the satisfaction of watching the dance which his nephew had been denied. He saw also the first performance of Sedaine's comic opera *Richard Coeur de Lion.*[12]

"On September 7 the Count d'Oels honored with his presence a sitting of the Royal Academy of Inscriptions and Belles Lettres," and on October 26 an assembly of the Royal Society of Medicine; and at each "the secretary opened the session with an address appropriate to the occasion."[13]

Consistently the visitor from Prussia lived up to his reputation as a friend of art and letters, a lover of the beautiful, and an enlightened prince. Nor was he unobservant. His letters to Frederick were filled with reports on provisions for the health of the French troops, particularly in tropical climates, on a French school for the instruction of deaf mutes, and theoretical discussions of the possibilities of aeronautics, electricity, and mesmeric cures.

Delighted with Paris though he was, the prince made little effort to extend his interest or his social activities to Versailles. The Austrian queen Marie Antoinette was not favorably predisposed toward her mother's ancient enemy, and strongly suspected him of anti-Austrian political activity. As for Prince Henry himself, he was not enough of a ladies' man or courtier to feel at home at a dancing party at Versailles, and he had always shared Frederick's aversion for women who meddled in politics. So although he was presented at court on August 22 as "Count d'Oels" with the ceremonial usual for ambassadors,[14] and dined occasionally with the king and queen and some of their ministers, Versailles saw little of him. The queen, he grudgingly conceded, was much prettier than he had been told she was. In his comments on the king he was much more enthusiastic, praising him extravagantly for his justice and

[12] Grantham, *Rococo*, 131; Larivière, "Le Prince Henri de Prusse à Paris," 338. Among the other friends he made in Paris were the Duke of Orleans, the Duc de Richelieu, Abbé Barthélemy, Abbé Sieyès, and Condorcet. Krauel, *Prinz Heinrich in Paris*, 14. Condorcet he singled out as the only public man in France who seemed unaware of his own merits. H. to F., September 13, in the Staatsarchiv, Rep. 96, 108, L.

[13] *Gazette de France*, No. 75, September 17, 1784; No. 89, November 5, 1784.

[14] *Ibid.*, No. 70, August 31, 1784; Goltz to Frederick, in the Staatsarchiv, Rep. 96, 29, G.

goodness of heart. No premonition of impending disaster clouded his few pen pictures of their court.

The Austrian queen of France was not the only one who suspected and feared that Henry had been sent to Paris on some secret mission. Frederick, expecting to be quoted, as of course he was, had once called that rumor ridiculous, saying roundly that if he had had any important business afoot in Paris — which he had not — he would certainly have sent someone other than Henry to transact it. But, as he would have been expected to say something to that effect as camouflage if the report were true, his denial was not found convincing. Count Mercy, the Austrian ambassador to the king of France, was as much agog as his royal compatriot the queen. Baron Bernhard Wilhelm von der Goltz, Frederick's minister to France, was doubly concerned: Prince Henry had forbidden him to report upon any but the public and social aspects of his visit, but Goltz felt certain that the prince was making use of his own special cipher to report directly to the king upon him and his activities.

Goltz was unduly alarmed. The prince was too prudent to be overreached by Vergennes or Count Mercy, as the baron broadly hinted to Frederick that he was in danger of being. He was scrupulously careful, moreover, not to undermine the minister's standing either with the French government or with his own king. Frederick, meanwhile, blandly refused to notice Goltz's eagerness to be commanded to send in a full report on matters that the prince had forbidden him to mention.[15]

The Austrians in France and in Vienna had better reason to be disturbed over Prince Henry's presence in Paris than the badly worried Baron von der Goltz had. Once more, by what can scarcely have been only a coincidence, the prince had chosen to go on his travels at a time when great events were impending and a new diplomatic revolution seemed not at all improbable. The fact that he had not been explicitly commissioned by Frederick to undertake any formal negotiation on behalf of Prussia would not have prevented him from dipping his spoon into any dish that looked promising, or his personal spoon from proving eventually to be a Prussian one if it had happened to bring out a morsel that the king of Prussia found appetizing or judged valuable.

All the continental nations, viewing one another as at least potential devils, were supping with especially long spoons in 1784. Catherine of Russia and Joseph of Austria and Hungary had been in official agreement upon a joint Near Eastern policy since 1780, but they were mutu-

---

[15] Staatsarchiv; the Goltz correspondence is in Rep. 96, 29, G, Prince Henry's with the king in Rep. 96, 108, L.

ally suspicious partners, and Frederick was hoping that Catherine might die soon and that her son Paul might then revive the Prussian alliance.[16]

"When one has lost one's old friends one seeks new ones," Prince Henry had written to his brother from Wittenberg as he began his journey.[17] Such a remark, as was so often the case with his statements, might have had only a personal significance; but Frederick was rather obviously expected to read into it a much broader meaning. Soon the two were engaged in an outspoken discussion of the possibility and the desirability of a French alliance for Prussia. The prince thought the alliance worth having and not unattainable. Frederick warned him that he would find France under Louis XVI only the hollow shell of the France of Louis XIV, and that the French ministers would merely use his presence to impose their wishes upon the emperor and would then quietly drop the subject of a Prussian alliance.[18]

The old alliance of France and Austria was still nominally in effect; but the interests of the two countries were by no means identical, so the alliance had already been under a serious strain for a year or more before Prince Henry left Rheinsberg.[19] In order to strengthen the strategical position of France for her perennial struggle against England, the French ministers were cultivating the friendship of the Netherlands with a view to the formation of an alliance. They found themselves therefore seriously embarrassed by the steadily increasing tension and threats of impending hostilities between their old ally, Austria, and their potential new one, the Netherlands.

Joseph II had been trying since 1783 to compel the Dutch to agree to the opening of the Scheldt river to navigation. Antwerp, in the Austrian Netherlands and on the Scheldt, would have profited by the change, and Joseph could argue eloquently on his city's behalf for freedom of access to the sea; but the control of the lower reaches of the river had been won by the Dutch in their war for independence from Spain, and the agreement granting it had been confirmed by the general treaties of

[16] Prince Henry's guess was that Catherine's indisposition was only temporary but that her estrangement from Prussia would prove to be permanent — and that Russia would be of no further use to Prussia in Frederick's lifetime. "My brother knows Russia better than I do," was Frederick's comment to Baron Goltz. Henry also knew Catherine better. She soon regained her health and her interest in life, and lived for twelve years longer without exerting herself again in Prussia's interest.

[17] *Oeuvres,* XXVI, 503.

[18] The Russians were of the same opinion, according to Frederick, but hoped that the necessity for caution with regard to France would force the emperor to show more consideration for Russia's interests. "The Russians are glad to have you in Paris," the king wrote to Henry in September. Staatsarchiv, Rep. 96, 108, L.

[19] He did not mention that fact as one of his reasons for going to Paris, but was almost certainly aware of it; and it was almost as certainly one of his principal reasons for going when he did.

Münster-Westphalia and Utrecht. So Joseph's *Summary of the Emperor's Claims,* in 1783, however logical or justifiable from the point of view of Antwerp, was highly disturbing to everyone else. The Dutch were defiant; the British, who had themselves hinted in Vienna in 1780 that the Scheldt ought to be reopened, were again at peace with the Dutch Republic in 1784; and the French were more willing to mediate the dispute than to support Joseph in it.

The dilemma of the French ministers was well appreciated by the veteran Prussian diplomat Baron Goltz. If they supported Holland too vigorously, they would offend the emperor as they could ill afford to do. If they failed to support her vigorously enough, France would lose face with the Dutch and would suffer a serious loss of prestige throughout Europe. It was indeed an awkward situation until Vergennes showed his colleagues that a way out of it might be found by taking advantage of Prince Henry's apparently fortuitous presence in Paris. Let the Austrian ambassador, the queen, and the emperor worry all they would over the apparent danger that, if Joseph carried out his threat to use force to open the Scheldt, France and Prussia would form an alliance and take the field in defense of the treaties and the *status quo.* The more they worried the more likely they would be to listen to reason, and the less likely France would be to become involved in troubles which she ought if possible to avoid.[20]

Vergennes was much too adroit, and knew too well the strength of the queen's party, to overbid his hand. He was careful not to be seen too frequently in conversation either with the closely watched visitor or with the recognized Prussian minister, but dealt with Prince Henry through intermediaries. Messengers were easy to find. Sometimes he used some of the older army officers whom the prince had handled so courteously while they were prisoners in his custody during the Seven Years' War. Another willing intermediary was the Duc de Nivernois, whose acquaintance Henry had made and cultivated in Berlin in 1756, and who had at that time convinced the princes if not the king of Prussia that a war with France was both unnecessary and unwise. The prince was an eager and responsive listener, and soon reported that all parties, even that of the queen's friends, were convinced that a *rapprochement* with Prussia had become necessary.

Frederick would also have been glad to be convinced; he had himself suggested a defensive alliance less than a year before but had been politely refused. So, perhaps half in earnest and half for the benefit of the

[20] Goltz to Frederick, September 8. Goltz suspected that Vergennes had foreseen some such crisis and had had the prince invited to Paris and held there in the hope of having him available for use in this fashion if needed.

French spies who he suspected would read his letter in transit, he wrote that France would indeed be wise to draw closer to Prussia, and might well do so if the ministers were men enough to oppose the queen and still retain their offices. But Prussia could wait, so the prince would do well to make haste slowly. After all, Hannibal was not at Prussia's gates; it was not as if she were being driven by any distress of her own to make an emergency alliance that day or the next.[21]

By the middle of October the prince, finding his traveling funds depleted by expensive living, and convinced by the friendly assurances of Vergennes and Calonne that his visit had prepared the way for a real *rapprochement* between France and Prussia, considered his purpose accomplished and had already planned his journey home.[22] But just then things began to happen which caused him to defer his departure. Joseph II ordered two small vessels to sail the lower Scheldt, one upstream and the other downstream, and not to permit themselves to be stopped; but stopped they were, when they were fired upon by the Dutch fortresses on the banks of the river.

At once a crisis developed. Austrian troops began to make a show of great activity and the emperor announced that he was sending sixty thousand men into the Austrian Netherlands to enforce his demands. The Dutch, confident of French support, were as defiant as ever, and the French were more than ever alarmed. Vergennes soon decided to renew his offer of mediation, and to lend weight to the suggestion by combining with it a threat to extend a hand to Prussia for joint action if Holland were attacked.[23]

[21] F. to Goltz, September 13. "Hâte toy lentement," he wrote to the prince on October 4. "Don't throw yourself at those fellows' heads," he had warned his brother on August 21; "it is more prudent to wait and watch them come on than to make the advances [yourself]." Staatsarchiv, Rep. 96, 108, L. But he never went further than to counsel caution, or wrote anything to deter his brother from responding as favorably as he saw fit to any advances the French might make, or to keep him from bringing off the alliance if he could. He was simply less sanguine about it than Henry was, and more careful to avoid the error of seeming overeager.

[22] He wrote to Frederick on October 11 that he expected to visit the Duke of Orleans at St. Assise, then to travel by way of Chantilly, Nancy, Strasburg, and Brunswick. His financial distress was relieved soon after his return home by a loan from the banker Laborde. Count Mercy, with the help of the Abbé Vermond, a confidant of Marie Antoinette, once managed to induce Laborde to refuse the loan after having promised it, but it was then guaranteed by Louis XVI himself and the money carried to Prussia at his order in the form of two sight drafts for 200,000 francs each. The messenger used was Laborde's son-in-law, Baron d'Escars, who pretended to have made the trip to attend the maneuvers of 1785. Although the loan was made for political reasons only, the prince treated it as a financial obligation and repaid it in full in 1787 with interest at five per cent. He had been practically forced to borrow abroad, if he was to borrow at all, by an order of Frederick's forbidding the Prussian bankers to lend any more money to any of the Prussian princes. His nephew the crown prince had borrowed from Joseph II even during the War of the Bavarian Succession. Krauel, *Prinz Heinrich in Paris,* 44.

[23] Meanwhile the Dutch applied not only to France but to Frederick for protection, but he "sent them back to Versailles." He had no alliance with them, he wrote to Baron Goltz

Prince Henry's presence in Paris had quickly assumed a new importance and a new value in the eyes of the French ministers. Dropping the curtain of secrecy behind which he had worked until then, and dispensing with the use of intermediaries, Vergennes consulted the prince both as to the form which the French offer of mediation should take and as to the advisability of "inviting" Frederick to add his voice to whatever warning France should send the emperor against any act of aggression. While the king, Vergennes, and Comptroller General Calonne were working in cabinet conference over the wording of the letter which Louis was to send the emperor, Calonne was sent twice to the prince to report progress and to carry back his comments.

On October 27, again thinking that his work was done, the prince went for the last time to supper with the king and queen and began to send off to Berlin some of the gifts with which they and others had loaded him down, and other objects of art which he had purchased. On October 31 he took his leave.[24]

Again he was delayed. On November 8 Calonne followed him in great haste to St. Assise, whither he had gone as the guest of the Duke of Orleans, to tell him orally the content of the letter the French king had finally decided to send "at once" to the emperor. The king of France, the message was to say, viewed with great alarm the emperor's preparation for an attack upon Holland, particularly at a time when he was himself about to form an alliance with that country and when he would therefore be especially sorry to see it driven into the arms of Britain. He renewed his offer of mediation but served notice that if that offer were refused he would be compelled to post on his own borders just as many troops as Joseph might send into the Austrian Netherlands. This declaration would be sent to Berlin and to other courts, and if it produced no effect, the king would then consult the king of Prussia with a view to joint action to preserve the peace of Europe.[25]

on November 15, and had not guaranteed their territory. Of course he did not blame them for seeking some stouter defenders than the French. "Your French are poor allies," he had written Prince Henry on October 24. Staatsarchiv, *loc. cit.; Oeuvres,* XXVI, 513.

[24] The gifts of the king of France were the carefully calculated equivalents, in some cases duplicates, of the paintings, porcelains, and tapestries given the Russian grand duke and the king of Sweden when they had visited Paris. The prince was sending home also, among other things, fourteen marble statues and six volumes of engravings, and had been promised portraits of Louis XVI and Henry IV. All these he hoped Frederick would admit into the country tariff-free. Goltz to F., October 27, H. to F., October 30, in the Staatsarchiv; *Gazette de France,* No. 89, November 5, 1784.

[25] H. to F., ciphered and sent by special courier from Paris, November 9, in the Staatsarchiv, *loc. cit.;* Krauel, *Prinz Heinrich in Paris,* 33. The prince said he had written down "word for word" what Calonne told him. Calonne admitted to Count Mercy that he had talked to the prince at St. Assise, but said he had told him only that France could not be indifferent to the fate of Holland and would keep Prussia informed of the emperor's further proposals as they became known, and of whatever decisions the French govern-

Marie Antoinette was able to delay the sending of the letter to her brother for another week, and before it was sent the king revised its wording so as to make it somewhat less peremptory in tone; but with those slight modifications it was sent essentially as Calonne had outlined it to Prince Henry. As Louis had hoped, the emperor stayed his hand and withheld his troops from the Netherlands. So the French king's threat to consult the king of Prussia never had to be made good. As Frederick had predicted, no Franco-Prussian alliance materialized, as the need for joint action did not then become imperative.[26]

Again Prince Henry had had the tantalizing experience of standing on the threshold of participation in events of vast importance, most of which had failed to happen; yet once more he had good reason to believe that he had done something to determine the outcome of a major diplomatic crisis, and so to shape the destiny of his country and of Europe.

He could go home well pleased with himself and with the people who had entertained him so royally. Day after day, as his carriage rolled and jolted eastward, he recalled and recounted the pleasant experiences of the weeks just past, reviewing his voluminous notebooks filled with lists of prominent people he had met, and regaling his traveling companions with repetitions of their conversation.

His hosts were careful to see that nothing disturbed the happy state of mind in which he had left Paris. Baron d'Escars, who was later to serve him so well in the matter of his loan from Laborde, was assigned the double duty of escorting him and of reporting every move he made.[27] At Nancy, Lunéville, and Strasburg elaborate military reviews were held in his honor while d'Escars plied him with questions and secretly noted down his answers and his comments. The baron's report on their military conversations was subsequently studied by Ségur, the French minister of war, and submitted to his staff as the basis of reforms to be effected in line with the prince's criticisms. Prince Henry presumably did not know that he was being used as a special inspector general of French troops, but might have been equally loquacious if he had known it.[28]

ment might make. The Austrian ambassador rightly suspected that Calonne was lying to him.

[26] When he was sounded out by the Austrian ambassador in Berlin, Frederick replied that he hoped for the sake of humanity that peace could be preserved in Europe that year, but that he could not be expected merely in the interest of peace to put any pressure upon the Dutch to induce them to submit to the emperor's demands. To Baron Goltz, though not to the Austrian ambassador, he said further that only an actual alliance with both France and Holland would make it worth his while to risk the safety of Prussia in any way by playing Don Quixote for the Dutch. F. to Goltz, December 6, 1784, in the Staatsarchiv, *loc. cit.*

[27] See note 22.

[28] Krauel, *Prinz Heinrich in Paris,* 37–39. D'Escars was himself the colonel of one of

Strasburg honored him with a civic celebration and a festival performance in the theater. Then the final bouquet was handed him at Kehl by Beaumarchais. In the publishing establishment of the local literary and typographical society, he was invited to try his hand at printing; and the press turned out under his hand a flowery poem by Beaumarchais in his praise.

After all that, a quiet visit with his sister in Brunswick and the usual conference with Frederick in Potsdam, although pleasant enough, must have seemed almost an anticlimax. Certainly the sands and pines of Rheinsberg looked dreary to him indeed when he returned there at the end of November. Only the afterglow of the brilliance of Paris was still about him as he settled down with his memories in the gloom of an early Brandenburg winter, to live it all over again in retrospect and to wonder when and how he could manage to revisit the scene of so happy an experience.

the Nancy regiments. He had received a part of his early military training in Prussia and had cultivated the prince's acquaintance in his Potsdam days. He had also been used by Vergennes as an intermediary between the ministry and the prince in Paris.

# CHAPTER XXIV

# Death of a King

*"The king of Prussia . . . is dying, and he will
have no successor."*— Mirabeau.

IN THE YEAR following Prince Henry's return from his first visit to Paris,
the king discussed political questions and international affairs with him
more frequently and more freely than at any other time after the War
of the Bavarian Succession. Henry's personal knowledge of the men
around the French king was put at his brother's disposal, as his acquaintance with Catherine II and her court had been drawn upon in previous
years. Meanwhile Frederick's increasing physical infirmities and continued lack of confidence in the nephew who was to be his legal successor caused him to fall back once more upon Prince Henry for such
sympathy and intellectual companionship as the prince could still offer
him.[1]

When Joseph II abandoned his attempt to force the opening of the
Scheldt, he turned to the alternative of offering Karl Theodore the Austrian Netherlands and the title of king of Burgundy in exchange for
Bavaria. Frederick checkmated him by forming the *Fürstenbund,* a
league of German princes, and kept Prince Henry informed of the
course of events.[2] Henry was not asked for advice, but he volunteered
the opinion that the league would be of little value to Prussia because
the princes composing it were so sadly deficient in spirit and so undependable. A French alliance would, he thought, be a far better guarantee
of Prussia's future peace and safety. The immediate danger which was
calling the league into being seemed much less serious to him than to
Frederick. He would wager his head, he wrote, that France would give

---

[1] While Prince Henry was in Paris the king had described himself once as only "a spirit
still dragging around a body that is already dead," and again as an old dotard who had
already sent most of his heavy baggage on ahead for the last journey he had yet to make.
"You will find it dull here after seeing so many famous places, attending the opera, as-
sociating with Academicians and other brilliant people, and I shall bore you with my
conversation and my ineptitude," he had written, "but remember that this old fellow loves
you more than do all the fine intellectuals there are in Paris." Letters of September 27, in
*Oeuvres,* XXVI, 508, and of October 17, 1784, in the Staatsarchiv, Rep. 96, 108, L.

[2] F. to H., February 18, 1785, in *Oeuvres,* XXVI, 517. Frederick took again the position
he had taken in the War of the Bavarian Succession and in the negotiation of the Peace
of Teschen: the German states ought to act in concert to protect their common interest
in the Germanic constitution, and Prussia would ask for no territorial gains as the price of
her leadership in such action. And this time he did not seek the help of any non-German
power.

no support to the emperor's proposal, and that without French support Joseph himself would not adhere to it in the face of Prussian opposition. Nothing good was to be expected of their restless Hapsburg neighbor, certainly; but he was only troublesome, not really dangerous — "always starting several projects at once and finishing none of them." If Frederick would only take the trouble to win the support of France, he need not then depend upon the minor German princes for the defense of Prussia's position, nor sacrifice his own freedom of action by tying himself up in any way to Hanover and Britain.[3]

Distrust of Britain had taken more complete and more permanent possession of Prince Henry's mind than of Frederick's, as a result of their experience in the Seven Years' War; but that was not his only reason for opposing the inclusion of the elector of Hanover in the league. He had never given up his old idea that Prussia ought to control the whole southern shore of the Baltic "from the Elbe to the Vistula," and he had added a new paragraph meanwhile to his program for the future expansion of Prussia: she must also control the whole German course of the Elbe, and for that she might need both Anhalt and Hanover.[4]

No one entertaining such grandiose ideas of Prussia's future could consistently hope that the league of German princes would be a permanent organization. While it stood, and while it included in its membership the rulers of Hanover, Mecklenburg, and Anhalt, it would prevent the acquisition by Prussia of any of those territories, as its members guaranteed one another's possessions. The secularization of the lands of the ecclesiastical states, about which the prince had already been thinking for nearly ten years, was prohibited by the constitution of the league. And the French alliance, which might have made territorial expansion possible without war, was also precluded.

The spring and early summer of 1786 were months of trial for Prince Henry, and of torture for the dying king. It was obvious to everyone,

---

[3] H. to F., letters of February 18, May 20, August 5, and others, in the Staatsarchiv, *loc. cit.* Frederick was willing to let George III, as elector of Hanover, have the honor of being named president of the league.

[4] Holstein, Mecklenburg, and Swedish Pomerania still lay along the shore of the Baltic between the Elbe and the Vistula. Denmark would have defended Holstein, of which the Danish king was duke, if that duchy had then been attacked; and it would not have been easy to wrest Pomerania from Sweden; but the prince had no idea of an immediate or ill-timed attack upon either. He revealed these opinions piecemeal in various memoranda and letters, most of which were written for the eyes of Frederick William II or his ministers after Frederick's death. Contemporary testimony that he held them before the old king died is offered by the reports of the French ambassador, d'Esterno, which are quoted from the archives of the French Ministry of Foreign Affairs by Henri Welschinger, editor of Mirabeau's *Histoire secrète de la cour de Berlin* (Paris, 1900), 119–121, and by G. B. Volz in his essay "Prinz Heinrich von Preussen und die preussische Politik vor der ersten Teilung Polens," *F. B. P. G.*, XVIII, 186. Dr. Volz cites also the *Diaries and Correspondence of James Harris* (London, 1845), III, 169.

himself included, that Frederick had but a short time left to live — and equally apparent to all observers that he would be king to his last conscious moment. Grimly noting from week to week the ground he was losing in the final battle of his life against a coalition of bodily ills — asthma, gout, and dropsy — he endured with amazing fortitude the added discomfort occasioned by the heroic but futile remedies he prescribed for himself or tried at the behest of his harassed medical advisers.[5] Yet he kept on at his work.

While Frederick was being torn apart in the tug of war between death and the doctors, his brother Henry was being similarly torn and tossed between his own better and baser natures. At his best he was genuinely sympathetic in his feelings toward the king — as on March 30 when he wrote him as "Doctor Henry" a letter full of solicitude and generous clinical advice.[6] At his worst, eight days later, he could confide to a friend that he was almost daily expecting "a great event" which, while it would "interrupt all his pleasures," would work a great change in his status.[7]

That the change in his status would be something more than the mere transition from the footing of the old king's younger brother to that of the new king's service-wise uncle, no one doubted. Just how much more, no one knew. Inevitably everyone speculated more or less on the question, and the prince was spied upon both by those who hoped to use him and by those who hoped to exclude him from the councils of the new regime.

One of the keenest, but certainly not the most friendly or the most honest, of such interested observers was the able but unscrupulous Frenchman Mirabeau.[8] Although not accredited as a diplomat, Mirabeau called twice on Frederick — once to account for his presence and once to take his leave. He left only for a tour to some of the other German capitals, however, and was back in Berlin to report on Frederick's death and funeral and the first months of the new reign. He was Prince

---

[5] One doctor, he wrote on June 28, had bedeviled him with *assafaetida*, the next with *dent-de-lion* (dandelion), neither of which had helped him much. *Oeuvres*, XXVI, 532.

[6] *Ibid.*, 526; Staatsarchiv, *loc cit.*

[7] H. to Baron Münchhausen, in the Hausarchiv, Rep. 56, II, I. One of the "pleasures" described in a previous letter to the same correspondent was drinking *Punsch* all evening and shouting "Goddam" in derision of the English. *Ibid.*

[8] Mirabeau was in Germany as an unofficial and unaccredited observer, apparently the confidential agent of Vergennes and Calonne. He had been sent partly because they were glad to be rid of him, even temporarily, and partly because they were not sure of the completeness or accuracy of d'Esterno's dispatches. With all his intelligence and gifts of expression, however, it cannot be said that his reports are any more reliable than d'Esterno's. His *Histoire secrète de la cour de Berlin*, purporting to be a compilation of his letters written in fulfillment of this mission, is such a spiteful collection of scandalous gossip and slanderous character sketches as only a misguided and malignant genius could have writ-

Henry's guest at Rheinsberg for several days just before the old king died, and saw him a few times afterward; but he was never on such intimate terms with him as he pretended to be, and got much of what he retailed as confidential information only through such devious and dubious channels as the prince's French secretaries and more menial servants whom he paid well for whatever scraps of gossip they brought him. It was Mirabeau who wrote of Frederick on July 12, 1786: "He is still king, and will be to the end." [9] Prince Henry he described in the same "letter" as "eternally expectant, without knowing just what he has to expect." [10]

One change anticipated by most observers was that Austria and Russia would make full use of the opportunity afforded them by Frederick's death to join hands for their further mutual aggrandizement at the immediate expense either of Poland or of Turkey, which would redound to the ultimate disadvantage of Prussia by disturbing the existing balance of power in eastern Europe. No one expected the new king of Prussia to be able to cope with such formidable rivals unless he should reveal after his accession a higher type of political wisdom, a greater capacity for resolute action, and more readiness to accept sound advice than he had yet given anyone reason to suspect that he possessed. "If the king of Prussia were ten years younger," wrote Mirabeau, "he would know well enough how to restore the balance; for he would take as much in Poland as the others took elsewhere; but he is dying, and he will have no successor." [11]

If the great king had no capable successor, then the trusted counselors of the new monarch would assume an unprecedented importance. D'Esterno assumed that Frederick's mantle would inevitably fall upon the waiting shoulders of Prince Henry, though his crown would be worn by "the nephew." Mirabeau evidently hoped that something of that sort would happen; for he was well informed, as indeed everyone in Prussia was or might have been if he had troubled to ask anyone, of the warmth of the prince's friendship for France and of his hatred of England. Because he so wanted the Francophile prince to gain control of Prussian policy upon Frederick's death, he was doubly critical of him. No fault

ten. The original two-volume edition (Rotterdam, 1789), and the author's notes for it, were burned by the public executioner in Paris almost as soon as it appeared, but copies were preserved and new editions appeared. An English translation was made in 1895. In 1900 Henri Welschinger, as editor, published a carefully annotated edition, to which the citations hereafter made will refer.

[9] Unless he added that to his "letter" later. There is reason to believe that his reports were not all written just when and where their date lines indicate, and that some if not all of them were revised and extended before printing.

[10] Mirabeau, *Histoire secrète*, Welschinger edition, 104.

[11] "Letter IX, from Berlin, July 31," *ibid.*, 154.

or blunder could be forgiven him if it impaired his potential usefulness to France.

Mirabeau saw, more clearly than d'Esterno did, the danger that the prince might, after all, fail them; but so long as his eventual ascendancy over his nephew seemed possible, whether probable or not, his friendship was to be sedulously cultivated; so the visiting Frenchman avidly accepted an invitation to visit him in Rheinsberg. For nearly two weeks, in early August, the guest subjected his host to a clever cross-examination on his political views and his aims for Prussia, keeping him meanwhile under the closest scrutiny and noting his every weakness. One of the most flagrant of those weaknesses was indiscretion. Another was want of the discernment necessary to recognize the unscrupulous character of the gifted visitor into whose hands he so delivered himself and his friends.

Mirabeau returned to Berlin on August 14 or 15, more fully convinced than ever that Prince Henry was "the avowed and fanatical defender of the French system." "This prince is, will be, and will die French," he wrote. "Will he have influence? That I do not know." He was too pompous and proud. He had talked too much about his "success" in Paris, and had "given himself too much of an air of divination about the new regime." Knyphausen, whom Mirabeau considered one of Prussia's ablest men if not the only really able man in Prussia, was his friend and ally; but Hertzberg was his enemy and would advocate a pro-British policy for that reason if for no other. If only Henry "had the character to dissimulate" with Hertzberg, he might learn to handle that minister; but he could not be depended upon to do that. He would be master of the ministry or he would be nothing.[12]

As for the new king-to-be: "Has he a system? That I do not know. A mind? I doubt it. Character? I know nothing [about that], and think that no one has the right either to deny or to affirm that he has." But he was determined to rule by himself. The Duke of Brunswick might be able to manage him but would not try. Prince Henry would try, by fair means or foul, but would probably not succeed. The *Illuminati* seemed likely to win in the long run, as the young prince's entourage had shown so far only weakness, confusion, and fondness for petty intrigue.[13]

Just before leaving for Rheinsberg, Mirabeau had written a lurid though not altogether unsympathetic description of the torment the old

---

[12] "Letter XIII, from Berlin, August 15," *ibid.*, 161–164. There are at least two versions of this letter extant, printed apparently from different drafts, largely but not entirely identical.

[13] *Ibid.* Mirabeau is the only known authority for a story, included in the same report, that Prince Henry had suggested to him that a new female favorite be found and used to

king was so stoically enduring. Although his legs were so frightfully swollen that they seemed about to burst, Frederick had for weeks been unable to lie in his bed because he could not breathe there. At best he could sleep but fitfully, half reclining in a chair. With impairment of his digestive and assimilative processes had come an abnormal appetite for highly seasoned and unhealthful foods; and his unwise indulgence of that craving, and the emetics necessitated by it, seemed only to aggravate his other ills.

All these things — told him by informers, for he had not seen the king again — the Frenchman presumably told his host at Rheinsberg. The prince had last seen his brother in Sans Souci in March, though letters had continued to come and go whenever Frederick was able to hold a pen.[14] While Mirabeau was with him he received his last letter from the hand of the king, confirming the most pessimistic reports. He wrote back at once expressing great alarm, but offering the sufferer by way of encouragement only the rather doubtful consolation of a reminder that their father had been in a very similar condition in 1735 but had recovered and lived five years longer "after his leg had opened" so that the poison could be drained out of it. He was eager to come to see the king again, he said, and was waiting only for permission to do so.[15]

The permission was never granted. Frederick was unable to answer. Early in the morning of August 17 he died in the arms of the orderly who knelt beside his chair. No member of his family was present. None of them had been summoned, and only Henry had sought the permission without which no one was expected to come. Old Fritz started his last journey, as he had started so many, before dawn and alone but for the presence of a body servant in soldier's uniform.

He had been king, and a soldier, to the end. If he had been interviewed just before his departure and could have answered with his usual lucidity, Frederick the king and soldier would have asked no more odds of death than he had asked of life; and Frederick the philosopher would

influence the heir to the throne. She should be blonde rather than brunette, not too slender, musical, amiable but not notoriously so, and intelligent enough to manage the young man without his knowing it and to make him think she was bestowing favors but soliciting none. Arriving as a stranger, she should pose as a foreigner but of course not as a French-woman; perhaps as an Italian. Such a suggestion seems more likely to have emanated from Mirabeau himself than from a confirmed misogynist such as Prince Henry. Mirabeau imported a woman spy later, but Prince Henry gave neither aid nor countenance to the scheme, and apparently knew nothing of it. It failed.

[14] One of the king's July letters bequeathed Henry beforehand the concertmaster of the royal orchestra, François Benda. Another acknowledged his grateful acceptance and profuse thanks. *Oeuvres,* XXVI, 532. Prince Henry's letter of March 7, to Baron Münchhausen from Berlin, indicates March 7 to 10 as the date of his last journey to Potsdam in Frederick's lifetime. Hausarchiv, Rep. 56, II, I. See also F. to H., in *Oeuvres,* XXVI, 526.

[15] H. to F., August 11, 1786, from Rheinsberg, in the Staatsarchiv, Rep. 96, 108, L.

have accepted no sympathy offered on the ground that he was about to die alone. All men are lonely in dying, if not in death, he would probably have said. Only Frederick the man would have confessed to years of unhappiness over his loneliness in life.

"The old king has been generous," commented Mirabeau after Prince Henry had told him the provisions of Frederick's personal will; and the comment was well justified. The widowed queen was given ten thousand thaler in one sum and an increase in her annual allowance, Prince Ferdinand fifty thousand in one sum and some Hungarian wine, the princess Ferdinand (probably for the sake of her children) ten thousand a year, the widowed Duchess of Brunswick and the other surviving sister Amelia like amounts, and Amelia all of Frederick's personal gold and silver plate. Many others, less closely related, received smaller bequests. The princess Henry's allowance was to be increased by six thousand thaler per year. All of these payments, it was expressly stated, were to be made out of the savings in the king's privy purse, not out of current state revenues.

Prince Henry's legacy was the richest of all: twenty thousand thaler in one sum, a diamond ring that the king had worn, a crystal chandelier valued at fifteen thousand thaler, an eight-horse carriage, two richly caparisoned saddle horses, and fifty casks of Hungarian wine — in addition to revenues already granted him and to the properties and perquisites to which he might be or might become entitled under the provisions of the general family settlement set up by his father's will.[16]

"I give back to nature the breath of life that she has given me, and my body to the elements of which it is composed."[17] It is easy to imagine the thoughtful king, lover of his land and skeptic as to immortality, sitting in his ground-floor study in Sans Souci as he penned those lines, looking out over that beautiful bit of garden only a few yards away where his dogs and his favorite horse lay in their carefully tended graves and where all his wartime wills had directed that he also be buried. More than once to others, and no one knows how often to himself, he had said in moments of weariness that only when he at last lay out there with them — then and only then — would he be truly *sans souci,* without care. So it is not quite incomprehensible that, turning his back upon

[16] Mirabeau, "Letters XV and XVI, from Berlin, August 18 and 22," in *Histoire secrète,* 178, 184; Bouillé, *La Vie privée,* 243ff. This will is not to be confused with any of the political testaments. Mirabeau professed to have been told by Prince Henry that it had been made in 1769.

[17] The opening sentence of the will, according to Bouillé.

the place that awaited him beside his father in the garrison church, he repeated his request that he be quietly buried in his garden.

That was the only provision of the will that his successor did not confirm and execute. Down a plank road blanketed in black and lined with troops with muffled drums, the king who had so often chosen to dispense with ceremony, and in whose life religion had filled so small a space, had to ride, whether he would or not, in a last ceremonial procession — to church, to make a national shrine of the tomb behind the chancel. In death as in life, duty dictated where he should go; and the king of Prussia defined his duty for him as he himself had done for other Prussians while he was king. Behind him Frederick William II walked alone; then Henry and Ferdinand, then the new Prince of Prussia (subsequently Frederick William III) with Ferdinand's son Louis Ferdinand, who was then fourteen, and who twenty years later was to die in battle against Napoleon. The whole church was hung with captured battle flags, and every pillar bore the names of two Prussian victories. Until the end of the service the royal insignia lay upon the coffin; then they were stripped from it and conferred upon the new king.[18]

The great king was dead. Prussia still lived, but it was a kingdom dependent upon its king. For good or ill, that was the way it was made. Mirabeau had been much impressed on the first day of the new reign as he watched the soldiers take the oath of personal allegiance; but that ceremony emphasized too much, he thought, the military aspect of the monarchy. "This seems to me to say," he wrote, " 'I am above all the king of the soldiers. I rely upon my army because I am not sure that I have a kingdom.' "[19]

The kingdom of Prussia had not asked itself the question that its uninvited critic suggested. It was wondering only whether it had a king.

[18] The description is based upon the accounts of two professed eyewitnesses, Mirabeau and Frederick's niece, Princess Anton Radziwill, *née* Louise of Prussia, daughter of Prince Ferdinand. See Princess Radziwill's *Forty-five Years of My Life*, 64ff., and Mirabeau, *Histoire secrète*, 222.

Prince Henry and his secretary had arranged the funeral music. Mirabeau mentioned the music but no minister. He praised the smoothness and efficiency with which the procession and service were managed, and the dinner that followed, but added the somewhat supercilious comment: "Nulle comparison pour la magnificence, le goût, la richesse, avec nos catafalques de l'eglise de Notre Dame; mais pour le pays, pour le temps, on a fait tout ce qu'on pouvoit faire."

[19] Mirabeau, *Histoire secrète*, 173.

# CHAPTER XXV

# Almost an Émigré

*"He will leave the country, go insane, or die."*
— Mirabeau, September 5, 1786.

"EITHER one must not presume to undertake the governance of states," Frederick had once written, "or he must make the high-hearted resolution to render himself worthy of the task and to acquire all of the skills that are a part of the education of a prince; and he must animate himself with the noble ambition to evade none of the labors and none of the cares which the business of governing demands of him." [1]

"The place of the king is always filled," wrote Prince Henry philosophically in October, 1786, to Countess Bentinck, a friend of his youth. [2] But desks were soon piled high with documents awaiting the king's attention, and it became increasingly obvious that, try as he would, Frederick William could not fill Frederick's place; and no one knew how long he would go on trying.

Meanwhile it became more and more apparent—even to Prince Henry, who closed his eyes to the unpleasant truth as long as he could— that the old prince was not to be permitted to step into the old king's place as preceptor. Frederick William daily made more manifest his need of tutelage by daily manifesting his fear of it. Kalckreuth, banished to garrison duty in Königsberg ever since the prince's separation from his wife, was brought back to Berlin, promoted, and treated with special favor. Karl Wilhelm, the reigning Duke of Brunswick, was promoted over his uncle Henry's head to the rank of field marshal. [3] On January

---

[1] Reinhold Koser, *Zur preussischen und deutschen Geschichte* (Stuttgart, 1921), 432.

[2] Hausarchiv, *loc. cit.* Mirabeau tried, tactlessly and of course unsuccessfully, to induce Frederick William to seek Prince Henry's guidance in all things. "One of your uncles," he wrote to the king on the first day of the new reign, "crowned with glory and success, possesses the confidence of Europe, the genius of a hero, and the mind of a sage. He is a counselor, a coadjutor, a friend, whom nature and destiny have sent to you at the moment when you have most need of him, at the time when the more voluntary your deference to him may be, the more infallibly you will be applauded."

[3] Karl Wilhelm was a nephew of the Ferdinand of Brunswick who had earned such fame in the Seven Years' War. The younger duke had also served with distinction under Frederick in the later campaigns of that war and in the War of the Bavarian Succession. He subsequently commanded the Prussian armies in their campaign of intervention in the Netherlands, in their invasion of France in 1791, and against Napoleon in 1806. He was killed at Auerstädt.

Frederick had never promoted Prince Henry beyond the rank of general of infantry, holding that it was improper for a prince of the blood to occupy a higher position in the

18, 1787, the new king who "had time for everything but business" celebrated Prince Henry's birthday with all the pomp and ceremony that
Frederick had made traditional; but within a week he had insulted the
great king's former comrade in arms and associate commander by refusing him the position of inspector general of the forces, which the
prince had offered some months earlier, through Bischoffwerder, to
accept.

Deeply wounded and as deeply offended by the rejection of his offer,
the prince was compelled at last to realize that he was not wanted in
any position in the government. He hoped, he wrote to the king, that
the country he had defended in the past, and such as were left of the
men he had once commanded, might prosper and be happy without him
(although the tone of his letter indicated that he did not expect them
to). Born a Prussian prince, he continued, he had never been capable
of indifference to Prussia's welfare; and the same sense of duty which
had guided him through life had impelled him to offer once more to
place his experience and his knowledge at the service of the state. By
so doing he had satisfied his own sense of honor; but the rebuff he had
met had convinced him that he was never again to be permitted to serve
the state; so he would retire to Rheinsberg as soon as possible and enjoy
his freedom as best he might.

The king replied, with malice ill concealed beneath the polite phrase-
ology of his letter, that he had been prompted solely by personal affection
for his illustrious uncle when he refused to permit him to endanger his
health by assuming so heavy a task. One so devoted to the state would
of course do what it asked of him, at whatever cost, but a recurrence of
the physical disabilities which had necessitated the prince's retirement
from the military service in 1779 might endanger his life. That was a
risk which his dutiful nephew could not permit him to run. His multi-
farious services to the state had earned him a rest.[4]

Thus it was that, early in 1787, Rheinsberg again knew its restless
master's presence. He had not chosen to return there, and he did not
choose to stay. Having found life in Berlin insufferable under the existing circumstances, he knew that nowhere in Prussia would he find hap-

military hierarchy; but he had been careful not to promote others past him. (Ferdinand of
Brunswick had been a field marshal, but he had always been Henry's senior both in years
and in military rank; and he was not the king's brother.) Mirabeau reported (*Histoire
secrète*, 439) that Frederick William had offered to promote his uncle along with the Duke
of Brunswick and that Henry, citing Frederick's ruling as his reason, had refused the promotion. This story is unconfirmed and seems unconvincing.
[4] Fr. Wm. to H., February 1, 1787, in the Hausarchiv, Rep. 48, I.; H. to Fr. Wm., *ibid.*,
Rep. 56, I; H. to Bischoffwerder and vice versa, *ibid.*, Rep. 56, II, I.

piness or peace of mind while his enemies governed the king and the king failed to govern the state. So he began methodically to make arrangements for a return to France, with a view to establishing his permanent residence there; but before his plans were complete another proposal, more fantastic still, had been tentatively made to him. Through General von Steuben, he was sounded out as to his readiness to accept the regency, or stadtholdership, of the United States!

He was approached by letter through General von Steuben, who was then living near New York. "Your letter of the second of the month of November has reached me," he replied to his one-time "apprentice" early in April, 1787.

I have received it with feelings of deepest appreciation mingled with surprise. Your good intentions are well worthy of my esteem; they seem to me to grow out of a zeal which I am happy to recognize, while my surprise arises from the news that I gather from one of your friends.[5] I confess that I can scarcely believe that anyone can seriously intend to change the principles of government [now] established in the United States of America; but if the entire nation should unanimously decide to establish others, and should choose as its model the constitution of England, I should say that in my judgment that is the one that appears to me to be the most perfect of all constitutions. It has the advantage that if, as in all human institutions, some fault is found, one can correct it and make such good laws for the better establishment of the balance between sovereign and subjects that neither he nor they can ever encroach upon the rights assigned to the other.

It is not possible for me to send you a cipher. You will understand that it would run the risks that letters do, and would stay in the hands of those who first got hold of it. [But] I am going this autumn to France; perhaps I shall find one of your friends there.

The French are up to now the true allies of the United States of America. It seems to me that nothing of great importance can be properly done among you without the concurrence of this ally. It will suffice, Sir, to let you understand that it is through this channel that I can [best] receive in the future the letters that you wish to send me.[6]

In other words, the cautious prince would have naught to do with any such anomalous position as that of stadtholder of a republic. Nothing less than a legitimate, though constitutional, monarchy would in-

---

[5] Apparently Nathaniel Gorham.

[6] The retained draft of Prince Henry's letter, in his own hand, is in the Hausarchiv, Rep. 56, II, I. It was printed with an article by Dr. Krauel in the *American Historical Review*, XVII (1911–12), 44–51. The prince was probably requested either to destroy or return the letters addressed to him.

The document was not paragraphed. Dr. Krauel, in preparing it for publication, modernized much of the prince's peculiar orthography and corrected many of his careless errors and omissions. One word he seems to have misread, transcribing *les droit assigne respectivement a chacun* as *les droits alloués respectivement à chacun*.

terest him; and he would not commit himself even to that unless he could be assured that it would have the wholehearted support of all or an overwhelming majority of the American people. The candidate must have also the cordial approval of the French. There, the prince coyly but indirectly suggested, he could qualify.[7]

Before Prince Henry's letter could have reached von Steuben and been transmitted by him to the unnamed person for whom it was intended, the Philadelphia convention was in session. Monarchist ideas were no longer negotiable instruments in American politics; and men who had entertained them asked nothing better than that the whole incident be quickly forgotten, as — by most people — it was.

The prince said nothing of it to anyone, as he had said nothing to anyone of the previous reports that he was to be made king of Poland or of Rumania. He had apparently taken none of the three proposals very seriously. Chimerical crowns such as those could have meant comparatively little to a man whose one consuming ambition, never realized,

[7] The evidence that Prince Henry was thus approached is incomplete but convincing. With the adoption of the federal constitution, the American or Americans responsible for the correspondence would presumably, for the sake of their own political futures, have wished that it all be destroyed. Until the present century it was only upon charges made for political reasons thirty or forty years after the event, accusing the old Federalists of monarchist tendencies, that the whole story had to rest. Most of these charges seem to be based upon statements made by James Monroe.

To General Andrew Jackson in 1816, for example, Monroe wrote that while he was a member of Congress under the Articles of Confederation he had become convinced that some of the Federalists were friendly to the idea of establishing a monarchy, but that, being unable to carry Washington with them, they had had to keep the whole discussion on a confidential and oral basis; so he could not prove his statement from the public documents. *Writings of James Monroe* (New York, 1901), V, 343. Printed in the *National Intelligencer*, May 7, 1824.

Joseph Gardner Swift, one of the earliest graduates of the United States Military Academy and superintendent of that institution from 1812 to 1817, quoted Monroe in his memoirs as having said to him in 1817 that "during the presidency of Congress of N. Gorham, that gentleman wrote Prince Henry, of Prussia, his fears that America could not sustain her independence, and asked the prince if he could be induced to accept royal power on the failure of our free institutions. The prince replied that he regretted deeply the probability of failure, and that he would do no act to promote such failure, and was too old to commence new labors in life." *The Memoirs of General Joseph Gardner Swift* (privately printed, 1890), 164.

Under date of May 10, 1824, Rufus King recorded in his journal a similar story which he had heard secondhand from Mr. Monroe: "Col. Miller this evening said to me, speaking of Mr. Pr. Monroe that he had told him that Mr. Gorham, formerly President of Congress, had written a letter to Prince Henry, brother of the great Frederic, desiring him to come to the U. S. to *be their king,* and that the Prince had declined by informing Mr. Gorham that the Americans had shown so much determination agt. their old King, that they wod. not readily submit to a new one; Mr. Monroe adding that Genl. Armstrong had given him this information and that the papers or correspondence was in the hands of General Hull." *Life and Correspondence of Rufus King* (New York, 1894–1900), VI, 643.

General John Armstrong lived in the same lodginghouse with von Steuben in the winter of 1787–88, and was his friend. General Hull had served under von Steuben in the war for independence and had participated in the suppression of Shays's rebellion in Massachusetts in the winter of 1786–87; so it is both possible and probable that whatever one of the three knew of the matter they all knew. Armstrong was secretary of war

had always been to make himself one day the uncrowned king in Prussia.

Financial and other difficulties made it impossible for the prince to return to France until a year later than he had planned. The king, moreover, was reluctant to give his uncle permission to go — perhaps because he knew that the French ministers themselves were less eager to have him come than they had been in 1784. A prince without influence in Berlin or Potsdam was not worth cultivating in Paris; and the presence of distinguished foreigners — a disquieting number of whom were already revealing their intentions to be present if they could — might be decidedly awkward if the revolutionary situation with which the French already knew themselves threatened should get out of hand. Characteristically they preferred to discuss their domestic affairs in the privacy of the family; guests would be less welcome then than at some other time.[8]

In the third week of October, 1788, using the same transparent incognito as before, "the Count d'Oels" set out again for France via Gotha and Frankfort. At Metz he was received with honor by the archbishop. November 1 found him in Paris, and he had an audience with the French king the next day.[9]

Although his French friends had not urged him to do so and both

when Hull was tried by court-martial in 1813 for his failure at Detroit the year before. A large part of Hull's papers were destroyed by fire in 1812. It seems quite improbable that Prince Henry's reply was among them, but it has never come to light. See, in this connection, Louise Burnham Dunbar, "A Study of 'Monarchical' Tendencies in the United States from 1776 to 1801," in the *University of Illinois Studies in the Social Sciences,* Vol. X, No. 1.

It may safely be assumed that von Steuben was pledged to secrecy, though there is reason to believe that he failed to keep the pledge. One of his earlier biographers accepted and quoted an anecdote told many years after the general's death by a man who had once been his secretary. This witness, Mulligan, himself an old man when he told the tale, said that before the adoption of the constitution von Steuben had been asked what kind of stadtholder Prince Henry would make if a government modeled on that of the Netherlands were established and if he were asked to become head of it. "As far as I know the prince he would never think of crossing the ocean to be your master," Mulligan quoted the old German as having replied. "I wrote to him a good while ago what kind of fellows you are; he would not have the patience to stay three days among you." Friedrich Kapp, *The Life of Frederick William von Steuben* (New York, 1859), xii, 584; General John McA. Palmer, *General von Steuben* (New Haven, 1937), 341.

[8] Comte de Montmorin, French minister for foreign affairs, to d'Esterno in Berlin, September 7, and d'Esterno to Montmorin, September 28, in the Archives of the French Foreign Office, Prussian Correspondence, 209; see also Chevalier de Larivière, "Le Prince Henri de Prusse à Paris en 1784 et en 1788," in the *Revue politique et littéraire,* 4ᵉ Serie, Tome XVI (1901), 394.

[9] *Gazette de France,* No. 90, November 7, 1788; Baron Goltz to the Prussian Ministry, from Paris, November 3, in the Staatsarchiv, Rep. XI, 89, 282; Thomas Jefferson to Mr. Cutting, from Paris, November 3, in H. A. Washington, *Writings of Thomas Jefferson* (Washington, D. C., 1853), II, 491. Jefferson called the new arrival "Prince Henry of Russia."

Baron Grimm and the Duc de Nivernois had tried to dissuade him, he had hurried his journey so as to be on hand for the reconvening of the Assembly of Notables on November 6. Fully appreciating the potential significance of the occasion and overoptimistic about the reforms which the notables might be expected to approve, he thought that he was witnessing or about to witness the dawn of a new era in the history of Europe. Knowing that the French people were not destitute, he saw no reason why their government, by identifying its interests more fully with theirs as the Prussian monarchy had always identified itself with its people, could not command their confidence — and enough of their resources to lift itself out of bankruptcy.

He quickly renewed his friendship with the new finance minister Necker, whose acquaintance he had made in Switzerland in 1784, and thought it a very moving spectacle when Necker, on behalf of the king, addressed the notables like a father speaking to his children. He studied Necker's report on the national finances and thought it a great state paper. He heartily endorsed the ministerial proposals to abolish the use of the infamous *lettres de cachet,* to establish legal ministerial responsibility, and to double the representation of the Third Estate in the Estates General soon to be elected. The proposed reforms, he thought, would quickly double the strength of France and make her again the most powerful nation in Europe. When the notables failed to read the writing on the wall and refused to consent to any change other than the surrender of their legal right to exemption from taxation, he was able to overlook their refusal to do more and to praise them for the little they had done.[10]

The Prussian and Austrian diplomats Goltz and Mercy, who had been so seriously perturbed by Prince Henry's political activities during his previous Paris visit, were relieved this time to find that he made only personal contacts with the king and his ministers, carefully avoided the company of known leaders of the opposition such as the king's brothers, was discreetly quiet about his own aversion to the queen, and contented himself with the distinctions that came to him as an individual. With Baron Grimm again acting as his social secretary and unofficial publicity manager, he received plenty of recognition.

Wherever he appeared, the public courtesies shown him were applauded by the public. At the Lycée Professor Garet, lecturing on the Gracchi in his presence, used him and Frederick as modern examples of civic virtue — Frederick as a king who was also a great man and Henry

[10] Letters to Ferdinand, in the Hausarchiv. See also Larivière, in the *Revue politique et littéraire,* 4ᵉ Serie, XVI, and Krauel, *Prinz Heinrich in Paris,* 55.

as a great man who might well have been a king and needed only a throne to make him Frederick's equal. At the Palais de Justice he regularly attended the sessions at which the case of Kornmann vs. Beaumarchais was being tried — and heard an elaborate eulogy of himself interpolated by Duverrier into his defense of the accused.

At a special performance of *Le Bourgeois Gentilhomme,* given in honor of him and of the Duchess of Orleans (mother of that Philippe Égalité who was one day to become King Louis Philippe), more eulogies of the prince were interpolated by Bouflers into the play; this time he was compared with his own most admired hero, Henry of Navarre.

While Henry was in Paris the 1788 edition of Frederick's works appeared there. Since Caesar's commentaries on his Gallic Wars, said Grimm, nothing had been written comparable to the Prussian king's *Histoire de mon temps* or his *Histoire de la guerre de sept ans.* The publication afforded new grounds upon which to congratulate the author's brother.[11]

There was less upon which to congratulate him in Mirabeau's *Histoire secrète de la cour de Berlin,* published in Alençon, which appeared anonymously in Paris in the middle of January, 1789.[12] The government ordered the police throughout France to suppress the book at once as libelous, but some twenty thousand copies of it were clandestinely sold. The foreign secretary hurried to inform Baron Goltz of the steps that had been taken and urged him to send an explanation quickly to Berlin and to recommend immediate measures there to keep the book from appearing in Prussia. A similar explanation and apology were sent to the king of Prussia through Count d'Esterno.

The Prussian ministers, both in Berlin and in Paris, demanded the apprehension and punishment of the author. Montmorin replied that certainly the publisher and the printer would be punished, and they were. If Mirabeau himself had been in Paris, said the French foreign minister, he could and would have been arrested again under a *lettre*

---

[11] Thomas Jefferson wrote to James Madison, from Paris on January 12, that he understood that only a badly garbled version of the work was available in Paris but he hoped soon to obtain an unexpurgated edition from Switzerland. H. A. Washington, *Writings of Thomas Jefferson,* II, 565.

Henry himself was more disposed to accuse Frederick of falsifying the record than the French of mutilating it; but he gave utterance to his opinion only some time later by writing it on the margins of that edition. Of his first Silesian war Frederick had written: "What contributed most to this conquest was an army that had been developed over a period of twenty years by an admirable discipline superior to that of the other military systems of Europe, generals who were true citizens, prudent and incorruptible ministers, and finally a certain good fortune which often goes along with youth and refuses to accompany the old."—"The only truth in the book," was Henry's comment. *Oeuvres,* 1788 edition in the Schlossbibliothek, Berlin, I, 230. See *supra,* page 36, note 6.

[12] For comment on this book, see *supra,* page 330, note 8.

*de cachet;* but as he was then out in one of the provinces, one already seriously disaffected and full of disorder, it was scarcely practicable to seize him there.[13]

Either the clamor aroused by the book did not spread to the provinces or the people of Provence cared little about it. Two Provençal cities, Aix and Marseilles, elected its author as their representative in the Estates General, and he chose to sit for Aix. Prince Henry saw him in Paris but refused to speak to him or to answer any of the three letters he received from him.[14]

Count Mercy predicted on February 7 that the book would be burned and the matter dropped, although he expressed the opinion that if the government "had a shadow of energy and dignity" it would not allow the author to go unpunished. The Prussian ministry expected the writer to be condemned by respectable opinion but not by the nerveless French government.

The Austrian and Prussian prognosticators were not far wrong. The advocate general Antoine Louis Seguier, himself a member of the Academy, demanded before a plenary session of the *parlement* of Paris that the book be torn by the hand of the hangman and publicly burned; but the author's anonymity, his repeated disclaimers of responsibility, and his popularity with the revolutionary elements among the population afforded him immunity. The government found it wiser not to establish authorship.[15]

Prince Henry himself showed no inclination to push the matter, and may have gained more than he lost in personal prestige as a result of it. His friends at least did all they could to salve his feelings. In his address to the *parlement* Seguier condemned the book most bitterly for having wronged Frederick and slandered Henry. Had not the prince, asked the speaker, proved himself to be a general worthy to command under his august brother, to second his views, and to execute his plans? Had he not been designated by the king of Prussia himself as the only

[13] Goltz to the Prussian government, January 16 and 23; the Prussian ministry to Goltz, January 30, in the Staatsarchiv, Rep. XI, 89, 282. The Austrian, Saxon, and Russian governments also protested. Many of the most prominent persons in Europe had engaged the attention of the character assassin, and few of those prominent in Prussia had escaped it.

[14] H. to Ferdinand, in the Hausarchiv, *loc. cit.*; Krauel, *Prinz Heinrich in Paris,* 64; Larivière, 396–397. Henry repeatedly warned Ferdinand not to buy, touch, or look at the book; but in doing so he may well have been trying to safeguard his brother's happiness rather than his own reputation. Mirabeau had written that Count Schmettau was generally known and openly conceded to have been the father of the princess Ferdinand's two sons. He had further characterized both Ferdinand and his wife as malicious but malleable persons, fond of spiteful gossip but possessing neither minds nor wills of their own.

[15] Goltz to the Prussian ministry, February 6, 10, and 16, in the Staatsarchiv, *loc. cit.*; Krauel, *Prinz Heinrich in Paris,* 65–66. The French *parlement* of that period, it will be remembered, was a court, not a legislative body.

one of his generals who had committed no blunder, suffered no defeat? Had he not combined the activity of a Hannibal and the prudence of a Fabius with the wisdom of a Scipio? Gentle and affable though he was in private life, had he not shown himself intrepid and at ease in action, humane and compassionate after the combat, and been therefore revered by officers and men, friend and foe alike? The insult put upon him must be avenged; and the vengeance ought to be carried out not by a mere magistrate, a man of peace, but by the French army itself! "The Chambers assembled, the Peers being present," the *parlement* pronounced sentence. A copy of the book was publicly torn up and burned by the hangman, and the seizure of all other copies was ordered.[16]

A little later, meeting Seguier in the king's apartments at Versailles, the prince is reported to have said to him: "I am very grateful to you and sorry for the trouble that has been taken over this matter. But is not the guilty party being done more honor than he deserves?" And to others: "Why should I worry about it? I was born into a position which puts me entirely at the mercy of historical truth. If what Monsieur de Mirabeau says of me is true, he has only got a little ahead of history, and there is nothing in that to bother about. If what he says is false, I should not trouble myself over it; history will avenge me."[17]

Far from attempting to keep the libel from falling under the eyes of his friends — except Ferdinand, to whom he refused to send it, saying that he had but two copies and would not lend one — he bought sixteen copies of the outlawed book and passed them around, asking his friends to tell him whether the portrait therein drawn of him in any way resembled its original. In November of that year, however, after his return to Rheinsberg, he refused to see a self-styled French nobleman for whom Baron Münchhausen was interceding unless the man could prove that he had not been Mirabeau's secretary or been in some other way connected with him, as people said he had been; and in April, 1791, writing in praise of one of Mirabeau's speeches, he remarked that "the wickedest man in the world could write the most virtuous discourse."[18]

As the miniature tempest over Mirabeau's book died down, and as the great storm of revolution loomed up ever blacker on the horizon — a storm the winds of which that same Mirabeau was to ride so briefly

[16] Mirabeau, *Histoire secrète* (1895 edition), I, xv, xx; Krauel, *Prinz Heinrich in Paris,* 59, 66ff. On March 6 the prince was given another compensatory public ovation at the Comédie Française.

[17] Larivière, "Le Prince Henri de Prusse à Paris en 1784 et en 1788," *Revue politique et littéraire,* 4⁰ Serie, XVI (1901), 397.

[18] H. to Münchhausen, in the Hausarchiv, Rep. 56, II, I.

but boldly while he hurled some of its most effective thunderbolts — the thoughts of Prince Henry turned again homeward. The idea of settling permanently in France, half formed in his mind but categorically denied to the king before he had left Rheinsberg, was given up, although while in Paris he had negotiated tentatively for the purchase of a house in the city and of a fine country estate not too far away.

The prince did not fully share the apprehensions of those already trembling before the revolution. The government might well be strengthened by reorganization, he thought, and win popular support by enlightened concessions to the justifiable demands of its people. He would have been glad to stay and watch the process. His friends, however, permitted him to realize that it would be less awkward for them if he should leave before the meeting of the Estates General; when it was known that he was leaving, Montmorin praised the departing guest by writing to d'Esterno that it would have been impossible for anyone to conduct himself more prudently than the prince had done throughout his visit.[19]

He had thought of going to Rome, and had asked through the papal nuncio in Paris whether he would be welcome there if "sometime, perhaps a few years hence," he should be able to come. The pope replied at once that he would be very welcome indeed, both for his own brilliant qualities and as a member of a family which the papacy had always held so dear and had reason to respect so highly.[20]

Not Rome but Rheinsberg was his destination, however, when on March 16 he took leave of Paris for the last time.[21]

At Metz he was entertained again, this time by the Dowager Duchess of Zweibrücken. Then followed a brief visit in Dessau, and the returning traveler reached Rheinsberg on April 8 without having stopped in Potsdam. Frederick William had not asked him to do that, and he would not stop without being asked. Nor had he reported regularly to the king by letter as he had done to Frederick during his previous tour of France.

He never again traveled farther abroad than to Carlsbad, Teplitz, or Brunswick; and even Berlin seemed more and more like a foreign land

---

[19] "He is accompanied by the regrets of all those who have had the good fortune to come near him during his stay here," was Goltz's report to Berlin. Staatsarchiv, *loc. cit.* Goltz had learned by then to respect and admire the prince, while the prince had formed a favorable opinion of the ability and integrity of the man whom Frederick had chosen as his representative in Paris and had kept there in that capacity so long.

[20] Goltz to his government, February 20, *ibid.* The prince wrote later to the young Count de Sabran that he would have liked to go to Rome but could never have been happy in a country where his path would have been constantly beset with priests. Krauel, *Prinz Heinrich in Paris,* 68.

[21] Goltz to his government, March 16, in the Staatsarchiv, *loc. cit.* On March 13 the *Gazette de France* had reported: "Le 8, le Comte d'Oëls a pris congé de Leurs Majestés et de la Famille Royale."

to him. He who had so nearly been an *émigré* came steadily nearer to being a hermit — in a rather elegant hermitage, to be sure. His brother Ferdinand, who never went anywhere except to Rheinsberg, advised him to travel no more lest he find himself unable ever again to be happy at home.

Farewell then to travel, and — for the thousandth time — farewell to politics! He would arm himself with indifference, he assured his brother. Since the only way to be happy under a despotic government was to know and to wish to know nothing, to be unable to read, write, think, or understand, he would seek happiness thereafter by retiring permanently to his sylvan retreat, thinking as little as possible, and saying less than he thought.

He remembered his resolution for several weeks.

# CHAPTER XXVI

# 𝔅𝔞𝔰𝔢𝔩

*"For me, to be silent would be cowardly."*—
Henry to Frederick William.

FREDERICK II could not have been happy if he had had to live in Prussia as a subject during the reign of Frederick William II; and it was much as if his mind had lived on after his death in the mind of his brother Henry — who was not much happier in Prussia during that period than Frederick would have been. Without ever acknowledging it and probably without realizing it himself, Henry judged and condemned the new king and the new policies, totally unlike Frederick and his ways, by standards not essentially different from Frederick's.

No matter what resolutions he might make or how often he might repeat them, he could not keep silent. On June 30, 1789, d'Esterno reported that he was "dead and buried"; but the earthquake known to history as the fall of the Bastille quickly disinterred him. When the news of that event reached Berlin, the king, who had permitted three months to pass without showing the slightest curiosity about the political information his uncle might have brought back from Paris, summoned him at once to ask what the new phenomenon might portend. In Berlin in midsummer and for more than a week in Rheinsberg in the early autumn the two were often and long in conference.

The old prince had survived too many cataclysms to be startled into mistaking the fall of the Bastille for the end of the world. The French monarchy, he thought, might well weather the storm by rationalizing and nationalizing itself; and the king of Prussia, if he chose them wisely, would find some useful new subjects among the *émigrés* as his forefathers had done since the time of the Great Elector. The French government, however, if it were to survive in any recognizable form, must, he thought, make an honest effort to conciliate public opinion; and the Prussian king must not permit the *émigrés* to persuade him to interfere in the face of that tremendous new social force.[1] And all this despite

---

[1] "La guerre ne peut dompter l'opinion." H. to F. W., September 11, 1789, in the Hausarchiv, Rep. 56, I. The prince at that time thought it probable that the French National Assembly would soon call home the *émigrés;* and he would have been heartily glad to see them go.

As the revolution went on to more radical measures his sympathy for it diminished. "My constant prayers for France seem to be useless," he wrote to Münchhausen in February, 1790.

the fact that many of the most eloquent of the fugitives were or pretended to be among the prince's best friends, went to Rheinsberg before going to Berlin, and brazenly imposed upon his hospitality by living under his roof unasked and unabashed while urging upon the Prussian government a policy of intervention which he steadily opposed.

The natural spokesman of the illustrious Frenchmen who had fled from France to find someone to fight the French for them was Charles Philippe, Count of Artois, the king's younger brother. That prince had no valid claim upon Prince Henry, who had pointedly evaded him in Paris because of his known opposition to the concessions Louis XVI had then been promising to make to those demanding reform. So he wrote first directly to Frederick William and turned to the king's uncle as intermediary only when his initial efforts had failed to get results.

The objective which the self-exiled French prince sought to attain was nothing less than immediate armed intervention by Austria, Prussia, and the Empire. From Turin on February 14, 1790, he appealed to Frederick William in a letter in which he assembled every argument and exerted every sort of pressure to move his man to action.

The time had not yet come, he conceded, when he could hope to see a formal and permanent alliance made between his brother and the king of Prussia; but it was rapidly approaching, for he was sure that Frederick William would want to join the other sovereigns of Europe in the noble enterprise of restoring to the king of France his throne and his liberty.

Britain, he hinted, was already about to intervene. The kings of Spain and of Sardinia, he said, had shown beyond question how well they realized that in their own interest and for the sake of their own peoples they must rescue France and its king from the most dangerous of all despotisms, that of the multitude.

The writer warned the apprehensive king of Prussia of the danger that all sovereigns and all governments would run if the poison which had infected France were given time to spread. So prompt remedial measures for the cure of France must constitute the only prudent course.

His brother the king could be rescued, he said, only by force, the one language the ungrateful and perfidious rebels could understand; and only so could the blinders be struck from the eyes of a people led astray by traitors. He would not attempt to conceal from the Prussian king that most of the French people had been won over to the side of the revolutionaries. The French monarchy was already gone forever unless the other powers hastened to restore it; but there were still a large number of "good Frenchmen" left who were waiting and longing only for a sign of help from abroad.

The most recent act of the king of France might indeed seem strange to the rest of Europe, but when viewed in the light of his situation, the count explained, it would be seen to be only a consequence of his captivity.[2]

That the revolutionaries were justified in questioning the sincerity of their king's acceptance of his new status was proved by Count Charles in his letter — unless Charles himself was lying for what he would have called reasons of state. He offered to submit documentary evidence of his brother's bad faith. "Before he did that," wrote the count, "I had in my hands absolute proof that his heart denied it, and that he regarded as null in advance all acts which the ill fortune of circumstances might extort from him."

Then, playing upon the Prussian king's presumed ambition to weaken the "house of Austria" — a wish which the writer professed to endorse and to share — he went on to say that there was every reason to suppose that a quick Prussian attack upon Austria would be successful. But meanwhile the fatal French revolution would every day gain in strength and would spread until no one could prevent it from overwhelming every king in Europe, even him who seemed strongest and safest.

So why should not the king of Prussia achieve two great purposes at once? By rescuing the king of France he could destroy the very germs of the pestilence that was ravaging that fair kingdom; by so doing he would acquire "immortal rights" to the gratitude of the French king and to an alliance with France, and thus would deal the house of Austria its most mortal blow.

The count concluded his letter with the usual polite professions of loyalty and devotion, and with thanks for a loan which he said Frederick William had offered him.[3]

Frederick William sent the letter to Prince Henry, who had already received a similar one from the count which he had sent on to the king. Each asked the other how he should answer, and Henry saw and approved his nephew's reply before it was sent. It was full of personal sympathy for the French royal family, but promised no political or military intervention. The loan referred to was to be made secretly through

[2] The act referred to was apparently the king's assent to the nationalization of ecclesiastical estates. That step was taken after the revolutionary mob had stormed Versailles in October, 1789, and carried him and the queen back to Paris with them. He had previously assented to the Assembly decrees abolishing the survivals of feudal privilege and to the Declaration of the Rights of Man.

[3] MS. in the Hausarchiv, *loc. cit.*, with Prince Henry's letters to Frederick William II; published by Bailleu in the *Historische Zeitschrift*, Bd. 74 (1895, Neue Folge, Bd. 38), 259.

Prince Henry, who held the count's signed receipt, countersigned by the Prince of Condé, for four hundred thousand thaler. He had to go on holding it so long that it had become embarassing to him before he was able to deliver the money. The king temporized until the end of June before making payment, and then gave the count only half of the amount expected.[4]

As he recovered somewhat from the first shock of the news of the revolution and learned to meet or to fend off the frantic demands of the *émigrés,* Frederick William asked his uncle less often for advice on those matters. On other matters — the attempt to secure Danzig and Thorn while Austria and Russia were engaged in Catherine's second war with the Turks; the humiliating agreement at Reichenbach by which, under Austrian and British pressure, he abandoned that project; and the Pillnitz declaration by which he and the emperor publicly identified themselves with the interests of the king of France in his quarrel with the French people — he neither asked for his erstwhile mentor's advice nor enjoyed his approval. Few indeed were those of whom in 1791 Prince Henry did approve.[5]

Throughout that quiet year he clung to his hope that there would be no war of intervention. Only Britain wanted war, he thought, and she wanted it only so that the trade of other nations would be destroyed. If the accursed English would only throw Pitt into the Thames, the Duke of Brunswick would be speedily cured of his war fever and Prussia might yet consult her own interests and remain at peace.[6]

It would have been better for Prince Henry's reputation if he had had more important things to do in 1791. Then he might not have found

[4] H. to F. W., March 18, April 2, 11, 12, May 12, and June 27, in the Hausarchiv, *loc. cit.*

[5] "Happily I can ignore here the existence of Berlin and Potsdam, of Frederick William, of King Bischoffwerder and King Wöllner, and of the blessed sisters in theology who have been planted in Berlin to introduce the new doctrine. . . . So long as I live Liberty shall be my device," he wrote in December to Count Henckel von Donnersmarck. Leo Amadeus, Graf Henckel von Donnersmarck, *Briefe der Brüder Friedrichs des Grossen an meine Grosseltern,* 55. His correspondent was one of his former adjutants. When Henckel died, early in 1793, the prince made himself responsible for the education of his younger son, having him tutored as a boy and then sending him to the University of Halle. Although he saw the boy but once, he supported him for years, and payments provided for by his will were continued even after his death by the royal commission administering his estate. His letters to the lad's mother are as full of concern for her welfare as for that of the boy, and are models of tactful generosity. They show a real but little-known facet of the prince's many-sided character. His protégé repaid him by making a good record at the university and in the civil service. The widowed countess's daughter Henriette was also provided for by the prince, who gave her an appointment as lady in waiting to his estranged wife, Princess Henry; and the countess herself lived at Rheinsberg for several years as unofficial mistress of the household.

[6] H. to Baron Münchhausen, May 3 and 7, in the Hausarchiv, *loc. cit.*

time to draw his own ugliest portrait by erecting on rising ground across the lake from Schloss Rheinsberg, where it became the outstanding feature of the landscape, his personal war memorial to the heroes of the Silesian and Seven Years' Wars — with the name of Frederick the Great omitted! Frederick's favorite generals, Winterfeldt and Fouqué, he also excluded; and he mentioned neither himself nor Ferdinand of Brunswick. Those who had been in any way neglected or who had been most severely criticized by Frederick were exalted; the last were made first. The place of greatest honor on the obelisk was given to the name and portrait plaque of Prince William, who died in disgrace in 1758.

The column was in reality a memorial to that beloved brother who Prince Henry still believed had been grievously wronged by Frederick during the campaign of 1757 and maligned in Frederick's own histories of the war. Or was it a monument to a lifelong sense of injury? "I wrote you long ago that I was going to do something for my brother, and I have done it," he reported to Henckel von Donnersmarck. "I have recalled to mind and heart all the names of which I could speak and of which the great Frederick in his lying memoirs says not a word." [7]

As Prince Henry viewed it, he was performing a long-delayed act of justice, redeeming the reputation of a brother he had loved. In his dedicatory address, read for him first in French and then in German by his adjutant Tauentzien, he praised Prince William without stint both for his personal virtues and for his military services, crediting him with having had a decisive part in winning the victory at Hohenfriedberg, and with having "commanded an army in 1757 under the most difficult conditions." He was not there paying a public debt, he explained; he was only fulfilling a personal obligation imposed upon him by his own heart. It was a king's task to erect a monument to Frederick worthy of his services, and history could never overlook so great a king, who had already written his own story of his deeds and therefore needed no further encomiums from his contemporaries.[8]

[7] Count Henckel von Donnersmarck, *Briefe*, 53; Hamilton, *Rheinsberg*, II, 128. The memorial was unveiled on July 4 before a large assemblage consisting largely of veterans of the Seven Years' War, both officers and soldiers. Frederick William II, whose father was being honored, was not present and expressed publicly neither approval nor disapproval.
[8] Heinrich von Bülow, *Prinz Heinrich*, 353ff; Hamilton, *Rheinsberg*, II, 127; Bouillé, *La vie privée*, 272ff.
Of the Duke of Bevern the memorial says in stone: "To him was due the victory of Lobositz in 1756."
Of Marshall Keith: "Killed at the surprise of Hochkirch, 1758."
Of Quartermaster General von Marwitz: "As he died at the age of thirty-six years, in 1759, his merits and his services would be forgotten if this monument did not preserve his memory."
Of Schwerin: "The 11th of April, 1741, he won the battle of Mollwitz."
Of Seydlitz: "On all occasions he covered himself with glory. Skill and intrepidity,

That misbegotten memorial has been a perpetual reminder of the ugly fact that Henry never forgave Frederick for his treatment of William. By erecting it he did Frederick no harm and William little good; but he gave his own reputation a heavy handicap to carry through history.

Meanwhile Prussia followed Austria into war against France. By the abolition of feudal privilege and by the secularization of church property, the French had violated certain treaty rights retained on the French side of the border since the Peace of Westphalia by some of the German princes and ecclesiastical states, members of the Empire; and as emperors the Hapsburgs had protested the violation.[9] The Imperial family had felt the same fear of a spreading revolution that the Count of Artois had so artfully tried to use to induce the king of Prussia to intervene on behalf of the Bourbons, while personal kinship with Marie Antoinette and an old alliance with Louis XVI made it impossible for them to view the revolution with indifference.

Yet it was revolutionary France, eying the Belgian Netherlands and the Rhenish border lands, that declared war on April 20, 1792 — on Francis as archduke of Austria, not as emperor. The king of Prussia then entered as an ally of Austria a war for which he had subsequently to continue to furnish a contingent of troops as a member of the Empire.

Few laurels were won on either side in the campaign of 1792. Eighty thousand Prussian and Austrian troops were assembled at Coblenz for an invasion of France. Not half enough, said Prince Henry. If the enterprise was to be only a demonstration designed to strike terror into the hearts of the French, it should be made with awe-inspiring numbers; if national resistance were encountered, as he was sure it would be, then more fighting strength would be needed.

On July 25, over the signature but against the judgment of the Duke of Brunswick, commander of the allied armies, a proclamation was issued announcing that the invaders were there to restore the monarchy, and threatening the people of Paris with dire retribution if any harm

combined with swiftness and prudence, made all his operations fatal to the enemy."

Of Wobersnow: "The battle of Kai was fought against his judgment; the Prussians lost it, and he died a hero."

Around the base of Frederick's splendid equestrian statue erected on Unter den Linden by Frederick William III, positions of honor were assigned in the following order: Prince Henry, Ferdinand of Brunswick, and Generals Seydlitz and Zieten on horseback at the four corners, Prince William on foot on the front face of the pedestal, between Henry and Ferdinand of Brunswick. See the illustration facing page 356.

[9] Joseph II was succeeded in 1790 by his brother Leopold II, who died early in 1792 and was followed by his son Francis II. Joseph and Leopold were brothers of Marie Antoinette.

should be done their royal family. Thus the enemies of France literally named its king as one of themselves, and the French people thereafter treated him as one. Marie Antoinette had been so classified in the minds of many of them for a long time.

By the time it reached Valmy the invasion had bogged down. There, on September 20, it suffered its first defeat at the hands of the French armies. Goethe, accompanying the Duke of Weimar who was there in command of troops, may have been the first to say in so many words that there, that day, began a new epoch in history; but the French National Convention was not far behind him. It decreed on September 22 that the monarchy was abolished, and the year I of the French Republic, one and indivisible, began in Paris with the receipt of the news of Valmy.

Prince Henry also realized better than most observers the potential strength of the new forces being roused to life in France. "This mass of men is terrible," he wrote on December 12 to his former adjutant Henckel von Donnersmarck. "Next year you can defeat fifty thousand men four times and still be destroyed without having accomplished anything."

How little had been accomplished, and how unlikely the invasion had been to accomplish anything, he put into bitter words in a satirical review of the campaign. The presence of the king of Prussia, wrote the veteran of three wars — at least two of which had been real ones — had been no great military advantage. One could have put behind any battalion a bag of wool with a crown on it and have found it just as useful both to that battalion and to the army as a whole when the enemy's guns opened fire.

The manifestos had ruined everything.

To march on Paris, leaving fortified towns and enemy corps in the rear of the army, had been "a folly which became a famine." Before the armies had passed Verdun, it had already become evident that French opinion was unanimously hostile, as no one declared himself in favor of the princes. Yet the march had been foolishly continued over roads made almost impassable by the early autumn rains until the troops found themselves far from their base of supplies, exhausted, hungry after going two days without bread, wet to the bone, and confronted by a well-posted army upon which they could not even train their guns to advantage.

In the cannonade at Valmy, about which — but not by which — so much noise had been made, perhaps as many as a hundred and forty men had been killed or wounded! Then the invaders were ready to negotiate and only too happy to retreat, quarreling like cats and dogs among themselves and ready to murder one another, each blaming the other for the defeat.

"There are regiments that have lost as many as three officers," wrote the survivor of Prague and Rossbach in disgust. "The king has lost some of his domestics; and, as in the army of the late king in Bohemia, *disputérie* has become epidemic. I do not know the number of the dead, but twelve thousand men are in the field hospitals. The guns are in Luxemburg without horses, and part of the cavalry is marching on foot. Meanwhile Custine has taken Mainz and Frankfort, and today's reports (which are not yet confirmed) say that he has taken Hanau." [10]

When writing directly to the king Henry showed more self-restraint in his choice of words, but he made his meaning equally clear. On the eve of the new year he wrote his nephew that he would like to be able to wish him a good New Year; if wishes would suffice, there would be nothing left to wish for. But with Prussia still involved in a purposeless war he could see little prospect of the good fortune he so ardently desired for the land he had served for the greater part of his life. Tactlessly but dutifully — as he saw it — he called attention to the risk to which the king was exposing the state, and to the fruitless expenditure of money and of men's lives that his policy had already entailed. Without the assured prospect of material gain for Prussia, he argued as always, neither risk nor expenditure was warranted. In the sharpest terms he contrasted the condition of the country and its finances at the time of Frederick William's accession with the sorry state in which the end of such a war would find them. Yet, since the state was apparently already committed to another campaign, if the king should see fit to make any use of an old soldier's knowledge of such things, the old soldier would gladly come to headquarters and lay before him certain suggestions as to strategy which he thought would be found valuable but which it would be indiscreet to put into writing. [11]

The offer was declined; but although as a subject he could not go uninvited to see the king, as a prince and the king's uncle he could still write unsolicited letters — which he soon had a new occasion to do.

On January 14, 1793, Prussian and Russian troops moved into Poland. In spite of his own connection with the first partition of that luckless land, this step toward a second seemed to him unwise to the point of utter irresponsibility. "You are the head of a great state," he wrote to Frederick William. "You are responsible to God and to the nation that is subject to you. A war is useful only when the interest of that state is

[10] Henckel von Donnersmarck, *Briefe,* 58.
[11] Hausarchiv, *loc. cit.* See also Krauel, *Prinz Heinrich als Politiker,* 6off., 187–189. The king's headquarters were then at Frankfort on the Main.

354

well served. . . . Your troops are invading Poland, your manifesto has appeared. I tell you frankly, my dear nephew, that I see in that only an extension of the labyrinth in which you already find yourself. That is all I permit myself to say. How I wish that I could have kept silent, that I could efface the present and the past, to see you in a happy land! But I am too closely related to you; for me to be silent would be cowardly, and my conscience is my law. Consider this carefully, my dear nephew: true rectitude requires me to speak to you as I have done." [12]

The campaigns of 1793 were but little less disastrous to Prussian arms than Henry had thought they would be. The end of the year found the allied armies east of the Rhine, with the whole left bank in the possession of the French. While he could not rejoice in the defeat, the prince found during that year some consolation in the thought that the Austrians were undergoing the same painful treatment and suffering an even greater loss of prestige, and in the hope that his nephew would soon muster courage enough to refuse to be made any longer the blind instrument of Austrian policy. His hopes rose when the king reported to him that the French National Assembly had adopted a resolution in favor of making a separate peace with Prussia.[13]

He was further heartened, rather than disheartened, by the king's declaration that without solid financial assistance Prussia could not go on, but must recall from the Rhine all but the twenty thousand troops that constituted her contingent to the army of the Empire.[14] He was therefore all the more bitterly disillusioned when he learned that by the

[12] Hausarchiv, *loc. cit.*; Krauel, *Prinz Heinrich als Politiker*, 63, 189–190. In agreement with Russia, on January 23, 1793, Prussia secured Danzig, Thorn, and Posen. Russia compensated herself generously at Poland's expense. Austria, more deeply involved than Prussia in the French war, was compelled to consent to the change, but did so only under heavy pressure and resentfully. Frederick William proclaimed in his manifesto that he had to intervene to protect the rest of Europe from the pestilential ideas of the French Revolution, which had gained such a wide acceptance in Poland as to constitute a menace to civilization.

[13] Hausarchiv, *loc. cit.* Under date of September, 1792, there is in the Archives Nationales in Paris a logically reasoned but unsigned memorandum headed "Question à résoudre au Conseil" in support of such a proposal. Interest alone, it reasons, had drawn Prussia and Austria together; then interest should be used to draw them apart. Austria would no doubt try to take some French territory to pay off Prussia; then let France buy her off with an offer of an offensive and defensive alliance and a cash indemnity to cover the costs of the war to date. The king of Prussia could easily find a way out of his obligations to the emperor by declaring that he had been tricked into thinking that he was entering a campaign against a disruptive faction only but had found himself at war with a free nation bravely defending itself against enemies both foreign and domestic. Archives Nationales Françaises, Relations Extérieures, 1792–An VIII. As the war went on and brought victory after victory with it, the French did not lose sight of the advantages of a separate peace with Prussia but saw less need of paying any very high price for it.

[14] This declaration was known to the French government, as witnessed by Bacher's reports from Switzerland covering both the king's statement and one already made by Prussia's spokesman in the Imperial Diet. Archives du Ministère des Affaires Étrangéres, Correspondance de Prusse (cited hereafter as French Foreign Office Archives, or Fr. F. O.), I, 36, 45.

Hague Convention of April 19, 1794, the Prussian army had been, as he said, "sold to the English and the Hollanders" and must not only keep the field but be used as the interests of the maritime powers might dictate.[15]

The Hague Convention could not be enforced. There was little reason why Britain should pay for the maintenance of troops which she could not use where she would; while the Prussians, whether subsidized or not, were disinclined to fight in any interest other than their own, or to leave the region of the middle Rhine where Prussian interests were more vitally involved than in the low countries.

Other events, moreover, effectively nullified the agreement. On March 24 Kosciusko had summoned the Polish people to revolt against Russian and Prussian domination. On April 18, the day before the Hague Convention was signed, Russian troops had had to evacuate Warsaw. In May, in response to a Russian call for help, Frederick William sent more troops into Poland; and in June, with his conscience reminding him that he had promised to command in person against the French and his ministers telling him that his proper place was in Poland, he went to Poland.[16]

He went without his uncle Henry's blessing. He had told the prince of his plan, and had been exhorted to give it up. He ought to liquidate both wars at once, Prince Henry urged, and work toward a general pacification of Europe through Prussian mediation instead of plunging deeper into such costly enterprises of such questionable utility.[17]

The king must remember his people, wrote the old prince, and learn to distinguish between his true friends and the false ones who were leading him astray. "True friends," he continued, "are not those who praise you and applaud your every act, but precisely those who, seeing you at the head of a great nation, recognize the close connection which must exist between the interest of him who governs and the peoples who are

[15] Krauel, *Prinz Heinrich als Politiker*, 63–64. The Prussian field army in the west was to be maintained at a strength of 62,000 men, and it was understood that the king of Prussia would command it in person. Toward its maintenance Great Britain would pay a subsidy of 50,000 pounds per year. Conquered territories were to be at the disposal of the maritime powers.

[16] Möllendorff, left in command of the Rhine army, refused to budge at the behest of the British, who discontinued payment of the subsidy. Hardenberg, for Prussia, denounced the unworkable convention on October 25, 1794.

[17] Hertzberg, who had retired from the ministry, took the same view and protested in the same fashion, but the coincidence did not lead to an immediate reconciliation between the two. "If Hertzberg had been so obliging as to die ten years ago, he would have done Prussia and Europe a great service; today it is of no consequence whether he lives or dies," was the prince's kindly comment when he heard that the former minister was ill in September, 1794. Krauel, *Prinz Heinrich als Politiker*, 65.

*Statue of Frederick II at the Foot of Unter den Linden, Berlin*

Prince Henry's is the figure on horseback at the right front corner of the base. The Staatsbibliothek is in the left background, and a corner of Prince Henry's former palace, now the University of Berlin, is at the right (see the note on page 352).

governed. One cannot be truly attached to you without being equally devoted to the state, and one cannot be devoted to the state without wishing that all your acts may contribute to its welfare. . . . May Heaven grant that the day may not come when you will recognize, but too late, the rectitude of my intentions!" [18]

Before his departure the king told his uncle sharply that by virtue of his position he considered himself personally responsible for all decisions, including the choice of counselors and of policies, and answerable to no other person for any of them; but by July differences of opinion among the ministers and generals, and the king's own indecision, had brought Prussia's affairs to a state of almost incredible confusion. Frederick William was with the troops besieging Warsaw. Haugwitz, the foreign minister, was in Berlin, restricted in action by the necessity of securing the countersignature of the other ministers to most of his correspondence and royal assent to steps of major importance. Hardenberg, young in the service, was posted in Frankfort on the Main with instructions to report perfunctorily to the whole ministry and confidentially and at length to Haugwitz only. Möllendorff, in command of the troops on the Rhine front, had been empowered to negotiate with the French for an exchange of prisoners, and was expected under cover of that negotiation to find out if possible on what terms Prussia could make a separate peace in spite of her two existing treaty agreements not to do so. With Möllendorff were Kalckreuth and Schulenberg; and the three fighters could agree on only the one point that they wished to do no more fighting. In Vienna Lucchesini was forbidden to mention peace officially, but was instructed to find out what he could personally about the possibility of its attainment.[19]

During September things went badly for Prussia in Poland. Austria refused the king's request for troops for the siege of Warsaw, and Russia threatened to withdraw hers; so Frederick William abandoned his attempt to capture the city. The new tone of the Russian and Austrian governments indicated that they expected to dictate the terms of any new Polish settlement or partition with very little reference to Prussia;

[18] Hausarchiv, *loc. cit.;* Krauel, *Prinz Heinrich als Politiker,* 191.

[19] Heinrich von Sybel, *Geschichte der Revolutionszeit 1789–1790* (Frankfurt-am-Main, 1882), III, 227–228; Hardenberg to Haugwitz, July 26 and 30, August 11 and 30, in the Staatsarchiv, Rep. XI, 89, 314. Both Hardenberg and Haugwitz would have been much more comfortable in their minds over a general peace, made in concert with their allies, than over a separate one; but, wrote Haugwitz, "Frieden müssen wir haben. . . . Man muss des Elends ein Ende machen, und der Winter muss uns Frieden bringen." *Ibid.*

On August 11 Hardenberg sent to Haugwitz a confidential agent, Gervinus, "Ihnen mündlich manches zu sagen das für die Feder nicht ganz geeignet ist."

and the king and his ministers feared that Austria would make a quick separate peace with France and transfer all her troops to Poland while the principal Prussian army was still tied fast in the Rhineland. If the thought was not father to the wish, it at least emphasized the need for haste if Prussia was to anticipate her ally and do unto Austria as she feared Austria was about to do unto her.[20]

Under such circumstances it was not surprising that the joint Austrian-Prussian counterattack for the recapture of Trier, in mid-September, failed. The Prussian commander Möllendorff had sabotaged it before it started. Through his *voyageur* Schmertz of Creuznach and another intermediary called "Chancellor Ochs," he had got word to the French secretary-interpreter Bacher, in Basel, that the attack was to be made and that the Prussian generals had not been able absolutely to refuse to participate in it, but that they and the French ought to be careful not to injure one another.[21] The Prussians would start out on the expedition with rations for only eight days and unless molested by the French would advance only to a designated line, where they would act merely as observers, content with defending themselves if attacked.[22]

Bacher cynically reported that Möllendorff was only seeking a pretext to withdraw across the Rhine without "a too apparent defection" and without the humiliation of being driven across by the French; yet he agreed to a *de facto* cessation of hostilities, a sort of undeclared armistice, if all Prussian troops were ordered back to the right bank — which was done on October 19. He promised also that Cleves and Guelders, Prussian provinces on the left bank occupied by the French, would be treated as leniently as possible in consideration of the proposed exchange of prisoners, of whom the Prussians held more than the French did. In September and October he repeatedly recommended that France convert these semiofficial conversations into a serious negotiation for a separate peace with Prussia. France had then, as he saw it, a superb opportunity to determine the destiny of Europe and to re-establish her own brilliant

[20] Spencer and Lord Grenville were in Vienna and Lord Malmesbury in Frankfort, making desperate efforts to hold Austria and Prussia to their alliance and to incite them to action. In September Lord Malmesbury was still professing to Hardenberg implicit confidence in the Prussian king, though he then said frankly that he had no faith whatever in the Prussian army. By October he was, Hardenberg said, "recht ärgerlich." Staatsarchiv, *loc. cit.*
[21] In an earlier message he had expressed some concern lest the French attack his troops around Kaiserslautern and "force them to abandon their inactivity." The French generals ought to act with "great circumspection," he wrote, and not sacrifice uselessly their brave soldiers who could be so much better employed against the Austrians. Schmertz to Ochs, September 3, and Bacher to Buchot, September 14, in the Fr. F. O., Pr. 1, 63, Correspondance de Barthélemy.
[22] Bacher to Buchot, September 16, *ibid.*

position of old as protectress of German liberties and a guarantor of the Peace of Westphalia.[23]

Major Meyerinck, Möllendorff's adjutant who as his emissary had dealt with Bacher during the first half of October, hurried to Frederick William and assured him that France was ready to listen to talk of peace. Further pressure was put on the king by the electors of Mainz and Trier, the Duke of Zweibrücken, the landgraves of Hesse-Cassel and Darmstadt, and the stadtholder of the Netherlands, all of whom urged him to make peace and then as mediator secure such terms as he could for them.[24]

So far had the peace movement developed without Prince Henry's being in any way officially connected with it; yet his position was never merely that of an interested outsider. Möllendorff had been his trusted and useful subordinate in the War of the Bavarian Succession; he had effected a reconciliation with Kalckreuth; and, sure of his support, they had let him know what they were doing. All through September his letters to Ferdinand took on an entirely new tone of cheerfulness and were filled with references to important business on which he was "working very hard"; but he knew his brother too well to tell him anything more definite than that. On October 25 he had dinner with the king at Sans Souci; and four days later, probably by prearrangement, he sent the king the first of another long series of political memoranda.[25]

The war had lost its point, he argued, since the death of Louis XVI, and had become only a series of useless sacrifices in which Prussia had already done more for both of her principal allies than her treaty obligations required of her. She therefore owed them nothing further and need not hesitate to abandon them as history had shown that they would abandon her whenever they thought that their own immediate interests would be best served by so doing.

But to treat with the French would not, he said, be an act of desertion or abandonment. The negotiations need be kept secret only long enough

---

[23] Bacher to Buchot, October 19, 26, *ibid*. When rumors of the negotiations reached St. Petersburg the Russian ministers gave Tauentzien to understand that they "hoped" the report was untrue, as nothing could hurt Prussia's standing with Russia so much. No fanciful tale could be farther from the truth, Tauentzien assured them, or a greater injustice to Prussia. Von Sybel, III, 270. Tauentzien had until recently been Prince Henry's adjutant.

[24] Von Sybel, III, 273.

[25] Hausarchiv, Rep. 56, II, F and I. He wrote to Haugwitz in the following January that he had been "initiated into these mysteries in October," but he must have had some confidential knowledge of them prior to his initiation. See von Sybel, III, 275.

Bouillé's version of the October 25 interview at Sans Souci is that the king threw himself into Prince Henry's arms crying: "My dear uncle, save me." *La Vie privée*, 307. As Frederick William was nearly twice as large as Henry, the story is as difficult to picture as it is to believe.

to ascertain that the French were ready to make peace and would accept Prussian mediation on behalf of the other powers; then it could be announced to all that Prussia was safeguarding the interests of all. The glory of the Prussian king would ultimately be enhanced rather than diminished as a result of the part he would have played in bringing about the general pacification already so generally desired.

As her first objectives Prussia ought to insist that the safety of her Westphalian possessions be guaranteed, that the French assent to her new acquisitions in Poland, and that no part of Bavaria should under any circumstances go to Austria.

As a negotiator she ought to send someone who knew the French language well and who had been long enough in France to be thoroughly familiar with the people and their ways.[26]

The first step which he was advising could be taken easily, urged the prince. The purpose of the whole move was the glory of the king and the interest of his state. God would take care of the rest.[27]

Encouraged by the favorable reception of his first memorandum, the irrepressible prince followed it four days later with another. France must be made, he said, first to see that Prussia had been unable to prevent the Russian aggressions in Poland, and second to realize that France herself needed a strong Prussia between Austria and Russia to hold them in check and keep Europe in balance.[28]

The third memorandum of the series, dated November 6, was prompted by a report that the elector of Mainz, in the Imperial Diet at Regensburg, had proposed that the king of Sweden, as a guarantor of the Peace of Westphalia, be asked to open negotiations on behalf of the German princes. The prince warned his nephew not to show his hand with reference to the treaties of Westphalia until he knew what attitude the French would take toward them. If France still wished to uphold that settlement he could remind her that he was also one of its guarantors and as proper a negotiator as the king of Sweden. If France, on the other

[26] Count Bernhard von der Goltz, minister to France from 1772 to the outbreak of the war, was obviously indicated, though not then named by the prince. Prince Henry himself might almost equally well have been indicated, but was disqualified as an active negotiator by his rank.

[27] "Réflexions sur l'état présent des affaires de l'Europe et en particulier des intérêts de sa Majesté Prussienne." Original in the prince's own hand and copy made by Baron Münchhausen, king's chamberlain, and certified by the prince ("copié exactement 29 d'8'bre 1794, Henri.") in the Hausarchiv, Rep. 56, II, I. Submitted through Struensee, who, in acknowledging it on November 11, wrote: "The minister named by you will be made plenipotentiary." *Ibid.* This and the other memoranda that followed it are discussed at length by Dr. Krauel in Chapter III of his *Prinz Heinrich von Preussen als Politiker,* and several of them are printed in the original French in the supplement to that useful little book.

[28] Hausarchiv, *loc. cit.,* Münchhausen's copy only.

hand, was ready to tear up those old treaties, Prussia should make no foolish effort to maintain them. If she did, she would find that every little prince in western Germany would soon be appealing to them for redress of real or fancied grievances.[29]

The third memorandum led to a series of interviews with Haugwitz, to which the king authorized his minister to invite the prince, warning Haugwitz, however, not to let himself be swept off his feet by his impetuous interlocutor. Running no risk of having the same thing happen to himself, he replied by letter that Meyerinck had been sent back to Basel to ask for an armistice, but that he could not consider a peace which would mean the cession of Prussian territories on the left bank of the Rhine.[30]

As soon as Meyerinck reached Basel he let Bacher know that twenty thousand Prussian troops, soon to be followed by others and by their artillery, were ready to leave the Rhine army. Without waiting for instructions from his own government, Bacher suggested to the French General Michaud that he seize the opportunity to negotiate his way into Mainz, and notify the Committee of Public Safety about it after the fact.[31]

Bacher himself reported on November 14 that the earlier mentors of the king of Prussia such as Lucchesini and Bischoffwerder, who had been "sold to the coalition," had lost all influence, while around Prince Henry were rallying the old ministers and generals of Frederick II who had always felt themselves dishonored by the coalition policy and the subservience to Great Britain and Austria which it involved.[32]

On December 1, moved by the advice of his ministers Haugwitz, Struensee, Finckenstein, and Alvensleben, by another memorandum from Prince Henry, and by word that the Netherlands was about to make peace with the French, Frederick William decided to send Baron Goltz secretly to Basel to establish contact with the French agents there. The prince's fourth memorandum, on November 21, had been written in the form of a set of instructions "for him who is to negotiate for peace"; but the king instructed the ministers to draft the envoy's instructions themselves, having him merely "for politeness" stop at Rheinsberg for a day "to hear the opinions" of the prince. Goltz was then in Magde-

---

[29] *Ibid.* Münchhausen's copy certified by the prince. Any serious revival of the treaties of Westphalia would have put a barrier in the way of the prince's plans, tentatively formed nearly twenty years before and never forgotten, to consolidate Prussia's possessions east of the Rhine by secularization of ecclesiastical states.

[30] *Ibid.*, Rep. 48, I.

[31] Fr. F. O., Corr. de Barthélemy, Pr. I, 91. The twenty thousand soldiers were ordered back to Möllendorff's camp within a week.

[32] *Ibid.*, 93.

burg. Convinced that the war was a bankrupt enterprise, the ministers were quite content to turn over to someone else the thankless task of liquidating it. So although they obeyed the king's instructions faithfully, even to the point of repeating to Goltz that it was "for politeness" that he was being sent to Rheinsberg, they added that he should talk freely to the prince and listen carefully to everything he had to say.[33]

Struensee and Bischoffwerder wrote to Prince Henry soon afterward that Goltz had been deeply impressed with the wisdom of the plan of peace propounded to him at Rheinsberg, and that his official instructions were in every way consonant with the views expressed in the prince's memoranda on the subject.

Their statements were only partially true. The prince had wanted the conference moved to Berne to get away from the crowds of Frenchmen and other intriguers, both aristocrats and democrats, that he said were overrunning Basel. The ministry dropped that proposal, which was perhaps just as well; for Goltz soon found that the French Committee of Public Safety was at first unwilling to treat anywhere but in Paris.

Prince Henry had also stipulated that French assent to new Prussian acquisitions in Poland must be secured. The ministry chose not to mention Poland rather than concede that France could properly have anything to say about what happened there.

In most other respects Goltz's instructions read very much as if Prince Henry had written them himself. He must seek an immediate armistice for Prussia, then neutralization of those states whose rulers had asked Prussia to mediate for them. He must safeguard the dynastic interests of the House of Orange, but might withdraw the previous Prussian objection to a French-Dutch alliance. He must see what terms could be secured for the *émigrés*, but must sacrifice no vital Prussian interest for their sake. He must demand the immediate restoration of French-occupied Prussian territories on the left bank of the Rhine (though it is impossible not to draw the inference that the demand was to be made chiefly for trading purposes and that compensatory gains on the right bank would be acceptable in exchange, provided that Austria did not apply the same principle and take Bavaria in exchange for the Belgian Netherlands).

For the sake of the negotiation he was to promise official recognition of the French Republic, but with the stated reservation that the recog-

[33] H. to Haugwitz, November 26; F. W. to Haugwitz, December 1; Haugwitz to Goltz, December 2, in the Staatsarchiv, Rep. XI, 89, 317. Goltz was at Rheinsberg December 9 and went on from there to Potsdam to see the king, carefully disguised and under an assumed name.

nition would become at once *"nulle et non avenu"* if the negotiation were ever broken off; he was not to let himself be drawn into any discussion of a Franco-Prussian alliance. To give the proceedings greater dignity, and because the Prussian ministers knew more about Barthélemy than about Bacher and had greater confidence in his integrity, Goltz was to ask that Barthélemy, an experienced diplomat of the old school and head of the French mission in Switzerland, be named as France's plenipotentiary. Harnier, Prussian secretary of legation at Basel, was to be retained and used by Goltz.[34]

While Goltz was on his way from Berlin to Basel, Harnier was riding the same road in the opposite direction bearing a blunt note from the Committee of Public Safety to the effect that its members had seen from the first that Major Meyerinck had not been dealing honestly with them, but that they hoped that the king of Prussia was ready to speak frankly and straightforwardly. If so, they were ready to listen to any proposition he might have to make, consistent with the interests and dignity of the French people; but they chose to do their listening in Paris. In the meantime Secretary Bacher would be in Basel to receive and transmit messages.[35]

Unwilling though they were to go to Canossa in such fashion at the behest of their arrogant republican adversaries, the Prussian ministers had no choice. Harnier was sent to Paris by way of Basel, where he was coached by Goltz and given his passports by Bacher. He was instructed to tell the French government that Prussia wanted peace, provided that France would accept Prussian mediation between herself and the states of the Empire. He was, however, to discuss only the general basis of the peace, not its specific terms, and was to return to Basel as soon as a French plenipotentiary — who the king of Prussia hoped would be Bar-

---

[34] Staatsarchiv, Rep. XI, 89, 317. Secretary Bacher had spent several years of his youth in Berlin and had received his military education there. He now reported to the Committee of Public Safety that he had at that time been put under heavy obligation by Prince Henry, "born protector of all the French." He wrote to Möllendorff that he could not die happy without paying his thirty-year-old debt to the prince, and again to Prince Henry himself in similar terms. Hausarchiv, Rep. 56, II, I. The Committee of Public Safety had already notified Bacher on December 5 that they expected to negotiate in Paris only, so would need to name no plenipotentiary. They were therefore leaving the correspondence in the hands of him who had begun it. If they should ultimately decide, however, to use an ambassador, Barthélemy would, they said, have a right to expect to be chosen for the task. Barthélemy, when notified, praised Bacher highly and asked for his help. Fr. F. O., Corr. de Barthélemy, 108, Pr. I, 116.

[35] Staatsarchiv, Rep. XI, 89, 317. The note was signed by Merlin of Douai, Carnot, Guyton, Cochon, Bréard, Delmas, and Petiet. Plain speaking was the committee's policy. On January 1 it sharply reprimanded Bacher for having failed to maintain the "austerity" of a free man, for having written in a too friendly and "unrepublican" tone to Möllendorff (whom he had known for thirty years), and for having written on political matters to General Michaud instead of to the deputy on mission.

thélemy — was named. As a pretext for being in France at all he should pretend, as Bacher had suggested, that he was there to inspect prison camps and report on the treatment of German prisoners of war.[36]

The French insistence that someone be sent to Paris, and the Prussian decision to send someone, indicated clearly enough that both teams of players knew which held the higher cards. Why should France negotiate for what she had already won or was about to win by force of arms, asked Merlin de Thionville, writing to Bacher from the headquarters of the French army of the Rhine and the Moselle on December 3. Why palaver over the fate of Cleves, Mainz, or the possessions of Rhineland bishops too weak to defend themselves and too pusillanimous to try? Prussia was in a desperate plight and knew it. She could trust neither her armies nor her allies, so was in no condition either to continue the war or to treat successfully for terms. Then why treat with her? [37] — Why, indeed!

On December 22, on motion of Archbishop Dalberg of Mainz, the Imperial Diet at Regensburg voted for peace and asked the emperor and the king of Prussia to act as mediators. Thugut of Austria advised his emperor to make no further sacrifices for the worthless states of the Empire but merely to fall back upon and consolidate Austria's own position as a power, letting Prussia, who seemed willing, assume the thankless task of mediation. If she succeeded in making an honorable peace, the emperor could confirm it; if not, let Prussia be blamed for the failure.[38]

Failure it was, inevitably, if the partially successful liquidation of a business already bankrupt can ever properly be called a failure. If Prussia had been in a better general position, her bargaining power would have been greater and some liquidating dividends might have been paid. If her king and ministry had shown half the cohesion and hardihood displayed by the Committee of Public Safety, something more might have been saved from the wreck; but they did not. If the able and experienced Baron Goltz had lived, he might have bargained to better advantage; but he died after a short illness on February 5, 1795, and young Hardenberg was less able than he to hold his own against such redoubtable opponents as Barthélemy and Bacher. If Prince Henry's advice had been

<hr>

[36] *Ibid.* The instructions were dated December 18. Prussia was still trying to keep the negotiation secret, and was publicly and officially denying in other European capitals that any was in progress. See J. Q. Adams, Dispatch No. 10, December 10, 1794, from the Hague to the Secretary of State, Department of State, Washington, D. C.

[37] Fr. F. O., Corr. de Barthélemy, Pr. I, 107. The Prussian ministry knew by December 19 that the third partition of Poland had been agreed upon by Russia and Austria, it being understood that Prussia might take what was offered her (16,000 square miles as against 20,000 for Austria and 44,500 for Russia) with no right of protest. It was that or nothing. Von Sybel, III, 286.

[38] Von Sybel, III, 292.

followed throughout the negotiation, the treaty might have borne a closer resemblance to the one for which he had hoped; but his influence virtually died with his nominee, Baron Goltz. The direction of Prussian policy had again slipped from his hands.[39]

To tempt his nephew to go into the negotiation that led to the Treaty of Basel, the prince had held up before him a glorified picture of himself not only as king of Prussia but as "Pacificator of Europe" and protector of northern and western Germany. He had himself gone into that enterprise with very little expectation that it would lead at once to a general peace, but in the hope that Prussia might be able to serve as mediator for the smaller states and would at least make peace for herself on better terms than she could secure by further fighting.

Such advantages as Prussia was finally granted by the treaty signed on April 5, 1795, had been specified by the prince in all his memoranda on the subject as minimum demands upon which the Prussian envoys must insist at all costs. Among them were the provisions that the cession to France of Prussian territories west of the Rhine should be considered temporary and provisional only, pending a general pacification, and that the French troops would meanwhile respect a line of demarcation which left northern Germany open to Prussian control. Another was a secret clause providing that, if the Prussian possessions on the left bank were retained by France in the ultimate general settlement, Prussia was to find compensation on the right bank. Just how much that right of compensation by "mediatization" was to mean, he did not then say; but he had already said enough at various times to indicate that to him it meant the absorption by Prussia of such ecclesiastical states and perhaps other minor principalities as were conveniently located and seemed worth picking up.

He was disappointed in the outcome. If the business had been better handled, more could have been made out of it, he thought. But Prussia

[39] He could and did continue to draft one memorandum after another, but with diminishing results. A partial list of those not already mentioned follows:

"Observations ultérieures du Prince Henri sur la négociation d'une paix avec la France," December 9, 1794, in the Hausarchiv, Rep. 56, II, I.

"Exposé sur la médiation du Roi pour l'Empire, et des moyens qui paraissent les plus utiles pour la conduite de cette enterprise," January 1, 1795, *ibid.*

"Réflexions sur l'état présent des affaires," January 16, in the Staatsarchiv, XI, 89, 315; Hausarchiv, *loc. cit.*

"Réflexions," January 23, *ibid.*

"Projet qui peut servir d'instruction au Ct. de Goltz," January 26, *ibid.*

"Exposé sur la guerre et la paix," February 1, *ibid.*

"Declaration à toutes les puissances coalisées pour être insérée dans les gazettes," March 8, *ibid.*

Those published by Krauel, in *Prinz Heinrich als Politiker,* 205–212, are printed from the prince's retained drafts in the Hausarchiv, some in his own hand, some copied by Baron Münchhausen.

was freed from the danger of wars on two fronts at once; and he had always regarded Austria rather as a rival and potential enemy of Prussia than as an ally. The charge of bad faith meant nothing to him. Austria, he said, had shown but little loyalty to Prussia, and Britain had never shown any. If he had been accused of having deserted the German cause in the face of a rising "national" menace, he would scarcely have realized what his accuser meant. Neither he nor any of his German contemporaries had any conscious sense of German nationalism. As always, it was Prussia he served; and it was Prussia that he thought he had saved.

# CHAPTER XXVII

# A Voice Crying

*"Politically, my papers will prove that I have
done my duty."*— Henry to Ferdinand of Prussia.

PRINCE HENRY's active interest in politics, and particularly in international affairs, lasted as long as he lived; but his influence waned from the day of the death of Baron von der Goltz at Basel. Each year he spent less time in Berlin or Potsdam and more at Rheinsberg, Wusterhausen, and Teplitz, his personal participation in the direction of public policy being confined to the writing of another memorandum at every important turn of events and an occasional conference with the king or one of his ministers for discussion of the latest memorandum. Increasingly pessimistic about the good he was doing, he went on, as he said, "from a sense of duty, writing as a patriot for the good of the state," and retaining with an eye to history a copy of every memorandum and of nearly every important letter he wrote, so that his papers would ultimately clear him of the charge of having lived in Prussia through those years, seen such blunders made and such opportunities wasted, and kept silent.

The king was prodded by his uncle into publishing on May 1, 1795, a statement explaining to the other German princes his reasons for making the Peace of Basel; but it was longer and much more diffuse in its wording than the model the prince had submitted, so Henry was not pleased with it.[1]

In a memorandum "on the situation of Prussia in the present state of Europe," November 27, 1795, Prince Henry urged that Prussia seek not a formal alliance but a ministerial *rapprochement* with France, and an agreement upon a common policy as to the character of the general pacification of Germany. Prussia needed some such agreement, he argued, to protect her against the danger of being left isolated between Austria and Russia.[2]

[1] H. to Ferdinand of Prussia, May 15, in the Hausarchiv, Rep. 56, II, F.
[2] More than five years later, when what the prince had feared had come to pass, John Quincy Adams wrote from Berlin to the American secretary of state that, as both France and Russia fully realized that their friendship was much more vitally necessary to Prussia than hers was to them, she was unable to influence them. They did not find it necessary even to be courteous to her. Dispatch No. 184, March 7, 1801, United States Department of State.
While in Prussia Mr. Adams visited Prince Henry and reported that he was the most

The worst mistake a king of Prussia could make, the prince continued, would be to listen further to the French *émigrés*. They would convince him if they could that revolutionary France was weak; the prince warned him that it was incomparably stronger than the old regime had been; nor would it ever return to the *émigrés* their lands that it had seized. They were loyal neither to France nor to the old monarchy, he thought. All that any of them wanted was to regain the lands and the position he had lost. For those selfish purposes they were willing to keep all Europe at war, regardless of the true interests of the states that had sheltered and aided them.[3]

Another twenty years would pass, he thought in 1795, before the monarchy could be restored in France; and when the restoration did take place it would be on a constitutional basis. Twenty years would be a long time to wait. Then why not learn to live with the French Republic, induce the other west German states also to make peace with it, and find compensation east of the Rhine, by secularization and absorption of ecclesiastical states and principalities, for lands lost west of that river?[4]

In February, 1796, the prince's "reflections on what may happen in the course of another campaign, viewed politically," reminded the king that in considering such a question there was only one book to read — that of national interest. It was in the interest of France to be able to use Prussia as a counterweight against Russia, especially since Sweden was no longer strong enough to be useful for that purpose; so if France were handled right she could be made to strengthen Prussia. It was not in Russia's interest or in Austria's to build Prussia up; so they could be expected to tear her down if possible. France, moreover, was likely to win. Then why not conciliate her? Why tie oneself to a corpse?[5]

No alliance with Britain, and no guarantee of the integrity of Hanover, would ever have his sanction. The British would always fail their

intelligent and best-informed member of the royal family he had met, knowing more about America than the king and all his ministers combined.

[3] In gratitude for favors done him in France, he was himself still housing at considerable expense a number of troublesome exiles; but he drew a sharp distinction between the obligations of personal hospitality, which he readily recognized, and the political support which they expected but which he did not feel in any way bound to offer them. It was not until in June, 1797, that he finally rid himself of some of the most troublesome of them, Seguier, Madame de Sabran, and the Chevalier de Boufflers. "Leur rage mérite le guillotine," he wrote to his brother Ferdinand on August 19, 1795. Hausarchiv, Rep. 56, II, F.

[4] Hausarchiv, Rep. 56, II, I. The prince had no use for "the mannequin Louis XVIII." He wrote to Ferdinand in 1797 that it did not matter in the least whether Prussia recognized the pretender to the French throne, and in February, 1801, that Louis would be lucky if he got out of Russia without having to go on a little trip to Siberia to hunt black foxes.

[5] *Ibid.*

allies in the pinch as they had always done, and the people who trusted them would only find their trade ruined without territorial gain to compensate them for the loss. As for Hanover: "If I were king of Prussia, Hanover would be mine tomorrow; but the king is too timid and too scrupulous for a king."[6]

On June 10, 1796, attempting to establish a basis for the joint policy he so earnestly wished to see France and Prussia agree to follow, the politically minded prince turned from his own government to the French and submitted through its Berlin agent Parandier a long memorandum which specifically suggested many of the steps subsequently taken by the French at Loeben, Campo Formio, and Rastadt. France and Prussia, wrote Prince Henry, mutually supporting one another's demands, should compel the emperor to agree in advance to any aggrandizement that might come to Prussia as a result of the secularization of ecclesiastical states and the absorption of the lands of the Imperial knights in the reorganization of Germany for which France should have a free hand. Britain must lose Hanover, and both Britain and Russia should be excluded from any conference on German affairs. Austria should be given Salzburg and a better boundary in Bavaria. Imperial elector Dalberg might be given a principality elsewhere if he acquiesced in the loss of his old archbishopric of Mainz. Three new Protestant electorates should be created, to constitute a Protestant majority in the electoral college. The House of Hapsburg might even be deprived of the Imperial title (as it was, in 1806).[7]

It was not Prince Henry's fault that no interview with his own king followed immediately after that with Parandier. For a month he sought one, only to be told at last that the king was about to go to Pyrmont to "take the waters" for his health, and could not tax his strength at such a time by granting an interview. So he rewrote another long memorandum already prepared, shortening it as much as possible so that the reading of it would not fatigue the king unduly during his water cure, and sent it to Frederick William by way of Bischoffwerder. The proposals

[6] H. to Duke Charles of Brunswick, April 26, 1796, *ibid.;* Raymond Tabournel, "Le Prince Henri de Prusse et le Directoire, 1795–1802," *Revue des études historiques,* LXXIV (1908), 21.

[7] Von Sybel, IV, 246; Tabournel, "Le Prince Henri," 14–24, based on Parandier's report to Delacroix, French minister for foreign affairs, in the Fr. F. O., Prusse, vol. 219, p. 152, and Archives Nationales, A. F., III, 76, dossier 315. On his return from an eight-day visit at Rheinsberg, Parandier described Prince Henry as "the first general in Germany." Although without political influence, according to his French visitor, he still had clearer ideas as to policy than anyone else in Prussia, combining the head and the vivacity of thirty with the experience of seventy-two. Talleyrand, Delacroix's successor, sent the prince on behalf of the Directory an elaborately ornamented pair of pistols with letter to match.

he made therein were substantially the same as those he had already made to the French Directory for a preliminary Franco-Prussian agreement as to the general character of the prospective reconstitution of Germany, and for a whole new system of alliances. It was his hope that a Franco-Prussian alliance, to be secretly planned in advance but to become effective only after the general pacification, might eventually be expanded to include Denmark and Sweden, and then be directed against Russia. As to the possible durability of such an alignment, he assured the king in an accompanying letter that the French Revolution might for all practical purposes be presumed to be permanent. An alliance would in any case endure just as long as both parties found it advantageous, and would be broken as soon as either found it hurtful.[8]

On August 7, 1796, France and Prussia signed a publicly announced treaty establishing a line of demarcation between areas occupied by their troops in Westphalia, and along with it a secret agreement looking forward to the remaking of the map of southwestern Germany along the lines recently suggested to both governments by Prince Henry. In the cooperation with France promised by that secret treaty, the prince thought he saw a golden opportunity for Prussia to add to her territory, regain her lost prestige, and lift herself into a position of preponderance among the German states such as she had never yet attained. If the king and his ministers let that opportunity slip, "no good citizen could keep silent."[9]

Thinking as he did that what hurt Austria would eventually help Prussia "if the fools in Berlin knew how to take advantage of it," the prince watched with all the interest of a nonbelligerent ally while Napoleon for the first time pushed the Austrians out of northern Italy. Duke Charles of Brunswick was amazed at Austria's defeat. Future gen-

[8] H. to Haugwitz, June 20, and to Bischoffwerder, June 24 and July 11, in the Staatsarchiv, Rep. 92, B, VI, 10; memorandum and letter to the king, in the Hausarchiv, Rep. 56, II, I. It was really too bad, wrote the prince to Bischoffwerder on July 11, to have to work in such underground fashion without knowing whether any of his suggestions would be adopted. He should have been permitted to explain his "great plan" orally, instead of having to present it in such an abridged form in writing. What was the use? Who knew that, even if it were accepted, his plan would not be bungled in its execution or abandoned when half finished as the negotiations at Basel had been?

To Baron Münchhausen on July 8 he had already answered his own question. He was worn out, he complained, from copying a memorandum on six pages of "long paper"; but, if others by their foolish blunders failed to carry out his recommendations, *his own papers would vindicate him* by showing that what he had recommended had been right and reasonable. Staatsarchiv, *loc. cit.* (The italics are the author's.)

[9] H. to Haugwitz, September 6, in the Staatsarchiv, *loc. cit.* See also von Sybel, IV, 247. Other memoranda submitted by the prince by way of "follow-up" were "On France and Russia," March 1, and "Reflections on the present situation of Europe," March 2, 1797. Their principal arguments were that, although the Russian alliance had been profitable to Frederick in its first fifteen years, there existed no longer any real community of interest between Russia and Prussia. Hausarchiv, *loc. cit.*

erations, he wrote, would find it incredible that Germany with her splendid armies had been so helpless in the face of the inexperienced generals and hastily raised conscript levies of France; but he recognized by August 10 that France needed "only a leader — a Richelieu or a Mazarin" — to make her again a menace to the peace of Europe.[10]

Prince Henry was neither surprised nor displeased by Bonaparte's early successes, seeing in the Peace of Campo Formio and later in the French plans for the Congress of Rastadt merely the fulfillment of the memorandum he had handed to Parandier in June, 1796. The profitable peace for which he had worked so long was, he thought, about to come to pass; and he was glad. All would yet be well! [11]

Another reason for the prince's optimism after November, 1797, was that Prussia again had a new king — and a queen. Frederick William III was a more attractive man than his father had been, and his great-uncle had more confidence in him. He was destined to go through dark days as king, but Prince Henry did not know that and fortunately did not live to see it. At the beginning of the reign he saw only a new king, one of sound character and unquestioned patriotism, cognizant of his responsibilities whether equal to them or not, coming to the throne at a moment when great opportunities as well as great dangers lay immediately before him. As Prince and Princess of Prussia, Frederick William and Louise had asked him two years before to be godfather to their infant son, and his relations with them had always been pleasant. They continued to be pleasant — but only that.

The incomparable queen Louise was so attractive and so kind to him, and her flaming patriotism so won his admiration, that he could almost have forgiven her — though he did not quite — for taking such an active interest in public affairs. Frederick William, he was sure, was an honest — that is, a devoted — king. Both treated him always with the greatest possible personal consideration, preserving and honoring him as a sort of living monument to a glorious period of Prussia's past, the dauntless spirit of which they hoped to revive. For him, as one French observer remarked, posterity had already begun; but, with the exception of the king and queen and Ferdinand's children, most of the younger generation found him too old, too eccentric, too critical, and too dictatorial to be listened to for long. His political influence continued to diminish. He had become, so to speak, a living legend.

[10] Charles to H., July 28, August 10, in the Hausarchiv, *loc. cit.* Apparently the duke had not yet noticed Napoleon, nor realized that those youthful French generals were gaining experience with every campaign through which he sat as an idle spectator, learning nothing. A more tragic surprise was in store for him at Jena.

[11] Letters to Ferdinand and Münchhausen, in the Hausarchiv, *loc. cit.*

True to his own tradition, however, he continued to express his opinions as freely as ever, and to record them in his own peculiar fashion by retaining copies of the memoranda by which he sought to induce the government to implement them. His comments on Russia, and on his former friend Paul who had become emperor when Catherine died, were more and more caustic. It would have been better for Prussia, he thought, to work for a reconstituted Poland than to let Russia retain the enormous territory she had annexed in the second and third partitions. A buffer state there would be useful; direct contact with Russia was uncomfortable. Russia's share in the victories of the second coalition in northern Italy in 1799 convinced him anew of her restless ambition to play a major part in European affairs, but did not shake his conviction that her military prowess had always been greatly overestimated. The Russians, he insisted, had been stopped before and could be stopped again either by Frenchmen or by Prussians — by anyone, in fact, who was not paralyzed by fear of them. As for Czar Paul, he was a fool. His head would make an excellent weather vane for a church spire; it turned with every change of wind.[12]

While Napoleon, after his return from Egypt, planned and fought in 1800 the campaigns that destroyed the second coalition, the Prussian government sought steadily, as it had done since August, 1796, to realize as a neutral the advantages which Prince Henry had promised would be the first fruits of an alliance with France. Neutrality did not suit the prince. It was unfruitful, unnatural, and dangerous, he wrote to the king. Unfruitful because in such a period of general upheaval a state could get only what it was strong enough to take, and Prussia was still weak; no one feared her, because she was known to be "afraid of war." Unnatural because, with its most vital interests obviously involved, no state could pretend to be uninterested in the outcome of any of the wars then being waged or about to be waged all around it. Dangerous because of the persistent enmity of Russia and Austria, and because Prussia's neutrality would prolong the war while an alliance with France might shorten it. It was merely a matter of national interest. What was an alliance,

[12] Kalckreuth, *Paroles,* 354 *et passim.* Kalckreuth, by combining political and military talents and activities, had become one of Prussia's foremost soldiers. Finding him prominent enough to be potentially useful, and hoping to learn what he could from any indiscreet disclosure his former adjutant might be led to make, the prince had taken the initiative in effecting a reconciliation. H. to Kalckreuth, July 2 and 17, 1795, *ibid.,* 336, and to Ferdinand of Prussia, July 3, in the Hausarchiv, Rep. 56, II, F.

Kalckreuth's *Paroles* were written after his dismissal from Prince Henry's service but before the reconciliation, so deal with the prince's reputation no more charitably than Mirabeau's *Histoire secrète.* His narrative ends with the events of 1764 and 1765, so sheds no light on his contribution to the troubles of the princess Henry or on his own career thereafter.

*The "Shell Room" at Rheinsberg,*
*the decorations of which date from 1763 or 1764*

*The Room at Rheinsberg in Which Prince Henry Died*

realistically viewed, that the king of Prussia should stand in awe of the very word itself? An alliance was nothing more than a formal recognition of the fact that the nations making it had, when it was made, certain interests in common. It did not and could not create those common interests; it merely stated and sanctioned them. When they ceased to give it life, it died. Thus the old alliance with Austria had died, whether denounced or not; thus a new one with France would endure while it justified itself. Longer than that no one would wish it to endure.

Finally, argued the prince who had once faced the Russians on the Polish frontier for a whole summer and yet survived, Prussia could never again by a negative policy of neutrality keep Russia out of Prussian Poland or out of German affairs. If the Hapsburg emperor preferred a Russian alliance and a continued war to a general German peace, let him have them; but France and Prussia ought then to form an allied front against him. With France to hold Austria in check, Prussia could deal with Russia on even terms, diplomatically or if necessary on the field of battle. She would be feared again when she ceased to be afraid.[18]

The alliance that the old prince wanted was never made. The audacity that he remembered from Frederick's day and to which he paid perhaps unconscious tribute by recommending it to Frederick's faint-hearted successors, forgetting how often he had criticized it in the old bold one himself, seemed too dangerous. A certain deference to Austria, which Henry could never understand, was still shown by the Prussian king and by some of his ministers. Although less aware than he of the hurricane strength of the winds blowing over Europe out of France, the men whom he sought vainly to counsel were more afraid than he to try to sail with those winds to glory. In the last two years of his life he resigned his position as volunteer — and unwelcome — navigator and weather prognosticator, and let himself drop out of sight in his quiet backwater at Rheinsberg.

The old warrior's last years resembled the calm after the storm. Distinguished guests still sought him out — Sieyès in 1798, who went away marveling at the clarity of his mind and the purity of his language; Lord and Lady Holland in 1800, sharing with him his hatred of Pitt; Louis Bonaparte in 1801, who was surprised by his iconoclastic remarks about the military genius of the great Frederick; but no guest, however prominent in his own sphere, disturbed seriously or for long Rheinsberg's regular routine.

[18] H. to Frederick William III — extract in the French Archives Nationales, Relations Extérieures, Prusse, 1792–An VIII.

Many things which had once infuriated Prince Henry seemed less important as he looked back at them from the vantage point of seventy-five. Great men and great events appeared smaller in historical perspective. Wars were still made as always by unprincipled rogues to satisfy their selfish ambitions, and won by the valor of soldiers who had not made them; but when wars and warriors had done their worst the rivers still ran downhill to the sea. National boundaries might be altered now and then, but the land and the peoples remained; and only the land and the peoples were, in the last analysis, important.[14]

Only friendship mattered to the lonely prince as much as it had done when he was young. He had long since composed his old quarrels with his former adjutants Kalckreuth and Henckel von Donnersmarck, and was still supporting the latter's widow, son, and daughter. No son of an an old army officer who had once served with him was ever refused any help that he could give. "His uncle was my friend and his father was a brave and gallant soldier" was the only reason he gave for asking Ferdinand to employ an admittedly worthless applicant, and it was considered sufficient.

Ancient grudges were permitted to die for want of sustenance. The embers of his wrath against his wife still glowed occasionally, when fanned by some new incident, but that fire too had burned itself out. He was grateful to others for any kindness shown his wife, and was himself more considerate of her wishes than formerly, especially after learning that she had openly taken his side in a quarrel with Haugwitz; but when "the good old queen" Elizabeth Christina's will revealed her wish that her palace at Schönhausen should go to the princess Henry after her death, he refused to pay for the maintenance of another palace. He no longer took the trouble to hate the princess, but he took no step toward a reconciliation and made no attempt to undo what had been done. The quarrel was not worth maintaining, but the marriage was not worth mending.

The person who meant most to him in his last years was his nephew Louis Ferdinand, one of the sons of Prince Ferdinand. That high-spirited and attractive but rather turbulent youth was a constant puzzle to his parents, who were scandalized by his extravagance and his escapades; but his uncle Henry was always ready to defend him, to help him pay off his debts, to explain that "vivacity" was a virtue in youth although it might be called folly by the young man's aged parents. Louis Ferdinand, he once wrote, was a genius and must not be subjected to a too

---

[14] H. to Kalckreuth, January 2, 1801, in *Paroles*, 356.

rigid discipline. He could remember that he had himself been a rebel in his youth.[15]

Louis Ferdinand was an impulsive youth, often unmanageable but easily imposed upon, and not much wiser in his choice of companions than his indulgent old uncle had been when he was young; but he knew enough to appreciate and to reciprocate the sympathy, understanding, and affection with which he was invariably greeted at Rheinsberg. Their common devotion to Prince Henry was almost the only thing he and his father had in common. Prince Henry, for his part, doted upon his nephew and made no secret of the fact that he looked upon him as his son and heir.

In June, 1802, Prince Henry permitted the fiftieth anniversary of his marriage to pass unnoticed. Only a few days before, he had entertained at a grand festival in celebration of his brother Ferdinand's recent recovery from an illness, and his guests had departed without noting any unusual sign of ill health in their host himself, although an apoplectic stroke in the previous December had left its mark upon him.

At the end of July he suffered another attack. With the finger of death upon him and with his own hand barely able to hold the pen, physical disability evident in every line, he scrawled a last message to his grand-nephew the king:

From Rheinsberg for the third of August, 1802.

Sire: I wish Your Majesty all happiness and contentment for your birthday. My health, which is a little deranged, has scarcely permitted me to scrawl four words of my love, being perfectly, Sire

Your Majesty's
completely devoted and faithful
servant and affectionate
uncle Henri.[16]

Two days later he was dead. Death came swiftly and mercifully, as he wished it to come. "I like attacks that make an end quickly," he had said. "I have no mind for the sort that only set you making grimaces, and I should hate to have them call me 'the idiot of Rheinsberg.' " Afraid that his medicine would keep him alive but leave him helpless, he looked at it and threw it away, remarking, "I do not choose to live on as an imbecile." [17]

---

[15] H. to Ferdinand, April 4, 1797, in the Hausarchiv, *loc. cit.*

[16] A facsimile is printed by Krauel with his "Prinz Heinrich von Preussen in Rheinsberg," in the *Hohenzollern Jahrbücher*, VI (1902), 34.

[17] Oral report of Prince Louis Ferdinand, who said he had been watching, unseen. Princess Anton Radziwill, *Forty-five Years of My Life*, 196, 200.

Louis Ferdinand and his sister, Princess Radziwill, had hurried to Rheinsberg as soon as they were notified of Henry's illness, and were there when he died. They and their brother August were the only members of the family present when the servants, following faithfully the detailed instructions found in the envelope with his will, carried him across the footbridge to the simple pyramidal brick tomb already built amid the trees a hundred yards from the Schloss. He had asked that he be buried in uniform — an old one. One simple wreath lay on the coffin, a tribute from his niece Louise, Princess Radziwill. Old Ferdinand was ill again and could not come. The court and army wore mourning for the usual fourteen days, and a memorial musical service — which Prince Henry would have appreciated much more than the official mourning — was held in the garrison church on September 16.[18]

Much of the property and the revenue the prince had been privileged to use during his lifetime was not his to bequeath to anyone. His Berlin palace reverted to the state, so was available for the use of the Friedrich Wilhelm University, more commonly called the University of Berlin, when that institution was founded in 1810. Rheinsberg and some allodial lands purchased out of income or inherited under the will of Frederick William I were to go to Louis Ferdinand; but Ferdinand was given a life interest in them, and his son died in battle at Saalfeld without coming into his inheritance.

A life income for the princess Henry had already been provided. In his will, rewritten apparently some years before his death and added to from time to time thereafter, her husband said of her: "I entertain no feeling of hatred for the princess my wife; reason and circumstances painful to me have forced me to live apart from her. I renounce all unpleasant memory and wish for her peace and everything good that in her old age she can still enjoy."[19]

All his servants were generously though unequally rewarded. Three thousand thaler were to be set aside for a school for children of officers of his regiment.

His decorations were to be returned to the governments that had given them to him: the Order of the Black Eagle to the king of Prussia, the Order of St. Andrew to Russia, and the Order of St. Seraphim to

---

[18] *Ibid.*, 202–204; Tabournel, "Le Prince Henri," 40; Krauel, "Prinz Heinrich in Rheinsberg," 13, 24. The prince had jokingly ordered while the tomb was being built that he should be buried facing the Schloss, so as always to be able to watch what went on there. In his written instructions he directed that his body should not "lie in state"; he refused, he said, to have people tormented by being required to view such an ugly inanimate thing as a corpse.

[19] Krauel, "Prinz Heinrich in Rheinsberg," 17.

Sweden. His books and papers he bequeathed to the last of his aides, Count de la Roche-Aymon; but they were taken over by the government.

It was about his sword that the soldier prince who had so disliked soldiering cared most at the end, because it symbolized his greatest and most generally recognized patriotic service. "The sword which I carried in the Seven Years' War," he wrote in the instructions that supplemented his will, "shall be put into the hands of the count de la Roche-Aymon. I ask that he go and find the king immediately after my burial to assure him of my last prayers for him and for the state, and to give him my sword, asking him in my name to have it preserved as a reminder of the fidelity with which I have served the state." [20]

He had written his own epitaph and had it ready, cut into the marble slab that closed the door of his tomb:

Thrown by his birth into the cloud of empty smoke that the vulgar call glory and grandeur but of which the wise know the emptiness; a prey to all the ills of humanity, tormented by the passions of others and made restless by his own, exposed often to calumny, the butt of injustice, and further afflicted by the loss of cherished relatives and trustworthy and faithful friends; but equally often consoled by friendship, happy in the recollection of his thoughts; happier when his services could be useful to his country or to suffering humanity: such is the short story of the life of Frederic Henri Louis, son of Frederick William king of Prussia and of Sophia Dorothea, daughter of George I king of Great Britain.

Passer-by! Remember that perfection is not found on the earth. If I have not been able to be the best of men, I am at least not to be numbered among the wicked. Neither praise nor blame can further touch him who rests in eternity; but the gentle Hope brightens the last moments of him who does his duty; she is with me as I die.[21]

Fifteen days after the prince's death the *Königliche privilegierte Berlinische Zeitung von Staats- und gelehrten Sachen* published the following tribute:

*An die Humanität,*
*Als der Prinz Heinrich den 3ten August 1802*
*gestorben war*

*Humanität, setz' Ihm ein Monument und drauf:*
*Im Schlachtfelde und in Kabinette*
*That er, was ich gethan, an seiner Stelle, hätte:*
*Das ist sein Lebenslauf.*

---

[20] *Ibid.;* Henckel von Donnersmarck, *Briefe*, 13. The sword was ultimately placed in the Hohenzollern Museum in Schloss Monbijou in Berlin.
[21] Tabournel, "Le Prince Henri," 41; Henckel von Donnersmarck, *Briefe*, 14.

*Die Muse Polyhymnia,*
*Die seine Freundin war,*
*Und die ihn sterben sah,*
*Die Sprach gerührt:*
*"Den zweiten Einzigen verliert*
*In Ihm Borussia!"* [22]

Ferdinand used fewer words for it than that: "Il a tout fait pour l'État." [23]

Six years earlier Prince Henry, in a letter to Haugwitz, had without realizing it written himself a less self-conscious and far better epitaph: [24]

In writing you this letter I am doing what honor prescribes for me so as to have proof in my possession of having left nothing undone up to the last moment for the happy outcome of an affair so important, . . . which may prove to be the basis of the welfare or the ruin of the state. It is as an honest citizen that I write to you, for if I were not one nothing could ever have made me, a prince, work so in obscurity to which I was not at all accustomed after having been not only employed but consulted by the late king in affairs of the greatest importance. No matter! I have done my duty; and one day, when all is known and I am no more, Prussia shall be my judge.

Prussia might well have judged him more kindly than she has done.

[22] Tabournel, "Le Prince Henri," 40.
[23] On a bust by Houdon, then in Ferdinand's palace "Bellevue," in Berlin.
[24] H. to Haugwitz, September 6, 1796, in the Staatsarchiv, Rep. 92, B, IV, 10.

*Exit filius patriae fidelis.*

BIBLIOGRAPHY
AND INDEX

# BIBLIOGRAPHY

## SOURCE MATERIALS

### MANUSCRIPTS

BRITISH MUSEUM. The Prussian correspondence of Sir Andrew Mitchell with the British ministers and with Prince Henry. Additional Manuscripts 6804–6871, 11260–11262 (Volumes I–LXVIII).

ARCHIVES NATIONALES, FRANCE. Originals of the correspondence of Bacher and Barthélemy concerning the negotiation of the treaty of Basel. Originals or extracts of several of Prince Henry's memoranda on Franco-Prussian relations.

ARCHIVES DU MINISTÈRE DES AFFAIRES ÉTRANGÈRES, FRANCE. Copies of French and Prussian diplomatic correspondence concerning Prince Henry's two visits to Paris and the negotiation of the treaty of Basel, including instructions from the Committee of Public Safety to Bacher and Barthélemy.

BRANDENBURG-PREUSSISCHES HAUSARCHIV, BERLIN-CHARLOTTENBURG. Prince Henry's correspondence with his brother Ferdinand, King Frederick William II, Catherine II of Russia, Duke Charles of Brunswick, the ministers Haugwitz and Struensee, Baron von Münchhausen, and others; many of his political memoranda; correspondence of the princess Henry.

GEHEIMES PREUSSISCHES STAATSARCHIV, BERLIN-DAHLEM. Prince Henry's correspondence with Frederick II not published in the *Politische Correspondenz Friedrichs des Grossen* and with Frederick William II and his ministers; other political correspondence of both kings and their ministers.

### PUBLISHED CORRESPONDENCE, DIARIES, MEMOIRS, ETC.

BERNER, ERNST, AND GUSTAVE B. VOLZ. *Aus der Zeit des siebenjährigen Krieges. Tagebuchblätter der prinzessin Heinrich und des königlichen Hauses (Quellen und Untersuchungen zur Geschichte des Hauses Hohenzollern*, Vol. IX). Berlin, 1908. Princess Henry's diary, a number of her letters, and some of Queen Elizabeth Christina's correspondence.

BIELFELD, BARON JAKOB FRIEDRICH. *Lettres familières et autres.* 2 vols. The Hague, 1763. Personalities and other trivialities of Prussian court life.

BISSET, ANDREW, ed. *Memoirs and Papers of Sir Andrew Mitchell, K. B.* 2 vols. London, 1850.

CAROLINE, LANDGRÄFIN VON HESSEN. *Briefwechsel der "Grossen Landgräfin" Caroline von Hessen. Dreissig Jähren eines fürstlichen Frauenlebens. Nach den im grossherzoglichen Hausarchiv zu Darmstadt befindlichen Papieren herausgegeben,* edited by A. F. Walther. 2 vols. Vienna, 1877.

FREDERICK II. *Politische Correspondenz Friedrichs des Grossen,* edited by Gustav B. Volz and Others. 46 vols. Oldenburg-Berlin, 1879–1939. Covers the period ending with March, 1782. Principally letters and dispatches written by Frederick, but the content of those written to him is often indicated by excerpts or summaries, especially since Dr. Volz took over the editorship-in-chief with Volume XXV. Some such letters are printed in full. See Professor Walter L. Dorn's article, written on the death of Dr. Volz, in the *American Historical Review,* XLV (1939–40), 469–470.

HENCKEL VON DONNERSMARCK, LEO AMADEUS, GRAF. *Briefe der Brüder Friedrichs des Grossen an meine Grosseltern.* Berlin, 1877.

HENRY, PRINCE OF PRUSSIA. "Considérations sur la guerre de sept ans," edited by Raymond Tabournel. *Revue des études historiques,* 1902, pp. 5–26.

HENRY, PRINCE OF PRUSSIA (pseudonym Maréchal Gessler). "Mémoire sur la situation présente de sa Majesté Prussienne, par le Maréchal Gessler du 19 Novembre 1753,"

# Prince Henry of Prussia

edited by O. Herrmann. *Forschungen zur brandenburgischen und preussischen Geschichte (F. B. P. G.)*, XXXIV (1922), 246–264.

HORDT, COMTE JOHANN LUDWIG DE. *Mémoires du comte de Hordt, gentilhomme suédois, lieutenant-général des armées de Sa Majesté Prussienne, écrits par lui-même.* 2 vols. Berlin and Paris, 1789. Useful chiefly for his account of Prince Henry's Swedish and Russian missions.

LEHNDORFF, REICHSGRAF ERNST V. *Dreissig Jahre am Hofe Friedrichs des Grossen. Aus den Tagebüchern des Reichsgrafen Ernst Ahaseurus Heinrich von Lehndorff, Kammerherrn der Königin Elizabeth Christine von Preussen,* edited by Karl Eduard Schmidt-Lötzen. Gotha, 1907.

————*Nachträge.* Gotha, 1910.

OPPELN-BRONIKOWSKI, FRIEDRICH, AND G. B. VOLZ. *Gespräche Friedrichs des Grossen.* Berlin, 1919.

RADZIWILL, PRINCESS ANTON (Princess Louise of Prussia). *Forty-five Years of My Life,* edited by Princess Radziwill, *née* Castellane, translated by A. R. Allison, M. A. New York, 1912.

## ARTICLES

BERNER, ERNST. "Die Brautfahrt des Prinzen Heinrich von Preussen." *Hohenzollern Jahrbücher,* VIII (1904), 75ff.

DORN, WALTER L. "Frederick the Great and Lord Bute." *Journal of Modern History,* I (1929), 529–560.

DUNBAR, LOUISE BURNHAM. "A Study of 'Monarchical' Tendencies in the United States." *University of Illinois Studies in Social Science,* Vol. X, No. 1. 1923.

FITTE, SIEGFRIED. "Prinz Heinrich und die deutsche Litteratur." *Vossische Zeitung,* January 19, 1896.

HERRMANN, OTTO. "Eine Beurteilung Friedrichs des Grossen aus dem Jahre 1753." *F. B. P. G.,* XXXIV (1922), 239–264.

————"Zur Beurteilung des Prinzen Heinrich von Preussen als Feldherrn." *Jahrbücher für die deutsche Armée und Marine,* No. 554–555 (1917).

————"Friedrich der Grosse im Spiegel seines Bruders Heinrich." *Historische Vierteljahrschrift,* XXVI (1931), 365–379.

————"Prinz Ferdinand von Preussen über den Feldzug vom Jahre 1757." *F. B. P. G.,* XXXI (1919), 85–105.

JANY, CURT. "Der siebenjährige Krieg. Ein Schlusswort zum Generalstabswerk." *F. B. P. G.,* XXXV (1923), 161–192.

KOSER, REINHOLD. "Prinz Heinrich und Generalleutnant von Möllendorff im bayerischen Erbfolgekrieg." *F. B. P. G.,* XXIII (1910), 187–204.

————"Die preussische Kriegführung im siebenjährigen Krieg." *Historische Zeitschrift,* XCII (1904), 239–273.

————"Unterhaltungen mit Friedrich dem Grossen. Memoiren und Tagebücher von Heinrich de Catt." *Publikationen aus den königlichen preussischen Staatsarchiven,* XXII (1884).

KRAUEL, RICHARD. "Briefe des Prinzen Heinrich von Preussen an die Königin Louise Ulrike, Gustav III, und die Prinzessin Sophie Albertine von Schweden, 1771–1797." *F. B. P. G.,* XVI (1903), 207–250.

————*Briefwechsel zwischen Heinrich von Preussen und Katherina II von Russland, 1770–1780 (Quellen und Untersuchungen zur Geschichte des Hauses Hohenzollern,* Vol. VIII). Berlin, 1903.

————"Original Briefe Friedrichs des Grossen, des Prinzen Heinrich, und der Prinzessin Amalie von Preussen an die Herzogin Charlotte von Braunschweig." *F. B. P. G.,* XIII (1900), 377–404.

————"Prince Henry of Prussia and the Regency of the United States." *American Historical Review,* XVII (1911–12), 44–51.

382

# Bibliography

————"Prinz Heinrich von Preussen in Rheinsberg." *Hohenzollern Jahrbücher*, VI (1902), 12–37.

LARIVIÈRE, CHEVALIER DE. "Le Prince Henri de Prusse à Paris en 1784 et en 1788." *Revue politique et littéraire*, 4ᵉ Serie, XVI (1901), 334–340, 393–398.

MAMLOCK, G. L. "Krankheit und Tod des Prinzen August Wilhelms, des Bruders Friedrichs des Grossen." *F. B. P. G.*, XVII (1904), 574–580.

MASCHKE, E. "Friedrich der Grosse und Prinz Heinrich von Preussen." *Jahrbücher für die deutsche Armée und Marine*, CXVII (1900), 66–86, 192–216, 276–298.

NAUDÉ, ALBERT. "Berichte des Prinzen Moritz von Anhalt-Dessau über die Schlachten bei Prag, Kollin, Rossbach, Leuthen, und Zorndorf." *F. B. P. G.*, V (1892), 232–245.

————"Aus ungedruckten Memoiren der Brüder Friedrichs des Grossen." *F. B. P. G.* I (1888), 221–269.

ROSE, J. HOLLAND. "Frederick the Great and England, 1756–1763." *English Historical Review*, XXIX (1914), 79–93, 256–275.

ROTHFELS, HANS. "Friedrich der Grosse in den Krisen des siebenjährigen Krieges." *Historische Zeitschrift*, CXXXIV (1926), 14–30.

SCHÄFER, ARNOLD. "Französische Friedensanträge an Preussen vom Jahre 1758." *Historische Zeitschrift*, XXI (1869), 112–124.

STUPPERICH, ROBERT. "Die zweite Reise des Prinzen Heinrich nach Petersburg." *Jahrbuch für Geschichte Osteuropas*, III (1938), 580–600.

TABOURNEL, RAYMOND. "Les Derniers Volontés du Prince Henri de Prusse." *Revue des études historiques*, LXIX (1903), 156–161.

————"Le Prince Henri de Prusse et le Directoire, 1795–1802." *Revue des études historiques*, LXXIV (1908), 5–41.

————"La Reine Louise et le prince Henri de Prusse." *Revue des études historiques*, LXXI (1905), 46–59.

VOLZ, GUSTAV B. "Friedrich der Grosse und die erste Teilung Polens." *F. B. P. G.*, XXIII (1910), 71–143, 225–226.

————"Der Plan einer Mitregentschaft des Prinzen Heinrich." *Hohenzollern Jahrbücher*, XX (1916).

————"Prinz Heinrich als Kritiker Friedrichs des Grossen." *Sonderabdruck, Historische Vierteljahrschrift*, XXVII (1932), 390–400.

————"Prinz Heinrich von Preussen und die preussische Politik vor der ersten Teilung Polens." *F. B. P. G.*, XVIII (1905), 150–188.

————"Prinz Heinrich von Preussen und die polnische Krone." *F. B. P. G.*, XVIII (1905), 188–201.

————"Prinz Heinrich und die Vorgeschichte der ersten Teilung Polens." *F. B. P. G.*, XXXV (1923), 193–211.

————"Das rheinsberger Protokoll vom 29 Oktober, 1740." *F. B. P. G.*, XXIX (1916), 67–93.

————"Die *Vie privée* und die ältere Literatur über den Prinzen Heinrich von Preussen." *F. B. P. G.*, XIX (1906), 423–462.

## BOOKS

ANONYMOUS. *Anekdoten, Charakterzüge, und Kriegsfahrten aus dem Leben des Prinzen Heinrich von Preussen.* Göttingen, 1803. Of practically no scientific value. Much of it merely a translation of Guyton de Morveau's unreliable *Vie privée d'un prince célèbre.*

————*Paul Petrowitz . . . und Prinz Heinrich von Preussen, und der Reise von St. Petersburg bis Berlin im Jahre 1776.* Riga, *ca.* 1777. Detailed description of processions, entertainments, etc.

ARNETH, ALFRED VON. *Geschichte Maria Theresias.* 10 vols. Vienna, 1863–1879. Volumes V and VI deal with the Seven Years' War.

# Prince Henry of Prussia

BERNHARDI, THEODOR VON. *Friedrich der Grosse als Feldherr.* 2 vols. Berlin, 1881. Available also in English translation. Based on the military *Nachlass* of Count Henckel von Donnersmarck and on Schöning (*q.v.*). Extremely critical of Prince Henry.

BÖTHLING, GERHARD. *Friedrich der Grosse und sein Bruder Heinrich in ihren Verhältnis als Feldherren.* Halle, 1929. Doctoral dissertation at Jena. Stresses their differences.

BOUILLÉ, JOSEPH L. A., MARQUIS DE. *La Vie privée, politique, et militaire du Prince Henri de Prusse.* Paris, 1809. Strongly partisan in praise of Prince Henry. Formerly attributed to de la Roche-Aymon.

BÜLOW, ADAM HEINRICH DIETRICH VON. *Prinz Heinrich von Preussen, kritische Geschichte seiner Feldzüge.* 2 vols. Berlin, 1805. Critical only of the king. Says that it was Henry, not Frederick, who "saved the Prussian monarchy."

CROUSAZ, H. VON. *Prinz Heinrich, der Bruder Friedrichs des Grossen.* Berlin, 1876. A laudatory memorial pamphlet.

DORN, WALTER L. *Competition for Empire.* New York and London, 1940. Indispensable for its discussion of the Prussian military and administrative systems, as well as for its brief account of the Seven Years' War.

ELDON, CARL WILLIAM. *England's Subsidy Policy towards the Continent during the Seven Years' War.* Philadelphia, 1938. Doctoral dissertation, University of Pennsylvania.

FAY, SYDNEY B. *The Rise of Brandenburg-Prussia to 1786.* New York, 1937.

FREDERICK II. *Oeuvres de Frédéric le Grand.* 30 vols. Berlin, 1846–1856. There are several editions.

GRANTHAM, A. E. *Rococo: Life and Times of Prince Henry of Prussia.* London, 1938. Devoted principally to the social diversions and literary and other cultural interests of the prince and his contemporaries.

DER GROSSE GENERALSTAB, KRIEGSGESCHICHTLICHE ABTEILUNG III. *Der siebenjährige Krieg.* 13 vols. Berlin, 1901–1914. Covers the period to the end of 1760.

GUYTON DE MORVEAU. *La Vie privée d'un prince célèbre, ou détails des loisirs du Prince Henri de Prusse dans sa retraite à Rheinsberg.* Berlin, 1784. Only a panegyric, but used by most of the others of the prince's early biographers. Prince Henry also had his Parson Weems.

HAMILTON, ANDREW. *Rheinsberg: Memorials of Frederick the Great and Prince Henry of Prussia.* 2 vols. London, 1880. Available also in German translation.

HEIDENSTAM, O. G. DE. *Une Soeur du grand Frédéric, Louise Ulrique, reine de Suède.* Paris, 1897.

HENCKEL VON DONNERSMARCK, GRAF VICTOR AMADEUS. *Militärische Nachlass.* 2 vols. Leipzig, 1858. Second edition. Valuable for chronological account of troop movements; unreliable on personal relationship between Henry and Frederick.

HENNERT, KARL WILHELM. *Beschreibung des Lustschlosses und Gartens Sr. Königl. Hoheit des Prinzen Heinrichs, Bruders des Königs, zu Rheinsberg.* Berlin, 1778.

JANY, CURT. *Geschichte der Königlichen Preussischen Armee bis zum Jahre 1807.* 3 vols. Berlin, 1929. Volume III covers the War of the Bavarian Succession.

KALCKREUTH, FRIEDRICH ADOLF. *Paroles du Feldmaréchal Kalckreuth.* Paris, 1844(?). Full of malicious gossip about both Henry and Frederick.

KOSER, REINHOLD. *Geschichte Friedrichs des Grossen.* Leipzig, 1884. 4 vols. in 3, Stuttgart, 1912–1914. Unsurpassed.

————*Aus dem Leben Friedrichs des Grossen. Denkwürdige Worte des Königs, mit kurzer Erzählung seiner Thaten.* Stuttgart and Berlin, 1916.

————*Zur preussischen und deutschen Geschichte; Aufsätze und Vorträge.* Stuttgart, 1921.

KRAUEL, RICHARD. *Prinz Heinrich von Preussen in Paris während der Jahre 1784 und 1788–1789.* Berlin, 1901.

————*Prinz Heinrich von Preussen als Politiker* (*Quellen und Untersuchungen zur Geschichte des Hauses Hohenzollern,* Bd. IV, Reihe III). Berlin, 1902.

# Bibliography

LONGMAN, F. W. *Frederick the Great.* London, 1917.

MIRABEAU, HONORÉ. *Histoire secrète de la cour de Berlin,* edited by Henri Welschinger. Paris, 1900.

OELRICHS, J. H. C. *Ausführliche Beschreibung der Reise des Grossfürsten Paul Petrowitz von St. Petersburg an den Kgl. Preussischen Hof.* Berlin, 1776.

PAULIG, F. R. *Friedrich der Grosse, König von Preussen. Neue Beiträge zur Geschichte seines Privatlebens, seines Hofes, und seiner Zeit* (Paulig's Familiengeschichte des Hohenzollernschen Kaiserhauses, Vol. III). Frankfort a. Oder, 1892.

REDDAWAY, W. F. *Frederick the Great and the Rise of Prussia.* New York, 1904.

SCHÄFER, ARNOLD. *Geschichte des siebenjährigen Krieges.* 3 vols. Berlin, 1867.

SCHÄFER, KURD WOLFGANG VON. *Der siebenjährige Krieg. Nach der Original-Correspondenz Friedrichs des Grossen mit dem Prinzen Heinrich und seinen Generalen.* Berlin, 1859.

SCHMETTAU, FRIEDRICH WILHELM KARL, GRAF VON. *Lebensgeschichte des Grafen von Schmettau.* Berlin, 1806.

SCHMITT, RUDOLPH. *Prinz Heinrich von Preussen als Feldherr im siebenjährigen Kriege.* 2 vols. Greifswald, 1885, 1897. Doctoral dissertation at Greifswald. Aims at objectivity, but frequently compares Henry's judgment favorably with Frederick's.

SCHÖNING, KURD WOLFGANG VON. *Militärische Correspondenz des Königs Friedrich des Grossen mit dem Prinzen Heinrich von Preussen.* 4 vols. Berlin, 1859. From the documents in the Staatsarchiv. Volumes I to III, first published in Potsdam in 1851–52, are on the Seven Years' War; Volume IV, first published in 1854, covers the War of the Bavarian Succession.

SYBEL, HEINRICH VON. *Geschichte der Revolutionszeit.* 5 vols. Frankfurt-am-Main, 1882. Fourth edition.

TSCHIRCH, OTTO. *Geschichte der öffentlichen Meinung in Preussen vom baseler Frieden bis zum Zusammenbruch des Staates (1795–1806).* 2 vols. Weimar, 1933.

VOLZ, GUSTAV B., AND MAX KUTSCHMANN. *Friedrich der Einzige. Ausgewählte Werke, Briefe, Gespräche, und Gedichte.* Berlin, 1933.

WADDINGTON, RICHARD. *La Guerre de sept ans.* 5 vols. Paris, 1899–1914. A general diplomatic and military history of the whole war.

WELSCHINGER, HENRI. *La Mission secrète de Mirabeau à Berlin, 1786–1787. D'après les documents originaux des archives étrangères.* Paris, 1900.

YOUNG, NORWOOD. *Life of Frederick the Great.* London, 1919. Contains much unsympathetic criticism of Frederick.

# INDEX

Adams, John Quincy, in Berlin, 313n; comment on Prussia's position, 367n; comment on Prince Henry, 368n
Aix, in Provence, 343
Albert, Prince of Saxony, Austrian general, 214
Alençon, 342
Alsace-Lorraine, 15. *See also* Lorraine
Alvensleben, Count Philip Charles v., Prussian minister, 361
Amelia, Abbess of Quedlinburg, sister of Frederick II, 6, 10; guest at Rheinsberg, 24; and Princess Henry, 26, 38n, 91, 92, 247, 248; musician, 28; and William, 46n, 49n; and Henry, 91, 92; at Frederick's home-coming, 235; in Frederick's will, 334
Anhalt, Heinrich Wilhelm v., Prussian staff officer, 174, 180, 181, 182, 186–187, 198, 206, 215n, 219, 222n, 242
Anhalt, principality of, 63, 329
Anhalt-Dessau, Prince Leopold of, in first Silesian war, 14; at Kesselsdorf, 16
Anhalt-Dessau, Prince Moritz of, at Hochkirch, 85n
Ansbach, visited by Henry, 23; succession to, 292, 299, 313. *See also* Frederika Louisa
*Antimachiavel,* 20
Antwerp, 322
Arensberg, Duke Karl Maria Raimund of, Austrian general, at Pretsch, 114
d'Argens, Jean Baptiste de Boyer, Marquis, letter to, 234
Armstrong, John, 339n–340n
Artillery, use in Seven Years' War, 97, 104, 139, 169, 201, 303; in War of Bavarian Succession, 303, 305
Artois, Count of, *see* Charles Philippe
Assembly of Notables, French, 341
Auerstädt, 336n
Augustus III, King of Poland and Elector of Saxony, 232–233, 239, 249–250, 251
Augustus William, Prince of Prussia, brother of Frederick II, *see* William
Aussig, Bohemian frontier town, 95, 304
Austria, relations with Prussia, 12ff, 233, 249, 254–256, 263, 265, 271, 292–308, 311n, 313, 328–329; relations with Russia, 41, 151; troops of, at Kunersdorf, 104, 107; plans for *1760*, 128; army reduced, *1762*, 176; war aims, *1762*, 189, 193–194; request for an armistice, 223; peace, 230–233; and the Bavarian succession, 292–313; and the Netherlands,

322–326, 328–329; feared in Prussia, *1786*, 331; *1800*, 372; and third partition of Poland, 356–358, 364
Austrian succession, *1740*, 12–16
Austrian war against French Revolution, sought by Count of Artois, 348–349; campaigns, 352–354, 355, 358; Prussian alliance, 352
Austrians, threatening Berlin, 103, 105, 107; in Silesia, *1760*, 130, 133, 135–137, 140–141, 143, 144, 146; *1761*, 162, 163, 166–170; *1762*, 195; in Berlin, 150–152; in Poland, *1770*, 269–270, 283

Bacher, Théobald, French secretary of legation, junior negotiator at Basel, 358, 359, 363–365
Bahr, Prussian officer, 211
Baireuth, Margrave of, 76
Baireuth, 63, 75, 76, 98, 198, 201, 236, 240; succession to, 292, 299, 313. *See also* Wilhelmina, Margravine of Baireuth
Baltic coast, Frederick to be "lord of," 263, 269, 329
Baltic Sea, British urged to send fleet to, 53, 55; mentioned, 129
Bamberg, bishopric of, 74, 84, 95, 97, 99, 222–223, 295
Bandemer, Colonel, Prussian officer, 197–198
Bar, Confederation of, 253
Barnitz, near Meissen, 173
Barthélemy, François, Marquis de, French ambassador to Switzerland, senior negotiator at Basel, 363–365
Barthélemy, Jean-Jacques, Abbé, 320n
Basel, negotiations at, 358–365; Treaty of, *1795*, 365–366, 367
Bastille, news of fall of, 347
Bautzen, 82, 85, 87, 101, 108n; Austrian base, 110, 112, 113, 173
Bavaria, Charles Albert of, and the Imperial succession, 14
Bavaria, in War of Austrian Succession, 14, 15; mentioned, 126, 360, 362, 369. *See also* Bavarian succession
Bavarian succession, question of, 275, 281, 292–302, 311–312, 328
Bavarian Succession, War of, 12n, 297, 303–308, 328
Beaumarchais, Pierre-Augustin Caron de, French dramatist, 320, 327
Beck, Baron Levin Philipp v., Austrian general, 173

387

# Index

293, 300–301; and Joseph II, 321–322; mentioned, 372

Catholics (Roman), in Poland, 252–253

Catt, Henri de, reader to Frederick II, 43n, 83n, 86n, 96n; with Henry at Schmottseifen, 109n; praise of Henry, 117n; stories about Maxen, 118–119, 120n, 123n; other anecdotes, 143n

Cavalry, at Mollwitz, 14; at Chotusitz, 15; at Rossbach, 59; in Poland, 135; commanders, 157; at Freiberg, 217

Chantilly, France, 324n

Charles, Margrave of Brandenburg, 224n, 236, 239

Charles VI of Hapsburg, Emperor, 12

Charles XII of Sweden, 122n

Charles Albert, Elector of Bavaria, and the Imperial succession, 14, 15

Charles Philippe, Count of Artois (later Charles X of France), brother of Louis XVI, 348–350, 352

Charlottenburg, 25, 151n, 241, 289

Chemnitz, near Freiberg, 154, 175, 197–198, 201, 222

Choiseul, Étienne François, Duc de, French minister of foreign affairs, 252n

Chotusitz, battle of, 15

Clausewitz, Karl v., opinion cited, 216

Clermont, Count, French general, 66

Cleves, Prussian province, 63, 207, 358, 364

Cobenzl, Count Ludwig v., Austrian minister to Prussia, 294, 295, 297–298, 317n

Coblenz, in war against France, 352

Cochon de Lapparent, Count Charles, member of Committee of Public Safety, 363n

Coeper, Frederick's secretary, 105

Collenbach, Heinrich Gabriel v., Austrian negotiator at Hubertusburg, 228, 233

Cologne, visited by Henry, 22

Committee of Public Safety, 361–365

Condé, Louis-Joseph de Bourbon, Prince de, émigré, 350

Condorcet, M.-J.-A.-N.-Caritat, Marquis de, 320n

Constantinople, 221, 257

Coronation day, in Hohenzollern family, 9

Cossacks, 131n, 132, 202

Cothenius, Christian Andreas, staff surgeon, 47n; with Henry, 94, 125, 162n; with Mitchell, 158n

Courier service, 82, 105n, 106n, 109, 111n, 116, 127, 135, 138n, 142n, 143, 222, 238, 268, 270

Crown prince, position of, in Prussia, 4

Culm, West Prussian town, 274

Custine, Count Adam-Philippe de, French general, 354

Czartoryski party, in Poland, 250

Czernichev, Count Ivan, Russian official, 269

Czernichev, Zachary, Russian general, in Silesia, 141, 142, 169; in Berlin, 151;

leaving Loudon, 194; with Frederick, 199, 202–204

Dahlen, near Hubertusburg, 224, 225, 233

Dalberg, Karl Theodor Anton Maria v., Elector of Mainz, see Mainz

Danube River, 223, 265, 268, 297

Danzig, defense of, 128; rumor about, 241; "sanitary cordon" and, 1770, 262; in partitions of Poland, 270, 281, 283–284, 350, 355

Daun, Count Leopold Joseph v., Austrian field marshal, at Kolin, 42; in Bohemia, 74; at Meissen, 1758, 82; at Stolpen, 83, 84; at Hochkirch, 85; in Saxony, 1758, 88, 305; in Bohemia, 1759, 96, 97, 98, 100, 101, 107; plans to crush Henry, 108–113; march to Saxony, 112–113; campaign in Saxony, 1759, 114–124; and Loudon, 133; and relief of Dresden, 1760, 140; at Liegnitz, 140–141, 147; at Torgau, 152–154; in Saxony, 1761, 161–163, 167, 170–173, 176; 1762, 177, 186, 210; blocks exchange of prisoners, 179; in Silesia, 1762, 198n, 202–203

Declaration of the Rights of Man, 349n

Delacroix de Constant, Charles, French foreign minister, 369n

Delmas, J.-F.-B., member of Committee of Public Safety, 363n

Denmark, neutrality of, 128, 189, 194, 235; and Holstein, 329

Dettingen, battle of, 15

Diderot, 282

Dijon, visited by Henry, 1784, 319

Diplomatic Revolution, 32, 33

Dippoldiswalde, near Dresden, 81, 119; abandoned by Austrians, 1759, 123; Austrian base, 1762, 197, 198, 221, 222

Directory, French, 369n

Dissidents, in Poland, 252–253, 267

Dittmannsdorf, near Burkersdorf, 203

Döbeln, Saxon village, 175, 196

Dohna, Count Christoph, Prussian general, 77–81, 96, 100, 101, 124, 132, 288

Dolgoruki, Prince Vladimir, Russian minister to Prussia, 249n

Dommitsch, Austrian base in Saxony, 114n

Dönhoff, Count Friedrich Wilhelm, 288

Dorn, Walter L., cited, 193–194n

Dresden, winter quarters of prince and king in, 37, 67, 91, 94; Prussian regime in, 64, 70; defense of, 69, 70, 78, 82, 88, 95, 100, 101, 107, 108; loss of, 110, 111, 113, 137; plans for recapture of, 114, 115, 175, 180, 195; siege of, 135–136, 139–140, 143; Austrian base, 153, 154, 162, 197, 199, 201, 204–205, 210, 214, 215, 220, 221, 222; in War of Bavarian Succession, 304, 310, 312

Dresden, Peace of, 16, 17

389

# Index

# Index

Michell, Abraham Ludwig, Prussian secretary of legation, later minister to Britain, 55, 126n, 192, 208
Mietzel River, 81
Minden, 65; battle of, 100–101, 123n
Mirabeau, Count Gabriel-Honoré Riquetti, 318n, 328; in Germany, 330–337; *Histoire secréte*, 342–344
"Miracle of the House of Brandenburg," 106, 107, 109
Mitchell, Sir Andrew, British minister to Prussia, arrives in Berlin, 32, 33; on origins of Seven Years' War, 34, 37; at Prague, 42; mediator between Frederick and William, 46n; mediator between Frederick and Henry, 149, 154, 155, 158, 225; and British fleet, 53; and British subsidy, 53–55, 79, 157–158, 189, 191, 241; praise of Frederick, 54, 55, 169, 230n; criticism of Frederick, 57, 74n, 85, 119–120, 125, 134, 139, 149, 190, 202, 208, 210n, 230n, 243n; criticism of Henry, 59, 129, 139, 149; praise of Henry, 66, 83, 88, 90, 91, 109, 113n, 116, 123, 172n, 185, 210n; fatigues of campaigning, 67, 113, 141, 149, 156; at Zorndorf, 80n; at Dresden, *1758*, 88; with Henry, 109–123, 149n, 150, 154, 162n; and Kolberg, 173; on treatment of prisoners, 179, 180; on conditions in Silesia and Saxony, *1762*, 184–185; on Russian-Prussian peace, 189–193, 195; estimate of Henry's army, *1762*, 200; comment on Schweidnitz, 207; in British-French peace negotiations, 207–209; and news of Freiberg, 219, 224; and news of Hubertusburg, 230n; on postwar conditions, 231, 236–237, 244n; at Frederick's home-coming, 235; on Polish succession question, 249n, 250
Mokranowski, Count Andreas, Polish general, 251, 252
Moldavia, 254, 265
Möllendorff, Wichard Joachim Heinrich v., Prussian general, 304, 308n; commands Rhine army, 356n, 358, 361, 363n
Mollwitz, battle of, 14, 351
Monbijou, residence of queen mother, Sophia Dorothea, 28; Hohenzollern museum, 28n, 377n
Monnot, French sculptor, 319
Monroe, James, 339n
Montmorin-Saint-Herem, Count Armand-Marc de, French minister for foreign affairs, 340, 345
Moravia, campaigns in, *1742*, 15; *1758*, 40, 48, 68, 74, 93; Loudon's retreat from, *1759*, 110, 116n; proposed invasion of, *1762*, 180, 182, 204; Frederick meets Joseph in, 259, 261; in War of Bavarian Succession, 304–305

Moscow, visited, by Henry, 268; by Catherine, 282
Moys, battle of, 60n
Muhle, 92
Mulde River, in Saxony, 196–197, 201, 213, 216, 217, 218
Mulligan, 340n
Müllrose, 91, 106
Münchhausen, Baron Karl Ludwig (or Chlodwig) Heino, 330n, 344, 361, 370n
Münster, 123n, 207

Nancy, visited by Henry, 324n, 326–327
Napoleon, allusions to, 84n, 96, 104, 335, 336; opinion of Henry's tactics, 175n, 216; in Italy, 370–371, 372
Natalie, Russian grand duchess, *née* Wilhelmina of Hesse-Darmstadt, 281, 284
Naumburg, 93, 94
Necker, Jacques, in Geneva, 318; in Assembly of Notables, 341
Neisse, Silesian fortress, siege of, *1741*, 14; relieved, *1758*, 87; threatened, *1761*, 163; mentioned, 220; Frederick meets Joseph at, 254–256, 257, 259, 292, 316
Netherlands, 235, 316; and the Scheldt question, 322–326; relations with Prussia, 326, 336n; reported seeking peace, *1794*, 359, 361, 362. *See also* Belgian Netherlands, Wilhelmina of Orange
Neumarkt, Silesian village, 141
Neuschloss, near Leipa, 304
Neustadt, in Moravia, Frederick meets Joseph II at, 259
Neustadt, in Saxony, occupied, 41
New Mark, Prussian province, 77, 78, 89, 131, 132, 262
New Palace, Potsdam, 238
Newcastle, Thomas Pelham-Holles, Duke of, 193n
Niemes, captured, *1778*, 304
Nivernois, Louis Jules Barbon Mancini-Mazarin, Duc de, French minister to Prussia, *1756*, 32; in Paris, 315, 323, 341
Nossen, near Freiberg, 118
Nugent von Waldosetto, Count Jakob, Austrian minister to Prussia, 262, 263
Nuremberg, 99, 201, 222–223

Ochs, Peter (?), intermediary at Basel, 358
Oder River, 40, 91, 93, 102, 105, 106, 107, 108, 129, 137, 141, 147, 151
Öderan, near Chemnitz, 197
O'Donnell, Count Karl, Austrian general, 153
d'Oels, Count, pseudonym used by Prince Henry in France
Oetscher, near Frankfort on the Oder, 103
Olmütz, location, 40; siege of, *1758*, 48, 68, 71, 72, 74, 76

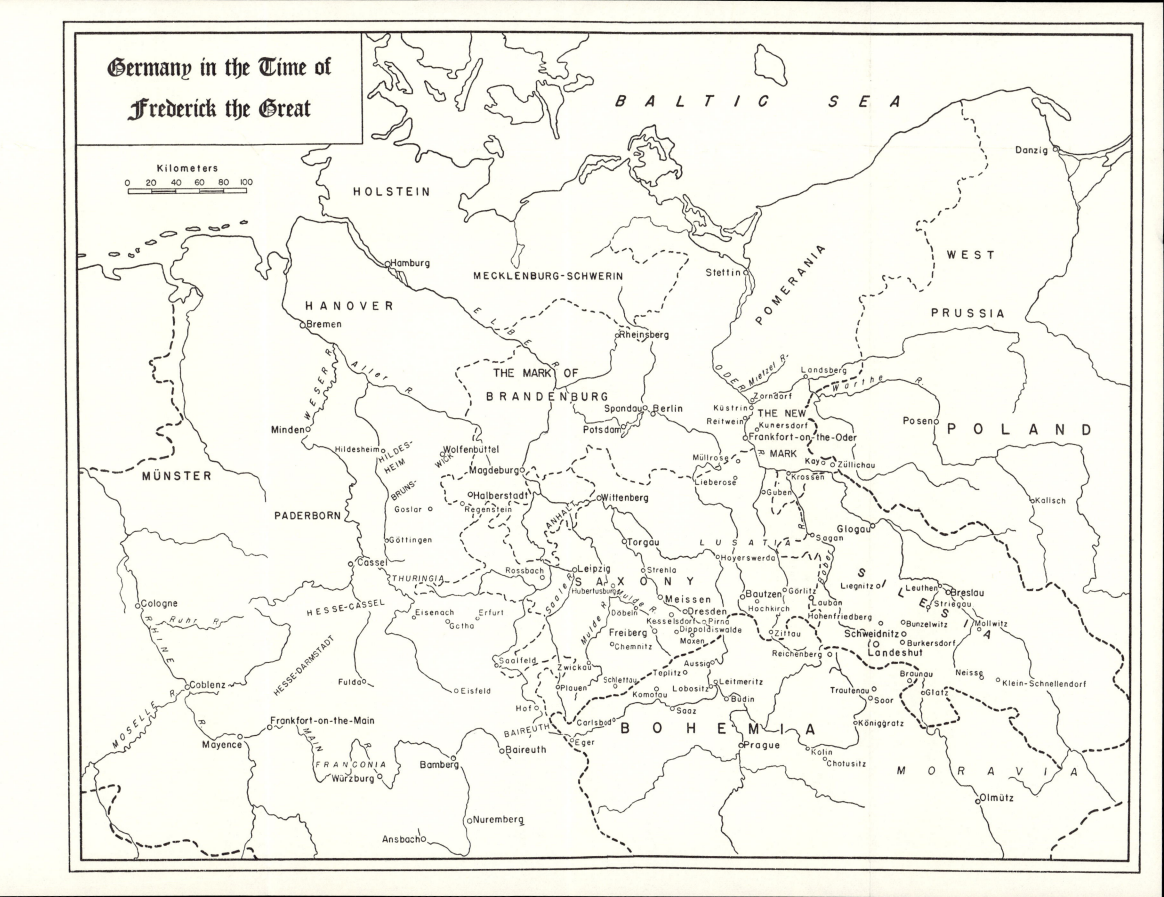

**Germany in the Time of Frederick the Great**

Kilometers
0 20 40 60 80 100

BALTIC SEA

HOLSTEIN

Hamburg

MECKLENBURG-SCHWERIN

Stettin

POMERANIA

WEST

Danzig

PRUSSIA

HANOVER

Bremen

Rheinsberg

THE MARK OF

BRANDENBURG

Spandau Berlin

Potsdam

Landsberg

Zorndorf

Küstrin

Reitwein

THE NEW

Kunersdorf

Frankfort-on-the-Oder

MARK

Poseno

POLAND

Minden

Hildesheim HILDES-
HEIM

Wolfenbüttel

WICK

Magdeburg

Müllrose

Lieberose

Kay Züllichau

Krossen

Guben

Kallsch

MÜNSTER

BRUNS-

Halberstadt

Wittenberg

Goslar

Regenstein

Glogau

Sagan

PADERBORN

Göttingen

Torgau

LUSATIA

Hoyerswerda

Bober

Liegnitz

Leuthen

Breslau

S

Cassel

Rossbach

Leipzig

Strehla

SAXONY

Meissen

Bautzen

Görlitz

Lauban

Striegau

Cologne

THURINGIA

Hubertusburg

Döbeln

Dresden

Hochkirch

Hohenfriedberg

L

E

S

I

A

Ruhr R.

HESSE-CASSEL

Eisenach

Erfurt

Kesselsdorf Pirna

Dippoldiswalde

Zittau

Bunzelwitz

Mollwitz

RHINE

Gotha

Freiberg

Maxen

Reichenberg

Schweidnitz

Landeshut

Burkersdorf

Coblenz

HESSE-DARMSTADT

Fulda

Saalfeld

Chemnitz

Zwickau

Aussig

Teplitz

Braunau

Neisse

Klein-Schnellendorf

MOSELLE R.

Mayence

MAIN R.

Eisfeld

Plauen

Schlettau

Komotau

Lobositz

Leitmeritz

Budin

Trautenau

Soor

Glatz

Königgratz

Frankfort-on-the-Main

Hof

Saaz

Carlsbad

BAIREUTH

Eger

BOHEMIA

Prague

Kolin

Chotusitz

MORAVIA

Baireuth

FRANCONIA

Bamberg

Würzburg

Olmütz

Ansbach

Nuremberg

WESER R.

Aller R.

ELBER.

ODER

Mietzel R.

Warthe R.

Saaler R.

Mulde R.

BOBER

45059